Feb. 8   U.S. Military C⟨...⟩ ⟨...⟩ ⟨...⟩ in Vietnam

March 19 Cease-fire in Al⟨...⟩

July 3   Algeria becomes independent

Oct. 20–Nov. 21   China invades India
Oct. 22–Nov. 20   Cuba-Soviet missiles crisis
Dec. 15–16   Rambouillet meeting between Macmillan and
             de Gaulle
Dec. 18–21   Nassau meeting between Macmillan and
             Kennedy. Polaris agreement

Dec. 28–29   Renewed fighting in Katanga

Jan. 29   De Gaulle vetoes U.K.'s entry into Common
          Market

Aug. 5   Nuclear Test Ban Treaty between U.S.A., U.K.,
          U.S.S.R.

Nov. 22   Kennedy assassinated

AT THE END OF THE DAY

At the end of the day: with Lady Dorothy in retirement at Birch Grove

AT THE END OF THE DAY

1961–1963

HAROLD MACMILLAN

* * * * * *

MACMILLAN

1973

First published 1973 by
MACMILLAN LONDON LTD
London and Basingstoke
Associated companies in New York
Dublin Melbourne Johannesburg and Madras

SBN 333 12413 8

Printed in Great Britain by
ROBERT MACLEHOSE AND CO LTD
The University Press, Glasgow

Contents

Appendixes

List of Illustrations

List of Cartoons

The first cartoon is reproduced by courtesy of Associated Newspapers Group Ltd, the second by courtesy of *London Express News
and Feature Services*

Acknowledgements

I HAVE to thank Her Majesty the Queen for permission to quote extracts from my letters to her during my premiership which are used in this and the preceding volume, *Pointing the Way*. I am also deeply grateful for her gracious permission to use her own letter to me on my resignation.

I have to thank Miss Christine Struthers and Miss Ann Macdonald for their careful work in typing and retyping.

I take the opportunity afforded by the publication of the sixth and final volume to give my special thanks to Miss Anne Glyn-Jones, who has for eight years worked with rare devotion in the preparation and arrangement of material from an immense collection of documents in my possession. No one who has not attempted anything of the kind can realise the complication and magnitude of such an undertaking. I owe her a deep debt of gratitude.

1 June 1973   H. M.

CHAPTER I

Europe and Britain

O<small>N</small> 27 July 1961 the Cabinet agreed that the British Government should make a formal application to accede to the Treaty of Rome. This was a necessary step in order to initiate negotiations for meeting the special needs of the United Kingdom, of the Commonwealth countries and of the other members of the European Free Trade Area. Should these prove successful it was our hope that the Community of the Six could be enlarged to include all, or almost all, the countries of Western Europe. This decision, which was announced to Parliament four days later (31 July 1961), can be regarded as a turning-point in our history.

In those fateful years when the rise of Hitler threatened Europe with an internecine and destructive conflict for the second time within a single generation, our philosopher historian, Arnold Toynbee, published some pregnant and prophetic words. After referring to the spectacular growth of the United States, he foresaw the rise of further giants of the same calibre.

When that day comes, the . . . countries of Europe, instead of being confronted by a single giant, will be encircled by half a dozen ; and these encompassing giants, who already overtop us as they grow in stature, all owe their gigantic strength to the currents of vitality that have been flowing into their frames, through one medium or another, from Europe itself. These gigantic countries of the extra-European World have either been colonized by European immigrants or they have been overrun by European conquerors or they have been opened up by European traders or else they have been spiritually irradiated by European techniques or institutions or ideas without any physical inoculation with European flesh and blood; but, whatever the process may have been, they have all been brought to life by being brought within the ambit of that Western Civilization of which Europe has been the fountain-head. And thus it would appear that—to invert a famous phrase—we Europeans have called a new world into being not to *redress* but to *upset* the balance of the old.

This situation, he continued, is a challenge to statesmanship.

> If the . . . states at the centre take no preventive action, it is obvious that the giant states on the periphery are bound to overwhelm them by sheer weight of metal; and this means that, on the political plane, the creators and sustainers of the common civilization will lose their power of initiative and perhaps their independence, and that the sceptre will pass to the outer 'barbarians' who are not yet fit to wield it. This will not only be a political calamity for the pygmy central states; it will also be a cultural calamity for Society as a whole. From every point of view, it is in the public interest that this calamity should be averted; and the duty of averting it devolves upon the statesmen of the central states whose political existence is threatened. It is for them to act, but how are they to perform their task? The solution manifestly lies in somehow transmuting political pluralism and political strife into political concord and political solidarity; but how is this miracle to be achieved?[1]

As all the world knows the miracle was not forthcoming; and the events of the Second World War accelerated, by many years, a situation already threatening. Yet even during the Second War there was one man gifted with the prophetic imagination to foresee the inevitable march of events. I have already described how Churchill, even in the midst of the great struggle, compiled a paper of outstanding importance regarding the need for European unity as part of a coherent effort to maintain peace and civilisation throughout the world.[2]

There followed, in the years immediately after the end of the war, Churchill's Zürich speech in September 1946, and in December 1947 the foundation of the European Movement. The Marshall Plan, the most generous act ever entered into by a great country, led,

[1] Arnold Toynbee, *A Study of History* (1934) III, p. 304.
[2] *Tides of Fortune*, p. 182.

as part of the European recovery programme, to the establishment in the spring of 1948 of the Organisation for European Economic Co-operation. A year later there was created the North Atlantic Treaty Organisation; and in May of that year the Council of Europe met in Strasburg. An invitation to Western Germany to join the Council of Europe was extended and accepted in March 1950. Thus, in no clear or logical pattern, and largely under British leadership, the movement began. Next came the launching of the Schuman Plan for coal and steel and the signing of the consequential treaty in April 1951 by six leading countries of Europe. The British Government, alas, decided not to participate. The next years were filled by an attempt to organise the so-called European Defence Community. Although this failed, a high degree of co-operation was created by the foundation, in October 1954, through the initiative of Eden as Foreign Secretary of the Western European Union which included a revived and rearmed Germany.

In the summer of 1955 the Six countries—France, Germany, Italy, Holland, Belgium and Luxembourg—jointly operating the Coal and Steel Community met in Messina to discuss the formation of 'a general common market'. During the following year, 1956, the British Government tried to persuade our European friends to adopt an industrial free trade area covering all the countries of Western Europe. Had this plan succeeded, many of the complications regarding British agriculture and the main interests of our Commonwealth partners would have been avoided. But in March 1957 the Six Messina powers signed the Treaty of Rome, which became operative on 1 January 1958. Nevertheless, during all this period negotiations proceeded with every hope of success to harmonise the interests of the two European groups. Unhappily, our proposals were finally rejected by the French Government under General de Gaulle, in November 1958.[1]

We then turned to what seemed a practical alternative, to protect ourselves and the other countries of Europe who were not members of the Common Market. The European Free Trade Area Treaty, covering seven European countries, was signed in November 1959. Nevertheless, I was deeply distressed at the division of Europe, or

[1] See *Riding the Storm*, chaps. iii and xiv.

what remained of Free Europe, into two groups and I spent much time and effort in 1960 in an attempt to win the support of the Germans for the unification of Western Europe, to enlist the sympathy of the Italians, and somehow to overcome the continued resistance of the French.

At the end of 1960, during the short Christmas holidays, I had prepared and circulated to my colleagues a memorandum on the state of the Free World and the need to organise all its forces, economic, political and military, to withstand the threats looming against us all over the world. This document, which became familiarly known in the inner circles of Whitehall as 'The Grand Design', was the basis of further efforts. I had already, in the closing months of 1960, tried to win the personal support of Kennedy, of Adenauer and of de Gaulle himself. It seemed to me now of vital importance to concentrate, among other objectives, on securing a real unity of the Western half of divided Europe, thus returning to the concepts which had inspired the Founding Fathers of the European Movement nearly fourteen years before.

At home, the chief practical difficulty concerned the future of British agriculture. Both Britain and the Common Market countries supported their agricultural industries, but in very different ways. Profound and detailed study would be required, in close co-operation with the agricultural leaders. Accordingly, early in 1961 I sent a memorandum to the head of the Cabinet Office, describing a talk with Butler—on whose judgement on these matters I specially relied.

I had a good talk with the Home Secretary [Butler] today at lunch and gave him the very rough details of what we have been working on recently. He did not seem unduly alarmed. He made, however, one important suggestion. If we are able to come anywhere near to negotiation on the Six and the Seven, he thinks it would make a great difference if the Farmers' Union Chairman and especially officials are brought into the discussions. We must work with them. . . . He says that their economist is quite sensible. It might even be worth somebody making contact with him now in broad discussion.

I was interested to see that the new Chairman made a much more sensible speech than one might have expected.

All this, of course, would have to be done through the Ministry of Agriculture.[1]

In the middle of April, I noted with satisfaction, after a long discussion, that the Minister of Agriculture 'is really getting down to a new study of the Agricultural Problem in relation to Europe'.[2]

Apart from the material objections and difficulties which we might expect from the members of the Conservative Party in both Houses, who had close links with the agricultural interest, there were doubters, and in the end opponents, whose hesitations were based on more traditional and perhaps higher motives. It was, after all, asking a great deal of the Conservative Party, so long and so intimately linked with the ideal of Empire, to accept the changed situation, which might require a new concept by which Britain might serve Commonwealth and world interests more efficiently if she were linked with Europe than if she remained isolated, doomed to a diminishing power in a world in which her relative wealth and strength were bound to shrink. It was clear, therefore, that before any formal application to enter E.E.C. the first need was to consult, as confidentially but as fully as possible, the Commonwealth Governments. There had been some purely exploratory talks during the meeting of Commonwealth Prime Ministers in London the previous autumn (20 and 21 September 1960) but these had been very guarded.

On 27 February, Heath, as Lord Privy Seal, acting with the full authority of the Cabinet, told the Council of Ministers of the Western European Union that Britain was prepared to contemplate 'a fundamental change of principle' in its approach to the Common Market and to participate in the political consultations with the Six if unanimously invited to do so. It was therefore becoming urgent that we should at least make up our minds about what *we* wanted to do. But here was a dilemma. I could scarcely urge my colleagues to enter on so novel and hazardous a course without at least some preliminary soundings in the Commonwealth, yet such discussions would prove fruitless, and even harmful, unless we in the Cabinet

[1] Memorandum to Sir Norman Brook, 24 January 1961.

[2] 13 April 1961. Quotations from my private journals and other personal memoranda are indicated by the date of the entry.

had already thrashed out the problem to the point of being convinced that Britain's power and influence would ultimately be
increased to the advantage of the Commonwealth itself by joining
the European grouping – itself the result of and the cure for some of
the troubles of the post-war world.

Unfortunately, the meeting of Commonwealth Prime Ministers
in March was almost wholly taken up with the problem of the
Union of South Africa. There was little opportunity for even
informal talks upon this larger issue. On 15 April 1961, following
my visit to Washington, I gave a report to the Prime Ministers of
Australia and New Zealand regarding the attitude of the Kennedy
administration. I had already had an opportunity to discuss the
question of Europe with the Prime Minister of Canada when I paid
a short visit to Ottawa on my way home. In my messages to Menzies
and Holyoake I explained that the Kennedy administration seemed
more ready than their predecessors to recognise the dangers of
a further political division in Europe. Consequently, they now
believed that it would be better if Britain were to join the political as
well as the economic associations of the Six. The economic advantages and disadvantages were difficult to assess; but in any case they
would have to be weighed against the broader issues which confronted the Free World. Holyoake, the Prime Minister of New
Zealand, not unnaturally dwelt upon the practical dangers to his
country. The maintenance of unrestricted and duty-free entry of
New Zealand's products into the United Kingdom was absolutely
vital. Menzies, though sympathetic, expressed similar doubts.

During the next few days there were important discussions in the
Cabinet on the whole question. The preliminary conclusion reached
was that it was in the interest of the Western World as a whole to
create a truly united Europe. If there was an economic price to be
paid in the short run by our going in, nevertheless, a much heavier
forfeit would have to be paid in the long run by our staying out.
There were, of course, doubts voiced by several Ministers about the
problem of sovereignty, and the ultimate effect on the future of the
Commonwealth. Moreover, the possible damage that might be
inflicted on British agriculture and Commonwealth trade was a
question of vital importance. Much would therefore depend upon

the issue of any negotiations. Certainly the Commonwealth aspects of the problem overshadowed all others – politically, economically and, above all, emotionally. The preferential trade arrangements, an important aspect of the Commonwealth link, had been a traditional part of Conservative policy for more than half a century. It was true, of course, that their practical importance had been eroded in recent years. Nevertheless, there were many doubts as to whether the Commonwealth fabric could stand the strain of the radical departure of policy which we were now contemplating. On the other hand it could hardly be denied that if the United Kingdom stayed out of Europe it might nevertheless not be possible to maintain indefinitely the present trade arrangements with the Commonwealth. It can readily be understood how difficult it was for a Conservative administration to weigh the pros and cons with any mathematical accuracy. If we were to succeed we must be able to obtain terms which would protect the vital interests of Commonwealth countries mainly concerned, especially New Zealand. We must also be able to convince our friends in the Commonwealth that the course we were proposing to follow would, in the long run, strengthen rather than weaken Britain and the Commonwealth as a whole. We had, therefore, not merely to search for advantageous terms in a business arrangement; we must obtain the genuine approval and sincere goodwill of, at any rate, the leading Commonwealth countries. Sometimes these discussions were held in full meetings of the Cabinet, sometimes with a number of Ministers mainly concerned.

> We have had long meetings of Ministers . . . about Europe – some progress is being made. But the position is very delicate. The Commonwealth and Agricultural interests are anxious, even alarmed.[1]

Parliamentary Questions were now building up about the intentions of the United Kingdom. I could only repeat, on 9 May, that our Commonwealth commitments and the interests of British agriculture must be

> regarded as preconditions. The problem remains. It is a very difficult and technical problem, as those who have studied the

[1] 14 May 1961.

details are aware, of whether this can be done. I have always thought that it could be done if there was a will on all sides to do it, but I recognise the difficulty and complication in any such negotiation.

Pressure in the House of Commons continued to increase.

> Parliamentary Questions—mostly about Europe and the Common Market. The pace is quickening and we have still no firm policy approved by the Cabinet![1]

On 17 May,

> we had a *very* good talk (for two hours) this morning at the Committee of Ministers on Sixes and Sevens. It was a kind of Second Reading of the Minister of Agriculture's paper. Butler had, naturally, anxieties and reservations about agriculture in United Kingdom; Sandys, although a keen European, about the Commonwealth. But all agreed that we now had a much clearer picture of what our negotiating position could be.[2]

Two days later I felt that

> the European problem has held the attention of Parliament, the Press and to some extent the public in the last few days. The Government's position is rather better understood. Some still accuse us of indecision; but more are beginning to realise the difficulties and complexities.
>
> As far as Parliament is concerned, Lord Privy Seal (Edward Heath) has made an excellent impression by three speeches—the first to the Foreign Affairs Committee [of the Party], which I am told was brilliant as an objective presentation of the problem; the second and third in opening and winding up the two-day Foreign Affairs Debate. . . .
>
> We had [only] five abstentions in the division. . . . But there are many very *anxious* Conservatives. It is getting terribly like 1846. Anyway, none of these . . . can be Disraeli to my Peel. The Press is divided. Beaverbrook's papers—*Daily Express, Sunday Express, Evening Standard* are already hysterical in opposition. Broadly speaking, all the rest of the Press (*Times, Daily Telegraph, Daily Mail, Daily Mirror*) are sympathetic. But it is clear that we are

[1] 16 May 1961.   [2] 17 May 1961.

approaching critical decisions, both for the Party and the nation. Opponents . . . are calling already for an Election, but I am not sure that they would really like one.[1]

I did not hide from myself the magnitude of the decision with which we were about to be faced. If we decided to make an application for admission to the Common Market we would indeed be taking one of those radical and almost revolutionary steps in policy which Conservative parties have so often had to make in the past. Nevertheless, I felt determined to make the effort for I felt daily more convinced that if we were successful the future not only of Britain but of the whole Free World would be far brighter.

There was now one of those tiresome incidents which served, at any rate, as a temporary distraction.

> Poor Rab [Butler] has been unlucky, caught by an old trick. He is on holiday in Spain. He attended a 'private' dinner, given by the Spanish Foreign Minister, while in Madrid on his way south. He made a little speech 'off the cuff' and, as he thought, 'off the record'. He said that 'it was a great shame that Spain has been left outside international life for so many years'. He went on to say 'Spain should be fully incorporated in the Western World', etc., etc. The Spanish Ministry of Information issued the full text of the speech, and so the fat is in the fire! The Press—especially the 'popular' Press—is very excited here. There will certainly be [a] demand for a debate or a vote of censure. All this will waste Parliamentary time and add to the sense that the Government has 'lost grip'. It is really very tiresome and very silly.[2]

A week later,

> The house met today; there were a large number of questions—ten or eleven—about Rab's Spanish escapade. I took them all together, and we had about a quarter of an hour of supplementaries. It was all pretty good-humoured with the exception of the 'fellow-travellers'.[3]

On 25 May a meeting of senior Commonwealth officials took

[1] 19 May 1961.   [2] 23 May 1961.   [3] 30 May 1961.

place in London. They were told that informal and exploratory talks were proceeding with individual members of the Six on the basis of which we would immediately begin conversations with the countries of the Commonwealth as well as with those of EFTA. Accordingly, on 30 May we took an important step. It would certainly be some weeks before the Cabinet could decide whether the arrangements we might hope to secure in negotiations with the European Economic Community would prove acceptable and whether the policy of seeking wider political and economic associations with Europe should be pursued or abandoned. Meanwhile, we felt that much would be gained by some personal discussions. Telegrams and messages could, of course, play their part, as well as close consultation with the High Commissioners. But something more was needed.

A long Cabinet—10.30–1.00 this morning. We agreed a message to Commonwealth Prime Ministers (from me) proposing a visit from Sandys (Australia, New Zealand and Canada) and to the others by some other Minister to discuss Europe and the Common Market. I feel sure it is right to *consult* them while the Cabinet is itself trying to reach a conclusion and *not* afterwards—for that is not really consultation. Moreover, only a Cabinet Minister can develop the whole argument, political as well as economic.[1]

Accordingly, I sent off messages to the Prime Ministers of all the Commonwealth Governments proposing such visits.

The spate of Questions in the House continued, as well as some anxious messages between London and Ottawa. I explained to Diefenbaker that we could not tell him exactly what arrangements for entry into the E.E.C. we envisaged. That was what we must discuss. Diefenbaker, although he assured me privately that he was satisfied with the visit of the Commonwealth Secretary, at any rate in the first stage, now made a public statement asking for a full meeting of the Commonwealth Prime Ministers. On 13 June when I made a full statement after Questions in the House, Gaitskell not unnaturally called attention to Diefenbaker's proposal. In reply, I

[1] 30 May 1961.

emphasised the importance of detailed and individual discussion, especially regarding the varying interests of the different members of the Commonwealth, before such a meeting could be profitable. Since the Leader of the Opposition and other Members used the phrase 'before decisions are taken', I explained that 'there is first a decision to negotiate, and then, much later, a decision, as a result of negotiations, to see whether any satisfactory arrangements can be made'. In a reply to further Questions, I tried to clarify the procedure.

On 13 June I told the House:

The first thing is to get these Commonwealth discussions before any further discussions between ourselves and the members of the Six. All that procedure must be gone through, as well as the meeting which is to take place at the end of this month with the EFTA Ministers.

I emphasise, because I think that the right hon. Gentleman and I are in a great deal of agreement about how this matter should be handled, that what we are really discussing is not whether to agree to some arrangement immediately, but whether to enter a negotiation. To decide that, it is important to decide what would be the necessary derogation from the precise working of the Rome Treaty as it stands from the Commonwealth point of view and from the British agricultural point of view on the economic side. Then there are even larger questions of the broad political future of the world—the free world—and how best this country can make its contributions.

All those questions must be discussed, and, therefore, I think that it would be far too crude to say that we must just sign it or not sign it. This is a great issue which we must handle carefully and effectively.

Since the Prime Minister of Eire had made it clear that if Britain went into the Common Market his country would probably wish to do so, I invited him to come for personal consultations in July. This would be convenient because our talks would take place during the period that United Kingdom Ministers were making their Commonwealth visits. I found Seán Lemass particularly helpful, and enjoyed my meetings with him.

The next stage was a European weekend at Chequers.

Ministers began to collect before dinner [on Saturday], and we had a most useful talk after dinner. (No officials till tomorrow.) Butler, Lloyd, Heath, Maudling, Macleod, Sandys. Next day (Sunday) a great number of officials arrived. I think we were twenty-five or twenty-six at luncheon. We talked all day – morning and afternoon. We got *somewhere* – but not very far.... At any rate, we agreed enough to allow the 'peripatetic' Ministers (or perhaps one should say the St. John the Baptists) to set out on their tour of Commonwealth countries. This is really quite a good plan. Duncan Sandys will go [to] Australia, New Zealand, and Canada. Heath will go to Cyprus. Lord Perth to West Indies. Peter Thorneycroft to India, Pakistan, Malaya, Ceylon. John Hare to Ghana, Nigeria, Sierra Leone, etc. This makes quite an impressive list.[1]

The discussions at Chequers were certainly valuable. The difficulty with the Six would centre on temperate foodstuffs and on manufactured goods from developed Commonwealth countries – Canada, Australia, New Zealand. We could probably negotiate satisfactory terms for tropical goods, raw materials and perhaps some manufactured items from underdeveloped countries. But, in the long run, even with satisfactory transitional arrangements it would be very difficult to preserve the Commonwealth's traditional rights in the United Kingdom market. We must persuade the Six of the value of the Commonwealth to the Free World, and the meeting concurred in the belief that neither the Commonwealth countries nor British public opinion would accept that Commonwealth interests should only be safeguarded during the transitional period. What Commonwealth countries might secure as a result of the proposed review at the end of the transitional period should not be left completely open. At the same time, we must make clear to them that even if Britain did not join the E.E.C. the Government could not guarantee permanent unrestricted entry of Commonwealth produce. It was agreed that Britain should seek to accede to the Treaty of Rome on conditions which permitted the present levels of Commonwealth exports to the United Kingdom to be maintained

[1] 17 and 18 June 1961.

in the transitional period; and they should be changed in the Common Market period only if this was necessary in order not to frustrate the purposes of the Community and would not damage the essential interests of Commonwealth countries.

We agreed to seek to retain the right for our Exchequer to continue to give some support to farmers for as long as we thought necessary. Otherwise British farming opinion would be implacably hostile. But, if we were to persuade the E.E.C. to accept such a provision, we should have to accept some sort of limitations—for instance by imposing a ceiling on the amount paid to our farmers, and by agreeing not to apply the policy in a way which would enable us to make extra agricultural exports to the E.E.C.

Finally, we agreed that our approach to the Commonwealth countries should stress the political aspects of our desire to accede to E.E.C.—and should seek Commonwealth views on the interests they wanted safeguarded. We could not yet tell what terms we were likely to get.

On 22 June the conclusions of the Chequers meeting were brought before the full Cabinet. 'After much discussion, broad approval was given to the "Directive" (on Europe, etc.) to be given to the peripatetic Ministers.'[1] This document set out the position in detail and gave full instructions as to the line which they should take. Their most important duty was to explain that so far our informal discussions with the Six had not enabled us to find out with any precision what would be the actual conditions of entry. The only way to do so would be by a formal application. But we were anxious to keep our Commonwealth friends fully informed and if we decided to negotiate there must be close and continuous consultation with them. The first purpose of the Ministers was to set out

> the broad political considerations which point to the conclusion that the most effective way of securing our political objectives in the world, and of averting the dangers of continued division in Europe which we foresee, lies in full United Kingdom membership of the European Economic Community. Ministers would say that the United Kingdom Government—on their own judgement of these broad political considerations as well as of the

[1] 22 June 1961.

general economic arguments – are minded to join the Six, provided
that satisfactory arrangements can be negotiated with the Community to safeguard the essential interests of the Commonwealth
(and also of United Kingdom agriculture and of our partners in
the European Free Trade Association).

The two final paragraphs ran as follows :

At the end of any negotiations, when we have a clear idea of the
terms on which membership of the European Economic Community is open to us, the United Kingdom Government will have
to reach a final decision – looking at the 'package' as a whole – on
whether or not the terms are such as to justify our joining the Six.
The Commonwealth will be fully in the picture and it may well be
that at that point a full Commonwealth Conference [of Prime
Ministers] will be desirable.

United Kingdom Ministers may be pressed to have a Commonwealth Conference before that – indeed to call one in the
immediate future. If they are, they would say that such a conference would have little value until there is a concrete proposition
to be discussed (which there will not be until negotiations with the
Six have gone some way), but they might undertake to find out
the wishes of the other Commonwealth countries. In general
United Kingdom Ministers would discourage any such suggestion
as far as they can.

The same afternoon

Cecil King (*Daily Mirror*) called, to talk about Europe,
Common Market, etc. He is, of course, one of the ablest . . . and
most successful of the tycoons.[1]

He assured me of his devotion to the cause of the European Movement and promised to put all the support of his papers behind him.
This promise has been carried out faithfully both by himself and by
his successors.

While my colleagues were travelling round the world a number
of messages naturally passed between myself and some of the leading
Prime Ministers. I explained once more to Holyoake, Diefenbaker

[1] 22 June 1961.

and Menzies that the Ottawa agreements could not be permanently guaranteed in a changing world. At the same time the problem remained–only formal negotiations could tell us whether we could obtain the terms that we required. To Menzies an old and trusted friend, I sent a special paper summarising the past history. The main points were that the E.E.C. was developing into an effective political and economic force, and the Community had acquired a dynamic of its own. When we decided at the end of 1955 not to take part in the negotiations for the establishment of the E.E.C. we were influenced by two considerations, in both of which we were to be proved wrong. We thought they would not succeed–or, if they did, that we could work out a satisfactory association. We realised now that it was all-or-nothing and, if we went ahead, it would be in order to discover what 'all' involved.

Some of our Commonwealth colleagues seemed chiefly alarmed at the political repercussions upon the survival of the Commonwealth, others were more insistent upon securing themselves against serious economic losses. An interesting point was made by Nehru who said if he were a European he thought he would probably be standing for closer unity in Europe. But Indians, he thought, would be anxious about the political effect on the Commonwealth, and the economic effect on themselves. Some doubts were also expressed about 'a getting together of the industrial countries at the expense of the developing ones'.

Meanwhile the House of Commons was beginning to take an increasing interest in 'The Great Debate'. On 28 June there was an interesting discussion on a Private Member's motion. Although no division was taken certain leading Members adopted positions to which they were afterwards to remain consistently loyal. Roy Jenkins ended a luminous speech by expressing the hope 'that the Government will move towards Europe a great deal more decisively than they have yet shown any sign of doing'. This debate was followed by a flow of Parliamentary Questions which I could only deal with by the recognised Parliamentary evasions. In reference to one of these occasions when a certain bitterness developed, my friend Edward Boyle wrote me a most valuable letter on 20 July. He pointed out that while the anti-Europeans were well organised, although without any real alternative to propose, the pro-Europeans had a policy but no organisation. He felt that the main difficulty was the uncertainty as to the Government's position. He emphasised with truth the dangers of prolonged hesitation.

I don't see how the Conservative Party can avoid some sort of split on this issue. But the example of Balfour after 1903 surely suggests that the attempt to avoid *any* split, on some hotly contentious issue, may simply result in a far greater and more damaging one (and in electoral disaster).

I replied the next day as follows :

Many thanks for your kind letter with which I agree. My son, Maurice, who has quite a good judgement in these affairs, feels that the worst thing of all would be to dither along.

The travelling Ministers had now returned and reported to their colleagues in full. Five Ministers had undertaken these arduous journeys and apart from the constant flow of telegrams were able to give us their personal impressions, so often more valuable than written messages. This gathering which took place in my room at the House of Commons on 22 July was indeed of vital importance.

At this meeting, which was fully attended (except Chancellor of Exchequer who sent Economic Secretary) and [in] which *every* member of the Cabinet took part, there was a *unanimous* decision in principle that I should announce on Monday next that Her Majesty's Government would *apply to enter the Common Market*.[1]

In accordance with my practice in taking decisions of high significance I encouraged everyone to speak and made no attempt to bring my colleagues to a premature conclusion. I had to be satisfied that all were now ready to make the plunge. On returning home that night I could not but feel that this was a great and perhaps historic decision. Nevertheless, I had a feeling of uncertainty as to the result.

Whether or not, having taken this momentous decision and communicated it to the Governments of the Six, we shall reach agreement on the vital points of (*a*) Commonwealth, (*b*) British

[1] 22 July 1961.

agriculture, I cannot tell. I should judge that the chances are *against* an agreement, unless—on political grounds—de Gaulle changes his mind. For I feel that he is still hostile and jealous.[1]

To those who feared the political effects of Britain's membership of Europe I felt it right to point out that once inside this body our influence should grow rather than be diminished.

After the decision was taken I informed President Kennedy, and a few days later sent to the Commonwealth Heads of State, as well as to the Prime Ministers of Eire and South Africa, the text of the statement which I intended to make in Parliament.

> On Monday [31 July], I made a statement which the Cabinet has agreed, announcing the intention of Her Majesty's Government to make a formal application for membership of the E.E.C. under Article 237 of the Treaty of Rome with a view to a negotiation on our special obligations, internal and external (British agriculture and Commonwealth trade). There were a lot of supplementaries, which I answered as well as I could, and the general effect was fairly good. But the Conservative Party is, naturally, anxious and rather jumpy.[2]

The President's reply of 28 July was certainly couched in most generous terms.

> I want to thank you most heartily for your message of 28 July communicating the bold decision which Her Majesty's Government has taken with respect to the E.E.C. We are wholly with you, as you know, and I admire your courage in moving ahead in the face of the difficulties you have encountered in the preparatory discussions. The good will and firm support of the United States Government are with you in this next stage of negotiations, and if at any time there are particular issues on which you think we might be helpful, I will count on you to let me know. In your relations with the great States of Europe and with the Commonwealth, the United States may not always be the best possible go-between, but in the ways in which we can be useful, within the framework of the discussions which our Governments have had in recent months, you can count on us absolutely. With warm personal wishes.

[1] 22 July 1961.   [2] 5 August 1961.

Since we had arranged a two-day debate for 2 and 3 August, questions following my statement of 31 July were fairly limited. The Leader of the Opposition, Gaitskell, was very fair and did no more than point out some of the difficulties and raise points regarding the proposed procedure. Grimond, the Leader of the Liberal Party, observed with conscious rectitude,

> may I . . . congratulate the Prime Minister on his conversion to the policy which we on these benches have long urged upon him in the interests not only of this country and of Europe, but of the Commonwealth?

The Common Market debate was on a motion in the following terms:

> That this House supports the decision of Her Majesty's Government to make formal application under Article 237 of the Treaty of Rome in order to initiate negotiations to see if satisfactory arrangements can be made to meet the special interests of the United Kingdom, of the Commonwealth and of the European Free Trade Association; and further accepts the undertaking of Her Majesty's Government that no agreement affecting these special interests or involving British sovereignty will be entered into until it has been approved by this House after full consultation with other Commonwealth countries, by whatever procedure they may generally agree.

In making the formal announcement of the Government's intentions on 31 July, I had contented myself with a short factual and carefully restrained statement. Since there had been some comments at the time, repeated by subsequent historians, that the announcement was 'brief and, considering the historic importance of the occasion, . . . delivered in a surprisingly uninspired way',[1] I thought it right, when it came to the full-scale debate, to make a considerable effort to raise the level of discussion to match the historic importance of so great an endeavour. Nevertheless, it was important to point out that the moment of final decision had not yet come.

---

[1] Miriam Camps, *Britain and the European Community – 1955–63* (Princeton, New Jersey, 1964).

What the House is now asked to do is to support the Government's proposal to initiate negotiations on the Common Market within the terms of the Motion. When these negotiations are completed one way or the other, the House will have to pass judgement.

After a résumé of the movement towards the unification of Europe in the years since the War, culminating in the present dichotomy, I went on:

I am myself convinced that the existence of this division in Europe, although it is superficially of a commercial character, undoubtedly detracts from the political strength and unity of Western Europe. If we are to be involved in Europe at all, then we have a duty—and so have all the other countries in Europe—to seek some means of resolving the causes of potential division.

I then turned to the instinctive anxiety and even suspicion of British people about the ambitious plan which the Government was now anxious to promote.

In this country, of course, there is a long tradition of isolation. In this, as in most countries, there is a certain suspicion of foreigners. There is also the additional division between us and Continental Europe of a wholly different development of our legal, administrative and, to some extent, political systems. If we are basically united by our religious faith, even here great divisions have grown up.

Nevertheless, it is perhaps worth recording that in every period when the world has been in danger of tyrants or aggression, Britain has abandoned isolationism. It is true that when the immediate danger was removed, we have sometimes tried to return to an insular policy. In due course we have abandoned it. In any case, who could say today that our present danger had been removed, or will soon disappear? Who doubts that we have to face a long and exhausting struggle over more than one generation if the forces of Communistic expansion are to be contained?

Further anxieties had been expressed about the precarious position in some of the countries with which we proposed to associate ourselves.

I have sometimes heard it asked, 'What would happen if one of the countries with which we might be associated in Europe fell into political difficulties, even went Communist? Would not this have a grave effect on us if we were members?' Of course, but the effects would be equally grave whether we were members of the Common Market or not. If a member of NATO or W.E.U. went Communist or semi-Communist, what would be the position of the other member States? If all the countries of Western Europe became satellites of Moscow, what would be the position of this island?

We have only to pose the question to answer it. We shall not escape from the consequences of such a disaster by seeking in isolation a security which our geographical position no longer gives us. Surely, from this point of view, it will be better for us to play our role to the full and use the influence we have for the free development of the life and thought of Europe.

Others saw a different danger. That we might be about to join a movement tending to isolate Europe from the rest of the world, to turn its back on the outer world and look inwards upon itself. It might, of course, be that there were some people who believed that this

small but uniquely endowed continent can lead a rich, fruitful and prosperous life almost cut off from contact with the rest of the world.

But I do not believe that such people, if they exist, are to be found among the leading men or the Governments of Europe. Certainly, this island could never join an association which believed in such medieval dreams, but if there are little Europeans, and perhaps there are, is it not the duty of this country, with its world-wide ties, to lend its weight to the majority of Europeans who see the true prospective of events? I believe that our right place is in the vanguard of the movement towards the greater unity of the free world, and that we can lead better from within than outside. At any rate, I am persuaded that we ought to try.

As to the method which we proposed to adopt, we must keep in closest touch with the representatives of British agriculture; with the Commonwealth countries, probably ending, if our negotiations with the Community seemed to justify it, in a Conference of Commonwealth Prime Ministers; and finally Parliament's approval must be sought. With regard to the wider issues, in the Commonwealth there were those who argued and believed with deep sincerity that by associating more closely with Europe in this new economic grouping we should injure the strength of the Commonwealth.

If I thought this, I would not, of course, recommend this Motion to the House. But let us examine the Commonwealth position. We make no binding decisions at the Commonwealth Prime Ministers' meetings. We follow no agreed foreign policy. We have no agreed defence policy. Some members of the Commonwealth are in the various defensive pacts of the free world, and some are unaligned. Yet, for all this diversity, the Commonwealth, although not strictly a political unit, has real life and unity. It is something precious and unique.

On the contrary I asked myself the question—how could we best serve the Commonwealth?

By standing aside from the movement for European unity, or by playing our full part in its development? By retaining our influence in the New World, or by allowing it to decline by the relative shrinking of our own political and economic power compared with the massive grouping of the modern world? Britain in isolation would be of little value to our Commonwealth partners, and I think that the Commonwealth understand it. It would, therefore, be wrong in my view to regard our Commonwealth and our European interests as conflicting. Basically, they must be complementary.

The changing pattern of trade that had followed the signing of the Ottawa agreement between the wars had brought about some startling changes.

First and foremost, British agriculture has been revived and now supplies our country with two-thirds of its temperate foodstuffs and with one-third of all its foodstuffs. All the Commonwealth countries have also developed a wider diversity of manufactured goods, partly for sale at home and partly for export.

As the House knows, this changing pattern of trade has presented us with certain difficulties in certain quarters and they will have to be dealt with whether we enter the Common Market or not.

I then went on to give a pledge that these negotiations would only be concluded if the special interests of the Commonwealth could be met. We had equally our obligations to EFTA. Finally, there was our determination to maintain, by one method or another, the strength and prosperity of British agriculture. But I pointed out that the actual machinery had already over recent years been subject to many changes. During the war and in the period immediately following we operated by bulk purchase of the produce of British farmers. We then moved to deficiency payments. It might well mean that we would have ultimately to shift from a system where much of the farmers' support came from the Exchequer to one 'in which arrangements are made to secure that the market itself provides a fair return to the producer'.

Turning then to British industry I admitted that the precise balance of gain or loss would be difficult to assess.

The protective tariffs set up before the war have given us some shelter from this competition in the home market. Many people feel that we have perhaps had too much shelter. However that may be, in the long run an island placed as ours is, where our need to export to other people will always be greater than their need to export to us, cannot maintain the high standards of life that we want for our people in an isolated protective system.

Yet I was convinced that the weight of opinion among British industrialists was that the balance of advantage lay in joining the unit whose market would be of a size comparable to, let us say, the United States or Russia. Finally, I turned to the question of sovereignty. I pointed out that in spite of the political overtones in the whole concept the E.E.C. was an economic community. Every treaty, of course, was to some extent a limitation of a nation's freedom of action. Nevertheless,

a number of years have passed since the movement began which culminated in the Treaty of Rome, and I am bound to say that I do not see any signs of the members of the Community losing their national identity because they have delegated a measure of their sovereignty. This problem of sovereignty, to which we must, of course, attach the highest importance is, in the end, perhaps a matter of degree.

There was certainly a keen federalist movement supported by some Europeans, but I doubted whether these had very deep roots. Parallels with the creation of the United States of America were based, in my view, on a false analogy.

The United States of America was originally born out of colonists with only a few generations of history behind them. They were of broadly the same national origins and spoke the same language. Europe is too old, too diverse in tradition, language and history to find itself united by such means. Although the federalist movement exists in Europe it is not one favoured by the leading figures and certainly not by the leading Governments of Europe today. Certainly not by the French Government.

The alternative concept, which one might call confederation, seemed to me more in tune

with the national traditions of European countries and, in particular, of our own. It is one with which we could associate willingly and wholeheartedly. At any rate, there is nothing in the Treaty of Rome which commits the members of E.E.C. to any kind of federalist solution, nor could such a system be imposed on member countries.

What were the chances of success? Failure would, of course, be a grave disaster. I could only repeat that I was more hopeful now than before.

The very deterioration of the situation in Europe must tend to increase the forces of unity. There is an old fable of the rivalry between the sun and the wind, as to which could make the traveller discard his coat. As the East wind blows, nations tend to draw together under a common cloak of unity.

When I spoke these words, members, of course, were aware of an acute and dangerous crisis developing over Berlin, and all of us were

B

living under the shadow of ever increasing nuclear armaments. I ended with these words.

> I think, however, that most of us recognise that in a changing world, if we are not to be left behind and to drop out of the main stream of the world's life, we must be prepared to change and adapt our methods. All through history this has been one of the main sources of our strength.
>
> I therefore ask the House to give Ministers the authority—not to sign a treaty—but to find out on what honourable basis such a treaty could be put forward for the decision of the House.

It has always been my experience in the House of Commons, that when one sits down one knows immediately whether the speech has been a failure, a moderate success, or something of a triumph. At any rate, both as to matter and to manner, I felt contented. In my own diary I wrote:

> Everyone, on both sides, listened to it without interruption. Many of my friends thought it the best speech I had ever made. The later evening papers (perhaps a little repentant of all their whispering campaign culminating in [my alleged] heart attack) switched right round. *Evening Standard*'s headline was 'Premier Rebounds—Back to Top Form', which (in view of Max Beaverbrook's position on Common Market, etc.) was generous. Anyway, it was lucky—for a failure or only a moderately good speech at this point might have been fatal.[1]

Gaitskell, in moving an amendment, sat firmly on the fence—a position which his successors in the leadership of the Labour Party were to maintain, varied by occasional frantic leaps down to one side or another. But his speech as always was able and delivered with considerable charm.

> Churchill sat through most of the speeches in the two days' debate and came into my room at intervals. This may (if things go well) crown his work as founder of the European Movement.[1]

The first evening, Maudling 'wound up' with a well-argued and effective contribution but the most brilliant speech of the debate was made by Wilson, who opened on the second day. He did not do

[1] 5 August 1961.

much in the way of discussing the Common Market; he was more intent on attacking the Government. But it was admirably done. Its only fault was that it seemed to come down too much against the European plan, but he retrieved this at the last moment and climbed back upon the official party fence by wishing well to the Government in their endeavours. This reluctant and somewhat disingenuous piece of generosity brought down upon him the wrath of Shinwell. Foot made a bitter speech, admirably answered by Duncan Sandys. I was very pleased with my son's contribution.

> Maurice made one of the best speeches of the debate and enormously increased his reputation.[1]

One of the most effective, and, in view of subsequent events, the most significant speech of the debate, was that delivered by Roy Jenkins. It was impressive both from the luminosity of the argument and from the sincerity of the speaker. He began by announcing formally that he belonged to 'the right side, the pro-Europe side of this controversy'. With regard to Britain's own position he declared

> if we stay out of Europe we will go on being economically weak. If by 1970 we are still a sluggish, crisis-ridden nation unable to provide substantial resources of development capital to the Commonwealth, whatever sentimental arguments the Commonwealth may produce during the months of negotiations, they will turn their backs on us far more than if they find that by being in Europe we are economically prosperous and dynamic and able to offer them the economic leadership which to some extent they need.

Turning to the argument on the loss of our independence, from whichever view it might be regarded, his remarks were equally effective.

> It must be obvious that if we say that we must at all costs preserve our right to do what we want with our own, whether it is done for imperialist reasons or in the name of Socialism, or simply for xenophobic reasons, this requirement of an absolute right to do what one wants with one's own is bound to produce

[1] 5 August 1961.

an inward-looking and a contracting-out attitude which is at variance with the international outlook of the Labour movement.

In his final sentence he reaffirmed his position clearly and dramatically.

> There is a real danger that we shall go into a kind of drab decline rather detached from the main currents of life in the world, blaming other countries for our misfortunes and occasionally deluding ourselves, but no one else, with illusions of grandeur. I believe that the best prophylactic against that rather dismal happening is that we should go into Europe.

When recalling the events many years later it is strange to see how the political groupings have remained pretty constant. At that time they seemed novel.

> The new alliance between the extreme Right and the extreme Left was very queer. It was ridiculed by someone who said he had lived to see 'Butskell' replaced by 'Silverbrooke'. (The first was the alleged similarity of position between Butler and Gaitskell, the second between Silverman and Lord Hinchingbrooke.)

Heath distinguished himself in a speech marked by his usual clarity and forcefulness. The two days' debate was one of the highlights of this Parliament. I listened to nearly all of it, and I have seldom heard a higher standard maintained.

> The official Labour amendment was fatuous, and was so like the Government motion in essentials, that a strong Speaker (like FitzRoy) would have refused to call it. However, it was voted on, and by some miracle we won by well over one hundred (one hundred and nine, I think).
> When it came to the Government motion, the Opposition abstained. A division was forced by the extreme Left—five voted against us, including one Tory. . . . About twenty to twenty-two Conservatives abstained. We expected thirty—so the Whips have done well. They abstained in both divisions.
> The Conservative abstainers are of two kinds—earnest Imperialists [and] the disgusted group (who oppose the Government in every trouble, whatever the subject). . . . But I see no Disraeli among them; not even a Lord George Bentinck.

Perhaps they will arise when the real crunch comes—that is, if we have successful negotiations and have to get Parliament's assent to a Treaty.[1]

In summing up the position to the Queen I wrote on 5 August:

Your Majesty will have seen the result of the two-day debate in the House of Commons and a similar debate in the House of Lords on the Common Market. The speeches made on both sides of this question reached a very high level in both Houses. As I anticipated there was a good deal of cross-Party feeling and this, of course, enhances the value and standard of argument. Instead of the usual rather dreary partisan reproaches or accusations which become very stale, Members in both Houses have to apply their minds to a new problem and become, temporarily at any rate, earnest seekers after the truth. As I told Your Majesty I was under some apprehension that the Conservative Party would be deeply split by the proposal that we should enter into negotiations with the Six European countries. Naturally sentiment and tradition make many Conservatives unwilling to associate themselves more closely with Europe. These Conservatives, in their attachment to the Commonwealth, I think are often thinking more of the old Commonwealth countries than of the new. Nevertheless they sincerely feel that there is a real conflict of interest between Britain as a Commonwealth and Britain as a European power. But I was gratified to find that the Conservative Party was fluid, ready to move with the times, and, especially among the younger men, anxious to seize new opportunities. The great majority feel that our position in the Commonwealth should we weaken industrially and economically would ultimately fade away. Could we in the second half of this century seize our opportunities and become, in association with Europe, a strong, active, and well-balanced country economically? We should become for that very reason a better member of the Commonwealth and more fit to lead it.

There now began a long, difficult and often tortuous series of discussions of which the first stage ended in October 1962, not without considerable hope of ultimate success. During all these months either by direct negotiation with E.E.C. or in our talks with

[1] 5 August 1961.

the Commonwealth and with British agriculturalists the British
Government was ably served. The recent reshuffle in the Cabinet
had led to two important Ministries—the Commonwealth Relations
Office and the Ministry of Agriculture—being in the hands of
Ministers who were keen 'Europeans'—Duncan Sandys and
Christopher Soames. They were to give, in addition to their many
other duties, notable assistance in the novel tasks which we had
undertaken. Moreover, Derry Heathcoat Amory, who had insisted
on retiring from the Government, was persuaded by me to go for a
period of at least two years as High Commissioner in Ottawa; an
appointment which was flattering to our Canadian friends and was
carried out with his natural tact and charm. The main negotiations
with the E.E.C. were in the hands of Edward Heath, appointed for
this purpose as a colleague with Alec Home at the Foreign Office
and holding the position of Lord Privy Seal. He was assisted by an
admirably chosen team of officials. Sir Pierson Dixon, the British
Ambassador in Paris, was made head of the delegation, and with
him served Sir Eric Roll and Sir Roderick Barclay; the Commonwealth Relations Office made available Sir Henry Lintott, and the
Colonial Office Sir William Gorell Barnes. All these had become
close friends of M. Marjolin and other European officials through
their work together on the O.E.E.C. and similar bodies. Never
before in our history had we mustered so powerful and intelligent
a number of men to serve so great an enterprise. Moreover, I
persuaded Butler to be in charge of the ministerial committee at
home which should oversee the negotiations and to which all
matters should be referred by any of our representatives. Many
points, through these months, were cleared in this way without the
necessity to bring them to the notice of the whole Cabinet. It would
be indeed impossible to set out in detail the course of this long and
sometimes painful story. Some notable accounts have already been
published, to which I can only add personal memories of the chief
incidents.

A few days after the debates in Parliament it became necessary to
prepare

the draft of a letter from me to Professor Erhard (President for the month) making Britain's formal application to join the European Community. This was not too easy to draft and everyone had different views. Lord Privy Seal (Heath) was acting for Foreign Office. Eventually a text was agreed. I signed it; it was sent to London and will go by bag to Bonn tonight. This is quite an historic affair. Six months after I concocted the Grand Design at Chequers after Christmas![1]

Our troubles were not slow to begin. At a meeting of the Commonwealth Economic Consultative Council in Accra on 12 to 14 September, the atmosphere was somewhat strained. This was largely due to the Canadian representatives, whose opposition to our move towards Europe was marked and even acrimonious. Nor was Nkrumah, although pleased to have the meeting in his capital, disposed to make himself complaisant. Although my relations with Diefenbaker were always pleasant enough, I could never quite discover the basis of his political thought. He seemed to me to be unduly influenced by internal political situations, which necessarily change from time to time, and to pay too little regard to the great underlying movements of world affairs.

A few days later I lunched with Eric Harrison, the Australian High Commissioner,

> to meet Harold Holt, Treasurer in the Australian Government. The High Commissioner is a good host. Holt held forth about the Common Market, and talked good sense, moderately and fairly. I was encouraged by this. He was very critical of the Canadian Government, who are (he says) out to smash United Kingdom Government by fair means or foul.[2]

Menzies, who was always loyal and helpful in all our difficulties, made the position of Australia quite clear in a letter of 6 October.

> We want the whole of our trade interests in the United Kingdom to be protected. These interests have their counterpart in United Kingdom interests in trade into Australia.[3]

In reply I said that Heath would begin by suggesting that there should be a continuation of duty-free entry into the British market,

[1] 9 August 1961.   [2] 27 September 1961.   [3] 8 October 1961.

but that it was unrealistic to believe that we could hope to keep everything unchanged. There must be some concessions. The real issue was that of judging our common interests.

A few days later, Jean Monnet

> came to luncheon . . . full of vigour as ever. He is very hopeful about the Common Market negotiations, and thinks that de Gaulle has changed his view about the question. Up to now, he has been hostile and this has been reflected all through the French bureaucratic hierarchy. But (so says Monnet) the mood has changed. I had to tell Monnet that I thought the difficulties here were growing—pressure from Canada and Australia; anxiety of farmers; Trade Union fear of 'competition', etc., etc. I therefore hoped that we could have a *quick* negotiation and get it over. If it dragged, opposition and pressure groups would grow in strength. Monnet agreed with this.[1]

On 10 October Heath made a formal declaration to the first official meeting of the Six in Paris. This was a most impressive paper prepared with all the joint resources at our disposal and was in effect a statement of our full case. Complete copies of the text were made available to the delegates, not only in English, but in French, German, Dutch and Italian. A fairly full summary was released to the Press and given to the Commonwealth and other diplomatic missions. The purpose of not releasing the full text was to avoid setting a precedent which might prove awkward regarding other documents as the negotiations proceeded. However, in the following weeks, from one source or another, the full document was leaked, and after some consultation with my colleagues I decided that it should be published in full.[2] On the whole I was glad of this incident because when the full paper became available there was general admiration for the masterly position of the British case.[3] Heath, at this opening meeting, gained that respect and even affection from his European colleagues which he has always retained.

Our next hurdle was at home. There had been much talk that the

[1] 8 October 1961.
[2] *The United Kingdom and the European Economic Community*, Cmnd. 1565 (H.M.S.O., November 1961).
[3] Camps, pp. 377–86.

opposition within the Party would soon show itself, especially at the annual Party Conference. In those days it was the custom of the Leader of the Party to appear only when the Conference was over and to deliver a somewhat pontifical oration with the purpose of summing up its results and inspiring the workers to new efforts. I received continual reports from my staff that

> the Common Market Debate this morning will be . . . difficult. Lord Beaverbrook and the *Daily Express* are making tremendous efforts to get hold of our chaps. Some (I fear) have fallen into the spider's web.[1]

However, all doubts were soon resolved.

> The Brighton Conference has gone very well so far. Yesterday the 'Common Market' received 'overwhelming' support. Only thirty or forty voted against, in a huge assembly of four thousand or more.[2]

At any rate we were on safe ground for the time being.

Meanwhile, before the main discussions could begin, there were some useful interchanges. Menzies was anxious for me to make an approach to the Common Market negotiators to allow Australia to be present when matters concerning their interests were discussed. Although I had much sympathy for his purpose, I could not believe that this proposal would receive a good response. I therefore told him that I thought the best way would be to arrange for the closest contacts between Heath and his team and any Australian or other Commonwealth representatives who should be available both in London and in Brussels. Towards the end of November I had an encouraging visit from the Canadian Finance Minister, Donald Fleming. Although his object was not altogether clear, it seemed that his real purpose was to express regret over some minor misunderstandings both in London and in Ottawa. I had always found Fleming most helpful; and, although I naturally did not express any sense of grievance, I was glad to have confirmation of his sympathy and understanding.

[1] 12 October 1961.   [2] 13 October 1961.

On 26 November General de Gaulle came to stay with me in my home at Birch Grove House. The visit is fully described in a previous volume.[1] Although our views as to the proper method of organising Europe were really very close, I was still left with doubts as to what his final position would be. I tried to impress upon my guest that the United Kingdom could not be expected to go on playing so great a part in the defence of Europe, involving such heavy expenditure across the exchanges, if she was permanently excluded from the Common Market and all the other institutions that might be expected to flow from a truly united European structure. To this he replied that the French were not opposed to the British but were concerned about 'the flock of British connections'. When I asked him what he meant by that, he said, America, the old Commonwealth, India, Africa, and so on. These would all want to rush in with Britain, thus swamping the very Europe that the Six were determined to preserve. I could not help pointing out that France had made very good arrangements for the countries of the old French Empire, and it was obvious that we could not cut adrift from the Commonwealth. Even if it were not an ignoble surrender of all we owed to history, this result would be worse from his own point of view. Canada, Australia and New Zealand would inevitably drift into the American orbit while the remainder would fall into Russia's lap. To this he made no answer; but I felt that while unwilling openly to oppose British accession to the Common Market he was relying on my proving unable to overcome the objections of the Commonwealth. He also asked me, on this as he was to do on subsequent occasions, whether I could really carry the Conservative Party into so revolutionary a position, contrary to all its traditions. It was clear that, while I was anxious to bring the matter to a rapid conclusion, he was much against any hasty action. I felt that speed was essential—he was for delay. This I knew would mean that the French would use all their skill in diplomacy to prolong the discussions and demand that every point of detail should be laboriously and minutely examined before it was finally resolved. So it was to prove. I naturally sent full accounts of our

[1] *Pointing the Way*, pp. 410–28.

discussions concerning the Common Market to my colleagues in Canada, Australia and New Zealand. I felt it important that they should learn directly from me the course of these talks.

An attempt to woo Lord Beaverbrook was not altogether successful. I wrote to him on 27 November:

> I had hoped to see you on Thursday at The Other Club last week. But I fear you were not able to come and I do hope you are better.
>
> Your papers continue to attack me with the 'rancour and asperity' appropriate to members of the Club.
>
> Nevertheless, I am proud to feel that I have your friendship.
>
> Let me know if there is a chance of seeing you – when do you leave England?

To this he sent a characteristic reply.

> It is most agreeable to me to hear from you. I was ill. Now I am well.
>
> Will you come to lunch with me one day? Any day you mention from next Tuesday to Friday.
>
> The newspapers are not backward in support for you. When you make an appeal to the country, they give full support.
>
> But there is unfortunately one situation on which you and they cannot be reconciled. That is of course the Common Market. This policy runs against the faith of the *Daily Express* in the Commonwealth, a traditional and ineradicable clause in our creed. As well ask us to repudiate the Presbyterian Church as give up this cause.
>
> My personal devotion to you remains unchanged. I have too many human defects, but lack of consistency in friendship is not, I am sure, among the number.[1]

The year ended with a message on 12 December from de Gaulle following his meeting with Adenauer. After giving an account of their views on the Berlin crisis he ended with these words:

> We also spoke about the Common Market, as well as the

---

[1] This letter and the one on pp. 516–17 are printed by kind permission of Sir Max Aitken and the First Beaverbrook Foundation.

question of the political unification of Europe. In both cases we reaffirmed our intention of pushing ahead, in the common hope that Great Britain might one day be able to join our organisation on the same footing as we are now.[1]

This somewhat enigmatic message could perhaps bear a hopeful interpretation. In the approaching mood of Christmas I decided to draw from it at least some encouragement.

[1] Nous avons également parlé du Marché Commun, ainsi que du problème de l'union politique de l'Europe. Aussi bien pour l'un que pour l'autre, nous avons ré-affirmé notre intention de faire avancer les choses, en souhaitant tous les deux que la Grande-Bretagne puisse se joindre un jour à notre organisation dans les mêmes condi-tions où nous nous y trouvons nous-mêmes.

CHAPTER II

The Pay Pause

O N the home front, 1962 began on a sombre note. In the words of the *Annual Register*:

> the year opened with the Government locked in direct conflict with the Unions over the Chancellor of the Exchequer's pay pause. Exactly on midnight, as the New Year began, the 160,000-strong Union of Post Office Workers began a month's work-to-rule in protest at the rejection on 18 November of their claim for a four per cent wage increase.[1]

Four per cent! One is astonished, a decade later, to recall the moderation of those years of 'Tory misrule'.

In order to make clear the situation with which we were confronted it is necessary to go back a few months. At the end of July 1961 the Treasury, supported or instigated by the Bank of England, had become seriously alarmed at the continued signs of inflation now reflected in an unfavourable balance of payments for the third year in succession. Although I was temperamentally opposed to some of the deflationary proposals which the 'authorities' seemed to think necessary, I was forced to agree to certain further measures of restriction. These involved new economies in public expenditure and more rigorous exchange control as well as deflationary steps calculated to curtail consumption, including the temporary raising of the Bank Rate to seven per cent. Nevertheless, it was already clear to me that the major problem which now confronted us was of a novel character. Our difficulties were not due to an attempt to run the economy at too great a rate or to the strains upon Government expenditure, whether at home or overseas. They were primarily

[1] *Annual Register*, 1962, pp. 1–2.

due to the simple fact that rising personal demand was not being met by rising productivity. This point was indeed emphasised by Selwyn Lloyd, the Chancellor of the Exchequer, in a statement to Parliament at the end of July 1961.[1] Wages and salaries had increased by eight per cent—national productivity only by three per cent—'a pay pause was now essential'. This explosion of wages, although comparatively modest at that time, has been a continuing problem facing successive post-war governments of whatever complexion. Nor have the orthodox methods of deflation and even of consequent unemployment brought the desired relief. Indeed within the last decade both the Labour and the succeeding Conservative administrations have been faced with the dual spectre of inflation and stagnation. The pay pause of 1961–2 was the first—no doubt amateurish—attempt to move towards what has afterwards become known as an 'incomes policy'. Since the concept was novel, and the leaders of the trade unions in Britain are conspicuous for their conservatism, the pay pause not unnaturally resulted in serious political difficulties and pressures as well as the prospect of widespread conflict involving bitter opposition to the Government of the day.

The financial situation was at any rate rapidly relieved. 'Sterling is strong and being supported by foreign buying.'[2] But this was only the beginning.

We must now face up to the wage battle. This will be decisive, one way or the other. Then there will be Government expenditure and the 1962–3 Estimates. We are bound to have trouble with the Ministers in the spending Departments—especially with Minister of Education. Nor will the Minister of Defence find it easy to make the economic cuts—especially the overseas economic cuts—which we must have. At the same time, what is the use of our scraping and scrounging to get £50–£150 million of 'economies', if the extra wage and salary bill of £1,000 million or more is presented again? If this happens, sterling must be devalued. Yet, if this is *not* to happen, there are bound to be one or more serious strikes.[2]

[1] *Pointing the Way*, pp. 377–80.
[2] 9 August 1961.

However, we must face 'the danger of strikes and how to keep services going (like electricity, gas, railways)'.[1]

In August I had been somewhat encouraged by the July figures which showed a substantial reduction in the trade gap. Although the final attitude of the trade unions was still uncertain, it was clear that their leaders were well aware that excessive wage claims would lead to inflation and consequently drastic measures of control. Unhappily, they dared not say this openly.

Meanwhile, the Chancellor of the Exchequer and I worked on a letter to be addressed to both sides of industry proposing the creation of the National Economic Development Council, drawn from trade unions, management and government who would participate in central planning advice. This imaginative proposal had been vaguely foreshadowed in Selwyn Lloyd's speech on 25 July. The discussion about this plan revealed

> a rather interesting and quite deep divergence of view between Ministers, really corresponding to whether they had old Whig, Liberal, *laissez-faire* traditions, or Tory opinions, paternalists and not afraid of a little *dirigisme*.[2]

However, after two long meetings my colleagues gave formal approval on 21 September. The letter was accordingly published and this institution, now commonly known as 'Neddy', has become an important and valuable part of our national machinery. Moreover, it has been fruitful in every sense of the word. For not only has it been a source of much valuable discussion and action at the top level, but it has given birth to a large number of so-called 'little Neddys' which industry by industry have contributed much to the greater improvement of labour relations as well as of productivity. To Selwyn Lloyd, supported by his advisers in the Treasury, belongs the credit for this forward-looking scheme.

As the autumn proceeded warning rumbles of trade union thunder grew louder and nearer. Yet on the whole the pay pause, the duration of which was expected to last until the following April, remained broadly operative. My colleagues decided, at the end of September, to stand firm on Civil Service wages. At the same time,

[1] 9 August 1961.   [2] 21 September 1961.

in the hope that confidence would be helped, the Bank Rate was reduced on 5 October to six and a half per cent. This cautious step was well received, and later, on 2 November, there was a further reduction to six per cent. But the struggle was only just about to begin:

> We are going to have trouble with the trade unions over the so-called M employees of the Government. We have 'imposed' a wages pause, as with other civil servants. But these men are in either Cousins's or Tom Williamson's Union, and they are threatening us with strikes.
>
> The position in the motor industry is curious. *Ford's* have not yet struck (over the tea-break). The unions are trying to get the men back at *Rootes'* Acton plant. This situation of 1,000 men is causing a complete hold-up of all Rootes factories, involving all their car production and thousands of men.
>
> In the building industry (including Mowlem's, who are doing No. 10 Downing Street) there are sporadic strikes, also about the tea-break in the morning. Meanwhile, our French, German and other European competitors are hard at work.[1]

Strange that tea, 'the cup that cheers but not inebriates', should prove industrially such a heady beverage! Naturally the political position of the Government began to be affected. There was a loss of popularity and confidence in the constituencies likely to be followed by a corresponding nervousness in the Parliamentary Party.

The Conservative Party had now been in office for ten years. It had won three consecutive General Elections with increasing majorities. Quite apart from the political and economic pressures, which were in fact no greater than normal, the public were becoming bored with the party and the party bored with itself.

> The trouble is that after ten years the Conservative Party has got pretty restive. There are too many ex-Ministers who had to be got rid of for incompetence . . . and too many young men still disappointed. Fortunately, I have got most of the ex-Ministers to the Lords, but those that are still with us are very critical and dangerous.[2]

[1] 8 October 1961.   [2] 30 November 1961.

One critic who had been one of the most incompetent Ministers in office that I could recall had suddenly become a great authority on the subject of which he had appeared almost ignorant when responsible. Another who had been a really bad administrator had become an admirable speaker – a quality which he had never shown when in office. A third, although still a bore and a complete failure at the minor post to which I appointed him on trial, had acquired a new authority below the gangway. What had once been regarded as pomposity was now hailed as profundity.

I had already been thinking, before the summer holidays, that some ministerial changes might be necessary and had talked this over with the Lord Chancellor, Kilmuir, early in August. But I knew that it would 'not be easy to get any vacancies without some painful decisions'.[1] In September, while struggling with the constitutional problems of Northern Rhodesia with all its complexities, and of the unresolved question of Berlin with all its dangers, I began to cogitate seriously about our affairs at home.

Philip de Zulueta came for luncheon. It was a fine day and we had a walk. In the evening, I dictated the first draft of a speech for the Conservative Conference in October. We have now begun to go rather badly *down* in the Gallup Poll. This was bound to happen at some point during this Parliament and I would prefer to have it now rather than later. It is due to *three* main causes.

1. Gaitskell's very patriotic and successful stand against 'Unilateralism' has undoubtedly increased his national stature.

2. Our economic troubles are attributed to the Government – the 'stop and go' policy, as they call it. Some critics say we ought to have *more* planning. Others say that we have never given the 'Liberal' economy a chance, because of our excessive fear of unemployment. The ordinary public are puzzled, and blame us.

3. The Foreign and Colonial problems have frightened people. They have not full confidence that we can handle them.

All this together means that (in the words of Churchill when he told a waiter to take away a messy pudding) 'We have no *theme*.'[2]

One of the immediate needs was to find a full-time Chairman for

[1] 7 August 1961.   [2] 16 September 1961.

the party. Butler with his usual good nature had agreed not only to shoulder the responsibility of his own difficult and even delicate office—he was Home Secretary—but to act as Leader of the House. Immediately after the General Election I had asked him to take on the Chairmanship of the Party, for I was anxious to give the progressive tone to our party which this appointment would assure. In addition to these already onerous tasks I now had to ask him to undertake the co-ordination of the work of Ministers concerned with the question of Europe and the Common Market. This fourth duty would be calculated to break the back even of so patient and unselfish a political camel.

> I have had a talk with Butler about all this and I have persuaded him to give up the Chairmanship of the Party to a younger man (if I can find the right one) who could devote his *whole* time to thinking, organising and speaking. We agreed that the right man for the job (if he can be persuaded to do it) is Iain Macleod, now Colonial Secretary. He could help me to recreate a sense of purpose—a movement—almost a crusade. The speech that I am preparing for the Conference would give the lead.[1]

The next step was to approach Iain Macleod.

> I had a long talk last night with Macleod about the future of the Party, and the idea of his taking on as Chairman. He is attracted by it; but I think he fears that he will be said to have been got rid of from the Colonial Office. This may be said by some; but, of course, for me to appoint him Chairman is a mark of complete confidence. I did not press the issue too far but asked him to reflect and talk to the Chief Whip.
>
> I saw the Chief Whip this morning (who is keen on the idea and goes further in thinking that Iain might perhaps lead the House as well, Rab becoming in fact, if not in name, 'Deputy Prime Minister'). Chief Whip and Iain will have a talk. Then Rab must be seen again. This is a very delicate affair and must not be rushed.[2]

On 21 September Butler came to luncheon after the Cabinet.

> The position reached after a most frank and helpful talk was

---

[1] 16 September 1961.   [2] 18 September 1961.

that he would think about it further this weekend. The new proposition is

1. Macleod to become Chairman of the Party and Leader of the House, with a sinecure office.

2. Butler to retain the Home Office.

It would be announced that owing to growing pressure of work, in foreign and home spheres, on the Prime Minister, Butler (by relinquishing the Leadership of the House and the Party Chairmanship) would have time to help me in Committees, Cabinet, etc. He cannot be appointed to the post of Deputy Prime Minister officially. There are three reasons for this. (I have had looked up all the precedents, including the recent one between Churchill and the Palace about Eden in 1952.)

1. The Queen has in the past rightly pointed out that there is *no* such official post, for which Queen's approval is required.

2. I must not let the Press say that I am failing in mind and health!

3. I must not be accused of trying to appoint my successor, and thus injure the prerogative or try to bind the Party.

Nevertheless, I think we can (following the Churchill–Eden precedent) find a form of words for the purpose of covering Rab's abandonment of two important posts. At any rate, I hope we can, for these moves will be of great value to the Party and our hopes of reviving our fortunes before the next Election.[1]

With characteristic generosity Butler informed me, within a day or two, of his agreement to this plan, and it was only necessary to discuss the consequential changes. Maudling would move to the Colonial Office in Macleod's place and would be succeeded at the Board of Trade by Freddie Erroll. These changes, when announced on 9 October, were well received by the Press.

> The significance of Macleod becoming Chairman is well understood. It means 'Progressive Toryism'.[2]

Among the changes was the revival in the Treasury of the old office of Chief Secretary, to which I appointed Henry Brooke, and to which by a curious chance my son, Maurice, was appointed in 1970. This double-backing of the Chancellor of the Exchequer

[1] 21 September 1961. [2] 10 October 1961.

received widespread support. I was a little anxious as to whether Butler waș wholly reconciled to the new arrangement, but was somewhat relieved to hear that so far from showing any ill-feeling he was claiming authorship of the new plan.

We were now approaching the period of the Conservative Conference, and I was grateful to Hailsham for sending me his suggestions. He felt that in my speech at the end of the Conference, rather than touching on the great variety of topics covered through-out the preceding days, I should be 'simple, direct and geared to action'. The trouble about this advice was that although admirably attuned to a position when one's policies have seen the light of day, it is not so valuable during the long period of gestation. We were committed to the pay pause; but we had scarcely begun to think out a coherent 'incomes policy'. When the Party Conference met the delegates seemed chiefly interested in the reference to the Common Market and to the problem of immigration, which was now begin-ning to exercise the public mind. Nevertheless, the question of the pay pause and the pending struggle on this issue was ever present. The Chancellor of the Exchequer was to take the main part in this discussion, and I ventured to send him a note on 3 October before the Conference met.

> I suppose you read the *Daily Worker*. It is much the best paper for us to study. The leading article today should give you great help, for it points out that Mr. Harold Wilson and Co. are not against the wage freeze; their resolution is against a breach of arbitration but not against wage restraint. Indeed, as the *Worker* rightly says, Mr. Wilson, introducing the debate on Signposts for the Sixties, argued that a Labour Government could get the people to agree to sacrifices and restraint better than the Tories. Their slogan, therefore, should be 'Vote Labour and bigger and more pauses'. I think there is quite a point to be made out of this, perhaps at Brighton. Anyway, I hope you read the *Daily Worker* every day.

Unhappily, these great issues are settled not by arguments but by events. The reactions of the Press to the discussions at the Conference were interesting.

> The Beaverbrook Press subdued; the *Guardian*, . . . chagrined

at the disappearance of Colonel Blimp. The *Herald* is more generous, especially about the Common Market. *The Times* has a leader on Butler and Crime, written in its most 'auntie' mood. The *Daily Telegraph* is fairly polite to the Government. The *Mirror* is very good, praising Her Majesty's Government and the Conservative Party about the Common Market. What particularly pleases me is (*a*) the *image* of the Party—as liberal (with small 'l'), progressive, modern, efficient—is restored; (*b*) its catholicity is emphasised—Aristocrat—Lord Home; Academic and Civil Service tradition—Butler; the new managerial type—Heath; the strong political character—Sandys; the progressive intellectual —Macleod; all of [whom] had equal success.[1]

On the industrial front, however, the signs were bad.

There is a new row in South Wales steel works as well as in Ford's and Rootes. The railways are threatening to strike. The 'rough' industrial winter which I feared has started. But it's better than just sliding into inflation and it's better to have it in 1961–2 than in 1963–4.[1]

Happily, before the economic debate in the House of Commons timed for 23 October, the teachers called off their threatened strike. Nevertheless, the labour situation remained dangerous.

The Rootes strike goes on at Acton, where 1,000 'unofficial' strikers are putting many thousands of men out of work in Coventry—with great loss to exports. Ford is better, and the strike is over. The steel strike in South Wales continues—15,000 men out of work over a silly dispute concerning 300-odd furnace bricklayers, whose wages are said to run from £35 to £60, or £70 a week![2]

A few days later another complicated question arose. This was

whether or not to agree with Lord Robens and the Coal Board, who want to raise the price of Scottish coal by 15s. 0d. a ton. Scottish coal is run at a heavy loss, year after year. Lord Robens wants to *reduce* demand and so help in closing the worst pits. But how do we reconcile this with (say) putting half the new steel plant with Colville's in Scotland—for social reasons—instead of in South Wales, for economic reasons?[3]

[1] 13 October 1961.　　　[2] 24 October 1961.　　　[3] 26 October 1961.

Meanwhile

the likelihood of a strike in the Power Stations is growing. Foulkes (the Electric Trades Union leader) has asked for £2 immediately. This is intolerable, both as to amount and date. But these 150,000 have the whole country in pawn. Owing to the greater interlocking and great complication of these plants, we cannot do what we did in the General Strike of 1926. We could produce little or quite insufficient power to meet the needs of a nation now wholly geared, industrially and domestically, to electricity.[1]

Today, with the experience of subsequent years, the problems and complications in any policy of wage restraint are well understood. No doubt when the Chancellor of the Exchequer first proposed this temporary alleviation of our economic difficulties in July 1961, neither he nor his colleagues had a clear picture of all that was implied. In any event our conception of the pay pause was an appeal to the common sense and patriotism of all concerned—employers, employed and the general public. But as the months passed we began to realise the complexities of a policy spread over such a wide field. In many industries there were agreements for automatic pay increases in accordance with any rise in the cost of living; in others agreements had already been made for a rise within the near future; in others negotiations were proceeding. In addition, arbitration agreements ruled over quite a wide field. Were these to be suspended or set aside? Similarly among the Government's own employees there were many different groups. With some of the Civil Service Associations there were arrangements similar to those in private industry either for automatic rises as the cost of living increased or for arbitration procedures. In others there had been a long understanding that certain groups of industrial employees of the Government, as opposed to administrative classes, should fall within the wage arrangements in allied industries. Finally, there were the large number employed by the nationalised industries. What authority should the Government attempt to exercise over their chiefs whose legal position in relation to the central Government was delicate and obscure? Could a general directive be issued?

[1] 26 October 1961.

Could a specific order be given? Or could we only appeal to a sense of patriotic duty? Moreover, since the pay pause was only conceived of as a temporary expedient, to be abandoned if the economy seemed to justify it or to be succeeded by some other system more carefully perfected, were we to accept the inevitable leakages, hoping that the temporary dam, in spite of its imperfections, might at least stem the flood?

All these questions, long simmering, came to the boil with the decision reached by the Electricity Board in a wage dispute with their employees.

> There has been the first serious breach in the Wages Pause. This is due partly to the weakness of the Electricity Board and partly to [that] of the Minister. . . . The negotiators, after eleven hours' argument, rang up [the Minister] late on Thursday night, and told him that they could see no alternative to a settlement on terms *far* worse than the Board had—informally but firmly—agreed with Ministers. This settlement gave 2*d*. instead of 1*d*. increase (per hour) and agreed to 28 January instead of 1 April. . . . [The Minister] protested over the telephone but *did nothing*. He should have urged the negotiator to break off the talks or adjourn them. He should have at once informed me, or the Chancellor of the Exchequer, or Lord Mills.[1]

The next day a hue and cry began both in the Press and in the Party. Even so normally balanced a journal as the *Economist* declared:

> the Government deserves the deepest censure for its contribution to the electricity wages surrender; and it is no good the Prime Minister wringing his hands like an impotent Pontius Pilate and saying that it was impossible for him and his Cabinet colleagues to avert it.

It can well be imagined that the more popular newspapers used even stronger language.

At a well-attended meeting of the Party there seemed to be a general feeling that the pay pause could not successfully be maintained without legal powers. Nevertheless, I felt it would be quite wrong to be rushed into any hasty decision. Nor did it seem fair to require the Minister's resignation. I dealt with the matter in the

[1] 20 November 1961.

House of Commons by making a carefully prepared statement which was not too badly received. It was my purpose to minimise the incident as far as possible. But the immediate repercussions were dangerous. Either the whole policy of the pay pause would collapse prematurely or we would be forced to take legal powers—a most hazardous course, at least at this stage.

> The Party are very worried—and rightly. The important thing is to steer them away from demanding foolish remedies.[1]

Partly as a result of this affair and partly because of the personal feelings against me entertained by some active spirits in the Right wing of the Party who had always viewed me with disapproval, the weeks before Christmas were not altogether happy.

However, when the day came for a full-dress debate, on 18 December, in spite of all the alarms, the Government obtained good support.

> The Economic Debate went very quietly. We got a majority of ninety-two (on a *two*-line whip) which shows that the Party is beginning to recover its balance.[2]

Indeed, the Congo crisis, which had suddenly blown up in the House of Commons, seemed to be more immediately alarming than the wage issue.[3]

Nevertheless there were the consistent *Frondeux* who took advantage of each successive opportunity to make trouble.

> There was revealed a hard core—ten to twenty M.P.s on our side—who are so bitter against me and my 'progressive' colleagues that they will use every difficulty or every critical situation to work up a large-scale revolt. They cannot normally attract the 'respectable' or 'middle' opinion in the Party. But they can get some of them in on a special issue—e.g. Queen's visit to Ghana; Congo; breach of Pay Pause by Electricity settlement; Immigration Bill; Loans to Coal Industry, etc. . . . But I think few want a dissolution or a break-up of the Government.[4]

On 13 December, before leaving to meet President Kennedy in Bermuda I sent the Queen a summary of the situation as it stood at the end of the year.

[1] 21 November 1961. [2] 18 December 1961.
[3] *Pointing the Way*, pp. 451–5. [4] 20 December 1961.

On the home front the economic battle continues. On the whole we have held the line on wages fairly well. As in any campaign, an action is lost here and there, but broadly speaking the position has so far been maintained. The Government servants have had the pause enforced upon them, whether industrial or non-industrial. A large number of settlements which the Minister has no legal right to hold up indefinitely have been at least put off from the early autumn until 1 January, and we have succeeded in maintaining this principle with the Firemen. Although this was misunderstood by the Press and was represented as a defeat in fact it was a victory, for the local authorities gave in to our threat that if they settled as they wanted to do—for an early date in October—we would not pay the extra grant concerned. The Electricians got away with it through the feebleness of the Board, which I publicly rebuked. However, if I may be quite frank with Your Majesty, it has the advantage that we have retreated, perhaps not in a very orderly fashion, but in any case retreated, from the one point in the line which it is in fact impossible to hold, for we have no technically effective method by which electric power could be produced on any reasonable scale in the event of a strike.

And so it goes on.

On the constructive aspect, the 'planning' proposals of the Chancellor, I am much more hopeful. I think the Trade Unions will come along sooner or later—there are some quite friendly signs. It would obviously be better if we could concentrate not so much on the battle of dividing up the tiny bit of additional cake available each year as on a real effort to increase the size of each new baking. I am sure that with a real effort by all concerned this could be done.

On the sterling front we have had one or two shocks but on the whole we have done fairly well. I do not yet know how December will work out but November showed a profit of £59 million, of which we used £50 million to repay some of our debt to the International Monetary Fund.

During the Christmas holiday, I recorded my thoughts in a somewhat gloomy mood:

The problems which now confront Britain, internally and externally, are really terrifying. No one seems to realise their complexity, although the public are dimly aware of the dangers and *resent* being the victims, when in so many ways life could be so agreeable.[1]

I was beginning to find that my constant journeys tired me more each time, and these discussions took a tremendous lot 'out of one'.[1] Nor was there much encouragement to be obtained from the Press which

> continues critical of the Government. *The Times* is particularly smug and irritating. Happily, I think the Press, with its gossip and sneering and pomposity and pettiness—as well as its downright lies—is losing influence every day. Television, I.T.V., Radio—these are the instruments. Kennedy told me that he was using the television to appeal to the people over the heads of a broadly hostile Press. I wonder whether a monthly Press Conference on American lines would be a good thing for me to try.[1]

These few days unhappily promised but little respite.

> It seems now agreed that I should go to Bonn on 8 or 9 January to see Adenauer. This is really quite unnecessary and may even introduce complications. But since everyone else has visited everyone (with this exception) in the last few weeks, this visit will complete the international quadrille.[1]

At the opening of the year 1962 the Government faced many complicated and baffling economic and human issues. We had to maintain at least until the spring the policy of the pay pause announced by the Chancellor of the Exchequer six months before. While we could not hope it would be a completely watertight system, we believed it might give the economy a temporary relief from those ills which were caused by the undoubted rise in wage costs without a corresponding increase in productivity. Although these were not upon the staggering scale to which we have since become accustomed, yet they were greater than we felt the country could stand. If the percentages were three, four, five or—at the very worst—ten per cent rather than twenty or thirty per cent and the sums involved a few shillings rather than several pounds, yet the effect of a continued wage inflation was likely to be equally disagreeable. We might have

[1] 23 December 1961.

to accept devaluation, to be followed, as the effects of the drug wore off, by large-scale unemployment. For myself, I felt devaluation more suitable to a Labour than to a Conservative Government. At any rate, it was no solution to fundamental problems. But the pay pause could only be temporary; and we must try to work out during the interval allowed us some other satisfactory and permanent system. In other words, we must become pioneers in the field of what is now generally called an 'incomes policy'—at that time an almost unknown concept, now for good or ill a household word. But I was equally determined that this negative policy should be accompanied by more positive action; hence my enthusiastic support for the Chancellor of the Exchequer's bold proposal—the National Economic Development Council. At the same time I was always anxious lest he should yield to the pressure for deflation exerted upon him by the officials in the Treasury and the Bank of England. I did not believe that the wage inflation, particularly at the comparatively modest levels of those times, could be cured by a general deflationary policy on the orthodox models recommended so consistently by Montagu Norman, and followed, so slavishly, by successive Chancellors of the Exchequer between the wars. We had already induced the authorities to agree to successive reductions of Bank Rate. At the beginning of 1962 it stood at six per cent. I hoped for further reductions and for a corresponding relaxation in the monetary system by the increase of banking facilities. At the same time we had to deal with a not unnatural sense of disappointment in the Party, inside and outside the House, and nerve ourselves against the inevitable by-elections in which Conservative seats would be difficult to hold and Conservative voters would either melt away into abstention or be deluded by the vague promises of a now reviving Liberal Party. If we could survive all these troubles and contrive a Budget which, while not being popular, could command respect, I felt little doubt that at the end of the summer our strength would be largely restored. In the immediate future, however,

> everything turns on (*a*) holding on to the wage *pause* for two or three more months; (*b*) being able to slide into 'wage restraint'; (*c*) getting started the machinery for a long-term policy.[1]

[1] 5 January 1962.

The struggle now began in earnest. Although it is strange to reflect that in the great majority of cases the increases demanded were all of an order which would now seem modest, yet the principles were important; and the issue was being watched by the whole world. As always in these matters there was a good deal of the ludicrous mixed up with the serious aspect. The Post Office workers were now 'working to rule'. The public, only mildly annoyed about the delay in the distribution of letters or parcels, was seriously alarmed at the possibility that the football pools traffic would be dangerously affected. However, this was happily avoided. Moreover, a typical national argument began about the difference between 'working to rule' and 'going slow'. The first could be justified on traditional grounds and, by a curious paradox, led normally to considerable overtime earnings. The second could be penalised with loss of wages. The Post Office Engineering Union followed their postmen colleagues on 20 January with similar action, and their protest was to continue until the middle of March. Both the white-collar unions and the industrial unions were watching the outcome of this dispute. But when the Civil Service Clerical Association announced on 4 January that they would follow the same tactics, the Chief Secretary, Henry Brooke, assured them that the Government intended to restore an unfettered system of arbitration *after* the end of the pay pause which was expected to be at the end of March. This led to the union leaders being able to control the militants and continue normal working.

The industrial unions were now beginning to press their own wage demands; as a preliminary to the campaign a number of one-day strikes took place in the tubes and the electrified railways. Similar action was taken over part of the engineering industry. Among all these troubles there was always some slight relief. In the words of the *Annual Register*:

> To send a final chill through the nation's heart, all 120 workers employed in the manufacture of cricket balls threatened on 26 January to come out on strike if they did not receive an extra 6*d.* an hour; this disaster at least was averted.[1]

[1] *Annual Register, 1962*, p. 2.

The Chancellor of the Exchequer, after a meeting with the leaders of the Trades Union Congress on 5 January, sent them an important letter asking for their co-operation in keeping increased earnings in 1962 within the limit set by the Treasury estimate of the probable rise in productivity. This was calculated at two and a half per cent; and this principle, which was to operate after the end of the pay pause, soon became known as 'the guiding light'—a curiously Victorian phrase, with all its implications. Although the official reply of the T.U.C. was by no means encouraging, yet the publication of the correspondence was well received by the public:

> A meeting with the Chancellor of the Exchequer. The letter to the T.U.C. has gone well. We are now faced with the wage demands of the Coal Miners and the Railwaymen (as well as Gas, Bus, and some other public employees). The 'go-slow' in the Civil Service is 'off'. (It has produced a great many bitter jests. How *could* the Civil Service go any slower?)[1]

My diary reflects the development of this strange and rather ragged battle.

> Chancellor of the Exchequer at 11.30. We agreed a statement on Railway Wages, to be issued by the Treasury to which Dr. Beeching has at last been induced (by the combined efforts of Lord Mills, John Hare and Ernest Marples) to agree. We hope this will lead to arbitration. But it is *not* a binding arbitration on either side. The Post Office 'go slow' is still going on, and the leaders are issuing threatening statements. But there are indications that the men are getting fed up with it.[2]

Amidst all these troubles, it was some encouragement to learn that the Economic Committee of the T.U.C. had agreed to join the N.E.D.C. Although they only consented to do so on the express understanding that their representatives were not expected to preach wage-restraint to their affiliated unions, yet their association with the productive and positive side of our policy would at least lead them to greater understanding of the real problems with which the nation was confronted.

At this time, before the meeting of Parliament, I felt that 'at

[1] 15 January 1962.   [2] 19 January 1962.

home ... we are making ground on the "pay pause" and the
economic front generally'.[1] On 24 January I delivered a broadcast
speech covering a wide range of topics, part of the theme being
devoted to the simple argument that whatever our policies might be
in any sphere of effort we had to *earn* our place in a changing world.
Although the speech was said to have been acceptable to the public
as a whole I did not feel satisfied. There was a mood of disappointment throughout the country, which would soon begin to show
itself not merely in increased industrial pressure but in a lack of
political support. Nevertheless, when Parliament met, the Party
seemed by no means discouraged.

> The Railway wages decision which we have taken has caused
> a storm of protest. This is the contrary to what we expected. We
> thought we should be attacked for weakness. We are being
> attacked for strength![2]

But the Cabinet, happily engaged in arguing about next year's
estimates, seemed firm and resolute.

On 29 January, a few days after the House met, there was not
unnaturally a Labour vote of censure of our wage policy; but it did
not appear to make a great impression either in the House or
outside. The most important statement made in this debate was the
announcement by John Hare, the Minister of Labour, on behalf of
the Government, that the end of the pay pause proper would come
on 31 March. Thereafter a new and slightly more flexible system
would begin to operate.

There were long discussions as to what form this new system
should take, and the Government's first thoughts were set out in
the Chancellor of the Exchequer's White Paper, *Incomes Policy:
The Next Step*.[3]

> This set down the criteria by which the Government intended
> to judge, and meant others including arbitration tribunals to
> judge, wage demands according to the national interest. Thus
> increases in the cost of living would by themselves be no justifica-
> tion for wage rises (an attempt to cut into one of the chief
> inflationary spirals of the post-war period); increased productivity

---

[1] 19 January 1962.   [2] 24 January 1962.
[3] Cmnd. 1626 (London, February 1962).

in an industry would not be sufficient reason unless it had been achieved by people accepting more exacting work, or more onerous conditions, or by a renunciation of restrictive practices; the principle of comparability would no longer be acceptable, since it meant that one inflationary increase was promptly followed by others; and industries should think of the national pattern before bidding up the price for labour.[1]

Although the sentiments were excellent, the publicity campaign which the Chancellor of the Exchequer and the Treasury were trying to run seemed to meet with little response. On the other hand there were some hopeful signs:

> The Post Office workers have given up their 'working to rule' – after a month. It is satisfactory that the P.M.G. had made *no* concession to obtain this. It looks as if the unofficial 'one day's' strike or go slow on the Railways and Tubes will be abandoned. So we *are* gaining some ground.[2]

At the beginning of February Lord Robens offered the miners four per cent, and Beeching three per cent to the railwaymen. Two of the three railway unions came to see me on 14 February in view of the threatened strike.

> We had a good deal of discussion amongst Cabinet colleagues and Treasury experts about what I was to say. Finally, a document was agreed, from which I did *not* repeat *not* depart. I gave the Union representatives no promise or commitment. But I tried (on this somewhat arid basis) to provide a 'gleam of hope'. Three hours' talk; much consumption of whisky; etc., etc. It was announced yesterday that there would be no strike. This was a great relief. The Press is very kind: 'Mac's triumph', etc., etc. How quickly it changes. Up till the debate in the House, the 'bomb' initiative, and the settled railway strike, it has been the ageing and feeble Premier.[3]

After the railway strike I wrote a note on 16 February to Lord Mills, who had been a tower of strength throughout these troubles.

> This is just to thank you for all your help about recent economic

[1] *Annual Register, 1962*, p. 3.   [2] 2 February 1962.
[3] 16 February 1962.

questions, especially the railway wage problem. It was a very great help to me to have you to lean upon.

What I am anxious about now is that we should not appear to let the railways down by being bullied into higher figures by other industries or groups over whom the Government has control. What, for instance, is going to happen about the gas workers? Will you keep an eye on [this]; for the railwaymen would have a legitimate grievance if we suddenly gave the gas workers four per cent.

Thus this somewhat ragged and inconclusive battle continued; but on the whole we could feel reasonably satisfied. The teachers were told that their salaries could not increase by more than three per cent, and they seemed to accept the situation. The nurses were offered two and a half per cent, and their representatives organised a protest campaign which, in view of the low scale of salary paid to nurses, naturally received much public support. Yet if Ministers were to abandon the general principle in the spheres in which they were especially responsible it would be hopeless to expect the rest of industry to make any effort. By the time the pay pause ended it could not be denied that the Government, although it had incurred much unpopularity, had gained at least part of its objective. The economic medicines had begun to work; the balance of payments for 1961 had turned out better than we had hoped, and the prospects for 1962 looked good. The first stage therefore was concluded, and some, though insufficient, thought had been given to the next phase. Meanwhile, the political situation during these months was, if not alarming, sufficiently unfavourable to encourage our critics and cause some anxious flutterings in the hearts of the less stalwart of our friends.

At the beginning of February I addressed a crowded meeting of the 1922 Committee, a body which includes all the Conservative Members of Parliament other than Ministers. The proceedings were supposed to be secret; but naturally, with an audience of between two and three hundred, this rule was more honoured in the breach than in the observance.

The newspapers today published long and very tendentious

accounts of this 'private' meeting. Chief Whip is naturally upset.[1]

The next day a new incident created quite a stir. An agreeable, but somewhat eccentric M.P., Sir Harry Legge-Bourke, made a speech, full of praise of me, but saying I should retire, exhausted, in favour of a younger P.M.[2] Naturally this outburst made a new sensation. Many of my friends wrote angrily in my defence; but those best acquainted with the House of Commons knew how little importance need be attached to such an affair. The public, however, was no doubt temporarily impressed by the importance given to what the popular Press called, in huge black lettering, 'the revolt against Macmillan' and to lurid accounts of the palace revolution which was preparing. Fortunately, there was an important Foreign Affairs Debate on 5 February, in which I felt sure that I had retained my position, at any rate in Parliament.

On the whole, yesterday was a good day. The Press (as usual) with the exception of the *Manchester Guardian*, makes *no* attempt at an objective account of the debate. The *Daily Mirror*'s headline is MAC FLOPS ($4\frac{1}{2}$ million). The *Daily Express* is MAC TRIUMPHS (also $4\frac{1}{2}$ million circulation). The *Daily Telegraph* is peevish.... *The Times* is 'wet'.... And so on. But one can always tell. I know that the House of Commons thought my speech was good—*not* a triumph, *not* rhetoric, but good, persuasive oratory. The Party were satisfied, and more—almost enthusiastic. There are the malignant opponents ... who will never be satisfied. There are the nice cranks, like Legge-Bourke, who now tells everyone that he did not see my broadcast or hear my speech to the 1922 Committee, yet has made these two incidents the ground for his attack on me.... Gaitskell opened, with a good speech. I followed. Harold Wilson wound up for Opposition in his usual style 'one long smear'. Ted Heath wound up for us, with a good slashing reply. Majority ninety-eight (four of our chaps, coming from Yorkshire, were two hours late—or we would have had one hundred and two). Churchill came and sat on the front bench by my side while the division was being announced, and we walked out slowly together (he leaning heavily on my arm) amid applause.[3]

[1] 2 February 1962.   [2] 3 February 1962.   [3] 6 February 1962.

c

The next night I had to address seven hundred bankers at the Guildhall, presided over by my friend, Walter Monckton. I have always thought that to face one banker is quite an ordeal; but in addressing seven hundred I felt like Daniel entering the lions' den. I had not had time to prepare a speech; although the draft that had been put into my hands was no doubt an admirable dissertation, I did not feel in the mood to read it out. I tore it up and spoke 'off the cuff'. As so often happens the obvious spontaneity was agreeable to an audience no doubt sated with academic essays. An intelligent commentator wrote in the *Daily Telegraph* the next day:

> the Prime Minister's emphasis on the strength of sterling and the rise in the reserves is the Government's answer to charges that the measures of 25 July, including the pay pause, have failed.
>
> Since then the reserves have risen by more than the amount of I.M.F. loan, of which £150 m. has been repaid. Home demand has fallen, imports have stopped rising and the index of weekly wage rates has advanced by little more than half compared with the corresponding period twelve months before.
>
> One of the Government's problems is to draw these favourable factors to the attention of overseas opinion without giving the impression at home that the economic battle is as good as won. Hence the complaint that Ministers, and especially Mr. Macmillan, veer between optimism and pessimism.

This was an accurate summary of a dilemma with which Ministers, in a democratic country, are often confronted, in peace and war.

A few days later I recorded:

> The broad political situation is unchanged. The Government has lost popularity; but the Opposition have not gained it. In the various 'Gallup Polls', the numbers of Liberal and 'don't-know' voters seem to grow. This is due to the natural swing away from a Government that has been ten years in power, while the Labour Socialist Party has no glamour and no theme. In the Government itself, many Ministers are tired; the older ones from natural causes, the younger ones because I don't think young people today have learned how to work. The really appalling burden—physical as well as intellectual—that falls on us nowadays would astonish a trim City tycoon. No 'working man' would stand it for a week. I am in fairly good health—for my age—but only by

taking great care of myself, resting (if possible in bed) whenever I can. Perhaps the most exhausting things are the personal problems—Cabinet disagreements, dark threats of resignation, etc. These have been rather more frequent lately than some years ago. This too is natural. In 1956 the ship was practically sinking and no one thought of anything but keeping it afloat.[1]

The important thing for me was to appear calm and good humoured.

Yesterday I came into the smoking-room and found myself at a table with Sir Harry Legge-Bourke. The poor man was very embarrassed, and tried to move away. But I got him talking; bought him a drink; and got a lot of friends to gather round. The news of the settlement of the Railway question had just been announced, and there were many congratulations from Labour as much as from Conservatives. Poor Harry seemed to be wondering whether the poor old Prime Minister was really past it after all, only fit to be put out to grass or sent to the knackers.[1]

In a number of by-elections—as I expected—the voters began to show their lack of confidence in the Government by voting not for the Socialist but for the Liberal candidate. Many of them no doubt thought that this was a way of giving a reproof to Ministers; it by no means indicated that this so-called Liberal revival would survive into a General Election. It is one thing to administer a warning to a Conservative Government with a majority of one hundred; it is quite another to risk at a General Election the return of the Socialists. On 8 and 13 March there were by-elections at Lincoln and Blackpool. In both the Conservative did badly—in the latter only narrowly retaining a safe seat against a Liberal challenge. At Middlesbrough East, on 14 March, Labour held the seat (as expected) but the Liberals moved into second place. Now, there came the staggering blow of Orpington. Considered one of the safest Conservative seats in the country, here a majority of nearly 15,000 was turned into a loss to the Liberals by some 8,000, the Labour vote virtually disappearing. The effect of this series of by-elections culminating in Orpington can well be imagined. Although the Labour Party could take only a moderate satisfaction from this result, the Liberals became almost hysterical. Mr. Grimond who

[1] 16 February 1962.

had described this success as 'an incredible result' was even believed
to be beginning to pick a new Government. Meanwhile the fifth of
the series, on 22 March at Pontefract, where, with no Liberal
standing, the swing from the Conservatives was minimal (less than
one per cent), seemed to confirm the view that the electors were
expressing their dislike of both the great parties and perhaps of the
Parliamentary system itself. In a word, what seemed to some critics
a proof of statesmanlike enlightenment appeared to others a sign of
incipient *poujadism*.

Largely in order to clear my own mind I put my thoughts on
paper.

The whole political situation has been dominated by a series
of by-election results which seem to indicate a dramatic change
(for the worse) in the fortunes of our party.... This has not
been due to the *Socialists*. They have held their own seats, without
change. But we have been swept off our feet by a *Liberal* revival.
Some say that this phenomenon is similar to what happened in
1956 – Tonbridge and Torrington. But it is far more pronounced,
and seems to indicate a real movement, representing or expressing
real grievances or emotions.... It is the revolt of the middle
classes or lower middle classes, who resent the vastly improved
conditions of the working classes, and are envious of the apparent
prosperity and luxury of the 'rich' – whether they live on office
expenses, capital gains, or capital. These white collar 'little men' –
clerks, civil servants, etc., have [in the past] voted Conservative
'to keep Labour out'. Now (especially at by-elections) they are
voting Liberal to 'give the Government a smack in the eye'. So
much for grievances – in this sense, it is (as *The Times* said) a
poujadiste movement.

Then there is fashion. It is getting dull to be a young Conservative. It is not at all smart to go Labour. Liberal is not in the
Establishment; has a flavour of 'something different'.

Most of all, it is a revolt against all the unsolved problems.
The Bomb (it favours the abolition of the British independent
deterrent); relations with Russia; NATO; Berlin; Rhodesia....
But it springs most from the Government's inability to keep the
economy on an even course of continuous progress. It deplores
'Stop and Go' or 'Acceleration and Brake'. It wants enormously
increased expenditure, and *reduced* taxation. It wants a larger

army, without conscription. It wants wage stability, without any restraint. In a word, it wants what we all want and know we can't have.

The Pay Pause—the Government's policy—has offended dons, schoolmasters, school-teachers, Civil Servants, clerks, nurses, public utility workers, railwaymen, and all the rest. But perhaps it is most resented by the doctors, dons, nurses, etc., who feel that they are *relatively* ill paid, compared to the high wages which they hear about coming in to the ordinary artisan's household. Anyway, it is a portent. And the Tories are very worried. Naturally, their disappointment must find an outlet. This must, in the long run, mean an attack on the Leadership of the Party.[1]

How would this situation develop?

So far, there has been a mood of loyalty in most of the Party. 'Keep your nerve', 'Take it steady', 'Don't be rattled' were the slogans of the Conservative Central Council, which met (by hazard) the day after Orpington and which I attended. . . . The temper was firm. I had to go on 15 and 16 March to Liverpool and Manchester—two speeches (nominally non-party gatherings but largely Conservatives) and they seemed steady enough. Tory M.P.s are divided into different groups. But the enemies of the Leadership, already numerous, have undoubtedly been strengthened. . . .

I went to Bromley last night (23 March) for the Conservative Association's Annual Meeting. The audience—all members— were quite as loyal as ever, but (I thought) rather shaken. . . . I have had long talks with Selwyn Lloyd (Chancellor of the Exchequer) about the Budget. It cannot be popular. It will keep taxation about the same (with some increases and some decreases). The proposed tax on speculative gain—Stock Exchange or Land— will in theory please those who don't indulge, but will be violently opposed by those rich men in our party who keep up their standard of living by dabbling in the market, without income tax. Our plan is right—but there will be trouble.[1]

Further thought did not change my conclusion.

The political situation at home will certainly get *worse* from our point of view in the next series of elections. It will also show

[1] 24 March 1962.

in some fairly startling national [opinion] polls. . . . Really the Liberal revival is *not* a revival of Liberalism. They have *no* policy and *no* principles. They are purely opportunist. It is an *anti*-party movement. 'A plague on both your houses' is the real slogan. This is understandable, perhaps healthy. But it is *not* easy to deal with. If only something could go right on the foreign front! (But when it does, it's forgotten—like Cyprus.) On the home front, two reductions of Bank Rate within a fortnight shows that the medicine is working.

Nevertheless, the Sunday newspapers are all at one in prophesying the ignominious collapse of the Tory Party and a Liberal revival to the point of perhaps forming the next Government. . . . We have some bad months ahead. Then will come the decision on Europe and the Common Market. Whichever way it goes, it may well transform the face of British politics.

The more I reflect on the political situation, the more perplexed I am. We must *not* abandon our economic policies, which will perhaps bring their results. But we must, even if we can 'expand' again with more vigour, try to impose our 'incomes policy'. Otherwise, we shall merely fall into another sterling crisis. If we could get some improvement in the foreign situation, it would help. I fear the truth is that after ten years of unparalleled prosperity, the people are bored. Or perhaps . . . we have killed the class war and the fear of Socialism. So, by removing their fear, we have made it possible for people to gratify their exasperation at minor difficulties by voting against the Government. In a word, we have made England safe for Liberalism![1]

There was now another by-election pending—this time in my old seat, Stockton-on-Tees. The accounts that reached me from Iain Macleod, the new Chairman of the Party, were discouraging. The Liberal tide still seemed to be flowing on. Contrary to the advice of some of my intimate friends, but supported by that indomitable fighter, Iain Macleod, I decided to make a breach in tradition and to go myself to Stockton. I might perhaps be able to secure that we should at least reach the second place. I had fought six elections at Stockton—three successfully and three unsuccessfully. My wife and I had spent twenty-five years of our lives among the people. We

[1] 25 March 1962.

loved them dearly, and I think we could feel, without boasting, that they had some affection for us. It was at Stockton that my first knowledge of practical politics began. It was here that I had been through the terrible years of the Great Depression which left indelible marks upon my mind and heart. So, although conscious of the serious effect of a complete failure, I decided to take the risk. Dorothy and I started off as in the old days to tour the streets all day with a great meeting in the evening.

The whole of Monday [2 April] was occupied by an electioneering tour—from 10.30 a.m. to 10.30 p.m. The speech, in the Palais de Danse, seemed well received by a large audience. The general view was that the Liberal would be second and that we should be a bad third. However, much to my relief, we were second—by a short head. The news came through at midnight on Thursday and was certainly a great relief. People had been very divided as to the wisdom of my going to Stockton. But it has been proved right. The Press (even the usually hostile Press, like *The Times* and the *Daily Mail*) has been full of praise of my 'courage'.[1]

I took the opportunity of my speech at Stockton, a place so dear to me, after justifying my efforts to find a middle way between Socialism and *laisser-faire* capitalism, efforts which had been crowned by the dramatic change which had taken place in the happiness, comfort and wealth of the mass of the people, to make clear beyond doubt my personal commitment to the policy of trying to join the European Common Market:

Of course, it has its risks, its pitfalls—all great transactions have.
What I can now do is to hold out to you the Government's hope of success. Success in securing our Commonwealth interests. Success in securing the interests of our manufacturers and farmers. Success—at the end—in achieving an ever more dynamic influence in the affairs and the future of Western Europe and the Western World. These are high stakes. As high as any that Britain ever contemplated. High stakes—and the prospect of

[1] 7 April 1962.

high reward ... of peace and security, of rising prosperity and happiness for the British people.

All the people—the people in the great centres of industry like Tees-side, the people in the farming belts like those nearby.

The Common Market presents us with a tremendous challenge —and a gigantic opportunity. The Government accepts that challenge. It has seized that opportunity. But, of course, we have set about our negotiations with care as well as confidence. With responsibility as well as resource. This is not child's play. This is high policy—and we know what we are doing.

Yet the Liberal Party, having no responsibility and apparently very little interest in the Commonwealth, make this claim: 'The Liberals have been the only Party to say Britain *must* join the Common Market.'

And they would have us join right away—like that—without conditions and apparently without negotiations. They do not care at all what is to happen to the interests of the Commonwealth—Australia, Canada, New Zealand and all the new Commonwealth countries. Nor do they seem to care at all what happens to British agriculture. They would have us just apply to join, sign on the dotted line and become members of the club.

The Socialists, on the other hand, like cautious bathers, have just put a timorous toe into the water and promptly withdrawn it.

If the Liberals have plunged, the Socialists have shivered. Meanwhile we have done what I believe every serious person thinks is right; we have entered into negotiations to see whether we can join the European Community without injury to, and with proper safeguards for, all those towards whom we have responsibility—the Commonwealth, our own farmers and our trading partners in the other countries of Europe.

Surely this is the only course which is at once prudent and honourable.

The Stockton result confirmed my own analysis as to the loss of confidence in the Government.

The general view is that this is based not so much on the policy mistakes of Ministers as to their failure in public relations. Of course this is the usual excuse. I have known it all my life. The traditional form was to blame the Conservative Central Office. Now (rather more fairly) it is Ministers who cannot 'put over' their cases. The back-bench M.P.s (who don't seem to realise that this is their job) join in the general scare. Last week it seemed to me to be getting quite out of hand, and might, at any moment, turn into a panic. The Party has had ten years of success. The young M.P.s, especially, have no experience of defeat or even of serious set-backs. 1957 is not a true parallel. Our position in 1962 is much worse than then. I felt it right to take the Stockton gamble in order to give a lead. It has, so far, paid off. But I am, of course, not so foolish as not to realise how deep-seated is the general malaise. The Socialists do not gain. The Tory discontented vote Liberal—not because of Liberal personalities or policies, but as a protest. Naturally, the economic policies we have had to follow have been very unpopular. Now that the results are beginning to come (strong pound, lower Bank Rate, and improving balance of payments) we may begin a political recovery. But this time it will not be so easy. They really are tired of us—of our faces, our caricatured faces, our appearance; above all, they want a 'whipping boy'. They are also bored. However, within a few months the great European issue will have to be fought out. This will bring a sense of reality and excitement.[1]

Meanwhile, on 2 April, I had received a valuable report from Iain Macleod in which he expressed his view, based upon a very careful analysis, of the position of Orpington.

One thing that emerges with absolute clarity is that the popular reasons, such as pensions, Schedule A, nuclear disarmament and Colonial policy, had nothing whatever to do with the result. Incomparably the leading factor was the dislike of the pay policy and general dislike of the Government, which I suspect more than anything else is also connected with this. I am sure it is true that as the pay pause begins to show results much of the dissatisfaction will be removed, but a great deal will hang both on the Budget itself and on the words that the Chancellor uses when he speaks. As far as the first is concerned, we must begin, I think, to show the light at the end of the tunnel; and as far as the second is concerned, it is essential to emphasise that what we really wish to see is a policy of growth and that our efforts will be directed towards this.

[1] 7 April 1962.

After the Budget the political trend seemed to change neither for the better nor the worse. At a by-election in Derby in the middle of April the Conservatives were pushed into the third place and so the movement seemed nationwide. Nevertheless it was little comfort for the official Opposition.

We had a bad electoral reverse in Derby by-election – we were third – the Liberals being a few hundred ahead (the reverse of Stockton). Our General Election vote of 20,000 dwindled to 10,000. In other words, the same emotion is all over the country – N.E. (Middlesbrough and Stockton) N.W. (Blackpool) London suburbs (Orpington) Midlands (Derby). It is a very extra-ordinary change in a very few months. Last autumn's elections were quite normal. It is now clear that this swing will go on – at least for the time.[1]

We have now become accustomed to sudden and dramatic changes of mood in an electorate which has become much more volatile than ever before. In recent years, in by-elections as in opinion polls, the swings have in one direction or another been violent and exaggerated. But at this time no one realised the new feature of modern politics.

All the leader writers, columnists, gossip writers are at sixes and sevens in their different explanations. The Party in Parliament is rather stunned. The Socialists don't quite like it (for the normal anti-Government feeling that must come aften ten years has gone to the Liberals, not to Labour). Even the Liberals are a bit aghast – they are as much surprised as anyone. On paper, it looks like complete disaster for Conservatives, who may emerge from the next General Election as the smallest party. As Leader of the Party I shall have led it to its greatest victory in 1959 and its greatest defeat in 1963 or 1964. It's very puzzling.[1]

Nevertheless, I took comfort in the thought that

in spite of the obvious unpopularity of the medicine, it *is* working. The pay pause, with all its unfairness, has given us a precious advantage. German and French costs are beginning to rise. Although exports have not risen in any spectacular way, the prospects are good and there is a steady improvement. Imports

[1] 21 April 1962.

are down. The Balance of Payments *results* for 1961 are *far* better than we could have hoped. The prospects for 1962 are very good. Bank Rate is down from seven per cent to five per cent. I have agreed to another half a per cent on Thursday next. There will be another 'boom' at the end of this year or the beginning of next. As long as we can prevent a ridiculous increase in wages, we should be in a good position. But will the public realise? Will they give us credit for our resolution and courage? Or will they continue to blame us for the disaster so narrowly averted as well as resent all the measures necessary for safety? Naturally, the whole political situation will change—perhaps for the better, perhaps for the worse—when we reach a definite point in the Common Market negotiations. This will be the most exciting political issue since 1845. All Party allegiances and formations may be radically changed. Yet we don't know at all what are the chances of a reasonable offer by the Six. Will they press us very hard? Will France refuse all concessions, especially about agriculture and Commonwealth interests? Will de Gaulle 'smile and smile and smile', but betray us after all? No one knows. I feel rather overwhelmed by the responsibility on me and rather lonely. The sudden change of political fortune is at once reflected in the ordinary intercourse of life. . . . If I were not so old, I would be very cynical. But it is the young who are cynical—or at least believe themselves to be so.[1]

From 25 April to 2 May I was in the United States of America and Canada. On my return I heard the detailed results of the Local Government Elections. These told the same story, of Liberal successes and alarming Conservative losses. It had now become the accepted rule that these local campaigns were fought not upon local but upon the national issues. The swing away from the Conservatives was spectacular. In the middle of May there was a by-election in Montgomeryshire made necessary by the death of a very old friend of mine, Clem Davies, a man of singular charm and at periods of great national crisis of considerable courage. Here the Liberal majority rose by some 5,000 votes.

Meanwhile the situation on the wages front showed a balance of failure and success. The Confederation of Shipbuilding and

[1] 21 April 1962.

Engineering Unions decided, by a great majority, against a strike in support of their wage demands. This was on 10 May; but on 12 May the dockers received an increase amounting to about nine per cent, against the so-called 'guiding light' of two and a half per cent.

> All the week the trouble in the docks has been boiling up. The employers (a very weak lot) promised us that they would offer *either* a three per cent rise *or* a forty-two hour week. On Tuesday they offered both. So they *started* with too high a bid and were ignominiously pushed on further still. For, although Mr. Cousins put these two concessions, with a slight advance—1s. to 1s. 2d.—to his delegates, on Friday they rejected [them]. We had made all the preparations necessary, troops, etc., and on hearing the news of the rejection of the employers' offer, I came back to London from Inverness (where I had gone for the annual conference of the Scottish Unionist Party).[1]

I immediately sent for the Chancellor of the Exchequer, the Lord Chancellor, and the Minister of Labour.

> We discussed the situation on the basis that nothing could now avert the strike, and that the Minister of Labour should *not* bring any pressure on the employers to improve their offer. On the contrary, as a member of the Government, he had already told them that they had gone too far.[1]

However, it was too late. The employers

> were already on the run and after eight hours' talk, they capitulated at 11 p.m. to Cousins. This is a *great* blow to our incomes policy, and makes it difficult to see where we go now.[1]

It was not easy to disguise the fact that it was the Government's own employees who were having to bear the brunt of wage restraint while private employers, wherever it suited their interests, gave way to the full demands. Nevertheless, I could not help noticing that while berating the concession to the dockers, everybody was, in fact, delighted with the fact that the strike was off. John Hare, Minister of Labour, who showed throughout both competence and courage, addressed a full meeting of back-benchers on 16 May, in which he

[1] 14 May 1962.

pointed out that, although here and there the voluntary barrier had been broken through, yet broadly speaking it had proved successful. In nearly eight cases there had been settlements of two and a half per cent, and what must now be decided was whether we should be armed with disciplinary powers or depend on mobilising public opinion behind government policy.

On the main items of the Budget the Chancellor of the Exchequer was in close consultation with both Butler and me. His proposals were fair and honourable, but not exciting. The Budget was 'neutral' and therefore pleased nobody. Some changes were made in the incidence of indirect taxation; but what was given away in one direction was taken back in another. Purchase tax was reduced on motor cars, television sets and washing machines. But it was now to be placed upon soft drinks, sweets and ice-creams. The first was popular, but the second much resented; thus the cry of 'taxing the kiddies' was effectively raised against us. I had hoped that it would be possible to abolish what was known as the Schedule A income tax—a tax much resented by owner-occupiers who felt it both harsh and inequitable. Unhappily, the Chancellor of the Exchequer could only undertake that this would be abolished next year. But this prospective benefit was balanced by what seemed to many an immediate evil, for the most important feature of the Budget was the levy on speculative capital gains—that is a capital tax on the profits arising from the sale of stocks and shares within a period of six months.

We had tried hard to find some method of controlling prices to correspond with the restraint on wages and salaries, but it was not practicable to do so. This new capital gains tax was at least a gesture towards the trade unions to encourage them to join whole-heartedly in N.E.D.C. and to persuade them to accept some measure of restraint. Although we believed this tax to be right in principle, its effects were not great. The capitalist class was annoyed; the trade unions were not impressed. Meanwhile, I had been continually pressing on the Chancellor of the Exchequer and the Treasury the need for a substantial reflation. At least we had been able to move away from the crisis Bank Rate of seven per cent established in July 1961, and by 8 March 1962 Bank Rate was reduced from six to five and a half per cent. But I was not satisfied and kept pressing for further expansionist moves. On 22 March Bank Rate came down to five per cent and to my great delight the Treasury and the Bank agreed to a further reduction to four and a half per cent on 26 April. In the same mood N.E.D.C. set a 'target' for growth of four per cent per annum. But I was also anxious for the system of Special Deposits to be modified with a corresponding increase of the total sums available for credit. This was done on 31 May when £70 m. of these deposits were released. Nevertheless, with the end of the pay pause and some expansion of credit, the major problem remained to be resolved – what kind of incomes policy and what kind of broad economic plan was to be adopted.

> In practice . . . the pay pause has been a success. We have gained a year; rises have been much less than they would have been; our 'wage structure' is getting nearer to that of France or of Germany (we may even have the edge on them) and so trade is beginning to 'boom'. Last month's figures are good – exports up, imports down. The money is still coming in and the reserves growing. So, while the Government is thought to have failed, the policy is succeeding.[1]

Although many Ministers were discussing, privately or collectively, some kind of workable incomes policy, I felt more and more dismayed at the lack of any energetic or imaginative suggestions coming from the Treasury. On 23 May I had to address a conference of Women Conservatives in the Albert Hall. Although the reception of my speech was less enthusiastic than last year the applause when we left was even greater than before. This helped the Press; for some could say I had a cool reception; others could say it was warm. Therefore all readers would be pleased. In fact, I felt the favour of the women delegates was shown more to Dorothy than to me. She captivated them with a charming little speech.

> She has not spared herself since I became Prime Minister. She has been *all over* the country, to simple and friendly meetings of women of all types. Now (when they come together at their conference) very many of them know her personally.[2]

[1] 17 May 1962.   [2] 23 May 1962.

But the Cabinet was still uncertain, and the Chancellor of the Exchequer gave no real lead. On 24 May

> most of the time was taken up by the discussion of an 'incomes policy'. All the Ministers argued and all put forward different and conflicting views. At the end of it all, there was a complete impasse![1]

My own little team of loyal advisers—the private secretaries—supported by the Cabinet Office—did their best to help.

> Worked all the morning on the two great issues.
>
> (1) *Britain and Europe*, in the light of my visit to de Gaulle next Saturday and Sunday.
>
> (2) *British Economy and an Incomes Policy*. Both intractable, obscure, and baffling problems.
>
> On (1) there seems an increasing impression that de Gaulle does *not* repeat *not* want us in Europe. (Although it seems as if Couve de Murville accepts our adhesion as 'a historical fatality'.) But the General may feel unable or unwilling to oppose our application *openly* and *directly*. His instructions to the negotiators are likely to be to obstruct, waste time, try to make everybody—including the British—lose heart. Alternatively, if this fails, the French will insist on terms so harsh for our farmers and for the Commonwealth that we shall be forced to withdraw. This, of course, is a dangerous game. French hegemony in Europe (or a part of Europe) may be maintained for a time. But the future will be insecure. What will Germany do *after* Adenauer? What will France be *after* de Gaulle?
>
> On (2) our Incomes Policy, the colleagues are all confused—so is the Party in the House. We must try to work out something rather more imaginative than we had done so far.[2]

Much of our attention was now directed to the deteriorating position in Laos and in South-East Asia generally. It was not until 28 May that I was able to expound at some length to my colleagues my ideas for a possible incomes policy. I had had much discussion both with Lloyd and Butler; but I was beginning to resent the

---

[1] 24 May 1962.   [2] 27 May 1962.

apparent readiness of all concerned to place the chief burden upon me for any new approach. I have still the notes from which I spoke on this occasion and since this great problem—whether or not an incomes policy is desirable or practicable—is still under discussion, it is perhaps worth while to give a summary of a statement which took well over an hour to deliver.

We had four objectives—full employment, stable prices, a favourable balance of payments and the expansion of the economy. So far as I knew no nation, at any rate no free nation, had succeeded in sustaining them all for any length of time. Yet either one of these objectives must be abandoned, which I thought unacceptable, or there must be some permanent form of incomes policy applying both to the private and the public sector. It was quite impossible to maintain the pressure on government employees if in the private area wage inflation was to run riot. How were we to persuade public opinion to so great a change from traditional methods as a permanent part of our industrial structure? The Press was no help—their policy was to preach restraint in theory but to surrender in practice to any demand made in Fleet Street. N.E.D.C. could scarcely fulfil this function. It was too new, too delicate a plant—and too specialised. An incomes policy must form part of an overall scheme seen to be fair all round, and seen also to be the *only* fair way. This meant a complete reappraisal of the relative status and conditions of employment of 'workers' and 'staff'. There must be proper contracts of employment for workers, and redundancy and retraining arrangements. There must be an impartial source of wage assessment operating over the whole field, in place of a series of *ad hoc* arbitrations when one group after another felt itself to be left behind. Action, if necessary taxation, must be used to prevent profits increasing their share of the national cake. Finally, to encourage growth there must be more stimulation of demand, as we could not expect *all* the growth to go into exports. This meant action over the special deposits, and the Bank Rate, and above all the long-term interest rate.

The Cabinet was somewhat stunned by this portentous address. Undeterred I took up the same theme a few days later with the back-benchers.

I went to the 1922 Committee, to which (according to some newspapers) I had been 'summoned'. I told them that since some of their number—or one—was employed by the Press I could not speak to them confidentially. They all cheered! Then I mentioned that one of the worst breaches of the pay pause was by the Newspaper Proprietors who had given a rise of eleven per cent to the Journalists—'I only hope this will be given to occasional as well as regular contributors.' They roared with laughter. I did fifteen minutes on Economics. Today the Special Deposits are being released to the tune of £70 m.; the Bankers are widening their conditions for credit; we have paid back another £25 m. to I.M.F.—the spring is late, but beginning at last! But we must have (after Pay Pause, Phase One and Pay Pause Phase Two) [an] 'Incomes Policy'. Don't underrate the difficulties. But let us try.[1]

I felt that after all these troubles I had the sympathy and support of the Parliamentary party as a whole.

In the early part of June there were two more by-elections somewhat more satisfactory.

We have lost (as we expected) the Middlesbrough seat to Labour, owing to the Liberals. But we are second, and only 2,000 off Labour. It is bad—but in the present political climate—not too bad. On the other hand, Aidan Crawley has held West Derbyshire for us by 1,200. Here the Liberals are second, and Labour third. The Liberals must have taken their votes mainly from us. But West Derbyshire is an old Liberal seat (Whig with the Cavendishes; Liberal with Charlie White)—and so this is a good result on the whole.[2]

In spite of some days in France and long discussions with Bob Menzies in London on the European Common Market, I was able, by the 19 June, to complete a draft on Incomes Policy which I discussed with three or four of my colleagues at Chequers:

If the Cabinet accepts my plans (based on my broad proposals to them before Whitsun) it will at least give us back some

[1] 31 May 1962.   [2] 7 June 1962.

initiative. I thought the Chancellor of the Exchequer rather chilly. The others seemed strongly in favour.[1]

But before embarking upon this phase in the life and work of the Government I was beginning seriously to think that we should require not only new measures but new men.

[1] 17 June 1962.

CHAPTER III

The Immigrants

WHILE my colleagues and I were still struggling against the rising tide of wages, we were almost immersed by an equally troublesome phenomenon – the sudden influx of immigrants, especially from the new Commonwealth countries. This problem was first brought to the attention of Ministers in 1954 during Churchill's last administration. At that time, the total coloured population was about 40,000, compared with about 7,000 before the war, but immigration was increasing dramatically. In 1954 the number of coloured immigrants entering the United Kingdom increased fourfold over 1953, and there was every prospect of the flow growing steadily larger. As can well be imagined, serious housing and social problems began to emerge, especially in the Midlands where a large number of the new arrivals sought work and homes. On 5 November 1954, in answer to questions in the House of Commons, the Minister of State for the Colonies said

> we are very well aware of the importance of the problem, of its urgency, and of the deep concern which it causes in many parts of the country, and we are determined to press on with our work and to see that a satisfactory solution is evolved.

Experts in Parliamentary phraseology could deduce from this delphic reply that nothing very much would be done about it now, but that something might have to be done about it some time or other.

Early in 1955, after some rather desultory discussions in the Cabinet, it was agreed that a Bill should be tentatively drafted. I remember that Churchill, rather maliciously, observed that perhaps the cry of 'Keep Britain White' might be a good slogan for the Election which we should soon have to fight without the benefit of his leadership. Yet both he and his colleagues instinctively shrank from any interference with the traditional freedom of movement between the countries of the Commonwealth and the Motherland. But the pressure continued; in 1955 the numbers arriving from the West Indies, India, Pakistan, Cyprus, Africa, Aden and Hong Kong rose to a total of 43,000.

In the summer of 1957 I asked the Home Secretary to look again into the question of instituting some control. But no action was taken until the matter was brought forcibly to public attention by the so-called 'race riots' which took place in 1958, first in the Midlands, at Nottingham, and afterwards in London, at Notting Hill. In this year, as in the subsequent year, the numbers entering the country were falling to 38,000 in 1958 and to 21,000 in 1959. Nevertheless, I felt that sooner or later we should have to grasp this nettle. Accordingly, on 2 September 1958, I sent a memorandum to the Home Secretary.

> I have no doubt you will be reporting to the Cabinet when it meets about the situation in London and elsewhere in what are called the 'race riots'. If I remember right, we agreed not long ago to look again at the immigration question in a few months' time. Perhaps we should look at it now.

At the same time a statement was issued to the Press, confirming that the Government was engaged upon a study of the whole problem, although no long-term decisions would be taken until after prolonged and careful consideration. The public rightly deduced from this that the Government still hoped to find some way of controlling the influx without legislation.

Meanwhile the judiciary were rightly determined to stamp heavily on any outbreak of 'racism'. After the riots severe sentences were handed out to a number of young men who had 'beaten up' some West Indians. In view of the fact that the nine youths concerned had no previous convictions and that their victims had made a complete recovery, these sentences might almost be regarded as savage; four years' imprisonment was the penalty imposed by the judge.

In September 1958, Norman Manley, the Chief Minister of

Jamaica, and several of his colleagues came over for discussions on this delicate issue. Our talks were friendly but inconclusive.

> Large luncheon party for Mr. Manley (Prime Minister of Jamaica) and other West Indian notabilities, who have arrived here in connection with the so-called 'racial riots'. Butler and Alan Boyd have been dealing with them, and seem to have got on well. We can, I hope, reduce the rate of immigration *without* legislation. At least, we must give this a trial.[1]

Unhappily, the drop in immigration which had shown itself in 1958 and 1959 was later reversed. In 1960 the numbers rose to 58,000. We perhaps insufficiently realised at the time the true reasons which lay behind the post-war movement. It was the reaction to a barrier suddenly erected against a more natural and traditional flow. To quote Lord Butler's words,

> in view of all that has happened since, it is necessary to see this Act in its true historical perspective. For decades, many thousands of West Indians, lacking opportunity, jobs and money at home, had emigrated to the United States. In 1952 Congress virtually blocked this channel when it passed the McCarran–Walter Immigration Act. Other countries on the American mainland were also operating immigration restrictions. Britain alone provided an open door for West Indians, as for all other Commonwealth peoples.[2]

At the same time, the conditions both of employment and, it should be added, of unemployment, were so much more favourable for immigrants in Britain than in any other country, including America, that the attraction of Britain and the British 'welfare state' continually increased. In 1961 the rate of intake seemed likely to double. In fact it was to reach 136,000 in the following year. It therefore became clear to me in the spring of 1961 that we could no longer rely upon the methods hitherto employed, by which many of the Commonwealth Governments had voluntarily tried to discourage emigration, or at least to confine emigration to those who

[1] 12 September 1958.
[2] Lord Butler, *The Art of the Possible* (London, 1971), p. 205.

would be likely to obtain employment on their arrival. Something more stringent and more effective would be necessary, however distasteful might be the decision to over-ride an established and highly prized tradition.

We were all conscious of the difficulty and significance of any change. For generations there had been free entry into the Old Country from any country of the Commonwealth. It is true that before the great extensions of the Commonwealth after the Second World War the movement had been largely the other way. It was the emigrants from Britain who had gone in their thousands to Canada, Australia, New Zealand and South Africa. Now a huge flow was beginning in the opposite direction and it was impossible without hypocrisy to conceal the fact that the difference of race involved many problems of employment, of housing and of what was known as 'integration' into our community. It was true that *all* the Commonwealth countries, old and new, practised a rigid control on immigration into their own countries. In Australia this was upon a frankly racial basis. 'White Australia' was a firm decision – almost a dogma – of the Australian people which neither party dared to challenge. Paradoxically enough, the new Commonwealth countries maintained a similar control. Even within the West Indian Federation there was no free movement from one island to another. Thus those very Ministers who were to plead so eloquently for the uncontrolled right of entry of West Indians into Britain did not practise what they preached. Nevertheless, when the Cabinet resolved to act it was a hard and disagreeable decision, taken reluctantly and as some may think too late. On 30 May there was

a long discussion on West Indian immigration into United Kingdom, which is now becoming rather a serious problem. There seemed to be a general agreement that we shall have to legislate in the autumn. Colonial Secretary (rather surprisingly) concurred. But we must keep a final decision till then and meanwhile ask Lord Chancellor and his Committee (who have already done a lot of work) to go on preparing the necessary measures. There are a great many complications – not the least of which is Irish immigration.[1]

[1] 30 May 1961.

Before Parliament rose at the end of the summer it was clear that the Conservative Party, becoming aware of the sudden growth of the figures, was seriously alarmed. It was now estimated that there were 350,000 coloured immigrants in the country; if a rate of 100,000 a year or more was to be accepted, it was clear that within a few years the consequential strains would be almost intolerable. The political pressure was renewed at the Party Conference in October.

Although Butler handled the immigration debate very skilfully, he had some difficulties on this and other issues with the members of the Conference, whom in my experience it was always best to treat firmly.

> He has brought much of his trouble on himself by an appearance of vacillation. This is not really fair on him. Like Arthur Balfour, he has a fine, academic mind, which I personally admire.[1]

In fact he told the delegates that legislation would be introduced in the autumn.

> It would carefully avoid race or colour prejudice and would be based on the principle that immigrants without independent means would have to satisfy the Minister of Labour that they had a job to come to or that there was a need in Britain for their services. Powers would also be taken to prevent the entry of immigrants with criminal records. The restrictions would have to be applied to immigrants from Eire and from the 'older countries of the Commonwealth'. The Governments of the countries concerned would be consulted.[2]

Accordingly, all the Commonwealth Governments were warned of our intentions, and the Prime Minister of the West Indies Federation, Sir Grantley Adams, was also informed. On 1 November the Bill was published—and the storm broke. It was clear from the first that the opposition would not be confined to Labour and Liberal members of the House of Commons, but would be widely and even violently expressed from many different and some unexpected quarters. Throughout the greater part of the Press, especially the serious Press appealing to the more educated classes, the attack was twofold—first an accusation of lack of consultation

[1] 13 October 1961.   [2] *Annual Register, 1961*, p. 45.

with the Governments concerned; secondly, and much more important, a reaffirmation of the principle of free entry into the Mother Country as vital to the continued strength of the Commonwealth and required by any decent and humane attitude towards religion and morals.

The first was an issue which Gaitskell made especially his own, beginning with Parliamentary Questions early in November, and culminating in a strange attempt to repeat a technique which he had used unsuccessfully on an earlier occasion.[1] Sir Grantley Adams had strongly protested against our action which he even declared to be no different to the system of apartheid practised in South Africa. But his logical position was not improved by the practice pertaining among the islands themselves. However, whatever might be the pitfalls which awaited me from the Caribbean I was usually able to avoid the traps so skilfully laid from Hampstead.

> As I was going out to dinner with the Press Club, I was given a letter from Gaitskell, in which he attacked our lack of 'consultation' with the West Indies, quoted a telegram from Sir Grantley Adams, and asked me to make a statement in the House of Commons. Gaitskell said that he was publishing his letter. This was the repetition of the technique he tried with me over the 'Offshore islands' some years ago. I was at Langwell, in Caithness. I beat him then, and I beat him again today. I got a reply prepared in my office, agreed with Colonial Office, delivered to him at Hampstead; and sent to press—all by 10 p.m. The letter was brought to me to sign during dinner.[2]

Such are the advantages of an ever vigilant and loyal staff. The next day, following our interchange of letters, Gaitskell came back to the same point with undimmed enthusiasm. I could only repeat what I had already told him.

> As I said in my letter, the Government provided information of their intention, invited comments, and sought the co-operation of the West Indian Government in implementing any scheme outlined. That is what I understand to be consultation. Perhaps the right hon. Gentleman is confusing consultation with concurrence.

[1] *Riding the Storm*, p. 553.   [2] 22 November 1961.

It was also suggested that we should have had a full Common-wealth Conference on this question, and this point was strenuously urged by some of the less responsible critics. It would indeed be difficult to conceive a meeting more calculated to break up the Commonwealth than one in which each Prime Minister was forced to explain to the others the extremely restrictive laws on immigration which he operated in his own territory. I could understand that it was necessary, especially for the West Indian Ministers, to take a strong position in public, although I felt sure that they understood and sympathised with the reasons which had forced the British Government most reluctantly to abandon a time-honoured practice.

This first question of consultation, although it played a great part in the propaganda battle now raging against us, was really a side issue. The second and major question involved far more grave and important decisions. If the publication of the Bill was followed by a storm, the second reading provided an opportunity for a regular typhoon. I have never seen the House of Commons in so hysterical a mood since the days of Suez. There was only this difference. I thought that, apart from the genuine convictions of Gaitskell and Gordon-Walker and others who felt strongly on the matter, some of the emotion was somewhat synthetic. It seemed a good line into which to harry Ministers already in some difficulty on larger issues; it was especially attractive to accuse of disloyalty to the Common-wealth a Party which had always been so devoted to the Empire. It was fortunate indeed for us that we had Butler in charge. His long-standing political reputation as a protagonist of liberal and progressive views stood him in good stead. Yet he was interrupted to an extent that is quite contrary to Parliamentary tradition when a Minister is introducing a Bill. But he remained calm, unmoved and good-tempered and gradually wore down the Opposition. He made it clear from the outset how distasteful the decision to introduce a control had been to him and his colleagues; but this principle of the 'open door', however ancient, had become impossible in modern conditions. The United Kingdom was already highly developed and highly populated, and although we were glad to be able to receive a reasonable number of fellow-members of the Commonwealth as well as other foreigners we must have regard to the actual facts of life. The recent and startling increase was clearly reaching a rate which was incompatible with the absorption of these newcomers into the life of the country. It was bound to produce and was already producing considerable social dangers. It accentuated the difficulties of housing, and would make it impossible to integrate the newcomers in any real sense with the existing population. Therefore this absolute right of free entry could no longer be maintained. Nevertheless, every possible safeguard would be made to secure that it was honoured up to the maximum point that we could find tolerable. The principle of the Bill was simple. Apart from those who could support themselves and their dependants from their own resources, Commonwealth citizens would be able to enter Britain in future in one of three ways. First, the Minister of Labour would issue vouchers to those who could show that they had a job to come to; secondly, vouchers would be given to those who possessed the training, skill and educational qualifications likely to be useful in this country; thirdly, there would be a quota system by which the Ministry of Labour would admit applicants subject to the limit which the Government might think necessary from time to time. For this third category the rule would be 'first come first served'. Special arrangements would be made for students. The measure was to be temporary, applicable for five years, and could not be renewed without an order in council subject to affirmative resolution by both Houses of Parliament.

A special problem arose about citizens of the Republic of Ireland. After much discussion within the Government it was found to be quite impracticable to make the clause covering control of entry apply to the Southern Irish. The large numbers who moved backwards and forwards both at harvest and for other purposes was well established and useful to both countries. The difficulty of imposing anything like wartime controls was clear. It would involve closing the border between Ulster and the Republic, and it would not be feasible in peacetime. Naturally this decision was a proof in the eyes of many members that the Bill was purely racialist in purpose; but it was a decision to which the Government was forced after a careful study of the difficulties. Yet in this exception lay the heart of the attack. Although the Bill was designed to regulate immigration from every part of the Commonwealth and thus to bring into force a system comparable to that which applied throughout the Commonwealth by its constituent members, yet in practice it was difficult to maintain that these measures would have been taken had there not been so great an influx from the West Indies and from the Indian subcontinent. There were many of the Government's supporters, especially those who were the greatest enthusiasts for the Empire and Commonwealth, who disliked the measure, and the Irish decision disturbed them greatly.

There was much talk of finding some other workable plan for the Irish Republic, but it proved impossible to do so.

> The situation about [the] Immigration Bill is no better. Ministers concerned are working on an 'Irish' plan – but it will be pretty thin, and I fear may not satisfy our critics. It will be a strange irony if Ireland once again brings down a British Government – and this time over a Bill which (according to Gallup) over ninety per cent of the people support.[1]

For, although we had a fierce opposition from the intellectuals, there was no doubt at all where the mass of the people stood. Butler's speech was violently attacked inside and outside the House, and the fair and realistic manner in which he presented his case, admitting the diffract points with his usual candour, were seized upon not as a sign of strength but as a confession of weakness. At the best the unhappy Home Secretary was accused of feebly conceding to his colleagues, who were well known to be guilty of racialism, reaction, Mosleyism and almost Hitlerism. To use Butler's own words,

> the Labour Opposition, led by Hugh Gaitskell, launched the most infuriated attack on the Bill which they labelled as cruel and brutal anti-colour legislation.[2]

One of the leaders in this campaign was *The Times* newspaper, which exceeded itself in its self-righteous and unctuous approach. A series of leading articles followed each other week by week like an artillery bombardment, with ever-growing intensity, culminating on 4 December with the statement 'it would be best if the Bill could

[1] 30 November 1961.   [2] Butler, p. 206.

be thrown out altogether'. It is strange how persistent has been the tradition of this great organ of the Press which has been exercising its power over successive governments for so many years. Mount Olympus was the name which Trollope gave more than a hundred years ago to the place from which Jupiter, the great Thunderer, issued

> those infallible laws ... which cabinets are called upon to obey; by which bishops are to be guided, lords and commons controlled,—judges instructed in law, generals in strategy, admirals in naval tactics, and orange-women in the management of their barrows.[1]

Through each generation these denunciations have been hurled and these decrees pronounced. The proprietors and the editors have changed—Amurath has succeeded to Amurath—but the style has remained. Fortunately, with singular integrity if with some lack of humour, a history of the paper has been published at appropriate intervals showing that in moments of extreme national importance the views put forward by the Editor of *The Times* have generally been wrong and often disastrous. However, undeterred by the mistakes of his predecessors, the then occupant of the throne discharged his thunderbolts on my colleagues and especially on myself with savage delight. It was therefore some source of comfort for me to read, in my retirement, this bland recantation published in the same great paper on 16 February 1967:

> There were widespread misgivings at the passing of the Commonwealth Immigrants Act in 1962. A good many people were reluctant to believe that such restrictions were necessary. Since then it has become evident that they are essential.

The battle at the committee stage was fiercely conducted. Although it was becoming gradually clear that the facts made some measure of control necessary, every suggestion put forward by the Government was equally objectionable. However, we struggled on, and the Bill received its third reading on 27 February 1962, after a fine defence by the Home Secretary. The Act came into force on 1 July. Persons born in the United Kingdom or holding passports

[1] Anthony Trollope, *The Warden* (London, 1891), vol. i, p. 133.

issued by the United Kingdom Government were to be exempt. The large category of Asians in African colonies who later, when their countries of residence became independent, preferred, under special provisions made at the time, not to register as citizens of their new countries, but to remain United Kingdom citizens, was subsequently to prove a source of difficulty and anxiety.

It is strange to reflect that the charge brought against my colleagues and myself a very few years later was one not of undue harshness, but of thoughtless leniency. In spite of all the noble sentiments and splendid protestations of the Labour Party in opposition, they were, in office, compelled to introduce measures which were far more stringent than those for which we were responsible. Perhaps there is comfort in the thought which the author of these reforms later expressed in his own hope that

> the two major parties, by drawing closer together in espousing the twin policies of control and integration, make it more difficult for the candidates of either to exploit colour problems for political advantage.[1]

This generous sentiment is certainly some consolation ten years later. But at the time it was rough going.

[1] Butler, p. 207.

CHAPTER IV

New Men and New Measures

DURING the summer months of 1962 the first if hesitating attempts were made to deal with a new problem which ten years later is still unresolved. Hitherto the orthodox theory, held with an almost religious devotion by the 'authorities' (that is, the chief pundits in the financial and banking world as well as in the Treasury itself), had proved a good working rule in spite of all its accompanying troubles and tribulations. If, as the phrase then ran, the economic system became 'overheated' it had to be cooled down by deflationary touches of various kinds, ranging from open market operations by the Bank of England to economies in government expenditure in every field. The signs of this malaise were said to be easily recognisable—over-employment, an unfavourable balance of payments, pressure on sterling, rises in wages unjustified by any increase in productivity and a corresponding increase in prices. If the conventional remedies recommended by doctors of the highest reputations were applied in time the patient could be expected to react favourably. With the removal of the deep-seated causes of the malady the symptoms would be relieved. But in 1962 for the first time there began to show itself a resistance—almost an immunity—such as the human body sometimes develops when it has become accustomed to a treatment too persistently applied. Thus doubts arose both as to the diagnosis and the cure.

During the previous twelve months the conventional and lowering regimen had been conscientiously applied; yet the pressures were by no means reduced. On the contrary, wages and wage demands seemed to be growing every day. I had an instinctive feeling that we were moving into a new situation where, as in the Einstein world, cause and effect seemed to follow different rules. One of the usual symptoms of a boom, that is unjustified wage demands, continued unchecked. For this unexpected persistence of high fever in spite of a low diet, a new term of art was later devised—'stagflation'. I have described in Chapter II my growing conviction that some better and more effective methods should be devised. I seemed to get little support from the practitioners of most repute, who appeared satisfied with the traditional forms of febrifuge—blood-letting, purging and the rest. I was therefore thrown back either on quack doctors or on an attempt, amid many other preoccupations, to devise some new treatment by my own efforts.

I have been trying to work on 'Incomes Policy: A New Approach'. There is a mass of paper and a large number of suggestions (mostly self-contradictory). . . . We have got through quite a lot of preliminary work. But I am still at a loss. There doesn't seem to be a way through the tangle. We had a useful meeting of Ministers concerned last Thursday—but there was very little progress. Hailsham has the best 'large' ideas—but no detail. The Treasury are not very imaginative. I have thought a lot, but cannot produce much. And the time is short.[1]

I was confirmed in my diagnosis by a friend on whose judgement I placed great reliance. But even he seemed to see no obvious remedy:

Roy Harrod thinks the economy is on the decline and should be expanded, but *without* increasing wages (which merely increases costs). There seemed no answer to *how* this was to be done.[2]

Meanwhile, I could only struggle on, helped by my own small staff. On 12 June, I felt that

we are making some progress with 'Incomes Policy: A New Approach'—but it's hard going. I dictated all yesterday, and had a meeting with Tim Bligh (my Principal Private Secretary) and two of the Cabinet Secretariat (Carney and Baldwin). We made a start with a new form of these proposals (especially for the

[1] 11 June 1962.   [2] 12 June 1962.

National Commission on Wages and Salaries) and with some of the other plans. It will now be necessary, with the help of the Treasury, Board of Trade, and Minister of Labour to produce a paper for the Cabinet to approve (or disapprove).[1]

The next morning

> Lord Hailsham came for a talk at 10.00 a.m. – very helpful. He has a fine brain and real imagination. Then Chancellor of the Exchequer – nurses, gas-workers, electricians, and all the rest of the wage claims. He seemed in some distress. But – equally important – what the 1962–3 baby is to be – Master Boom or Miss Slump? Even the Treasury are not now so certain.[2]

The result of the West Lothian by-election was not encouraging. This was a traditional Labour seat in which, of course, we had no chance of success; but both the Conservative and the Liberal candidates lost their deposits. This was an indignity to which the once powerful Liberal Party was now accustomed; but it was a serious blow to us. Once more I urged upon the Chancellor of the Exchequer the need to get long-term interest rates down, not only from social and political motives, but also as an encouragement to industrialists to increase investment. Although I was still working hard at my paper, a Conservative fête on Saturday, 16 June, in my own constituency, Bromley, made a pleasant change, in spite of the hazards:

> After the fête, we had some trouble in getting away, owing to the Anti-Bomb brigade, who lay on the ground in front of our car. Dorothy (who was driving) was very calm and nobody was hurt.[3]

I remember that the police were lost in admiration of the idiomatic language with which she rebuked these genteel protesters.

After further talks with Hailsham, Macleod and Selwyn Lloyd, as well as with Michael Fraser (of the Conservative Research Department), I succeeded in finishing my draft.

There were four main elements in the plan. First, the 'guiding light', the principle which had been propounded at the beginning

---

[1] 12 June 1962.   [2] 13 June 1962.   [3] 16 June 1962.

of the year, must be maintained. The rise in personal incomes must be related to the increase in national wealth, which was estimated at about two and a half per cent per annum. As the rate of increase changed, so could the 'guiding light'. Next, I proposed a Standing Commission on Pay—not an *ad hoc* arbitration commission, but a permanent body, whose duty it would be to examine and pronounce on the relative merits of different claims, bearing in mind the national interest as defined by the 'guiding light'. Its advice would not be binding; there was no question at this time of a statutory incomes policy in the modern sense. But public ventilation of the full facts would be secured. To protect the consumer, I wanted to tackle the problem of prices by abolishing resale price maintenance; and I thought we should give more publicity to the efforts we were making to reduce tariffs and to investigate monopolies and restrictive practices, though on the second point it would probably not be wise to initiate legislation until we knew the outcome of the Common Market negotiations. I also proposed the setting up of a Consumers' Council, and the introduction of legislation on weights and measures. Based on advice from the Ministry of Labour, I made a number of suggestions to improve the status and security of people at work, both wage and salary earners, covering such matters as training and redundancy. A Shops and Offices Bill intended to give white-collar workers the sort of protection already enjoyed in industry should be introduced as early as possible.

The problem remained of how to make the Commission effective. The Government would seek its advice so far as public servants were concerned; but how could the Commission ensure the co-operation of industry? Of course, we could try compulsion. This would require statutory provision that existing wage and salary agreements should be registered with the Government, and new claims notified. The Government would then be empowered, subject to certain criteria for deciding the national importance of the claim, to refer the matter to the Commission. It could be a criminal offence, subject to appropriate penalties, to increase an agreed wage or salary rate which had been referred by the Government to the Commission, until the Commission's advice on it had been published. Or there might be a fiscal penalty, such as the imposition of a tax

D

on the pay roll of the industry or firm concerned. A trade union which disregarded the Government's request that a case should be considered by the Commission could be deprived of the protection of the 1906 Trade Disputes Act, and thus risk actions for damages resulting from strike action. But all these measures would be open to severe criticism, notably that there would be an arbitrary element in the Government's choice of which disputes to refer to the Commission. In any case, much industrial action was 'unofficial', and thus beyond the control of the unions. Yet it was evident that an entirely voluntary system would probably fail, because it could easily be ignored.

A third possibility was to inject an element of compulsion by providing that where an award or agreement above the 'guiding light' had been made, the industry involved could be summoned to a full enquiry of its circumstances, which would expose any inefficiencies, restrictive practices, over staffing and collusion to pass on higher wages in the form of higher costs. Collective bargaining would thus continue, but settlements would involve full public disclosure of the facts, and be subject to public castigation. At least let us try the 'open air cure' which seemed effective in treating other ailments.

Such was the ambitious, if still in some respects nebulous, programme which, in default of any other suggestion, I decided to propose to my surprised, but loyal, colleagues. At the same time it was important that this plan, especially the Incomes Commission, should not be thought of as an isolated or temporary measure intended to impose upon an unwilling people disagreeable but short-term *restrictions*. It was to be represented as closely connected with the *expansion* of the wealth and strength of the nation. If its authority could become gradually recognised as representing the broad national interests, it would allow successive governments to devote themselves to the maximum expansion of the economy. In other words, the Incomes Policy must not be an instrument of deflation but a weapon for more rapid growth.

I was now to be concerned with an equally serious but much more delicate and unpleasant question—the personal factor. The preparation, and even the launching, of large policies is an agreeable exercise enjoyed by all politicians and their friends. But matters of high ministerial posts, above all when changes in the Cabinet itself are concerned, involving many old and tested friendships—all these throw upon the head of an administration an uncongenial and often almost intolerable burden.[1] A talk with Lord Cromer, the Governor of the Bank of England, convinced me that there was a real risk of a world deflation.

> This makes . . . an effective 'incomes policy' more important. At present we dare not re-inflate, because our system is open at both ends—wages, and imports. Increased wages mean (without increased productivity) more imports and less exports.[2]

On 21 June, while I was turning over all these questions in my mind, Butler came to lunch—as always calm and helpful.

> He feels that the present grave political position is due entirely to the bad handling of the economic problem (or rather its bad presentation) by the Chancellor of the Exchequer and the Treasury. He felt that drastic action was necessary to save the situation. This means the problem (an immense human and political problem) of replacing the Chancellor of the Exchequer.[3]

On 22 June there was a preliminary talk with some of my colleagues on the Incomes Policy paper which I had now circulated.

> A very good but very critical discussion. We shall have to do a lot more work on it. This makes me all the more angry with the Treasury and the Chancellor for their delay and lack of initiative. A whole year gone, and then the P.M. has to do it himself, at the last minute.[4]

There was one pleasant interruption in my now almost constant struggle with the dual problem of economic policy and Cabinet reconstruction. On 24 June I dined with the Foreign Secretary at Carlton Gardens. Dean Rusk—the American Secretary of State—and some of his brilliant team were present.

[1] See *Pointing the Way*, pp. 31–3.   [2] 20 June 1962.
[3] 21 June 1962.   [4] 22 June 1962.

I'm afraid I was indiscreet. But I could not resist some reproaches. The President had called Makarios a 'famous fighter for Freedom'—which was a remark which many English people felt very wounding. I said that I proposed to describe Castro as 'that famous fighter for Freedom'. Rusk (who took it quite seriously) begged me not to do so.[1]

When we turned to wider issues I remembered the current saying in Washington that the way to get on in life was to go to Harvard and then turn Left. I only wish this had really been true; but the Americans were at this time very conservative in economic matters.

We also had words about wood and glass and other tariffs; about shipping policies, etc. It is sometimes a good thing, in my view, to talk straight to the Americans. But poor Sir Harold Caccia, etc. were upset. Worse still, we had an argument about money, and I trotted out again my heretical views on gold.[1]

But it was all too soon—before the Almighty Dollar had begun to topple from its throne.

On the morning of 6 July I had a further meeting of selected Ministers on the incomes policy.

My plan was approved, with minor changes. It is now in a state to go to the whole Cabinet. Much depends on this, and I have already made good progress with the speech.

I am still very worried about Government changes, but Butler and Chief Whip are very helpful. The Treasury is still the great problem.[2]

There now followed some of the most unhappy days of my whole administration. Great national troubles, even disasters, can be faced with calm and equanimity by Ministers of courage. There is even a strange exhilaration which follows in their wake. But personal difficulties, involving, as they often do, the breach of long and happy associations and comradeship, are a burden on an altogether different plane. They bring bitterness, even anguish, into private life and friendships. Churchill found the changes in the High Command which he felt it his duty to make during critical moments in the war more onerous and more exhausting than even

[1] 24 June 1962.   [2] 6 July 1962.

the many military set-backs which we were doomed to suffer. As usual I will tell the story of the reconstruction of the Government largely from the words I wrote down at the time.

> I am sure it is necessary to make the vital change at the Treasury. Selwyn—of whom I am very fond and who has been a true and loyal friend since I became P.M. seems to me to have lost grip . . . . Lately, he seems hardly to function in some vital matters—e.g. this Incomes Policy affair. The Pay Pause started a *year* ago, exactly. By the end of the year, it was clear that it was to be succeeded by a more permanent policy. In spite of continual pressure from me, *nothing* at all was done, except long and fruitless discussions in [the] Economic Policy Committee and in Cabinet. These I brought to a head and in despair wrote the new policy myself during the Whitsun holidays, with the help of two young men from the Cabinet Secretariat and Tim Bligh. I am still doing all this, and naturally enough there are a lot of questions and details to be settled. But the Chancellor of the Exchequer *ought* to have got going at least after the turn of the year (that is after six months of Pay Pause—Phase One). Had he done so, the Incomes Policy plan would be now in better shape.[1]

There was another matter which caused me much concern. At this time there had been much talk about a possible devaluation of the dollar. If that were to occur

> whereas the dollar and sterling, and probably other currencies, would move together, we have *gold* debts (or debts in terms of gold) which would become twice as onerous. So we ought to pay them off in dollars as soon as we can.[1]

Yet

> in the *vital* matter of getting our *gold* obligations reduced (repayment to the I.M.F. of our borrowings) nothing had been done until I sent for the Governor himself (rather improperly) and found that he agreed with my apprehensions.[1]

In effect Selwyn Lloyd was suffering from the effects of carrying too heavy a burden over too many years. He had undergone all the disappointments of the long Egyptian negotiations and suffered

[1] 8 July 1962.

from the tortuous methods of the American Secretary of State all through 1956 until the crisis of Suez. He had served splendidly through that time, especially by his grand defence of our position at the United Nations. When I succeeded—after Eden's illness—to the difficult, almost desperate task, I retained Selwyn as Foreign Secretary and then he had loyally, at my request, transferred in July 1960 to the Treasury. Here he was met with new and growing difficulties. He had held office since 1951—eleven years—and the highest offices since the end of 1955. Alas, such are the cruel conditions in which politics have to be carried on that none of the methods available for dealing with such a situation in other occupations are practicable. A Foreign Secretary or a Chancellor of the Exchequer cannot take six months' holiday and then return, as would happen in a business enterprise or an academic post. This problem, with its painful implications, weighed heavily upon me at the time.

> It will be personally terrible, and I shrink from it. It will be said to be a 'panic' measure. I will be accused of gross 'disloyalty'. Yet all those I trust . . . agree that it is right. I am to talk with [Lloyd] on Thursday, and try to give him forewarning.[1]

I had now fully made up my mind where my duty lay; yet in looking back many years later upon this period, I recognise now that I was led into a serious error in attempting to mask the blow to the reputation of one Minister, and especially one with whom I had worked so closely, by combining this move with a general reconstruction of the Government. It would have been wiser to have made only the change at the Treasury and to have left wider alterations in the administration until Parliament had been adjourned and the operation could have been carried out in the autumn quietly and without any sense of undue pressure. I had long thought that it would be wise, after so long a period, to bring some younger men into the administration, and the general principle upon which a reconstruction of the Government as a whole should be based would be simple. I must ensure that whether or not the Party was successful in the next General Election (and this would be hoping

[1] 8 July 1962.

for an unprecedented term—four Elections in a row) the front
bench should be strong enough, whether in Government or in
Opposition, to fulfil its duties. I remembered occasions in history
when a Party lately in office had come back shattered and without
effective leadership. Some of the older men had resigned or accepted
peerages; others had suffered political defeat; and many years were
spent in Opposition in providing the nucleus of a new government.
This was broadly Mr. Balfour's mistake in 1905, and I was determined not to repeat it. Nevertheless, in retrospect I am sure that it
would have been better to separate the two operations. I was partly
persuaded not to do so because of the vital importance of carrying
through the Conservative Conference in October the great European
plan on which everything was to be staked. A change of Ministers
early in October, just before the Conference, might have led to the
impression that these Ministers had resigned voluntarily because
they could not agree to the bold European project. Nevertheless, it
would have been the better risk, and I was wrong.

Acting on the principle of protecting the future, I asked all, or
most, of my colleagues what they intended to do at the end of the
Parliament. Unless they were ready to stand again at the General
Election I thought it right to suggest to some of them that they
should resign now and either accept a peerage immediately or when
the Parliament ended. Some were ready enough to fall in with this
idea and never showed the slightest resentment. This category
included Mills, Watkinson and Maclay. In the case of the Lord
Chancellor, Kilmuir, one of my oldest and dearest friends, I thought
it right to accept his often repeated readiness to make way if I
thought the time had come. It seemed to me that since the Attorney-
General, Manningham-Buller, had served us so long and so
efficiently, it was fair that he should succeed to the position of
Lord Chancellor before the Parliament ended. David Eccles,
Minister of Education, to whom I offered the Board of Trade,
preferred to retire with an immediate peerage. On the Saturday I
recorded the story:

I am writing in bed at Birch Grove, feeling exhausted, almost shattered by the events of the last two days. On Thursday

morning, we had a Cabinet, the chief item on the agenda being a paper of mine (the result of many recent meetings and talks) on the Incomes Policy problem. It was a most unhappy meeting. Whether Selwyn had heard rumours, or whether it was an advanced form of the strange kind of apathy which has overcome him recently, I cannot tell. There was a good discussion, especially good points were raised by Macleod, Hare, Maudling and Hailsham. Selwyn took little part. Brooke (Chief Secretary) seemed embarrassed, but was – of course – useful and sensible.[1]

Six o'clock had been arranged as the time for my talk with the Chancellor of the Exchequer.

I did my best – but it was a terribly difficult and emotional scene. It lasted three-quarters of an hour. Naturally, I tried to persuade him of the need for a radical reconstruction on political grounds; that he had filled with distinction the two highest posts – Foreign Secretary and Chancellor of Exchequer – and that (unless he aspired to leading the party, which he had often told me that he had not) now seemed the time for him to start that third concern in business about which he had often talked to me. But it was of no avail. I'm afraid the truth is that these events are always very bad and perhaps the worst of all the duties of a Prime Minister. Selwyn refused a peerage; said he would stay in the House and support his financial policy (or, I suppose, criticise any deviation from it).[1]

After seeing Henry Brooke, a man in whose probity and honour I had the most confidence, I was somewhat comforted. He felt that, loyal as he was to his chief at the Treasury, the decision was right. This long and harassing day ended almost farcically.

It was then time to dress hurriedly, and go to the Savoy – for a dinner given *by* President Tubman [of Liberia] to the Queen. We got there just before the scheduled time for the Royals to arrive – Princess Royal, Princess Margaret, Duchess of Gloucester, Dowager Duchess of Kent, Duchess of Kent, Queen Mother, Queen. But somebody was late, and dinner began at 9 p.m.! Again I was lucky, sitting between Duchess of Kent and Duchess

[1] 14 July 1962.

of Hamilton. It was a fantastic scene—we all sat round an immense circle—small and narrow tables, one side only occupied. In the middle of the large open space thus formed, were three immense wreaths! Dorothy and I managed to get away when the Queen left, and *before* the reception.[1]

The next day, 13 July, it was clear to me that so much had leaked (from what source I never discovered) about the changes in the Government and so dangerous might be the political results following various Parliamentary intrigues and the speculations of the weekend Press that it was necessary to act rapidly.

The most important change, from the public point of view, was the appointment of Reggie Maudling as Chancellor of the Exchequer in place of Selwyn Lloyd. The others, although old friends and well-known public figures, had held less powerful positions in the Government.

In the end, things worked out pretty well. David Kilmuir, Harold Watkinson, Maclay, Percy Mills, as one would expect, did not think of themselves but only of me and the best course for the country. I got an earldom for David, a Viscounty for Mills; and C.H.s for Watkinson and Maclay. I told Tim Bligh to ring up Selwyn and say that in the emotion of our talk, I had forgotten to offer him a C.H. Would he like it? I was glad to hear that he accepted.[1]

I am still happier to reflect that Selwyn Lloyd has since been able to crown a distinguished career by election to the high office of Speaker of the House of Commons.

Maudling's change from the Colonial Office to the Treasury allowed me to make a reorganisation which I had long been anxious to achieve. I therefore decided to amalgamate the Commonwealth and Colonial Offices, both to be in the hands of Duncan Sandys. Among the new Ministers whom I was able to bring in was Sir Edward Boyle, for whom I had a high regard, who went to the Board of Education and 'another clever young man—Sir Keith Joseph—is to go to Housing and Local Government'.[1] Thorneycroft became Minister of Defence, and Deedes replaced Mills as Minister

[1] 14 July 1962.

Without Portfolio. Since Butler was now fully engaged in the difficult and unenviable task of taking full responsibility for Central Africa, he preferred to leave the Home Office, to which I appointed Henry Brooke. Julian Amery took Aviation, but not in the Cabinet.

> It was a dreadful day (I think I saw twenty people–some twice) but we got the list to the Queen (who was leaving the Garden Party) by 6.10 p.m.–with all the various changes, peerages, decorations, etc., and these went to the Press in time for 7 p.m. news. Selwyn thought fit to write a letter (rather stiff) to which I replied. These also were given to the Press. No other letters–I really thought *seven* or *eight* would be rather absurd. . . . Motored to Birch Grove arriving absolutely exhausted about 11 p.m.[1]

My correspondence with Selwyn Lloyd was as follows:

Dear Prime Minister,
    You have told me that you would like me to resign and this I willingly do.
    I realise that the policies with which I have been associated have been unpopular. On the other hand I believe that they have been right and have had a considerable measure of success. In my view our currency is stronger and our economic prospects on a firmer basis than for some time, and we are in a better position to face any difficulties which may come.
    I am also glad to have been associated with certain new departures, such as the development of an incomes policy and the creation of the National Economic Development Council. My primary aim has been to strengthen the country's competitive power and lay the foundation for sound growth.
    I know that you are well aware of my concern that these policies should be continued, and also of my anxiety that the growth of public expenditure, so much of it highly desirable in itself, should not outstrip our resources.
    I am very grateful to you for the many personal kindnesses which you have shown me.
                                        Yours ever,
                                                Selwyn

[1] 14 July 1962.

Dear Selwyn,

Thank you very much for your letter.

Your courageous policies at the Treasury have always commanded the support of your colleagues. You can rest assured that we intend to continue on the path that you have prepared. I am certain that this is the only way in which we can, in your own words, build growth upon a sound basis.

I am sure you realise the need in the present situation for a broad reconstruction of the Government with a view to the future, and I am grateful to you for facilitating this.

I am touched by your reference to personal kindnesses. We have worked together for a long time through many difficulties, and I am deeply grateful to you for your friendly support and encouragement.

Yours ever,

Harold Macmillan

The Saturday papers varied in tone—some purely sensational, and others more responsible. It was clear that a storm of some violence was to be expected.

The dangers are:

(*a*) A rally of extreme restrictionists to Selwyn. This has already started with a bitter letter to *The Times* from Nigel Birch.

(*b*) Sense of 'panic' measures. It was unfortunate that Leicester by-election—where we were third, beaten by Liberal—was announced on Thursday night.

(*c*) Accusations against me of 'disloyalty'. I have saved my skin by throwing my colleagues to the wolves. This will be pressed in spite of six years during which I have been accused of just the opposite.

(*d*) *More serious.* Effect on market and sterling if the idea gets about that we are going to reverse engines and go in for a dangerously 'expansionist' policy. After discussion with Governor of Bank, I got Maudling to issue a statement last night, to reassure in particular foreigners, etc. Here the continued weakness of the dollar does not hurt us, at least temporarily.[1]

On Saturday morning I confess that I felt shaken. It was clear that some who were stout-hearted in theory were beginning to weaken

[1] 14 July 1962.

in practice. But I was more shaken by the personal experience. I felt that I would prefer to go through a battle rather than face again such dreadfully painful and poignant scenes.

> Well, it's all over. I am in bed, in mother's old bedroom, looking out into the garden and the woods. It is all very peaceful. Dorothy is here with me—otherwise we are alone. Dorothy is very robust over all this—but it's very sad. I was particularly sorry to have to ask David Kilmuir to make way. Of course, he was splendid about it. But he is one of oldest, staunchest and most loyal friends, and I shall miss him very much.[1]

I made one minor change in my plans on the Saturday night.

> On reflection, I decided later in the day to send *formal* letters to each of the Ministers (to be published in Monday's papers— the Sunday Press is unsuitable for this anyway) and I have written long *private* letters to each—Kilmuir, Eccles, Watkinson, Maclay, Hill—I feel this will help.[1]

The next day we were able to fill up all the minor posts without much difficulty. I felt that the new team of Ministers would certainly make a good impression. Altogether we had ten new faces in the administration and this in the long run would help the Party.

In reporting to the Queen on the completion of the whole operation on 14 July, I wrote:

> The chief problem was whether to make the reconstruction immediately or, as is more normal and in many ways more convenient, at the beginning of the Parliamentary Recess. I would have advised Your Majesty that this course should be followed had it not been for the importance of completing and introducing the new form of the incomes policy upon which I have myself been engaged for some weeks. This must be presented to Parliament and the country before the Recess. Yet it seemed unrealistic that it should be in the hands of the Chancellor of the Exchequer whose replacement I had already decided to recommend to Your Majesty. Therefore, the only thing seemed to be to act now and that the new Chancellor of the Exchequer

[1] 14 July 1962.

should speak in the Debate when the time comes to develop the second stage of the incomes policy.

After explaining the painful character of my first interviews and the leakages in the Press,

I formed the view that there might be a Parliamentary or Party intrigue which might lead to a real danger to the Government. This would be enormously added to by the weekend Press and all its speculations. It might, therefore, well be that unless action were taken rapidly, action would be too late, and that by the early days of next week the Government might be found unable to maintain itself.

I therefore decided to get the whole thing done within the day, and I am most grateful for Your Majesty's co-operation.

In reference to my own feelings I added:

It is hard to say how much I have been worried by the nervous energy and emotion which this sort of operation implies. All the friendships of many years may be temporarily or perhaps permanently destroyed. Some of course, as Your Majesty may well imagine, are most co-operative and friendly. There are always Ministers who are only making way to give place to younger men . . . but there are Ministers who have ambition of higher things and who are rather badly wounded. All this, which involved I think twenty interviews in a space of about six hours, has left me very tired, but I went to my home in Sussex, from which I am writing to Your Majesty and where I am resting for a day or two.

Finally, I turned to the situation ahead.

What the future may bring is uncertain. There are so many grave problems and so many difficulties. One of my anxieties, I hope, will be successfully relieved by the repayment to the International Monetary Fund of the large debt which we have. Since this is a debt of £250 m. or more in terms of gold, it is very hazardous to have it weighing upon us in the light of the un-certainties as to the possible devaluation of the dollar. With the co-operation of the Governor I think this matter may be regulated by the end of next week.

I think Your Majesty may rest assured that the new Ministers will serve Your Majesty well. Mr. Maudling, although young, is experienced, able and balanced. I have been very glad to have had the opportunity to bring in men like Sir Edward Boyle and Sir Keith Joseph who represent active and energetic youth; all this is to the good.

Nevertheless, I cannot conceal from Your Majesty the dangers in our political situation if the present run of opinion continues as exhibited in the by-elections. I shall do all I can to help the position; it will require both courage and skill and I believe I can look to the support of my colleagues and Parliament as a whole. There is always, of course, a danger of intrigue and splits but this is not the normal practice of the Conservative Party; for all its weaknesses it is essentially loyal.

The new Cabinet met on 17 July. I got the feeling that

there *was* a sense of freshness and interest.[1]

In the afternoon

I entered the House of Commons at 3.10 p.m. for my questions. No applause from our side, jeers from Opposition. During my answers, a lot of laughter and barracking from Opposition. Our side quiet, except for one or two who tried to come to my help but did (as so often) more harm than good. It was clear to me that the storm is going to be quite hard to ride. Curiously enough, those most vociferous for change seem now to be the chief critics.[1]

Within a day or two the atmosphere began to improve.

It would seem that the Party is calming down. (Indeed, this is reflected in *some* of the Press.) P.Q.'s went off very quietly—indeed the Opposition were almost subdued and our side friendly to one or two little ripostes which I made in a light and bantering vein.[2]

Later that day, at the 1922 Committee,

There were two hundred and fifty Members present. I spoke very . . . simply—chiefly on the personal aspect of the changes. There was no 'panic'. A radical reconstruction was necessary and

[1] 17 July 1962.   [2] 19 July 1962.

I had decided on it in principle some time ago. The problem was timing. There were strong arguments for now—before outcome of Brussels negotiations; before Party Conference; and before shape of departmental estimates and therefore next year's Budget was fixed. I paid tributes to Selwyn and other colleagues. One or two questions (not hostile) and I returned to Admiralty House, where we had a party for one hundred and ninety constituents. I felt . . . satisfied. I had a good and sympathetic reception. I felt that feeling was now moving definitely towards me and my action. (If the letters which M.P.s are receiving are anything like those which we are getting at No. 10, this may have affected them. Ours are ten to one in favour.)[1]

Although widely different reports of this 'private' meeting were published, I had no doubt that the crisis was surmounted. *The Times* gave an absolutely correct report. The *Telegraph* and the *Guardian* were both fair and friendly. The *Express* was extremely hostile but curiously enough the *Evening Standard* took a completely different line. It was no longer a 'humiliation' for me but a 'triumph'. Perhaps new orders had come from Lord Beaverbrook.

The new Cabinet had now to review and approve the latest form of the Incomes Policy. In essence, this followed the lines of my original suggestions, the emphasis being on an overall approach covering status and security at work, consumer protection, the 'guiding light' and the proposal to set up a Standing Commission on incomes. However, we had come to the conclusion that the principle of the guiding light had got to be modified to allow for more flexibility in assessing claims in relation to the national interest—for instance it might be desirable to strengthen the man-power in a particular sector relative to other sectors. On the Standing Commission, we decided to abandon any compulsory reference of wage claims. Nevertheless, where a settlement had been reached without reference to the Commission which appeared to conflict with the national interest, the Government would ask the Commission to conduct an *ex post facto* review and it would be given power to send for papers and persons, and to make constructive as well as negative criticisms in its report.

[1] 19 July 1962.

On 26 July the House of Commons met for a full-dress debate on the whole situation. The Opposition put down a vote of censure in the following terms:

> That this House declares that Her Majesty's Government no longer enjoys the confidence of the country, and accordingly calls upon the Prime Minister to advise Her Majesty to dissolve Parliament so that a General Election can be held.

This was quite strong meat, and quite unusual excitement was worked up in and outside Parliament. I well knew that everything would turn upon the discussion and the vote that was to follow. My error in combining the change at the Treasury with a general reconstruction of the Government had undoubtedly obscured the fundamental purpose which I had in mind. The sensational news headlines 'Mac the Knife', 'Panic in Whitehall' and all the rest, made it attractive for the Leader of the Opposition to concentrate the vigour of his attack upon the personal issues. His opening words were as follows:

> This debate takes place in the shadow of ... sensational events. ... The terms of the Motion are their direct consequence, for what happened then was the most convincing confession of failure which could have been offered by the Government, and the most complete vindication of the charges and criticisms put forward by the Opposition.
>
> Of course, in all Governments incompetent Ministers are from time to time dismissed. In all Governments some older men retire. In all Governments reshuffles occur and resignations on political and personal grounds sometimes take place. But in all the flood of comment which has appeared since 20 July I have not seen a single suggestion that there is a precedent for the removal of no fewer than seven Ministers, one-third of the whole of the Cabinet, the curt dismissal of the Chancellor of the Exchequer, the man who had previously held the other highest office in the State under the Prime Minister, that of Secretary of State for Foreign Affairs, together with eight other Ministers in the Government.

He described the changes as the

act of a desperate man in a desperate situation, and the desperate situation was the steady, remorseless and steep decline of the Conservative Party's fortunes in by-election after by-election.

The whole of his speech was on the same note and fully justified, in all the circumstances. But Gaitskell was a lecturer by nature, not an orator. When he came to realities, his references to the economic situation were neither effective nor profound. He ended with some bitter words:

> The great Governments of the past have often been composed of men of different views and outlook, but they have been bound together by some common purpose. Prime Ministers who have lived in history have set more store by their policy objectives than by the time they remained in office. This was true of Peel, of Gladstone, of Churchill, of Attlee. It was true of Lord Avon, however mistaken we may think the policy was.
> It is not true of the right hon. Gentleman the Prime Minister. His Government will be remembered not for the leadership they gave the nation, but as a conspiracy to retain power. Men and measures have been equally sacrificed for this purpose.

In replying I thought it best to deal immediately with these accusations. I began by saying,

> The right hon. Member the Leader of the Opposition, in moving the Motion, has dealt partly with personalities and partly with policies. I am bound to say that he did not say much about policies. He soon came back to the personalities. No doubt he found it much easier.

I went on, in a short passage, to defend my own record and to give the reasons for the Government changes.

> I am not at all abashed by the accusations of disloyalty or lack of courage or panic. These taunts are natural. Obviously, they are very easy to make; but, curiously, two exactly opposite attacks have been made on me since I became Prime Minister. I have been accused during my years in office of excessive loyalty to old friends and colleagues and unwillingness to introduce new blood

into the Government. I have also been accused of a detachment amounting almost to disdain. Now I am accused of taking violent action in a moment of panic.

These contradictory accusations do not move me. I am content to be judged by those with whom I have worked during nearly fifty years of active life – in the Army, in business, here in the House of Commons and in Government.

But what has distressed me is having to make a number of decisions which are unhappily necessary from time to time, affecting long friendships. My right hon. and learned Friend the former Chancellor of the Exchequer has worked with me in close partnership for six years. He has held the high offices of both Foreign Secretary and Chancellor of the Exchequer. We all recognise the courage, single-mindedness and patriotism that he has shown. Last July, with my full support, he embarked upon an operation made necessary by the fierce pressures on sterling which were then being developed. That phase of the battle is over. We have achieved a sound basis for growth and we must confirm that and move to a new phase.

I have decided that for this new phase there must be some new commanders. These decisions are, as all those who have held this office know, one of the greatest burdens that fall upon a Prime Minister. I can assure the House that they are much easier to evade than to make. There is no inconsistency in all this. To take the decision and to face its consequences does not detract in the slightest degree from the sincerity of my tribute to the work of my right hon. and learned Friend, which, I believe, will be shared by all hon. Members on this side of the House.

I devoted the rest of my speech to a review of the economic situation and to the philosophy which must guide the national effort in the modern world. In a country like ours where there was, broadly speaking, full employment and certainly no massive reserves of manpower as in the case of some European countries, 'expansion can be achieved only in two ways, by the rapid transfer of manpower where it is available from declining to expanding industries, and by the removal of any obstacles to growth'. We must therefore look to the National Economic Development Council for the most efficient use of management and labour in exploiting the vast complex of machinery and techniques which modern science had made available. Yet we must accept the fact that

> if the nation as a whole pays itself in increased wages, salaries and dividends more than is justified by increasing production, it is surely accepted that costs will rise and exports fall. In that event even the increase in individual incomes will be but Dead Sea fruit.

I made therefore a declaration to which I still adhere. 'An incomes policy is, therefore, necessary as a permanent feature of our economic life.' I next referred to the various attempts to exercise some control on wages and salaries.

> Even in war—with controlled prices, rationing, the direction of labour, one hundred per cent Excess Profits Tax and post-war credits to reduce the impact of increasing wages and the rest— we did not have a wholly successful incomes policy. One of the results is the immense debt [which] we now carry.

After 1945, although the Labour Government had inherited a highly controlled system brought about by the siege economy inevitable for an island in war, they were baffled by the same problem.

> Many of us could recall how at that time the Labour Ministers resorted as we have, to appeal and exhortation and many of us remember the immense energy and enthusiasm which Sir Stafford Cripps devoted to this purpose. (Hon. Members: 'Hear, hear.') But even he was not successful and now that we have a much freer economy it may be that the task is more difficult. I freely admit that.

Yet all these efforts had not been in vain. Public opinion was beginning to understand what must happen if one sector tried to gain an undue advantage over the rest and how fatal would be the result if all insisted in pursuing increasing money incomes without regard to their real value. In the last year, by the Pay Pause and other methods, a respite had been gained. Yet what we now needed was a new machinery and a new advance.

I then set out both the structure and the functions of the National Incomes Commission in accordance with the form agreed by the Cabinet.

Our experience over the past year has shown clearly that it is not enough for the Government to offer guidance in general terms. What we need is an impartial and authoritative view on the more important or difficult pay questions given by a body which can see these questions both as they affect individual interests and the nation.

The Incomes Commission would be a permanent body; but there was, of course, no intention to deprive any man of his right to sell his labour or to hire other men's labour as he might wish. Free negotiation, the machinery of arbitration, the wage-council system would all continue. Nevertheless, the Commission would have an important part to play.

It will be given terms of reference requiring it to inquire into and to express views on claims of special importance. In so doing it will take into account not only the circumstances of each claim but also the wider considerations of national interest such as the need for increases in incomes to be matched by increases in production. It will carry out this work, so far as possible, in public. It will publish its findings and its reasons for them in full. . . . This is important, for one of our main needs today is to mobilise and inform public opinion.

Much that happens now in the sort of dim industrial twilight might well be brought into the clear light of day. The Commission will deal not only with problems in industry but also with public and other services, the value of which cannot be measured by purely commercial considerations.

Since the time was not yet ripe for any compulsory system the Commission would depend on its sanction for the power of public opinion. It

will consider specially important pay claims or disputes which may be referred to it by the agreement of the parties concerned. But there may well be cases from time to time in which, although one side or the other is reluctant to agree to the reference of a claim to the Commission, the Government may nevertheless form the view, on representations from one of the parties, or on wider grounds, that the Commission should consider the question in the public interest.

I cannot believe that in practice the parties would not give weight to the Government's expressed view, and I cannot believe that either side would disregard it. But if it did, the public would form its own conclusion.

After giving further details of the plan with all its difficulties, but with all its hopeful prospects, I thought it right to say something about profits and dividends.

I have spoken of increases in wages and salaries. But I am not unmindful of the widespread and natural feeling that restraint in profits and dividends is no less important. It is vital that people should not feel that their acceptance of the restraint implied in a national incomes policy is merely going to give someone else a larger profit or dividend. This is to a large extent in the hands of the Government, and the Government will, by fiscal or any other appropriate means, restrain any undue growth in aggregate profits which might follow from restraint in wages and salaries.

In most economies, I think the right hon. Gentleman will agree, profits are usually drawn hand-in-hand with rising wages; and restraint in wages and salaries would be accompanied by falling profits. Nevertheless, I give this formal pledge.

I then turned to various other reforms—consumer protection, the Shops and Offices Bill, the need for retraining, the need for proper contracts of service, and other allied questions. In conclusion I stated:

I confidently ask the House to reject the Motion. Since its return to power in 1951, the Conservative Party in office has faithfully carried out its programme. It was elected to office in 1951, and its mandate has twice been renewed and fortified. With the support of the House, we intend to carry on and complete our work.

So, on a tentative—and as yet voluntary—basis, the Incomes Policy was launched. This bark, constructed with so much labour and pain, was destined to meet with, and almost founder in, some stormy seas. It is, temporarily at any rate, in dock.

The debate, like all these highly advertised debates worked up by the Press, was rather a flop. Gaitskell made a very *bad* speech, quite unworthy of the occasion or of himself. My reply was not at all good oratorically. But I managed to put forward my proposals and get them listened to. Maudling (the new Chancellor of Exchequer) wound up. His matter was good, but his task was made difficult by persistent heckling and jeering. Our majority was ninety-eight—not an abstention from our side. (Our formal majority is now ninety-four.)[1]

I was particularly touched to learn that a number of our supporters had returned from abroad or given up important engagements to be present at this division, always at much inconvenience and often at considerable expense. When I got the list of all those who had shown their loyalty so conspicuously I wrote each a personal letter of thanks.

At any rate the debate did much to clarify the real issues. We were now definitely set upon an expansionist course, and the whole purpose of the changes at the Treasury was to ensure that this should take place without further delay. Unhappily, owing to my error in confusing the issue by the large-scale reconstruction of the Government, this vital objective had been at first obscured. The debate made it plain. This expansion was in fact pursued not without success during the rest of my tenure of my post. We regarded the Incomes Policy as essential in order to sustain expansion without incurring the evils which inflated costs following inflated wages had brought in the past and might, if unchecked, bring in the future. With all the painful tribulations of this search for new men and new measures my main object had been attained. It is true that the Trades Union Congress declared that they would have nothing to do with any Incomes Policy. That first reaction was to be expected; but I noticed with pleasure that there were a number of the more responsible leaders who said little, and from whom I believed we could expect quiet and uneffusive sympathy.

[1] 29 July 1962.

It took a little time to find a suitable chairman for the National Incomes Commission, to be commonly known as 'Nicky', and to formulate the terms of reference. Much to my delight, Sir Geoffrey Lawrence, Q.C., accepted the arduous post, and by 5 November the formal terms of reference were announced. This body which was, of course, a first attempt to deal with these baffling problems, operated with varying degrees of success until it was replaced, under the Labour Government, in March 1965, by the Prices and Incomes Board. Much has followed since then, with many hopes and many disappointments. But I remain convinced that our initiative in 1962 was right and that in the long run, if the four great objectives—full employment, steady prices, a strong currency involving a favourable balance of payments, as well as continued economic growth—are to be achieved and maintained, some form of incomes policy will be found necessary. By a curious paradox, a Labour administration became converts to this view, although, like the Conservatives, they subsequently lapsed or even apostasised.

This episode, if painful, was unavoidable. Its conduct was not made easier for me because of the other distractions of these months —the East—West complications and the growing Soviet pressure, soon to culminate in the Cuba crisis; the European negotiations reaching an apparent deadlock in Brussels; and the approaching breakdown of the Central African Federation. Although in tracing and describing the various themes in my story each must be recorded separately, the reader must not forget that all these difficulties are apt to occur simultaneously. While accepting in principle the thought in Cowper's line 'Variety's the spice of life' I sometimes felt that the flavouring could be a little overdone.

CHAPTER V

Europe and the Commonwealth

In spite of these distractions at home – the relentless pressure of wage inflation, the new problem of immigration, and the painful necessity of Cabinet reconstruction – my colleagues and I recognised that the year 1962 would prove a turning-point in the story of Britain's relations with Europe.

The Government changes left undisturbed the team of Ministers mainly concerned; indeed, the succession of Maudling to the Treasury gave us the advantage of his long, if somewhat unrewarding, experience in similar negotiations. Butler continued to preside over the small group of Ministers dealing with day-to-day work, while Heath carried the burden of long and fatiguing discussions in Brussels, supported by his team of experts. To defend the interests of the Commonwealth there was Duncan Sandys, who, as one of the founders of the European Movement, was admirably suited to the task of marrying the two themes. Christopher Soames, as Minister of Agriculture, was a keen European, but an equally firm defender of the claims of British farmers.

In this tangle of interests there were four main strands to be unravelled. First, the American position, which was broadly sympathetic. Secondly, the European attitudes, as revealed both in my talks with the leaders of the Six, particularly de Gaulle and Adenauer, and in Heath's prolonged meetings with the Ministers and officials of the Community. These were complicated by the fact that the members of the Community had still much ground to cover to complete their own internal arrangements. Thirdly, the feelings expressed in our interchanges with the Commonwealth leaders culminating in the dramatic Prime Ministers' Conference in September 1962. Fourthly, there were the pressures and manoeuvres within the Conservative Party leading up to the Conference in October.

President Kennedy himself was helpful and sympathetic throughout. When we met in Bermuda at the end of December 1961, we were mainly concerned (as I shall describe in the next chapter) with the threats and frustrations arising from Russian policy. Nevertheless, we had some talk about the Common Market and found ourselves in broad agreement. Apart from the President, the Americans generally, both official and unofficial, accepted with sympathy our theme of European unity. At that time they relied so unhesitatingly on the firm and unassaulted citadel of the dollar as to show little alarm about possible consequences. Individual parts of the American machine were no doubt anxious about the competitive power of a united Europe in the years ahead. There was also the constant rivalry between the Pentagon and our Ministry of Defence, each struggling to secure the maximum orders arising from the rearmament of Germany; and there was always Mr. George Ball of the State Department who seemed determined to thwart our policy in Europe and the Common Market negotiations. Nevertheless, both at our personal meetings and by constant messages of encouragement, Kennedy showed his full appreciation of our purpose, basing himself partly on economic advantages to the Free World, but still more upon the enhanced strategic contribution which a united Europe could make. He expressed these sentiments in a notable speech on 4 July, when he took up and underlined my old theme of the interdependence of the nations of the Free World and the partnership which must be maintained between Europe and the United States. When I read his speech I was much moved and sent him the following message on 9 July:

I must send you my warmest congratulations on the Interdependence Speech made on Independence Day. I feel especially gratified because I made a small effort to scratch rather than blaze the trail at Boston last year. Now everything depends on the Brussels negotiations. Europeans are in rather a touchy mood. But I am quite hopeful of the ultimate result. It may be best to let things go on quietly for a bit.

As regards the Common Market countries, it must be remembered how many vital points were left unsettled and uncertain by the terms of the Treaty of Rome. It is true that in some respects these engagements were more precise and detailed than most of us British might have desired. Nevertheless, much was decided only 'in principle' and a great deal had to be worked out 'in practice'. This was especially true when the methods of applying the single market to agriculture had to be agreed and meetings lasting over many months, with a full quota of all-night sessions, were devoted to the various details of this immense field of endeavour. Moreover, and perhaps from our point of view even more disturbing, there was a certain ambivalence of approach and aims inherent in the whole history of the Movement. There were the enthusiastic federalists, who believed that something like the United States of America might rapidly be brought into being in Europe; there were the cynics who, while accepting the general idea of European unity, regarded it in effect as a convenient instrument for their own ambitious national policies. In between, there were the moderates, who believed that, once economic unity was brought about, a gradual but cautious approach could be made to central decisions on matters of defence, foreign policy and the like, but without involving any high degree of 'institutionalism' for these purposes.

Curiously enough, de Gaulle himself took up a position which on the surface resembled our own. He was a confederalist, not a federalist. Nevertheless, I was always conscious that the very feelings of tradition which led him to oppose the federalist dream were the instinctive cause of his reluctance to accept British membership, which might even develop into British leadership.

On 14 January 1962, after weeks of discussion and almost continuous sessions, day and night, the Six ultimately agreed the next stage of their agricultural policy. Only now could negotiations begin with the British delegation on the problem of temperate foodstuffs. A few days later, on 18 January, the Fouchet Committee resumed its talks on political union—a dangerous subject—but one in which I knew that our own views would be very close to those of the French.

On the same day the Italian Prime Minister, Amintore Fanfani, together with the Foreign Minister, Antonio Segni, paid a visit to London.

Yesterday was an all-Italian day. Meetings in morning and afternoon. Luncheon at Italian Embassy for us; dinner at Admiralty House for them. The talks were useful but not dramatic. Both Ministers [Fanfani and Segni] are able, courteous and well-informed. Their chief anxiety is as NATO members. They don't want to be exposed to dangerous courses over Berlin. . . . On Europe, they will be helpful – but they have rather 'federationist' ideas. I went to the Embassy this morning to say goodbye.[1]

Early the following month

Ted Heath came to luncheon and gave me his impressions of the Common Market negotiations, their difficulties and their prospects. The hope is to finish by the end of July – but I doubt it. If it does, we should have to aim at Commonwealth Prime Ministers in late September or early October. This could be followed by Party Conference and then Parliament. But I fear that the negotiations may drift on. However, it all opens up a fascinating autumn.[2]

Encouraged by his report we made a firm application to start negotiations for entering the European Atomic Energy Community and the Coal and Steel Community. The usual squabble about the support costs of our troops in Germany did not seem to introduce any discordant note, for we were accustomed to these annual disputes.

By March I felt hopeful about the proceedings in Brussels. However, I was beginning to be concerned by a new dilemma.

The great problem, which looms ahead, is how to arrange for the meeting of Commonwealth Prime Ministers on Europe. The negotiations for Britain's entry into the Common Market are going on well in Brussels. Although they are at present of a preliminary character, they will come to the crunch during the summer. We may expect to know by the end of July on what sort of terms, as regards EFTA countries, British agriculture, and the

[1] 18 January 1962.　　　　[2] 7 February 1962.

Commonwealth we can join the Six. In fact, we are having the closest consultation all the time with Commonwealth officials. We have had visits from and to individual Ministers. But everyone will pretend the opposite (if it suits them) and nothing will be regarded as constituting 'consultation' except a meeting of Prime Ministers. So the question arises, when? It could be in *May*, just *before* the real negotiation starts, or in *September*, just after. If in May, some of them will say such things about the Europeans . . . that the negotiations will be wrecked. If we have them in September, the Tory Party 'loyalists' (Walker-Smith, Turton, Lord Salisbury) will say they have been presented with a *fait accompli* and they may swing the Party Conference in October and the Party [in] the House of Commons when Parliament meets.[1]

Early in April, following a cease-fire in Algeria, a referendum was held in France and de Gaulle received an overwhelming victory; ninety per cent of the voters gave him their confidence. I thought this would be helpful because the Algerian revolt touched a most delicate chord in his sensitive character. Accordingly, I wrote to him on 16 April to send my congratulations on his success.

Quite a lot has happened since I had the pleasure of entertaining you at Birch Grove House last November. I am hoping that the satisfactory settlement of the Algerian problem and the massive support which you have received from the French people will make it possible for you now to turn your mind increasingly to the political, economic and defence problems of Western Europe.

On our side I am hoping for real progress by the end of the summer towards a successful conclusion of the Brussels negotiations with all that that implies.

If you are agreeable, I would like to find some moment which was convenient to you in which we might renew our discussions on all these vital subjects. I have arranged to go immediately after Easter for a short visit to the United States and Canada. Is there any chance of you giving me a day in the early part of June?

We are all sorry to lose Monsieur Chauvel [outgoing French

[1] 24 March 1962.

Ambassador] but equally, as you know, Monsieur de Courcel [incoming French Ambassador] will be very welcome.

On 15 May, at a Press Conference, de Gaulle stressed his opposition to a supranational political development of Europe and his preference for a Community of national states. The fact that five of his Ministers who favoured federalism resigned from his Government as a result was encouraging for us. Nevertheless, it still left the problem of how we could persuade France to support British entry. Our adhesion could not be very attractive from an economic point of view, for it would add a strong competitor to the Market. We could not offer a nuclear bargain, because of our agreements with the United States of America. Was it perhaps the long-term doubts about the future of Germany which might make forward-looking French statesmen look to Britain as a loyal and dependable ally? Much therefore would turn on my meeting with de Gaulle, and careful preparations had to be made.

During these months, within the Commonwealth, especially the old Commonwealth countries, doubts, criticisms and some degree even of suspicion not unnaturally emerged. At the beginning of January 1962, Heath had visited Canada and done his best to calm the somewhat emotional situation which had begun to develop. I sent him a note on 11 January to express my gratitude:

I should like to tell you how pleased I am at the results of your most successful visit to Canada and the United States.

Judging from the reports, you seem to have made considerable progress in Canada. Both Government circles and indeed public opinion generally now seem to be in a much calmer frame of mind about the Common Market. Many congratulations.

Derry Amory, our High Commissioner, also sent me an encouraging report on 15 January:

The newspapers here are almost without exception sympathetic and understanding in regard to our European efforts. Ministers too are really trying quite hard to change their rigid attitude of hostility to the idea for something more constructive and friendly. They have a real and perhaps natural apprehension of either getting squeezed between a combined Europe and the United

States or swallowed up by the latter. Ted Heath's visit was most helpful from every point of view.

Although Diefenbaker on 20 February emphasised the need for a meeting of Commonwealth Prime Ministers before any final decisions were taken, he was of course forcing an open door. The only point of doubt was the best moment for the conference to be held. It was obviously premature in February. On 26 March, Diefenbaker renewed his pressure and Menzies was also expressing some anxiety. It became, therefore, necessary to make a definite decision. Accordingly, on 30 March I sent a message in similar terms to the Prime Ministers or Presidents of every Commonwealth country. After explaining that our first idea had been to suggest a meeting some time during the next two or three months, we had now come to the conclusion that if the real purpose was to consider together the pattern which was to emerge from the negotiations at Brussels, a somewhat later date would be more useful. I therefore definitely proposed that we should, if possible, hold a week's meeting in London beginning on 10 September. I also suggested that the Prime Ministers might wish to bring with them their Finance or Trade Ministers. I added, 'although the formal business of the meeting would be mainly concerned with the subject of our relations with the E.E.C., Commonwealth Prime Ministers would no doubt wish to take this opportunity to discuss together the world situation'. Naturally a conference of this kind, to meet the convenience of some sixteen busy politicians, needs a good deal of arranging. I therefore counted myself fortunate that by 19 April I was able to announce the precise date–10 September–in the House of Commons.

Meanwhile, John McEwen, the Deputy Prime Minister of Australia, had made us a visit and had also undertaken a full tour of Western Europe.

He has been to Paris; Bonn; Rome; Brussels; and *well* received by the leading personalities. De Gaulle was very gracious to him and Mr. McEwen was much impressed. On the whole, we were encouraged both by Mr. McEwen's general attitude to the Common Market and by the sympathetic reception which he

had received from European statesmen. The same was true of
Hallstein.[1]

This was good news, for McEwen, a powerful figure, represented
the Country Party, an essential element in the coalition on which
Menzies relied. A skilful and determined negotiator, he was a man
who fought hard and spoke his mind in a forthright and sometimes
even contentious manner. I had great regard for him, for he was
straight and honourable; if he once gave his word, he would never
go back on it.

From 29 April to 3 May I was in Canada. Since the Canadian
General Election was now under way, I had to tread very warily.
Nevertheless, the speech which I gave to the Canadian Press in
Toronto seemed acceptable to the audience.

The references to Britain's double duty—to the Commonwealth *and* to Europe—were well understood and well received.[2]

Diefenbaker's attitude of hostility toward our great plan was not
disguised, but I felt that it was

not shared by the *serious* people in Canada . . . I was particularly
struck by the broad views of the bankers and businessmen whom
I met in Toronto.[2]

Indeed,

I did not find any antagonism among ordinary folk. When I was
given the Freedom of Toronto, I got a tremendous reception
from a very large crowd.[2]

On my return home, I sent a message to Holyoake in New
Zealand urging him to send one of his Ministers to London. I was
glad to have an enthusiastic reply agreeing to send Jack Marshall,
the Minister in his Government most closely associated with these
questions.

It will be seen, therefore, that both in Europe itself and in the
Commonwealth, as well as in Parliament and in public opinion at
home, we were making steady progress. But I knew that, as we
approached the final stages, the atmosphere would become more
tense.

[1] 12 April 1962.　　　[2] 6 May 1962.

The next important event must clearly be my meeting with de Gaulle. On 19 May I had a long talk with Heath to discuss tactics.

> The strange feature of the present situation is the paradox that de Gaulle wants the kind of Europe we would be able readily to join, but he doesn't want us in it (*L'Europe à l'anglais sans les anglais*). Sir Pierson Dixon, who has the most subtle mind in Whitehall, thinks that de Gaulle has now definitely decided to exclude us. But he believes that, if we play our cards well, we can put him into an untenable position which even he will not like . . . Sir Pierson Dixon thinks that—with patience and good temper—we can outwit him. Others (and I am one) do not feel so sure that de Gaulle has definitely made up his mind. I think he may still be torn between emotion and reason. He *hates* England—still more America—because of the war, because of France's shame, because of Churchill and Roosevelt, because of the nuclear weapon. Yet it is a sort of 'love–hate' complex. We shall see—and soon.[1]

Heath's own view was that de Gaulle and his entourage hoped that the negotiations would break down in such a way as would make it possible to blame Britain, either because we would be confronted by terms which we could not accept or because, even if our negotiators reached agreement, it would be on a basis which the Commonwealth and the British Parliament would reject. He also felt that there was a genuine fear on de Gaulle's part of admitting Britain as a kind of Trojan horse which would either disrupt the present system or prevent French domination. There was no doubt resentment about our close relations with the United States, especially in the field of defence. A long discussion followed as to how we might try to meet de Gaulle's suspicions and antagonism. At any rate, a few days later

> some very interesting evidence is beginning to come in about de Gaulle's fears, anxieties, inhibitions, and jealousies. All this confirms what I have said all along—this is not an economic problem. It's a political problem.[2]

My thoughts travelled round and round this almost insoluble puzzle.

[1] 19 May 1962.   [2] 22 May 1962.

There seems an increasing impression that de Gaulle does *not* repeat *not* want us in Europe. (Although it seems as if Couve de Murville accepts our adhesion as 'a historical fatality'.) But the General may feel unable or unwilling to oppose our application *openly* and *directly*. His instructions to the negotiators are likely to be to obstruct, waste time, try to make everybody – including the British – lose heart. Alternatively, if this fails, the French will insist on terms so harsh for our farmers and for the Commonwealth that we shall be forced to withdraw. This, of course, is a dangerous game. French hegemony in Europe (or a part of Europe) may be maintained for a time. But the future will be insecure.[1]

Before leaving for Paris, I had a chance of a private and informal talk with Menzies, who had come to London to see me and my leading colleagues.

A long talk – two hours – with Bob Menzies, chiefly about the international situation and the *political* purpose of our joining Europe. I thought him impressed by my arguments, but not persuaded.[2]

The next day he and Marshall, the New Zealand Minister, issued a joint statement about the Common Market

which has hit the headlines. I thought Bob seemed rather ashamed today, and he pretended that he had no idea it would have such publicity. This is, of course, absurd, since Bob is an old hand. What the effect will be, it's too early to tell. Fortunately, they have concentrated on their weakest point – free entry of *manufactured* goods under the Ottawa agreement. No mention is made . . . of how the British preferences have been whittled away over the years, and the many discriminating measures taken . . . against British trade.[3]

The same afternoon Dorothy and I left London at two o'clock. Philip de Zulueta came with us. On landing at the airport, where we were met by M. de Courcel, the French Ambassador in London, and Bob Dixon, we drove to Château de Champs. It was always a great event to be received by the General. He was a charming host

[1] 27 May 1962.   [2] 1 June 1962.   [3] 2 June 1962.

E

with his natural courtesy and old-world manners. The Château de Champs suited him to perfection. It was a lovely eighteenth-century house of modest size

> which belonged to Madame de Pompadour and was bought, restored, and presented to the State by a rich Jew. It has a wonderful garden, by Le Nôtre, in the classic style—avenues of cut limes, statues, fountains, etc., etc. The furniture is good and the rooms reasonably comfortable.[1]

The first talk took place between 6 p.m. and 7.45 p.m., when only four were present: the General, with his Private Secretary, M. Burin des Roziers; I brought Philip de Zulueta. Earlier in the week, de Gaulle had had a general conversation with our Ambassador, in which he had set out the political and economic difficulties as he saw them and these he now repeated. 'I tried to answer these, point by point, with a mass of detail as well as with argument of principle.'[1] A small family dinner followed, which was very agreeable, with de Gaulle in the role of a stately monarch unbending a little to the representative of a once hostile but now friendly country.

The next day was Sunday and before we resumed our conversations I reflected on what had passed so far.

> I felt reasonably satisfied. The General did not show the rather brutal attitude which had been attributed to him, and predicted as likely. On the other hand, it is clear that he is *not* really keen on having us in Europe for two main reasons.
>
> (1) It will *alter the character* of the Community, both in the economic and the political field. Now it is a nice little club, not too big, not too small, under French hegemony. With us, and the Norwegians, and the Danes, etc., it will change its character. Is this to France's advantage?
>
> (2) He thinks that, apart from our loyalty to the Commonwealth, we shall always be too intimately tied up with the Americans. De Gaulle regards American alliance as essential, but he feels that America wants to make Europe into a number of satellite states.[2]

[1] 2 June 1962.   [2] 3 June 1962.

As so often before, I found it difficult to fathom the character of this strange and enigmatic man.

I find it difficult to be sure about de Gaulle's attitude. My talks with him have certainly convinced him that H.M.G. regard it as, on the whole, a British interest that we should enter the European Community, if reasonable terms can be made, especially for the old Commonwealth countries. I think he is persuaded also that we put as much, perhaps even more, weight on the political as on the economic arguments. He was impressed by my review of this unhappy century, and how a close Anglo-French alliance, really effectively managed from day to day, would have avoided both wars and all that has flowed from them. Nevertheless, I am not at all sure how far de Gaulle and the French really feel it to be in France's interest to have us in. It cannot be done without much discussion and negotiation or without disturbing some of the agreements so painfully arrived at by very hard bargaining between the Six. Moreover, it means the end of French hegemony.[1]

One point emerged clearly: the General wanted a nuclear deterrent force for France. But he seemed to understand that, while we might co-operate in some of the details which were within our own control, we could not part with those secrets which we only received from America as heirs of the original founders of nuclear science in the war. In a letter to the Queen on 5 June, I tried to summarise my impressions of the visit:

[General de Gaulle] was very frank about our difficulties concerning our application for entry into the Six, and he pointed out that this would change the character in the Community both economically and politically. The economic consequences did not seem to trouble him, but he was clearly much more perturbed about the political results. He said he thought a united Europe would be able to hold up its head and look the Americans in the face. There should be a European policy not only for Europe but all over the world. In order to ensure the possibility of this there will also have to be a European defence without which no government has any responsibility or authority. I think that I was able to explain some of the economic effects to de Gaulle and to

[1] 3 June 1962.

dispose of certain doubts which he had about the possibility of the United Kingdom joining the Community. On the political and defence side, I could not but express a good deal of sympathy with his point of view, while being careful to defend the United States as a good and indispensable ally, a thesis from which de Gaulle did not dissent.

I returned to find the usual minor crisis in the financial world:

A new worry is that the collapse in the New York Stock Market is beginning to affect sterling. I suppose Americans are selling their British investments to pay for their losses on Wall Street.[1]

At the same time, the Common Market controversy was working up at home.

Lord Beaverbrook has now got Lord Montgomery, whose views are being disseminated in large . . . advertisements in all the newspapers. The Conservative opposition (led by Sir Derek Walker-Smith, Mr. Turton, Lord Hinchingbrooke, etc.) is getting under way. The Labour Party is uncertain – a new battle *against* Gaitskell, who has been deserted by Healey and (probably) Harold Wilson.[1]

At the Opposition's request, there was a debate arranged on Europe; but it took place on the adjournment, and there was no vote.

Heath . . . made an admirable opening to the debate – lucid, firm and showing a great grasp of all the complicated details. Gaitskell was engaged in his familiar role of sitting on the fence.[1]

Yet the situation was delicate. At the Australia Club dinner on 12 June, where Menzies was chief guest,

I had to propose the toast, and did so quite effectively, I think. Bob was in great form – but much more reasonable than I had expected about the Common Market. He was obviously trying hard to play the game, and his talks with all of us have helped.[2]

Naturally, the *Express* has completely misrepresented both my speech and Bob's. Sentences are taken out of their context and printed in heavy type. The qualifying sentences are suppressed. Jokes are turned into serious points and *vice versa*.[3]

[1] 6 June 1962.   [2] 12 June 1962.   [3] 13 June 1962.

Into this somewhat tense situation, Robert McNamara, the United States Defence Secretary, now threw an explosive bomb of his own. In a speech at Michigan, he condemned all national nuclear forces as 'dangerous' and 'lacking in credibility'.

> McNamara's foolish speech . . . has enraged the French. . . . All the Allies are angry with the American proposal that we should buy [their] rockets. . . . This is not a European rocket. It's a racket of the American industry.[1]

The trouble with American Cabinet Ministers is that they are generally drawn either from the board room or from the common room. But neither tycoons nor academics are very skilful or sensitive in politics, especially the politics of other countries.

Early in July I noted that

> the *Daily Express*, as part of its campaign against the Common Market, is now suggesting that there *will* be an Election about it in the autumn. The next stage, of course, will be to claim that there *must* be an Election about it.[2]

On 16 July I received a message from Adenauer giving an account of his visit to France:

> In our conversations, President de Gaulle and I also dealt with the question of the United Kingdom's accession to the European communities. There was agreement between us that the British decision is to be welcomed, that it should be supported, and that it would be a contribution toward the strengthening of Europe. At the same time it seemed necessary to us that all questions raised by the accession of such an important partner should be thoroughly considered.
>
> With regard to the European political union, President de Gaulle and I were agreed that the Six should in the near future take up this matter again, which has been pending since the summer of 1961, in order to bring it to a positive conclusion. We also agreed that, as hitherto, the British Government should be kept informed continuously of the progress of these endeavours.

[1] 19 June 1962.   [2] 7 July 1962.

Although on the surface this letter was satisfactory, it was in very general terms. I therefore replied by asking him not to encourage protracted negotiations which were damaging to the cause of unity and would only create difficulties for us in view of the approaching Conference of Commonwealth Prime Ministers. However, his reply was again rather unhelpful. He told me that so far as he could learn from Brussels the negotiations had a very long way to go and would last well into 1963. This confirmed the impression that had already been formed by our representatives about the tactics being adopted. All this caused me concern, and I felt that the Germans were making no real effort to prevent the dilatory tactics of the French. I thought it as well to remind him of some of the past history.

Ever since you and I decided in 1960 that the wheels should be set in motion again to see if Britain could accede to the Common Market, I have felt that you agreed with me that Britain's participation represents as it were the other half of the pattern of European Unity, with which your name will ever be associated, and to which I know that you attach such great importance. I was therefore very glad to see that you and President de Gaulle agreed about the importance of Britain's participation in order to strengthen Europe.

We have been watching with sympathetic interest the efforts of the Six to move towards greater political union and I can assure you that once the Brussels negotiations are successfully concluded, we shall wish to join whole-heartedly in this task.

Meanwhile in the negotiations there are, as you say, many problems to be overcome. I do not underestimate the difficulties we shall have to face in our negotiations during the coming weeks. I thought I would give you a brief outline, which I append as an annex to this message, of where I think we stand on the main questions at issue and how they might be resolved. In doing so, I should like to repeat my firm conviction that, given the political will, we shall be able to find solutions within the framework of the system which you have built up under the Treaty of Rome.

My main concern is that we should all agree that speed is essential and that we must bring the negotiations to a clear issue so that it is possible for [our] Government to see whether the elements exist for a settlement which we can commend to the Commonwealth and to our own people. Only then shall we be in a position to decide, in the light of the discussions I shall be having with the Commonwealth Prime Ministers early in September, whether it is possible to proceed or not. I am convinced that if no clarity can be obtained on these lines by August, we shall all be in serious trouble. A great opportunity will have been missed and I would not like to say how soon it would be possible to repair the damage.

Naturally, as we approach the point of decision, every sort of influence and vested interest against change can be counted upon to make itself felt. Those who oppose the unity of Europe, those who put narrow interests first, are sure to make their voices heard in the coming weeks and there will be doubts cast on the motives of all of us. We must not allow ourselves to be side-tracked by these diversions or let our great enterprise fail because of them.

Unhappily, my fears were soon to be confirmed. On 29 July I heard of the failure to reach any agreement at Brussels about temperate zone foodstuffs. This meant that there would be no hope of finishing even the preliminary negotiations before the holidays.

The new crisis is the failure to reach any agreement at Brussels about the Commonwealth problem on temperate foodstuffs. The French were successful in forcing a rather negative attitude on the other five. After three days' talk, the meeting was adjourned till next Wednesday. This, of course, destroys the . . . chance of concluding the whole preliminary negotiations before the holidays.

Heath and Bob Dixon came to Chequers at 5 p.m. on Saturday (direct from Brussels). Alec Home stayed on from luncheon, and we had a talk about the next steps. The situation is very complicated, and I fear that all this intransigence will harden opinion here. All the same, the Europeans point out that we are asking guarantees for the Old Commonwealth countries which we have never been willing to give them ourselves![1]

Heath now reported to us on the situation in some detail, and

[1] 29 July 1962.

accordingly the Cabinet agreed to some modifications which he put before the Ministers on 3 August; but no comprehensive agreement followed. Even an all-night sitting could not break the log-jam, and on 5 August we could only accept the adjournment. Nevertheless, by this time, some progress had been made, as a historian of the period acknowledges:

> All the points affecting the Commonwealth had been discussed in enough detail, so that the British had a clear idea of the arrangements they would be able to negotiate. And many pieces of the jigsaw were already in place, or almost in place. The principles that would be applied to temperate-zone agricultural imports were settled, although many loose ends, and some very important loose ends, remained to be tied up. The arrangements for manufactures from the developed countries of the Commonwealth had been agreed. The arrangements to be made for imports from India, Pakistan, and Ceylon were largely agreed. With a few exceptions, it was clear which Commonwealth countries would be offered association, and the Six were far enough along with their own associates in agreeing on the terms of the new association convention, so that it was reasonably clear what, in fact, 'association' meant. Apart from the important nil duty requests, on which little progress had been made, and the treatment to be given to certain processed foodstuffs, in particular canned and dried fruit and canned salmon, those aspects of the negotiation that particularly affected the Commonwealth countries had been largely settled. Thus, although Mr. Heath's objective of an 'outline' agreement had not been reached, there was plenty for the Commonwealth Prime Ministers to discuss.[1]

In spite of all the troubles of this summer the Conservative Party, both in and out of Parliament, remained on the whole firm and loyal. The pay pause, the wage freeze, the Cabinet reconstruction, at home; the ever-darkening situation in Berlin and the terrifying Russian nuclear tests, overseas—all these made a confused and rather gloomy picture. I could only comfort myself with the thought that my predecessors had been through still darker days. From now on until the late autumn, while de Gaulle was to remain

[1] Camps, pp. 411–12.

enigmatic and Adenauer ineffective, the chief interest naturally concentrated on the reaction of the Commonwealth and the Conservative Party to the European element in the 'Grand Design' to which I and my colleagues were now committed.

On 11 August, I sent a message to all Commonwealth Prime Ministers giving them a general account of the situation which we had reached in Brussels.

When we were trying to find the best date for the Prime Ministers to meet I was conscious of two factors which we had to bear in mind. First it was not going to be easy to find a date suited to the different political commitments of no less than sixteen Prime Ministers. I am deeply grateful to you and our other colleagues for falling in with the date which seemed to be generally convenient. The second difficulty was to foresee, six months ago, the date by which the negotiations would have reached the point at which this Commonwealth Meeting would be most fruitful. In the event I think that things have worked out reasonably well. I have always wanted to avoid a situation in which we might have appeared to be presenting some cut and dried scheme. On the other hand, I have always felt that the Meeting would be of little value if the proposition were so little defined that there was nothing that anybody could really get hold of. I am glad to think that, as things have turned out, we have steered successfully between Scylla and Charybdis.

We have not yet been able in the Brussels negotiations to bring matters to a provisional conclusion on every one of the issues which would have to be settled before we could take our final decision about joining the European Economic Community. But we have been able to reach provisional conclusions on most of the important sectors which are of concern to other Commonwealth Governments, and we have had useful preliminary discussions on most of the remaining topics. We shall thus be able to put before you and the other Commonwealth Prime Ministers at our meeting in September a reasonably comprehensive outline of the terms on which we might be able to join the Community if we decided to do so.

After a short holiday in Yorkshire I returned to London to keep a long-standing arrangement for a talk with Rab Butler.

E2

This was at Buck's, to which he invited me to come as his guest. The engagement was made in July. It was clearly to be an occasion. And it was. He told me that in spite of *(a)* the farmers; *(b)* the Commonwealth; *(c)* the probable break-up of the Conservative Party he had decided to support our joining the Common Market. It was too late to turn back now. It was too big a chance to miss, for Britain's wealth and strength. But we must face the fact that we might share the fate of Sir Robert Peel and his supporters.[1]

This helpful, if somewhat belated, declaration gave me great encouragement, and when the Cabinet met the next day nearly three hours were devoted

to a report by Butler's Committee on [the] Common Market, which had been in session on Monday and Tuesday. The views of the Ministers on the Committee (including Commonwealth Secretary and Minister of Agriculture) were unanimous. The Cabinet accepted their decisions, after a long, clause by clause, discussion of Lord Privy Seal's paper. (I was much struck by modest but impressive contributions by some of the new members –Boyle, Keith Joseph, etc.)

Butler then made his declaration of faith, in the same terms as he had to me at Buck's last night. It was quite an occasion. I rather trailed my coat, with some remarks about Peel, Lord George Bentinck and Disraeli. But Rab was firm, if rather gloomy. This gloom was shared to the full by Soames (Minister of Agriculture) who prophesies great trouble from our farmers.

All the afternoon 3–5.30, meeting of Ministers on how to handle the Commonwealth Prime Ministers Conference. A broad tactical line was agreed.[2]

The sense that we were now approaching a decisive stage in this great issue filled us all with a feeling of romance and drama. Even the news that Lord Beaverbrook had written to the Chairman of the Central Norfolk Conservative Association suggesting that they should run an anti-market candidate at a by-election did not cause me any undue alarm. It seemed rather like playing again an old

[1] 21 August 1962.   [2] 22 August 1962.

film which I remembered so well from the days of 1930. Nor was I unduly concerned about

> a ridiculous television performance by Dr. Adenauer, rather critical of me and referring to my private letters to him; the attack has recoiled on the German Chancellor and I think the air is cleared. The German officials and public are obviously incensed by his indiscretions. Even the *Express* seemed to take my side.[1]

The Prime Ministers began to assemble in London. On 5 September Bob Menzies came to dinner alone, and we had a very frank and useful talk.

> I formed the impression that he is going to try to take a constructive line – not break up the Conference or appeal to the British people over our heads. I told him that I thought he had the *power* to prevent Britain joining Europe. But I thought it a terrible responsibility before history.
> Bob Menzies is really the key to the situation in my judgement – not Diefenbaker . . . Bob Menzies is a survivor of the great Imperial statesmen of the Second World War.[2]

Everything was now ready for the opening on 10 September. However, 7 September proved to be

> a very long and tiring day. Two and a half hours in the morning with the Australians – Menzies, Holt and McEwen. I was supported by Sandys and Heath. Two and a half hours in the afternoon with New Zealanders. Holyoake and Marshall for New Zealand; I had same team. We made quite good progress with Australians. New Zealanders were very gloomy.[3]

I also saw all the representatives of the new Commonwealth, for most of whose countries we hoped to obtain 'association' with the Common Market. On 8 September I spent two hours with Nash, the leader of the Opposition in New Zealand – for it now seemed that not merely the Prime Ministers but the leaders of the Opposition were flocking to London, a procedure which was likely to add to the confusion. However, I had a useful talk with my old friend

[1] 30 August 1962.   [2] 5 September 1962.   [3] 7 September 1962.

'ranging from butter to Utopia. I think it did good'.[1] President
Ayub of Pakistan came to luncheon.

> He will be reasonable. He wants better terms for textiles—or
> rather, thinks India has been treated too generously. He is a fine
> character and easy to talk to—a stage product of Sandhurst and
> the Indian Cavalry, with all language and phrases of the cavalry
> officers' mess.[1]

On 9 September, the day before the Conference was to meet,
Gaitskell threw what was intended to be a bombshell into the
already delicate situation. He,

> with the support of, or after conferences with, Commonwealth
> Labour leaders, has issued a statement *against* entering Common
> Market on present terms and demanding a second Conference. . . .
> He also demands a General Election on the issue if the parties
> are not agreed.[2]

Happily, this proved a completely damp squib. On the next day

> the Press . . . is *very* critical of Gaitskell. *The Times*, the *Guardian*,
> the *Daily Mail* are all very scornful of his 'political' manoeuvre.
> The *Daily Mirror* which is *pro*-Common Market but violently
> *anti*-Government, tries to explain it away. The *Daily Telegraph* is
> good. The *Daily Herald* . . . (*pro*-Common Market) is hard put to
> it and confused. Of course, he may have struck a timely and fatal
> blow. Or he may have made a fatal error. Only time will show.[3]

Meanwhile I had a long luncheon with Diefenbaker alone.

> He kept his cards very close to his chest and gave me no
> indication of what he proposed to say in the great debate. He was
> *very* pleasant; talked chiefly of internal politics . . . I thought him
> somewhat subdued by his electoral reverses and financial crisis.
> But this may easily result in his trying to recover ground by
> a great Commonwealth demonstration at the Conference, on
> Beaverbrook lines. Later in the afternoon came [Sir Alexander]
> Bustamante (Prime Minister of Jamaica) and Dr. [Eric] Williams
> (Prime Minister of Trinidad).[2]

[1] 8 September 1962.   [2] 9 September 1962.
[3] 10 September 1962.

The Conference met at Marlborough House, which, by the bounty of the Queen, had been handed over as a centre for Commonwealth meetings. In its new decoration the old building was marvellously adapted to its purpose, and all those present felt a sense of obligation to the generosity of the royal donor. After a few procedural formalities, which filled the morning of the first day, I took Home and Nehru back to luncheon at No. 10. 'N. looked old and tired – with little to say.'[1]

In the afternoon, I opened with a carefully prepared speech which lasted over an hour.[2] My address was followed by 'an hour and a half from Heath. This left them exhausted – and I hope impressed.'[1] I had never before heard so remarkable an effort as Heath's. His

> exposition today was really a masterpiece – from notes, and not from a script. The temper was good, the knowledge of detail was extraordinary, and the grasp of complicated issues affecting twenty countries and many commodities was very impressive.[1]

The next two days were devoted to speeches by the Prime Ministers in different tones of warning or protest.

> We have now had two days of Commonwealth speakers. It has been a broadside attack upon us, led by Diefenbaker on the first day . . . Menzies wound up the first day with a very able and *very* damaging speech. Holyoake said New Zealand would be ruined. Nehru (who seemed painfully weak physically) was peevish. The Africans, who get everything they could want by 'association' are too proud . . . even to ask for it.
> Actually, the second day was better – Trinidad (able Dr. Eric Williams) talked good sense at great length, and Malaya was friendly.[3]

On reading through the minutes of the discussion, I think perhaps these comments, written in the height of the debate, are somewhat over-strained; nevertheless I feel them worth recording as at least being written without hindsight. Naturally, with so great a concourse of foreign statesmen, Prime Ministers and Ministers of Finance, to which must be added members of the opposition in

[1] 10 September 1962.   [2] Appendix 1.   [3] 12 September 1962.

their own parliaments, there was much activity among the reporters, and a vast number of interviews and leaks from a nominally private meeting. On 12 September I noted that

> the Press this morning 'went to town'. Max Beaverbrook's papers were violent to a point of hysteria. The general view is that the Government must bow to Commonwealth and abandon the project. *Times, Daily Telegraph, Financial Times* are more sober. *Daily Mirror* is still enthusiastically *pro*-European. But this is the editorial staff. The 'news' is presented much more dramatically. It's Mac's Waterloo.[1]

After the first day, there was a dinner for all the Commonwealth Ministers at Admiralty House, followed by a large party at Lancaster House.

> A very tense atmosphere everywhere. Gaitskell going about smiling . . . as if he had just kissed hands. . . . Curiously enough, the political argument is used almost as much as the economic. The Commonwealth will never survive. . . . It is ironical to hear countries which have abused us for years now beseeching us not to abandon them. The thought that U.K. might declare herself independent seems so novel as to be quite alarming.[1]

I was struck by the fact that many of the Commonwealth representatives

> seemed to think that we were deciding whether or not the E.E.C. should be formed, not accepting its existence. It does exist and the only question is 'What are we going to do about it?'[1]

On the evening of 12 September, I certainly felt rather shaken. But on reflection I comforted myself with the thought that the immediate reaction was bound to be hostile. It would only be after a day or two that we would settle down to serious discussion. In other words, the first speeches were 'second reading' efforts; we should soon get to committee stage.

On 13 September I went to

> Marlborough House at 10.30 for a talk with Bob Menzies. This meant missing the Cabinet—which was a good idea. The

[1] 12 September 1962.

Press could hardly play it up as a 'crisis' Cabinet if I was not there. Before the Cabinet I had a talk with Butler at Marlborough House. He was calm and quite firm. There was a good deal of routine business anyway, and he would give them a general account of the Conference, which he has attended throughout. He afterwards told me that, with a few exceptions, Ministers were pretty calm.

Menzies was obviously rather distressed and seemed anxious to find a way out. I thought it better to let him talk. He would see whether he could not work out some thoughts for the final communiqué. After a luncheon for Sir Milton Margai (Sierra Leone) and Sir Alexander Bustamante (Jamaica) which was very jolly, I went back to Marlborough House and had useful talk with President Ayub. Later Mr. Diefenbaker came—with little to say, but I think also a little alarmed.[1]

I now proposed to the Conference to set up what we termed 'special groups' to deal with particular issues: temperate foodstuffs, Asian problems, African and West Indian problems and so forth. They met all day on Thursday, 13 September, as well as continuing on Friday and Saturday. This admirable arrangement had been proposed by Sir Norman Brook, and the British Ministers specially concerned, with their civil servant advisers, took charge of each study group. This plan not only brought the Commonwealth Ministers down to realities, but it also enormously lowered the general temperature.

The Queen's dinner was held on 13 September and was very well done.

The system of round tables, each presided [over] by a member of the Royal Family, is far better for the purpose than a long formal banqueting table, when all the seats go by protocol.[1]

I noticed already a change in the Press which, with the exception of the Beaverbrook papers, was becoming calm and even helpful.

In the late afternoon of Saturday, 15 September

Sandys, Heath and Norman Brook came for a conference on 'tactics'. It seems that some of Prime Ministers will wish to

[1] 13 September 1962.

speak again–I hope more moderately. It may be best to let them do so on Monday morning. Read *Kenilworth*–a splendid story.

Philip de Zulueta and I worked all the evening on the [final] speech, so as to have a version ready for the morning. Unfortunately, owing to weddings, holidays and colds we were rather short in the Garden Room. I dictated a long and splendid passage to one girl who seemed to take it down all right. But when it came to decyphering her own shorthand, she could not do so, but had a nervous *crise* and burst into tears. However, we finished before midnight.[1]

Sunday was nominally a day of rest. The Press was definitely good, with the exception of the *Sunday Express*. But I got the impression that even this paper was 'anxious not to *bore* their readers too much. There is less Commonwealth and Common Market than I would have thought.'[2]

On Monday, 17 September, the Conference resumed its work at 10.30 in the morning.

Several Prime Ministers accepted my proposal to speak again. The 'groups' have now covered three full days instead of two allowed for in the original plan. On Saturday they went on from morning to night. This shows that the Prime Ministers, Ministers and officials found them useful.[3]

On reflection on the general situation, it seemed to me more fluid: India and Pakistan were doing pretty well under the proposed plan, and, although they would bargain up to the last point, as was indeed proper, they would in the end be satisfied.

In the case of the Africans, the economic conditions of 'association' are almost too good to be true. But they shrink from the word. It is neo-colonialism to associate with a white man! Australia is anxious, but Bob (hard pressed by McEwen) is playing politics. All the same, they have *some* ground for anxiety. New Zealand merely say that they trust us to get them something special. Canada is just playing a sort of political game, based on Diefenbaker's strange *mystique*.[3]

[1] 15 September 1962.   [2] 16 September 1962.
[3] 17 September 1962.

After five or six of the Prime Ministers had spoken, I began my final speech at 12 noon and finished it before 1 p.m.[1] I had been provided with some admirable material, and the figures which I was able to give of the changing conditions of British industry seemed to convince the assembly that Britain could not alone in the world remain a free market for Commonwealth goods.

The afternoon meeting was devoted to a debate on world affairs, opened by Home as Foreign Secretary, and this was continued throughout the morning of 18 September, finishing at lunch time. All the Prime Ministers took part, and the debate was lively and vigorous. Then came what is for all conferences of this kind the critical moment – the drafting of the communiqué.

> After luncheon, the first session on the draft communiqué. This lasted from 3.30 to 5 p.m. By then, it was clear that the communiqué (although broadly agreed by officials last night) was going to prove a real difficulty. At one time, I feared that there would be more than one issued – with nothing like even 'agreement to differ'. The text which was put forward was based on that which I prepared myself a week or more ago.
>
> It set out the four *general principles* which had been the main theme of my winding-up speech and which had been well taken up by the Press. But each Prime Minister wanted to add his particular illustration to the general principle – so that the communiqué would be a sort of 'shopping list'. Bob Menzies (obviously under pressure from McEwen) was difficult. All the others followed. I felt it useless to go [on], but proposed that the officials might meet in the evening and prepare two drafts – one the original draft with some of the major amendments of principle which had been mentioned in the discussion; the other, a draft with all the particular reservations, etc., affecting their own countries which delegations sent in. So we adjourned.[2]

This was a pretty sticky period and

> I was very depressed, and so was poor Ted Heath. However, my scheme (really suggested to me by the incomparable Norman Brook) may work out. When they see the *long* draft, with

[1] Appendix 2.   [2] 18 September 1962.

a reference to every country's demands, they may realise its absurdity.[1]

The next morning,

the Press very gloomy. Mac's failure. Mac's collapse. Mac's test. The Conference in ruins. The best were the *Daily Telegraph* and *Times* [which] said that there was still hope of an agreement.[2]

This proved to be true. Once again an interval for reflection had brought all the members of the Conference to face the realities. Agreement

was, in fact, reached in one-and-a-half [hours] and the Brook–Macmillan tactics succeeded. The 'long' draft was rejected at once; we worked methodically and amicably through the 'short' draft. There were one or two difficulties, but a wholly different atmosphere from yesterday. Diefenbaker's deafness helped, and I was able to pass from one clause to another fairly rapidly. There was an African wrangle again. Ceylon and India helpful. Pakistan good. Menzies (having, I suppose, made a sufficient demonstration for home politics) was reasonable. He reverted to his favourite sport of teasing Diefenbaker.[2]

As a result of this new mood

the whole Conference ended before luncheon yesterday, in a very correct and even friendly mood. I made a little speech about Sir Norman Brook. This is his twelfth and last conference. The Prime Ministers spoke warmly and feelingly about him. Then Diefenbaker moved a vote of thanks to me, in very generous terms. And so goodbye![2]

The communiqué was issued at 2.15 p.m. It was, from our point of view, satisfactory. For, if it did not disguise the anxiety of certain Commonwealth countries on particular points, it accepted the broad policy which Britain was determined to pursue.[3]

[1] 18 September 1962.   [2] 19 September 1962.
[3] *Meeting of Commonwealth Prime Ministers—Final Communiqué, 19 September, 1963,* Cmnd. 1836 (H.M.S.O., 1962).

In my letter to the Queen on 21 September summarising the story, I felt bound to admit

> Nevertheless it would be wrong to disguise from ourselves the great problems which still await us. We can only try to face them with imagination and courage. I am very conscious that the problem of the Common Market and its impact upon the Commonwealth has raised difficulties which I would have wished during my Premiership to have spared Your Majesty. It must be very difficult and painful for Your Majesty, as the Monarch of the Old Commonwealth and as the Head of the new Commonwealth countries, to find these territories in disagreement, or partial disagreement, with Your Majesty's Government in the United Kingdom. . . .
> Broadly speaking then, Ma'am, I can only say that the Conference has gone off better than I expected. It might of course have been better still, but it might have been far worse. I do not feel that the Commonwealth is shaken or that there is any talk at all of disruption if it should prove possible for Britain to enter the European Community.

I went on to discuss some of the wider stresses and strains to which the Commonwealth was likely to be subjected, observing that this European problem had at least served the purpose of obscuring or delaying their emergence.

The immediate reactions of the Press were interesting:

> *Daily Express* is violent to a degree hardly believable—quite like the Press of the early nineteenth century. The Liberals (who seemed to be hedging) have come down in their conference quite firmly *for* the Common Market. . . . The *Manchester Guardian* still hedges—it represents the kind of attitude which Lord John Russell spent his life in promoting—always willing to wound and afraid to strike—and always essentially priggish and slightly dishonest. The *Daily Mail* is good. *The Times* and *Daily Telegraph* remain firm. *Yorkshire Post* good. *Daily Mirror* attacks me personally but supports my policy.[1]

Gaitskell, in the course of a television broadcast,

[1] 21 September 1962.

went much further than before. He criticised the terms, but he
also seemed now to [be] against going in on *any* terms. England,
he declared, would be like Texas. (Yet he wishes us to abandon the nuclear deterrent and throw ourselves altogether into
American arms !)[1]

But I was comforted by Bob Menzies, who sent me a very
friendly message; though naturally he had to consider his political
position at home. With his long experience and wisdom he recognised that the movement towards European unity was inevitable
and that Britain's isolation could not, in the long run, benefit the
Commonwealth.

Negotiations in Brussels could not now be resumed until the late
autumn. Interchanges of messages with all the members of the
Commonwealth had culminated in the Commonwealth Conference
with its acquiescence in, if not approval of, our policy. There
remained the internal conflicts both between and with our parties at
home. It is of course a serious inconvenience to Party Managers
when a novel issue arises on which the Party alignments have not
yet been strictly taken. The political organisers, pamphleteers and
popular speakers much prefer the well-trodden paths so that they
can repeat on each side without too much intellectual strain their
parrot-like but well-polished arguments. Up to now the idea of
European unity had been almost academic. It is true that Churchill
in his old age had initiated its birth in a series of dramatic efforts;
but he had not been able, in his last administration, to make any
very practical contribution towards its development. Moreover, to
some of the more rigid Tory partisans, Churchill was not really a
Conservative. It is true that for the purpose of winning the war he
had been necessary; but in their hearts they yearned for the more
respectable figures that held power in times of peace. If this uncertainty had been to some extent resolved by the action of the
present Government and the decisions which they announced, yet
many questions still had to be settled and a long and difficult
negotiation brought to a conclusion. Thus, while there was no
immediate enthusiasm in support of the European concept, there

[1] 22 September 1962.

were strong forces beginning to organise themselves against the whole plan both on economic and on political grounds resting on time-honoured feelings of patriotism and Imperial tradition.

On the Left, where one would have expected the traditional internationalism which had inspired the Socialist movement in its early days to be put firmly behind the European ideal, yet in fact the trade unions were dominated by protectionism and almost isolationism. Hence the leaders of the Parliamentary Party found themselves in some difficulty. Intellectually, they tended to be pro-Europeans; but the pressures against them led them to hesitate. I was not therefore surprised to find their leader in a continual condition of uncertainty. On 29 September

> Gaitskell seems to be engaged in climbing back on to the European fence. If so, it is rather a blow to his prestige.
>
> Gaitskell produced last night (with the help of the Labour Executive) yet another (but I suppose more authoritative) statement on Europe and the Common Market. It goes back on 'Texas' and 'a thousand years of history' which were the features of Mr. G.'s broadcast—that is, against Europe *in principle*. Now the line is that there's a lot to be said both ways; that 'on the whole' Europe is a good idea for us *if* we get much better terms than seems likely. Then there is a rather vague demand for a General Election *unless* there is general agreement on the terms. It is difficult to assess what all this amounts to at present. My first impression is that this is a pretty clever document, which should unite the Labour Party sufficiently to get them through their Conference.[1]

All the same I felt that the issue would finally be settled by many forces of greater authority than our own political parties.

> What does Germany want? What will Adenauer try to do? Is de Gaulle determined to keep us out? And so forth. The *terms* are important; but not so important as the spirit of the age![2]

A few days later the Leader of the Opposition with exquisite skill executed a slight change of position. His line now seemed to be not to reject the European idea in principle but demand such conditions

[1] 29–30 September 1962.   [2] 30 September 1962.

as to make it impossible for us to conclude any arrangement in practice.

My own task was to prepare my speech for the Conservative Party Conference. Since by tradition this was made after the Conference was ended, I was in some difficulty. I must find some way of influencing the delegates beforehand. I therefore compiled and published a pamphlet entitled *Britain, the Commonwealth and Europe* which summarised the whole argument. This was largely based upon the two speeches that I had used at the Commonwealth Conference. This publication, which appeared at a very opportune moment, undoubtedly had considerable effect. Nevertheless, I had to prepare my speech

> without knowing the outcome of the debate tomorrow (Thursday) on the Common Market. I spoke on the telephone to Ted Heath in the afternoon. He is a little anxious about the amendment, which will confuse the audience. But he says that the general spirit seems favourable. It is odd that the only person not able to take part in this critical discussion (which, if it went wrong, would be fatal to the Government of which I am the head) is myself![1]

Happily, on 11 October, I received the good news that

> the Conservative Conference had rejected the Turton–Walker-Smith amendment on the Common Market by an overwhelming majority—only fifty or so out of 4,000 voting for it. Butler and Heath seem to have made excellent speeches.[2]

It was therefore in a happy mood that I left for Llandudno, armed with the final, indeed the eighth, draft of my speech. This was shorter than customary, and perhaps for that reason enthusiastically received. As usual, my wife received a tremendous welcome.

At the end, therefore, of this second stage of the wooing of Europe my colleagues and I had succeeded in overcoming the obstacles in which General de Gaulle expected—and no doubt hoped—that we should be helplessly entangled. The Commonwealth Conference had been a clear success for the British Government, and provided negotiations were reasonably successful on the detailed points the leading figures in the Commonwealth would be

---

[1] 10 October 1962.   [2] 11 October 1962.

satisfied, if not enthusiastic. We had also surmounted triumphantly any hostile opinion in the Conservative Party. If, therefore, either General de Gaulle or Chancellor Adenauer were depending on our British horse falling at one of these formidable jumps they had been disappointed. We were now 'in the straight', and if we were to be prevented from reaching the winning-post somebody would have to trip us up and take the full responsibility for our fall. The Brussels negotiations must be made to fail; or, if that proved impossible, some grounds, however slender, must be found to justify a veto.

CHAPTER VI

The Nuclear Challenge

URING the second half of 1961 the political and military
confrontation between East and West became increasingly
alarming. The Russian pressure on Berlin took a new form.
In addition to the threats of a unilateral peace agreement with East
Germany, there was the new injury arising from the building of the
Berlin wall, with its stark brutality. This crude material representation of the deep spiritual gulf that lay across Europe profoundly
affected the imagination and shocked the conscience of the Western
World. At the same time there seemed no break in the dark clouds
cast by nuclear armaments, daily increasing. Discussions continued
under the aegis of the United Nations on the possibility of at least
a halt in the series of explosions which threatened ever increasing
pollution to the atmosphere. But these, though prolix and protracted,
proved hopelessly negative. The Soviet Government treated the
interminable debates on disarmament like Mr. Jorrocks, by 'adding
to the theory, with as little practice as possible'.

Meanwhile the Russians had embarked in the autumn of 1961
upon a large-scale series of tests of a peculiarly 'dirty' kind. I was
able to assure the House of Commons, with the full approval of the
President, that neither Britain nor America would start a new series
of tests purely for retaliation. Both our Governments would be
guided solely by the necessity to maintain the balance of deterrent
power.

Perhaps the weakest part of our position consisted in the difference
of view, or at least of emphasis, in the Allied camp, as to our best
tactical reply to the Russian political offensive. At first the Americans
seemed to agree with the line adopted by France (and, under de
Gaulle's pressure, accepted by Germany) that we should confront
the Russians with a bold face and make no move towards negotiation

on the Berlin issue. As regards the renewal of American tests on a massive scale, France especially was indifferent. But before the close of the year the Americans had moved towards the British position in respect of Berlin. We believed in strength; but we thought our policy should be flexible. We should at least seek to explore the possibilities of further and perhaps fruitful negotiations. It was amidst these confused moods that 1961 drew to its close. It was clear both to Kennedy and to me that a meeting between us was now both necessary and urgent.

Before I left for Bermuda on 19 December there had been two new developments. On 13 December, after long discussions, the Americans and the Russians agreed to promote and take part in an 'Eighteen-Nation Committee' to resume talks on disarmament, both conventional and unconventional. In this strange diplomatic contest it seemed of value to the cause of peace to keep in being mammoth negotiations of this kind, however sceptical everyone might be as to their likelihood of success. Each age enjoys its own methods of international discussion. If we sometimes are apt to read contemptuously of the elaborate ceremonies and prolonged diplomatic courtesies of earlier centuries, we must not forget that we follow today very similar, if less elegant, procedures. I knew, of course, that if we were ready to reach some conclusion we would have to revive the methods which had come to grief so tragically in the fatal summit meeting of May 1960. Nevertheless, the kind of international circus now proposed gave a certain amount of relief and did little harm.

On the same day, 13 December, Khrushchev sent me one of his long periodical bulletins on the subject of reducing tension in Europe. The main theme was not changed. Peace treaties must be signed with the two Germanys. The troops of the occupying nations must be withdrawn from West Berlin. If, however, the Western Powers insisted that their troops must remain in West Berlin, then Russian contingents must be included. No similar arrangements, of course, were suggested for East Berlin. If the West refused to agree to Russian contingents sharing their duties in West Berlin, then the only way would be to replace them all by United Nations troops; but the best hope of a prosperous West Berlin would be the removal of troops of whatever nation. The asperities of this rather specious argument were as usual softened by the covering of treacle in which they were buried. I could only send copies of this communication to Kennedy, Adenauer and de Gaulle for their information together with a short acknowledgement to Khrushchev. Although, as I told him frankly, there was much in his letter with which I could not agree, I hoped that after my meeting with the President it would 'be possible to resume . . . the efforts which were begun during Mr. Gromyko's recent visit to the United States and to this country to find an acceptable basis for negotiation'.

Meanwhile the Nuclear Test Conference, another of the many diplomatic quadrilles that were being solemnly performed at Geneva, was suspended—whether for the Christmas holidays or because no progress could be made was left prudently obscure.

19 December was a busy day.

> A long Cabinet—covering Foreign Affairs, Congo, Kenya, etc. A good discussion, but it is hard to see even a chink of light anywhere.[1]

The diary continues:

> Parliamentary Questions—only three. The House seemed very jumpy. Defence committee 4.30–7.30. Then a talk with Chancellor of Exchequer till 8.30–about the problem of Railway Wages. These men really *do* deserve a small increase. But how can we prevent a small stream becoming a flood?[1]

At midnight we left London Airport

> in a B.O.A.C. Britannia. Foreign Secretary; Sir Norman Brook; Sir William Penney; Sir Evelyn Shuckburgh; and Philip de Zulueta made up the main party—also Samuel (Parliamentary Secretary to Lord Home) and Russel (Foreign Office News Department). Sir John Richardson (my doctor) also came.[1]

We arrived the next day, 20 December, at 6 o'clock local time. On arrival we heard that the President's father, Mr. Joseph Kennedy,

[1] 19 December 1961.

had had a stroke and that it was doubtful whether the President could come.

    After we had arrived and settled down in the Governor's house (which is *extremely* comfortable) I sent a telegram to the President, offering to go to Palm Beach or Washington—or any other plan which might suit him. Later in the day, we got a message that Mr. Kennedy senior was a bit better, and that the President hoped to stick to the original plan—i.e. come to Bermuda tomorrow, 21 December.[1]

Those who know the beautiful island of Bermuda will realise what a pleasant relief was involved in exchanging the dark and gloomy surroundings of a British winter for the bright and cheerful atmosphere of this Atlantic colony. It was said that the first settlers to reach Bermuda were, in fact, on their way to America; but, having made a landfall in error, they wisely decided to remain contented with their discovery. It has even been argued that the adventure of these Elizabethan pioneers provided Shakespeare with the setting of *The Tempest*. At any rate nothing could have been more agreeable than the few days that we spent there, enjoying the hospitality of the Governor, an old Grenadier friend, Major-General Sir Julian Gascoigne. When the President arrived, the Governor very properly received him in full dress and with all appropriate ceremonies. Kennedy was at first rather amused by the somewhat antique form of the Governor's military costume, cocked hat, feathers, sword and gold spurs; but he soon began to realise the real quality of our host.

Our talks continued almost without interruption for two days. As regards the first problem discussed, the President seemed determined to negotiate with the U.S.S.R. and to find a solution to the problem of Berlin. This position having recently been adopted was maintained with all the fervour of a convert. He

    has had some secret correspondence with Khrushchev. He showed it to me and Lord Home. No one but Rusk (Secretary of State) and McGeorge Bundy has seen it. I showed him the long letter which I received the other day from Khrushchev and my

[1] 20 December 1961.

proposed reply. I got the feeling that the President is getting impatient with Adenauer and really angry with de Gaulle. He does *not* intend to risk war about Berlin, although outwardly and publicly he talks big.[1]

On the question of whether or not to resume atmospheric nuclear tests, the Americans fielded a large and distinguished team of experts who produced a massive series of papers, most of which were to me unintelligible. Sir William Penney was more than a match for them all. It was the first time that the President had met this remarkable man, a worthy successor to Lord Rutherford. He was deeply impressed by his humour and his sense of proportion, as well as by his profound knowledge. Nevertheless, we had to agree that

the last Russian tests are rather alarming. We know that they are working very hard on an 'anti-missile' missile. They have built a town of 20,000 people wholly devoted to scientific work in this sphere. In addition, the one hundred megaton is not just a stunt. . . . It would scorch with fire half France or England if dropped. What then should we do?[1]

I made a strong appeal to the President

that we should make another effort—in spite of the Russian trickery and bad faith—to put a stop to all this folly. We have agreed only now to make some *preparations* for renewed tests—probably at Christmas Island—on this anti-missile development. But we will hold our hand—to see whether in the next few months we can make some progress, both on Berlin and on Disarmament.[1]

As regards the Congo, the

Americans support Adoula, but recognise that United Nations leadership, civilian and military, had made great mistakes. We must work for a genuine reconciliation of all non-Communist Africans in Congo and try to stop the fighting from breaking out again.[1]

[1] 23 December 1961.

Finally, we discussed the Common Market and the freeing of world trade. At this point, having no financial advisers to hinder me, I tried to expound some of my ideas on monetary reform. Kennedy sympathised, but I knew that he too would be impeded by the spiritual heirs of those who had frustrated the full acceptance of the policies of Maynard Keynes. I was ten years too soon.

On this occasion we were able to issue a communiqué which was welcomed by the Press because, contrary to the usual custom, it really said something definite.[1] Apart from these questions,

> we talked also of the future of United Nations; of Goa and Indonesia; of Cuba; of China. On the latter, the President practically admitted that American policies are and have been absurd. But he cannot change too quickly on too many issues.[2]

On my return I was able to go straight to my home in Sussex and enjoy, amid a host of messages, cables, telephones and boxes full of papers, what was called the Christmas holidays. One of the pleasant parts of this meeting in Bermuda was that I felt that Kennedy and I had become even closer friends than before. One impression I noted:

> There is a marked contrast between President Kennedy 'in action' on a specific problem (e.g. Congo, West Irian, Ghana), and his attitude to larger issues, (the nuclear war, the struggle between East and West, Capitalism and Communism, etc.). In the first, he is an extraordinarily quick and effective operator–a born 'politician' (not in a pejorative sense). On the wider issues, he seems rather lost.[2]

As usual, I sent full accounts to the leading personalities in the Commonwealth as well as messages to Adenauer and de Gaulle. In my letter to the Queen of 24 December after setting out in some detail our discussion on Berlin, the Congo and the proposed tests at Christmas Island and on other matters I added:

> I think it might interest Your Majesty to have some impressions of the President on this, my fourth meeting with him. He was naturally suffering from the blow of his father's sudden illness, for the Kennedys are a very devoted family. The President

---

[1] Appendix 3.   [2] 23 December 1961.

owes a great deal to his father and is obviously very attached to
him. Moreover, it is a great shock to see a man perfectly fit one
day and two days later struck down and permanently immobilised.
I also thought the President's own health was not good. He is
very restless owing to his back. He finds it difficult to sit in the
same position for any length of time. I noticed the difficulty he
had in picking up a piece of paper that had fallen to the floor. We
produced a rocking chair, which was of some comfort to him. It
is really rather sad that so young a man should be so afflicted, but
he is very brave and does not show it except, as I say, by his
unwillingness to continue to talk for any length of time without
a break. He is also a very sensitive man, very easily pleased and
very easily offended. He likes presents—I gave him one, and so
did my niece, Debo Devonshire. He likes letters, he likes
attention. To match this he is clearly a very effective, even
ruthless, operator in the political field. I thought he was more
interested in short-term than in large and distant problems—but
that is perhaps natural from his present experience. He is a most
agreeable guest and carries the weight of his great office with
simplicity and dignity.

The President spoke to me several times about Your Majesty
and asked after you with genuine interest and affection. He talked
a good deal about Ghana and Your Majesty's experiences there.
He felt that gallantry demanded that he should match Your
Majesty's contribution as best he could with his own. If I might
venture to suggest it, Madam, I think he would welcome very
much an occasional letter from you on any matter of partly
international, partly political, and partly more personal interest.
He is fond of writing letters and, I think, of receiving them.

I also sent, on 22 December, a full reply to Khrushchev's last
message which I had only briefly acknowledged. After welcoming
his initiative in writing to me, I felt it necessary first to rebut his
accusations against Western Germany.

The phrase which struck me most in your letter was your
statement that the main aim of the Soviet Union is to exclude
the possibility of war with Germany or over Germany. I can
assure you that every man and woman in this country would
approve this aim. I can also state that the British people would

fully recognise the concern of the Soviet Union for its security against aggression, from whatever quarter. I do not of course share your views as to the revival of revanchist and aggressive sentiments in the Federal Republic. I believe these accusations to be quite contrary to the facts and I find it most regrettable that they are maintained by you. I believe I am entitled to say that in the close day-to-day association in defence matters which we maintain amongst allies in the North Atlantic Alliance we have received every evidence that the Federal Government is devoted to a policy of joint defence on a basis of integrated international forces, and that the NATO system provides a sure guarantee against independent adventures. The forces on the continent of Europe are under international command and their employment is subject to decisions agreed in common. This means that the United States and the United Kingdom amongst others, must approve every action of the alliance, and I can certainly speak for the United Kingdom in saying that we would never permit any one member nation to divert the forces of the Alliance to tasks which were not compatible with this defensive purpose. Moreover, as you know, there is the additional safeguard, in so far as nuclear weapons are concerned, that the United States retain control of all such weapons.

I went on to say that the ultimate solution of the German situation lay in a peace treaty with a freely elected Government representing all Germany as contemplated in the Potsdam Agreement. However, I fully recognised that this was at present unacceptable to the U.S.S.R. Meanwhile, we must find a practical plan involving the recognition by each side of what the other regarded as essential.

I note with satisfaction your statement that you think it might be possible before the Soviet Union concludes any peace treaty, to have an agreement on certain questions. This is the procedure which I think we should follow. As you rightly say in your letter, prestige counts for a great deal. Therefore, just as we do not seek to upset the existing order in Eastern Europe, though we cannot approve of it, so you for your part should respect the existing positions of the Western Powers. This means that, until such time as we can reach agreement on a permanent solution for Germany, neither side should seek to frustrate the arrangements and the policies which are vital to the other. It should be possible to devise mutual and collective guarantees against aggression and surprise attack which will permit us all to live at peace with each other and open the way to a real improvement in our relations. For us, this must include respect on the part of the Soviet Union for the Western position and for Western responsibilities in West Berlin.

I next turned to Khrushchev's proposal for a free city for West Berlin. This plan seemed very one-sided. East Berlin was fully integrated into Eastern Germany while West Berlin would be cut off from its legitimate links with the West and the rights of the Western Allied Powers would be abrogated.

Any plan for a free city in the sense you describe ought to be applied to the whole of Berlin. A whole city, of the importance of Berlin might perhaps be satisfactorily established as a 'neutralised free city' in certain circumstances. But half a city, surrounded entirely by territory controlled by some other authority, and prohibited from maintaining legitimate links with, or from relying for defence upon, its natural friends, could not possibly be a viable proposition. I ask you to consider this in all seriousness, so that you will understand the objections which I see to this proposal.

What then could be done? Surely the sensible course was that both sides should accept the facts of the existing situation and respect each other's rights and prestige. A *modus vivendi* could thus be negotiated.

The main point at issue here is the problem of access to West Berlin. We are willing to discuss ways in which the existing arrangements might be improved; and when I say improved I do not mean simply made easier for us and more difficult for you. We have no thought of asking the Soviet army to act as traffic policemen and we realise that traffic arrangements are of direct concern to the authorities who exercise responsibility in the territory over which the traffic runs. What interests us is to receive the Soviet Government's assurances, which we should reciprocate, that arrangements providing free access to the city will be maintained in all circumstances. It ought certainly to be possible to devise practical formalities which would give rise to the minimum of friction in their application. I should like to add in this connection that if we are to have stability in Berlin itself, and to avoid the daily occurrence of dangerous incidents on the sector border, some means must surely be found of restoring reasonable freedom of movement between the two parts of the city. This is a matter which could, if the responsible Powers expressed the necessary will, be easily arranged locally on a practical basis.

If we could reach an understanding in principle on these matters we could then widen the range of our discussions and open up more hopeful prospects. After ten years it seems possible that an agreement may be reached on the lines here outlined.

I naturally sent copies of my reply both to Adenauer and to de Gaulle as well as to Kennedy. The General was still opposed to negotiations on tactical grounds, but he raised no objection and showed no ill-will. His attitude and that of his leading colleagues was one of an amicable, if somewhat patronising, contempt felt by the most professional diplomatists in the world for the somewhat amateur efforts of London and Washington. This pose of detachment was safe enough; for in the long run Britain and America would not shrink from the defence of Europe.

In the days following Christmas I was confined to bed with a severe chill but

I pondered and brooded in bed and produced by last night a new plan for trying to get a general détente between the West and Communism, in which all the questions which seem insoluble by themselves might be subsumed into a new and general approach—a return to the Summit concept, before the breakdown of May 1960.

Today, I went through the document—some twenty foolscap pages—with Sir William Penney (to get the nuclear parts correct), Philip, Tim Bligh and Freddie Bishop. Then (after luncheon) with Sir Norman Brook, Sir Frederick Hoyer Millar and Sir Harold Caccia (who takes over from Sir Frederick Hoyer Millar on Monday). To my surprise, they were not as shocked as I expected. The draft goes to Foreign Secretary in Scotland tomorrow, if I can get all the amendments done in time.[1]

[1] 28 December 1961.

F

On 3 January my paper, which had been approved by the Foreign Secretary, was discussed by the full Cabinet.

Ministers had, of course, received full reports of the Bermuda talks. While these had covered a wide range of urgent problems which had to be dealt with, much of our deliberations was concentrated upon the East–West issue. As regards Berlin there was a general sense of relief that the President was now so personally committed to the policy of negotiation which the Americans had previously rejected. It seemed to be the general view that so long as negotiations of some kind could be kept in being, even Khruschchev's impetuous nature could hardly lead the Soviet Government to take any action to impede Western access to the city. There would be threats; there might even be an agreement with the Government of East Germany; but it seemed improbable that there would be such military interference with Western traffic as to provoke an immediate physical response.

However, the only immediate decision which the Cabinet had to make concerned the use of Christmas Island for a fresh series of nuclear tests. As my colleagues knew, I had told Parliament after the last Russian series that the Western Allies would not hold any further tests out of a mere sense of pride or anger. We would only do so for sound military reasons. The Americans considered, and it was difficult to disagree with them, that new tests were necessary for two purposes. In the first place, in order to maintain the balance of the deterrent, we must be sure that we could match the immense magnitude and widespread destructive effects of the new Russian super-bomb. Secondly, in order to develop a new defensive system involving the anti-missile missile, atmospheric tests would equally be required.

The Cabinet discussions lasted all the morning and a great part of the afternoon.

> Sir William Penney came to Cabinet after luncheon, and gave them—in a quarter of an hour—a simple but brilliant exposition of the problem.[1]

Our deliberations were excellent in form and matter, and full

[1] 3 January 1962.

agreement was reached as to the reply that I should now make to the President.

After the discussion was over, I had to start reshaping the letter to meet the views expressed. This will take a little time.[1]

The Cabinet agreed that we should take the necessary steps to put the installations in Christmas Island in such a state that the nuclear tests could be resumed if and when both Governments decided to do so. But they also wished for some new disarmament initiative to be taken and given wide publicity. My colleagues were particularly anxious that any announcement of the use of Christmas Island for further tests and of a new disarmament effort should be made simultaneously. Accordingly, in informing the British Ambassador, David Ormsby Gore, of the Cabinet's decision on 5 January, I wrote:

While I do not wish to make the President's agreement to the disarmament initiative a condition of granting facilities for United States tests at Christmas Island, I do, of course, very much hope that the President will agree to act as I suggest; and if he does not, I could not agree to make the facilities of Christmas Island available without consulting my colleagues again. I should also have to consider what other action we could take on disarmament, perhaps as an independent initiative.

My considered message to the President took the form of a letter sent by diplomatic bag. I knew the strong pressure being brought upon him by the Pentagon and the atomic scientists to resume tests immediately. I knew also the grave disadvantages which we might suffer if we 'dragged our feet' unduly or gave an absolute refusal to provide facilities which were essential to the American experiments. At the same time I knew that Kennedy was desperately anxious to postpone the day of resuming tests, which he regarded as a confession of failure in the diplomatic field. Like me he longed for some breakthrough towards peace. My purpose, therefore, was to provide him with the necessary ammunition and to urge upon him a new effort to deal with the problem as a whole.

[1] 3 January 1962.

The letter ran as follows:

I

When we met in Bermuda I undertook to consider as soon as possible with my colleagues your request for us to join with you in preparing Christmas Island for further atmospheric nuclear tests.

I have now discussed this question fully with the Cabinet. We recognised that the programme of tests now proposed seemed, so far as we could judge at present, to fall within the definitions of permissible nuclear tests which you and I made in the autumn. In these circumstances, whether we join with you in preparing Christmas Island or not, we should feel morally bound to support any decision which you might make to carry out this programme. My colleagues and I therefore agreed that it would be right to make available to you the facilities at Christmas Island which you require, subject, of course, to the conclusion of an agreement on scientific and technical collaboration as well as about the financial and administrative arrangements. As a contribution to scientific collaboration we would wish to place at your disposal certain United Kingdom techniques and experience, for example in observing nuclear weapons tests, which we believe would be of some value.

We made this decision on two assumptions. The first is that we can be satisfied, from the advice of our scientists working with yours, that the programme of tests proposed do indeed fall within our definitions of justifiable tests. From what I heard in Bermuda I do not in fact anticipate any difficulty here. Secondly, as I am sure you would agree, we should expect full consultation before a decision to start tests from Christmas Island is actually made. This is of special importance in the light of the proposals regarding a political initiative which I set out below. We think that in any announcement about the facilities at Christmas Island it would be better to state firmly that we had jointly decided that further tests were militarily necessary rather than saying only that we had agreed to make preparations for tests against a possible decision to hold them. At the same time, however, as you will see from the last section of this letter, we believe that an announcement in these terms should be accompanied by a determined new initiative towards disarmament and that it should indicate that the timing of tests could, to some extent, depend upon Soviet reactions to our proposals. From what you said in Bermuda I believe that you yourself would take into account the general international situation at the time before making a final decision to resume tests and I hope therefore that you will agree with this general approach.

II

In our discussions the Cabinet considered the probable progress which the Russians in their latest tests have made in the field of anti-missile work, and the danger that without some similar effort on our side we might one day find ourselves at their mercy. Of course at the very moment when we are beginning to work in this field we have to consider that the one-hundred-megaton weapon seems not merely to correspond with Mr. Khrushchev's natural instinct for magnitude but also to have valuable potential military importance and to pose a further difficult requirement for a defence system, at a time when it is not yet clear that defence will be possible even against missiles which must come much closer to their target before exploding. Even without this complication nobody knows whether either side will really be able to solve the immensely complicated problems of an anti-missile defensive system, towards which these are the first halting steps. Our scientific advisers, you will remember, said that, if it were not a matter on which national survival itself was at stake, they would say that it was impossible. But if, for such a stake, sufficient resources were developed and devoted to it, they could not definitely say that anything should be regarded as impossible. Yet, if we do what we are now contemplating, we shall be entering upon a new phase in this endless struggle, with all that this implies. When one adds to this the thought of the expenditure in money terms which will be necessary—and money terms are merely a convenient method of stating the vast resources, human and material, which are involved—it would really seem to any ordinary person who reflects calmly upon it that humanity is setting out on a path at once so fantastic and so retrograde, so sophisticated and so barbarous, as to be almost incredible. It certainly seems a strange irony, Mr. President, that I should have spent Christmas Day reflecting in what terms and by what arguments I should commend to my colleagues the dedication of Christmas Island for this purpose.

There are three aspects of this problem about which I am concerned. First, if we make these tests—modest in their size, without any serious effect on the pollution of the atmosphere and adding little from this point of view to the harm already done—undoubtedly the Russians will continue not only with preparing but with carrying out their next series. We shall later be forced to do the same; and so this contest will continue more or less indefinitely, each side trying to get the lead. But so heavy will be the expense, and so vast the claim upon resources, that I greatly fear the end may be what has nearly always been the end in these armament races—one side or the other, when it thinks it has the moment of superiority, will be temped to put the issue to the test. The second point we ought to consider is whether there is any real justification on technical grounds for believing that an effective anti-missile system could be developed. For our small island, of course, there can be none; for if even eight or nine missiles of the present size were to get through there would be little left of us. For you or for the Russians the situation is a little different because of the sheer size of the territory. Nevertheless, I would imagine that with all the counter-measures, the decoys, the electronic devices and all the rest of it, it must be very doubtful indeed whether a defence system can be achieved which will provide the minimum protection. Thirdly, there is the position of all the other countries. If the test programme of the Great Powers goes on there is no hope of dealing with what you call the nth country problem. Some countries will develop powerful systems, probably the Chinese and eventually the Germans—and, of course, the French. Nothing can stop them if the Great Powers go on. Others will develop nuisance systems—but they will be very formidable nuisances. And if all this capacity for destruction is spread about the world in the hands of all kinds of different characters—dictators, reactionaries, revolutionaries, madmen—then sooner or later, and certainly I think by the end of this century, either by error or folly or insanity, the great crime will be committed.

These are thoughts, Mr. President, about which I feel that you and I should ponder a little further. I ventured to put some of this to you in our short talks in Bermuda and it was because you were so responsive to the motives that lay behind that I am encouraged to send you this further analysis.

III

In Bermuda we covered a wide range of subjects. Apart from those mentioned in the Communiqué—Berlin, Nuclear Tests, the Congo, the European Common Market—we touched on a number of other points of almost equal importance. These included Laos and Vietnam and the general position in the Far East; the confused and always uncertain situation in the Middle East; Africa, where almost equal dangers may follow 'Colonialism' persisted in too long or abandoned too soon; the future of the emerging States like Ghana; and the likely development of the United Nations in its present form and under its present influence.

Running through all these discussions there was one common thread. All of these problems in their different ways reflect the great division which has dominated the world since the end of the Second World War. At every point and on every issue is the contest between Communism and the Free World, each struggling to contain the other and to attract the support of the so-called unaligned nations.

The more I reflect on all these problems the more I am led to the conclusion that none can be satisfactorily dealt with singly. But if, on the other hand, there could be some genuine improvement in the underlying malady from which humanity suffers, fairly rapid solutions of the particular problems would follow. In recent years there have been two attempts to break through the deadlock which seemed at one time to present some hope. The first was the Geneva negotiations for the abolition of nuclear tests, and the second was the series of efforts, including the interchange of visits between statesmen on both sides of the Iron Curtain which led up to the Summit meeting in Paris in 1960. Both these attempts ended in failure. Looking back, I think one must agree that the major blame for both these failures lay with the Soviet Government although the Allies were not wholly free from responsibility. For instance, I am personally convinced that an agreement at Geneva could have been reached on the basis of the abolition of tests above the threshold. That would have given us the enormous advantage of the introduction of at least an elementary system of inspection and control in a field where from its very nature the Russian suspicions or accusations of espionage were less plausible.

Similarly, the Summit meeting in Paris was the culminating point of a long and carefully prepared sequence of events, all of which seemed to afford some expectation of a genuine *détente*. Yet it not only failed, but broke up in a disorderly and discreditable way, in which we had to carry some of the blame. At the time no one seemed able to understand the excessive importance which Mr. Khrushchev attached to the U 2 incident. But I am inclined to think now that there was more connection than we then believed between Geneva and Paris. Mr. Khrushchev may have felt a genuine sense of shock at the discovery of how much we knew about the positions of their large rockets, on which they were depending so greatly. This in turn may have affected their attitude in Geneva and, combined with the remarkable success of the United States with nuclear submarines and Polaris missiles, may have led to the Russian decision to carry out their recent tests, on the preparation of which they had of course been long engaged.

At any rate, whatever the cause, the only two big diplomatic attempts which promised any success proved a disastrous failure. There is however this degree of comfort to be drawn from what happened. Mr. Khrushchev originally announced his decision to sign a peace treaty with the East Germans as long ago as November 27, 1958. At the time of my visit to Moscow in February, 1959, he deferred this threat; and, although he renewed it after the Paris débâcle, he is still showing some degree of moderation by refraining from implementing it even at the end of this year. I know there are some who say that this springs, not so much from a desire to appear reasonable towards the Western Allies and the world at large, as from his unwillingness to entrust dangerous decisions to Mr. Ulbricht and his friends. However that may be, we have been given a breathing space; and I know that it is your intention, in spite of all the difficulties inside the Western Alliance, to make full use of it.

The difficulty, as we all know, is to decide what to do. The somewhat sombre thoughts which I have developed can have no purpose unless they are intended to lead to at least some proposals for finding 'a way out' of the maze in which we are set. It may be that there is no way out. It may be that we are condemned, like the heroes of the old Greek tragedies, to an ineluctable fate from which there is no escape; and that like those doomed figures we must endure it, with only the consolation of the admonitory and sometimes irritating commentaries of the chorus, the fore-runners of the columnists of today. On the other hand, it may be that even those who cannot accept so pessimistic a view would feel it wiser to avoid any attempt to bring about a dramatic change of events and to rely upon 'something turning up' and somehow postponing at least for a period a fatal crisis. All my life there have been two views about the best way of dealing with this sort of problem. I can remember these arguments before the first war; they were of course in full flush between the wars; and they are still subject to much debate. One line of argument suggests that we should keep patiently at work trying to chisel away the excrescences which deface the body politic of mankind, and hope by this method to remove one by one the major dangers, whether local or general, arriving eventually at a point when an effective all-round settlement can become practical politics. The other view has been that there are moments in history when it is better to take a bolder choice and put a larger stake upon a more ambitious throw. A similar dispute has gone on recently between those who would wish to narrow and those who would wish to widen the discussions on Berlin. Chancellor Adenauer and his friends, after some hesitation, seem to have come down upon the side of narrowing any negotiation so as to deal only with access and the minimum amount of recognition of the D.D.R. required for practical purposes, thus avoiding such larger issues as the Oder–Neisse Line, or the ultimate future of Germany. General de Gaulle, on the other hand, has seemed to argue that without a general *détente* over a wide field any limited agreement on Berlin is hardly worth the paper it is written on.

All these arguments of detail must not be allowed to obscure the basic fact that the balance of power and continued peace in the world is maintained by the deterrent power of the United States and the United Kingdom on the one side against that of the U.S.S.R. on the other. The future of the uncommitted world, which tries to remain neutral on this great issue, is in fact dependent on the outcome. This lays a very great responsibility upon our two countries and I know, from our talks in Bermuda, that you feel as strongly as I do the over-riding need to find some way of breaking the deadlock between East and West. On the one side we have the problem of Berlin, on which we are now trying to find a basis for an understanding, and on the other the grim problem of the nuclear race, a new phase of which is opening before us and threatens to exhaust the resources of both sides.

We cannot tell at present how the Berlin exploration will go but at least we have a plan of campaign designed to test out the possibilities of agreement. We shall know in the next few weeks or months what prospects there are on this and it will certainly affect our whole approach to the question of relations with Russia. But in the meantime, I believe we should make a supreme effort to make progress in the field of disarmament and nuclear tests, in which we at present have not worked out an effective plan of campaign. My idea is that you and we might agree upon a scheme of policy designed to give new impetus to the disarmament negotiations and to unlock the present log-jam. With great respect, I would propose the following procedure and I beg you to consider it carefully and sympathetically.

IV

It has been agreed between us and the Russians that there will be an Eighteen-Power Conference on Disarmament beginning in the middle of March. We must build on this. But there is no doubt that this rather unwieldy, heterogeneous group of countries is not likely to achieve results unless it is given impulsion and leadership by the main nuclear powers. My idea would be that you and I, who are in the lead on the Western side, should take the initiative and invite Mr. Khrushchev to concert with us, before this committee meets, on the best methods of ensuring that practical progress is made. We might, for example, propose a conference of the Foreign Ministers of the three nuclear powers (perhaps joined by the French) backed by scientific as well as official advisers to meet before the opening of the Disarmament Commission in order to discuss the possibility of working as a team for its success. The purposes of this three- (or four-) power meeting would be:

(1) to reconcile our desire for adequate control over disarmament with the Soviet fear of espionage;

(2) to try to determine rapidly the conditions in which a permanent abolition of nuclear tests could be agreed;

(3) to discuss measures for ensuring greater security for the two sides pending an agreement on controlled disarmament;

(4) to issue a joint declaration to implement the Irish resolution passed at the last session of the United Nations assembly which enjoined nuclear powers not to relinquish control of nuclear weapons or to transfer knowledge relating to their manufacture to non-nuclear powers.

In proposing this meeting I suggest that we should make a declaration that we intend to make the success of the Disarmament Conference a major plank in our foreign policy, that we will take personal responsibility for the conduct of the negotiations and perhaps that we or our Foreign Ministers will personally attend the first meetings of the Commission.

If you should agree that a programme along these lines was desirable the next question would be how to present it both to our own public opinions and to the Russians. So far as I can judge opinion in the United States, there has been a very natural inclination to resume tests following the large-scale Russian tests. Yet I would also think that there will be a growing feeling of despair if nothing can be done to stop the present drift in the world. As regards my country, while our partnership with you in all this goes right back to the days of the Second World War and is highly valued, a decision to resume tests and to make British territory available for the purpose will not be readily understood unless it is accompanied by some public indication that we were making a new move to influence events. For that reason I would want to be able to announce at the same time the broad lines of this proposal and the decision to make available facilities at Christmas Island. On the other hand, if we are to achieve anything practical with the Russians, we must not handle this as a matter of public statement only but must approach Khrushchev direct and make it clear to him that we have a genuine desire for his co-operation in checking the nuclear arms race. Moreover, it would be important not to give him the impression that by a proposal of this kind we were seeking to avoid the issue of Berlin on which, as we well know, he is determined to achieve some settlement. My suggestion would be, therefore, that in addition to a public statement of our intentions, we should make a private communication of a rather more detailed kind to Khrushchev urging him to co-operate with us in a genuine effort to give impetus to the Disarmament Commission's work and to join in a meeting of Foreign Ministers of the nuclear powers on the lines described above. The purpose of the private approach to Khrushchev would be to indicate that we were genuinely concerned to save humanity from the threat and the wastage of a new competition designed to provide immunity against nuclear attack, a competition which we believe would almost certainly be fruitless and which could distort the whole economic life of the world.

It would be necessary of course to inform General de Gaulle and Dr. Adenauer of what we had in mind and perhaps to invite the French to take part in the initial approach to Khrushchev.

I suggest that we could meet the need to carry public opinion with us if we could make public statements on the following lines shortly after our approach to Khrushchev. We would say that:

(a) in our view the present technical situation justifies and indeed requires the West to make a further series of nuclear tests for purely military reasons. For this reason the United States and British Governments have decided to make preparations for such a series in various places including Christmas Island;

(b) we recognise that further tests by the West may be followed by more Soviet tests and so the cycle will continue indefinitely. Nevertheless, we see no justification here for abandoning our present plans but we are deeply concerned at the situation in which we find ourselves and for the future of mankind if a halt to the nuclear arms race cannot be called;

(c) we are therefore determined to make every effort to pull the world out of this rut and are making proposals to the Russians to this end (of which we can give a short outline); we hope that the result of our proposals will be to enable the nuclear Powers to stop testing altogether as the first move towards general disarmament.

If you agree with the above, I think the first step is to set up machinery for urgent discussions between our two countries on the programme envisaged and on the technical problems involved. This could include not only the question of tests and a disarmament programme but also, perhaps, of measures to ensure greater security in Europe and possibly elsewhere, including anti-surprise attack measures (notification of major military moves, observation teams, etc.) and, if we can overcome the doubts of the French and the Germans, limitation and

inspection of armaments in specified areas not limited to particular countries. I would like David Ormsby Gore to take this on
for us with such assistance as he requires. After that we should
have to try to bring the French in and perhaps other Allies; all
this in preparation for the Eighteen-Power Disarmament Commission's work. As there is very little time I would hope that we
could get on with this work straight away.

As I said, all this will be affected by the progress of the discussions on Berlin. If the probe is unsuccessful and we have to
hold a negotiation in a bad atmosphere, we in the West will not
be in a good situation. But, as you told me in Bermuda, this
would not be the end of the attempt to reach an understanding
with the Soviet Union and it might be that the approach which I
am proposing on disarmament would help us in making a new
move to negotiate with the Russians on the serious situation
which would then have arisen in Germany. If, on the other hand,
the Berlin explorations go well and seem likely to lead to a
negotiation between Foreign Ministers on that subject, there
again general prospects might be improved by the other initiative
and we could perhaps link the two negotiations with one another.
We might possibly envisage a Summit meeting later on, to
conclude a series of agreements covering these two major problems
and thus pave the way to a general improvement in East–West
relations.

It is, of course, easy to do nothing or to do nothing in particular. But, on the whole, it is not the things one did in one's life
that one regrets but rather the opportunities missed.
January 5, 1962.

On 8 and 9 January I paid a short visit to Bonn. This was not
really necessary except as a matter of courtesy; but Chancellor
Adenauer seemed to attach importance to these interchanges. On
hearing my account of our talks with the President he seemed quite
willing for negotiations about Berlin to proceed so long as they
were not taken at too rapid a pace and did not affect his close
relations with de Gaulle. On reporting this to Kennedy on 13
January, I added:

[Adenauer] was, however, more mellow about the Russians
than I have ever known him and spoke at some length about the

changing character of Soviet society in which the rise of a new intelligentsia or middle class may prove helpful in reaching a détente. He was interested in the idea of a new initiative about disarmament the importance of which subject, as you know, he has always stressed.

I thought it worth bringing to Kennedy's notice this last point for it was in conformity with the general policy outlined in my long message. Fortunately David Gore enjoyed the closest friendship with Kennedy, and their discussions were always frank and intimate.

On 14 January, I received the President's reply; the first two paragraphs ran as follows:

> We are giving the most urgent consideration to your letter of 5 January and to the additional comments made on it by David Ormsby Gore. I find myself in deep agreement with nearly all of what you say about the dangers of the arms race and the boldness of action required from those of us who bear primary responsibility in these matters. We must do all that we can to turn the nuclear spiral downward, and to save mankind from the increasing threat of events of surpassing horror.
>
> Whatever may be your final decision about Christmas Island, or mine about American atmospheric testing, I can assure you that we are ready to examine with you the possibilities for new efforts toward disarmament, on the most urgent basis. We are eager to work out together an initiative which might, if successful, mark a significant step forward and which would demonstrate, at a minimum, that we are continuing to press in every possible way to bring the arms race to an end. Dean Rusk is seeing David Ormsby Gore in order to determine how best to proceed. We have questions about some of the tactical aspects of your proposals. But we have no differences at all on the importance and urgency of the effort for progress.

The first difficulty involved the proposed meeting of Heads of Government. The President was not unexpectedly somewhat averse to this. Nevertheless he recognised the force of the argument that it would be damaging to us if the Russians jumped in with such a proposal of their own. This, in point of fact, was exactly what they were to do within a few weeks. He was also anxious lest any close link between the success of a general disarmament or a test ban treaty with the renewal of the Christmas Island tests might lead to the Russians merely prolonging the negotiations—'stringing us along' as he expressed it—in order to prepare a new series of their own experiments and thus get a lap ahead of us.

After an interchange of telegrams in which the Ambassador warned me that great pressure was being put on the President to have a formal agreement with us about Christmas Island, I put the whole correspondence before my colleagues on 18 January. After a very good discussion we settled upon our reply. In fact 'we agree to make Christmas Island available for tests; he agrees to my new initiative to try to bring them to an end'.[1]

Meanwhile, the Test Ban Conference which had been 'recon- vened' in the New Year broke up on 29 January in total deadlock and mutual recrimination.

In view of our long friendship, I thought it right to inform de Gaulle exactly where we stood. I told him of our willingness to allow the United States to use Christmas Island, but our determina- tion to make some new initiative in preparation of the opening of the Eighteen-Power Disarmament talks. Would he help us? His reply was characteristic. The first paragraph of his letter of 6 February ran as follows:

> Your letter of 28 January interested me greatly because of the information and proposals it contained on the immense question of atomic armaments. It has moreover touched me because of the emotion that you so justifiably show both as a statesman and a Christian in the face of the dangers which hang over the human race as a result of the nuclear peril.

He went on to note the decision on the proposed renewal of tests and our co-operation.

> On this question I must tell you that after the truly provocative series of recent Soviet explosions it seems to me very natural that, on the western side, one should be anxious not to allow a dangerous gap to be created or extended. Besides, we French are determined

[1] 18 January 1962.

to pursue our own tests as far as our means allow and however limited these means may be at the moment.

When, however, it came to the question of disarmament, he regarded this as only useful if all existing bombs and means of delivery were to be destroyed.

Obviously, if it was only a question of preventing any nuclear tests in future while permitting the enormous armaments accumulated to continue to exist, France would not subscribe as far as she is concerned—you are aware of the reasons—without, however, making any objection to the Three Powers, Britain, the United States and the Soviet Union who have already created and would keep their own armaments, undertaking in future to abstain from new explosions. However, as for expecting anything impartial or effective in this realm from the Committee of Eighteen, that seems to me in advance to be quite hopeless. The source of this committee, that is to say the General Assembly of the United Nations, as well as its own composition, have in my opinion too marked a demagogic and irresponsible character for one to be able to take towards it any other attitude than one of complete reserve.

I was not unduly disappointed by this reply, nor did I regret having consulted him before making my public announcement.

On 7 February the President and I sent a joint appeal to Khrushchev inviting him to join with us in a really sustained effort when the new negotiations began in Geneva. In the past such negotiations had been 'sporadic and frequently interrupted':

It should be clear to all of us that we can no longer afford to take a passive view of these negotiations. They must not be allowed to drift into failure. Accordingly, we propose that we three accept a personal responsibility for the part to be played by our representatives in the forthcoming talks, and that we agree beforehand that our representatives will remain at the conference table until concrete results have been achieved, however long this may take.

Our Foreign Ministers should attend at the beginning and make themselves available whenever circumstances required. It might be useful if they were to meet for a preliminary discussion a few days before the Conference began. The message set out in some detail the proposed system of work and ended with both an appeal and a request for a speedy expression of Khrushchev's views.

On 8 February I made an announcement to the House of Commons. I reminded the House of

the claims, true or false, made by Russian military leaders at the time of their nuclear test series last autumn that they have solved the problem of destroying ballistic missiles in flight.

I continued:

I felt myself bound to accept, therefore, the military and scientific arguments in favour of preparations for a resumption of tests [Hon. Members: 'Shame'.] and when President Kennedy asked for the use of facilities at Christmas Island for them, Her Majesty's Government thought it right to agree. Accordingly, an agreement is being discussed in Washington at the moment under which Her Majesty's Government will allow the United States the use of facilities at Christmas Island for a limited period and for a specific programme of tests with which we shall of course be associated. On this point, [an] announcement is being issued immediately in London and in Washington.

I went on to say how reluctant the President and I were to accept the need to prepare for further tests and how deeply distressed we were at this necessity and the future position of the world if a halt could not be called to the nuclear arms race.

When I was in Bermuda I made this point strongly to the President, who was very receptive, and accordingly, on my return after consulting my colleagues, I made a definite proposal to President Kennedy that the Western Powers should make another determined effort to reach some agreement with the Soviet Union on the question of disarmament. We have already agreed to join in the work of the Committee of Eighteen which meets in Geneva on 14 March, and I believe that this will offer an opportunity for renewed serious discussions.

I am glad to say that President Kennedy very much welcomed the idea of trying to give special impetus and effectiveness to this conference. Accordingly, the two Governments have today communicated with the Soviet Government, and have invited them to send their Foreign Minister to a tripartite meeting to assemble before the Geneva meeting and to begin this meeting also at the level of Foreign Ministers. I have addressed a personal letter to Mr. Khrushchev appealing to him to agree to this proposal and President Kennedy has done the same.

I had of course already informed the Prime Ministers of Canada, Australia and New Zealand by personal messages, and sent similar notification to the other members of the Commonwealth.

My statement in House of Commons . . . went very well. The 'two-pronged approach' made the whole difference. If I had merely announced the agreement to provide Christmas Island for the American atmospheric tests . . . without the joint letter from President Kennedy and myself to Khrushchev, urging a new and urgent approach to the disarmament question, it would have been much more difficult. I 'got away' with the announcement of our own underground test at Nevada, and I was not cross-examined too closely on the point which had caused so much concern to the Cabinet—that of who had the veto. The emphasis on close consultation was accepted. This affair has certainly caused more trouble to Gaitskell, for it reopens the old wound between the unilateralists and the multi-lateralists. I think the Government got credit from the handling of a difficult problem.[1]

The next day, as I had expected, Khrushchev made a more spectacular proposal. He

is now also trying to get ahead of us, by proposing an immediate 'Summit' meeting of Eighteen 'Heads of Government' in Geneva, without any preparation or any experts. This of course is pure propaganda, but we have to deal with it cautiously, or we shall be accused of 'dragging our feet'. We have sent off quite good replies, which will serve for the time being; but I think that once more I must try to press the . . . President on. He is good, but *very* cautious.[1]

My reply to Khrushchev on 14 February expressed gratification that we had been thinking along similar lines and promising to take a part personally at any stage in the Conference when it seemed

[1] 16 February 1962.

useful. President Kennedy and I had already said that we would associate ourselves closely with the work.

> I feel, however, that a meeting . . . will be more likely to be practicable and fruitful when the main problems have been clarified and some progress has been made. Meanwhile I think that meetings at the Foreign Ministers level would be the best instrument for achieving the progress at the opening stages.
> A special responsibility for the success of the Conference clearly devolves on our Governments as nuclear Powers and it was for this reason that the President and I suggested to you that the Foreign Ministers of the United Kingdom, United States and U.S.S.R. might meet in advance of the Conference in order to concert plans for its work. I trust that you will give your most serious consideration to this suggestion and that it will be acceptable to the Soviet Government.

In a telephone conversation the next day, President Kennedy expressed his full agreement with my reply and said that he would answer in similar terms. Meanwhile, we might bring as much pressure as possible on the countries of the eighteen powers to support the proposal of a preliminary meeting of Foreign Ministers. I felt strongly that, although Heads of Government might have to meet again, we could not afford another failure like the lamentable Summit meeting in Paris in 1960.

Meanwhile, the position in Berlin showed no improvement. The so-called diplomatic 'probe', the talks between Rusk and Gromyko which had started in the autumn of 1961, had produced no result nor had the follow-up in Moscow.

> The Russians are 'hotting up' the troubles in and around the city; 'buzzing' our aeroplanes; threatening to shoot them down, etc., etc. This is very tricky.[1]

Indeed it became necessary for Kennedy and me to discuss quite urgently the action that might be taken should the situation seriously deteriorate.

On the disarmament question, various people began to come into the act for or against the Anglo-American plan. In spite of a fresh

[1] 16 February 1962.

appeal, de Gaulle maintained his attitude of detachment. The only states, in his view, who could do anything positive about nuclear disarmament were those in possession of nuclear weapons. The Eighteen-Nation Conference seemed merely an opportunity for propaganda.

On 23 February Khrushchev replied. His answer was, as usual, very long—ten foolscap pages. He maintained that only the Heads of Government could take the necessary decisions—a point which, of course, we had never disputed—but he also argued that they ought to be present throughout the important part of the negotiations.

> As for myself it has been my rule in life to be present where the main work is being carried on, where it is most important of all to achieve success.

As his argument proceeded it deteriorated in tone. Was my reason for preferring a preliminary meeting of Foreign Ministers because I wanted them to take the blame for a negotiation which I did not hope would succeed? However the crucial part of his reply was that relating to control. He regarded any form of international control, whether of nuclear or conventional disarmament, as a form of espionage, and it was this position that the Russians took throughout. Indeed, it was this problem of providing an efficient system of detection which occupied us for many months. I was myself persuaded that our scientists could apply this even to underground tests of any significant magnitude without actually visiting the location; but the Americans were never convinced.

All this time, the battle of notes went merrily on. On 26 February, I assured Khrushchev of my willingness to come to Geneva either if agreement seemed to be likely or if a specific disagreement had been uncovered. In my view, only patient and detailed work could reveal the measure of possible success. However, I reiterated the value of the preliminary meeting of the Foreign Ministers.

On 28 February, the President informed me that he had decided that an announcement about the American resumption of tests must be made before the disarmament conference began. It would be more politic to do so than to wait until after it had started. At the same time he would announce an offer that, if the U.S.S.R. would sign a comprehensive test ban treaty with control provisions as tabled in April 1961, then the tests would not proceed. Otherwise they would be resumed on 15 April. I told him, on 1 March, that while I accepted a military need for tests I hoped he would give a longer period of warning, thus allowing more time to try to achieve an agreement with the Russians.

> The President . . . has gone some way to meet me. He has agreed to postpone his statement till tomorrow night. This is much more convenient for us. He has agreed to inform France, Italy and Canada (our partners in the Committee of Five) and also NATO. He had forgotten altogether about this, which makes me think that the State Department has not been in on this to any extent. He has agreed to saying 'towards the end of April' – which gives some chance of talks with the Russians first. The Cabinet felt we must accept the situation.[1]

While I was wondering how best to present the President's position in Parliament I got a welcome message that Krushchev had at least yielded on the point of procedure.

> I was rung up early by the Foreign Secretary, who told me that Khrushchev had now agreed to the procedure which we and the Americans had proposed for the Geneva Conference, including the prior meeting of the three Foreign Ministers to discuss in particular the nuclear test problem. This helped very much with my statement in the House of Commons on the American resumption of tests and the use of Christmas Island. The statement, on which we worked all the morning, went off very quietly. Mr. Gaitskell . . . was very helpful, and even shot down Grimond for me. Supplementaries very few. The left-wingers and fellow-travellers seemed stunned by the news of Khrushchev's acceptance. (Since this only came out on the tape at 2.30, it was news to most members.)[2]

The disarmament plan which we proposed to lay before the Conference was explained in detail by the Foreign Secretary to the Cabinet. I was somewhat alarmed by the signs that the American

---

[1] 1 March 1962.　　　　[2] 5 March 1962.

position was now beginning to harden. I therefore wrote to the President on 9 March suggesting a simple control provision believed to be now scientifically feasible—national monitoring systems supported by an international authority which could both collate seismic data and have mobile inspection teams to visit and investigate suspected violations. I thought that this plan might overcome the Soviet dislike of control posts on their soil—the 'espionage' argument. (On the other hand, as Kennedy pointed out, the idea of mobile investigators might upset them even more.) Nevertheless, although it could be argued that the Russians were being merely obstructive, I felt myself that their extreme sensitivity and their distrust of many of their own leading scientists, combined with their inherited xenophobia, were genuine emotions which we must somehow meet and overcome.

When Home and Rusk met at Geneva they had a very good talk and worked together with their usual friendliness. But Rusk told the Foreign Secretary that the American scientists were now beginning to question the effectiveness of a national detection system even if it were spread, as we had proposed, over all parts of the Commonwealth and in other friendly countries. Nor was the recent Soviet action in stepping up the harassment of our traffic to Berlin very encouraging. On 14 March Home reported that Gromyko categorically refused to accept any form of international inspection whatsoever.

We then made a new proposal which certainly was a test of Russian good faith. We asked the Russians whether, if we were to accept their own plan of national detection, they would admit any form of verification of unidentified explosions. Their refusal, although disappointing, put us in a very strong moral position. Nevertheless, I felt that there must be some clearer proof of our sincerity and Russian evasiveness before the American tests were resumed. At first, I thought of proposing a meeting between the President, Khrushchev and myself. But David Gore warned me that this would be hopeless. Various other plans were put forward including the proposal that Kennedy, in his formal announcement, should say that even now if Khrushchev would accept the principle of international verification the tests would be delayed.

Throughout I had the greatest help from our two experts—Sir Solly Zuckerman and Sir William Penney. After a meeting on 12 March I noted:

> The real argument now is whether *national* detection systems could detect underground explosions in Russia, without *any* actual stations on Russian soil. If that can be accepted, we can force the Russians out of their 'espionage' argument. If, without any permanent stations in Russia, they object to half a dozen or so inspections—of perhaps a few days' duration, by an international team—then it is clear that the Russians want not to avoid espionage but to preserve the right to cheat.[1]

But all our efforts were to prove fruitless.

> We have had a very rough ten days—in every field. The Geneva Conference has made no progress at all. Every day there have been telegrams to and fro from Geneva and Washington. Telephone messages to President as well. I sent Solly Zuckerman and William Penney to Washington.

They were cordially received, but I found that the American scientists were somewhat sceptical about the possibilities of detection.

> Unfortunately, although they were impressed, they were not wholly convinced that *national* instruments could detect underground tests in Soviet territory with any certainty. This is a pity—and worse. For if we could have offered to do without the *stations* in Russia, and only ask for *occasional visits* by teams which could be neutral, we would really be in a position to show up the hollowness of the Russian fear of espionage. Fortunately (in a way) Gromyko has declared over and over again at Geneva that even occasional visits are unacceptable. They have thus gone right back on what they said during the Geneva Test Conference and what Khrushchev proposed (or accepted) with me in Moscow in 1959. There seems therefore no way of preventing the starting of the American tests at Christmas Island after Easter. The Foreign Secretary (who came back last night) had a long talk with me this morning. He still has a lingering hope that the Americans will *postpone*. It is clear that the President is as unhappy as I am about the whole situation. But, of course, he is

[1] 12 March 1962.

under great pressure, from the Pentagon and from Congress. Here all the pressure is the other way.[1]

On 30 March I made one more effort. I proposed that either the President or I or both of us should ask Khrushchev to answer a simple question. Is the principle of international verification acceptable or not? In Kennedy's reply on 3 April he told me frankly that he saw no prospect of success in a direct appeal to Khrushchev. Moreover, American opinion would be hostile, but that should not, in his view, deter me nor would he have any ill-feeling if I acted alone; alternatively, if I preferred, he would agree to a joint statement rather than an appeal and sent me the text of such a statement.

I had at this time many preoccupations with home policies as well as with difficult and complicated issues in Africa. Nevertheless I pursued, with perhaps unjustifiable obstinacy, what was no doubt something of a will-o'-the-wisp. Kennedy throughout showed the greatest patience, partly because he fully understood my political position and also sympathised with my ideals and hopes. He resisted the pressure put upon him as long as he could, and had Khrushchev made the smallest gesture to meet us I am certain that Kennedy would have risked everything to follow it up. But I had often to admit to myself that there was little real hope of this.

A lot of telegrams; teleprinter messages; telephone calls between Washington and London have gone on all the week. I have kept the Cabinet informed all through. The position is really rather sad. If only science had made a little more advance, we might have been able to make an offer to Russia which she *might* have accepted, and which she could only reject by losing all sympathy in the neutral world. Our own scientists would (I think) feel that the politicians might take the risk. Some of the American scientists feel the same. It is now called 'International Minus' as a code name. It means that we would definitely abandon the idea of listening stations to detect illegal underground tests on *Russian soil*. We would only ask for *occasional* visits by neutral scientific teams to look at unexplained seismic events. However, owing to the Russian intransigence at Geneva, and the fact that both Gromyko and Zorin have rejected over and

[1] 24 March 1962.

over again any form of visiting teams or occasional inspection inside Russia, from a purely propaganda point of view, we are on sound ground. I have now agreed a statement which President Kennedy and I will make jointly on Tuesday. I shall also write myself a letter to Khrushchev, asking him to accept the principle of international verification in some form. But I am sad, because if the West could have made it quite clear that we would abandon permanently stationed posts, I think it's just possible that the Russians might have accepted occasional visits—which Khrushchev agreed with me in Moscow in 1959. Of course, in Geneva they accepted both fixed posts and spot checks.

My comfort lies in the view, for which there is a good deal of . . . support, that the Russians have another Test series ready and that as soon as the Americans start theirs, the Russians will follow—larger, and more alarming! If that is so, there never has been much hope. Yet it may well be that both Mr. Ks. are similarly placed and that both have to deal with military and political pressures.[1]

On 9 April, a joint statement from President Kennedy and myself was handed to the Soviet Government. Its last paragraph ran as follows:

We continue to hope that the Soviet Government may reconsider the position and express their readiness to accept the principle of international verification. If they will do this, there is still time to reach agreement. But if there is no change in the present Soviet position, the Governments of the United States and the United Kingdom must conclude that their efforts to obtain a workable treaty to ban nuclear tests are not now successful, and the test series scheduled for the latter part of this month will have to go forward.

At the same time I sent a personal letter to be delivered to Khrushchev, and on the next day I informed Parliament. Gaitskell was sensible and helpful, although both he and Grimond fell into the trap of Khrushchev's proposed Summit Conference—of Eighteen Heads of State—almost as multi-headed as the Hydra. In reply to Gaitskell, I said:

[1] 7 April 1962.

If there is any question of a Summit Conference in the sense of three or four Heads of Government—not twenty, thirty or forty—I want to be quite sure that it is timed in such a way as to be most likely to be fruitful and upon perhaps a fairly wide range.

As I feared,

the neutrals in Geneva are now turning against us and U.S.A. The Russians have (rather cleverly) proposed another 'moratorium'. I suppose they (the neutrals) have forgotten what happened during the three years. Indeed, the moratorium would still have been in existence, if the Russians had not made their autumn series—suddenly, out of the blue.[1]

On 14 April, Khrushchev's reply arrived. He answered

my short and temperate letter with a four-thousand-word effusion, covering a great deal of ground, making wild charges against us and the Americans—and generally taking a very polemical tone. The view of the Foreign Office is that he is really rather embarrassed. But he has managed to frighten the neutrals at Geneva, who are now threatening to 'walk out' of the Disarmament Conference if the tests go on. They were not so robust last autumn, when the Russian tests were made. It is a case of 'double standard' again.[2]

Yet hope springs eternal in a neutral breast!

The great Nuclear Test debate continues. I thought Mr. Khrushchev's letter to me had rather clinched it. But the 'neutrals' at Geneva have worked out a so-called compromise. This, The Times falls for, in a very disingenuous leading article. The fundamental point—the Russian refusal to allow any inspection on the sacred soil of Russia—is *not* met at all by the neutrals. The Times says it's only the difference between 'could' and 'should'. But that *is* all the difference in the world.[3]

In my statement to the House of Commons, I said that the tests must now definitely go ahead, and this was accepted with very little hostile comment. Accordingly, on 25 April, the series of tests at Christmas Island began. I had, of course, given due warning to all the Commonwealth Prime Ministers.

[1] 13 April 1962.   [2] 14 April 1962.   [3] 17 April 1962.

For the next four days I had to be in New York and Washington, followed by a short visit to Ottawa. Naturally the European Common Market was the theme chiefly in my mind, but there was much talk upon our relations with the Soviet Government. It was clear that President Kennedy was really anxious to see some way of stopping the tests after the present series. As regards disarmament, he made a prophecy which proved to have some substance. He felt that when both sides had sufficient weight of nuclear weapons, enough for a 'portentous mutual over-kill', then at last disarmament talks might begin in full seriousness; but this would be a matter of some years ahead.

The interchange of telegrams and memoranda between British and American scientists continued gaily all through the summer. Scientists, who are the poets of the twentieth century, seem to be subject to the most conflicting moods. At one stage I received a message to say that the President now thought that the United States scientists were completely revising their ideas about identifying underground tests. It might well prove that they would be able without difficulty to distinguish them from natural seismic phenomena. Three weeks later this report was negatived. Some kind of outside inspection would still be required, and this was still the great stumbling block. Yet on 27 July there came a message to me among a whole stream of constantly exchanged thoughts in which there could be found the germ of the Treaty ultimately reached. If on-site international inspection continued to be ruled out by Russian suspicions, could we not go for the second best solution—a Treaty banning tests in the atmosphere and under the water? It was this alternative that we were to pursue until its final fruition in the following year.

Meanwhile, the Berlin 'probe' had continued from time to time but without much result. Also there were alarming rumours reaching us through various sources about an impending Russian action. It was even suggested that all the Russian fuss about nuclear tests was an elaborate cover plan for a decisive move in Germany. However, in the course of these interminable talks between Rusk and Gromyko, the latter never seemed anxious to set any time-limit. But some of my doubts were resolved when on 5 August the news came of a new series of tests by the Russians. These must have been prepared for many months before, and even our most captious critics could hardly maintain that their explosion was the direct result of the American resumption of tests.

The summer months passed in a mood of uncertainty. As regards Berlin,

> the general view now is that nothing will happen in August. After that (when Khrushchev gets back from his holiday) there may be some dramatic moves. A congress of 'peace-loving peoples' (i.e. Russian satellites) to inaugurate a Peace Treaty with the East German Government. Perhaps some neutrals or unaligned might be induced to join in – Yugoslavia, Egypt, etc. Sir Frank Roberts seems to think something on these lines likely (Frank Roberts is our brilliant Ambassador in Moscow). Others feel that the economic situation in East Germany is so bad that Ulbricht will not risk cutting off supplies of all sorts of necessities from West Germany.[1]

Anxious as I was to make some forward movement, it was vital not to do anything to injure the Brussels negotiations on the Common Market. Thus, one suggestion followed another with a growing sense of despair and the war of words continued.

During a short visit to Bolton Abbey in August, where David Gore was one of the party, he gave me a vivid picture of the difficulties with which the President was surrounded. He

> wants to *do* something big; but doesn't know how to do it. On Berlin, tests, etc. – he can make little progress. On the economic front, he is equally constricted by the political situation internally and the American dread of unorthodox policies.[2]

By the end of August, we had agreed to offer the Russians an option either of an atmospheric ban or of a total and comprehensive ban with a reasonable number of inspections. On 5 September, Khrushchev made a somewhat ambiguous reply; thus as autumn came, the controversy ran tediously on, losing itself like some great river in the sands and never reaching the sea.

Yet all the time, immersed as I was with the problems at home

[1] 5 August 1962.   [2] 21 August 1962.

and the paramount issue of our entry in the Common Market, involving long and apparently somewhat fruitless negotiations at Brussels, as well as the heavy burden of a Conference of Commonwealth Prime Ministers on this outstanding question, I felt instinctively anxious lest the President and I were being deceived or lulled into a false security. What lay behind Khrushchev's manoeuvrings, sometimes threatening, sometimes friendly? Was there some new plot hatching? Were we to wake up one morning faced not merely with verbal disputations but by actions which might prove the terrible prelude to the Third World War?

CHAPTER VII

On the Brink

I did not have to wait long; before the leaves had fully turned and the oaks and beeches at my Sussex home taken on their autumn glory, my dire forebodings were dramatically fulfilled. I was working quietly in my room in London on Sunday evening, 21 October, when about 10 p.m. I was handed by the duty clerk an urgent message from President Kennedy informing me that a serious crisis was rapidly developing between the United States and the Soviet Union. We had already received, two days before, some warning from the British Ambassador, to whom the President had spoken in guarded terms. Although David Gore gave no details, he sensed that the alarm in the White House was 'probably about missiles in Cuba'. So the blow was destined to fall not in the East, but in the West—not in Germany, but in the Caribbean.

The relations between the United States and Cuba formed indeed a tangled story. Originally conquered from the Spaniards (or 'liberated' as the phrase goes today), the island became independent in 1902. Although there was occasional need to send in American troops to restore order, the liberal policy of Washington was maintained. The economy of the island was developed and enriched by the American Government, and large American investments were made, covering sugar, oil, transport and fruit-growing, which were at once helpful to the economy and a source of envy to the inhabitants. Unhappily, no very satisfactory form of native government had developed. Each successive régime had seemed more incompetent and corrupt than its predecessor. When the rule of Batista was finally overthrown in January 1959 by Castro's revolutionary guerrillas, a violent swing to the Left was unavoidable. President Eisenhower was worried, shocked, but not yet convinced that a purely Communist system must necessarily follow. Yet the ex-

propriation of American property; the sale of the sugar crop to the
U.S.S.R.; the trade agreement with Poland—all seemed dangerous
and inescapable evidence of Cuba's political and economic orienta-
tion. At the end of May 1960, American 'aid' to Cuba was terminated. In July, the Shell refinery at Havana was seized, against
which the United Kingdom Government made a formal but in-
effectual protest. All the Americans could do in retaliation was to
reduce still further the Cuban sugar quota into the United States.

Khrushchev then got into the act in his usual boisterous and
boastful manner by issuing a dramatic warning 'in case of necessity,
Soviet artillery can support the Cuban people with their rocket fire'.

But Eisenhower remained calm. Indeed, during the first six
months of Castro's rule, he tried to adopt a co-operative attitude.
But in the following period it had become clear that Castro was
wholly committed to the Russian bloc. Eisenhower could now only
rely on economic pressure, in which he urged us to join, to rally the
Cuban people against their new oppressors. While accepting the
President's analysis, I expressed doubts as to whether economic
hardship would encourage opposition to Castro, especially if it could
be blamed on the Americans and mitigated by Russian help. Nor
could I agree to operate any blockade, whether of tankers or other
ships. In peace time, we had no legal power to prevent tankers
taking Russian oil to Cuba. I might have added that we had encountered quite a lot of difficulty in operating a blockade even
during two world wars.

So matters had drifted on, with occasional wrangles in the
Security Council and the Assembly of the United Nations. I had
even suffered myself from these, having listened to some parts of
Castro's famous five-hour oration. But nothing effective could be
done. It was impossible to unseat Castro, difficult to live with him.

Then had followed, early in President Kennedy's régime, the
famous incident of the 'Bay of Pigs'. Once more Castro had
triumphed; and only Kennedy's innate courage and resiliency had
enabled him to survive a staggering blow to his prestige.

All these thoughts and recollections passed through my mind
as I began to read the long and alarming telegrams which began
slowly to emerge from the 'machine' on that calm Sunday night.

Kennedy's message had been preceded by a few hours by a further warning from the Ambassador:

I have just come from seeing the President. He will be sending you an extremely important message on Cuba by teletype machine to Admiralty House at about 10 p.m. today London time. I think it essential you should be there to receive it immediately. The President particularly stressed that not only are the contents of the message confidential in the highest degree but that the fact that you are receiving a message at this time should on no account become known.

The President's message ran as follows:

I am sending you this most private message to give you advance notice of a most serious situation and of my plan to meet it. I am arranging to have David Bruce report to you more fully tomorrow morning, but I want you to have this message tonight so that you may have as much time as possible to consider the dangers we will now have to face together.

Photographic intelligence has established beyond question, in the last week, that the Soviet Union has engaged in a major build-up of medium-range missiles in Cuba. Six sites have so far been identified, and two of them may be in operational readiness. In sum, it is clear that a massive secret operation has been proceeding in spite of the repeated assurances we have received from the Soviet Union on this point.

After careful reflection, this Government has decided to prevent any further build-up by sea and to demand the removal of this nuclear threat to our hemisphere. When he sees you tomorrow, Ambassador Bruce will have at hand the substance of a speech which I will give on Monday evening, Washington time.

This extraordinarily dangerous and aggressive Soviet step obviously creates a crisis of the most serious sort, in which we shall have to act most closely together. I have found it absolutely essential, in the interest of security and speed, to make my first decision on my own responsibility, but from now on I expect that we can and should be in the closest touch, and I know that together with our other friends we will resolutely meet this challenge. I recognise fully that Khrushchev's main intention may be to increase his chances at Berlin, and we shall be ready to take a full role there as well as in the Caribbean. What is essential at this moment of highest test is that Khrushchev should discover that if he is counting on weakness or irresolution, he has miscalculated.

I venture to repeat my hope that the nature of this threat and of my first decision to meet it be held most privately until announcements are made here.

Although we ourselves had received indications that trouble might develop regarding Cuba, we had only a general report that Soviet build-up of arms and technicians was continuing throughout the late summer. In early September, the President had issued a statement making it clear that the introduction into Cuba of surface-to-surface offensive missiles or of any other significant 'capability' whether in Cuban hands or under Russian direction would raise issues of the gravest kind. He had repeated this warning at a news conference on 13 September:

> If at any time . . . Cuba were to . . . become an offensive military base of significant capacity for the Soviet Union, then this country will do whatever must be done to protect its own security and that of its allies.

But we had little further information, and, with so many other preoccupations, I had observed without any alarm or incredulity the Russian disclaimers. Indeed, it was only on 14 October that the first evidence became available to the Americans through aerial photography that the offensive missile sites were actually being prepared. These were not the SAM (surface to air missiles) which might perhaps be represented as defensive armoury against air attack; they were ballistic missiles directed on the great cities of the United States and capable of spreading destruction and death on a colossal scale within a few minutes.

In reading and re-reading the President's words, I noted particularly the vital third paragraph; although the sites were in an advanced stage of preparation, few, if any, of the missiles themselves seemed yet to be in position. Hence the decision of the American Government 'to prevent any further build-up by sea'. I did not of course then know that this declaration came only after a long and

G

even bitter debate among the President's own advisers as to the appropriate reply to the threat which had been revealed. Some, indeed the majority, as we now know, recommended an immediate military strike followed by an invasion and occupation of the island. Had the President and his team known what only became clear a few days later, that the missiles themselves were largely in position and that the force deployed represented a great part of the available nuclear strength of the whole Russian economy, Kennedy might not have been able to resist the arguments in favour of immediate and decisive action. It is a tribute nevertheless to his calm wisdom through these dangerous days that, largely influenced by his brother, Robert, he was determined to find a method by which Khrushchev himself could, should he wish it, retreat, without too much loss of face, from the perilous position which he had occupied.

There was little for me to do this Sunday night except to await the meeting with Ambassador Bruce; yet it was difficult at so dangerous a moment to reconcile myself to inaction. After some reflection I decided, at this stage, not even to warn the Foreign Secretary; it would be better to wait until the Ambassador came.

The next day, Monday 22 October, is best described by my notes at the time:

> The first day of the World Crisis! Ambassador Bruce called at noon. He brought a long letter from President Kennedy, as well as a great dossier to prove that (contrary to *specific* assurances given by the Russian Government and by Gromyko in particular) there had now been secretly deployed in Cuba a formidable armoury of M.R.B.M.s and I.R.B.M.s (short and moderate range missiles) which were a pistol pointed at America (and Canada and South America) and which could not be tolerated. The President was going to speak later today (7 p.m. Washington time; midnight London time) to the nation and the world. Text of speech would be delivered to me immediately—by 12.30 or 1.
>
> Ambassador Bruce, in his detached and quiet manner, did not attempt to conceal the excited, almost chaotic, atmosphere in Washington. The photographs revealing the full extent of the offensive missile deployment in Cuba had only become available

about 17 October. The President had hurriedly cancelled his election tour, and returned to Washington on Saturday 20th. All the decisions had been taken on Saturday and Sunday. He felt sure that the decisions were not yet final—hence the delay in getting me copy of speech. The Ambassador thought that the President's proposed action (which seemed to be to impose a 'quarantine' or blockade on all ships, Russian or neutral, carrying arms to Cuba, and to threaten a more complete blockade if necessary) would not satisfy the 'war' party in U.S., and yet would have great dangers of precipitating a clash. We speculated a little about the likely response by Mr. Khrushchev. Would it be words or deeds? in the Caribbean or in Europe?[1]

I had already acknowledged the President's telegram and promised to send a message immediately I had seen Ambassador Bruce, which, owing to the difference in time, should reach him in the morning. The Ambassador brought me a further and more detailed account from the President:

We are now in possession of incontrovertible military evidence obtained through photographic reconnaissances, that the Soviets have already installed offensive nuclear missiles in Cuba, and that some of these may already be operational. This constitutes a threat to the peace which imperils the security not only of this hemisphere but of the entire free world. You will recall that last month I stated publicly that the Government of the United States would consider the presence of ground-to-ground missiles in Cuba as an offensive threat. In response to my remarks, the Soviets stated that such armaments and military equipment as had been shipped by them to Cuba were exclusively of a defensive nature, and this was repeated to me only last Thursday by Gromyko under instruction.

The foregoing has created a highly critical situation which must be met promptly and fearlessly. This evening at 1900 hours Washington time I shall be making a public statement of which Ambassador Bruce will be giving you a draft together with this message. This text is not necessarily final in every detail, but the essentials of the problem, and the means by which I intend to meet it, have already been decided as set forth in the present text.

[1] 22 October 1962.

Ambassador Bruce will also be prepared fully to explain to you the evidence on which we have based our conclusions. I am also writing to Chairman Khrushchev to bring home to him how perilous is his present course of action, but expressing the hope that we can agree to resume the path of peaceful negotiation. I am quite clear in my mind that these missiles have got to be withdrawn, and you will see that I intend to state this publicly in my speech as well as telling Chairman Khrushchev this in my letter to him.

The object of the quarantine, which will be put into effect immediately, is to prevent the Soviet Union from introducing additional missiles into Cuba and to lead to the elimination of the missiles that are already in place.

I shall also be sending a personal message to Prime Minister Diefenbaker, General de Gaulle, Chairman Adenauer, and Prime Minister Fanfani and have sent Dean Acheson to Paris to assist Ambassador Finletter in briefing the North Atlantic Council shortly before I make my public statement. However, I wanted you to be the first to be informed of this grave development, in order that we should have the opportunity, should you wish it, to discuss the situation between ourselves by means of our private channel of communication.

This is a solemn moment for our two countries, indeed for the fate of the entire world. It is essential that the already great dangers before us should not be increased through miscalculation or underestimation by the Soviets of what we intend to do, and are prepared to endure, in the face of the course on which they have so recklessly embarked.

I need not point out to you the possible relation of this secret and dangerous move on the part of Khrushchev to Berlin. We must together be prepared for a time of testing. It is a source of great personal satisfaction to me that you and I can keep in close touch with each other by rapid and secure means at a time like this, and I intend to keep you fully informed of my thinking as the situation evolves.

In the meanwhile I am also requesting an urgent meeting of the United Nations Security Council. I have asked Ambassador Stevenson to present on behalf of the United States a resolution calling for the withdrawal of missile bases and other offensive weapons in Cuba under the supervision of United Nations observers. This would make it possible for the United States to lift its quarantine. I hope that you will instruct your representative in New York to work actively with us and speak forthrightly in support of the above program in the United Nations.

As soon as the Ambassador left, I arranged for the Foreign Secretary and some of his chief advisers to come over to discuss the position. Later, we got an analysis of the material from the Air Staff. There seemed no doubt as to the facts. But I was still awaiting David Gore's report, on which I knew I could rely for accuracy and full understanding of the President's mind. Meanwhile,

in spite of all the promises, no copy of the President's speech. This finally arrived about 5 p.m. Alec Home came over and together we worked out a reply to the President. I think it was a pretty good document.[1]

This was not altogether easy to draft. One could, of course, promise support in general terms, but I had to remember that the people of Europe and of Britain had lived in close proximity to Soviet missiles for several years. Nor was it very clear what kind of blockade was intended—was it merely to keep out ships bringing missiles and armaments, or was it to be a total blockade? Moreover, was it not likely that Khrushchev's real purpose was to trade Cuba for Berlin? If he were stopped, with great loss of face, in Cuba, would he not be tempted to recover himself in Berlin? Indeed, might not this be the whole purpose of the exercise—to move forward one pawn in order to exchange it for another? All these points I had put to the Ambassador. Nevertheless, it was important that our reply should show no hesitation or weakness. Indeed, in my first draft, I had thought of advising him to seize Cuba and have done with it; at any rate to avoid drifting into the situation which we had done at Suez. In addition, I was alarmed lest Kennedy

'miss the bus'—he may *never* get rid of Cuban rockets except by trading them for Turkish, Italian or other bases. Thus Khrushchev will have won his point.[1]

[1] 22 October 1962.

I also reflected that

> the blockade is to be of 'arms', that will prevent *more* rockets reaching Cuba. But only an intensified and complete blockade can bring down Castro's Government. But this will be long (at least 3 months) and will (since it is patently 'illegal') cause a great deal of trouble with neutral and even with friendly countries.[1]

Nevertheless, we had to act quickly and our reply was sent off in the following terms:

> Ambassador Bruce called to see me this morning and gave me evidence of the Soviet build-up in Cuba. I quite understand how fiercely American public opinion will react when it knows these facts. I have this moment received through our teleprinter the text of your proposed declaration tonight. Let me say at once that we shall of course give you all the support we can in the Security Council. I hope that you will provide us immediately with the best legal case that can be made in support of the broad moral position so that our representative can weigh in effectively. Of course the international lawyers will take the point that a blockade which involves the searching of ships of all countries is difficult to defend in peace time. Indeed quite a lot of controversy has gone on in the past about its use in wartime. However, we must rest not so much on precedent as on the unprecedented condition of the modern world in a nuclear age.
>
> If, as I assume, the Security Council resolution is vetoed the only appeal is to the Assembly. What the result will be there no one can tell, but I doubt whether they will be in favour of any conclusive action, or even if they are I do not see how they will enforce it. What I think we must now consider is Khrushchev's likely reaction. He may reply either in words or in kind or both. If he contents himself with the first he may demand the removal of all American bases in Europe. If he decides to act he may do so either in the Caribbean or elsewhere. If he reacts in the Caribbean his obvious method would be to escort his ships and force you into the position of attacking them. This fire-first dilemma has always worried us, and we have always hoped to impale the Russians on this horn. No doubt you have thought of this, but

[1] 22 October 1962.

I would be glad to know how you feel it can be handled. Alternatively, he may bring some pressure on the weaker parts of the free world defence system. This may be in South-East Asia, in Iran, possibly in Turkey, but more likely in Berlin. If he reacts outside the Caribbean—as I fear he may—it will be tempting for him to answer one blockade by declaring another. We must therefore be ready. Any retaliatory action on Berlin as envisaged in the various contingency plans will lead us either to an escalation to world war or to the holding of a conference. What seems essential to me is that you and I should think over and decide in what direction we want to steer things within the alliance and elsewhere. We should take counsel as soon as we have the Russian reaction.

While you know how deeply I sympathise with your difficulty and how much we will do to help in every way, it would only be right to tell you that there are two aspects which give me concern. Many of us in Europe have lived so long in close proximity to the enemy's nuclear weapons of the most devastating kind that we have got accustomed to it. So European opinion will need attention. The second, which is more worrying, is that if Khrushchev comes to a conference he will of course try to trade his Cuba position against his ambitions in Berlin and elsewhere. This we must avoid at all costs, as it will endanger the unity of the alliance.

We were still without any direct news from the Ambassador. For some reason his telegram did not reach me till after 10 p.m. Although it would have helped in drafting our reply to the President, both Home and I felt that it was imperative not to delay in sending him our thoughts.

As soon as the Foreign Secretary left, I

sent for Chancellor of Exchequer and put him in the picture. His advice was sensible. He would see Governor of Bank. There would be heavy buying of gold and a general fall of all stocks and shares—but no panic.[1]

On this evening I was due to give a large dinner in honour of General Lauris Norstad, now Supreme Allied Commander in Europe,

[1] 22 October 1962.

an old and valued friend. This, although a tiresome distraction, at least

> gave me a chance of a private talk with General Norstad. Washington . . . have been urging a NATO 'Alert', with all that this implies (in our case, Royal Proclamation and call-up of Reservists). I told him that we would *not* repeat *not* agree at this stage. N. agreed with this, and said he thought NATO powers would take the same view. I said that 'mobilisation' had sometimes caused war. Here it was absurd, since the additional forces made available by 'Alert' had *no* military significance.[1]

Indeed, apart from certain precautions affecting the Royal Air Force, we maintained this position throughout the crisis. Since Gaitskell was at the dinner, I thought it best to tell the main facts as I knew them. I took him to

> Cabinet room and showed him all the documents, and the President's speech. He did *not* take a very robust attitude. He thought his party 'would not like it'. I doubt if they would like any decision – firm decision – on any subject.[1]

About 10.30 p.m. I was told that Gore's telegram had at last arrived. It was long and illuminating, and I was indeed glad to be able to read it before answering a telephone call from the President, which had been arranged for 11 p.m. The Ambassador's account ran as follows:

> I know that David Bruce had instructions to put us in the picture at midday today in London, but it may be useful if I give an account of my talk with the President yesterday. He asked me to come unseen to the White House just before lunch. We were quite alone, and he told me that no one else outside the United States Government was being informed of what was going on.
>
> He then said that the situation with regard to Cuba had completely changed during the course of the last week. A major photo reconnaissance effort by U2 aircraft had now shown that Cuba was obtaining two types of medium-range offensive missiles. One type on fixed sites had an estimated range of two thousand

[1] 22 October 1962.

miles. The other type was mobile with an estimated range of fifteen hundred miles. He was not very specific with regard to figures, but he thought that there were perhaps thirty to forty missiles already on the island and they now knew that more were on their way by ship. They had to assume that these missiles would be armed with nuclear warheads. They would be more or less useless without them, but the Americans had no firm information at this time as to whether nuclear warheads had arrived. They did, however, know of the construction of underground storage facilities. He said that this new information posed a very serious problem for the United States. He had made his position very clear on September 13 when he had said, among other things, that if Cuba became an offensive military base of significant capacity for the Soviet Union, then the United States would do whatever must be done to protect its own security and that of its Allies. This straightforward differentiation between defensive and offensive capacity constituted a clear warning of where the United States would draw the line. In these circumstances and in the light of this latest information, the Administration had had to decide what action they could appropriately take.

The President said that they had come to the conclusion that there were two alternatives open to them:

(1) They could order an all-out air strike first thing Monday morning to take out all the known missile sites and the missiles themselves insofar as they had been able to pinpoint their present whereabouts. The military authorities estimated that such a strike would eliminate at least fifty per cent of the Cuban missile potential, but it would inevitably cause a large number of casualties to Russians as well as Cubans. The strike would be followed by the imposition of a blockade of Cuba.

(2) They could impose almost immediately a blockade without first carrying out an air strike. They would stop and search all ships suspected of carrying goods which would help to build up the military potential of Cuba. This would mean leaving the Cubans with their present offensive capacity, such as it was, but would demonstrate America's determination not to allow the build-up to proceed any further.

The President then asked me for my views as to which of these two courses I felt was the correct one. I said that I saw very serious drawbacks in the first course of action he had outlined to me. Very few people outside the United States would consider the provocation offered by the Cubans serious enough to merit an American air attack. I thought that in the circumstances America would be damaged politically, and in any case I could not believe that the missiles so far landed constituted any significant military threat to the United States. Even with these weapons in existence on Cuba the United States could presumably overwhelm the island in a very short time if they decided at some future date that this had to be done. I thought we ought also to bear in mind the possible repercussions on the Berlin situation. American action of this kind might well provide a smokescreen behind which the Russians might move against Berlin under favourable conditions. Therefore, of the two alternatives he had put to me I would certainly favour the second, although this too would have far-reaching political implications including the probability of a major Russian reaction perhaps in the Berlin context.

The President said that he and his colleagues had come to the same conclusion and they therefore intended to carry out the second course of action. He added that he supposed that there was a third course and even a fourth course open to them. They might, for instance, use the latest developments as an excuse for a full-scale invasion of Cuba and so finish with Castro once and for all. They might never have a better opportunity for such action. Again, they might do nothing at all and go on as before, but he thought that this was not only politically impossible but was in any case too dangerous. It was now clear that their present actions in Cuba constituted a direct challenge by the Soviets to the United States. They knew perfectly well what his own position and that of the United States Government was and if, when confronted by this provocative challenge, he did nothing, his friends and Allies would come to the conclusion that he was afraid to move and Khrushchev would be bound to assume that the Americans, for all their tough words, would be prepared to sit supine and inactive whatever he, Khrushchev, did. This would have its effect in other areas all around the globe and especially in respect of Berlin.

In answer to this, I said that I was sure that an invasion at this time would be most unwise. I had seen no evidence that the conditions in Cuba were such that the Americans could expect any widespread popular support for their action and history indicated that an invasion without internal popular support usually led to endless trouble. The idea of a puppet régime kept in power by American marines was not a happy prospect. In any case, this could provide the Soviets with the opportunity to take over West Berlin at a moment when United States political stock would be at a very low ebb and the Americans could be blamed for triggering off this exchange of pawns in the most reckless manner. Nevertheless, I could well understand the political dangers and the internal difficulties of doing nothing, but I supposed that the blockade itself would give us many headaches and we would now have to prepare for vigorous Russian reactions to it.

I then asked the President under what authority they would institute a blockade of Cuba. He said that it would be under the terms of the Rio treaty and that a meeting of the O.A.S. would be called urgently and they would expect to get a two-thirds majority in favour of the course of action they were taking. I said that I feared that the invocation of the Rio treaty would not help us very much as I presumed that the United Kingdom had no legal obligations under its terms. Our traditional attitude with regard to the freedom of the seas would put us in an awkward position. Here the President commented that he understood that most of the British shipping taking part in the Cuban trade was not operated by the more respected companies. He also made it clear that shipments of P.O.L.[1] would be denied to Cuba. Such shipments would be regarded as assistance to the military potential of Cuba and in any case, in view of the action they were taking, there seemed to be little point in adopting half measures. Certainly the denial of P.O.L. to Cuba would have the most disastrous effects on the Cuban economy.

The President finally said that he could not help admiring the Soviet strategy. They offered this deliberate and provocative challenge to the United States in the knowledge that if the Americans reacted violently to it, the Russians would be given an ideal opportunity to move against West Berlin. If, on the other hand, he did nothing, the Latin Americans and the United States' other Allies would feel that the Americans had no real will to resist the encroachments of Communism and would hedge their bets accordingly.

The President impressed upon me how vital it was to keep all

[1] Petroleum, oil and lubricants.

this information secret until they were ready to act. He wished that only you and your closest advisers should be informed of what was happening. I said that in these circumstances I thought it would be better if I did not report through the usual channels but rather that he should send you a personal message later in the afternoon by teletype machine.

At 11.30 p.m., the President came on the telephone – the special secret line which was so carefully guarded by our Security Officer. This was the first of many conversations during the Cuba Missile Crisis; they were a great comfort for me, since I felt all the time intimately informed of each changing aspect of these terrible days. Conversation, owing to the peculiar mechanism of the machine, was not easy but we soon learned to manage the technique. Sometimes the President rang as many as three times in the day. Unluckily, he forgot that his last call, which was at midnight his time, was at 5 a.m. our time. However, Alec Home and I sat up cheerfully through several nights, as the crisis deepened, attended by relays of devoted secretaries and constant refreshment. Of this first of our Cuba conversations, I recorded:

He seemed rather excited, but very clear. He had just finished his broadcast. He was grateful for my messages and for David Gore's help. He could not tell what Khrushchev would do. He was rather vague about the blockade (it is clear that all kinds of plans have been all day under discussion). He is building up his forces for a *coup de main* to seize Cuba, should that become necessary.[1]

But there was more to be done that night.

One of the tasks which occupied us late into the night was the sending of appropriate messages to various friends. All need careful and separate drafting. De Gaulle, Adenauer, Fanfani in Europe. Diefenbaker . . . Menzies, Holyoake – *and* then Nehru and President Ayub. (I also sent a warm personal message to Nehru about his troubles. The Chinese are pressing on victoriously all along the front. We are giving India lots of ammunition, light arms, etc.) Then, in more or less identical terms, to the African P.M.s, etc.[2]

[1] 22 October 1962.   [2] 23 October 1962.

The Cabinet met the next morning, 23 October, and

> I explained the whole Cuban situation, and read out aloud (but did *not* circulate) the vital documents—viz: (*a*) the President's confidential message to me; (*b*) the Ambassador's *démarche* and the summary of the evidence about the missiles in Cuba; (*c*) my replies; (*d*) summary of our telephone talk. Ministers seemed rather shaken, but satisfied.[1]

Of course, by now I seemed to have been living with Cuba, day and night, for a prolonged period, dreaming and thinking of little else. To my colleagues, it was a bolt from the blue. Anyway, the pound was stable, even if the heavens were about to fall. The Chancellor of the Exchequer

> gave me a message at Cabinet as follows: 'Sterling steady this morning. Gold market very active. We sold $22 m. gold, but recouped it all in Foreign Exchange. $ opened weak but has steadied.' But of course the stock market is much down—mostly, perhaps, due to jobbers marking down shares rather than due to any great volume of selling.[1]

After luncheon, General Norstad came to take his leave. 'He had little to say, except the good news that he had persuaded Washington to be more reasonable'[1] about mobilisation of NATO powers. It was already clear to me that the situation was not one which required such old-fashioned mechanisms. Either the bombs would fall, or one side or the other would recoil. As Secretary Rusk was to say, 'We looked into the mouth of the cannon; the Russians flinched.' Although it was perhaps not quite so simple as that, there was no need to anticipate the horrors of nuclear warfare by observing all the traditional, almost ritual, preliminaries to conventional combat.

Later, I saw Gaitskell again, at his request. He brought two of his colleagues.

> At 5 p.m. Gaitskell, Brown and Wilson came. They hadn't much to say. Brown was more robust than G. . . . Fortunately, they all distrust each other profoundly.[1]

[1] 23 October 1962.

Next came my audience with the Queen. I tried to explain the dangers of the situation, without exaggerating them. She was, as usual, calm and sympathetic.

Meanwhile, the American administration had gone into action with remarkable skill and energy. The Organisation of American States had already met and demanded 'the immediate dismantling and withdrawal from Cuba of all missiles and other weapons with any offensive capacity'. It also called on all its members to take all measures necessary to prevent continued supply of military material from Sino-Soviet powers. This was indeed a personal triumph for Kennedy, whose standing was high with the Central and South American States.

On the same day (23 October) the Security Council met, and the Russian representative, Zorin, in reply to the excited accusations of Adlai Stevenson, had the effrontery to deny that there were any missiles or launching pads in Cuba. This was too much for the impassioned American idealist. Armed with enlarged photographs, admirably presented, he was able to confound his adversary and prove, even to the most sceptical or hostile observer, the strength and accuracy of the American complaint. This incident had a profound effect in Britain and throughout the world. It was of real importance, because, as I had already warned Washington, it was essential that the actual photographs should be made as public and as intelligible as possible—those supplied to me by Ambassador Bruce required expert interpretation to be convincing. However, the demonstration in the Security Council was widely reported. Moreover, all doubts were subsequently to be removed by Khrushchev himself.

During the night of 23 October, there was little that I could do but await events. A further telegram from the President warned me that the critical moment would come if and when the Russian ships met the large blockading forces which the Americans had rapidly mobilised.

Our Naval Commanders are instructed to use the very minimum of force, but I know of no sure escape from the problem of the first shot. Our best basic source is firmness, now.[1]

[1] 23 October 1962.

I learnt later that, in conversation with the President, David Gore observed that the interception line at eight hundred miles distant from Cuba was too far out. If the object was to give Khrushchev a chance of reconsidering his position, the more time afforded him the better. At his suggestion, therefore, the President shortened the distance to one of five hundred miles.

The next day, 24 October, the blockade went formally into effect. At the same time the President decided on a further release of photographs to the Press of the world, and these continued to be made available day by day as the American photographic aeroplanes flew over the island. Each day they disclosed that the work was continuing. This accumulation of proof was of vital importance, and the President was very conscious of this. On Wednesday, 24 October, I received a telegram from the British Ambassador on this point:

> I had another long talk with the President after a private dinner at the White House last night. He asked me about the reaction to his speech in the United Kingdom. I said that I thought it was most important that the Americans provide really convincing evidence to the general public of the Soviet offensive build-up in Cuba. He quite understood, and after he had sent for a batch of photographs he gave instructions as to which of them should be published and he emphasised the importance of clear explanatory notes being attached to them. I had pointed out that without such explanatory notes the uninitiated would have no means of telling whether the missiles depicted were six feet long and therefore defensive or sixty feet long and therefore offensive. The President said that they had carried out a very low-level photo reconnaissance flight during the course of the day and they hoped that this would provide them with some useful close-up pictures of the missiles. He called for a report on Zorin's speech in the Security Council and was told that Zorin had not specifically denied the presence of long-range missiles in Cuba. Zorin's argument had been that Cuba had no offensive designs and therefore all weapons in their possession were defensive.

We now knew that twenty-five Soviet ships were approaching Cuba, fourteen of which were believed to be carrying rockets. The first clash must thus soon come. The President had wisely decided only to seize the missiles; ships with minor arms, after being searched, would be allowed to proceed.

U Thant now made an appeal both to Kennedy and to Khrushchev suggesting that both the blockade and the shipment of arms should be suspended for two to three weeks while negotiations proceeded. The first news I had of this was from the President the same night.

No further news came to us that day, 24 October, except the rumour that some of the Russian ships had turned back. At 11 p.m. (London time) the President telephoned. The conversation was indeed a strange one. Yet, had I been able to make use of it in Parliament, it would have certainly dispelled the accusation that there was no 'special relationship' between London and Washington. After some preliminary greetings, Kennedy turned to the vital question of the Russian ships.

> *President Kennedy:* As you have probably heard, some of these ships, the ones we're particularly interested in, have turned around—others are coming on, so we ought to know in the next twelve hours whether they're going to try to run it or whether they're going to submit to be searched. So we'll be wiser by tomorrow night, but maybe not happier.
>
> *Prime Minister:* You don't really know whether they're going back or whether they're going to try and make it, do you?
>
> *K:* Some of the ships that have turned back are the ones that we were the most interested in and which we think would have given us some material. Others are continuing, I think they're just tankers that are continuing. Now, I don't know whether they are going to make us sink these or whether we are going to be permitted to search them. That's still in question.

At this point I said that the turning back of the ships seemed a definite success. But the President was uncertain.

> *K:* Some of them are coming on and the ones that are turning back are the ones that we felt might have offensive military equipment on them, so they probably didn't want that equipment to fall into our hands. That's the reason they're turning back, but

MISSILE-READY TENT

LAUNCH POSITION

MISSILE ERECTOR

A medium-range ballistic missile base in Cuba, late October 1962

A Russian ship with eight canvas-covered missiles on her decks

Adlai Stevenson in the Security Council

we still don't know whether the other ships will respect our
quarantine or whether they will make us take action, military
action, against them. That we don't know and we won't know
that for overnight.

P.M.: That's very interesting. But now what do you think it
means? If they're turning back it means he's frightened a bit,
doesn't it?

K: No, he may be turning back these, the little ones, to avoid
our possession of them because they have either missiles or
supporting equipment which is either secret material or because
it would give him a bad position in the world. So these ships—the
five or six which we're particularly anxious to get a hold of—they
have been turned back, but the others are coming so we still
don't know whether we're going to have an incident, which is
possible, with a ship which doesn't have anything of military
importance on it. That may be what our problem is going to be,
but we won't know that, as I say, until tomorrow.

I then asked him what he was going to do about removing the
rockets that were already in Cuba.

K: Well, if we go through Stage I as I say, and if they respect
our quarantine then we've got this problem of the rockets on
Cuba and the last 24 hours' film show that they are continuing to
build those rockets, and then we're going to have to make the
judgement as to whether we're going to invade Cuba taking our
chances or whether we hold off and use Cuba as a sort of hostage
in the matter of Berlin. Then any time he takes an action against
Berlin, we take action against Cuba. That's really the choice we
now have. What's your judgement?

P.M.: Well, I would like to think about that. I think it is very
important because I suppose the world feels that we shall some-
time or other have to have some sort of discussion with them, but
we don't want to do that in such a way that he has all these cards
in his hands.

K: He has Cuba in his hands, but he doesn't have Berlin. If he
takes Berlin, then we will take Cuba. If we take Cuba now we
have the problem of course of these missiles being fired or a
general missile firing and we certainly will have the problem of
Berlin being seized.

P.M.: Yes, I agree with that. It needs thought.

In a broadcast in reply to a letter from Bertrand Russell, Khrushchev had said that he wanted a Summit meeting, and I wondered whether the President knew any more about it.

K: Yes, I saw that, but he said that there would be no point in a Summit if we continued our piratical actions. The implication was that he would be glad to talk but not if we continued our quarantine or if we carry it out. It wasn't very precise.

He also told me that U Thant had asked him to suspend the quarantine for two weeks, but that he could not agree to that unless the Russians agreed to stop work on the missile bases.

I supported him in this. 'But all the same,' I added, 'I think he is a bit wondering what to do, don't you?'

K: Well, I think that they certainly have not been very precise in the last 24 hours. The question I would like to have you think about, Prime Minister, is this one. If they respect the quarantine, then we get the second stage of this problem and work continues on the missiles. Do we then tell them that if they don't get the missiles out that we're going to invade Cuba? He will then say that if we invade Cuba that there's going to be a general nuclear assault and he will in any case grab Berlin. Or do we just let the nuclear work go on figuring he won't ever dare fire them and when he tries to grab Berlin, we then go into Cuba. That's what I'd like to have you think about.

I said I should like to think about it and send him a message later. He agreed and asked me if I was having any trouble with the Opposition in Parliament.

P.M.: All I have to do is to make a short statement and they ask a few questions. It won't last more than half an hour and then we prorogue the Parliament. So tomorrow should be fairly simple. I shall just make a statement of the facts and supporting you and just leave it at that. Of course they will ask me whether I propose to intervene, and all that kind of thing, but I shall say the time's not ripe for that yet.

K: That's fine. . . . The two important points seem to me (1) my statement in early September saying that we were opposed to taking any military action in Cuba unless they indulged in offensive capacity and the second was their statement that they would never put rockets into Cuba, so this deception seems to me to be so indefensible from their point of view. And I assume you have all that material in case you were being pressed at all by the Labour Members.

P.M.: Yes, very kindly you've given me that. Ambassador Bruce gave me that this morning and I think we've got all that into the statement. This big issue of which you have just spoken is the one I would like to think about. And then we must consider how we handle the Europeans and who will begin to get a bit excited – de Gaulle and Adenauer and Co. – and how we take the next steps. But I feel myself pretty sure that we ought not to do anything in a hurry. We ought just to let this develop a day or two.

K: Right, Prime Minister. As I say we are mobilising our force so that if we decide to invade we will be in a position to do so within a few more days.

We then turned to the question of the United Nations, and I asked him exactly what U Thant had said to him.

K: The Secretary-General's proposal was that no aggressive arms be shipped into Cuba, number one; and number two, the quarantine be suspended for two weeks and that there be negotiations during that two weeks. We're sending back an answer saying that this does not provide us with any assurances. If we withdraw the quarantine we have no assurances that arms won't be sent in there, number one; and number two, if we could get reasonable assurances that they wouldn't be sent in there that would be satisfactory, but there's also work on the missile sites would have to stop, and that the missiles that are presently pointing at us should be subjected to inspection. So that's what we'll come back with, and then we'll see what he says.

P.M.: Will that be all public, or is that a private message to you?

K: I think he's probably reporting it to the Security Council. I haven't seen it on the ticker yet, but he's sending it to Khrushchev, so my judgement is he'll release it, and our answers will be released.

P.M.: I think that's rather tiresome of him [U Thant] because it looks sensible and yet it's very bad.

K: Well, yes. I think the fact that work on the missile bases will continue – I'll read you his message. I am just informed that he has not made a public statement yet. He has just given us a copy of the prospective public statement that he is going to make. Now it may not be finally made but I'll read it to you. [The President then read the text slowly at dictation speed.]

'I have been asked by the permanent representatives of a large number of member Governments of the U.N. to address an urgent appeal to you in the present critical situation. These representatives feel in the interests of international peace and security that all concerned should refrain from any action which may aggravate the situation and bring with it the risk of war. In their view it is important that time should be given to enable the parties to get together to resolve the situation the present crisis presented and normalise the situation in the Caribbean. This involves on the one hand the voluntary suspension of all armed shipments to Cuba and also the voluntary suspension of the quarantine measures involving the searching of ships bound for Cuba. I believe that the voluntary suspension for a period of two or three weeks will greatly ease the situation and give time to the parties concerned to meet and discuss with a view to finding a peaceful solution to the problem. In this context I shall gladly make myself available to all parties for whatever services I may be able to perform. I urgently appeal to Your Excellency for immediate consideration of this message. I have sent an identical message to the Chairman of the Council of Ministers of the Soviet Union. (Signed) U Thant.'

Now we don't know whether that's what he's finally going to do but that's what he was indicating he was going to do half an hour ago.

I thought that this was a very dangerous message and that it was most important that the President should send a good reply.

K: Yes. Well, we're just getting it ready and we'll point out the deficiencies in it, that there's no guarantees against a breach of the quarantine and also the work on the missile sites will continue, and the danger will be greater within two weeks. So we'll point that out and send it right back to him the minute we get an indication that he's going to send it to us.

P.M.: Well now, how do you think we shall get out of this in the long run? Do you think we ought to try and do a deal, have a meeting with him, or not? What initiative do you think ought to be taken and by whom?

K: Well, I think probably at the end of this 24-hour period when we understand more of what he's going to do on the quarantine, I think we shall probably judge it better. As I say part of that answer, Prime Minister, seems to me to depend on the answer to the question that we were originally discussing, which was whether we ought to wait and let this build-up continue in Cuba, because otherwise we risk war and equally important, at least of some importance, we risk the loss of Berlin. Otherwise, we can keep on the quarantine, the build-up of missiles will continue, and then we would threaten to take action in Cuba if they go into Berlin.

Until we had decided what to do there was no point in having a meeting. What should we discuss? Khrushchev would merely offer to dismantle the missiles if we neutralised Berlin. How should we reply? It was a difficult political problem which we ought to be thinking about.

I would certainly think about it. Meanwhile I wondered whether it would be helpful if I were to go and see him.

K: Why don't we talk on Friday when we know what we're going to do with this quarantine. Then if it looks like we're going to have a period of halt, then I think it would be very good. But why don't we talk Friday and then we shall see what looks like our best timing.

P.M.: I think that's a very good idea. We'll have a talk on Friday night. Is that the best we can do?

K: That'll be fine, Prime Minister, unless you're going to be away on Friday night.

P.M.: I shall stay in London, but I think it very useful if we can have a brief talk each evening if it's not inconvenient to you, then we can just compare notes as to how things are going on.

K: Good, I will call you then, tomorrow evening, Prime Minister at 6.00 my time.

P.M.: That'll do me fine. Good night.

K: Good night, Prime Minister. Thank you.

It was now necessary to reply to the vital question which the

President had put. 'Should we take out Cuba?' I did so the next morning in the following terms.

I have been thinking over the sixty-four thousand dollar question which you posed on the telephone. After much reflection, I think that events have gone too far. While circumstances may arise in which such action would be right and necessary, I think that we are now all in a phase where you must try to obtain your objectives by other means.

I am going to make the point today in the House of Commons that if you had let the Russians get away with it after your September statement none of the American guarantees to the free world would have had any value. This is the vital point of justification. I am also going to make the second point that in view of the Russian duplicity we cannot rest on mere words in any arrangements, we must have verification and confirmation. In these circumstances, I would suggest that in the reply which you make to U Thant today, which will be of vital importance and subject to the closest scrutiny by our friends and neutrals as well as enemies, you should concentrate on the point that there must be some system of inspection if the quarantine is called off. Such inspection must make sure that ships with arms do not in fact enter the ports. We cannot rest now upon the Russian promise. That is the first point.

You must also demand that there should be some inspection by the United Nations or other independent authority to stop the work on the major military installations so long as the negotiation lasts. This would enable you to say that you had in fact obtained your objectives. For if there are no ships arriving, then the purpose of the quarantine is served; and if there is no more construction the purpose of largely immobilising this threat is also served. In other words, such an approach as I suggest fits in with the answer to last night's question which I feel I must give.

At the same time you will no doubt continue with your military build-up for any emergency. This may be as important a factor for persuading the Cubans to accept inspection as in other directions.

Not unexpectedly, Khrushchev accepted the Secretary-General's proposal. But the President was too wise to fall into the trap. He made it quite clear that the offensive weapons must be removed from Cuba. U Thant now made a further move. He wrote to Khrushchev hoping that the U.S.S.R. 'may find it possible to instruct the Soviet ships already on their way to stay away from the interception area for a limited time only in order to permit discussions'. To President Kennedy he wrote asking the United States to avoid direct confrontation. To this Kennedy adroitly answered that if the Russian ships did in fact keep out of the area there would be no confrontation.

On the same day, 25 October, the House of Commons met, happily only for the purpose of being prorogued. Since the new session was not to start until 30 October, we had at least the good fortune to escape daily questioning with all the embarrassment involved. However, I arranged with Gaitskell to make a short statement at 11 a.m.

> The Conservative benches were packed. Opposition pretty full, especially *below* the gangway. Statement well received on all sides. Gaitskell, as usual, said he would ask two questions and proceeded to ask ten. But his tone was helpful. By the time (after one or two Conservatives, including Selwyn Lloyd) we got to the Communists or Fellow-Travellers it was getting on to 11.30. I had settled with Gaitskell that we would put off Black Rod from 11 a.m. (usual time for Prorogation) but not beyond 11.30. There was a mild demonstration, but it amounted to very little.[1]

Parliament, the Press and the public remained remarkably calm, at least at this stage.

I sent messages to leaders of all the Commonwealth countries and also to de Gaulle. I emphasised strongly to the old Commonwealth countries the need for America to act firmly, if confidence in American support was to be maintained among her allies. The lesson of Russian duplicity would at least serve to show that disarmament could not be left to depend upon Russian assurances.

The President and I had a further conversation at 11 p.m. He immediately asked about our position in Parliament.

> *P.M.:* We did very well. The House was very good. I have sent you the text of what I said and I think it was very well accepted.

[1] 25 October 1962.

I made all the points I could especially the one you gave me about your statement on September 11 and the deception which the Russians have made. That was very well received.

K: Prime Minister, we got a second message from U Thant which you may be familiar with which asks Khrushchev to keep his ships out of there and asks us to avoid a confrontation. Now we are sending back a message saying that if he keeps his ships out of there of course we will avoid a confrontation. As you know today 14 ships turned around and they were probably the ones with the aggressive cargo. One tanker we stopped and we asked where it was going and it said it was coming from the Black Sea to Cuba and the cargo was oil. It was obviously a tanker and we passed that. We have tomorrow two or three vessels including particularly an East German vessel which has probably six or seven hundred passengers. It stopped in Leningrad on its way and it may have 6000 tons of cargo on it. So we are going to have to stop that we think. That's what we are now discussing. Now we have got two tracks running. One is that one of these ships, the selected ships which Khrushchev continues to have come towards Cuba. On the other hand we have U Thant and we don't want to sink a ship and then right in the middle of when U Thant is supposedly arranging for the Russians to stay out. So we may have to let some hours go by but sooner or later probably by tomorrow evening we'll have to accost one of these and board it. Now we got a message last night from Mr. Khrushchev which I'll make sure you get if you haven't gotten it already which said that this is piratical and that their ships are going to go through and not submit to this and that if we do stop them they have the means of action against us. That's last night. So that's about where we are.

I had seen his message to U Thant, which I told him I thought was very good. It was not only ingenious, but also firmly insisted that the problem was to get rid of the weapons and that it would be up to Stevenson and U Thant to discuss how this could be done. I was interested to know what line Stevenson would take.

Meanwhile the President had further news.

K: We had a message from U Thant about a half hour ago which goes somewhat further than the first one went.

The Secretary-General now said that he was specifically asking Khrushchev to keep his ships out of the quarantine area—which he had not done in his first message. The President welcomed this, and repeated that if the ships kept away there could be no incident.

K: On the other hand we do point out in our response to him that Soviet ships still are coming. Now that's that. Now if these conversations begin, we're going to point out that in the beginning once we get this matter of the ships straightened out, because we still haven't had our first search yet and that's going to be a very important event and we will then know what the Russians are going to do. But that will come tomorrow. Then if we begin the conversations we are going to begin by pointing out that work is going on and that work must stop or otherwise we've got to extend this blockade and consider other actions to stop it. But I think that's at least 24 hours away. I think the next thing for us to do is to figure out how we will handle this first search in view of the fact that the U.N. is involved in this now. In other words I don't want to have a fight with a Russian ship tomorrow morning and a search of it at a time when it appears that U Thant has got the Russians to agree not to continue. I hope that by tomorrow afternoon it will be clear either that the Russians are just continuing their shipping during these preliminary conversations or if they're not, then the responsibility is on them.

P.M.: I think that's very good about the ships but you will be pursuing the question of immobilising the weapons in Cuba which is your major point isn't it?

K: Yes, as I say the first problem we have is the circumstances under which we will search the first Russian ship on the basis of two things.

Khrushchev was still insisting that the ships must not be searched, and U Thant was appealing for a suspension of shipping while the talks went on. If the Russians halted their ships that would ease the situation, but if the Russian ships continued the President would have to face the risk of searching and perhaps sinking a ship some time on the following afternoon. And if we overcame this first problem satisfactorily, and we got talks going, we had also to insist that work on the sites, which was still going on, must stop. Otherwise we should have to tighten the blockade and perhaps take other

action as well. This would be one of the first points to be made in
the talks.

K: But even if the talks don't begin, we are going to begin to
say it on Saturday anyway.

P.M.: Yes, I quite understand that. I think that's what you
must do. But I quite see that it's in two stages. First question is
the ships and then the actual question of the weapons in Cuba.

K: As I say, the fourteen ships that have turned back are
obviously the ones that have the sensitive cargo that he does not
want us to be able to produce. The ships that are continuing
probably are the ones that don't have anything important in them
but we cannot permit him to establish the principle that he
determines which ships will go and which will not. But as I say
I think tomorrow night we will know a lot better about this
matter of the U.N.'s actions and Khrushchev's attitude about
continuing his shipping and also what attitude he will take in
regard to our searching them.

P.M.: Well, I think that's a great help. Perhaps it would be a
good thing if I could give you a ring tomorrow night, Mr.
President. Would that be all right?

K: We will know tomorrow night whether Khrushchev will
accept U Thant's proposal to cease all shipping going to Cuba
during the period of these talks, number one. Number two, if he
doesn't do that, we'll know what their reaction will be to our
searching of a vessel. So I think I could call you tomorrow
night at the same time if that's not too late for you.

P.M.: That's very nice indeed and it'll suit me very well. I am
very much obliged to you. We'll have a talk tomorrow night.
Good night.

K: Good night, Prime Minister. I'll send you Khrushchev's
message of last evening. Good night.

On Friday, 26 October, a mass of messages kept coming backwards and forwards. Although Khrushchev informed U Thant that
he had ordered the Soviet vessels bound for Cuba but 'not yet
within the area of the warships' piratical activities' to stay out of the
interception area, he states in his memoirs (assuming these to be
genuine) that 'our ships, with the remainder of our deliveries to
Cuba, headed straight through an armada of the American navy'.

Meanwhile, aeroplane observation revealed the alarming fact that the emplacements were being finished and missiles being put into position at great speed. I noted in my diary

two *long* telephone talks with the President. The situation is very obscure and dangerous. It is a trial of will.[1]

The second of these conversations led to some new ideas.

P.M.: The idea that you have just mentioned is that Cuba might be made like Belgium was by international guarantee—an inviolable country and all of us would guarantee its neutrality and inviolability. Is that a possibility?

K: That is a matter which seems to me we ought to be thinking about and we will be talking about that in the next twenty-four hours as to whether there is any room for a settlement on that basis. Probably with Castro in power it would leave the Russians perhaps free to ship in a good deal more offensive equipment and they have shipped in a good deal. We now find a good many self-propelled armoured vehicles with very sophisticated special equipment and so on but it may be a possibility. I shall probably give you more information about that tomorrow night but at least there have been a couple of hints but not enough to go on yet.

P.M.: Yes, now I thought another possibility was that U Thant might himself propose to the United Nations, which I believe they would accept, that he should go with a team and ensure that these missiles were made inoperable during the period of any conference or discussion.

K: Yes, that is correct. There would have to be some technical way of determining that these weapons were being made inoperable and that work on the sites was ceasing during these conversations, that is correct.

P.M.: Yes, but do you think that U Thant . . . I am quite sure that Hammarskjöld would have done such a thing. Mightn't he suggest to the United Nations that he would do this? He would go and do it with a team and see that they were not operable during the period of the talks.

K: Yes, there is some suggestion of that. Also they want to inspect some of the refugee camps in Florida and Nicaragua, Guatemala and Swan Island. That was the summing up of the

[1] 26 October 1962.

conversation with the Governor [Stevenson] and I am looking into it. I don't think we have got anything going there that would be difficult to inspect but this is all part of the political proposals which are now being looked at in view of the Governor's conversation. So I would sum it up, Prime Minister, by saying that by tomorrow morning or noon we should be in a position of knowing whether there is some political proposal that we could agree to and whether the Russians are interested in it or not. We will know a little more I think by tomorrow afternoon. In the meanwhile the quarantine stays, if he doesn't send ships in. We let a ship pass this afternoon but there are no other ships within 48 hours or so, so we don't expect any problems on the sea. The problem that concerns us is the continued build-up and I issued a statement on that today.

He promised to send a more detailed report of the political proposals and of U Thant's conversation with Stevenson so that I could have it in the morning.

P.M.: There is just a third point that occurred to us. If we want to help the Russians to save face would it be worthwhile our undertaking to immobilise the missiles which are here in England during the same period—during the conference?

K: Well, let me put that into the machinery and then I'll be in touch with you on that.

P.M.: I think it is just an idea that it might help the Russians to accept.

K: Sure, Prime Minister, let me send that over to the Department. I think we don't want to have too many dismantlings but it is possible that that proposal might help; they might also insist on Greece, on Turkey and Italy but I will keep in mind your suggestion here so that if it gets into that it may be advantageous.

P.M.: Yes, I don't see why they should ask for more because there wouldn't be as many in Cuba.

K: Yes, that is correct. After listening to Adlai Stevenson's report you will have that in mind in the conversation.

P.M.: Well now, if there are any other suggestions that we can make you will probably send me a message tonight and we can get in touch with you tomorrow.

K: That is correct, Prime Minister. I think we will just have to wait until we have analysed this conversation. I haven't seen the entire conversation but I think that the prospect of a trade of these missiles for some guarantee for Cuba is still so vague that I am not really in a position to say that there is any possibility of an easing up. Maybe by tomorrow evening at this time I'll know better.

P.M.: Yes, because of course at this stage any movement by you may produce a result in Berlin which would be very bad for us all. That's the danger now.

K: Well, we are not going to have any problems because he is keeping his ships out of there and as I say we let one ship pass today for the very reason that you have named. On the other hand, if at the end of 48 hours we are getting no place and the missile sites continue to be constructed then we are going to be faced with some hard decisions.

P.M.: And, of course, in making those decisions one has to realise that they will have their effect on Berlin as well as on Cuba.

K: Correct, and that is really why we have not done more than we have done up till now. But of course, on the other hand, if the missile sites continue and get constructed and we don't do anything about it then I would suppose that it would have quite an effect on Berlin anyway.

P.M.: Yes, I think that is the difficulty, but anyway there are these political plans which we have now got going and if I may I'll send you a message concerning them and you will send me the result of U Thant's conversation.

K: I'll send you a memorandum based on the topic of the conversation Stevenson had with U Thant. I will also keep in touch with you tomorrow at this time, or otherwise I'll send you a message tomorrow or maybe I'll send you a message unless we get something immediate. And number three, we will not take any further action until I have talked to you in any case. I won't bother to call you tomorrow because I may be away from here tomorrow evening and I assume you may be too, but I will send you a message if there is anything new and in any case I'll talk to you on the phone before we do anything of a drastic nature.

P.M.: Thank you. I'll be here all day so you can get me any time of the day tomorrow or Sunday.

The President then digressed for a moment from these weighty matters in order to let me know that he was going to send me a formal request to extend General Lauris Norstad's tour of duty at NATO until the end of the year so that he could have a sixty-day overlap with his successor, General Lemnitzer, 'to be sort of adjusted to his new responsibilities'. I think he was more anxious that de Gaulle, who, he said, 'is very sensitive in these NATO matters', should make no difficulties than concerned about my reaction. Certainly I had no objection to what seemed a sensible plan.

K: Well, I will be in touch in [the usual] way with you tomorrow on that matter and I'll send you tonight the memorandum of the U Thant conversation. And I hope all goes well.

P.M.: Well, thank you very much and of course Bundy can always ring up de Zulueta here. They can speak to each other so it is quite easy to have a talk.

K: Fine, Prime Minister. And I'll be in touch with you very shortly. Thank you and goodnight.

P.M.: Goodnight.

The Russians now made a rather dangerous but specious proposal. They tried to bargain the missiles which they had put into Cuba against the American rockets stationed in Turkey. The weaker brethren, at home and abroad, naturally fell for this. Fortunately, early on Saturday, the President issued a statement declaring that proposals concerning the security of nations outside 'this hemisphere' could be explored as soon as 'the present Soviet-created threat is ended'. The crisis was entirely caused by offensive weapons in Cuba. Work on the bases must stop; offensive weapons rendered inoperable; further shipments must cease and all this must be done under effective international verification. This reply was adroit and convincing.

While I was ready to agree, and indeed to propose, that during the period of a conference the missiles in the U.K. might be temporarily immobilised, pending the success or failure of a general negotiation, this was only an attempt to find some escape for Khrushchev. I should never have consented, in spite of the arguments which might be urged about the obsolescence of the missile base in Turkey, to this as a permanent deal. All America's allies would feel that to avoid the Cuban threat the U.S. Government had bargained away their protection. Kennedy, in spite of some pressure among his advisers, never wavered on this issue.

Yet strangely enough the letter from Khrushchev, proposing the exchange of the Cuba missiles for those in Turkey, and drafted in severe and somewhat formal terms, followed a long and diffuse communication which had arrived on the preceding night, couched in very different language. In this, written in the impulsive and highly emotional style characteristic of Khrushchev's personal messages, the Soviet leader appealed to Kennedy to save the world from its impending doom, the inevitable result of nuclear warfare. At the same time, he somewhat naïvely declared that the ships at sea carried no missiles, since these had already been delivered to Cuba— the first admission of their existence, contrary to the repeated protestations of the Soviet Ministers. However, in the letter, Khrushchev proposed that if Kennedy would give assurances that the United States would not 'participate in an attack on Cuba and that the blockade would be lifted', then he would agree to send in no more weapons and to allow those already in the island to be withdrawn or destroyed. This, in effect, met Kennedy's demands in full, and amounted to complete capitulation.

The second letter cancelling or withdrawing the first arrived on Saturday morning. It was accompanied by other events which caused the deepest anxiety. It was reported by the American security police that Russian personnel in Washington and New York were destroying their confidential documents. An American pilot was shot down in Cuba by a SAM, and this deliberate action put at risk the whole system of reconnaissance which was essential to protect American interests. It seemed, therefore, that on Saturday the climax had now been reached, and that the Americans could have no alternative but to launch an attack, at least to destroy the SAM sites.

If the next thirty-six hours were agonising in Washington, they were almost equally so in London. Yet even at this stage there were some signs of Russian weakening. In the last two or three days some rather devious approaches had been made to the Foreign Office, alleged to come from a member of the Russian Mission. The suggestion made was that if the British Government would issue an appeal for a Summit conference to settle the issue, the situation might still be saved. This proposal was repeated directly to me through a Conservative Member of Parliament of high character and standing on Saturday afternoon. Home and I agreed to regard the earlier approaches as mere attempts to drive a wedge between London and Washington. Even this last appeal seemed to me likely to conceal a trap. But, as we now know, a similar approach was made in Washington in the course of Saturday, again through an intermediary.

All through that critical day we waited for news while the President and his advisers struggled to find some alternative to military action. It was only late on Saturday night that, at his brother's suggestion, Kennedy made an adroit and, as it proved, a successful move. He decided to make one last effort and, ingeniously ignoring Khrushchev's second letter, he sent a message welcoming and accepting the suggestion made in the first. On Sunday morning, before any further news could reach us

> I decided (Butler, Home, Thorneycroft and Heath agreeing) to send a message to Khrushchev. We *supported* the American demand that the missiles should be taken out of Cuba. I appealed to him to do this, and then turn to more constructive work—disarmament and the like. Our message was sent off at 12 noon. As we were all finishing luncheon together, the news came (by radio) that the Russians had given in![1]

So it was all over! Khrushchev's reply indeed amounted to a complete surrender. He agreed to dismantle and withdraw the missiles under adequate supervision and inspection. In communicating this historic decision, which in effect brought the crisis to an end, the Russian Ambassador in Washington informed Robert Kennedy that Khrushchev 'wished to send his best wishes to the President'. So, almost with a sense of anti-climax, after days during which it was difficult to restrain yet necessary to conceal our emotions, on that Sunday afternoon my colleagues and I were able to share the feeling, if not of triumph, yet of relief and gratitude. We had been

[1] 28 October 1962.

on the brink, almost over it; yet the world had been providentially saved at the last moment from the final plunge.

Although there were still difficulties, they were of a minor character. U Thant went to Cuba to discuss the technical details, and Castro at first refused to allow the missiles to be withdrawn or the bombers to be given up. Khrushchev had then to send Mikoyan to reason with him. At last the work on dismantling the sites began, while the blockade was still maintained. By 12 November, forty-two missiles were removed, the Soviet authorities allowing visual inspection from planes and ships. Yet when, on 14 November, I had a further conversation with Kennedy, there were still some anxieties:

> *K:* We are still not too far along on the Cuba matter and the bombers.
> *P.M.:* What about the bombers?
> *K:* We might get the bombers out but they want us to withdraw the quarantine and the over-flights and have inspection of Florida as well as Cuba. We do not want to crank up the quarantine again over the bombers. The only question is whether we should do that or take some other action. For example, we might say the whole deal is off and withdraw our no invasion pledge and harass them generally. I think what I will do, Prime Minister, is to send you a message about what we propose to do in Cuba. I should be grateful for your judgement. I will send you a message tomorrow and we could perhaps have a telephone conversation on Friday.
> *P.M.:* I would be grateful. You must not give in to him.
> *K:* The question is whether to continue the quarantine or over-flights. But I will send you a message about that.

After much manoeuvring on both sides, and in spite of some pressure on the President to let the Russians off the hook, by 20 November the Russians had formally agreed that the bombers would be removed and the blockade was finally lifted. The last of the bombers actually left on 6 December.

On 4 November I tried to compile my own impressions:

> The trouble about a first-class crisis is that it is physically impossible to keep the diary going, just when it would be really interesting ! . . .

H

It's now a week away—still difficult to realise . . .

[This] week has seemed rather unreal, compared to the week before—with all those messages and telephone calls, and the frightful desire to *do* something, with the knowledge that *not* to do anything (except to talk to the President and keep Europe and the Commonwealth calm and firm) was probably the right answer. I still feel (with all the other work of the week) tired out. One longs for some days of continued rest, which is impossible. At 68 I am *not* as resilient as when I was a young officer. Yet this *has* been a battle in which everything was at stake. I am at home (at Birch Grove) and I must try to analyse my feelings. (I gave a pretty good account of actual events in my House of Commons speech on Tuesday.) . . . The only unlucky thing was that we decided to send our message to Khrushchev through *diplomatic* channels. This meant that it was not published till the very moment when the Russian *radio* message of 'climb-down' came through. It almost seemed as if we had sent the telegram backing the horse *after* the race. Otherwise, I think we played our part perfectly. We were 'in on' and took full part in (and almost responsibility for) every American move. Our complete calm helped to keep the Europeans calm.[1]

Naturally there was considerable alarm throughout Europe.

But they *said* and *did* nothing to spoil the American playing of the hand.

The following seem to be the main questions and thoughts that occur to me.

(1) *Why did Khrushchev [send in] the Cuban missiles?*

The general view is that he thought he would be able to complete the job without being found out, or by denying the facts (as he did, followed by all other Communist states, as well as by the *Tribune*, the *Manchester Guardian*. Even *The Times* was rather sceptical at first).

He hoped to finish the job; go to United Nations at end of November; threaten about *Berlin*, and then reveal his Cuban strength, pointing at the 'soft underbelly' of U.S.A., three minutes warning instead of fifteen. (Of course, to us who face [many] of these missiles in Russia trained on Europe, there is

[1] 4 November 1962.

something slightly ironical about these twenty to thirty in Cuba. But, as I told the President, when one lives on Vesuvius, one takes little account of the risk of eruptions.) This explanation of Mr. K's motives would seem to account for his continued references to making no trouble about anything till after the American elections (early November). He meant, till after the missiles were safely installed in Cuba.

(2) *What did it cost K?*

Quite a lot – probably £300–£400 m. Over one hundred ships had to be chartered or made available. We think there were some 10,000 Russian military personnel on the island. Besides the *offensive* weapons, there are a lot of ground to air missiles (SAMs) which of course could not be managed by any but Russians. There is also a great deal of other military material – tanks, guns, etc.

(3) *Why did he make the offer to swap Turkey (American base) for Cuba (Russian base) on Saturday?*

This rather specious argument about the bases was one which gained much support among all the weaker brethren, both here and in neutral and unaligned states. Of course, there is no comparison between the NATO and Warsaw Pact forces, which have faced each other for fifteen years or more in Europe and the *sudden* introduction of missile threat into the Western hemisphere . . . K must have been aware that he could get a lot . . . of support. It did involve *admitting* the existence of the ballistic missiles – hitherto denied. But the American photographic air reconnaissance was too good and too persistent to be laughed off altogether. The Turkey–Cuba deal would of course have been greatly to the advantage of U.S. The Turkey base is useful, but not vital. Cuba was vital. I suggested to President that if anything of the kind was to be done, it would be better done with our [missiles]. For British opinion could stand up; the Turks would feel betrayed. (This offer, though it was not necessary, was useful.) However, it became clear [to the Americans] on Saturday that anything like this deal would do great injury to NATO.

(4) *Why did he suddenly abandon the Turkey–Cuba deal, and send the telegram of Sunday, in effect throwing in his hand?*

This is the crucial question, and on the answer much depends.

Why did he not make some counter-move, for instance, on Berlin? Will he make it quite soon? Or on Turkey, or Persia? This is, of course, still a mystery, and every Ambassador and Foreign Office expert has a different theory. The general view is that he realised that the Americans were serious and would invade Cuba and capture it. (This they intended to do on Monday morning. The invasion was always timed for the Monday 29th. The President told me earlier in the week about 23rd or 24th that the 'build-up' would take a week from the day he made his speech—Monday 22nd.) *This American invasion could not be stopped by conventional means.* Therefore the Russians would have to use nuclear, in a 'fire first' attack. This they would not face— and rightly. But if the Americans attacked, they would do three things: (i) destroy Castro and the Communist régime; (ii) deal a great blow to Russian prestige; (iii) capture the missiles. So, by his apparent 'cave-in', Khrushchev at least avoided all these disadvantages. On (i) Castro is going to be a tremendous nuisance. On (iii) the Russians will get back their missiles. On (ii) there is a loss of prestige, in the sense that the expensive little flutter has failed—but not so great a loss as an American invasion, which Russia could not or dare not prevent. So he decided to cut his losses.

(5) *What are the strategic lessons?*

May they not be that, under the cover of the terrible nuclear war which nobody dares start, you can get away with anything you can do by *conventional* means? You can take Cuba. The enemy can only reply by all-out nuclear war. But this applies to Berlin. The Russians *can* take Berlin by conventional means. The Allies *cannot defend* or *re-capture* it by any conventional means. (The conclusion to be drawn is rather sinister.)

(6) *What is going to happen in Cuba, etc.?*

U.N. (U Thant & Co.) and U.S.A. are going to find it quite difficult to deal with Castro. He is naturally making a lot of trouble for the Russians and they have had to send out Mikoyan to deal with him. But this is only about the ballistic missiles. The other *defensive* weapons will remain *in situ* (SAMs, etc.) and Cuba will remain as the base for Communist propaganda throughout Central and South America.

(7) *Conduct of crisis*

President Kennedy conducted his affair with great skill, energy, resourcefulness and courage. He answered the Communists with their own weapons—for they always use several and even divergent means to secure their ends. (*a*) He played a firm *military* game throughout—acting quickly and being ready to act *as soon as* mobilised. . . . You cannot keep an 'army of invasion' hanging about. It must invade or disperse. President K. did not bluster—but everyone knew that (if no other solution was found) there would be an invasion. (*b*) He played the *diplomatic* card excellently. The European and other Allies had no real grievance about non-consultation. The flying visit of Dean Acheson to Europe and the information to NATO Council was more than correctness demanded. (*d*) He played the *United Nations* admirably . . . Kennedy mobilised a lot of U.N. opinion and used *Stevenson* . . . to keep U.N. quiet. If it had come to the point, U.S.A. would *not* have had majority support in the *Assembly*. So they wisely never let it get out of the Security Council. In Security Council the Russians made the fatal mistake of bare-faced lying. Zorin was still denying the existence of the missiles in Cuba, when Khrushchev's message was published offering to swap them for those in Turkey!

Altogether the President did wonderfully well—and he was well served—by Rusk, by Stevenson, by Bundy (as well as by our British representatives, Gore and Dean).

(8) *Anglo-American relations*

In the debate [last] Tuesday (when Gaitskell took this line) and on Wednesday (when it was developed by Harold Wilson) the Opposition (supported by some of the Press—especially the 'columnists' and gossip writers)—have been making out that the Americans not only failed to consult us, but have treated us with contempt; that the 'special relationship' no longer applies; that we have gained nothing from our position as a nuclear power; that America risked total war in a U.S./U.S.S.R. quarrel, without bothering about us *or* Europe. The reasons for this attitude are (*a*) ignorance of what really happened; (*b*) desire to injure and denigrate me personally; (*c*) argument against deterrent; (*d*) annoyance at the success—or comparative success of Cuba enterprise; (*e*) shame—for they let it be known that they would oppose force, or threat of force. In fact, of course, the President and Rusk (and, above all, the President's 'chef de Cabinet', McGeorge Bundy) were in continuous touch with Alec Home and me. David Gore was all the time in and out of the White House. The whole episode was like a battle; and we in Admiralty House felt as if we were in the battle H.Q.

The teleprinter *and* telephone (direct secret line to the White House) worked admirably—without a hitch.

Actually, our secrets were almost too well kept; so this opposition or critical line is rather dangerous. We are doing something to let the truth be known. . . . It will gradually seep through from Whitehall to London society and thence pretty generally. But it is rather a bore, and has some dangers. The British people must not feel themselves slighted.[1]

The most curious finale to this terrifying episode was provided by a letter from Khrushchev to me on 27 November, in which he said:

I fully share your view, as well as that of President Kennedy, that the Cuban crisis has led to a better understanding of the need for a prompt settlement of acute international problems.

An admirable sentiment—but leaving quite a lot unsaid.

[1] 4 November 1962.

CHAPTER VIII

The Changing East

I. INDIA AND CHINA

I T is a vulgar, but illusory, belief that sovereign nations which share the same fundamental principles necessarily pursue in practice a common policy in their international relations. History shows that even during such periods as the religious struggles following the Reformation, the great Catholic powers, Spain and France, were prevented by mutual jealousy from joining wholeheartedly in the attack upon the schismatic and heretical governments of England, Holland and Germany. It was largely by exploiting their rivalries that Queen Elizabeth secured her survival. Even the Papacy, as an Italian power, was subject to these conflicting pressures. A strange example was an occasion in the time of Paul IV, when the Duke of Alva was advancing upon Rome with loyal and devoted Catholic troops and threatening a second conquest and perhaps sack of Rome, while the Pope was defended by German Protestants, rough and ribald soldiers, 'who mocked at the images of saints in the roads and churches, laughed at the mass . . . and committed a hundred acts for which the Pope would have punished every one of them, under other circumstances, with death'.[1]

These days passed, and in succeeding centuries leading European nations waged war on grounds of their material interest or the dynastic ambitions of their rulers. Even in the wars which followed 1789, although in the early stages revolutionary ideals were in conflict with established and 'reactionary' concepts, not many years passed before the struggle developed into one between the expansionist dreams of France and her ruler, and the independence of the threatened nations of Europe, fighting for survival. Similarly,

[1] Ranke's *History of Papacy*, 1842, vol. i, p. 229.

in the great contest which has been raging since the First World War, the conflicting principles of Communism and Nazism did not prevent a conspiracy between Stalin and Hitler to despoil their neighbours. The Russians still retain their share of the loot. The Germans over-reached themselves and lost all and more than all their gains. After the Second War, when Soviet Russia emerged triumphant and full of plans for expansion, both in the ideological and material fields by the spread of the religion of Marx, it might have been supposed that their great leader would have welcomed the effort of the Chinese Communists to complete the conversion of that vast and densely populated area. In fact, the opposite was the case. Stalin, whether through innate distrust, so marked a feature of his morose character, or remembering the independence displayed by another leader, Tito, who after obtaining the mastery of his country in the name of Communism then turned against the infallibility of Moscow, Stalin showed little enthusiasm for the Chinese Communist generals and seemed almost to fear their success. It is true that, when the issue was decided, the two great Marxist powers continued for some years in apparent harmony. If they nurtured some suspicions about each other's claims and ambitions, they concealed these unworthy doubts in a common denunciation of the capitalist world. Yet, as the territorial ambitions of each began to appear—as memories of Peter the Great and the expansionism of Tsarist tradition began to dominate Russian policy, and as the Chinese leaders began to recall, often a trifle ungraciously, the losses they had suffered not only in Tibet to British India but in Manchuria to Tsarist Russia—relations became first chilly, and then painfully strained.

Moreover, under Khrushchev's leadership, fashion had begun to change in Moscow. The doctrine of 'peaceful coexistence', which was there current, must have been specially distasteful to Peking. To the Chinese, rigid Calvinists of Marxism, Russian latitudinarianism must have appeared reprehensible 'back-sliding'. Indeed, Khrushchev's memoirs clearly reveal the ill-feeling between Russian and Chinese leaders that was building up in 1959 and the early part of 1960. Before the end of that year, the Russian technicians were withdrawn from China, a step of considerable importance both materially and psychologically. Yet, by a typically oriental device, in spite of bitter arguments in the Press, in speeches and on radio, both powers avoided identifying each other. The formula, as stated clearly by Khrushchev, was for the Russians to mask their attacks on the Chinese giant by directing them against the Albanian pigmy. For Albania, whether from interest or conviction, rigorously adhered to the most rigid form of orthodox dogma. The rift became virtually open, although Albania continued to be the official target. Thus 'face' was honourably saved. However, at the Twenty-Second Party Congress in Moscow in October 1961, Khrushchev's criticisms became so severe that the Chinese walked out of the meeting and returned to Peking. On this, the U.S.S.R. broke off diplomatic relations not, as one might suppose, with China but with Albania. As Khrushchev recalled,

> It was at the Twenty-Second Congress that we rejected the main tenets of Mao's position. I had run out of patience with him.[1]

By this time, the Russian leader, forgetful of Stalin's atrocities, had become almost respectable. He writes sorrowfully:

> The Chinese don't recognise any law except the law of power and force. If you don't obey, they tear your head off. And they do this very artfully: they strangle you in the middle of a square in front of thousands of people. What sort of 'politics' is that? You can't even call it barbarism. It's something more than that.[1]

These developments made it clear to me even at the time that the old lessons of history were once again proving true. Ideological agreement led no more on the Communist side to automatic co-operation than it did among the nations of Europe in the sixteenth and seventeenth centuries.

During these years, the relations between India and China had become equally strained. The unhappy circumstances in which the Indian sub-continent received the benefits of independence involved the partition of that great area so long united first under

---

[1] N. Khrushchev, *Khrushchev Remembers* (London, 1971), p. 478.

Mogul and then under British rule. This led inevitably to a situation in which India and Pakistan found it increasingly difficult to pursue any policy in common. They were held together by the slender tie of membership of the Commonwealth; but they were bitterly divided, not merely by religious but also by territorial disputes, in which the claim of Pakistan to Kashmir remained as a grievous and ever-festering wound. It was with difficulty that the efforts of the British Government, backed by the World Bank, had brought about some kind of co-operation even on the question of the Indus waters, so vital to each country. Thus, although both depended for their economic as well as their military strength on the generous aid of the British and American peoples, yet it was natural that in the Sino–Soviet dispute India and Pakistan should begin to take separate sides.

The relations between India and China deteriorated in 1959, following the Chinese suppression of Tibet, which they claimed as part of the Chinese Empire. The so-called Tibetan rebellion was mercilessly put down; and the flight of many devout Tibetans, including the Dalai Lama, into India, followed by incursions of Chinese troops across the frontier, caused deep emotion throughout India. Whatever may be the rights and wrongs of the frontier question, with the conflicting arguments about the delineation of the various lines, there can be no doubt that the brutality of the Chinese behaviour deeply shocked Indians of all castes and classes. It certainly had an almost traumatic effect upon Nehru himself, who both wrote and spoke to me in bitter terms of complaint about the Chinese Communists.[1] During all this time, I always felt that this affair was a mortifying blow to Nehru. On the one hand he had previously urged me to support the not illogical claim of the Chinese Communist Government to a seat in the United Nations. On the other hand, he was profoundly shocked and distressed by the materialism as well as by the 'double dealing' of the Chinese leaders. The vague principles of oriental mysticism, which had been supposed to lead to automatic peace between peoples, had been rudely shaken. Since the independence of India, Nehru had obtained a world position by preaching peace, and in support of this

[1] *Pointing the Way*, p. 173.

thesis had been scrupulous to avoid 'alignment' in the cold war between Communism and the Free World. Now he saw Mao, pacifist in principle, imperialist in practice, demanding the re-instatement of Chinese authority over all territories where at any time in their long history they could claim some kind of ancient power or even suzerainty. All this was a grievous blow to him and a source of bitter complaint.

Nonetheless, at the end of 1961, the Government of India took a significant step along a similar path. In August, India annexed two small and insignificant Portuguese territories. Before the end of the year, Indian troops were massed on the border of Portuguese Goa; and on 11 December Nehru announced, in phrases to which we had become all too accustomed, that 'India's patience was becoming exhausted'. While I recognised the strong and natural feeling that after the end of British rule it was something of an anomaly that even a tiny area should remain in European hands, I tried hard to deter Nehru from what seemed an act of pure aggression. In appealing to him, on 13 December, to hold his hand and try to obtain his purposes by negotiation, I expressed my full understanding of the pressures upon him and his desire to bring an end to what seemed an unjustifiable survival.

> But I feel deeply that there is an even wider world interest involved in your decision. India has established for itself under your leadership during the fourteen years of independence a world position of unique respect as a country which, however great the provocation, does not believe in solving problems by the use of armed force and will do its utmost at all times to find an alternative. This has given and continues to give you a stature which enables you to influence international relations for good in a way which has been of the utmost value to us all. The opinion of India's friends in this and many other countries will be that that unique position is jeopardised if with the greatly superior force that you possess you move into Goa.

I went on to say:

> What worries me most of all is that events are accustoming people to the use of force in order to carry out policies, and there

is a danger that people will think increasingly of a resort to arms as being the best way to obtain what they think is right. The great defence against such thinking in the last decade has been the stand which you have consistently taken in world affairs against resort to force. Your example has had an incalculable influence on many other countries. If we now lose this one safeguard I do not know where it will lead. I feel sure that President Sukarno would then consider himself justified in making a military attack on New Guinea, and I fear that many of the new African states would have recourse to the same methods in order to solve their feuds and jealousies.

But Nehru, in a long and courteous explanation, claimed that after fourteen years in which Indian public opinion had shown 'extraordinary patience' he could now no longer hold his hand. Accordingly, on the night of 17 December, Indian troops invaded Goa. A resolution put forward in the Security Council calling for a ceasefire was vetoed by the U.S.S.R. Goa surrendered two days later, and the long and not ignoble story of what Portugal had brought to India by way of religion, education and commerce was brought suddenly and brutally to an end. The lesson was not lost. As I feared, the incident led not merely to imitators in the Far East, but to an opening which Moscow was not slow to take.

Early in May 1962 rumours began to circulate that the Government of India was about to turn to Russia for fighter aircraft—the famous MIGs. I naturally asked Nehru about the truth of these stories, and he replied stating frankly that in view of the military strength of Pakistan and the growing tension between the two countries, he must find some rapid method of augmenting his air force. No final decision, however, had been taken as to the source of supply. The Americans became seriously alarmed, and the President intervened personally, offering to help in any way he could. Our difficulties were partly technical and partly financial. Our new machines, then the Lightnings, were only just entering production. Moreover, the costs would be very high. If we were to accept the risk of delaying our own re-equipment (which the Air Command naturally resisted strenuously), would the United States be prepared to help us financially? The indefatigable Commonwealth Secretary, Duncan Sandys, was on a visit to India and held several conferences with Nehru and his Ministers. Krishna Menon – no doubt for ideological reasons – was anxious to pursue the Russian deal; M. R. Desai, the Finance Minister, wiser and more experienced, was very sensitive about the possible repercussion of any flirtation with Russia on American aid, on which India was largely dependent.

Although Sandys reported on 19 June that Nehru seemed much shaken by the strength of both British and American reactions, he would only agree to postpone the decision. A British team was accordingly sent out to discuss the whole problem – the supply of British fighters to be followed by arrangements either for assembling or manufacturing further machines in India. But the negotiations dragged on without any satisfactory result, and by the beginning of August I was forced to warn the President that the Indians seemed to be set upon a deal with the Russians. On 17 August the Indo–Soviet agreement was officially announced. Russia would give, apparently free of cost, twelve MIGs; in addition, India would be allowed and helped to manufacture Russian jet engines for Indian-built planes. Although in fact only six MIGs were delivered, and these twelve months later, the political effects of this agreement were considerable. Public opinion, both in Britain and in America, was alarmed by this apparent drift of the Indian Government into the Soviet camp. The Americans, not yet sustained by the same experience of ingratitude as the British, were pained and even angry.

Yet within a very few days, a new crisis arose – if Delhi had made her peace with Moscow, there was no corresponding gesture of amity from Peking. On the contrary, on 8 September 1962, after months of interchange of diplomatic notes and some trifling border incidents, Chinese troops crossed the frontier in the high uplands of Tibet. After a lull of some weeks, a major Chinese offensive was launched, and the Indian troops were forced back all along the frontier. Nehru, in quite a different spirit from his recent detached neutralism, sent an urgent appeal for help. I had already sent him a short message of sympathy, thinking it better to forget the immediate past and emphasise the solidarity of the Commonwealth. In his reply of 24 October, while thanking me warmly for my friendly words, he referred to the 'recent extraordinary acts of aggression by the Chinese' in terms of wounded protest:

> We have, throughout the last five years of progressive Chinese aggressive intrusions, sought to resolve the differences by peaceful talks and discussions but the aggression started by the Chinese from 8th September, and the invasion by vast Chinese armies along various parts of the frontier since 10th October, 1962, have left us no choice but to resist. This will impose very heavy burdens on us but we are resolved not to submit to aggression.
>
> Your kind message and the assurance that you will do everything in your power to help us has further heartened us in our determination to resist this blatant Chinese aggression.

This was indeed a different tone from that adopted by the protagonist of non-resistance and 'non-alignment'.

These messages passed while we were in the middle of the formidable Cuba crisis. Even so, I did not neglect to take what steps were possible to give some assistance. Nehru was now making patriotic appeals to his people as well as world-wide requests for help. In an audience with the Queen, after explaining the Cuba situation, still unresolved, I gave her a full account of the developments of the Indo–Chinese war. I also noted

> the transformation of Nehru from an imitation of George Lansbury into a parody of Churchill. But I'm afraid the Indians are having a bad time. We are sending a lot of small arms, automatic rifles and ammunition. Although reports are scanty, my guess is that they are doing a bit of a Dunkirk. But when they get more into the plain and abandon the high mountains, the Chinese advantage should not be so great.[1]

On 27 October there came a long message from Nehru explaining what had happened and appealing for the support of all countries,

> not only because of their friendly relations with us, but also because our struggle is in the interests of world peace and is directed to the elimination of deceit, dissimulation and force in international relations.

[1] 23 October 1962.

We had already begun to send out supplies to the best of our ability. On 30 October the matter was raised in the Debate on the Address. Gaitskell, giving an account of the points of conflict over the frontier and supporting strongly the Indian view, made an appeal that the British and Western Governments should come to India's succour. In reply I referred to the immediate past:

> Although it is true that Chinese troops entered into Tibet in October, 1950, relations between India and China remained friendly. Indeed, in 1954 the famous Five Principles were announced, and the high peak of that amity was scaled. This was confirmed at the Bandung Conference, a year later.
>
> In the subsequent years, although there were some border incidents, they were not of great consequence and it was not until 1959 and 1960 that serious clashes took place. Even then the Indian Government, with characteristic moderation, tried to solve their differences by arranging a meeting between Mr. Nehru and Mr. Chou En-lai. The talks were successful.

After pointing out that with winter closing in, both in the Western sector and on the Eastern sector along the McMahon line, hostilities on the present scale could scarcely persist, I continued:

> The British people have seen with the deepest sorrow the heavy stresses to which the Government and people of India are now subjected. Our connection with India, covering so many generations, was not severed by the constitutional changes of 1947. There are still, happily, the most intimate links in trade and commerce between our countries. Indian students come to our law schools and universities in even greater numbers than before. Recently, all Britain rejoiced at the tumultuous welcome given by the Indian people in their thousands, their hundreds of thousands—almost their millions—to the Queen when she made her historic visit as head of the Commonwealth.
>
> Britain has given much to India—unity, the defence of her frontiers, the development of a Civil Service of high quality, a judicial system based upon our own and a Parliamentary and democratic Government. It is true that there have been divergencies, or some divergencies of thought and policy on some of the great issues which have dominated politics in the last fifteen

years. We have not always agreed, but we have always had, I think, a deep respect for each other's point of view.

Those of us who have had the privilege of personal contact with Mr. Nehru must know how keenly he feels the importance of these moral and spiritual values for which he has striven. If some of us doubt whether the Indian point of view has been sufficiently realist in the past; if, carrying as we have the heavy burden of defence, we are sometimes impatient of what is called neutralism or non-alignment, we must in fairness remember how deeply based in Indian philosophy are some of these concepts.

We therefore feel the tragedy which has come to the Prime Minister, a tragedy which he himself expressed in some very poignant phrases, when after all his efforts to build with the new Chinese Government and with the Chinese people a friendship based upon high and moral ethical principles he found the sudden, brutal and ruthless application of policies based upon the most naked and realist concepts of power.

Naturally, Ayub Khan, the President of Pakistan, took a more detached view. He pointed out that China was not likely to press beyond the frontier, on which she had some not unreasonable claims –the old frontier, before it had been defined and perhaps extended by British power. He also observed that since most of India's troops remained concentrated against Pakistan, there was no need for the Western countries to rush to help. I naturally tried to re-assure him, but throughout this affair the division of the India sub-continent, so fatally charged with dire menaces for the future, remained the dominating feature of the whole problem. If India was to lean on Soviet Russia, would not, sooner or later, Pakistan look to China as her friend? So, indeed, it was to prove.

Meanwhile, throughout November, Nehru sent agitated reports both to me and President Kennedy pleading for an immediate delivery of equipment. The Americans regarded these requests as showing 'a state of panic', since they were 'far-reaching in the extreme'. I was naturally in close touch with the Commonwealth countries, especially Australia and New Zealand, and all agreed that unless some way could be found of achieving an understanding between Pakistan and India—in other words, a compromise over

Kashmir—it would be difficult for America and ourselves to increase our supply of arms and material beyond a modest level.

At this point, on 21 November, Peking suddenly announced a cease-fire, stating that on 1 December Chinese troops would withdraw behind 'the lines of control which existed in November 1959'. A few days later it appeared that so far as the Ladakh–Kashmir frontier was concerned, the position that they intended to occupy was that established *after* the recent offensive. Their purpose was, of course, to develop a strategic road for the delivery of aid to Pakistan. After consultation with Menzies and Holyoake, as well as with Kennedy, my colleagues and I still felt so uncertain as to the real situation that it seemed best to ask Sandys to go out again to investigate. We should also be receiving reports from Mr. Tilney, the Under-Secretary at the Commonwealth Relations Office, and Sir Richard Hull, Chief of the Imperial General Staff, who had been able to go to Delhi ahead of him.

Admittedly the Chinese offer of a cease-fire and withdrawal had somewhat relieved the situation, but the political consequences of a successful Chinese invasion of India would be most serious. Sandys' visit to Delhi and Rawalpindi would be invaluable both for his assessment of the situation and so that we could try to find ways to assist in bolstering India up. Naturally, if in the aftermath of the Chinese invasion we could bring about a solution of the Kashmir problem it would greatly ameliorate both the military and the economic situation, and this would be one of Sandys' main objectives.

While I was awaiting all three reports I received a message from Menzies containing the shrewd appreciation that the Chinese withdrawal would probably make any attempt to reach agreement over Kashmir more difficult. Nevertheless, he would do everything possible to help, including sending a contingent to a Commonwealth Brigade to be stationed in Kashmir, if such a plan proved generally acceptable. Sandys' visit was successful to the extent that, after his talks, a joint communiqué was issued on 29 November by Nehru and Ayub Khan announcing their readiness to resume talks upon the problem of Kashmir. This at least was a move forward. The meeting of the two leaders reminded me of the famous conference

in Casablanca and the reluctant handshake between Giraud and de
Gaulle.

> Commonwealth Secretary came later in day, after a successful
> statement in Parliament. He has certainly done a good job and
> has *forced* Nehru and Ayub at least to meet. Whether any child
> will ever be conceived and born after this shotgun wedding I
> rather doubt.[1]

At the same time, the Chief of the Imperial General Staff returned
from India. His report was, on the whole, encouraging:

> The *Army* had . . . fought well enough and in some instances
> with great gallantry. The *Command* was feeble.[1]

While awaiting the opening of the discussions between Nehru
and Ayub Khan, Kennedy and I interchanged many messages about
the problem of organising the defence of the Indian sub-continent.
There was no air defence and crowded cities lay open to aerial
bombardment. How could he give the necessary aid to India without
making an overt condition that concessions should be made on the
Kashmir question? This would only bring about an angry reaction.
Nevertheless, after my meeting with Kennedy at Nassau, I sent
messages on 23 December 1962, both to Nehru and to Ayub. I
proposed to Nehru sending a joint U.S.–U.K. team to study the
whole question of air defence. Apart from the re-equipment of those
divisions of the Indian Army which were likely to be deployed on
the Chinese frontier, I explained to him the anxiety which the
President and I felt

> regarding the protection of your civilian population against
> bombing attacks. Kennedy and I have accordingly decided that,
> if it is agreeable to you, we would be willing to send a joint British–
> United States team to India to study with your air staff the problem
> of strengthening your air defence system.

I explained also how anxious we felt about the successful outcome
of his discussions with Ayub Khan. I continued:

> In our talks here in Nassau, Kennedy and I have not thought
> of our present military aid to help you meet the immediate Chinese

[1] 3 December 1962.

threat as conditional in any way on the settlement of outstanding differences with Pakistan. However, it is not necessary to explain to you how difficult it is for us to help you on the scale we would like without gravely damaging our relations with Pakistan. We also have to consider our own public opinion in Britain and America. There is great sympathy among our peoples for India in this time of danger and a sincere desire to help. At the same time, their enthusiasm is bound to be a little dampened if many Indian resources are immobilised on the Pakistan border which would otherwise be available for defence against China.

In my message to Ayub Khan, I stressed the need to avoid precipitate conclusions.

In a dispute which has been going on for so many years, it is too much to hope that an agreed solution can be found at once. As seen from the outside, the first necessity would seem to be a readiness by each government to explore patiently with the other any proposals, however unpromising they may at first appear. As discussions proceed, a greater understanding of one another's problems may emerge; and there may develop between the negotiators a measure of mutual respect and confidence which could prove a valuable asset in reaching agreement. It is very desirable that the negotiations should not be dragged out unduly. On the other hand, it would be tragic if the possibility of success were lost through either side rushing prematurely to the conclusion that agreement is impossible.

In the rest of my message I did my best to calm the natural anxieties which any increased aid to India must cause to the people of Pakistan.

The year ended, therefore, with the temporary withdrawal of China, apparently satisfied with the sharp lesson which they had taught their neighbours, and with at least the hope that the negotiations between the two parts of the great sub-continent might lead to some agreement over the dispute which had poisoned all their relations since the first days of independence.

These talks began just before the end of the year. They were rapidly adjourned until January 1963. The Indians appeared to be angered because Pakistan had come to an agreement with China about the frontier on the section in Kashmir and Sinkiang under Pakistani control. Since this part of the Kashmir border was only held as a result of the truce, the Indian Government regarded it as an 'infringement of sovereignty'. Nevertheless, the talks were resumed, and during the next few months we lived at least in the hope that some agreement might be reached, although the reports that reached us were not encouraging. As I feared would happen, the negotiations finally broke down on 16 May 1963.

This unhappy and apparently irreconcilable dispute immensely aggravated the difficulty of providing a defence for the sub-continent. While the negotiations proceeded, the Americans, obsessed with their anxiety about the aggressive intentions of 'Red' China, had not ceased to press for some positive steps. The American Ambassador in Delhi, J. K. Galbraith, took the view that India must feel secure enough to confront China and so take their minds off Kashmir. I felt very sceptical about this, and told the President frankly that in my view it would have the reverse effect: the more secure the Indians felt, the more intransigent they would be with the Pakistanis, who would then turn to the Chinese.

It was finally agreed that an Anglo-American Air Defence mission should be sent out, in which Australia was to participate. It was difficult to handle the conflicting interests. Both Kennedy and Menzies were disturbed about the position of Pakistan, a valuable member of the SEATO Pact. On the other hand, I was anxious not to become involved in 'open-ended' commitments beyond Britain's power to meet. After the breakdown of the negotiations between Nehru and Ayub Khan, Kennedy became more insistent. On 22 May 1963, he sent me a message saying that if we were unwilling to involve ourselves by sending a squadron to India, perhaps the United States had better 'go it alone'; but he would much prefer to act in concert with us. All this was discussed in great detail, and it was finally agreed by the Cabinet at the end of May that we should send a fighter squadron which would be regarded as merely a visit 'for training purposes'. We would make it clearly understood that our presence would not imply any commitment to operate in any renewed conflict with the Chinese. Kennedy, on 1 June, agreed with this view, adding an important qualification.

The President did not disguise his view that if the Chinese were to make a large-scale attack upon India, and especially if undefended Indian cities were put at risk, the reaction of American opinion would be serious. However, there was no need now to make any firm commitment. After some persuasion, both the Australian and Canadian Governments agreed to send a representative on the air mission at the same time as two fighter squadrons, one British and one American, were to be dispatched.

By the end of the year all these plans reached fruition. Joint air defence exercises took place in India, including British and American fighters as well as Australian bombers. Nehru loyally respected the understanding—he made it clear that these exercises were purely for training purposes, not in order to constitute an air umbrella against possible Chinese attack.

Looking back on this episode, it is curious to compare British scepticism with American alarm. Our advisers rightly believed that the Chinese forces would not advance beyond the line which it suited them to hold. They had made a raid in order to obtain, in these high mountain areas, a more convenient frontier. They would not embark upon wholesale invasion. My colleagues and I accepted this view; but Washington was more nervous than London, for Chinese expansionist policies were believed to be responsible for all the troubles in South-East Asia. It was this fundamental mistake which later led America into so many years of trouble. We, with our longer experience, felt convinced that while it would be Chinese policy to take advantage of any troubles or difficulties in any adjacent area they would not themselves advance on an adventurous policy. All through, we were concerned in trying our best to bring about some solution in the underlying tragedy which followed independence in the Indian sub-continent. The chief risk seemed to us not the invasion and occupation of India by vast Chinese hordes. The real danger lay in the breaking up in disorder of the fragile structure which we had left behind when we retired so hurriedly in 1947—the partition of India. Subsequent events have tragically confirmed our judgement.

II. INDO-CHINA

IF the grant of independence to the sub-continent of India brought with it the grave injury of partition, nevertheless the long years of British rule left behind a legacy of efficient local, provincial and central administration, based on an increasingly Indian-recruited Civil Service. It was therefore comparatively easy for the successor governments under the wise discretion of their first leaders to maintain the structure of law and order and to continue effectively the system of which they were the heirs. In India, the overwhelming authority of the Congress Party, especially in the early years, combined with the brilliant leadership of Jawaharlal Nehru, held out high hopes for the economic and political development of the country. Pakistan, first under Jinnah and then under Liaqat Ali Khan, made a good start; and if the uncongenial system of parliamentary government was subjected to many tribulations, nevertheless under the military leaderships which followed there seemed good prospect of steady evolution. Indeed, had it not been for the running sore of Kashmir, the relations between the two states might have remained good; and each, enjoying the generous material aid and genuine sympathy of Britain and the United States, might have looked confidently to the future. Moreover, the various peoples of India, partly by tradition, partly by experience of the long period of peace and progress under the British rule, were broadly patient and obedient.

In Indo-China, where the French had been the imperial power, a very different situation existed. From the very start of independence in 1949, there followed confusion and internal weaknesses, coupled with unrelenting external pressure under Communist direction. All this led gradually but inevitably to the terrible and protracted struggle between North and South Vietnam, involving the United States in what has amounted to a ten-year war.

During my period of office, however, only the first stages of the conflict in Vietnam had begun. There still seemed hopes of stabilising the position. The North Vietnamese infiltrations were as yet on a minor scale. Indeed, our chief anxieties were to prevent them involving the neighbouring countries of Cambodia and Laos, and using the latter for the passage of supplies and guerrilla forces.

In May 1954, by Eden's brilliant and tireless diplomacy, the first Geneva Conference, which took place about the time of the French disaster at Dien Bien Phu and the final withdrawal of French troops, led to an agreement between all the powers concerned— Britain, France, America, Russia, China, Vietnam, Laos, Cambodia, as well as representatives of Viet Minh, the Communist organisation in control of the northern part of Vietnam. Although the United States did not sign the agreement, they declared that they would 'respect the settlement'. Nevertheless, the fact that Foster Dulles took so sullen and unhelpful a position was a grave, even disastrous error which made a deep impression on all the other governments. The agreement called for an armistice line on the seventeenth parallel of Vietnam, pending the holding of nation-wide elections within two years. The parallel is still nominally the line of demarcation—the elections have never been held.

Later in the same year, the American Government used its influence amid all the contending factions for power in Vietnam to promote the success of that led by Diem. In October 1954 his régime was recognised by the British, French and American as well as by some other governments. But Diem remained a passionate opponent of the Geneva Agreement on the grounds that it had partitioned his country; and he steadfastly refused to take any steps towards allowing arrangements to be made for the International Commission to hold the elections.

In 1961, the main difficulties arose in Laos, for it was the capture or infiltration of Laos which was strategically necessary for the Northern Communists—then called Viet Minh—to achieve. In May 1961, however, a cease-fire was arranged in Laos between the Government and the Communist forces, and another Geneva Conference opened, consisting of representatives of all the countries which had taken part in the 1954 Conference, with the addition of India, Canada and Poland as members of the International Control Commission, as well as Burma and Thailand. This Conference continued until 23 July 1962, when agreement was reached, at least in words, to protect Laotian neutrality. All foreign troops were to be withdrawn and an International Commission consisting of the same powers was entrusted with supervising the carrying out of the undertaking. But during this long interval, there was continual Communist pressure, not only in Laos but also in Cambodia and Thailand. Since the latter was a member of SEATO, its interests and integrity must be defended, even while the Conference was in session.

In the autumn of 1961, in spite of the cease-fire, Viet Cong—Communist irregular forces—began once more to infiltrate through Laos in order to attack posts in South Vietnam. It became necessary to consider some plan to maintain at least the *status quo*. I noted on 15 June 1961:

> No settlement in sight. The Communists are now breaking the cease-fire.[1]

But while uncertainty continued in Laos itself, the three Laotian Princes—Prince Boun Oum for the right, Prince Souvanna Phouma for the neutralists, and Prince Souphannouvong for the Pathet Lao—continued, with superb detachment, their protracted discussions in the calmer atmosphere of Switzerland.

All this time I was chiefly anxious to find some method of keeping the cease-fire in being, or at least turning a blind eye to minor infractions. I wrote to the Foreign Secretary on 5 July 1961:

> It would suit the Russians very well to see the West bogged down in other problems just as Berlin is coming to a head. Let us try to stall the whole Laos problem for the moment by keeping the Conference going as long as possible.

Not unnaturally, the Americans began to get restless, and I feared that while nothing good seemed to be coming out of Geneva, either from the Princes or from the Conference itself, the war party in Washington would gain the upper hand. In the talks I held with the President in Key West in March 1961, I had warned him of the danger of being sucked into these inhospitable areas without a base, without any clear political or strategic aims and without any effective system of deploying armed forces or controlling local

[1] 15 June 1961.

administration. I now felt, and so informed him, that any provisional agreement reached with him had lapsed. If there was to be any United Kingdom commitment, fresh Cabinet approval would be required. I expressed my anxieties at this period in a letter to the Queen on 15 September which summarised the somewhat tangled situation:

> When we come to the question of Laos the dualism of American policy is much worse than it is in Europe. In Europe the President and Mr. Rusk seem gradually to be getting control. In the Far East, while Secretary Rusk, supported by the President, is, I think, perfectly honourably following the policy of trying to get a neutral Laos which has been agreed between us, part of the State Department and Americans on the spot are deliberately trying to sabotage its success. Proposals for a new Plan Five (to give it its official nomenclature)—that is a plan for an intervention by SEATO forces, in order to secure that at least part of the country is in non-Communist hands—have been refused by the Military, and these will soon leak, as they are intended to, to General Phoumi. This will have the effect of making this key figure more and more unwilling to agree to any reasonable settlement and more and more hopeful that a military intervention will follow a breakdown of negotiations. Mr. Harriman, acting with perfect integrity, knows what is happening and is doing his best to deal with it, but I fear the harm may have been done. We are thus threatened with the possibility of being asked to intervene militarily in the Far East, just at the time the European crisis is deepening.

I was accordingly relieved to receive a message from the Foreign Secretary on 16 September which was reassuring. With so many problems and difficulties 'on his plate', it was clear that the President was reluctant to get involved in military intervention in Laos. His view was that we should give firm diplomatic support now to Phouma. Whether the officials on the spot would carry out the President's instructions was another matter. However, the next news was that the three Princes had returned to Laos and agreed that Prince Phouma should be appointed Prime Minister. However, with all the deliberation and apparent unwillingness to face a critical position which sometimes characterises parliamentary leaders in more advanced countries, they were unable to decide how the various portfolios should be distributed. Thus, although the Prime Minister had been selected, the Government could not be formed.

When de Gaulle visited me at the end of November 1961 we discussed the situation at some length. But he had little advice to offer—France would retain a military mission in Laos and do her best to bring about some agreement. But now the Americans took a step which was the beginning of their long and painful experience. As so often, a quite small intervention led to a long and inextricable entanglement. On 11 December 1961 American helicopters and training aircraft together with four hundred service personnel arrived in Saigon. These were, of course, merely intended to assist the South Vietnamese Government in their efforts to create an efficient force. At the time, I did not foresee any more grave developments and in reporting to the Queen on 13 December I wrote:

> Meanwhile the position in South Vietnam is deteriorating and the Americans are giving all the support they can short of actual military operations—which in any case are not suitable to deal with this kind of infiltration.

But the first step was followed more rapidly than I had feared by a further move. On 8 February the formation of a new American Military Assistance Command for Vietnam, employing four thousand men 'for training purposes', was formally announced in Washington.

Meanwhile the situation in Laos remained confused and uncertain. The Russian Government seemed to be alarmed by possible developments. Accordingly, at the beginning of 1962, Gromyko and Home, as co-Chairmen of the original Geneva Conference, issued a joint statement urging the three contending groups, under the princely leaderships, to form a joint government and complaining that while full agreement had been reached on Laotian neutrality, the creation of a stable administration was still held up by their rivalries. At the end of March the United States issued a statement supporting the principle of coalition government in Laos under Phouma.

In May 1962 there was renewed fighting, and the Communist forces captured a major Laotian town and advanced to the Thai border.

> The situation in Laos has got suddenly worse. After months of arguing and no result (owing to the intransigence of the American stooge, Phoumi, who has turned out a rebellious stooge) the Pathet Lao—the Communists—have broken the truce and made a considerable advance, at one point to the Mekong river and the Thai border. The royalist Laotians *all* ran away, as fast as their legs would carry them, leaving their equipment (American) for the Communists to collect.[1]

These threats to Thailand introduced a new complication and one in which the British Government was much more closely involved.

The defeat of the Laotian Government's forces at Nam Tha caused great alarm in Thailand. The way seemed to be open to an invasion by the Pathet Lao and their Communist supporters. Thailand, as a loyal member of the SEATO alliance, was entitled to support in case of need. The Americans were very ready to extend their help.

> The President has started to move a fleet and to land marines. But (so far) this is on the basis of the *bilateral* undertakings between U.S.A. and Thailand. But, of course, if there is not a fairly rapid negotiation, I fear SEATO will be brought in and this means the Commonwealth Brigade and more British troops.[1]

I immediately informed both Menzies and Holyoake that if we received a formal request for help we would send a squadron of Hunters. Menzies replied very properly that Australia would be ready to send jets to Thailand if the Thais made a request, but he was most anxious that any action should be taken in the name of SEATO and the obligations under that Treaty, even if some SEATO powers made no contribution. Holyoake made a similar reply. He was willing to send a small force of 'jungle troops, transport freighters and perhaps a frigate'. He added, with his usual

[1] 14 May 1962.

good sense: 'We appreciate that the objective is to show as many flags as possible in Thailand.'

Accordingly, after a long discussion in the Cabinet,

> we agreed to send a more or less token force into Thailand, should we be asked to do so by the Thai Government. A squadron of Hunters of the R.A.F. could go back. They have recently been in Thailand on an exercise. But I have my doubts as to whether the Thais really want us, now that they have beguiled the Americans to send substantial ground forces in. Anyway, the Cabinet agreed, and the Australian and New Zealand Governments have done the same.[1]

It was of course necessary to make a statement to this effect in the House of Commons, which I did the same afternoon. It led to a fine row on the usual basis.

> The Labour Left (supported by the *Liberals* !) tried to adjourn the House, under Standing Order 9. The Speaker, with his usual indecision, first refused to accept the motion and then agreed. (He was, I think wrong in his first decision.) However, only 36 stood up, and on division the motion to have a debate at 7 p.m. was defeated.[1]

However, success in the House of Commons does not necessarily improve economic or political situations six thousand miles away, and although we acted quite properly in accordance with the Treaty I felt much more anxious to press on with the Geneva Conference. If only Laos could be stabilised and Cambodia kept reasonably quiet, the position of Thailand would be rapidly improved.

On 12 June the Princes at last reached agreement for a Provisional Government of National Unity in Laos with Phouma as Premier and Minister of Defence; Prince Boun Oum was to retire, but Phoumi, also a member of the Right-wing party, was to be Deputy Premier as well as Souphannouvong. This unexpectedly successful negotiation in Geneva, after months of frustration, was the preliminary to the winding-up of the Conference with agreements on neutrality and arrangements for the withdrawal of troops. So anxious seemed the Russian Government at this time to keep things

[1] 17 May 1962.

stable that this led to an agreeable interchange of telegrams between me and Khrushchev. In view of what was coming to us over Cuba a few months later, the terms of an enthusiastic message from Khrushchev certainly illustrate the versatility of his mind and the uncertainty of his moods. He wrote on 12 June:

> Good news has come from Laos. As a result of the successful conclusion of the negotiations between the three political forces in Laos, a Coalition Government of National Unity headed by Prince Souvanna Phouma has been successfully formed. Undoubtedly this act can be a turning-point both in the life of the Laotian people itself and in the cause of consolidating peace in South-East Asia. The formation of the Coalition Government of National Unity of Laos opens up a path towards bringing to an end in the very near future the work carried out at the Geneva Conference regarding the peaceful settlement of the Laotian question and towards giving force to the agreements worked out at this Conference which constitute a good basis for the development of Laos as a neutral and independent state. The example of Laos indicates that if there is a desire to solve complex international problems on a basis of collaboration with mutual consideration of the interests of all parties, such collaboration brings its own rewards. The results achieved in the settlement of the Laos question also strengthen the conviction that collaboration along the same lines may achieve success in the solution of other international problems which now divide the states and create tension in the world. As regards the Soviet Government, they have always maintained and continue to maintain this line, which in the present circumstances is the only correct course in international affairs corresponding to the interests of peace. In conclusion, I wish to express my satisfaction that the collaboration of the Governments of the U.S.S.R. and Great Britain as the co-Chairmen of the Geneva Conference has played its own useful role in clearing the paths towards a peaceful solution of the Laos question.

I sent an appropriate message reciprocating all these agreeable sentiments.

The Cambodians now began to come into the picture. Prince Sihanouk complained that both the Thais and the South Vietnamese were constantly violating Cambodia's frontiers. He wanted an international conference to guarantee his country's territorial integrity. In support of his plea he sent a long and well-argued personal protest to me, to which I could only reply that, while fully sympathising with Cambodia's desire for 'independent neutrality, unity and territorial integrity', I felt that in the first instance agreement should be sought both with Thailand and South Vietnam. The Russians and the French joined in supporting Sihanouk's proposal, but both Kennedy and I felt that we had better see how things worked out in Laos. Here, at any rate, United States forces were evacuated in accordance with the recent Geneva Agreement, and it was stated that the Pathet Lao had withdrawn as well. But there were many charges and counter-charges of breaches of the understanding.

As regards Thailand, the situation improved sufficiently for our forces to be withdrawn on 16 November 1962. In this we were followed by our other allies, in consequence of the Laos settlement. Nevertheless, the situation remained uncertain, and Kennedy and I had a long talk on the telephone. This was just after the settlement of Cuba, and therefore we both felt more relaxed. I noted:

> Another long talk on the telephone last night. The new machine is (*a*) better—you talk as on an ordinary telephone; (*b*) safer—it would take ninety years to break the code; (*c*) British. A score for us![1]

We both felt some concern that the Laos settlement was going to break up. A part of our conversation was about Cuba, where I urged the President to remain firm on the removal of the bombers. On Laos,

> we will try to get Malcolm MacDonald (now travelling in S.E. Asia as a private citizen) to go to Laos and try to get some spark into Souvanna Phouma. This is the 'moderate' leader, who is the key to the whole settlement. He is said to be losing heart and threatening to return to Paris where his treasure is—and his heart (in the shape of his daughters).[1]

Sihanouk kept pressing for an international guarantee for Cambodia, but my colleagues and I, although ready to make some

[1] 16 November 1962.

sort of declaration, were very anxious about its wording. Guarantees, without the power to implement them, are dangerous expedients.

Thus 1962 came to an end, and the first months of 1963 passed in a condition of comparative calm in South-East Asia. But in the spring of 1963 there was a steady deterioration in Laos. There was no sincere co-operation between the three groups. The Right-wing forces held the lowlands of the Mekong River; the Pathet Lao were in command of the northern and eastern hills, while the neutralists kept a precarious hold on Vientiane, the administrative capital. There were a number of assassinations and some sporadic fighting, while the Control Commission was hampered in its work by disagreements between the Poles on the one hand and the Canadians and Indians on the other, and by the Pathet Lao's refusal to co-operate with either. The Russians, on the other hand, still seemed genuinely anxious to avoid trouble, and accordingly Gromyko and Home were able to arrange on 21 April for at least a short cease-fire. Talks reopened at the beginning of July 1963 between the Pathet Lao and the neutralists, but these soon broke down in mutual recrimination.

In South Vietnam there was a new form of disturbance—the ruling group, under Diem's somewhat remote control, who were said to be Christian converts, clashed with the Buddhists with some loss of life and much bitter feeling. Before the summer was over, in spite of attempts to reach some accommodation, these troubles were renewed.

Before I left office in October 1963, the situation was broadly as follows: in Thailand there was relative quiet. In Cambodia, Prince Sihanouk was anxious and even suspicious, more especially at the violations of his frontier, which he asserted, probably with good reason, came from Thailand and South Vietnam. In Laos, there was sporadic and inconclusive fighting, with the Pathet Lao generally on the offensive, backed of course by the North Vietnamese Government and Viet-cong guerrillas anxious to keep open their supply lines through that country. In South Vietnam, owing to the weakness of the Government—its internal dissensions, its lack of any effective co-ordination of effort—the prospects looked gloomy for the prosecution of any successful defence against the Communists from the North.

In the following years, American involvement was to increase steadily until she found herself committed with immense forces without effective control of the local government and with the grave strategic difficulty of fighting a war of containment. This development, which has had important effects both on the internal morale and the external prestige of the United States, belongs to a later period. American policies produced the very situation against which I ventured to warn President Kennedy at my first meeting with him in Key West. But it is not for the British people, who have so often found themselves in a similar situation, drawn relentlessly into commitments which they did not originally foresee, to indulge in captious criticism. A mood of respectful sympathy for the troubles of our loyal ally seems more fitting.

III. MALAYSIA AND INDONESIA

I F the transfer of power from Britain to the successor governments in the Indian sub-continent resulted, at least after the first fearful period of terror and slaughter, in relative stability, the collapse of French authority in Indo-China was followed by a struggle for power, which, in Vietnam at least, still continues. In Malaya, a similar contest against Communist aggression resulted, by the summer of 1961, in a sufficiently encouraging situation to enable us to lift our eyes to wider horizons.

Malaya reached full independence within the Commonwealth in 1957, and Singapore was granted internal self-government in 1959. As a result, I had been able to make the acquaintance, which soon broadened into friendship, of the remarkable Prime Minister of Malaya, Tunku Abdul Rahman, generally known as 'the Tunku'. His contributions to our discussions at gatherings of Commonwealth Prime Ministers were always lively and generally wise; and if I had occasionally to accept that his passionate devotion to Association football led him at times to acts of truancy from a session, particularly when the subjects under discussion did not seem greatly to affect his people, my colleagues and I were always delighted by his company and assisted by his experience and sagacity. Similarly, I had got to know that most remarkable figure, Lee Kuan Yew, the most powerful Prime Minister of Singapore under the new régime.

The relatively quiet condition of Malaya was the result of a long and sustained effort, covering some twelve years from the middle of 1948 until the end of June 1960, when the state of emergency was officially ended. This remarkable achievement, in the face of baffling difficulties similar to those later encountered by the Americans in Vietnam, was due almost entirely to the courage, determination, and resourcefulness of the British authorities—political, police, security and military—under the glowing leadership of General Sir Gerald Templer. At a cost, in fatal casualties, of some ten thousand, including two hundred and fifty British soldiers, the revolution was quelled. Peace, or comparative peace, was established, greatly to the advantage of all the inhabitants, whether Malayan or Chinese. If, in order to maintain these conditions, it was necessary to continue the power of detention of subjects without trial, this was a small price to pay.

In Singapore the situation was not easy. Lee Kuan Yew always looked forward to the possibility of closer association with Malaya, and for this purpose tried to curb Chinese chauvinism among his mixed population and to foster larger loyalties. Nevertheless, in the early months of 1961, the underlying tensions could not be disguised. It was difficult for the non-Malay population, mainly Chinese, to forget their roots and their connections with their old home and to develop a genuine allegiance towards a country so recently established under leaders of a different race. When, therefore, on 27 May 1961 the Tunku declared in a notable speech that it would be necessary for his country to build closer political and economic ties with Singapore and with the British territories in Sarawak, Brunei and North Borneo, this ambitious plan, generally interpreted as a demand for a Greater Malaysia, seemed to mark the beginning of a new era. Reaction in Singapore was by no means unfavourable, and when questioned in the House of Commons on 20 June I thought it wise to give at least a guarded welcome. These

I

peoples, emerging into the perils as well as the pleasures of independence, had at least this claim for our support; they needed it. Yet, in spite of the enthusiasm of the Tunku and his urgent desire for a rapid decision, it was not until 8 July 1963 that the final agreement could be reached. The reasons for this delay were twofold. First arose the vital question of defence, involving the rights and responsibilities both of Britain and the chief Commonwealth powers in the area, Australia and New Zealand. There was also involved the interests of other SEATO allies, primarily the United States. The second cause was the need to persuade and not coerce the peoples of those countries, for which Britain was still responsible, to enter the new organisation.

On 3 August, as a result of long discussions in London, I sent the Tunku a long message in which, while welcoming his ambitious and imaginative proposals, I tried somewhat to restrain his impetuosity.

> On defence, the question of the continued use of our important bases and facilities in Malaya and the other countries concerned raises very large issues. Certainly the present difficult state of affairs in South-East Asia, and the need in all our interests to maintain confidence there, makes it very important that nothing should be said which might cast doubt on the maintenance of British defence capabilities in the area. Our mutual friends in Australia and New Zealand are of course also directly concerned, and we shall wish to consult with them.
>
> As regards the Borneo Territories, I hear that you have just been visiting Brunei and Sarawak yourself. You will thus have been able to form some preliminary impressions about the situation there, and the state of opinion on a wider association of the kind you have in mind. Our impression is that the idea of finding their eventual political future in some kind of link with Malaya is seen to have attractions. This suggests that, if the ground were carefully prepared, and the advantages of any wider association became generally recognised, the Borneo Territories would be ready to come in as free and willing members. I am sure you will agree that it is most important at this initial stage, and in view of the doubts and hesitations which have been expressed publicly in the territories over what close political association would in-

volve for the various races there, that we do not give the impression that we are deciding on their future without regard for their own wishes.

I had learned caution from some unhappy examples of ill-prepared schemes of Federation. I certainly did not want a shot-gun wedding.

In reply the Tunku made it clear to me that while he was willing, in order to contain the Communist threat, to include Singapore in the new Federation and to do so quickly, he could hardly face the addition of so large a number of Chinese voters unless the imbalance could be corrected by the addition of Malays; these could only be provided from the three Borneo territories. Consequently, we must make up our minds as to whether we were prepared to relinquish sovereignty both over Singapore and the Borneo states. On defence, while he felt that some arrangements could be worked out within the context of the existing defence agreement, he was not so precise.

A Committee of Ministers, in which the Commonwealth and Colonial Secretaries both played their full part, was set up to study the whole affair. But progress was necessarily slow. I recognised of course that Lee Kuan Yew might be forced, in order to anticipate a possible Communist *coup*, to demand or seize full independence for Singapore. If the merger could not be put through rapidly, this was a real danger. Nevertheless, I was not prepared to be rushed upon either issue. We had our obligations to the inhabitants of the territories we had so long and so effectively governed; we had also our duty to the Commonwealth, especially Australia and New Zealand, whose defence interests were so vitally affected. Accordingly, I invited the Tunku to come to London as soon as possible for a full discussion. Owing to his many commitments, he was not able to arrive until the last weeks in November; but this delay at least gave the opportunity for an interchange with Menzies and Holyoake on both issues. The Australians had, of course, a particular interest both in Borneo as well as in the larger question of defence. Menzies's message of 18 October was therefore significant. I had sent him full information of how matters stood.

Thank you for your message of 4th October telling me what

you have said to the Tunku on the Greater Malaysia Plan. I completely agree with your handling of the matter and am heartened that the Tunku will soon meet you in London.

I note in particular your emphasis on the free association with Malaya of the peoples of the Borneo Territories. Any suggestion that the United Kingdom or the Malayan Government is prepared to allow other considerations to override the principle of self-determination could, I believe, have the most damaging effects, most immediately in Borneo. These could prejudice the prospects of achieving the wider association and would in any case undermine its stability if it were formed. Consultation with the Borneo Territories must, as your draft announcement states, precede any commitments in respect of transfer of sovereignty. I feel that your comments to the Tunku on this point were both prudent and timely.

No doubt the effect of Greater Malaysia on the Commonwealth strategic reserve's participation in SEATO exercises and operations will occupy a large place in your discussions with the Tunku. I look forward, therefore, to having an early indication, in as concrete terms as possible, of your proposed aims in negotiations on this subject and of the minimum conditions which you feel would be acceptable to the United Kingdom.

As a preliminary to further discussion, I sent him, and also to Holyoake, a résumé of an important paper on our defence strategy, with particular regard to the likely impact on SEATO of impending developments in Malaysia. In addition, I reminded both Prime Ministers that we had to face the fact that, with few exceptions, the overseas bases in our hands depended on the goodwill and support of the local government and population. Singapore was a case where these were vital to us; and political and economic strategy would have to play a greater part and the old-fashioned military methods a smaller role in future defence tactics. On the other hand, the growing mobility of our forces would be a partial compensation. At the same time, I proposed that Lord Carrington, First Lord of the Admiralty, in whom I had the greatest confidence, should visit Canberra and Wellington and, on the way back, Washington, for urgent defence talks before the discussion with the Tunku. Unhappily, this plan proved impracticable owing to the imminent general election in Australia. However, I was well informed through constant interchange of messages, of the main anxieties in the minds of these trusted friends and colleagues, before the Tunku arrived for the discussions on his ambitious design.

These, on the whole, went well. The Tunku, always ebullient, was in a particularly confident mood. The talks were carried on chiefly by the Commonwealth Secretary and other Ministers. By 22 November I was able to hold a

> meeting with Tunku and the Malayans, to sign the agreement which has been reached about *Greater Malaysia* and the *Singapore Base*. The Defence part of the agreement is quite satisfactory (which is better than we expected).[1]

Although Malaya and the Greater Malaysia Federation, when it came into being, would not be formally associated with SEATO, nevertheless Singapore would continue to offer full access and facilities. The fact that there were to be no restrictions was a great success for our negotiators, especially in view of some of the earlier statements made by or attributed to the Tunku.

The main political difficulty, however, remained—how to ascertain the views of the peoples of the new territories to be associated in the Federation. However, a machinery was devised to which both we and the Tunku agreed. My letter to the Queen of 22 November sums up the result of all these negotiations.

> Your Majesty will know that the Tunku has been visiting London this week to discuss the proposal to create a 'Federation of Malaysia' embracing Malaya, Singapore, North Borneo, Sarawak and Brunei. These talks have been very friendly and agreement has been reached. The main political problem is how to ascertain the views of the peoples in North Borneo and Sarawak. To meet this it has been decided to set up a Commission appointed by both the British and Malayan Governments who will try to find out what the peoples of these territories think. The main defence problem was to make certain that if there were a merger between Singapore and Malaya Britain would have the continued ability to fulfil her Commonwealth and international obligations. We are now reasonably satisfied that we should be able to use our

[1] 22 November 1961.

Far East bases under a Federation of Malaysia for all the purposes for which we think we might need them.

Apart from a certain apprehension felt by the Australian and New Zealand Governments as to the long-term dangers, a more immediate concern arose from the hostile attitude of the Indonesians. Sukarno, whom I had met some years before when we were both guests of Nehru in Delhi, fully lived up to the unfavourable impression which I had formed of him at that time; vain, ambitious, truculent. The ideals of the patriot seemed already to be lost in the outward trappings of the popular dictator. His rule was not destined to be permanent; yet during his period of power he was a perpetual menace, not only to many classes of his own countrymen but to his immediate neighbours, as well as to the outside world. Indeed it was largely because of the pressure from the controllers of Indonesia, as well as from the Communist movements on his eastern flank, that the Tunku was so anxious for a forward move in consolidating his position.

Sukarno now began to issue threats of an attack on Dutch West New Guinea and, by proclaiming it to be a new province of West Irian at Christmas 1961, added to the sense of uncertainty in the area. On Christmas Eve this was one of a number of troublesome problems which broke into the few days' rest.

A lot of telephoning all the morning on (*a*) Congo (*b*) West Irian–Indonesia (*c*) Kuwait.

On (*a*) the Adoula–Tshombe agreement looks like breaking down. This will be very bad, and we shall be back in the political dilemma from which we escaped with difficulty last week.

On (*b*) an attack by the Indonesians (encouraged by Goa) seems likely in the very near future. This, naturally, much excites and alarms the Australians.

On (*c*) there are strong rumours of an attack by Kassem, the head of Iraq. We have alerted troops, etc., in case the Kuwaitis call us in to support the Arab League forces who relieved us a little time ago.[1]

Such are the minor worries of a modern Prime Minister in the festive season.

[1] 24 December 1961.

However, we decided to press on, and although the whole of this Malaysian plan seemed to move with oriental deliberation and perpetual delay, yet the first step was taken with the appointment, at the beginning of February 1962, of Lord Cobbold as the Chairman of a joint Commission of Enquiry to investigate the attitude of the peoples of Sarawak and North Borneo to the new plan, now to be known as Greater Malaysia. To my great delight, Lord Cobbold, so long a notable Governor of the Bank of England, was ready to undertake this ungrateful task. My letter to him of 3 February ran as follows:

> With the concurrence of the Prime Minister of the Federation of Malaya I write to confirm your appointment by the British and Malayan Governments as Chairman of the Commission of Enquiry which is to visit Sarawak and North Borneo.
>
> The terms of reference to this Commission will be as indicated hereunder.
>
> Having regard to the expressed agreement of the Governments of the United Kingdom and the Federation of Malaya that the inclusion of North Borneo and Sarawak (together with other territories) in the proposed Federation of Malaysia is a desirable aim in the interests of the peoples of the territories concerned:
>
> (*a*) to ascertain the views of the peoples of North Borneo and Sarawak on this question; and
>
> (*b*) in the light of their assessment of these views, to make recommendations.
>
> Tunku Abdul Rahman and I are most grateful to you for agreeing to serve as Chairman of this most important Commission of Enquiry, the advice of which will be of the greatest importance to the British and Malayan Governments in deciding the further steps to be taken.

The Commission duly set out and was able to complete its report by the beginning of July 1962. One of our most valuable advisers on all this was Lord Selkirk, the High Commissioner in Singapore. Owing to his experience of government at home, in which he had held many important posts, I could rely greatly upon his advice.

Lord and Lady Selkirk and the R. A. Butlers to dinner. A long talk about Malaysia which is going to present us with some pretty awkward problems when the Tunku arrives next month.[1]

Whatever the Commission might report, there were bound to be difficulties about the implementation of the scheme.

On 4 July we received the recommendations of Lord Cobbold and his colleagues. There was unanimous support for the objectives of Greater Malaysia, but serious differences emerged between the British and Malayan members over the form of administration for Borneo and Sarawak during the necessary transition period. It was clear that the Tunku would not like the proposal to retain British expatriate officers in Borneo and Sarawak with full authority over internal domestic affairs until the time came when suitable substitutes could be found from local sources. On the other hand, it did not seem to us to be right that Malayan officers, without knowledge of the local customs and people, should be imposed upon these areas immediately on Greater Malaysia coming into being. However, the Cabinet agreed that we would support the objectives of Greater Malaysia on the understanding that acceptable solutions on the transitional problems could be found which would fully protect the interests of the inhabitants of the Borneo territories. I was not altogether looking forward to renewed discussion with the Tunku for, in a somewhat sharp message, he had indicated that if he could not take on the internal administration of the new territories with his own officials, he would prefer not to accept formal sovereignty. However, our first meeting went well.

11–12, Tunku. A talk alone about the problems of Greater Malaysia's birth. After quite a relaxed talk (his threats seemed to have been withdrawn), we were joined by Ministers and officials on both sides and a scheme of work was agreed. Luncheon followed.[2]

The negotiation was in the skilful hands of Duncan Sandys, who now combined the posts of Commonwealth and Colonial Secretary. After some ten days of discussion, good progress was made, and by 1 August Sandys was able, in his new role, to make a full statement to the House. At the same time, the report of the Cobbold Com-

---

[1] 29 June 1962.   [2] 17 July 1962.

mission was published. Sandys announced that the new Federation of Malaysia was to come into being not later than 31 August 1963, that is, within a year. At that time the British Government would transfer the sovereignty of Sarawak, North Borneo and Singapore to the new Federation. The Sultan of Brunei, who had not yet formally adhered, had publicly declared his support of the creation of the new Federation.

The Commonwealth Secretary, in making his statement to the House of Commons, emphasised the fact that although agreement had been reached in principle, a period of detailed negotiation would now be necessary in order to cover all the points in the plan, including the necessary safeguards as to matters of

religious freedom, education, representation in the Federal Parliament, the position of the indigenous races, control of immigration, citizenship and the State constitutions.

He went on to say:

In order that the introduction of the new Federal system may be effected as smoothly as possible and with the least disturbance to existing administrative arrangements, there will be, after the transfer of sovereignty, a transition period, during which a number of the Federal constitutional powers will be delegated temporarily to the State Governments.

An Inter-Governmental Committee will be established as soon as possible, on which the British, Malayan, North Borneo and Sarawak Governments will be represented. Its task will be to work out the future constitutional arrangements and the form of the necessary safeguards for the two territories.

The Minister of State for the Colonies, Lord Lansdowne, who will be the Chairman of this Committee, and the Deputy Prime Minister of the Federation of Malaya, Tun Abdul Razak, will proceed shortly to Sarawak and North Borneo to conduct discussions.

In order to maintain the efficiency of the administration, the British and Malayan Governments are agreed on the importance of retaining the services of as many of the expatriate officials as possible. The Minister of State will discuss with the Governments of the territories and with the staff associates how this best can be done.

12

Towards the end of the year, a minor revolt was staged by some Malays in Brunei against the Sultan.

> There is trouble in Brunei. Some two to five thousand rebels have seized the Shell refinery and tried to throw out the Sultan. No doubt this is fomented from Indonesia by Sukarno. I always feared that once the West New Guinea question was settled and the Dutch 'ousted', he would start in Borneo.[1]

We acted rapidly to suppress the insurrection and, soon after the despatch of three thousand British troops, I was able to record

> The Brunei local situation is in hand, but Indonesia threatens us with intervention. I suspect that they want to force us into a position where they can confiscate our enormous investments. Having squeezed the Dutch dry, they will turn on Britain.[2]

There were rumblings and even threats.

> We have had very alarming reports of Indonesian schemes against Borneo. They seem about to 'hot-up' the Brunei rebellion again; to infiltrate across the Borneo borders in *large* numbers (it is all jungle country) and perhaps to attack openly by sea. We have alerted some more troops and aircraft and let it be known as publicly as possible that we are doing so. It may have a good effect locally.[3]

Somewhat surprisingly, the Filipinos now put in a claim to North Borneo; but on our curt refusal to entertain this monstrous effrontery they seemed to subside. Meanwhile it was clear that the new Federation would have no friendly welcome from its neighbours.

> Indonesia and Malaysia are very confused. There is danger— but more of infiltration and subversion than full-scale war.[4]

At the same time, the troubles in Brunei were beginning to spread, with increasing bitterness between the pro- and anti-Federation parties in Singapore, Sarawak and in Malaya itself. By April, armed raids from Indonesia were being sent into Sarawak, and it was necessary to move some British and Gurkha reinforcements to the

[1] 9 December 1962.　　[2] 24 December 1962.
[3] 28 January 1963.　　[4] 17 February 1963.

border. Sukarno now retaliated by an attack on the oil companies in his own territory.

> The Indonesians are going to seize Shell–£50 m. gone in a day. There is, it seems, no remedy, except war. The Americans don't mind. American Administration cannot face a 'Suez', and American (local) oil companies will be quite pleased. What will happen when Venezuela goes Communist and seizes all the American plants and concessions? Texas and Canada will be the beneficiaries, for I doubt if as much oil will actually be produced, unless Russians come in to help.[1]

On 27 May I sent a message to Sukarno telling him that the proposed legislation affecting Shell was of a 'confiscatory nature' and would, if enforced, have a 'profoundly damaging effect on Anglo-Indonesian relations'. Meanwhile negotiations with the oil companies seemed to be proceeding not unhopefully.

We made up our minds not to be deterred by foreign pressure, and on 8 July 1963 the Malaysia Agreement was signed. The Sultan of Brunei did not feel able to agree on any terms of accession; the Federation would therefore consist of Malaya, Singapore, Sarawak and North Borneo (now termed Sabah). This result was due entirely to the persistence of the Commonwealth Secretary, Duncan Sandys. Patient, laborious, courteous and imperturbable, he carried through this difficult project almost entirely by his own will and force of character.

> I went to Marlborough House at midnight to sign the Malaysia agreement. It was quite a moving occasion. Everyone has 'come in' except Brunei. The Sultan of Brunei is very obstinate and rather remote from the modern world. He has only 80,000 subjects, and no form of constitutional reform. But he has £10 m. a year or so from oil. So [he] is a desirable *parti*.[2]

There was now proposed a so-called 'Summit Meeting' between the heads of government of Indonesia, Malaya and the Philippines, which was to take place between 30 July and 5 August. I felt fairly sure that the Tunku would not allow himself to be outwitted.

To add to the confusion, President Kennedy intervened and made an appeal that the date for the formal constitution of Greater Malaysia should be postponed from 31 August, otherwise he thought the summit meeting might be 'torpedoed'. The Foreign Secretary – Home – thought it might be wise to accept this in order to keep the United States 'friendly', but he admitted that it would make little difference to Sukarno. I was not prepared to win or confirm my friendship with the President by appeasement. Nor was it necessary or even prudent. I therefore replied firmly to Kennedy that we must leave the question of date to the Tunku's judgement. We felt sure that Sukarno's real objective was to stop us using the South-East Asia bases and thus prevent us from fulfilling our role in SEATO, in which America was vitally interested.

> The news of the so-called 'Summit' on Malaysia is obscure. I fear that the Tunku may have had to yield to the Indonesians (which is what the Americans wanted). The President and the American machine are rather 'sold out' to the Indonesians, although their eyes have been opened a little by the recent Indonesian threat to the American as well as to the British oil companies. However, I felt sure it was right to resist President Kennedy's attempt to make *us* propose a postponement. The Tunku would be quite ready, in that event, to shift the blame for failure on to us.[1]

In the event, the outcome of the meeting at Manila was an agreement to postpone the start of Federation while the United Nations were asked to conduct an assessment of opinion in Sarawak and North Borneo (Sabah) in the presence of 'observers' from Malaya, Indonesia and the Philippines. I felt anxious about this, but it was impossible for us to reject what the Tunku had himself accepted. I therefore asked Home to say that we would agree to the Manila decision, provided the United Nations report was ready by 31 August, and was not subject to confirmation either by the United Nations itself or by the three governments who sent observers. U Thant readily accepted the second point, but he asked for an extension of time, promising that the United Nations assessment would be ready by 14 September. In spite of my fears, the Secretary-General faithfully carried out his undertaking, and Sandys, with

[1] 5 August 1963.

unrelenting persistence, went himself to Malaya to give encouragement to the Tunku.

It was fortunate indeed that he had taken this step, for on 31 August Lee Kuan Yew, either losing patience or determined to exploit the delay, announced that he was taking over the reserved powers and declared Singapore wholly independent of Britain.

> Telegrams rather bad from S.E. Asia. I have told Duncan Sandys to stay in Malaysia till the [inauguration] day. But (a) What will U.N. say? (b) What will Singapore Chinese do? Once again, how much more difficult it is to get rid of an Empire than to win it.[1]

Fortunately, the Commonwealth Secretary remained perfectly calm. With Nelsonic imperturbability he turned a blind eye to Lee Kuan Yew's blatant breach of the constitution and succeeded in keeping things quiet—coaxing the situation along, he called it—until the inauguration, on which all parties now seemed determined. He was highly successful in this manoeuvre, and on 14 September the United Nations report to U Thant was published. The findings were clear—the Mission had no doubt that the great majority of the people of Sabah and Sarawak supported the Malaysia Federation. Accordingly, the Federation was formally inaugurated on 16 September 1963, to be known in future as 'Malaysia Day'.

Both Indonesia and the Philippines at once refused recognition and severed relations. In Djakarta the mob was let loose, and the British Embassy, as well as many houses occupied by British citizens, was wrecked. In different parts of Indonesia, trade unions, no doubt on Sukarno's orders, tried to seize control of British commercial companies. On 20 September, not content with further damage to British property in Djakarta, the Indonesian Government placed all British companies under 'protective supervision'.

With the loyal help of both Menzies and Holyoake, it was clear that we could rely on Australian and New Zealand forces to cover any threat from Indonesia and to protect Malaysia from direct or indirect attack. All this we could do without any breach of propriety at the invitation of the Tunku and his Government.

[1] 7 September 1963.

So matters drifted on without any more serious military damage than could be easily contained by British and Gurkha troops, in support of the growing armed forces of Malaysia itself. Nevertheless, there was one aspect of these troubles which caused me both anxiety and grave disappointment. I was informed on what seemed good authority towards the end of September, that two American oil companies were about to sign agreements with the Indonesians without reference to and excluding the interests of Shell. In view of the close co-operation with which the President and I had worked so long over so wide a field, I felt hurt. Accordingly, on 23 September, I sent a message in protest. I had hoped that there was a good chance of final agreement being at last reached between the three foreign oil companies and the Indonesian Government as to their future operations. Although the American Ambassador was urging the Indonesians to sign with the two American companies, Caltex and Stanvac, simultaneously with the British company, Shell, it now seemed likely that Shell would be excluded; and that, in such an event, the two American companies were being advised to sign for themselves.

This had much disturbed me. It was the strong American stand taken in the negotiations with Sukarno in Tokyo which had achieved two objects—the safeguarding of British oil interests and a useful demonstration of Anglo-American solidarity. The good effect of this would be thrown away, and the future for foreign investors in Indonesia would be bleak indeed, unless we all kept firmly together. But I was not only thinking of commercial interests. We were facing a dangerous situation in South-East Asia. It was clear that Sukarno was out to destroy the new Malaysia. In view of our deep commitments, we could not stand by and watch. Britain was morally involved. But Sukarno would only be stopped if he clearly understood that the Western powers were at one in opposing his acquisition. I therefore appealed for a reconsideration of the advice which was being given to the American companies. If Shell were excluded they should refuse to sign.

The President's reply was not altogether satisfactory, and I sensed that he was somewhat embarrassed. It seemed that the American Government had told the two American companies to 'use their own judgement' of the risks involved including their own prospects for the future if Shell were forced out. But they wanted to go ahead alone and it would be difficult—and perhaps expensive—to force them to act against their judgement. However, the President was ready to instruct the American Ambassador to do all he could to ensure the full execution of the agreement in Tokyo. He would also give a further warning to the American companies as to the ultimate effect of allowing the oil interests to be divided.

At the same time, the Ambassador sent me a personal message informing me that Kennedy's apparently unhelpful attitude over this matter was due to the fact that he had been assured that the Shell company would be included in any new deal. This seemed rather lame. Nor was I much comforted by the American attitude on the broader question. Washington seemed determined to appease Sukarno and appeal to me to use my influence with the Tunku to do the same.

Sukarno, it seemed, was now prepared to attend a meeting without any preconditions. Although I thought it right to inform the Tunku of this fact, I felt that even under American pressure, which was now being applied to him direct, he would not yield. I had told the Americans firmly that, although the Tunku would wish to work for a *détente*, he could not be expected to meet Sukarno while his Government was not formally recognised.

Thus matters stood in the closing days of my Administration. Greater Malaysia had been achieved but at a considerable price. Although I have no doubt that Sukarno in any case would have seized foreign property in Indonesia in pursuance of his combination of communism and chauvinism, the Malaysia Federation had certainly provided him with a convenient excuse. Thus, although we had done our best, it was not on an altogether happy note that my connection with the affairs of South-East Asia was to terminate. Nor was it pleasant to reflect on the rift between me and the President, although I fully realised the pressures to which he was subjected.

It is perhaps right to give a brief summary of subsequent events.

The inclusion of Singapore in the Federation of Malaysia proved uneasy. In an atmosphere of strong tension in South-East Asia,

Malays accused the non-Malays of siding with Peking and with Indonesia, and the non-Malays (that is, the Chinese) of Singapore accused the Central Government of economic discrimination against them. On 9 August 1965, the Singapore Government announced its decision 'under pressure' to secede from the Federation. Singapore then became an independent country and a member, both of the Commonwealth and of the United Nations. With the British rundown of forces in the Far East, the Governments of Malaysia and Singapore have overcome their mutual antipathy and begun to cooperate over defence and other matters. Sarawak and Sabah have remained loyal to the Federation. Only the Sultan of Brunei, with the apparent approval of his subjects, decided to stand aloof and to continue enjoying all the advantages of 'imperialism' as a 'British-protected State'.

In Indonesia, an attempted *coup d'état* by Communists was suppressed in September 1965 and followed by a terrible and widespread massacre. President Sukarno, whom the Communists had intended should be their head of state, remained nominally in office, but without power. In March 1966 he degenerated, if one may presume to measure degrees of incapacity, into complete impotence. For on that date General Suharto took over effective control. The Communist Party was banned. As a result, on 11 August 1966 the 'confrontation' (or state of undeclared war) with Malaysia was finally terminated. On 12 March 1967, General Suharto became 'acting President' with full powers. Thus, in spite of all its accompanying horrors, the counter-revolution in Indonesia has at least brought peace and increasing prosperity both to Indonesia and to Malaysia.

CHAPTER IX

Arabia Infelix

GIBRALTAR, Malta, Alexandria, Aden—on this great string of fortresses long depended the power of Britain throughout the Mediterranean and the Middle East. Gibraltar was the pivot on which hinged that deployment of Anglo-American forces in North Africa which proved the turning point in the Second World War. Malta, surviving by a kind of miracle the fearful onslaught to which she was subjected, played a historic role through the bitter years when the route from West to East was virtually closed. Alexandria and the control of the Canal was the safety line of survival. Aden, as port, refuelling station, and air base, played almost as important a role. In the years of which I am now writing, the essential links were still unbroken. Gibraltar, in spite of Spanish claims, coud be preserved in good heart and strength by wise and courteous diplomacy. We did not then think it necessary to prove our devotion to our own democratic ideals by heaping vain insults on the proudest people in Europe. Malta, although perhaps of diminished importance, was still available. The Cyprus base, the successor, at least as regards air power, to Alexandria, after long and patient negotiations with Archbishop Makarios, seemed well established by a firm agreement; and it was from Cyprus that we were able, in a somewhat hazardous adventure in 1958, to answer King Hussein's appeal for help in Jordan.[1] From Aden we could command the Gulf and offer succour to the Sheikdoms with whom we were allied, as we did to Kuwait in 1961.[2] It was Aden, therefore, which was now destined to attract the envious hostility both of Nasser and of those countries of the Arab world which had fallen under his baneful influence.

The colony of Aden contained the port, the docks and workshops,

---

[1] *Riding the Storm*, chap. xvi.   [2] *Pointing the Way*, chap. xiii.

the air base and the vital territory surrounding these precious installations. The neighbouring states had long been under British protection. Six of these emirates were brought, by the efforts of Alan Lennox-Boyd, when Colonial Secretary, into a form of combination which it was hoped would make their life easier and improve their prosperity. They were known under the romantic names of Beihan, Audhali, Fadhli, Dhala, Upper Aulaqi, and Lower Yafa, and they were formed in 1959 into a loose, though effective, Federation. Later in the same year they were joined by Lahej. The Emirs each sent six members to the Federal Council, which was responsible for their joint affairs, and entered into a new treaty of friendship with Great Britain, which remained the protecting power. At the same time, a step forward in self-government was taken in the colony, since the majority in the Legislative Council dealing with internal matters became elective. In the next year, 1960, three further states, Lower Aulaqi, Dathina, and Aqrabi, were admitted to the membership of the Federation.

On the whole, conditions remained reasonably stable within their own borders. Nevertheless, it became necessary to mount an operation on a considerable scale to prevent the supply of arms to rebel tribesmen in the Aulaqi Sheikhdom. These weapons we knew to be of Czechoslovak origin (Czechoslovakia was the normal cover by which Russia-financed supplies of this character were brought in) and they came, of course, through Nasser's United Arab Republic.

The Yemenis meanwhile continued their hostility in spite of sincere efforts to improve our relations by our able representative, Sir William Luce, the Governor of Aden. The Royal Government of the Yemen was inspired not by Communist but by irredentist motives. Yet, in spite of the normal stream of abuse on the radio and some minor clashes on the frontier, there seemed little to fear. In the colony itself, there was a dangerous series of strikes fomented by the Arab Trades Union Congress, a political body resting upon the support of Nasser. Yet much material progress was made, and large sums of money devoted not only to the improvement of the harbour facilities but to social advance. A free health service was introduced, schools grew rapidly, supported by a technical institute and two teacher-training centres.

Unhappily, Nasser's pressure in this direction did not exhaust his malice, the subversion of the Arab Kingdom of Jordan becoming his main ambition. The King's position was indeed precarious.

> King Hussein to luncheon. Poor man, he is brave, but I fear for him. There is no doubt that his life is threatened, either directly by Egyptian agents or indirectly by Cairo stirring up trouble in Jordan.[1]

But, as always before and since, the King seemed undaunted.

The large and mixed populations of workmen inhabiting the colony of Aden proved an easy prey for agitation. Here was a 'proletariat' offering simple targets for the joint attacks of Communism and pan-Arab propaganda. The colony was vital to us politically and militarily; yet its internal condition was disturbing. In the hinterland the Emirs, living in a simpler and sometimes almost patriarchal world, were broadly friendly. A plan was therefore put forward to increase the stability of the colony by the influence of the Federated Sultans.

> A long and very important discussion about Aden Colony and the Protectorates. Two schemes will be prepared for us to consider. The real problem is how to use the influence and power of the Sultans to help us keep the Colony and its essential defence facilities.[2]

A few days later,

> we agreed about Aden. The line should be to merge the Colony with the Federation of Rulers and give as much power as we can to the Sultans who are on our side.[3]

At the end of 1961, in a mood of disgust at Yemen's lapse into comparative moderation, Nasser dissolved the Union of Arab States, a loose organisation of the United Arab Republic with the Yemen. The ostensible grounds were that the rulers of the Yemen had become 'reactionary'. He even ventured, relying on the same disingenuous slogan, to pour a wave of poisonous propaganda against the rich and powerful Saudi Arabian Government. All this

[1] 12 October 1960.   [2] 5 May 1961.   [3] 16 May 1961.

was satisfactory from our point of view, since it showed weakness rather than strength.

Meanwhile, in the course of the next year, in spite of the foundation of Egyptian money and agents of the so-called 'People's Socialist Party' in Aden colony to oppose Federation, as a result of long negotiations it was formally announced that on 1 March 1963 the union of the colony with the Federation would take place under a form of 'responsible' government. The elected members would have full internal control. But the Governor, now to be called High Commissioner, would be armed with reserved powers over external affairs, defence, security, the police and the civil service.

At this point, on 9 September 1962, died Imam Ahmed, the Ruler of Yemen. For fourteen years his rule had been notorious, even in an age which has become accustomed to terrorism and brutality, for cruelty and despotism on a truly oriental scale. He was certainly no friend of Britain's—we had suffered much from Yemeni pressure exercised against us by all means in his power. Nevertheless, he had kept the country together in a combination of medieval squalor and obedience. Three weeks later his son, Muhammed el Badr, whom he had named as 'Crown Prince' the previous year, was overthrown by the Army. Although the unhappy successor had tried to present himself as a 'modernist, friendly to President Nasser and co-operating with Russia, China and the United States of America in accordance with positive neutrality', his reforms were either too late or premature. The Army would have none of him. On 27 September, six tanks surrounded the palace and, in spite of a desperate resistance by the royal guards, Colonel Abdullah el Sallal declared himself President and Prime Minister of the emerging Republic. Although, as we learned later, the young Imam had succeeded in eluding his captors, Sallal was to all appearances in control. I had no doubts that he would prove sufficiently 'progressive', but I was less sure of his sentiments of universal brotherhood, or even of 'positive neutrality'.

All the afternoon and evening on the situation in the Yemen, which is developing very badly for us. If the new revolutionary Government is established, the pressure on the Aden Protectorate and then on the Aden Colony and base will be very dangerous.[1]

There was only one advantage to be gained. Our relations with Saudi Arabia had been strained since the Buraimi incident;[2] now there was a new danger facing this rich and proud country:

> We are hoping to get into better relations with the Saudi Government, which is much alarmed. Owing to the defection of some of their aeroplanes to Cairo, their whole air force is grounded (they are also short of spares).[3]

The young Imam, Muhammed, with the help of his uncle, Prince Hassan, recently returned from the less agitated atmosphere of the United Nations Assembly, now began to organise resistance. Since Sallal had appointed as Deputy Prime Minister Abdel Rahman el Baidani, a close adherent of Nasser, it was clear that if Nasser had not actually organised the coup he was ready to support it. Indeed, large forces from the U.A.R. soon made their appearance and were successful in a number of encounters. But in spite of a series of 'victories', the royalists were still unsubdued. Moreover, greatly to the surprise and chagrin both of the State Department and the Foreign Office, the new 'liberator' seemed almost as unpopular in many parts of the Yemen as the old tyrant. Although the new ruler tried to gain popularity by making violent verbal attacks on Britain and Saudi Arabia, this approach, although well received in the capital and the chief towns, seemed less effective in the more distant and less sophisticated areas.

During the month of October 1962, in spite of more immediate dangers elsewhere, I felt gravely concerned about our position in Aden. On 5 and 6 October, urgent meetings took place with my colleagues in charge of the Colonial Office, the Foreign Office and the Ministry of Defence. We agreed to prepare defensive measures in case Aden or the Protectorates were openly attacked and meanwhile to take such other action as might seem justifiable. Although we were under no illusion about the 'reactionary' character of the royalist 'rebels', our vital interests were more threatened by the

---

[1] 5 October 1962. [2] See *Tides of Fortune*, p. 641.
[3] 8 October 1962.

revolutionary régime. My letter to the Queen of 7 October summed up the situation:

> I must tell Your Majesty that we are very much worried about the situation in the Yemen. We are doing what we can . . . but I fear very much that the new revolutionary Government will get control. This means great danger to Aden. First to the Aden Federation, the various notables who govern these territories coming under our general surveillance, and next to the Aden Colony. . . . We have so far been able to maintain our position in the Gulf better than we had dared to hope. Our operation in Kuwait, for instance, was very successful. But so much depends on Aden and if we were to be driven out of Aden or faced with serious revolutionary troubles in Aden which might make the base useless, our whole authority over the Gulf would disappear. We have spent many anxious hours discussing what can be done and we have put certain action into operation. Nevertheless I fear that we shall have great difficulty.
>
> It is rather sad that circumstances compel us to support reactionary and really rather outmoded régimes because we know that the new forces, even if they begin with moderate opinions, always seem to drift into violent revolutionary and strongly anti-Western positions. Nasser, of course, is openly supporting the revolutionary forces in the Yemen. . . . It is a confused position which causes me, at the moment, more anxiety than many other questions which seem on the surface more immediate.

The Saudi Government were equally alarmed, though temporarily almost powerless, chiefly because of the lack of any effective air force.

On 22 October the Governor of Aden, at my request, came to London for consultation. Fortunately we had in Sir Charles Johnston a representative of quite exceptional power and authority—able, courageous, patient, determined. He explained to me the situation in the Yemen in terms familiar from Scottish history: the new Government held the capital and most of the lowlands, but the highland tribes, or clans, controlled the mountainous areas, amounting to a third of the whole country and were making serious raids upon the territory held by the nominal authorities. They were continually cutting communications as well as ambushing large numbers of Egyptian troops, unused to this sort of warfare. The

Governor thought it likely that, if Nasser persevered, he and Sallal would in the end succeed. But he made a strong plea that, although eventually recognition of the new Government might become necessary, it should be delayed. It has normally been our practice to give diplomatic recognition to a new government so soon as it can claim to be *de facto* 'in effective control'. In the present circumstances it could scarcely be argued that this was true of Sallal. Moreover, the Governor explained that we needed more time

> in order (*a*) to give Hassan and Co. a last chance to see what they could do; (*b*) to make it apparent to the rulers of the Protectorate that the Royalists had really [been given] a chance . . . (*c*) to get our friends to realise that recognition was unavoidable and give us at least a chance of getting on some working basis with the new republican Government.[1]

This discussion took place in the afternoon. That very morning Ambassador Bruce had called upon me to explain the opening stage of the Cuba crisis. Nevertheless, I was not disposed to be hurried into any premature decisions on the Yemen. If the Cuba situation went wrong, the world would be plunged into the total destruction of nuclear war; it would not then be necessary to worry too much about Aden and the neighbouring territories. If, on the other hand, the crisis in the Caribbean were resolved, it would be still important to maintain our position in Arabia.

The situation in the Yemen was having adverse effects upon the security of Aden and the Aden Protectorate. The Governor, Sir Charles Johnston, came on more than one occasion to discuss the problem with me and the Foreign Secretary, and I felt it important to give him every support in his difficult position. However, apart from any action that we might take to defend our interests, a great struggle now began about the question of recognition. In the intervals of messages all over the world regarding the Cuba missiles, I had a further talk with the two responsible Ministers on this tricky question.

In the early afternoon, a meeting with Foreign Secretary and Commonwealth Secretary about Yemen. The news is obscure

[1] 22 October 1962.

and the decision very difficult. If we *recognise* the new revolutionary Government, we shall lose all our friends in the Aden *Protectorate* and the *Colony* may get quite out of hand. If we do *not*, we lose our Embassy (in due course) and all chance of having some influence on the Government.[1]

The Foreign Office favoured recognition, but I was not convinced, especially having regard to the violent threats that Colonel el Sallal was now broadcasting against us—a virtual invitation to the inhabitants of Aden to revolt against the British. I felt reluctant to take a step from which I could see little advantage. It would be better to delay, all the more so since we were still able to retain our representative in the capital and to receive at least some communication from the centre. Accordingly, I began what was to prove a prolonged argument with Washington by a message to the President. In effect, Sallal was being supported by Egyptian forces on an ever-increasing scale. It could not be to the advantage either of the Americans, who were chiefly interested in Saudi Arabia, or the British, whose position in Aden and the adjoining territories was so delicate, to allow Yemen to become a tributary or occupied country of Nasser. In an opening shot in this campaign, I asked Kennedy on 14 November at least to delay formal recognition.

It seems to me that the big cards which you have to play in the Arabian area are recognition and financial aid. You want of course to save the Saudi régime and we both want to keep Jordan out of the struggle. In addition we have a vital interest in Aden where we fear that the local rulers may lose heart or go over to the other side. Of course the loss of Aden would have a disastrous effect on the whole Anglo-American position in the Gulf. I think you would agree with all this but the question is what should we do. . . .

The danger seems to be that if you play your cards, above all recognition, too soon in exchange for mere words, you may lose all power to influence events. I therefore feel that you should get something more than words before you give recognition and money. I quite recognise that the Royalists will probably not win in Yemen in the end but it would not suit us too badly if the new

[1] 26 October 1962.

Yemeni régime were occupied with their own internal affairs during the next few years.

I therefore suggest that you should not give recognition until the precise programme for withdrawal including a timetable and the final date for completion has been announced and certain specific steps have been taken. You might insist as a first step on the withdrawal of the U.A.R. air force from Yemen. This would have considerable effect: it would be easy to do, easy to detect and would remove an exacerbating feature from the local scene. An additional suggestion might be that United Nations observers might be introduced, perhaps at a later stage, to supervise the disengagement.

The President responded immediately; for as soon as he received my message he asked for a telephone discussion. There was little new to be said about Cuba; but the White House and the State Department were clearly anxious to go ahead with recognition of the new Yemeni Government, although it could certainly claim no *de jure* rights and was not *de facto* in control of the country.

With his usual charming frankness Kennedy began by disclaiming any knowledge of Yemen. 'I don't even know where it is.' But he was anxious to achieve two things; to get the Saudis and the Jordanians 'off the hook' and to induce Nasser to withdraw. He felt that the substantial American aid programme to Egypt, combined with the bait of 'recognition' of Nasser's Yemeni friends should do the trick.

While I agreed with Kennedy's objectives, I felt sceptical about the methods. Surely it would be better to get a definite timetable for Nasser's withdrawal, and when that was completed quicken up the aid and grant recognition. That was the right sequence especially in dealing with Nasser.

Kennedy, rather weakly, asked what would happen if, failing American recognition, Nasser refused any commitment to withdraw. I replied that Nasser would certainly continue his intervention and refuse any commitment to withdrawal, unless the Americans took a strong line. They could delay recognition and hold up aid. Any weakness would immediately affect our position in Aden, in the Gulf, and many of the Sheiks and peoples who trusted to our protection. After a little pause Kennedy asked if it would really help us in Aden if the United States Government refused recognition.

This was the question I was waiting for, and I had my reply ready: the rulers in the Protectorate were waiting to see which way the cat would jump. If ever they thought that Britain could be indefinitely 'pushed around' they would draw their own conclusions. If we lost authority in the Protectorate, we should be left with Aden. But Aden was not like Gibraltar, which could be defended (and without which, incidentally, we could not have won the war). If we lost the Protectorate, and were in serious trouble in Aden, still worse if we lost Aden, then we would be deprived of all means of defending our own and our clients in the Gulf. This was another trial of strength. Nasser must at least agree to a 'phased withdrawal'. Abyssinia, Morocco, Sudan, Libya, Jordan and the rest were watching. I begged him to think about it. It was not just the Yemen. It was a matter of prestige throughout the Arab world.

Kennedy, although clearly being prompted by the State Department advisers (to whom he referred from time to time) promised to reflect on the matter and communicate with me further. But I was not very hopeful.

On 15 November the Governor sent me a message reporting that recognition would spread consternation among our friends in Arabia, particularly in the Aden Protectorate, where it would be assumed that Britain was not sufficiently resolute to be dependable, or to resist American pressure. Recognition, he declared, must be conditional on the withdrawal of the Egyptian forces, which now amounted, apart from the air force, to something of the order of thirteen thousand troops, organised into three large brigades.

On 17 November I received a long but discouraging message from Washington. The President declared that the United States 'reading of the situation' was that Sallal and the revolutionaries were bound to win; that Nasser was totally committed to ensuring that they did win, and that to delay recognition was merely to encourage them to turn to Soviet Russia. 'The pro-royalist dabblings of the Saudis and the Jordanians are damaging to themselves.' It was to the Western interest to terminate the civil war. Nasser would not agree to withdraw his air force, 'his ace against the tribes', and the sooner the Americans granted recognition, the sooner they could exact pledges from Nasser and Sallal by which the withdrawal of Egyptian troops could be achieved with an assurance not to interfere with Aden and Saudi Arabia. I was very sceptical of all this, and in a further telephone conversation on 18 November I made our position clear. I followed this appeal with a message pleading for the delay of recognition for as long as possible. We were now at the stage of constitutional reform with the merger between the Aden Colony and the Protectorates in full swing. This would be a delicate operation, and its success depended on our commanding general confidence.

Kennedy was naturally more taken up with his recent terrible experiences over Cuba than with the problem of the Gulf. Nevertheless, he undertook to wait a few days and obtain a definite statement from Nasser and Sallal before granting recognition. Nasser would be asked to commit himself to withdrawal and Sallal to accept the 'normalisation of, and friendly relations with, all neighbouring areas'. He would be reminded that Aden and the Gulf were not merely a British interest but one in which America was deeply concerned. All this sounded very fine, and I could almost visualise the expert in the State Department drafting these high-sounding phrases. However, I thought it wiser to send a conciliatory reply, although I was still unsatisfied. I reflected that

> If the Americans can get a promise from Nasser to withdraw 'by stages'; if they can get a reasonable statement out of Sallal . . . repudiating his threats against the Aden Protectorate and Colony, then American recognition may not be too bad. In any case, it is hard to see what else we can do. We cannot make any overt intervention. The Saudis are very weak, internally. The Jordanians can do little (the defection of two 'Hunters' and their Air Commander to Cairo is a terrible blow to King Hussein). The Egyptians, although rotten soldiers, can put in a good deal of stuff to help the Yemeni rebel Government, and they have an air force which can be relied on to bomb the Royalists, who have no means of defence. But I am very concerned about Aden, where the position may easily get out of hand.[1]

[1] 17 November 1962.

Within a day or two my fears were justified.

> I'm afraid the American plan about Yemen is going to fail.
> Nasser is being very wary and I doubt whether he can afford to
> disengage from Yemen. So the Americans will risk paying the
> price (recognition) without effecting the purchase (Egyptian dis-
> engagement). This will make our position worse in the Pro-
> tectorate.[1]

When I saw de Gaulle on 16 December, he and I discussed this
matter briefly. He shared my anxieties and made it clear that
France was certainly 'not in a hurry to recognise the Republic'.
Before the end of the year the State Department got its way; but the
Foreign Office was beginning to doubt the value of recognition. The
official United States recognition followed an impudent broadcast
from Sallal announcing the formation of the Republic of the whole
Arabian Peninsula, thus implying a demand for revolution in Saudi
Arabia, Aden and the Protectorates, and the Persian Gulf states.
Certainly the Yemeni pupil was quick to learn from his Egyptian
master.

The next stage was naturally the demand for large loans of £20
million or more, to which the Americans made a cautious response,
preferring to despatch some forty thousand tons of maize; it had
been a good harvest that year in the United States.

At this period, the position of the rebels certainly seemed to be
weakening, and the advance of the Egyptian forces on Marib, near
the Aden Protectorate frontier, together with the arrival of rockets
in Sanaa with a range calculated to reach Aden, created some
anxiety. But the Colonial Secretary remained firm: no recognition
unless mutual. Sallal must acknowledge our position in Aden and
the Protectorate if we were to accept his as *de facto* Government of
Yemen.

The unresolved problem continued into the New Year. I was not
prepared to be rushed and asked the Governor, for whose judgement
I had such great respect, once more to come to London.

> Sir Charles Johnston . . . arrived on Monday night, and at all
> convenient intervals between other business we have had tre-

[1] 26 November 1962.

mendous discussions about whether or not to recognise the new 'republican' Government of the Yemen. It is a most difficult decision to take, for the argument is nicely balanced as between wider considerations (our relations with Nasser, etc.) and the immediate effects in the Aden Protectorate and Colony. We finally decided to bring home our envoy (and thus gain some weeks) and try to complete the Aden 'merger' or 'Federation' as soon as possible. This in itself will call out violent attacks from Nasser, etc.[1]

The Governor still counselled delay. However, there was another and brighter side to the picture; for the Saudi Arabians, feeling themselves under great threats, on 16 January 1963, renewed diplomatic relations with Britain which had been severed at the time of the Suez crisis in 1956.

Amid many other troubles I did not forget the Yemen. On 28 January I recorded:

We have brought back Gandy (our Minister) for consultation, but as he at once went down with influenza, we have not made any progress. There is still a violent division of opinion about recognition between Colonial Office and Foreign Office–Ministry of Defence siding with Colonial Office.[2]

A little later President Kennedy suggested to me that, now that the Aden merger was accomplished and our diplomatic relations with Saudi Arabia restored, British recognition of Yemen would be 'a constructive move'. A large number of messages passed but they were inconclusive. A little later, however, the question resolved itself. The President of the Yemen, Sallal, asked for the withdrawal of the British Legation, which had remained all this time at Taiz. Since we had enjoyed the advantage of having an observer on the spot without formal relations with the Government, we could hardly complain. I was not altogether sorry at this almost ludicrous solution of a problem which had been engaging us for so long.

The Yemen problem (like so many) has settled itself! The Republicans have got tired of waiting for recognition and have closed the embassy. The Foreign Office and Foreign Secretary

[1] 11 January 1963.   [2] 28 January 1963.

are rather upset. The Colonial Secretary is triumphant—so is Minister of Defence. I think it's the best thing 'in the short term', for we would have lost the confidence of all our friends in the new Aden Federation. In the long run, it may bring us trouble. But Arab politics change with startling rapidity and one can never be sure.[1]

I sent a message on 14 February to the President explaining our situation and ending with a conciliatory phrase, for I felt he was somewhat ruffled by our intransigence:

> I am sorry that the result is that you and we should now seem to be somewhat out of step in our Yemen policy, but as I see it this is due more to differences in our circumstances than to divergence in objectives.

Not surprisingly, Nasser did not honour his engagement with the Americans. Indeed, Egyptian troops continued to pour into the Yemen and by the beginning of March

> the position in the Yemen is deteriorating rapidly. There are now twenty-eight thousand Egyptians (one-third of all Egyptian active forces) in the Yemen. It is getting pretty clear that the Egyptians mean to use Yemen as a jumping-off ground for Saudi Arabia—a great prize. They are dropping arms inside Saudi Arabia, and obviously are in touch with subversive elements there. What is ironical is that the Americans, who accepted the threat to Aden and the Federation with some equanimity (especially an old colony!) are now tremendously excited and alarmed about Nasser going for Saudi Arabia and all the vast American oil interests involved.[2]

At the same time, the royalists seemed to be weakening. 'The tribes, like the Scottish clans in old days, are rallying to the winning side.'[3]

Serious violations were now made by the Yemeni of Aden territory. These were met without difficulty.

> The invaders have been chased off our ground. But what are we to do next? The Egyptians are heavily committed and will be difficult to dislodge by diplomatic means, although the Americans are trying to do so.[4]

[1] 17 February 1963.   [2] 7 March 1963.
[3] 8 March 1963.   [4] 28 February 1963.

With singular impudence Sallal now complained to the United Nations of British aggression, but I did not feel unduly concerned. Nevertheless, things were not going well in the Middle East.

> Of course, the Egyptians have a great capacity for being disliked. So, in the longer run, even the Yemenis may turn against Nasser. Meanwhile, he has gained a pro-Egyptian Government in Syria.[1]

However, the Americans were now beginning to have second thoughts. In spite of their traditional support of the republican states of the Middle East, they could not forget that the chief monarchy, Saudi Arabia, was vital to their oil interests.

In March 1963 Dr. Ralph Bunche, after a visit to Aden and Cairo on behalf of the United Nations, announced that Nasser had given his promise to withdraw troops if the Saudis would first stop helping the royalists. A month later, on 29 April, Egypt, Yemen and Saudi Arabia announced an agreement to end hostilities and to accept a United Nations team of 'observers' to enforce the truce. However, by the time they arrived, on 13 June, the war was continuing in full swing. I could not help reflecting on the curious bias of the United Nations.

> For instance, Nasser is bombing Yemen and Saudi Arabia day and night with powerful Russian bombers, and is using poison gas. Nothing happens. No protest. No Afro-Asian resolution in Security Council or Assembly. Imagine what would happen if we were doing one twentieth of this from (say) Aden.[2]

Within a few months my responsibility was to cease, but it is perhaps worth recording briefly some further stages of these sad events. In the Yemen, Egyptian troops had been increased by 1965 to seventy thousand, when a split developed among the republicans, some turning fiercely against the Egyptian intervention. This power struggle between the pro- and anti-Egyptian factions, continued through 1966 with great violence and was followed by widespread executions on both sides. Undoubtedly the strain on Nasser throughout these years was heavy, and his prestige was soon to be fatally injured by the Six-Day War with Israel in June 1967.

[1] 11 March 1963.　　　　[2] 16 August 1963.

Meanwhile, events in Aden and the surrounding territories began to deteriorate seriously in 1965, and in 1966 the fatal decision was taken to evacuate the Aden base. Even this withdrawal, with all its dangers, was carried out in a method calculated to produce the maximum of trouble and peril; for more than a year was to elapse before the evacuation in November 1967. At this date our friends were to be abandoned and our enemies comforted. In the event, the Federal Government and Army crumbled away; we found no successor government to whom to hand over our responsibilities, and we were forced to leave under strong naval cover at the end of November 1967. The shame of this sad event, with all its inherent dangers for the future, was to some extent redeemed by the courage and devotion of the small remaining British forces.

CHAPTER X

African Maze

I. CONGO

THROUGHOUT the first and stormy years following the Independence of the Congo, one of the chief anxieties of the Western Governments was to prevent that vast territory and its resources from falling into Communist hands or under Communist control. In order to achieve this, the British Government were in full agreement with the American in securing the services of the United Nations, hoping by military and economic means to restore some kind of order and to preserve or renew under a federal structure the high degree of unity and prosperity which the Belgians had brought to these primitive populations, with all their diverse tribal and regional jealousies. Although agreed in principle, we were confronted with many difficulties in practice. Moreover, the United Kingdom Government was continually subjected to different pressures which, without careful handling, might have led to a serious schism in the Commonwealth.

By the end of 1961, however, it seemed that the crisis had been overcome. Cyrille Adoula, the Prime Minister of the Central Government, a man of considerable ability and courage, acting with the loyal support of Joseph Kasavubu, the unruffled and unquestionably legitimate President, was beginning to establish his authority, with the help of the United Nations, at Léopoldville and the immediately surrounding areas. He had even succeeded in overcoming the power of Gizenga and his self-elected Communist minority established in Stanleyville. For by the beginning of January 1962 the Central Government, with United Nations support, arrested Gizenga and defeated his armed forces. All this seemed to be 'progress' on the right lines. There remained, however,

K

the vital question of the future of Katanga. This great territory, with its enormous resources of copper, amid all the turmoil and confusion of the surrounding provinces, remained, under the control of Moise Tshombe, relatively quiet and orderly. Tshombe not unnaturally enjoyed the moral support of Welensky and the Government of the Central African Federation, who were anxious to see a reasonably settled régime in a territory limitrophe with Northern Rhodesia. Other European interests, particularly the investors in the important copper mines, chiefly operated by the Union Minière, were equally concerned. It was, therefore, with great relief that we learnt that on 20 December 1961, after the 'occupation' of some important towns of Katanga by United Nations forces, Tshombe and Adoula had signed an agreement to end the secession. For if Katanga were allowed to develop as a wholly separate state, there could be no economic future for a Congo deprived of Katanga's wealth.

Rifts, however, soon began to appear. Nevertheless, I was glad to learn that 'the Americans on the spot are getting a little worried and are now trying to urge Adoula not to press Tshombe too hard.'[1] When, therefore, I heard that the Katanga Provincial Assembly were willing to accept the terms of the agreement, I felt happier about defending in Parliament the twelve-million-dollar subscription which the Cabinet had reluctantly agreed to make towards the expenses of the United Nations in this adventure. But my hopes were soon to be disappointed. Tshombe, with not unnatural suspicion, was unwilling to integrate his gendarmerie—the only effective native force—with that of the Central Government which was still in disorder, at least until the issue of the rights of individual states in the new Federal Constitution had been definitely settled. Adoula was equally anxious to prevent another separatist movement by getting control of the forces of law and order.

On 26 April 1962, when I was in New York, I discussed the situation with U Thant, then Acting Secretary-General.

[He] was very pleasant and seemed sensible enough.
He is anxious to get U.N. out of the Congo commitment if he

[1] 24 December 1961.

can. But these particular Africans seem really impossible to deal
with—Tshombe and Adoula are equally difficult.[1]

President Kennedy expressed a similar view and on 3 May I told
the Foreign Secretary that Kennedy felt that it was time we had an
Anglo-American-Belgian policy agreed which could then be imposed on everyone else. He was inclined at first to talk exclusively
in terms of pressure on Tshombe but did not dissent when I pointed
out that pressure on Adoula would also be necessary and that the
loi fondamentale would have to be amended. It seemed likely that
the Americans would agree to our trying to work out a joint
policy in London, with David Bruce as their representative. I felt
that we ought to follow this up as it seemed to augur well for the
future.

As time passed, neither Tshombe's talks with Adoula nor the
discussions between American and British officials reached any real
conclusion. I suspected that Tshombe was overplaying his hand;
but I made it clear to Kennedy that we should deplore further
military action. No good could come of destroying Tshombe; we
must make him join a Congo federation while persuading Adoula
to pay due respect to state rights. Thus I found myself in the
peculiar position of trying to persuade Washington that the only
solution for a country embracing a great area with many local
traditions was a federal constitution in preference to a unitary state.
For some reason, the Americans appeared to regard this as a somewhat rash and even novel proposition.

On 26 June 1962, Adoula declared that all peaceful means to a
solution were now exhausted. On 6 July, the Foreign Secretary
came to discuss the situation with me.

> No real settlement seems likely between Adoula (at Léopold-
> ville) and Tshombe (at Élisabethville). The U.N. threaten
> military action, with all its dangers. We cannot accept this.[2]

Fortunately, U Thant was himself most reluctant to embark upon
new measures of force. On 31 July he issued an appeal to all
member states to use their influence to bring about a peaceful

[1] 26 April 1962.   [2] 6 July 1962.

settlement. If all persuasion failed and Tshombe maintained an unreasonable attitude, then he gave the warning that economic measures might be necessary. Although my reflections at the time represented, perhaps, a somewhat prejudiced view, they are typical of the exasperation which we were now to feel. Before the Communist danger had been happily overcome, we had worked in harmony; now that it had been removed, we seemed to be drifting apart.

> Congo has quietened down a bit. The reason is that the Advisory Committee (which U Thant and the U.N. staff have to consult) represents the nations which have troops in the U.N. forces in Congo—Indians, Irish, Swedes, Ethiopians, etc. A year ago they were all for firm action. But having got a bloody nose, they have not [much] stomach for any more fighting. So now the Americans want 'economic sanctions' against Tshombe—i.e. refusing to allow the export of copper. Cynics observe that (since most of the world's copper which is not in Africa, is in American hands) the effect of such a boycott will benefit the Americans and American shareholders. (They have little or no holding in Union Minière.) Our real concern is that Welensky might be driven by United Nations' folly to some folly of his own. He might reach a merger or armed alliance with Tshombe. It would be tempting. The Katanga and the N. Rhodesian copper belts really form a single system.[1]

U Thant, however, showed exemplary patience and on 20 August outlined a programme of constitutional revision on federal lines, defining a proposed division of revenue, arrangements for a unified currency, and other matters. If this failed, then the United Nations must either withdraw or enforce its plan 'by all necessary measures'. The Katanga Government accepted these proposals on 3 September, and I felt again encouraged by the hope that Tshombe would be reasonable. Indeed, six weeks later, on 16 October, the new Federal Constitution was formally inaugurated. But with obstinate folly Tshombe now repudiated the whole plan. We were now therefore faced with a new crisis involving all the difficulties of the previous year.

[1] 5 August 1962.

Congo is boiling up again. U Thant (backed by Kennedy) wants to bring military pressure on Tshombe. This is *not* tolerable for us. They may be content with 'economic' sanctions – which we might have to accept, although only to the point of *not* increasing our purchases of copper.[1]

However, no definite action followed until my meeting at Nassau with Kennedy in December 1962. It was always a great benefit for us to be able to meet and talk frankly together, and in the course of a crowded agenda we had a full discussion of the whole situation.

The issues seemed nicely balanced. On the one hand the President argued vigorously that Adoula's position was becoming steadily worse, almost desperate; that if he failed altogether the way would be open for the Russians to return with all their sinister influence. Adoula was strongly anti-Communist and should be backed at all cost. Up to now the situation had been preserved by the steadiness of President Kasavubu and of his series of Prime Ministers, of whom Adoula was the best. It would be wrong if the stubbornness and intransigence of Tshombe were to destroy the chance of any sound and moderate solution.

There was a certain good sense in all this. Nevertheless Home argued strongly that we ought to work for some federal solution, with Katanga paying over a proper share of revenue to the central fund. Against this, Mr. Ball, the American representative, replied that Tshombe continued to demand impossible conditions. At the end, we were driven to accept the position that, without early and firm agreement, there must be a military operation to overcome Tshombe's resistance and to give strength to Adoula at the centre. In the event, United Nations forces established control over the main Katanga towns before the end of the year and Tshombe, under pressure, agreed to negotiate once more.

Naturally these events threatened fresh trouble in the Conservative Party.

Apart from Congo, where U.N. forces – aided and abetted by U.S. forces – have defeated Tshombe and produced an internal

[1] 27 November 1962.

crisis in the Tory Party, there has been a lot of routine work, ministerial meetings, etc. My chief hope is that the Union Minière will switch to Adoula—and that means [the interests which] are so heavily involved in Tanganyika Concessions, itself a large shareholder in Union Minière. Even in Africa *pecunia non olet*.[1]

A few days later,

Congo continues, partly farce, partly tragedy. Tshombe has gone off again to N. Rhodesia, but is ready to return for a final negotiation. The great Union Minière installations are mined, and the vital dams may be destroyed at any moment. The only man who has any restraining influence is the British Consul at Élisabethville. Characteristically, Adoula (Congo Central Government) has ordered him out of the country.[2]

But Tshombe was to prove a broken reed even to his fervent supporters. He could make an agreement, but he could never keep it. Thus we were soon forced by circumstances to admit that the American policy had at least the advantage of being clear and effective. During the next few months a chaotic situation prevailed throughout this vast area of the Congo, with a general state of political and economic collapse. It was therefore essential to maintain the United Nations presence, both militarily and administratively, in order to avoid complete chaos.

The departure of Tshombe, who fled to Europe on 14 June 1963, ended this stage of the long dispute, and conditions began to improve. Towards the end of July Adoula came to London for a short visit. I took great trouble to show him special courtesy and found him interesting and easy to talk to.

Motored to London Airport, to meet M. Adoula. He speaks good French. Madame Adoula, two Ministers, and a large staff came with him—also, Rose, our new Ambassador, was back from his post.

The situation is quiet—which means that the great provincial wars (with Tshombe, for instance) are over, at least for the time.

[1] 11 January 1963.   [2] 12 January 1963.

But since there are no police (who have mutinied and become armed bandits) there is no order. Except for a few cities, the Government's writ does not really run in this vast area.[1]

Adoula was engagingly frank with me and did not attempt to disguise the degree of political and economic disintegration which had been reached. He had, however, hopes that if he could get rid of Parliament, he might be able in the end to restore order and some degree of prosperity. It was parliaments that caused the great trouble. Although I had some natural sympathy for his point of view, I felt bound to repress it. But I was not surprised to learn in the autumn that a 'state of emergency' had been declared and Adoula, who showed considerable resolution, had established his authority. The Communist leaders escaped to the former French Congo; and by the end of November, after two Communists, albeit diplomatists, had been arrested and beaten up, the entire staff of the Soviet Embassy was deported. It remained to be seen how far the new Government could establish itself. The decision that the United Nations forces should remain until July 1964 seemed wise.

So ended at least a stage in the complicated and troublesome story which began several years before with the withdrawal of the Belgians. As so often, both in Africa and in Asia, the changeover from European administration to independence proved difficult and bloody. The readiness of the European Governments to hand on their authority was not matched, at least in the early stages, by any effective native authority able to take up the burden. The whole country thus became a convenient arena for the rivalries, ambitions, and fears of the great powers. The Communists undoubtedly intended, by turning the Congo into a satellite country, to form this territory, so rich in resources and, if properly organised, so powerful, into a base from which to spread Marxist gospel throughout the continent. The Americans and British were equally determined to circumvent these plans. In a sense, the task of the British Government was the more complicated because, although in full agreement with Washington's purpose, London was more affected by various

[1] 22 July 1963.

conflicting interests. It can at least be said that through this somewhat painful journey we managed to avoid the main dangers, both
internally and in the Commonwealth.

II. KENYA

I N their determination to bring about the gradual transference of
their own authority in various African colonies to the representatives of the native inhabitants, the British, like the other
European governments concerned, were faced with varied and
complex difficulties. In some, like the Congo, the mere size of the
territory was almost overwhelming, coupled with the tribal and
provincial rivalries as well as the shortage of trained African
administrators. In others, like the Central African Federation, where
far greater progress had been made in the development of local
institutions and a local civil service, the major embarrassment,
which led to its ultimate dissolution, arose from the basic difference
between two of the partners, Northern Rhodesia and Nyasaland, as
they were then called, and Southern Rhodesia. In the first two
cases, the European populations were small and partly transient. In
the second, the Europeans, almost entirely of British or Afrikaaner
descent, formed a large and prosperous element in the population
and had already achieved almost complete self-government on the
South Africa lines, so admired of Liberal politicians in the early
years of the century—that is, with almost complete disregard of
African interests.

In Kenya, together with the familiar problems with which we
were confronted in other territories, there was the special case of a
small but wealthy and intelligent European population which, by its
pioneering efforts, had achieved a high degree of agricultural
efficiency, followed by considerable commercial and even industrial
development. The Europeans, nearly all of British descent, were
broadly of two classes. There were the original settlers, one might
almost say explorers, who, under the leadership of such men as Lord

Delamere and Lord Cranworth, had discovered the virtually un-
inhabited highlands which, before their coming, only saw occasional
visits of wandering nomad tribes. Here, some six thousand feet
above the sea and almost on the equator, large farms, skilfully
managed and enjoying substantial capital equipment, had reached
a high degree of success. These estates were responsible for providing a surplus, whether for local consumption or for export.
They also produced certain specialised and valuable crops, such as
pyrethrum, which commanded a high price. These adventurous
men, often sufficiently wealthy to make frequent visits to Britain
and to educate their children at home, belonged to a period before
and after the First War. They were followed after the Second War
by a number of younger settlers, mainly officers from the forces
who were encouraged by the government of the day to invest their
small savings or gratuities on a less ambitious scale. Both these
classes of European settlers, who had brought with them investment,
knowledge and determination, brought about by the success of their
farms, the growing prosperity of Nairobi. For the rest, the immigrants consisted of some Arabs and a very large number, some
170,000 or more, of Indians. The main population was African,
divided into various tribes, large and small, who carried on a long-
standing tradition of rivalry and enmity.

It was not necessary to 'hold up a candle to the daylight' to
discern, even in the early days, that if and when the British Government began to hand over control, the position of the non-Africans,
and especially of the Europeans, would become increasingly
insecure. Indeed, as far back as 1923, the Colonial Secretary of the
day (the Duke of Devonshire) issued a famous declaration which
made it abundantly clear that it was the intention of the British
Government, in any conflict of interest, to regard that of the Africans
as 'paramount'. I well remember in the early years of my marriage,
many of the Duke's friends and relations, who had decided to make
their lives and risk their fortunes in the Kenya highlands, reproach-
ing him, sometimes bitterly, for this policy. Nevertheless, he stuck
manfully to what he considered right and obtained the full support
of Bonar Law's Cabinet and its successors. The doctrine of 'para-
mountcy' was never seriously challenged.

K2

After the Second War, the Colonial Office began to develop the processes of education and African participation, which were the normal preliminaries to independence, whether this should come early or late. The years from 1952 to 1956 were marred and progress correspondingly retarded by the tragic Mau-Mau rebellion with all its horrors and barbarism. Yet neither the Colonial Secretary, Oliver Lyttelton, nor his successor, Alan Lennox-Boyd, although giving the most loyal support to the responsible authorities to stamp out this dreadful outbreak, wavered in their long-term purposes. Accordingly, there were, especially after 1956, progressive amendments and changes in the structure of governments in the Colony which increased the share of the Africans. These reforms, although naturally regarded as inadequate by the leaders of the activist parties, were the essential foundations on which the road to independence could be built.

On 12 January 1960, the 'state of emergency', which had lasted for over seven years, was formally brought to an end. A conference was summoned, which met in the last half of January and the first weeks of February to consider constitutional reform. The Colonial Secretary, Iain Macleod, brought all the idealism and resourcefulness of his ardent nature to this task. The Governor, Sir Patrick Renison, and forty elected members of the Legislative Council took part—the latter representing all the various groups, European, Asian, African. There were, in addition, the usual quota of officers and advisers. This Conference was generally regarded as signalling the end of the Mau-Mau nightmare. While I was travelling in Africa, Macleod sent me a number of telegrams describing the difficulties of reconciling the African demand for a system which would give them ultimate power with the anxieties of all the other groups. The Colonial Secretary was convinced that power must eventually go to Africans; but he hoped and believed that their leaders might be open to persuasion on the timing of the constitutional changes, in order to bring other communities to recognise the inevitability of the final stage.

On my return to London, Macleod asked me to see Mr. Michael Blundell and his Committee of the New Kenya Party. Blundell represented the moderate and progressive element among the

European settlers and was a man of high ideals. He brought with him some British, some African and some Asian members of his group.

> I gave them drink and encouragement. The Conference has been going well on the Constitutional side, but is now threatened with disaster over the Land question.[1]

In the end, the Conference was successful, only Captain Briggs, of the extreme European Party, being unwilling to accept the report. The next task was to implement the agreed plan, which envisaged a Council of Ministers with four 'officials' and eight 'unofficials', of whom four were to be African, three European and one Asian. There was to be a Legislative Council of sixty-five; fifty-three to be elected directly by qualified voters, the qualifications being literacy and an income of £75 p.a., the other twelve to be elected indirectly on a racial basis. In the event, three of the Africans who were offered positions on the Council began by refusing, although two ultimately accepted.

By the beginning of the following year, the first elections became possible. But tension was growing, especially among the Africans. Two African groups were formed—Kenya African National Union, commonly known as KANU, and Kenya African Democratic Union, commonly known as KADU. These, unhappily, were based on tribal lines. At the same time, European alarm was becoming widespread, and I received many letters from friends and others who feared that African self-government, and still more African independence, would make their position untenable, especially in the highlands. I recalled with regret the vain effort that I had made nearly twenty years before when I was Under-Secretary for a short period at the Colonial Office. I had then put forward a proposal that the large European farms should be purchased by the Crown and run as State companies, either in their present shape or grouped into larger units, with their present owners as managers. The Treasury naturally obstructed the plan, even though the sums involved would have been small compared to the daily expenditure of the six years' war.[2] Now we were left with a land problem which

[1] 17 February 1960. [2] See *The Blast of War*, p. 177.

was to become more pressing and more baffling every day. 'The
world is indeed a comedy to those who think, a tragedy to those who
feel.'

At the beginning of January 1961, I had a long talk with the
Lord Chancellor (Lord Kilmuir).

> We both feel anxious about Kenya. In some ways this is more
> difficult *at home* even than Central Africa. People are not yet
> accustomed to the idea that, sooner or later, we shall have to
> accept independence in Kenya. . . . 'Sooner or later'–the Colonial
> Office are thinking in terms of 1964, which seems to many of us
> *too* soon. From the Party point of view, Kenya is going to create
> a big problem. We might even split on it. Lord Salisbury and
> Lord Lambton could easily rally a 'settler' lobby here of con-
> siderable power. The Kenyan settlement has been aristocratic
> and upper middle class (much more than Rhodesia) and has
> strong links with the City and the Clubs.[1]

On 1 March the Governor decided that he could not release
Jomo Kenyatta, the leader of the KANU Party and popular hero,
from the 'restriction' to which he and a number of Mau-Mau
leaders had to conform. KANU therefore refused to join the
Government, which had to be formed under Mr. Ngala's leadership
with the support of KADU and Blundell's New Party group. But
of course this could only be a temporary measure, for Kenya without
Kenyatta was like *Hamlet* without the Prince of Denmark.

> A formula has been found about Kenyatta, on which one of the
> African parties will agree to form a Government. But it has been
> made quite clear to them and to the Press by the Governor that
> there is *no* change in the position about Kenyatta's eventual
> release. This will continue to be governed by the conditions in
> the Governor's broadcast of March 1st. I think this will do; but
> of course the Party here are very suspicious.[2]

The conditions in fact involved the return to a reasonable degree of
law and order and the relaxation of the pressures which political
excitement was causing.

[1] 20 January 1961.   [2] 18 April 1961.

The British are indeed a people of short memories, at any rate concerning injuries done to themselves. Even so, to remove any form of control over Kenyatta and his principal colleagues so soon after the terrible events of the four years' Mau-Mau war was asking a great deal. Of course, we knew that this step must eventually be taken; but it must be at the right moment. During the summer, Kenyatta was allowed to return to Kikuyu territory, and the months passed uneasily with a series of meetings, walk-outs, accusations of intimidation and all the rest, on behalf of both African parties. The new Government faced a steady drain of capital, growing unemployment and the need to fulfil its election promises, particularly on education, and land for landless Africans. Election promises haunt the minds of Ministers equally in all parliamentary systems, new and old. Perhaps they are the reason why relief is so often sought in single-party government or military autocracy.

Meanwhile, mounting demands on the part of the Somalis in the northern province for freedom to join the Somali Republic became an increasing threat. In November, Reggie Maudling, who had now become Colonial Secretary, visited Kenya and, in the hope of reaching a solution of all these difficulties, arranged for a conference to open in London in the following year. I reflected rather gloomily:

> If we have to give independence to Kenya, it may well prove another Congo. If we hold on, it will mean a long and cruel campaign – Mau-Mau and all that.[1]

All my colleagues here were fully informed before the conference met.

> We have had long Cabinet discussions. Maudling seems to be both prudent and robust, and ready for trouble, if it has to be faced. The trouble is that Kenya is at the moment bankrupt (deficit is £30 m.) and (with self-government followed in a few months by independence) may become a bloody shambles.[2]

This was to prove a somewhat pessimistic mood, since, although the conference resulted in a virtual deadlock, it was agreed that a

---

[1] 19 December 1961.   [2] 16 February 1962.

coalition of all parties should be formed 'to work out further details', especially as regards regional powers and boundaries. With this typically British attempt to escape from an impasse, Kenya had, for the present, to be content. However, as so often happens with a compromise, each party interpreted it in its own way. Mr. Ngala, on his return, said that 'regionalism had been obtained', which Mr. Kenyatta hotly denied. Indeed, only the framework of a constitution was secured; 'all the details' had subsequently 'to be worked out'.

Kenyatta was now moving more and more into the controlling position, with Tom Mboya rising at his side in reputation. Other leaders were eagerly contending for power. All these internal conflicts resulted, of course, from the intense rivalries between the various tribes. Maudling went again to Kenya on 10 July 1962 and did his best to produce some order out of chaos. Perhaps the most important announcement that he was able to make was a declaration, to which the Cabinet had agreed, regarding African settlement in the European-owned highlands. Since the development of this area, Africans had naturally been attracted in large numbers as farm labourers and foremen; now in view of the land hunger throughout the colony, it was clear that some measure must be taken to provide African holdings. This was not wholly a racial question, for these *latifundia*, apart from the race to which their owners belonged, had become jealously regarded by smallholders who wished to see them broken up. Even if they had been in the hands of Africans, a native Gracchus would have arisen as a tribune of the African people. The announcement, therefore, that Britain would finance the purchase of a million acres for African settlement over a period of five years was well received.

Complications in making the constitution, with all the various interests concerned and the difficult demarcation of regions, including the coastal strip and the Somali area, led to months of delay. It was not until April 1963 that the Constitution could be published; on 18 May the elections were held.

Meanwhile, some wider issues had been raised. The representatives of Tanganyika and Uganda, which hoped to form an effective Federation with Kenya as soon as Kenyan independence was reached, were beginning to show impatience at the slow rate of progress. Both these countries were already self-governing and independent and showed natural pride in their new status. Duncan Sandys, the Minister now responsible both for the Commonwealth and the Colonies, showed extraordinary patience in dealing with them.

> I have had to spend several hours being reproached (and almost insulted) by . . . Mr. Kawawa and Mr. Obote, of Tanganyika and Uganda. However, it all ended amicably and they accepted a very harmless communiqué. They were complaining about the slow march of events in Kenya—which is only their affair to the extent that they are all there in the East African Organisation.[1]

More serious was the demand of the Somalis for secession, which we attempted to meet by arranging for a separate region for the Somalis in the north-east. Nevertheless there was a certain amount of rioting, and tension grew. The Somali Republic, which had not long been constituted, decided to break off diplomatic relations with Britain; but no armed attack seemed likely. It had by now become clear that any further delay towards internal self-government would be a grave error.

As a result of the May election, in spite of the defection of one or two important tribes, Kenyatta's Party were triumphant, receiving nearly two-thirds of the total votes. He was therefore able to form a strong Government with wide tribal representation and to become Kenya's first Prime Minister, with the inauguration of internal self-government on 1 June 1963. It is indeed strange to reflect that this man, so feared and hated as the leader of a rebellion with all its appalling features, within a very short time began to command not only the loyal affection of the majority of Africans but the respect and admiration of the Europeans. He has continued to hold this position continuously, year by year. Indeed, many of the fears still felt about Kenya's future are based upon the inevitable loss to the whole community that will follow Kenyatta's death or retirement.

It was now clear that independence must soon follow internal self-government. Nothing could be gained by delay; everything

[1] 28 January 1963.

might be won by a sign of confidence. Accordingly, I authorised independence talks to be opened in London before the end of September. These were duly held and after much hard bargaining as between rights of the regions and those of the Federal Government, followed by a threat of the KADU leaders to form a breakaway KADU State, agreement was finally reached. On 12 December 1963 Kenya became fully independent.

In the decade that has followed there have been gains and losses. The pressure upon the European landowners has increased, and by one means or another a large number of such European farmers have been bought out by the Government in order to meet the land hunger of the growing African population. While the terms have not been generous, they have not been altogether unreasonable. One aspect of the policies followed by the Government of Kenya which has caused the greatest dismay in Britain, even among those who most closely sympathise with African aspirations, has been the extreme nationalism displayed by their legislation against so-called 'non-citizens', mainly Asians. As a result of the refusal of work-permits, a mass departure to Britain of Asians, chiefly Indians and Pakistanis, has led to considerable tensions, and at the beginning of 1967 it was found necessary by the Home Secretary of the day, James Callaghan, to introduce legislation to control what otherwise would have become an overwhelming flood. It is one of the strange delusions of many Europeans that all non-Europeans must have a liking for each other. This, of course, is by no means the case; and the normal African feeling about Asians is often exaggerated by the suspicion that they are more intelligent, more thrifty, more adapted to commerce and therefore more successful. Indeed, the retail and much of the wholesale trade passed into their hands together with a great deal of money-lending and the like. They became, therefore, treated as the Jews of Africa and roused the jealousy and hatred of the African people. The policy of what amounts to mass expulsion has been cruel, even if understandable.

In other respects Kenya has been fortunate, for under the powerful leadership of Kenyatta, in spite of many economic difficulties, progress has been steady and peace secure.

III. RHODESIA

THE concluding years of my premiership were haunted, not to say poisoned, by the growing tensions in the countries constituting the Central African Federation and the bitter feelings aroused while the seemingly hopeless struggle to reach some acceptable solution continued. The story is made all the more tragic by the high character and earnest feelings of the protagonists, each devoted to what appeared to him as the path of wisdom and equity, and often unable to understand the deep emotions underlying these sad but perhaps inevitable conflicts.

In order to make the sequence of events intelligible, it is necessary to go back to the period following my return from Africa in February 1960.[1]

An Advisory Commission on the Review of the Constitution of Rhodesia and Nyasaland under Lord Monckton had been safely launched, after some preliminary difficulties, at the end of 1959. Its task was to prepare for the 'review' due to be held during 1960 by considering 'the constitutional programme and framework best suited to the achievement of the objects contained in the Constitution of 1953, including the Preamble'.[2]

While the Commission was taking evidence and preparing its report, I began to realise how delicate and even dangerous the position had become. For instance, when towards the end of April 1960 Sir Edgar Whitehead, the Premier of Southern Rhodesia, called on me in London, it was apparent how diverse were the interests of the leading figures. I was determined, as a matter not merely of policy but of honour, to do all that was possible to support the continuance of the Federation. It was quite true that I had already entertained some doubts as to this possibility in view of the rapid development of African nationalism throughout the continent. Indeed, it was abundantly clear that those who formed the imaginative

---

[1] See *Pointing the Way*, chap. vi.
[2] *Report of the Advisory Commission on the Review of Constitution of Rhodesia and Nyasaland*, Cmnd. 1148 (H.M.S.O., October 1960), para. 2.

design of linking together in a single federal union Southern Rhodesia, Northern Rhodesia and Nyasaland, with all its advantages from the point of view of trade and economic progress, would have hesitated had they known in 1950 with what sudden force the wind of change would blow through Africa and reach almost the force of a hurricane. Nevertheless, we were pledged to do our best; we must not wantonly throw away a system which had already brought such obvious gains to all the territories through the import of capital, the development of industry, the constitution of a common market and the important projects, of which the Kariba dam was an outstanding example, followed by substantial, even startling, increases in the standard of living, not merely of the European but of the African communities.

If Sir Edgar Whitehead was beginning to have doubts, Sir Roy Welensky, the Prime Minister of the Federation, had none. He was not only devoted to its maintenance but had genuine pride in its achievements. He firmly believed that in the course of time a multi-racial system might develop which would afford a fair place to the Africans and enhance their sense of loyalty to this novel but in-spiring concept. Yet in spite of his enthusiasm and devotion—indeed, perhaps because of these qualities—he was inclined to adopt a some-what rigid approach. The Constitution of the Federation had been made by the British Government. In his view, it was inviolable. He enjoyed a substantial majority in the Federal Parliament and regarded any criticisms based on the emotional tide which was sweeping across Africa as a sign of future betrayal. Thus, in spite of his strong and determined character, he did not find it easy to deal with the new problems with which he was now confronted. For the Federal Parliament was in fact a Parliament representing only Europeans, modified to a slight extent by a few African members. Nor, unhappily, had he the power—perhaps it would have been impossible for any man in all the circumstances—to attract the sym-pathy even of more moderate Africans. Yet he was devoted to the cause of multi-racialism and honestly believed that the maintenance of the Federation was essential if this high purpose were to be achieved.

Meanwhile, seeing the steady advance to independence already made, or about to be made, in other British colonies in Africa, the

African leaders in Northern Rhodesia and in Nyasaland naturally looked forward to reaching a similar status within their territories, where the European settler population was relatively small. At the same time, the Government and Assembly of Southern Rhodesia, representing the large body of European settlers, was beginning to wonder whether their interests would not be better served by a break-up of the Federation, allowing Southern Rhodesia to achieve the juridical independence which, under European rule, it had enjoyed in practice since 1923 with few, if important, limitations.

Nevertheless, Whitehead's proposals were something of a shock to me.

> He ... is introducing a new complication into an already difficult position. He demands the 'abrogation' of the reserved powers which U.K. Government has on (*a*) land (*b*) discrimination against Africans. He does not seem to realise the political difficulties here, in Africa, and in connection with the Monckton Commission.[1]

After talks with my leading colleagues, I told him that we were

> ready to consider whether an *equally effective* alternative can be devised—a Court or a Bill of Rights, or a Second Chamber, half African. He agrees that this is reasonable, but so far has only produced the embryo of a scheme. He threatens to go home and dissolve the S. Rhodesian Assembly and go to the General Election on the cry of 'Secession' . . . from the Federation.[1]

This would presumably lead naturally to 'independence' for Southern Rhodesia.

In the same way, although the release of Dr. Hastings Banda and the ending of the state of emergency in Nyasaland had improved the situation, events in the Congo naturally had their reaction. In Southern Rhodesia, signs of trouble arose. On 19 July 1960, three African political leaders were arrested, and protest demonstrations followed. On 24 July, there was rioting in Bulawayo, combined with looting and arson. Before order could be restored, eleven Africans were shot. Welensky professed a fear of further outbreaks in both Rhodesias as well as in Nyasaland.

[1] 26 April 1960.

In this somewhat agitated atmosphere there was one happy event. The conference on constitutional developments in Nyasaland opened in London on 25 July, and full agreement was reached on 4 August. There was to be a Legislative Council with an African majority and at least three out of the ten Executive Council were to be Africans.

> As a relief to this dark picture, the news came of the success of the Nyasaland Conference – a great triumph for Colonial Secretary [Macleod]. If this holds, it will immensely ease the whole Federation problem, on which the Monckton Commission is shortly to report.[1]

Yet my optimism was ill-founded, for of course it was clear that under any new constitution Dr. Banda would carry the support of the whole population and would soon himself seek secession from the Federation. Any Government in Northern Rhodesia which represented African feelings would doubtless make the same demand. Similarly, Whitehead, conscious of the danger of his party being weakened by the residual powers which remained with the United Kingdom Parliament, would become increasingly insistent that the protective shield of the British Government, on which Africans relied, should be relaxed or removed. For he believed that unless this could be done, more extreme pressures would result in the rise of a demand for total independence, with the European community preserved in a similar position to that of South Africa.

In spite of my apprehension, when the Monckton Commission's report was made available to me at the beginning of September, I still felt not without hope that some accommodation might be reached. The report, as might have been expected, was not unanimous; but all but two out of twenty-six members considered that Federation had proved of great economic value to all concerned, while recognising that the weight of African opinion was strongly opposed to its preservation. This was partly due to nationalist intimidation; partly to a failure to understand the importance of the economic advantages; and partly because of a conviction that Federation had been impeding African political advance and, by

[1] 4 August 1960.

virtue of the power of Southern Rhodesia, was perpetuating and even extending racial discrimination.

> The strength of African opposition in the Northern Territories is such that Federation cannot, in our view, be maintained in its present form.[1]

> African distrust has reached an intensity impossible, in our opinion, to dispel without drastic and fundamental changes both in the structure of the association itself and in the racial policies of Southern Rhodesia.[2]

Changes were therefore recommended in the Federal Constitution to give Africans a much higher proportion of the seats (though not a majority) in the Federal Assembly; swift moves to constitutional advance in Northern Rhodesia were proposed, with an African majority in the Legislature, as in the Nyasaland constitution recently agreed; discriminatory legislation in Southern Rhodesia should be amended or repealed; a Bill of Rights should be enacted, with a Council of State in each territory to check that new legislation did not infringe the Bill of Rights. But in the last resort 'we have reached the conclusion that Her Majesty's Government should make a declaration of intention to consider a request from the Government of a Territory to secede from the Federation'.[3] The minority report submitted by two members thought that the majority greatly overestimated the economic benefits of federation, especially for the Africans, and called for the institution, by the forthcoming Review Conference, of a referendum to discover whether the inhabitants (enfranchised or not) wished to continue with the Federation. 'Our own view remains this: that the Federation of Central Africa should be dissolved forthwith.'[4] These members also called for a Constitutional Conference on Northern Rhodesia to precede the Federal Constitutional Review, and the granting of 'self-government' to both Nyasaland and Northern Rhodesia.

Protracted argument now arose with Welensky. He maintained that the report was little more than 'an essay in the appeasement of

[1] Cmnd. 1148, para. 49.   [2] Ibid., para. 74.
[3] Ibid., para. 300.   [4] Ibid., minority report, para. 31.

African nationalists', and he regarded the references to the secession of some of the territories as outside the terms of reference and excluded by the assurances which he had been given. On the contrary, I felt that the report would not necessarily have to be accepted or rejected—it was a contribution to the problem and was presented for the consideration of the Review Commission, to which all were committed.

What was now clear was that the Federation could only be maintained by its own merits and by the necessary concessions. It must depend on persuasion, not on force. Unhappily, a day or two before the publication of the report there was serious rioting at Salisbury and Gwelo, followed by repressive legislation which led to the resignation of the Federal Chief Justice. It was therefore with considerable anxiety that I faced publication, which took place on 11 October. The report was well received by the Press, and although it could not be denied that from a narrow, legalistic point of view, Welensky had a certain case for total rejection, on the ground that the terms of reference had been exceeded, it was clear to me that we were approaching a situation which required a broader and more dynamic approach. Somehow or other we must get the Conference launched. This became my first purpose.

In the Debate on the Address, my speech on this was well received at home; but, as I expected, Welensky insisted that the original assurances which he had received and my recent statements in Parliament could not be reconciled.

> He does *not* think my speech fair and will reply next week, saying that he is willing for our telegrams to be published 'to let the world judge'.[1]

I could not accept this procedure.

> I cannot wait to be 'challenged' by Sir Roy Welensky. I have telegraphed offering to publish the relevant telegrams *forthwith* (i.e. on Monday) but asking him to think again before the first breach is made in the personal and confidential telegrams between Commonwealth Prime Ministers. . . . In every other way (except the evil precedent) I do not think publication will

[1] 2 November 1960.

injure me. After all, *I* did not alter or extend the terms of reference. It was because I did not do so, that the Labour Party refused to be represented on the Commission. I am not responsible for what the Commission actually did or the way in which they interpreted their terms of reference. I could only have suppressed the report—which would have been unthinkable.[1]

In the event, somewhat to my chagrin, in spite of my recognition of the principle of keeping private messages strictly private, Welensky withdrew his demand. He

now does *not* want to publish the letters which passed between us. I am glad, because I think it would be a very bad precedent. But Lord Salisbury has revived the charge of 'bad faith' in a letter to *The Times* (if not directly at least by innuendo) which is rather a bore, as I cannot now answer it by publishing the text.[2]

Fortunately, Welensky, although often somewhat impetuous, had a generous mind. When, at the end of November, he came to London,

we had a good talk after dinner. He was *most* friendly, although rather pessimistic. He in effect withdrew all his accusations (or imputations) of bad faith against me, although he still feels very bitter against Lord Monckton. He cannot answer the question 'Why did *all* the Europeans from Rhodesia sign the report?'[3]

The stage was now set for the opening of the Conference on the future of the Federation, which was to meet at Lancaster House on 5 December 1960. Through the next few weeks the Conference followed the usual erratic course to which I had by now become accustomed. The two Secretaries of State, Sandys for the Commonwealth and Macleod for the Colonies, were in charge, Sandys being responsible for the Federation as a whole as well as for Southern Rhodesia; Macleod's two wards were Northern Rhodesia and Nyasaland.

I opened the Conference with a short formal speech (Press, Radio, T.V., etc.) at Lancaster House this morning at 10.45 a.m. (having arrived at 10 a.m. for 'coffee-housing' where I saw the leading delegates, including Dr. Banda). Afterwards, the Press

[1] 3 November 1960. [2] 7 November 1960.
[3] 26 November 1960.

etc., left, and we settled procedural and other matters. To my surprise, all went off agreeably, and we adjourned till 3 p.m. tomorrow, when the 'General Debate' will start.[1]

I recorded:

> All still goes well with the Conference up to date, but I heard that later this afternoon Dr. Banda stormed out in a rage (and held a 'Press Conference'—which they all do, Europeans and Africans, on the slightest provocation). It is not thought that he will stay away altogether.[2]

Meanwhile, the United Nations Assembly, not content with the Congo situation, which was deteriorating day by day, had begun to take a hand.

> I ... sent a vigorous telegram to President Eisenhower, to protest against the American decision to vote *for* a monstrous Afro-Asian resolution at U.N. on 'Colonialism'. Secretary Herter called it 'a most nauseating document'—and yet, to curry favour, instructed the Americans to vote *for*. President replied very quickly, promising to reconsider this decision.[2]

I arranged for all the delegates to go to Chequers, which I had put at their disposal for the weekend. On Sunday evening I drove there to join the party for dinner, when there were

> a few little speeches, all very sincere and in good taste. Roy Welensky and Banda both spoke well.[3]

It was indeed a strange gathering—apart from the British Ministers and their Private Secretaries there were Sir Roy Welensky, Winston Field (Opposition Leader in the Federal Assembly), Sir Edgar Whitehead (Prime Minister of Southern Rhodesia), Mr. Harper (Leader of the Opposition in Southern Rhodesia), Dr. Banda of Nyasaland, Kenneth Kaunda of Northern Rhodesia and Joshua Nkomo of Southern Rhodesia.

> Whatever may come of it, the 'weekend' has certainly been worth while. Many of the guests had not known each other at all.
> Dr. Banda and Duncan Sandys read the first and second Lessons—which was thought quite symbolic.[3]

[1] 5 December 1960.   [2] 9 December 1960.   [3] 11 December 1960.

However, the Sunday spirit did not last. The next day the three chief African leaders

> without any intimation of their intention . . . 'walked out' of the Federation Conference at the end of this afternoon's meeting—this time, as they said in their respective Press Conferences and T.V. interviews 'for good'.[1]

After talking over the situation with the two Secretaries of State, I decided to put out a statement on behalf of the British Government

> 'postponing' the Territorial Conferences until the situation is clearer. This, of course, Dr. Banda does not mind—for the Nyasaland constitution is agreed and elections take place in the spring. But the N. Rhodesian and S. Rhodesian territorial conferences *are* much desired by the Africans. So this move *may* perhaps bring them to their senses.[1]

On the next day, 13 December,

> I had a luncheon arranged for the Nyasaland Group—three or four Europeans and six or seven Africans—including Dr. Banda. It seemed very unlikely that they would turn up—but they did, and brought along another African who had not been invited! We had a very agreeable party. At the end, I preached them a little sermon, which they seemed to take in good part.[2]

Both Sandys and Macleod worked hard to restore the position for the various conferences. There followed

> A most wearisome afternoon and evening, lasting till 2 a.m., on the rows and squabbles . . . in the Central African Conference.[3]

One of our main troubles was the fierce light of publicity. The participants were constantly exposed to the blandishments

> of the Press and T.V. (B.B.C. as bad as I.T.V.) who offer them free publicity—a 'Press Conference' or a T.V. stunt, at any time of day or night.[3]

[1] 12 December 1960. [2] 13 December 1960.
[3] 14 December 1960.

When I went to bed in the early hours

> nothing was settled as to whether the main Conference would now be boycotted by all the Africans or what would happen to the Territorial Conferences.[1]

On the following day the Cabinet was to have met at 11 a.m., but I put it off to noon.

> Sir Roy Welensky, Sir Edgar Whitehead, and the two Secretaries of State came round at 10 a.m., and we argued at considerable length. Sir E. Whitehead (without telling Welensky or Sandys) has sent a letter to Nkomo (the chief African figure in S. Rhodesia) dismissing him from his delegation. This is because Nkomo walked out of the main conference. But it also prevents him from attending the S. Rhodesian territorial conference—as he would probably like to do. Whitehead is in a very bad . . . mood. He gets blinder and deafer every day. Poor Sir Roy stayed behind and poured out his soul to me quite freely about his difficulties with Whitehead.[2]

In the morning of 17 December, the whole Federation Conference met.

> Sir Roy Welensky 'wound up' the general debate in a speech which, though hard-hitting, was reasonably fair. He sent me a draft last night and I had persuaded him to omit some of his attacks on the African leaders. Duncan Sandys then summed up for H.M.G. He gave an admirably balanced account of the various views expressed. He tried to find the points of agreement, as well as of disagreement. Federation is not really objected to by Africans *as such*; but because it is at present run exclusively by Europeans, it is therefore a political problem. Sandys then . . . proposed that we should (*a*) get on with the Territorial reviews (*b*) leave it, in light of progress made in (*a*) for the Governments to·reconvene [the Federation Conference] at the right time.
>
> I finished, giving full support to Sandys, and after a few desultory remarks (and one dangerous moment) by some delegates, I adjourned the Conference. Sir Roy Welensky came to luncheon alone. We had a good talk. He is a very attractive man—but like so many heavy, fat, solid-looking characters,

strangely mercurial. He cannot refrain from continual attacks on H.M.G.—although we are, in fact, almost his only friends.[1]

We had at least avoided a complete breakdown. The Federal Review Conference was to be reconvened when the Territorial conferences had made sufficient progress. Meanwhile the Southern Rhodesian and Northern Rhodesian conferences met and adjourned before Christmas; the Southern Rhodesian was to reopen in Salisbury in the New Year, the Northern Rhodesian in London.

This somewhat detailed account may give some impression of the alarms and excursions which took place continually over these African conferences. Yet the critical moment was still to come. How could a compromise be agreed between Africans demanding a majority on the Legislative Council both in Northern and Southern Rhodesia, while the Europeans refused even to consider parity in the former and proper African representation in the latter.

Meanwhile the question of any revised constitution for the Federation remained in abeyance. For the next fourteen months the struggle was concentrated on the separate arrangements for the various territories. Nyasaland was excluded, the new constitution having been already agreed. The only developments were Dr. Banda's triumphant success in August 1961, followed by his formal demand for secession from the Federation in 1962. Nyasaland remained quiet, and Dr. Banda began to win the confidence of Europeans, official and unofficial, by the openness and charm of his own character. Attention, therefore, was concentrated upon the two Rhodesias.

So far as Southern Rhodesia was concerned, Sandys reported to me at the end of January that feelings were running high. However, by his skilful management, the Commonwealth Secretary was able to obtain almost complete understanding on general principles at the Conference in Salisbury by 7 February 1961. The Dominion Party, that is the extreme European Party, alone dissented. Further negotiations with members both of the Government and of the various parties took place during the next few months, and final agreement of the details of the new constitution was reached on

[1] 17 December 1960.

1 June and accordingly announced in the British Parliament. The plan involved a complicated system for electing a Legislative Assembly of sixty-five members, fifty representing constituencies and fifteen representing electoral districts. There were to be two voters' rolls with different qualifications and an ingenious method of 'weighting' the votes, which was intended to ensure a definite, although minor, advance in African representation. Much more important, it left the door open for further progress as the Africans advanced in education and wealth. Equally important were the arrangements to protect the future. There was to be a Declaration of Rights, and any law passed after the enactment of the Constitution would be invalid if it infringed the Declaration. The courts would be the sole interpreters. In addition, a Constitutional Council would be created to advise the Legislative Assembly as to whether any proposed legislation was in conformity with the Declaration of Rights. At the same time, the existing native reserves and the native area would be regarded as Tribal Trust Land under an independent Board of Trustees. Finally, the basic clauses of the Constitution could only be amended either by a two-thirds majority in the Assembly together with the agreement of the European, African, Asian and Coloured communities, expressed in separate referenda, or by reference to the British Government.

This Constitution, which stood the test of time until its illegal amendment in recent years, was a great triumph for Sandys. Naturally, since it made only a modest advance in African representation, it was subjected to criticism from European sympathisers of high standing such as Sir Robert Tredgold and Garfield Todd. It was also violently attacked by some of the African groups. Nevertheless it revealed genuine progress.

As part of the understanding, a referendum was to be taken of the existing voters in Southern Rhodesia. This was duly held on 26 July, and resulted—much to our relief—in overwhelming support for the new proposals. Although a certain amount of unrest followed, which induced Whitehead to introduce a ban for two months on all political activity, the new Constitution was passed without difficulty through the British Parliament and received Royal Assent on 23 November 1961. It was only to become effective after the necessary changes in the franchise, which were made in the Southern Rhodesian Assembly on 13 December. Thus, for the time being, at any rate, the constitutional problems of Southern Rhodesia, like those of Nyasaland, were removed from public controversy.

Over Northern Rhodesia, alas, a fierce battle was joined and continued to rage for many months. A few days after the conference, on 9 January 1961, I suggested to Welensky a plan for giving sixteen African seats as against fourteen Europeans. Anything less would fail to satisfy reasonable African demands or meet outside opinion. Moreover, the addition of a number of *ex officio* members would ensure reasonable stability. I set out my views as follows:

> In the last few days, despite a good many other distractions, I have been thinking about the Northern Rhodesia Constitutional Conference which is due to start again on January 30th. I think we both agreed at our last talk that a great deal depends upon the successful outcome of this Conference. If it reaches, however painfully, reasonable agreement, the whole character of our problem in dealing with the future of the Federation is enormously improved.
>
> Of course there is a very wide gap to be bridged between the aims of the Africans as they will put them forward and what we can regard as reasonable. I have had several talks with Iain Macleod, Alport[1] (in Duncan Sandys' absence) and Alec Home, who has had a long experience of these matters; and I am sending you herewith an outline of our proposals. This allows for thirty elected members in the Legislative Council, plus about six nominated official members and two or three nominated non-official members, of whom at least one would be an Asian. There could also be some Chiefs, although this is still subject to local discussion. If they were included, we envisage them as non-voting.
>
> The main point to settle, therefore, is what is to be the precise ratio between the elected Africans and Europeans? As I understand it, although we shall avoid communal rolls, the franchise will, in fact, be such that we can get the numerical balance we want without racial reservation. When you and I had our last talk here, we felt that we should have to give parity or something

[1] C. J. M. Alport, Minister of State at the Commonwealth Office, and later, as Lord Alport, High Commissioner in the Federation of Rhodesia and Nyasaland, 1961–3.

like it. But I assume that the Africans will go to the Conference
with a demand for a big majority and will want nearly all the
thirty seats. It will be quite a job to beat them down from this
position. Actual parity would be fifteen a side. A token African
majority might be sixteen Africans to fourteen Europeans. But
either ratio would give the same result in practice in the sense that
it would leave the Africans, even if supported by the nominated
non-official members, in a minority compared with the Europeans
plus the official members. This, together with the nature of the
Executive Council which we have in mind, should ensure that
effective government remains in responsible hands.

I have a feeling in my bones that if we could give the Africans
a bare majority of elected members (although this might be very
difficult for the Europeans to accept) it would perhaps help to
bring them down from their more exaggerated demands and
enable the Conference to succeed. On the other hand, I do see
that fifteen–fifteen would be more acceptable to the Europeans
and that it would require all your authority and that of your
friends to get even this ratio through.

It was round this question that a long and bitter conflict was to
continue. Welensky replied setting out all the arguments from his
point of view. He denied altogether that he had ever contemplated
an African majority or even parity; either would 'mark the end of
Federation'. It would be the abandonment of the Europeans in
Northern Rhodesia and allow future African nationalist domination.
It would be the end of the partnership concept. This message, well
constructed and fortified by many powerful appeals, clarified the
real issue. Welensky and his colleagues in the Federal Government
were prepared in the last instance to let Nyasaland secede; or, at any
rate, to tolerate there African control. But Northern Rhodesia was,
from its large mineral resources and its great economic potential,
an essential part of the federal concept. Northern Rhodesia, therefore, must be kept under European control just as Southern
Rhodesia was still to be. Only on such a basis could the Federation
continue and flourish. The discussion soon began to become
embittered. I tried to impress upon Welensky that public opinion
would require parity or something like it. Welensky replied that our
plan was a blueprint for racial extremism.

Meanwhile the Northern Rhodesian Conference opened in London at the beginning of February 1961. The United Federal Party of Northern Rhodesia and the Dominion Party refused to take part.

Macleod is having the Northern Rhodesian Conference in London, boycotted by Welensky's Europeans, though not by Sir John Moffat's Liberals.[1]

In a somewhat pessimistic mood, much exaggerated by the gravity of the situation, but perhaps worth recording as a contemporary account of my thoughts, I summed up the position as follows:

Fundamentally, the problem is simple. The Europeans don't really want *any* African advance, but will accept something *less* than parity of representation for Africans in the Legislative Council of Northern Rhodesia (less in Southern). Africans demand 'one man one vote' but would accept some advance in the franchise to give *parity* (or, if possible, African nominal majority–to be discounted by *official* members). There will be *no* agreement. Her Majesty's Government must decide. If we lean too much to the European side:

1. [African] confidence in Her Majesty's Government will be undermined.

2. There will be serious disorder in Northern Rhodesia, perhaps spreading throughout the Federation.

3. [Some Ministers] will resign.

4. Our Government and Party will be split in two.

If, on the other hand, we make a decision which, without satisfying African demands, goes in their general favour

1. Europeans will have no faith left in Her Majesty's Government.

2. Sir Roy Welensky will declare Federation to be 'independent' and will try to take over Government of Northern Rhodesia by force or bluff or both.

3. If the Governor defends his position, there will be civil war– Europeans versus British officials, troops and Africans.

4. [Other Ministers] will resign.

5. Our Government and Party will be split in two.

[1] 4 February 1961.

We must try to find a way out—by the end of next week. I confess I do not see the way as things are.[1]

However, some progress was now made, and I began to feel more hopeful. In my letter to the Queen of 15 February I set out the position which we had now reached:

Since I last wrote to Your Majesty on February 7 I have had to devote nearly all my time to the Northern Rhodesia Constitutional Conference. The main point of difficulty has been the composition of the Legislative Council, although of course there are other important matters on which agreement has yet to be reached on the franchise, the composition of the Executive Council and so on. The Monckton Commission had recommended that in the new Legislative Council there should be either parity or an African majority amongst the elected Members. This idea was quite unacceptable to Sir Roy Welensky and the United Federal Party of Northern Rhodesia. It was the knowledge that Your Majesty's Government were thinking along these lines that caused the United Federal Party to boycott the Conference.

After a considerable number of meetings and as a result of a tremendous amount of work by the Commonwealth Secretary and the Colonial Secretary, we were able to prepare the outlines of an ingenious scheme under which the Legislative Council will have the elected Members divided into three groups:

(a) those elected by the Upper Roll, namely those with the higher franchise qualifications;

(b) those elected by the Lower Roll, namely those with a qualified franchise; and

(c) a number of seats in which the voting will be done by electors from both Rolls and in which a candidate to be successful must obtain at least a certain percentage of the votes of both Rolls. This means that extremists of either side will stand no chance of election.

There will also be a certain devaluation of Lower Roll votes (which will be about three times as numerous as the Upper Roll votes) in order not to weight the scales too heavily in favour of Lower Roll candidates.

[1] 4 February 1961.

After a series of exchanged telegrams and a number of telephone calls Sir Roy Welensky and Sir Edgar Whitehead were persuaded that this was basically a good scheme and the Colonial Secretary has now put this to the Northern Rhodesia Conference. Although it falls far short of the demands of the African parties there is nevertheless some hope that some sort of agreement will be reached.

After approval by the full Cabinet, this solution was propounded in a White Paper[1] as the British Government's own proposal. In putting it forward, I did not conceal from my colleagues the dangers: the Europeans might take matters into their own hands or the Africans promote serious disorder amounting to revolution; for, like all such judgements attempting to hold the scales even, ours was bound to be met by violent repercussions from both sides. For Welensky's more moderate attitude did not last.

We are preparing for the worst event in Rhodesia—that is, open rebellion. We are drawing up the necessary . . . plans, if the worst should occur.[2]

Yet, greatly to his credit in spite of what he regarded as a fatal decision from his point of view, Welensky refrained from going to any extreme. He remained, as he has always remained, a loyal subject of the Queen.

Welensky's motion in the Federal Parliament (at Salisbury) is *not* in such violent terms as I had feared, although it could be used as the basis for violence. It does *not* demand independence, but it calls on Federal Government to resist constitutional changes (i.e. *pro* African) in Northern Rhodesia 'by every means at its disposal'.[3]

Meanwhile I received

a good telegram from Whitehead—who remains calm, rather enjoying Welensky, whom he clearly regards as a bull in a china shop. (It might be John Morley about Harcourt.) We still must wait for Welensky's speech.[4]

---

[1] *Northern Rhodesia: Proposals for Constitutional Change*, Cmnd. 1295 (H.M.S.O., February 1961).
[2] 24 February 1961.   [3] 25 February 1961.   [4] 26 February 1961.

L

Fortunately he was about to arrive for the Commonwealth Prime Ministers' Conference, and there would soon be an opportunity for personal talks, and perhaps at least a measure of agreement.

Welensky came a few days before the beginning of this traumatic meeting, at the end of which, after exhausting every effort to preserve South Africa in the Commonwealth, I had reluctantly to accept the loss of that great and historic country rather than see the total break-up of the Commonwealth itself. It may be imagined, therefore, that these were not days in which negotiation about distribution of seats and voters rolls in a proposed new Constitution for Northern Rhodesia formed a very agreeable digression from the main theme. Fortunately, however, when Welensky came to dine with me alone,

> he was pleasant enough. . . . I asked him to produce some alternative plan, if he didn't like ours, for the Northern Rhodesian constitution. He had, after all, agreed to the *principles* behind our plan. If our proposals did not—as they stood—carry out these principles, or would work out quite differently from expectation, let his officials meet with ours to agree on a *factual* appreciation, and let him put in alternative schemes. He did this on March 14th (a week after his arrival) and proposed three or four schemes. We discussed them on March 18th, and I practically persuaded Sir Roy Welensky to accept that negotiations would go on at Lusaka, although we could not accept any of his plans as they stood. Parts of his scheme were quite helpful, but we could *not* accept a scheme, the sole purpose of which was to ensure a 'built-in' majority for his party. In any election there must be *some* element of uncertainty, however small. (This idea seemed to shock him.)[1]

I sent a full report of our talk both to Sandys and to Macleod, and it was finally arranged that there should be further negotiations in Lusaka. Welensky, while in London, tried to rally the support of prominent Right-wing Conservatives, led by Lord Salisbury in the Lords and by Lord Lambton in the Commons. I heard that he had addressed two hundred or more Conservative M.P.s, making a bitter attack upon the Commonwealth Secretary. Like so many

[1] 24 March 1961.

impulsive orators, he did not understand that 'those who play at single-stick, must bear a rap on the knuckles'. However, what concerned me more than his imputations against my colleagues and myself was my fear that his activities might injure Whitehead's chance of winning the referendum on the Southern Rhodesian constitution, which was all important. Fortunately this did not prove to be the case. Nevertheless, I did fully understand Welensky's difficulties. He must have known that if there was ever to be a *coup d'état* it would be in Southern Rhodesia and lead to independence—legal or illegal—of that State. It would not save the Federation; on the contrary, it would mark its final doom.

I tried very hard to persuade Sir Roy that about the only friend of Federation is Her Majesty's Government. The Socialists and the Liberals here are against it. *All* the Africans in the three territories are against it. Moffat and other Liberals in Africa are against it. Sir Edgar Whitehead is ready at any moment to abandon it to save his own skin. Why does Sir Roy insult Her Majesty's Government; quarrel with me and my Ministers; incite my Party to revolt; stir up Lord Beaverbrook, etc., etc? If Her Majesty's Government falls, they will not be succeeded by Lords Salisbury and Lambton. His *only* friends who have any effective strength will have gone. . . .[1]

The arguments and struggles about amendment or improvement of our proposals continued until the beginning of May, both Africans and Europeans being dissatisfied with the plan put out in the White Paper. The Africans wished for amendments favourable to them; equally, the Europeans thought our proposals went too far. The Governor of Northern Rhodesia, Sir Evelyn Hone, was for standing firm. The two Secretaries of State, Sandys and Macleod, although men of sufficient quality to take a broad view, were naturally subject to diverging pressures. Macleod was moved throughout by a high idealism and a deep sympathy with African aspirations. Sandys, no less conscious of the inevitable march of events, sought with unfailing diligence some means to secure progress without disaster. On 8 May, the two Ministers at last agreed and sent off

[1] 24 March 1961.

some amended proposals to Welensky, which he immediately rejected. Sandys, Macleod and I

> agreed on the next approach to Welensky. At present everything which the Governor of Northern Rhodesia will agree to does not go far enough to satisfy Welensky. Everything which satisfies Welensky, is unacceptable to the Governor of Northern Rhodesia. I am more and more astonished that we ever agreed to so difficult a project as 'Federation'—which involved two Secretaries of State being responsible for the same territories.[1]

In all these troubles, Lord Alport, who, since March 1961, had been High Commissioner in Salisbury, gave the fullest information and served as an admirable link.

In the course of June, the atmosphere both in Africa and in Whitehall was beginning to grow dark indeed. After long meetings on Sunday, 4 June, I began to feel that we were approaching resignations; but an accommodation was again reached.

> I am persuaded that no scheme, even if devised by the Archangel Gabriel, would meet with general support or even acquiescence by all the parties concerned. . . . This means that we shall within a fortnight or so or at the most three weeks have to make our own decision.[2]

Accordingly I noted:

> So our internal situation goes on, for the present. But Colonial Secretary (although a brilliant and most likeable man) is not an easy colleague. He is a Highlander—which means that he is easily worked up into an emotional mood; it also means that he is proud and ambitious. But he has great qualities—a soaring spirit and a real mastery of Parliamentary speaking. . . .
>
> Sandys is a great contrast to Macleod. As cool as a cucumber; methodical; very strong in character; has gradually mastered the art of Parliamentary speaking; tremendously hard-working; not easily shaken from his course.[2]

On 18 June I received some alarming messages from Alport showing that Welensky was again in a difficult mood. He had heard of our determination to remain firm upon our latest proposals, that

---

[1] 8 May 1961.   [2] 4 June 1961.

is an equal division between Africans and Europeans on the Legislative Council. He therefore threatened to come to London to organise opinion in Britain on his behalf in order to make a final stand against the erosion of the European position in Central Africa. All this was reported in detail by our representative, but in spite of the serious character of his messages I felt little doubt that my colleagues would refuse to be intimidated.

> Meeting at Admiralty House (Africa Committee). This meeting includes wise old birds like Lord Chancellor, with his great experience, and some very able and sensitive characters like Foreign Secretary (Home). We all agreed . . . to stand firm on a 'package' deal with Welensky, based on a fair interpretation of the White Paper. The real issue, in Northern Rhodesia, turns on 'Upper Roll Predominance'. Sir Roy Welensky and his friends demand this; Sir John Moffat (Liberal) and the Africans, while in theory demanding 'democracy' or 'one man one vote', will accept equality of strength between Upper and Lower Roll in electing the national seats. In other words, it is fifty–fifty (as the White Paper says) or sixty–forty (as Sir Roy Welensky demands). There are, however, points where we can fairly meet the Federal Party.[1]

On the same afternoon I felt it necessary to put the whole position before the full Cabinet.

> Ministers have been very good about letting a few of us try to manage this tiresome Central African affair. But I felt that we had now reached a point at which they must be properly informed. It was a long Cabinet–for there were many papers and telegrams to be read, and the discussion was prolonged. I was much impressed by the quality and tone.[1]

Alec Home dined with me alone to talk over this among other wearisome problems. I made no attempt to minimise, I even exaggerated, the dangers. Fortunately Sandys had now gone out himself to Rhodesia and was able to bring his influence to bear.

> The culminating scene was at Salisbury–Welensky, waiting to board the London Comet, to bring him here, and urged to do

[1] 19 June 1961.

so by Greenfield's[1] persistent telephone calls. Another aeroplane, smaller but more seductive, was also awaiting his will—he could go to Northern Rhodesia, to rest and fish. Finally, he was called to the telephone box in Salisbury airport and solemnly adjured by Duncan Sandys . . . *not* to come. If he came, all our concessions would be back in the melting pot. 'That sounds like a threat,' said Welensky. 'It is,' said Sandys.[2]

I was now, under Sir John Richardson's order, taking a few days' complete rest; but my treatment was brutally interfered with on the third day of the plan. I was dozing quietly at home in Sussex when the telephone rang.

> Welensky presses for more concessions. I have said *no*. Of the original four points he asked for, we have now given him two—the major two. It is now absolutely vital to make the announcement and stop further argument. At last this seems to have been achieved, and at 7 p.m. tonight I was told that everything was settled, and the Colonial Secretary would make the statement tomorrow.[2]

In spite of the anxieties which this long struggle had created, I was still not without hope that things might turn for the better.

> *If* Sir Roy Welensky *acquiesces*; (and does not either crow or lament); if he makes no foolish threats; if Southern Rhodesians see in the Northern Rhodesian settlement nothing to alarm them but rather a sensible and fair settlement; if they consequently vote *for* Whitehead's new constitution in the Referendum; if confidence returns and with it capital and capital expenditure throughout the Federation; if the British House of Commons is reasonably temperate, the Socialists accusing us of a 'sell-out' to Welensky and *The Times* accusing us of a sell-out to Kaunda and the Africans; if all these things happen (and they may do), then these terrible weeks of strain will have been worth while. It's gone on now (with little intermission) since February. The Ministers are all 'on edge'. . . . Macleod, with many faults, has been persistent, imaginative and ingenious. Sandys has been most loyal to me and absolutely tireless. Nor have we, in making some concessions to Welensky, surrendered any principle.[2]

---

[1] J. M. Greenfield, Federal Minister of Law.   [2] 25 June 1961.

The formal announcement of our amended proposals for the Northern Rhodesian Constitution were made on 26 June. They received, if not the approval, the acquiescence of Parliament and the Press.

> By a miracle, we have achieved a solution of the immediate crisis. Both Sandys and Macleod have agreed and so—under pressure—has Welensky. So the Conservative Party . . . are calm and united on this issue.[1]

Unhappily, towards the end of August, violence in Northern Rhodesia made it necessary for the Governor formally to ban Kaunda's Party which was demanding immediate independence with 'one man one vote'. The Colonial Secretary was equally under pressure from Kaunda to make some new changes more favourable to the Africans. But I rejected any alteration which would merely seem a concession to violence. Nevertheless, Macleod was impressed by the strength of African opinion, supported by moderate Europeans, and on 14 September we agreed to publish a statement that if order were rapidly restored the Government would be willing to hear what anyone had to say before actual legislation on Northern Rhodesia's Constitution. On my return to London from a few days' holiday, I met the two Secretaries of State and we finally agreed what both Sandys and Macleod

> thought a fair statement, declaring that we could receive no representations about our plan while disorder and violence took place, but that if order were restored, we would be willing to hear what anyone had to say before actually implementing our scheme. This is, of course, denounced with equal vigour by Welensky and Kaunda ![2]

There was now a change in the Ministers chiefly concerned involving some reconstruction of the Government. On 9 October 1961, it was announced that Butler would relieve me by undertaking the control of the work of all Ministers concerned with the Common Market negotiations. He would retain his duties as Home Secretary but give up the leadership of the House of Commons and the Chairmanship of the Conservative Organisation. In the two

[1] 8 July 1961.   [2] 15 September 1961.

latter positions he would be succeeded by Iain Macleod, admirably
fitted for both of these important tasks. When I first put this plan
to Macleod, he was naturally torn between his deep and genuine
interest in the colonies, to which he had committed so much of his
genius, and the glittering prospect of the leadership of the House
of Commons which necessarily brought him into the top ranks of
the Administration. He also felt proud to be asked to accept the
Chairmanship of the Party Organisation, which he had long served
in other capacities. After some consideration he accepted my
proposal. This change made it necessary to find a successor; and in
Reggie Maudling I was fortunate in obtaining a Minister of equal
ability. However, had I thought that there would be some relief in
the pressure from the Colonial Office, I was doomed to disappointment—I soon found that Maudling was quite as 'progressive' as
Macleod. Indeed, in some respects he seemed *plus royaliste que le
roi*.

In November 1961 Welensky came on a so-called 'unofficial'
visit during which he addressed both the Institute of Directors and
the back-bench members of the Conservative Party in the House of
Commons. The first was indeed a strange affair, for I was due to
speak after him. His address seemed to me extraordinary,

> a sort of parody of a parody of what Rudyard Kipling was
> supposed to believe. I spoke *after* him. Curiously enough, we
> *both* received tumultuous applause.[1]

All this time, of course, we were both struggling with the critical
affairs in the Congo, in which Rhodesia was so deeply involved.
However, our relations were still friendly, and that night I gave a
men's dinner for him, consisting of many notabilities of many walks
of life, political, industrial, legal and ecclesiastical.

Affairs continued reasonably secure in Southern Rhodesia, in
spite of the need to ban Nkomo's National Democratic Party. But
the pressure on us to make amendments in the proposed Constitution for Northern Rhodesia continued relentlessly. Throughout
January 1962 efforts continued to find some reasonable compromise.
It is rather sad now to reflect how unreal were the differences—we

[1] 13 November 1961.

were attempting to create a constitution which would preserve a reasonable degree of confidence, both among the Europeans and the Africans, and to provide the basis for further progress. The niceties and complexities of the various plans would be tedious to describe in detail and seem almost incomprehensible today. In a style worthy of the Abbé Sieyès one formula followed another in the attempt to reach agreement. Should there be an Asian seat to represent the small Asian community, or was this in itself a negation of the multi-racial principle? How should the different hurdles, which successful candidates had to overcome, be so devised as to ensure that minimum support for any candidate must come from each race or each roll of voters? It was upon such refinements that at one time even the stability of the British Government seemed to depend. Yet they were to prove but transient phantoms in an unreal dream.

On 30 January 1962 there was a meeting of Ministers concerned, who, after a long discussion, accepted an amended plan which they would recommend to the Cabinet.

> Lord Chancellor took charge of drafting the various documents, telegram to Alport—for talks with Welensky, etc. It will be put before Cabinet on Thursday, and (if agreed) Alport will act at once. Sandys will go out next week to Salisbury, and try to talk sensibly to Welensky. We shall have trouble here from Lord Salisbury, etc. But our plan is *fair* and honourable. So at least say Lords Home and Kilmuir, and they ought to know.[1]

Sandys did his best, but also reported that Dr. Banda was now quite adamant about the need for Nyasaland's secession from the Federation. On his return, towards the end of February, there were further prolonged discussions. I received, in all these perplexing troubles, great assistance from Butler, who remained throughout calm and impartial—almost detached. But I was beginning to feel that, although we might eventually succeed in finding an acceptable solution for the Constitution of Northern Rhodesia, 'all this is only a preliminary to the hideous trouble awaiting us, when first Nyasaland and then N. Rhodesia demands "secession" from the Federation'.[2]

[1] 30 January 1962.   [2] 23 February 1962.

L2

The security situation in the North was again threatening, and now we had to face a fresh menace from New York. I sent a memorandum accordingly to the Foreign Secretary on 24 February:

> I see a new horror—the United Nations and Southern Rhodesia. A group of countries, of which Poland is one, is to enquire into liberty in Southern Rhodesia!

On 26 and 27 February the Cabinet discussed the future in the light of what now seemed the inevitable disintegration of the Federation. The meeting on the first day lasted for two and a half hours—from 4.30 to 7 p.m.

> It was an *excellent* discussion in tone and content. We began with a general review of the whole situation in the Central African Federation and the grim future ahead. Nyasaland was already demanding 'secession'. As soon as N. Rhodesia got any kind of right of self-expression, the Legislative Council there would do the same.[1]

On the next day 'the discussion continued . . . everyone being in favour of some early announcement on the N. Rhodesian Constitution'.[2] For in spite of the various threats at home and abroad, including even the possibility of drastic action by the Government of the Federation, my colleagues now agreed that we must reach a final decision and announce it forthwith. I was still uncertain as to the attitude of the Colonial Secretary:

> after some three quarters of an hour's discussion, Colonial Secretary said—very quietly—that he felt the Government and the country were faced with such great problems in every field that—whatever it might be—he would *accept* the decision of his colleagues. This was a dramatic moment—certainly for me.[2]

The necessary telegrams were immediately sent to Welensky and Alport, who had represented us so ably in Salisbury. All through this critical time I received the greatest support both from Butler and Macleod.

[1] 26 February 1962.   [2] 27 February 1962.

But now new schemes began to be floated, especially by White-head, who had arrived in England accompanied by Welensky. Sir Roy called upon me on the evening of 28 February.

> He was calm—rather subdued. He tried to make a grievance about the delay in the telegram, but this was really not a great point. There was no need for him to come about N. Rhodesia anyway. He complained also about H.M.G.'s treatment of him for many years and informed me that he had now decided to go back and have a general election. He would ask for 'a Doctor's Mandate' to 'save the Federation'. I did not press him on how he intended to do this, or whether he contemplated force. He had already complained about the Press picking up the expression 'Fight'—so I assumed that this was a way of withdrawing his threat.[1]

On the same day the Colonial Secretary announced the Government's decision in the House of Commons, where it was well received. In fact, the alterations which had caused so much argument were of minor importance, for we all knew in our hearts that we were about to face a much larger issue.

I had reached a conclusion which the Cabinet, whether consciously or unconsciously, seemed generally to accept. The last two years had shown me that with all the goodwill and with all the loyalty which Conservative Cabinets can generally command, the system by which the Federation as a whole and the area of Southern Rhodesia fell under the Commonwealth Secretary, whereas Nyasa-land and Northern Rhodesia were the province of the Colonial Secretary, made the conduct of affairs almost impossible. Moreover, quite naturally, all the local notabilities took advantage of this now obsolete division of power, and it became impossible to conduct negotiations without accusations of lack of good faith or conflict of policies. I therefore made up my mind that the only way out was to put the whole of this great area under the responsibility of a single Minister. On reflection it became clear to me that I must try to persuade Butler to accept this onerous and distasteful task. He has described himself the spirit in which he accepted this burden and

[1] 28 February 1962.

has given an account of the methods by which he carried them out.[1] Both Secretaries of State loyally accepted this solution, and Sir Norman Brook, with his usual quiet efficiency, arranged for the technical details to be rapidly completed. On 9 March Butler formally accepted my proposal.

The announcement was well received,

> after an initial burst of derision in House of Commons, by the Press and by thinking people. Fortunately Welensky, Whitehead, Banda, and even Kaunda seem pleased.[2]

Indeed, it is possible that if Welensky had not acted so precipitately he would not have called the Federal election which in any case became somewhat farcical. The African and Liberal parties boycotted it because of their objections to Federation, while the other European parties did the same because they considered it unnecessary. Even the extreme Right-wing party, who united to form a Rhodesian Front under Winston Field, determined to concentrate on Southern Rhodesia and to take no part in the Federal election. Welensky's party was therefore virtually unopposed.

Butler has described the processes by which he handled the concluding stages of this long story.[3] After his visit in May 1962, he made it clear to his colleagues that the Nyasaland demand for secession could not be delayed much longer. On the other hand, the Northern and Southern Rhodesian economies were so interdependent that every effort should be made to find some form of association. On 28 June he was able to announce that a team of experts would visit Nyasaland to examine the economic and financial consequences if Nyasaland withdrew.

During the interval I noted with gratitude that Butler

> has certainly succeeded in giving us a quiet six months. But with the Nyasaland Conference in November, and the Northern Rhodesia elections, things will begin to move towards a new crisis.[4]

---

[1] Lord Butler, *The Art of the Possible* (London, 1971), p. 210.
[2] 24 March 1962.   [3] Butler, pp. 210–30.   [4] 9 October 1962.

It was an enormous relief to me to be spared the almost daily flow of telegrams in and out and the continual and divergent pressures which had operated under the old system.

At the end of October elections were held under the new Constitution in Northern Rhodesia, and on 14 December an African coalition government took office.

> The A.N.C. (Nkumbula), after making a sort of deal with U.F.P. (Welensky), seem likely to join in a coalition government of Africans with U.N.I.P. (Kaunda). This may not be a bad thing, and they may begin to learn something of the responsibilities of government instead of merely enjoying the luxury of opposition.[1]

In the middle of November, the Nyasaland Conference met in London and agreed the next stages in an advance to independence. So skilfully did Butler manage this affair that the question of secession was not openly discussed.

> But there will be a row from Welensky when we announce that we are prepared to give Nyasaland the right of secession.[2]

On 10 December three Federal Ministers, Barrow, Caldicott and Greenfield, came to London at Welensky's request

> to bring pressure on us about Nyasaland and about N. and S. Rhodesia. On the first, we can give them no satisfaction. The Cabinet has decided that if Nyasaland wants to leave the Federation (as Dr. Banda and his party certainly desire) she must be allowed to do so. This announcement will be made on December 17th, *after* the elections in N. Rhodesia and in S. Rhodesia have been concluded. As for the future of the two Rhodesias, we can assure them that we mean to work for some association. But we cannot pledge ourselves (as Welensky wants us to do) to any precise form. It's all very sad. The Federation *was* a good idea. But it has been wrecked by two things. (*a*) The 'wind of change' which has swept through Africa with unexpected force (unexpected, at least, ten years ago). (*b*) The policies first of Huggins —now Lord Malvern—and secondly of Welensky, which have made the Federation in the mind of Africans a symbol of white domination. Poor Sir Edgar Whitehead has been the victim.[3]

[1] 12 December 1962.   [2] 26 November 1962.   [3] 10 December 1962.

As I feared, the elections in Southern Rhodesia led to a victory for the Rhodesian Front led by Winston Field—the Central African Party, the most liberal of the European groups, was completely routed. We had, therefore, reached the situation which I had tried so long to avoid, but which was by now inevitable. The Federation was doomed.

> The election in S. Rhodesia (ejecting Sir Edgar Whitehead and substituting Winston Field) is, on the face of it, a retrogade and reactionary vote. But it may really simplify the situation for Butler since none of the three Provincial Governments is now in favour of the Federation. But, of course, the real danger is increased. We may see S. Rhodesia forced to join S. Africa. So, multi-racialism will have failed. The white man will be driven to extremism everywhere in Africa, in order to fight African extremism.[1]

I was deeply grieved by Whitehead's defeat, for he had represented, to the best of his power, a tradition of moderation and even of liberalism, and wrote to him on 16 January 1963.

> I did not send you a message after the Southern Rhodesian election because it is, as you will understand, contrary to the traditional practice between us all, but you were very much in my thoughts, and I would like to take the opportunity of Rab's visit to Rhodesia to send you this little personal line.
>
> The ups and downs of politics are very strange and sometimes very wounding. You at any rate can take to your comfort that the work you have done has been quite outstanding; nor do I think it will have been in vain. You have put into the minds of many people thoughts and aspirations which you alone were able to promote. If for the moment you have failed electorally, you can look back upon the great services you have rendered from the moment that you entered into the world of government. I do not believe that this service is at an end and I hope very much that in the future you will be able to play a valuable and constructive part. At any rate I recall with pleasure the moderation and understanding which you have always brought to discussions with us here. I hope you feel the same.

[1] 26 December 1962.

On 19 December Butler announced the British Government's agreement that Nyasaland should secede from the Federation. This naturally led to a furious attack in the Federation Parliament for our treacherous conduct and for abandoning the agreements made at the outset and during the existence of the Federation. These accusations were unjustified, but fully understandable. For it was clear that the end was approaching.

Butler reported to me from Rhodesia on 22 January 1963 that he hoped to demonstrate that the demand for dissolution of the Federation came not from the British Government but from each of the three territories. At the same time, he felt that the atmosphere in Nyasaland was much improved, and on 1 February internal self-government was granted to that territory with Dr. Banda as Prime Minister, and its future as an independent country was thus assured. In effect, all had now abandoned the Federation except the few Federation Ministers, whose devotion to what they felt to be their duty remained unshaken.

In the spring, the most important event was the arrival in London of Winston Field. He was here from 21 to 29 March. He came to lunch with me and we had some private talk.

He seems a sensible man, tough but not conceited. His other Minister, Dupont (Minister for Justice) is an English solicitor—clever but not impressive. . . . Field says that the Federation can't go on—but I fancy that he is trying to avoid saying this openly himself and is trying to make us (Her Majesty's Government) say it for him. He does not think that Welensky will try a *coup d'état*. He feels that Welensky has lost support now even of the Europeans. I warned Field that Welensky might try a referendum of his own (Federal) constituents, who are—in effect —the constituents of the Southern Rhodesia Parliament. If the question were loaded, he might win a great majority and claim a success for himself and a defeat for Field. The Southern Rhodesian Prime Minister seemed sceptical about this, though I thought he was somewhat alarmed. Of course, as Winston Field frankly said to me after luncheon, the Southern Rhodesians want 'independence'. . . . But he admitted that the question of election to the Commonwealth was rather tricky. However, if the Commonwealth and Her Majesty's Government would not have them, they had good contacts with South Africa and would work with them in defence, economic development, etc. Northern Rhodesia would not then be vital to her.[1]

I made it clear that the independence of Southern Rhodesia, like that of the other two territories, could not be finally settled until the complicated steps had been taken for the dissolution of the Federation and the substitution of whatever economic and other arrangements were agreed to be in the general interest. This must take a considerable time. There must also be proper safeguards for the African community. A few days later,

> Mr. Kaunda and Mr. Nkumbula to luncheon – African leaders of the two parties which form a coalition Government in Northern Rhodesia. We had Butler, Lord Chancellor, Macleod and Keith Joseph to meet them. A very sticky luncheon. After luncheon poor Rab had his meeting with them. They demanded immediate acceptance of 'secession'. When he demurred to this, they walked out. This news reached me late in the evening.[2]

I did not pay great attention to this episode. Kaunda was an able man and knew that he had only to wait.

After full discussion in the Cabinet on 28 March, I recorded my impressions:

> The Rhodesian problem was the chief item. Things are moving to a climax. . . . The Northern Rhodesian situation is fairly simple. They want the 'right to secede' to be granted. On that basis, they are willing to come to a conference to discuss the links between the territories, chiefly economic, which should follow the dissolution of the Federation. They recognise that the process of disentanglement will take perhaps a year. After that, they expect to move through the processes first of full internal self-government and finally of Independence (like Ghana, Nigeria, etc.).
>
> The Southern Rhodesian position is more complex. They have had independence – in effect – for forty years, except for Defence and Foreign Policy. It has been a convention respected by the British Government that we do not interfere with their domestic affairs. As a result, they have had *no* African representation in

[1] 22 March 1963.　　　　[2] 25 March 1963.

their Parliament up till a year ago, when Whitehead—under great pressure from Sandys—agreed to fifteen Africans, elected on a very restricted franchise. Of course, they have relied for defence on Welensky's federal forces, as well as their own police. Ultimately, the Federal territorial divisions (which consist of European farmers) are there for S. Rhodesia's defence, internal and external. Sir Edgar Whitehead (who was defeated at the last election) was an educated and liberal-minded man. Mr. Winston Field is a plantation owner . . . not without a certain charm. . . . The Federal Government, with Welensky the dominating figure, wants the present system to go on, but realises (I think) that the game is up. So Welensky and Field are playing a curious game. Welensky's friend, Whitehead, has lost out to Field. Field's friends are reactionaries and determined to 'keep the black man in order'. Whitehead was pledged to remove discrimination, even —vital test—in land. He had begun the process. Field and his party are reversing all this. For the moment there is a strange kind of alliance between Field and Kaunda (and even Banda). They want to end Federation. But there is, now that the die is cast, likely to be an alliance between Welensky and Field. Southern Rhodesia demands (with a certain show of reason) that if the Federation is to break up, S. Rhodesia also must be independent, and Welensky will support this claim. Actually, H.M.G. have no *physical* power to take any part in the affair. But we have a *legal* position and some *moral* influence. S. Rhodesia is a Government of several million Africans by 200,000 whites, among whom the planter interest predominates. Are we to give this country, with this constitution and now under Field . . . formal independence (and, presumably, financial help)? If we do, we shall be blamed by all progressive and even moderate opinion. If we do not, we shall do *no* benefit to the Africans and we shall force S.R. into the hands of S. Africa. This will mean a bloc of White power from the Cape to the Zambesi. Is this a good thing or not? These are the questions that pose themselves now.[1]

During this period, these leading figures, being now in London, addressed the back-bench members of the Conservative Party at well-attended meetings. I naturally received reports of what happened. On 21 March Winston Field was the speaker. He said

[1] 28 March 1963.

that he had always suspected Federation would prove unworkable, but had nevertheless tried to make it work. Now that it was obviously going to be abandoned by the United Kingdom, Southern Rhodesia would seek methods of co-operation with the other territories, but would insist on independence. Kaunda addressed the 26 March meeting, stressing the North's insistence on secession. On 28 March Welensky spoke. He said he was blamed by the British for the series of occurrences which were in fact due to territorial not federal action; but he was made the scapegoat for everything. There would be great economic problems ahead, 'the future is very bleak', and it would be the British Government that would have to pick up the pieces. If the United Kingdom Government broke up the Federation, he would throw his whole weight behind Field's demand for independence.

On 29 March, Butler, on behalf of the Government, made a press statement and broadcast. In this he declared our aim of preserving some association between the territories. At the same time he announced our conclusion that no territory could be kept in the Federation against its will. A conference would be necessary, preferably in Africa, to work out the new relationship. He has himself described the painful meeting in which he informed Welensky and his Ministers of this decision.[1]

There now began a new and dangerous conflict. Winston Field, in a formal letter to me, wished to make Southern Rhodesia's independence a condition for attending the dissolution conference. I was conscious of a division of opinion throughout the Party on this grave issue. There were some who felt that it was unrealistic to refuse an independence which we could not in fact prevent. There were others who were deeply concerned about the future of the African population and felt that even if we were powerless we ought not in honour to grant independence without effective safeguards for African progress. Discussions in the Cabinet continued on this question, one more of conscience than of reality. Alport had reported that Field and his colleagues seemed to think that they could maintain Commonwealth preferences, British investment and all other advantages of the British connection even if they moved to

[1] Butler, p. 225.

independence on their own. I made it quite clear that they must be told that they could not 'have their cake and eat it'. If they became rebels, they would be treated as rebels. Eventually, after much thought, we sent off a reply to Winston Field in firm but courteous terms. On 20 April, after much delay, the Southern Rhodesian Government sent their formal reply.[1]

> We have had a very long, argumentative, and unyielding reply to our letter about 'independence'. They want it without negotiation and without conditions. If we do not grant it, they will take it. All the same, the tone of this letter is better and the fact that they took ten days to concoct it is perhaps a good sign. Field is very inexperienced, and may learn some of the difficulties he too has to face. Meanwhile Whitehead has come out with a very good statement—liberal, moderate and against rash action.[2]

The situation at this time may best be summarised by my letter to the Queen of 15 April:

> The other problem which has occupied Your Majesty's servants recently has been the question of the winding up of the Federation of Central Africa, and the claim of Southern Rhodesia to immediate independence. The Cabinet has met several times [and there have been] many meetings of the Ministers chiefly concerned. Your Majesty may have seen the interchange of letters which were published as a White Paper on Thursday last.[3] I think our reply is sound and not in any way provocative. From the latest telegrams I have hopes that we can keep the correspondence going and lead eventually to some kind of conference. Whether at a conference the Southern Rhodesian Government will be willing to make any concessions to African opinion I cannot tell. Certainly it would not need very much for me to be able to carry an Independence Bill through the House of Commons with the assent of the great majority of the Conservative Party. But I cannot say, frankly, that it will be easy to carry independence unless some concession is made by Mr. Field and his colleagues. The trouble is that both the Prime Minister and the new Ministers are extremely inexperienced. Although I

---

[1] *Correspondence between Her Majesty's Government and the Government of Southern Rhodesia April–June 1963*, Cmnd. 2073 (H.M.S.O., June 1963).
[2] 23 April 1963.   [3] Cmnd. 2000.

formed quite a good opinion of Mr. Field, I thought he showed little understanding of the development of world opinion or even of the demands of Africans in the Rhodesias. What we have got to do is to get Southern Rhodesia and Northern Rhodesia, together with Nyasaland, to discuss seriously the economic links which are essential for the well-being of them all. But just as it has proved impossible to combine two countries with an African Government and one country with a purely European Government in a political union, so I fear it may be difficult to get them to work together in an economic union, unless some concessions are made on all sides. However, the only course to pursue is one of patience and try to gain a little ground slowly but surely.

Naturally the African leaders, both individually and through the United Nations, began to bring pressure upon us to stand firm. Fortunately Menzies, for whose help I had appealed, did his best to bring a moderating influence to bear. On 9 May Field somewhat changed his position. He now no longer demanded immediate independence but only from the date of the formal dissolution of the Federation. But he felt there should be preliminary discussions without delay and suggested that talks should begin on 27 May. Butler, with the full support of the Government, agreed to this. He pointed out that, if it proved impossible to complete the talks before the dissolution conference, they could be resumed at the earliest convenient date. Field accepted the invitation, and the talks began accordingly. My colleagues were all this time much distressed at the dilemma which we must face. But it was clear to me that unless African interests could be guaranteed in a formal and binding form not only the Asian and African members of the Commonwealth would be deeply disturbed, even to the point of leaving the Commonwealth, but the old Commonwealth countries—Canada, Australia and New Zealand—would be almost equally critical. Parliament was duly informed of the two sets of talks which it was proposed to hold on Southern Rhodesian independence and on the dissolution of the Federation.

I left the negotiations entirely in Butler's hands.

'Rab' gave a report of his first talks with Winston Field, P.M. of S. Rhodesia. It is clear that he is beginning to find out something of the facts of life. The great thing is to give him nothing, at this stage, but to press Field to tell us what *he* is prepared to do to 'liberalise' his régime.

I had Field to luncheon, and to meet him Lords Cromer and Chandos, as well as Australian High Commissioner. Field is a nice man, but seems rather out of his depth.[1]

In the event, Field, after returning to Salisbury, informed us on 13 June that, although the talks had failed to produce a basis for independence, Southern Rhodesia was prepared to attend the dissolution conference. This was duly arranged to take place at the Victoria Falls on 28 June 1963.

Butler has himself described the result of this conference, which he conducted with great resourcefulness. The officials worked hard, and by 2 July complete agreement was reached; the Federation was to be brought to an end on the last day of 1963, and all the complicated details had been satisfactorily worked out in order to preserve at least some of the practical advantages of the old union. I sent him accordingly a telegram on 4 July in the following terms:

> The Cabinet at their meeting this morning asked me to send you their warmest congratulations on the way in which you have handled the Victoria Falls Conference. It was not a happy occasion—the ending of a noble experiment—and it might well have ended in a mood of bitterness and determination not to co-operate. But your skill, experience and resourcefulness have won the day. You have instilled into the Governments taking part in the Conference a sense of dignity and a sense of responsibility. If in the future the countries of Central Africa grow closer together this will be due to your conduct and leadership.

In effect, this was the end of my connection with these great affairs. The autumn was chiefly taken up with a number of resolutions in the Security Council and the Assembly of the United Nations, the first of which we vetoed and in the second of which we refused to take part. The protests against the policies which the British Government had followed since the War towards British colonies and dependencies could carry little weight with impartial men. In most cases they were designed for internal rather than external use.

[1] 28 May 1963.

The rest of the sad story as regards Southern Rhodesia is well known. I still ask myself with regret whether by some means or other concessions to African opinion could have been obtained which would have justified a British Government in granting full independence to Southern Rhodesia. But at the time when I left the direction of affairs this issue was still in suspense, for it had been agreed that no final steps should be taken during the lifetime of the Federation—that is until January 1964. It is nevertheless melancholy to reflect upon the opportunities that were missed, and the mischief which followed. Yet, if it is easy to see the errors which were made by the European leaders in Africa, it is equally proper to admit the faults of which we at home were no doubt guilty. What remains in my memory is the immense amount of time and trouble taken over the future of the African territories amidst so many other baffling problems, internal and external, with which we, like every other Government, had to contend. If, as mortals, we could not command success, we might almost claim to have deserved it.

CHAPTER XI

The French Veto

IN the autumn of 1962 we were approaching the last stages of the negotiations for Britain's entry into the Common Market. Although the French representatives had done their best to procrastinate, yet their tactics had been largely outflanked by the skill and determination of Heath and his colleagues, ministerial and official, as well as by the obvious desire of the other five countries to make every practicable concession in order to ease the British difficulties. The talks, which had been postponed for the holidays, were resumed on 8 October; many of the hurdles had been steadily overcome, and it must now have been clear to de Gaulle that within a few months he would have to make a definite decision. Moreover, with the help of my colleagues and the loyalty of the Conservative Party, I had successfully overcome the obstacles which he thought likely to prove fatal. The Commonwealth countries, relying on certain concessions which seemed likely to be made, had been persuaded at the September Conference to accept the view that Britain's entry into the Common Market would be likely to strengthen her own economic power and consequently the authority of the Commonwealth as a whole. The opposition of the 'anti-Marketeers', as they would now be called, had proved a complete, almost ludicrous, failure. In a series of by-elections at the end of November the swing against the Government, although marked, was ascribed to other factors. Only in South Dorset was a seat lost on account of the European issue. Here the retiring member, Lord Hinchingbrooke (who had succeeded to the earldom of Sandwich, an honour which he was subsequently to discard), championed an independent Conservative candidate who, by obtaining some five thousand votes on an anti-Common Market basis, brought about the defeat of Angus Maude—the official Conservative—and the loss of a constituency which had long been held in the Tory interest. Nevertheless, this event, together with the swing against us in other seats and the loss of one in Scotland, led to some failure of nerve in some of our less valiant followers.

> The Press on Saturday and today have been quite hysterical and prophesy a revolt against me in the Parliamentary Party. The only thing to do is to remain calm and go on with our work.[1]

I had no doubt at all that if we could succeed in Brussels we could carry Parliament without difficulty. I knew, of course, that de Gaulle would seek some reason, or, rather, excuse, if he was to exercise the right of veto which each of the Six enjoyed against the extension of their number. As I feared, he was to find it in a familiar grievance. Earlier in the year, from the best of motives but using the worst of all possible methods, the heavy boots of the American Secretary for Defence had trodden firmly and repeatedly upon the sensitive French toes. If there were two subjects which were to de Gaulle like the traditional red rag to a bull, these were NATO and the Anglo-American nuclear power. NATO my old friend regarded as a kind of survival of A.F.H.Q. in North Africa and SHAEF in Western Europe. The physical presence of NATO headquarters in Paris was a source of continual distress, almost of humiliation. France, although ready to rely upon American and British divisions in the defence of Europe's frontiers, with ultimate dependence upon nuclear power, wanted to forget these unpleasant facts. At any rate, the General preferred to ignore them. At a NATO Ministerial Council held in Athens at the beginning of May, Robert McNamara, Defence Secretary, delivered a speech which although nominally 'secret' soon began to 'leak'. Its main burden was repeated openly at a meeting in Michigan at the beginning of June. He could hardly have done anything more calculated to upset both his French and his British allies. He put forward with equal vigour and clumsiness a powerful condemnation of all national nuclear forces, except, of course, those of the United States. All others he attacked on the dual, if somewhat contradictory, grounds that they were 'dangerous' and 'lacking in credibility'.

[1] 25 November 1962.

This sweeping condemnation of British and French policy was not alleviated by being combined with a demand that all the NATO Powers should spend large sums upon the purchase of expensive American rockets, the control of which would remain in American hands.

McNamara's foolish speech about nuclear arms has enraged the French and put us in a difficulty . . . I shall have a chance to tell Rusk on Sunday what terrible damage the Americans are doing in every field in Europe. In NATO, all the allies are angry with the American proposal that we should buy rockets to the tune of umpteen million dollars, the warheads to be under American control. This is not a European rocket. It's a racket of the American industry. So far as the Common Market is concerned, the Americans are (with the best intentions) doing our cause great harm. The more they tell the Germans, French, etc., that they (U.S.A.) want Britain to be in, the more they incline these countries to keep us out. Finally, at a time when the dollar is weak and may, in due course, drag down the pound and bring all Western Capitalism into confusion, they go round the European capitals explaining their weakness and asking for help. So gold price (and gold shares) go up. It's rather sad, because the Americans (who are naïve and inexperienced) are up against centuries of diplomatic skill and finesse.[1]

If the French were indignant, British defence authorities and our leading industrialists were equally concerned about the forceful salesmanship which induced most of the NATO Powers to buy a short-range Army surface-to-surface missile called Sergeant on the favourable terms more commonly arranged for vacuum-cleaners or washing-machines. This, in effect, brought to an end a better weapon known as Blue Water which English Electric had independently developed. The sales pressure was irresistible, and led to a situation which forced us by the middle of August to cancel our own weapon at considerable loss. No wonder, to British eyes, the concept of interdependence with the United States seemed to be becoming a somewhat one-sided traffic. The performance of Blue Water was admittedly higher; but the pressure exerted by American

[1] 19 June 1962.

military diplomacy was, in this contest at any rate, more effective. So Sergeant was imposed, though not preferred. In spite of my protests to the President, little could be done. Moreover, there were important considerations of policy to be borne in mind as to the role of weapons of this kind. When they were first conceived, they were regarded as a kind of superior artillery; now, with a range of five to six hundred miles, carrying a terrifying load of explosive power, the so-called 'tactical' nuclear weapon was hardly distinguishable from the 'strategic'. The President, on whom I pressed this view, substantially agreed; but he claimed that his Government was 'actively engaged in re-educating NATO, which was one of the purposes of McNamara's speech'. But unhappily, while most of the boys in the NATO school contented themselves with a mild protest against the clumsiness of the master, the French, conscious of their unique military history and traditional leadership in the life of Europe, were almost speechless with indignation.

But, regardless of French susceptibilities, the Americans continued their campaign for what was called 'the principle of non-dissemination of nuclear weapons'. Accordingly, I sent a message on 26 September 1962 to the Foreign Secretary, who was in New York:

> I am sure that we must keep firmly before us that our first priority now should be the Common Market negotiations. Consequently I think that we should keep out of this nuclear weapons question and let the Americans paddle their own canoe. As the United States Administration seems so anxious that our negotiations should succeed, I would think that you could explain this position in a frank and friendly way to Rusk.

A few days later, Heath, who was in Rome, reported that Fanfani and his colleagues were very anxious to support Britain's accession to the Six, but had warned him that Adenauer, now an easy prey to suggestions, however fantastic, had been persuaded that it was our purpose to disrupt the E.E.C. from within once we had become a member of that body.

A few days later, on 10 October, de Gaulle dissolved the French Assembly following the defeat of the Government which had supported his request for a referendum to amend the constitution in order to allow the President of the Republic to be elected by universal suffrage. There were, of course, long memories in France, and the use of the referendum for this purpose had some unhappy precedents.

> The French political situation is obscure. De Gaulle has challenged the political parties and the Parliament on a majestic scale. My guess is that he will win the referendum (but perhaps with something less than his usual majority). When the Parliamentary elections come, he may fail to get a majority to support a Government. Then he may be forced to take a further step, to abolish the Parliament or to alter the Constitution again. But this will reveal in its nakedness a 'dictatorship' which he has always been at pains to obscure. The sixty-four thousand dollar question is this—will all this commotion make him *more* difficult to deal with over Europe or *less*? I fear the former.[1]

In fact, the referendum was held with splendid disregard for the Parliament's vote on 28 October and, although there were disputed interpretations of what the results implied, the change in the constitution was duly made.

Nevertheless, Heath reported from Brussels that he was by no means depressed and thought that the French could not openly oppose our entry, although they would still employ delaying tactics.

In the middle of November, President Kennedy, conscious of the many unsolved problems which were piling up in many fields, suggested a meeting before Christmas.

> Another telegram from President K., suggesting a meeting on 19 and 20 December. This is good; but I want to see *de Gaulle* first, in accordance with my plan discussed a day or two ago with Alec Home. If I do not at least propose this, de Gaulle will be very suspicious.[2]

Meanwhile, contrary to many informed predictions, the French general election held at the end of November resulted in sweeping gains for the Gaullistes.

[1] 10 October 1962.   [2] 17 November 1962.

The de Gaulle and Kennedy meetings are now arranged for the second half of December. I fear that de Gaulle will be grander and more patronising than ever, since his sweeping victory at the polls. He will commiserate with me, in a most infuriating way, in my recent failures. But he will be rigid both as regards Common Market and as regards a possible *détente* with Russia.[1]

De Gaulle was not slow to show the result of his strengthened position.

Ted Heath came about 6.30, and we had a good talk before and after dinner. The *French* are opposing us by every means. . . . For some reason, they *terrify* the [Five]—by their intellectual superiority and spiritual arrogance. . . . *But* they are afraid of being pilloried as the destroyers of European unity.[2]

A day or two later I reflected:

After his victory both in the referendum and the Parliamentary election, de Gaulle's position is now very strong. He is a sort of mixture of Louis XIV and Napoleon—certainly in his own estimation. This means that he will be more mystical and remote, pontificating in general terms. At the same time, to protect the material interests (and short-term interests) of French agriculture and commerce, he will bargain as hard and as selfishly as any old French housewife in the market. The Brussels negotiations are dragging—but I suppose the crunch must come in February or March, at the latest.[3]

All this time the Government was coming under heavy criticism on a number of internal issues, as always happens after a long spell in office. I did not take too seriously the predictions of the professional psephologists. If I could succeed in Europe, I felt sure I could carry both Parliament and the people. On 6 December

the Italian Ambassador called at 5. I gave him a letter to Fanfani. The Italians want me to arrange a visit to Rome (in view of my visit to de Gaulle and meeting with Kennedy). I think the best thing is to arrange a date (say, in March) and announce it now.[4]

[1] 27 November 1962.   [2] 1 December 1962.
[3] 5 December 1962.   [4] 6 December 1962.

As a kind of prologue to the two vital meetings, a sudden storm burst over a speech, no doubt of a meditative and philosophical kind, which had been delivered by Dean Acheson, the former American Secretary of State. Acheson certainly did not mean to be offensive and perhaps hardly realised what effect in such a delicate situation would be caused by his words. He declared that in his view Britain's role 'was played out'. Put in some historic context, in reference to the relative growth in power and strength of Russia and America, no doubt his argument could have been made discreetly and without offence. I did not regard the violent reaction at home as a good sign

(for we ought to be strong enough to laugh off this kind of thing). Public opinion (if you trust the Press) is upset. . . . Lord Chandos, Sir Louis Spears and others from the Institute of Directors have written me a formal letter of protest, which they have put on B.B.C. news, T.V., and published in the Press last night and this morning. So I thought it best to use this as a peg for a reply. This I compiled early this morning, and after getting Sir Harold Caccia's approval on behalf of Foreign Secretary, I had it put out. I think it will please the Conservative Party and the 'patriotic' elements in the country. But it sticks firmly to the principle which I have been preaching all these post-war years—that is, the doctrine of 'interdependence'.[1]

My letter of 7 December to Lord Chandos ran as follows:

I have just received the letter which you and two of your colleagues have sent me on behalf of the Institute of Directors in connection with a lecture delivered at West Point by Mr. Dean Acheson, who was formerly American Secretary of State.

I have only seen the various Press reports of this speech. If those are accurate, in so far as he appeared to denigrate the resolution and will of Britain and the British people, Mr. Acheson has fallen into an error which has been made by quite a lot of people in the course of the last four hundred years, including Philip of Spain, Louis XIV, Napoleon, the Kaiser and Hitler. He also seems wholly to misunderstand the role of the Commonwealth in world affairs.

[1] 7 December 1962.

In so far as he referred to Britain's attempt to play a separate power role as about to be played out, this would be acceptable if he had extended this concept to the United States and to every other nation of the Free World. This is the doctrine of inter-dependence, which must be applied in the world today, if Peace and Prosperity are to be assured.

I do not know whether Mr. Acheson would accept the logical sequence of his own argument. I am sure it is fully recognised by the U.S. administration and by the American people.

This curious prelude being safely over, it became possible to concentrate upon our real difficulties – they were formidable enough.

Two meetings had now been arranged, the first with General de Gaulle at Rambouillet on 15 and 16 December and the second with Kennedy at Nassau from 18 to 21 December. Both would be of vital importance; and over both now hung dark and disturbing clouds. My purpose in going to France was to make a final appeal to de Gaulle to withdraw his opposition to Britain's entry into the Common Market. I could claim that my colleagues and I had overcome the obstacles presented by the Commonwealth and with the Conservative Party, on which de Gaulle had previously laid such stress. There could be little doubt that an agreement, if reached, would be ratified by the British Parliament. The Brussels negotiations showed that, on the economic level, arrangements could readily be made for a transition period to meet the needs of British agriculture and for longer arrangements to take care of the special interests of the Commonwealth countries. On the political issue, on which he relied so much, it was surely right that with the growing strength of the Russians on the one side and the Americans on the other, and in view of some alarming tendencies in American policy, Europe should grow closer together to defend its widest interests – in defence, in foreign policy and in economic development. Nor could he deny that the French people as a whole would welcome British entry. The European movement, following the Second War, had been founded by leading figures in Britain and France. It had been the means of reconciliation with Germany. In the fruitful co-operation of all the countries of Western Europe, an enlarged community could play a decisive role.

I still hoped that it might be possible to deploy arguments of sufficient strength to convince the General that he should yield at this decisive moment in European history. Yet I knew well that apart from his isolationist instincts, he viewed recent developments of American policy with displeasure and even with anger. McNamara's fervent denunciation of the dangers of the 'dissemination of nuclear power' was an ill-disguised attack upon the determination both of Britain and of France to maintain, at any rate in the foreseeable future, their separate, independent nuclear forces. While I could argue the benefits of broad strategic and even tactical planning through NATO, the final control of their individual forces must depend upon each separate government. I was therefore disturbed when I saw that at the NATO Council on 14 December McNamara had made a further move. No doubt with the purpose of isolating Britain and France he proposed that 'in recognition of the views of some other member states' America would be prepared to consider 'possible arrangements for a multilateral nuclear force in which NATO allies would share in the actual operation, employment, and support'. He went on to say that such a missile force should be 'under NATO control'. What precisely this phrase meant or how such a control was to be exercised was left undefined. I knew of course that General de Gaulle would regard this speech, even if innocently made (as perhaps it was), as further evidence of a plot to hinder the development of the French nuclear force on which his heart was set and on which the French Government had already incurred expenditure on a very large scale.

My meeting with President Kennedy, although it was intended to cover the whole field of world politics, must in fact be dominated by a new and embarrassing development, vitally affecting the future of the British nuclear deterrent. In order to make clear the gravity of this question, it is necessary briefly to recapitulate the decisions taken in March 1960. Following the earlier agreements made with President Eisenhower, our scientists had been able to accelerate the development of a nuclear warhead. In return, they had been able to give substantial assistance to their American colleagues. But, if there was no difficulty about making the bomb or warhead, for the means of delivery we still relied on the bombers and on free-falling bombs.

Yet greater sophistication in the art of defence had made it necessary to develop a method of firing the bombs from the aircraft. Thus, by a device known as Blue Steel, it had been possible to reach two hundred (and perhaps by perfecting such a mechanism three or four hundred) miles for the bomb beyond the position of the aeroplane. At the same time, we had started to develop, and spent substantial sums on, a ground-based rocket known as Blue Streak. Although there were the usual difficulties and setbacks in its development, undoubtedly this instrument of warfare could have been successfully perfected. Yet, partly because of the objection then felt by the Chiefs of Staff to installing these fixed-site rockets near the large centres of population in so small an island, and partly because of the high degree of efficiency which the Air Force had reached, the Government had decided to rely upon a mobile weapon. Accordingly, in March 1960, I had reached an agreement with President Eisenhower that he would supply us with a new device to be launched from the bombers on which the Americans had made great progress. It had been named Skybolt. This differed from Blue Steel and other similar techniques since, although fired from an aeroplane, it was a rocket going up into the atmosphere in the same way as a ground missile. It therefore seemed to us to combine all the advantages for our needs. It could be operated from the airfields by the Air Force; it involved no great and well-publicised ground bases; it preserved the essential mobility on which our advisers were so insistent. The arrangement about Skybolt was not merely a verbal understanding but a formal and binding agreement. At the same time and partly in return for our making bases on the west coast of Scotland available for the American Polaris submarine, which fired nuclear rockets, President Eisenhower gave us a firm, although not legal, assurance that if by some mischance the development of Skybolt proved unsatisfactory we would be able to obtain in substitution the essential elements of Polaris to be fitted to submarines of our own construction.[1]

There had since been some disquieting rumours of technical difficulties in relation to Skybolt; but President Eisenhower and subsequently President Kennedy had assured me that these would

[1] See *Pointing the Way*, pp. 251–5.

A visit to Rambouillet, 15 December 1962

Nassau, December 1962, for talks on Skybolt and Polaris

'Although the arguments were fierce . . . I was happy to feel . . . there was no change in the relations between Kennedy and myself.'

be overcome. As late as April 1962, the Minister of Defence, Peter Thorneycroft, had felt it possible to assure the House of Commons that he had no evidence of any unforeseen setback. Indeed, by 10 July, after a number of meetings with the Defence Committee, agreement was reached as to the number of Skybolt rockets that would be required and the number of warheads to be manufactured in Britain, and a formal order was placed and accepted in Washington. Nevertheless, as the year went on these rumours grew and such information as our representatives could obtain was disturbing. No doubt the conflict was partly one between the Service interests in the Pentagon. The Navy would naturally like to concentrate on Polaris; the Air Force would cling with all their strength to Skybolt. But in view of the implications of McNamara's speech in Michigan and again at a NATO meeting in Paris in December it was difficult to suppress the suspicion that the failure of Skybolt might be welcomed in some American quarters as a means of forcing Britain out of the nuclear club.

On 12 December Thorneycroft came to report his talks with McNamara in Paris. They had been wholly unsatisfactory; and the Minister of Defence had little doubt that the Americans meant to drop Skybolt altogether. I recorded laconically:

> There will be a great row in both countries. And it means a great battle with President Kennedy next week.[1]

On the next day a public announcement was made in Washington that Skybolt's future was uncertain, owing to unforeseen technical difficulties and rising costs. Although there were to be further talks and a final decision would be taken at Nassau, not unnaturally this statement caused a great furore in Britain.

> The Skybolt row is being fanned into something like hysteria by the 'popular' Press, led by Lord Beaverbrook. The so-called 'responsible' Press is a bit better. The President has stated that no decision will be taken definitely until after our talks in the Bahamas next week.

Meanwhile, the House of Commons was fairly quiet at

[1] 11 December 1962

M

Parliamentary Questions, but I sense a strong wave of anti-Americanism may start at any moment. Lord Beaverbrook and the anti-Common Market lobby are (curiously enough) leaders in this. They are, at heart, complete isolationists.[1]

I immediately sent a message to our Ambassador in Washington on how the Nassau meeting should be handled. It seemed to me that it ought to start right away with the Skybolt question.

> My difficulty is that if we cannot reach an agreement on a realistic means of maintaining the British independent deterrent, all the other questions may only justify perfunctory discussion, since an 'agonising reappraisal' of all our foreign and defence policy will be required.
> I would hope anyway to mention this to the President on Tuesday evening when we must have some personal talk about the agenda – perhaps after dinner.

It was therefore with a somewhat heavy heart that I set about the two tasks which now awaited me. I would have, of course, to inform de Gaulle in some detail about these troubles and our own determination *coûte que coûte* to maintain an independent nuclear force. On this, at any rate, I knew I would have his sympathy. Nevertheless, I felt that this evidence of American disregard for our interests could be used by him as an argument against the policy which I had so long maintained of close association with successive American administrations. He would, no doubt, take as much pleasure in Anglo-American disagreements as he was apt to take umbrage at their close alliance.

Dorothy and I left for Paris on the afternoon of 14 December. As so often before, Philip de Zulueta was my chief adviser and secretary. On arrival, after inspecting the usual Guard of Honour, we

> drove straight to Embassy, where we dined quietly with Ambassador and Lady Dixon. Alexander Macmillan [my grandson] (now at Sorbonne) came to dinner and seemed very well.
> Peter Thorneycroft and Alec Home came in at different times, to report on NATO matters. In spite of all the rumours in

[1] 13 December 1962.

the Press, things seem fairly quiet. McNamara (U.S. Defence Minister) made his offer to sell nuclear rockets (without warheads) to the Europeans. They did not seem very much attracted.[1]

I found it difficult to believe that McNamara's offer could have been quite so clumsy. It would be like giving a shotgun to a boy as a Christmas present on the understanding that he never had any cartridges. However, no doubt we should learn more at Nassau. About Skybolt, my colleagues had clearly formed the view that the Americans had made up their minds to kill the project but whether on political or military grounds was still obscure.

On the next day, 15 December, the formal visit began. At 8.30, leaving Dorothy to follow on later, I drove with the Ambassador, Bob Dixon, to Rambouillet. We were to begin with a pheasant shoot.

We were received by de Gaulle and the shoot started about 9.30, lasting till 12.30, when we came in, changed and had luncheon. It was rather cold, with some rain, but not too bad. I had never seen this strange mixture between sport and drill—it was fascinating. We had four drives—all short—and the birds flew reasonably well, considering the flat woods, with no cover except the sort of strange flushing points (made of low-cut hedges) near the end of each drive; and the fact that (except in the last drive) all the birds were being driven away from home. The beaters were soldiers, in white smocks; the loaders were game-keepers in a sort of military uniform (and very efficient); there was a good deal of trumpet work and much excited shouting. '*Ah! un double—bravo—un double!*' (meaning a right and left). Of course, lots of the birds flew very low, but with the strong wind and the fact that in most drives it was a cross wind, there were plenty of swinging birds which were both difficult and amusing. The birds had been shot *twice* before; I should think that at the first shoot they would hardly fly at all. The guns were very close together, which is awkward. . . . There were no dogs (the dog pick-up is done next day) but lots of 'pickers up'. All the birds were counted and attributed to the different guns. We got about four hundred head (about 385 pheasants) and I was alleged to have shot seventy-seven! It was an extraordinary and strangely

[1] 14 December 1962.

old-fashioned ceremony. I should imagine that Edwardian shoots in England . . . were not dissimilar. General de Gaulle does not shoot. He came out to watch the last stand.[1]

The other guns included the British Ambassador, M. de Courcel (the French Ambassador to London), M. de Boislambert (an old 'Resistance' friend of de Gaulle, whom I had known in Algiers), Commandant de Gaulle, the General's son, and one or two others. I was informed that the affair had been organised by M. Vidron, 'Director of State Shoots'.

The formal discussions began at 3.45 in the afternoon. There was no one present but the General and myself, together with our two Secretaries, des Roziers and de Zulueta, and an interpreter in case of need. A full record was kept of this long discussion, which continued for three hours and covered a wide field. The General began by observing that we had plenty of time, 'both today and tomorrow' and 'our present position is rather like that of two countries which need not be in a hurry'. This somewhat enigmatic remark was not encouraging since, as regards the Brussels negotiations at any rate, speed was of the essence of the problem. I replied that I would like to discuss three matters. First the world situation after Cuba; then the European situation as it affected France and Britain; and finally, and most urgent of all, the Brussels negotiations.

On the first question, the world scene, the General expatiated with his usual broad sweep. He had been astonished at Khrushchev's 'audacity' over Cuba; he had been equally surprised that he had retreated so quickly and wondered why this was. No doubt he had been aiming at blackmail and not at war, hoping to frighten the Americans to such a degree that they would abandon Berlin. He wondered whether Khrushchev would survive the loss of prestige involved. Here I called the General's attention to an important point: 'The United States could take Cuba by conventional arms, and the Russians could only reply with nuclear weapons. In Berlin the situation would be reversed.'

While we both agreed that we ought to seek some kind of *détente*, the question of how and when was not advanced by our discussions.

[1] 15 December 1962.

De Gaulle contented himself with saying that the Western countries should organise themselves better for peace and for war, and then one day it might be possible to negotiate effectively with the Russians.

On European defence, the first point that arose was that of nuclear weapons. I referred to the confused talk that had taken place about a NATO nuclear force. Until there was something more precise to go on, it was difficult to reach a decision. Meanwhile, Britain already had a considerable nuclear force, and we were determined to preserve this as 'independent' in the sense that its ultimate control would be under a British Government. I felt that this force was important for Britain, just as a similar force would be for France. It was the symbol of independence and showed that we were not just satellites or clients of America. This was one aspect and a vital one. At the same time, we ought to organise our forces jointly with our allies, including the Americans. For it would be absurd to have an alliance without plans for the joint use of its power. For this reason we had made tactical arrangements to use our force with that of the Americans to the best advantage. However, in the last resort we should have ultimate control in case we ever had to face a position of peril on our own. I thought the same could be true of France.

I then went on to explain the difficulty which had arisen about the means of delivery of nuclear weapons; the story of the bombers, of Blue Steel, of the abandonment of the ground-based rocket, Blue Streak, and the arrangement to buy Skybolt, a rocket fired from an aeroplane. If the Americans, as now seemed likely, decided to abandon Skybolt on whatever pretext, it would mean that in five or six years' time, British bombers would not have the power to penetrate deeply into enemy territory. We had relied on the Skybolt missile and had placed substantial orders for it. Until I had seen President Kennedy I could not tell the precise position. But of one thing I wished to assure the General—we were determined to maintain our independent deterrent. I would explain to the President that, if Skybolt broke down, I must have an adequate replacement from the United States, such as Polaris—otherwise Britain would have to develop her own system, whether submarine or aerial, in spite of the cost.

This declaration has a certain importance, because it was after-wards suggested that the General's reason for applying his veto at the Brussels negotiations was due to my agreement with President Kennedy a few days later to purchase Polaris in lieu of Skybolt. It was even put about in some French circles, though not, of course, authorised by General de Gaulle, who would not stoop to such meanness, that I had deceived him over this matter by concealing my intentions. The General was in no doubt as to my intentions, and indeed subsequently confirmed to various of my friends that I had told him at this meeting that if the United States administration cancelled Skybolt I would try to obtain Polaris in its place.[1]

De Gaulle said he was glad to hear my opinion about an in-dependent nuclear force. He, too, felt that this was necessary for France. It would not be enormous; but its power would be sub-stantial. We then discussed various methods of co-operation between Britain and France which were already proceeding. I said that we could do everything short of disclosing secret information which we obtained from the Americans on the warhead itself. On the need for a joint plan and joint targeting among the Allies, the General, in effect, accepted my argument. When I remarked that in the modern world independence was not an object in itself but a method of playing a worthy part in an alliance, he seemed to agree. But he observed mournfully that in truth at the present time only the Soviet Union and the United States counted. One day he hoped that Europe would count too; but he did not see how to organise this because the States of Europe did not have much resolution. All this I knew reflected the ill success of the Fouchet Commission, in which the French had put forward some ideas for political development between the Common Market powers, which had not been well received by the other members of the E.E.C. De Gaulle had taken this in very bad part.

We then turned to the Brussels negotiations. I made a strong plea for their rapid conclusion. I added that I quite understood the

---

[1] When the same allegation was repeated in Britain in March 1966, I issued a full statement giving the facts, to which I added these words: 'I have verified my recollection from my personal files. A complete record was made at the time and no doubt exists in the official archives.'

special position and importance of agriculture for France. In the same way we had some difficulties to overcome. But I wished to impress upon him two main points. First, delay was bad for everyone; a great deal of investment was being held up and this position was retarding economic growth. Secondly, Britain had fully accepted the Treaty of Rome, in spite of difficulties such as the common tariff, the end of Commonwealth preferences, and perhaps some disadvantages for the Commonwealth. None of the concessions for which we were asking were outside the Treaty of Rome. Finally, when I had met the President at Champs, he had expressed doubt as to whether I could carry the Commonwealth and my own Party. It had not been easy, but I had succeeded. The British people realised the importance of an expanding market; the Commonwealth understood the new situation by which the old colonial territories were building up their own industrial strength and also the importance of a united Europe for the general interest of the Free World. The main Commonwealth objections had been overcome, subject to some particular points. For example, the position of New Zealand was a very special one: it was 'an English farm in the Pacific' and must be dealt with in a special way. Of course, as regards our own position, the Government had taken risks; but anything was better than that a Europe already divided by the Iron Curtain should be split up a second time into the Six and Seven and thus be further balkanised. From the political even more than from the economic point of view, a united Europe was essential to the strength of European ideals.

The General's reply was discouraging. He doubted the value of the Common Market as a political organisation: it was an economic agreement and no more. It was true that the Treaty of Rome had envisaged political development, but it had failed even to make a start. Our proposal would make a great difference in the whole concept, as envisaged hitherto. He did not say that British membership was excluded. But in reality the Common Market would be quite changed by Britain's entry. France and Germany had similar economies, both industrially and agriculturally. But Britain had a different sort of economy, and if she entered there would be a new Common Market. Moreover, in addition to Britain there would be a lot of other new members like Ireland and Denmark and all the rest. On this rather pessimistic note the first discussion closed.

The evening ended, after an agreeable dinner attended by one or two of de Gaulle's Ministers and their wives, with the usual display of films. The next morning, Sunday, 16 December, the talks were resumed at 10 a.m. After recapitulating the previous day's discussions on international affairs and defence policy, the General passed to the main subject—what he rather obscurely called 'the European affair'. He complained that what he had tried to do for the political unity of Europe had yielded no results. The other five countries were unwilling to develop a genuine common policy. Of course, they used different pretexts—some that the Americans would not like it; some that the British would object, and so forth. But in reality there was a lack of will. Even if Britain joined, there would be little difference. To have any reality, common policy must be concerted with some definite purposes. He could see nothing practical about which agreement could be reached. As for the discussions in Brussels, they were bound to be prolonged. Perhaps the arrangements inside the Six were too rigid to suit British needs. I said frankly that I was astonished and even wounded by what the General had said. Six months ago, at Champs, he had asked if Britain would ever be European and had spoken of an economic agreement as mainly important as the basis on which the political unity of Europe might be built. He had expressed the fear that our ties with the Commonwealth would make all this impossible. I had overcome these obstacles and now, merely because the Fouchet Plan had not been at once accepted, the General was saying that the whole European idea had failed. I went on, somewhat emotionally, to describe the ideals and even the passions which lay behind the European movement when it had first been founded by Churchill. De Gaulle seemed slightly taken aback by this counter-attack. Although he defended his position in some detail, I felt that he was for once a little thrown off his guard. I continued to reproach him for his change of front. He said that, even if Britain's efforts were to fail now, they would not fail for ever. I replied that history showed that with nations, as with individuals, great opportunities once lost were seldom if ever recaptured. Once the chance had been missed, other paths were inevitably followed and the decisive moment passed. So it had been between the two wars with Britain and France. At Champs the General had told me that Britain would not wish to join Europe and that the country and the Commonwealth were not ready. I was deeply hurt to be told now that just because the other countries had not readily accepted the Fouchet Plan everything was changed.

At this point our talk became something of a wrangle. This was very unusual in our relationship. However we soon passed to some more detailed analysis of British and French agriculture, and the note of reproach, although underlying the remainder of this visit, was temporarily muted. Perhaps the most revealing statement which de Gaulle made was when we returned to the political issue. Supposing that one day a political organisation could be made in Europe, comprising some ten countries, on what subjects could they possibly have a common policy? I answered that if this was impossible, then the influence of European civilisation, which had dominated the world for 2,500 years, must now be regarded as at an end. Could we not devise common policies as regards defence, Russia, the Middle East, the Far East, Latin America, Africa and all the manifold questions which were continually forcing themselves on individual governments? Hitherto our policy had seldom been concerted; and for this reason we had failed. At this point the conversation turned to a number of detailed questions regarding these very issues—the Congo, India, China, South-East Asia, Africa, Egypt and the like.

We broke off at 11.45 till noon, when I was joined by the Foreign Secretary, Lord Home, and the British Ambassador, Bob Dixon. M. Pompidou, M. Couve de Murville and M. de Courcel were in support of de Gaulle. De Gaulle began by summing up the result of our discussions, explaining in a somewhat patronising way the subjects we had discussed and the conclusions we had reached. This was pleasant enough, although somehow slightly irritating. When he turned to Europe, de Gaulle referred to the difficulties of any political advance, owing to the failure of the Fouchet Plan. The truth was that the European countries did not dare to do anything without the United States. He therefore could not see any basis for any true European organisation. Moreover, if Britain joined, then Norway, Denmark, Ireland, Portugal, perhaps even Spain, would want to be included. Perhaps one day something might be worked out, but only gradually. Britain was certainly on the right road, but she should be patient. The Brussels negotiations were not finished and there were still many difficulties, especially regarding agriculture. For France it was important that the Common Market should remain unchanged for the present—there was no hurry. At this melancholy position, put forward in such a negative and defeatist way, I noticed that Pompidou seemed displeased and even de Courcel somewhat alarmed. De Gaulle then referred to discussion of other subjects, such as the Congo, China, Africa, South-East Asia, and stated that we were fully agreed on these matters. He ended up with a strange remark, again in the tone of a headmaster addressing an intelligent but somewhat pushing boy. It was important, he declared, that Britain should get nearer to Europe, and France was very pleased that she had come so far. The progress hitherto made was entirely due to my leadership. He then asked me if I had anything I wished to add.

I felt obliged to reproach President de Gaulle with his pessimism. The Brussels negotiations were well on the way to reaching agreement. We should push on—and without delay. If people of European race and tradition were to play a role worthy of their past, Europe must be united. Only so could we stand up to the colossi of America, Russia and perhaps, soon, China. The Fouchet Plan had been quite acceptable in principle to Britain. We believed, at this stage at any rate, in Confederation, not Federation. Nor should there be any question of a single country having a hegemony in Europe. After Brussels we would certainly work with France to create a sound political base. In the economic field, there was much to be done; for instance, could there be a common monetary system? There were questions of defence; and our relations with the Soviet Union and the United States. But if we did not soon begin the task, it would be too late. There might not be a disaster, and life would continue, no doubt, for all our peoples. But a breakdown in these negotiations, to which all Europe was looking, would be a tragic failure to match the level of events. I had myself taken great political

risks for this policy, because I believed it my duty to history, to my
country and to Europe. De Gaulle replied with a curious remark.
He graciously said that he was impressed by my words but he must
recall that, at one stage of the War, Mr. Churchill had said to him
that he would always choose Roosevelt rather than de Gaulle.
Slightly startled by this observation, I retorted that at that particular
time the United States alone had the overwhelming financial,
economic and military power which was essential for Mr. Churchill
to use. Our money had been spent, we depended on Lend Lease and
accordingly we were, in the closing years of the War, weaker than
our American ally. Anyway, I said, when Britain had the choice, she
stood alone for many months to defend the independence of Europe,
including that of France. All this de Gaulle acknowledged, rather
ungraciously. He then reverted to the difficulties at Brussels. In the
Six, France could say 'no' against even the Germans; she could stop
policies with which she disagreed, because of the strength of her
position. Once Britain and all the rest joined the organisation,
things would be different. Moreover, the rest of the world would
no doubt demand special arrangements, and the enlarged Common
Market would not be strong enough to withstand them. A sort of
world free trade area might be desirable—but it would not be
European.

At this point there was a pause. Collecting my thoughts, I said
with indignation that what President de Gaulle had now put
forward was a fundamental objection in principle to Britain's
application. If that was really the French view, it ought to have
been made clear at the start. It was not fair to have a year's negotiation and then bring forward an objection of principle. De Gaulle
seemed rather shaken by this and said I had misunderstood him.
At this awkward moment M. Pompidou observed that it was 'a
question of dates'. After a little talk about Berlin, in which the
Foreign Secretary joined, the meeting ended for luncheon.

The British Ambassador afterwards told me of a curious conversation between Couve de Murville and himself. Couve took him
aside and said that I had misunderstood General de Gaulle's
meaning, and he seemed almost to apologise for de Gaulle's
apparent change of front. In the end he admitted that he was not

really sure what was in de Gaulle's mind. He thought he was chiefly concerned with the agricultural difficulties which would arise in the enlarged community. On this depressing note our conference ended.

In trying to summarise my impressions after our return to England, which took place the same afternoon, I made a record as follows:

On foreign and defence policy, the talks were satisfactory. The General and I were broadly in agreement about the immediate policy towards Moscow. We also agreed the need for a wide *détente* at the right time.

On NATO and on the nuclear we also agreed. The General was as sceptical as we are about the great battle to be fought with conventional forces in Germany. He thinks (as I do) that it would last three hours, or at the most three days. On the nuclear deterrent, he thinks it should be independent, but that we should work together. Can these be reconciled—independence and interdependence? We shall see in Nassau.

But on economic policy—the Brussels negotiations and the entry of Britain into E.E.C.—de Gaulle was very intransigent. The French have got their agricultural pound of flesh out of Germany, and they are going to stick to it. On the political implications of the E.E.C., de Gaulle took a startlingly cynical line. The Five had independently rejected the 'Plan Fouchet'—so he (de Gaulle) had now lost interest in Europe. He rejected Europe! He would substitute a French hegemony of the Six and wanted no new members. (All this was either blatantly stated or dragged out in discussion. At one point, even Pompidou and de Murville were shocked and tried to re-interpret the General's words. But he was quite brutally frank and seemed surprised that we did not accept him in his role as Louis XIV with more enthusiasm.)

I thought the discussions about as bad as they could be from the European point of view. The only glimmer of hope lies in the French unwillingness to be held up to all the world as having openly wrecked our entry and having never really tried to negotiate sincerely. The agricultural interest, is, of course, very great. But I think jealousy of Britain is an even stronger motive. The French (or rather de Gaulle and his friends) want the Six dominated by France. They do *not* want a Europe of eight, nine or ten states, with an equilibrium of power. This is (I think) very short-sighted. . . . But their pride and natural isolationism makes them afraid of larger concepts. It was a very depressing experience, the brutal truth, of course, cleverly concealed by all the courtesy and good manners which surrounded the visit in all its details.[1]

If this visit had been, from my point of view, unfruitful and depressing, it left me in no doubt that de Gaulle would, if he dared, use some means, overt or covert, to prevent the fruition of the Brussels negotiation. I had always had such a high regard for this great Frenchman that it saddened me to feel that, either because of the natural isolationism of his temperament or from the effects of his personal and almost despotic control of France without the restraint to which parliamentary Ministers are daily subjected, in spite of his charm, his good manners and his courtesy, his character had changed—and not for the better.

We returned to London on 16 December, with rather heavy hearts. On the same afternoon there was a meeting of Ministers and officials concerned with Skybolt, which went on till late. On the next day Thorneycroft gave an account to the House of Commons of his talk with McNamara, together with a clear warning that the future of Skybolt was in jeopardy. George Brown suggested that it was time we gave up the attempt to have an independent nuclear deterrent. This did not seem altogether convincing; but it gave an indication of the attitude which even moderate Labour opinion would be likely to take.

On the same day, I set out for Nassau. Lord Home as Foreign Secretary and Peter Thorneycroft as Defence Minister came with me. Duncan Sandys, Commonwealth Secretary, came later. We occupied a beautiful house, put at our disposal by the kindness of the proprietor, Mrs. Holt.

It was on a little promontory, with the sea on both sides, with nice rooms, a pretty garden, and every conceivable comfort.

[1] 16 December 1962.

I lived there, with Tim Bligh and Philip de Zulueta. Foreign
Secretary and Minister of Defence were at the Club. (Commonwealth Secretary at Government House.) It was a great comfort
to have all these Ministers with me.[1]

All this, combined with the agreeable weather, meant that, however
difficult the negotiation, we should at least meet in the most pleasant
surroundings. The President was housed in another beautiful
property, with the usual elaborate security precautions.

The first meeting was at 9.50 a.m. on 19 December. Home and
Thorneycroft were with me, as well as the British Ambassador,
Ormsby Gore, and the two Private Secretaries. The President was
accompanied by McNamara, the Defence Minister, George Ball of
the State Department and two Ambassadors, David Bruce, the
American Ambassador in London, and Thompson, who had long
been Ambassador in Moscow; also McGeorge Bundy, whom my
staff had got to know very well and with whom they could work
closely.

I opened the conference by saying that unhappily the talks about
great world issues to which we had looked forward had now been
overshadowed by this question of the Skybolt missile. I quite understood the apprehension which the American Government had about
doing anything which might be displeasing to their NATO allies.
But we must not forget the historical background. I was one of
the few who could remember the early days of nuclear weapons.
The project then known as 'Tube Alloys' had been developed
originally by British scientists. It was on grounds of safety as well as
convenience that Churchill had agreed with Roosevelt that further
development should be joint and carried out in the United States.
But European countries knew perfectly well that Britain had been
first in the field and might be said, up to the end of the War, to
have had an equal share in the equity with America. After the
War, Anglo-American co-operation, which had not previously been
covered by any precise or binding legal agreements, was stopped
by the passage of the McMahon Act, certain clauses of which
President Eisenhower had told me frankly he regarded as dis-
honourable. The troubles caused by the notorious cases of espionage

[1] 23 December 1962.

continued to prevent amendment of this Act until 1958. Since then there had been complete co-operation between our two countries. Our scientists had been able to contribute a great deal to the joint stock and we had scrupulously maintained secrecy. We had developed Blue Streak and spent upon it something like two hundred million dollars. It was a powerful weapon, which we could have perfected. But for a number of reasons we decided to abandon it if we could get something better. At Camp David in 1960, President Eisenhower had discussed with me both Skybolt and Polaris. We accepted Skybolt because it would seem the best way for us to prolong the life of the bomber air force and utilise the advantages of its long experience. In return the British Government had made Holy Loch available for the Polaris base, which enormously enhanced the range and capacity of the submarine weapon. If Skybolt were definitely to fail us, we should have to find an alternative. President Eisenhower had assured me that, if necessary, we might rely on obtaining Polaris.

Whatever might be the outcome of the Common Market negotiations, I was quite certain that they would not be affected by the problem of delivery systems for nuclear weapons. The doubts and hesitations which de Gaulle had expressed were based on quite different considerations. In any case, it did not seem to me that a switch from the lame horse Skybolt to what seemed the new favourite, Polaris, would upset France or Germany. A mere change from a missile propelled through the air to one fired from beneath the sea was one of technique, not of principle. I felt bound to add a final point: if the difficulties arising from the development of Skybolt were used, or seemed to be used, as a method of forcing Britain out of an independent nuclear capacity, the results would be very serious indeed. It would be deeply resented both by those of our people who favoured an independent nuclear capability and by those who opposed it. It would offend the sense of national pride and would be resisted by every means in our power.

Kennedy seemed somewhat taken aback. He said at once that the decision to abandon Skybolt was not made for political reasons. He made the rather startling proposal that the American Government should pay half of any further development cost and the British the other half, the total being estimated at a further two hundred million dollars. In that case we would have the right to buy the missiles but the Americans could not undertake to do so. After making this somewhat astonishing suggestion, he referred to the difficulty for America in letting us change to Polaris. In spite of what I had said, he believed that it would add to de Gaulle's distrust of the United States and strengthen his accusation that they wished to maintain a domination of Europe.

After much discussion, often rather heated, in which the Americans continued to maintain that the change from Skybolt to Polaris was one of principle to which they were not even honourably committed, the President argued that his offer on Skybolt would put us about where we had been a month previously. I observed that although the proposed British marriage with Skybolt was not exactly a shotgun wedding, the virginity of the lady must now be regarded as doubtful. We were being asked to spend hundreds of millions of dollars upon a weapon on which the President's own authorities were casting doubts, both publicly and privately.

As the argument proceeded, the Americans found themselves in the difficulty that they were resting upon two conflicting arguments. On the one side they said Skybolt would fail; on the other, they said that it could be made to work but they did not need it because of the development of Polaris. They were prepared to sell it to us—on terms.

At this point discussion turned to the 'multilateral nuclear force', which the Americans wished to develop. When we met in the afternoon, it was clear that both Kennedy and his advisers attached immense importance to this plan, which they fondly believed would be very attractive to their NATO allies. What was envisaged was a force not only financed by different NATO countries, but also involving multinational crews. Apart from the difficulties of a complicated warship of this kind, with its incredibly sophisticated machinery, both for the propulsion of the vessel and for the firing of the rockets, being operated by a crew drawn from eight to ten countries, there was the question of the authority under which this multilateral force would operate. I myself thought that the best solution might be to have a joint force, with contributions assigned by the United States, Britain and perhaps France. In such circumstances it seemed reasonable to hope that other countries would not bother to build a nuclear force.

Much, of course, would turn on the meaning of the word 'assignment'. If we eventually did get Polaris, how could we prove our devotion to the cause of interdependence, of which I had been so long one of the protagonists? I remember saying at one stage that I interpreted the word 'assignment' as referring 'to a force operating under allied command in normal times but available for national use in time of emergency'. I remember also reminding the President of the force which we had assigned in this sense to the Anglo-French armies at the beginning of 1940. With our few divisions we had formed merely a corps under the French command of much larger armies. Yet Lord Gort had had no hesitation in exercising his rights as an independent commander when it became clear that General Gamelin had lost control of the battle. In fact, I was to argue all through that unless and until a single supranational state was formed there would have to be a combination of independence and interdependence.

Finally I repeated our urgent request for Polaris as a substitute for Skybolt. I understood the President's anxiety. Yet my proposal did not exclude his concept of multilateralism in due course. I sympathised with the Americans, who could not understand what the Europeans were worrying about. The Americans were willing to defend Europe and had the means to do so. Would they always have the will? America must realise that the great nations of Europe, with their different histories and varying responsibilities, would demand a reasonable degree of dignity and security. Certainly Britain with her world-wide commitments must continue, for the present at any rate, to have some independent nuclear force.

A number of proposals had by now been made which tried to combine our points of view. The President did not want to give us Polaris on political grounds, for fear of upsetting all the European nations who, with the exception of France, had no nuclear development. On the other hand, I was determined to get Polaris and felt that we had a right to it. In return we would be prepared to make it clear that in normal circumstances we would regard our nuclear power as available to NATO and thus add to its strength.

The discussions continued all through the morning of 20 December, when a drafting committee of the British and Americans was set up to prepare the text of a formal document. Finally, on 21 December, agreement was reached at a full meeting, and there was time to discuss a number of other points of varying importance; the most urgent of which was how to take up, in due course, an effort to reach an understanding with the Russians to abandon further nuclear tests.

The arrangement finally agreed was that we should be supplied with the Polaris missile, we making our own warheads, which we were quite able to do. In return, our nuclear fleet was to be 'assigned' to NATO, except in cases 'where Her Majesty's Government may decide that supreme national interests are at stake'. This meeting, in which the arguments were much more violently contested than in any previous one, was an exhausting experience.

> Three days hard negotiation – nearly four days in reality. The Americans pushed us very hard and may have 'out-smarted' us altogether. It is very hard to judge.[1]

Throughout the conference we sent full reports to our colleagues in London, and the draft agreement and communiqué as soon as they were prepared were subjected to comments from the Cabinet. Their amendments were all embodied in the final texts.[2]

> The discussions were protracted and fiercely contested. They turned almost entirely on 'independence' in national need. I had to pull out all the stops – adjourn, re-consider; refuse one draft and demand another, etc., etc. Whether Parliament and the country will think we have done well or badly I cannot tell yet.[1]

Although the arguments were fierce and sometimes painful, I was happy to feel at the end that there was no change in the relations between Kennedy and myself. Both he and McNamara seemed sometimes strangely ignorant of the immediate past. In this I, who had lived through it all for over twenty years, had an advantage.

The President had intended to leave early on Friday, 21 December, but hearing that Diefenbaker was coming to Nassau I

---

[1] 23 December 1962.   [2] Appendix 4.

persuaded him to remain for luncheon. This, under great pressure, he agreed to do. The rest of my time in Nassau was spent in talks with Diefenbaker on all the questions of the day. At last we managed to get away during the night of 22 December and arrived home the next morning, Sunday, 23 December.

By a curious chance, one of the main uncertainties which had dominated the whole conference, the effectiveness of Skybolt, seemed suddenly to be re-opened.

A very successful test was made on the day after our conference ended. Did the President and McNamara know about this or did they expect another failure? But, whatever the test may have shown, it is clear that the American *Defence* Minister *and* the White House have decided—on wider grounds—to concentrate on Minuteman (the Intercontinental Rocket) and Polaris (the submarine weapon). It is also clear to me that they are determined to kill Skybolt on good general grounds—not merely to annoy us or to drive Great Britain out of the nuclear business. But, of course, they have handled things in such a way as to make many of us very suspicious. Nor do we yet know what will be the effect of the successful test of Skybolt in American politics. The President is clearly alarmed. The Air Force 'lobby' in Washington, as well as the 'Douglas' lobby, will be much strengthened. All this may have repercussions on the general agreement which we reached and published at Nassau on Friday, December 21st.[1]

The Press reception of the communiqué and especially of that part of it dealing with the future of the nuclear deterrent was mixed; as usual it was also self-contradictory. Some attacked us for 'selling out Britain', others criticised us for obstinately clinging to a nuclear force which had no purpose. At the time I noted:

Broadly, I have agreed to make our present bomber force (or part of it) and our Polaris force (when it comes) a NATO force for general purposes. But I have reserved absolutely the right of H.M.G. to use it *independently* 'for supreme national interest'.

These phrases will be argued and counter-argued. But they represent a genuine attempt (which Americans finally accepted) to make a proper contribution to *interdependent* defence, while

[1] 23 December 1962.

retaining the ultimate rights of a sovereign state. This accepts the
facts of life as they are. But I do not conceal from myself that the
whole concept will be much knocked about by controversy at
home. The Cabinet (which met on the Friday morning and was
kept fully informed throughout) did not much like it, although
they backed us up loyally.[1]

Immediately on my return I sent personal messages to Menzies
and Holyoake. I had already, of course, explained everything to
Diefenbaker in Nassau.

Looking back on this affair after many years, it seems incredible
that anyone could have raised doubts as to the reserved power of the
British Government. After all, a nuclear weapon is not one which is
used lightly, whether independently or interdependently. Its use, if
ever such a horror came, must result as a time when supreme
national interests are at stake. However, I could only wait for the
meeting of Parliament and the development of events.

While we were at Nassau I had asked Sir Pierson Dixon to
explain to de Gaulle what we were doing from day to day, and in due
course the General received from Kennedy an offer of Polaris, on
terms similar to those agreed for Britain. All I could do was to hope
that the Americans would not frighten the French with too much
talk about their multilateral scheme, but give them time to consider
the Polaris offer, which could be a great advantage to them.

In other respects, the year concluded on a somewhat difficult
note—the Nassau agreements would be opposed on widely divergent
grounds, and the prospect of France taking a helpful view on
Europe seemed now remote.

Meanwhile, I had been much encouraged by a gracious letter
from the Queen, which I received on Christmas Eve, written in her
own hand. I had, of course, kept her informed of the progress of the
conference and had sent her a full account at the end.

On 3 January 1963 the Cabinet met in the morning. Our first
task was to say goodbye to Sir Norman Brook, who was about to
retire. Although his place was to be admirably filled by Sir Burke
Trend, I felt the loss deeply. For many years I had enjoyed the

---

[1] 23 December 1962.

friendship and the loyal support of this remarkable civil servant who commanded the confidence and affection of all my colleagues.

> I made a short speech about him and he replied; I have sent him a nice piece of plate, as a mark of esteem.[1]

The disposal of routine business lasted the whole morning, chiefly schemes for increasing pensions, insurance payments and other social benefits.

> We met again at 5 p.m. for two hours, to discuss the Nassau agreement. After a very full and very good discussion, the Cabinet approved what we did.[1]

There was still a last hurdle to be overcome before the final agreement could be signed, but I assumed that this would be a mere formality. I was therefore much concerned to hear, towards the end of the month, that the American Government were now asking us to contribute to the research and development costs of Polaris, a point which had never been mentioned at Nassau, where we had assumed that Polaris missiles would be available on the same basis as Skybolt—that is, 'actual end cost'.

> The American Defence Minister has been very grasping. I have refused to agree to his demands and have been forced to appeal to the President direct. I heard yesterday that he accepted my proposals. The trouble has been about a possible contribution by us to *future* 'marks' of the Polaris missile (not A1 or A2, which is in service, but A3, which is under development). I have refused to make an open-ended contribution to an unknown bill for Research and Development. But I have offered, in lieu, to add five per cent to the retail cost. So, if we bought fifty million pounds of missiles, we would pay fifty two and a half million pounds. Not a bad bargain. But it has caused me some sleepless nights.[2]

Everything, therefore, was in order for the debate, which was arranged for 31 January. Unhappily, by this time, there had been discouraging, even disastrous developments over Europe. Although when Heath came to see me on Sunday, 6 January, he was 'still hopeful of a successful outcome to the negotiations',[3] I could only

[1] 3 January 1963.   [2] 28 January 1963.   [3] 6 January 1963.

'watch and pray'. Thus the Government began the year in a difficult, if not actually dangerous position.

There is a general view that the Socialists will win the General Election. The country is in a dissatisfied and petulant mood. My own popularity has gone down a lot. There is a wave of anti-European and anti-American feeling.

There is trouble about growing unemployment. The Press is, with scarcely an exception, hostile. The T.V. is critical. Altogether, we are at a low ebb. Can we recover in 1963 and 1964? I don't know. But I mean to have a good try.[1]

I noticed that in the first Sunday of the year, the Press was

very hostile and prophesies my early departure and the fall of the Government! Happily, since I was not unduly elated by the extravagant praise of two years ago, I am not unduly depressed by this change of mood.[2]

I was now entering my seventh year as Prime Minister and received a great number of encouraging messages, together with some abusive ones.

On the face of it, the political and economic situation seems bad—some people feel desperate—so far as the life and future of the Government are concerned. But I do not share this view. Much depends on the Brussels negotiations. If these succeed, we can let loose a great pro-European propaganda, which we have [up till] now restrained, but [have] ready to unleash. Private investment will leap ahead, both British and American, in the U.K.[3]

I noticed that the French Press, no doubt under official direction, were working up the idea that if Britain were to join the Six American control would creep in by our side. Our Ambassador in Paris, in whose judgement I had great confidence, reported that much would depend upon how far de Gaulle felt able to challenge the undoubted desire of the other Five to welcome Britain's

[1] 1 January 1963.   [2] 6 January 1963.   [3] 11 January 1963.

adhesion to the Treaty. Thus the Brussels negotiations were about to be resumed in a somewhat tense atmosphere.

French propaganda against us . . . is developing on familiar lines. I am not discouraged. They often do this as a prelude to an agreement.[1]

But at the same time Christopher Soames, our Minister for Agriculture, had reported a conversation with his French counterpart, who had said to him:

Mon cher. C'est très simple. Maintenant, avec les six, il y a cinq poules et un coq. Si vous joignez (avec des autres pays), il y aura peut-être sept ou huit poules. Mais il y aura *deux* coqs. Alors—ce n'est pas aussi agréable.[1]

When the blow finally fell and de Gaulle exercised his veto, many explanations were made to account for the French hostility—the Polaris agreement, the plan for some multilateral nuclear force in NATO, as well as other, even less reasonable explanations. I wondered whether perhaps the French Minister of Agriculture had not found the true answer.

On 14 January, the very day when the Brussels talks resumed, de Gaulle gave one of his famous Press conferences, with all the *corps diplomatique* present. He laid great stress upon the essential difference between Britain and the E.E.C. countries, and how dangerous any enlargement of the community would be, since it would ultimately be dominated by an Atlantic community under American leadership. France was determined on complete independence and would have nothing to do with any of the arrangements that had been discussed at Nassau. He even asserted that our right to the independent use of our nuclear capacity would prove an illusion.

Following the conference, which was in de Gaulle's most majestic and 'Louis Quatorze' style [the Press were] putting round every kind of lie about us and about me. The reasons given for de Gaulle's sudden decision (of which not even Couve de Murville had been informed) are so diverse as to be ridiculous.[2]

[1] 12 January 1963.   [2] 28 January 1963.

I sent an immediate message to Kennedy, informing him that we should go on quietly with our work at Brussels and allow the five the opportunity to play their hand.

The General's *démarche* to the world was followed by Couve de Murville going to Brussels to demand that the negotiations must now stop. This caused anger (but, alas, impotent anger) among the Five, who are just beginning to realise the real inwardness of French policy. De Gaulle is trying to *dominate* Europe. His idea is not a partnership, but a Napoleonic or a Louis XIV hegemony.

All these two weeks have been taken up with a vast amount of coming and going; meetings, telegrams, etc. Our Cabinet has been very good—quite firm and sensible. But it is a great blow to all our hopes. It is the end—or at least the temporary bar—to everything for which I have worked for many years. As far as *internal* politics are concerned, it is another blow.[1]

On 17 January the French delivered a demand, almost an order, from the General that the conference at Brussels should be adjourned *sine die*. However, the other Five had at least sufficient strength to resist this, and the conference was to be resumed on 28 January. This gave some chance for the Five to take a strong position. Heath, who kept marvellously cool, wanted it to be made clear that, if the negotiations had been adjourned for technical reasons, there were no technical difficulties which could not be and indeed had not already been solved. If they were to be halted for purely political reasons, then it was at the will of one man.

By an unfortunate chance, a visit of Adenauer to Paris had been arranged for 20 January. The German political parties brought much pressure on the ageing Chancellor to keep the negotiations going. Unfortunately, he did nothing to help, but he contented himself with signing a Franco-German treaty. At the same time, rumours were put about by the French that Kennedy and I had made secret arrangements about the future of Europe.

I took the opportunity in a speech at Liverpool, which dealt largely with unemployment and other internal questions, to emphasise our position. De Gaulle's attempt to block our entry

[1] 28 January 1963.

into the Common Market was a setback, 'I trust and pray not a fatal setback'. I continued,

> Recrimination is useless, but the truth should be known. If there was an objection in principle to Britain's entry, we should, surely, have been told so from the start.

I denied altogether any suggestions that I had not treated General de Gaulle with absolute sincerity. It was false to allege that there were any secret undertakings given at Nassau. On the contrary, the General and I had discussed the whole question of defence in detail. 'I explained to de Gaulle at Rambouillet in December that if the Americans decided to abandon Skybolt, I would do my utmost to obtain an effective alternative.' In our view, there should be no question of hegemony in Europe of any country. America was allied to all the European countries mainly concerned, through NATO. The time was past for any concepts of dominance of a single country. As regards the Commonwealth, I pointed out that 'the French have themselves retained special links with their former overseas territories. So we in Britain believe that we can be loyal Europeans without disloyalty to our great Commonwealth tradition and duty'. Nevertheless, I sensed that de Gaulle could not be moved. In a moment of something like despair I recorded:

> All our policies at home and abroad are in ruins. Our defence plans have been radically changed, from air to sea. European unity is no more; French domination of Europe is the new and alarming feature; our popularity as a Government is rapidly declining. We have lost everything, except our courage and determination.[1]

When the talks re-opened in Brussels, there was much discussion between Heath and the other Five, privately assisted by Jean Monnet, as how best to proceed against de Gaulle. In the event, the Five agreed that the Commission be asked to report both to the Six and to the British Government on the situation, after which the negotiations would resume. The French, however, wanted a report from the Commission 'on the consequences of enlarging the community' without any commitment to continue the discussions.

[1] 28 January 1963.

On 29 January, when the Six powers met in Brussels, the French refused to accept the plan put up by the Five for such a mandate to the Commission. Heath was then formally told that the 'proposal had been rejected by France and the negotiations were therefore at an end'. After this, Heath wisely decided to concentrate the discussions on preserving the community from developing in a way which would make more difficulties for Britain's next bid for entry.

I felt instinctively that, although I myself might not take a part in the ultimate unity of Europe, yet I might, if I lived, be a witness of final success. However bitter our feelings might be, we must not allow ourselves to be misled into statements which would endanger the future. Meanwhile, I was particularly sorry for Heath.

> No one could have been a better negotiator and ambassador— but French duplicity has defeated us all. The final scenes took place Monday and Tuesday. The end—or at least long delay, whether prolonged or final—in all our European policy has had a curious effect. At home, there is the return of the old feeling 'the French always betray you in the end'. There is *great* and *grievous* disappointment (among the younger people especially) at the end of a fine vision.[1]

Letters of sympathy came pouring in from statesmen of all countries and from friends of the European Movement, among them one from Paul Reynaud, who recalled Churchill's offer of Franco-British union in 1940. These gave me much comfort. In the circumstances I thought it best to make a broadcast on 30 January on the breakdown of the Brussels negotiation.

> What happened at Brussels yesterday was bad, bad for us, bad for Europe, and bad for the whole Free World. A great opportunity has been missed. It is no good trying to disguise or minimise that fact. For what we and our friends were trying to do at Brussels was something very imaginative and dramatic. We were trying to strengthen the unity of Western Europe in a way which would spread out all over the whole Free World. We British didn't enter these negotiations in a half-hearted way or even, as some people think, only for our own ends. Of course the question everyone is asking is, 'Well, what do we do now?' But

[1] 4 February 1963.

before I come to that, I want just to say a word about what we were trying to do. Let me tell you as simply as I can.

For many centuries Europe has been the cradle of civilisation. All has spread outwards from Europe. Yet it has also been the scene of many bitter struggles. In the last fifty years in two wars Europe nearly destroyed herself. These great conflicts have generally been brought about by the attempts of one nation, even of one man, to dominate the whole of Europe, to create a sort of sham united Europe, not by agreement or partnership, but by power. We want to stop this happening again; we want to heal the divisions between Europe by a real unity through co-operation and then we want to see this freely united Europe use her strength and prosperity to help the outer world.

What has happened has revealed a division. France and her Government are looking backwards. They seem to think that one nation can dominate Europe and, equally wrong, that Europe can or ought to stand alone. But Europe cannot stand alone. She must co-operate with the rest of the Free World, with the Commonwealth, with the United States in an equal and honourable partnership. That is why we in Britain mean to stand by the Atlantic Alliance. After all, the story of the last seventeen years has been one of reconstruction and reconciliation.

I know there are a lot of people in this country who have been anxious about our application to join the Common Market. They felt that our special links with the Commonwealth might be weakened, that Commonwealth trade would be reduced. In our view with the pattern of Commonwealth trade already changed so much, our membership of the Common Market would open up new opportunities for the Commonwealth in a prosperous and expanding market. That at any rate was one of the things the negotiations were about. They have been long and complicated. But I am afraid that (in spite of assurances to the contrary) the only explanation for what has happened is that the French Government hoped the negotiations would fail in one way or another—hoped that the Commonwealth would turn them down; or perhaps that the Conservative Party at their Conference would turn them down; or else that the talks would be so indefinitely prolonged as to run into the sand. When in the last few weeks it became clear that the remaining points could be settled, then the French brought the negotiations to an end.

To us the economic side is important, because we all felt that, by the creation of an enlarged market of the European countries equal in strength to that of the United States, we could develop more wealth for everyone than we could separately. It has also been our purpose, shared by at any rate most of the European countries, that this system should be what is called outward-looking. We don't want it to shut itself up inside a fortress. We need to create new wealth to share with the poorer nations, the less developed and the under-developed nations. However, it is no good arguing about this now. The negotiations have broken down. What *we've* got to decide is what we are going to do next. People naturally ask if there is an alternative. Well, certainly not in the sense of a ready-made plan which is better than the one we have been pursuing.

What we do must be creative and constructive, not vindictive. It must be in harmony with our purpose and not against it. Of course, if it had been possible to create a common market like the European community, inside the Commonwealth, why, we would have done it years ago. It would have been very attractive for reasons of history and sentiment. No, there isn't an alternative in that sense, easy and ready-made. But there is a lot that we can do and must do. We consulted the Commonwealth countries all through the Brussels negotiations, and now we shall take counsel with them as to what is best to be done. And the same with the EFTA countries. And also the United States. We must work for lowering of tariffs all round, for that is one of the best ways we can increase trade throughout the world. We can do this in the tariff negotiations for which the preparations are now being made, and in which all will take part including the Community.

We certainly will not let the breakdown of the negotiations weaken our resolve to master the problem of expansion without inflation at home. That means we must rely upon our own determination, our own vigour and our own resources. We must be ready to accept change, to modernise, to adapt, to replace obsolete plant and methods which are outdated; to work together, all of us. Is this a gloomy prospect? Not at all. We've been in this kind of situation before. It's always drawn out the best in us. It will again.

By a curious chance I had recently been re-reading one of the volumes of Lloyd George's *War Memoirs* where, referring to Jules and Paul Cambon, the great French diplomats, he writes as follows:

They were intensely patriotic. France was their faith—their shrine—their worship—their deity. The first commandment of the true French patriot is: 'Thou shalt have no other gods but France.' It is a type or quality of patriotism which springs more naturally from the soil of France than that of any other land. Are Englishmen also not patriots? Yes, they are, but with them patriotism is a duty, with Frenchmen it is a fanaticism. Great leaders of men prove their gift of leadership by the appeals they address to those who under their command are called upon to fight against odds. Nelson's call to the English sailors was to respond to England's expectation that they should do their duty. Napoleon's appeal was to the glories of France. It was a love of country planted and raised during the torrid summer of the great Revolution, when the integrity and independence of France were threatened by all the monarchs of Europe, and matured whilst the French legions under Napoleon were tramping through the streets of every capital (except one) where these monarchs reigned. They were beaten in the end by a combined Europe. But national greatness does not depend as much on victory, as on the grandeur of the struggle put up by a people. No other country possesses the experiences of France, and one has always to remember, in dealing with French statesmen, that this great era of their national glory is at the roots of their policy. In negotiating with them it is a complex which interferes seriously with any attempt to secure a reasonable accommodation which takes the interests of other nations into account. It is always obtruding itself at inconvenient moments.[1]

Nevertheless I felt that while these emotions might sway de Gaulle and his contemporaries, the younger men of France, who were looking to the future, were earnest supporters of the European movement. In the years before us we must rely upon these forces.

After sending full reports to the Prime Ministers of the leading Commonwealth countries, the question arose as to whether we should attempt to organise even more strongly a combination with the EFTA and Commonwealth countries. But I felt all this to be a

[1] Lloyd George, *War Memoirs* (London 1934), vol. iv, pp. 2028–9.

mistake. We must wait in patience, our relations with France being one of cautious reserve without intimacy. By great misfortune, arrangements had been made for Princess Margaret to visit Paris at this time. Both the Foreign Office and the Ambassador advised postponement.

> Their fear was that de Gaulle would turn her 'private' luncheon with him into a great demonstration—guard of honour, all French Cabinet and many ambassadors, etc., etc. If this would be mis-understood in France (and regarded as Britain 'coming to heel') it would leave the Five (and indeed all other European countries) utterly bewildered. So I agreed to cancel it. We have had a great row ever since—in the Press, in the House, and in the Party—but I think we have weathered it.[1]

These fears were perhaps soundly based; but looking back I feel that our decision was wrong. It would have been more dignified to allow the Princess to fulfil a long-standing engagement.

In these anxious weeks I had to take part in two great debates. The first, on 30 and 31 January, was on the Nassau agreements. With the preparation for this as well as the final debate on the Common Market, the days were full enough. There were also to be dealt with the growing problem of unemployment in certain areas, the question of the Yemen and the alarming reports of aggression by Indonesia against Brunei and Malaysia. There was in addition the everlasting question of Sir Roy Welensky and Central Africa. On the defence issue,

> I decided that it was a time to try to rally the country and the Party. So I both opened and wound up the Polaris debate with vigorous speeches. The first was long but well-argued and impressive—a massive effort, to which the House listened for an hour without interruption. The wind-up was good and (in a noisy House) I was able to deal with Gordon-Walker, Brown and Wilson fairly effectively. Wilson was 'thin' and not as good as usual.[2]

In my winding-up speech I took the occasion to refer to the rumours

[1] 17 February 1963.   [2] 4 February 1963.

mentioned by Grimond that somehow the Nassau agreement had a damaging affect on the Brussels negotiations.

I have said this before, and I repeat it now. I discussed this with President de Gaulle and made quite clear what I wanted to get if Skybolt faded out. I do not think that this agreement was the reason for the failure of the negotiations. Indeed, during the last few days and weeks so many and such different reasons have been given for the sudden change of French policy—that England was an island, that we were not really sufficiently European, that there had been such a long delay in the negotiations, and so on. Every conceivable reason has been put forward. I do not think that I have anything on my conscience on this point. Indeed, when I first communicated with General de Gaulle, as I did immediately when at Nassau, I received a very sympathetic reply.

In spite of the fears of the whips, we had a good division with a majority of over a hundred. But I had now to make a speech in the Common Market debate. In this I had to meet immediate political needs, keep the record straight and, above all, not jeopardise the future.

I had already made, with the Lord Privy Seal, a short visit to Rome at the request of the Italians. While it was helpful for the European cause as a whole, it could bring us no immediate satisfaction. I found the Italians bitter against de Gaulle; but they realised that there was little that they could do.

I rather fear that the French calculation is right. All this indignation, they believe, will blow over and they will be left undisputed masters of the field.[1]

Before leaving Rome, I had an audience with Pope John.

I was shocked by his appearance. He had lost a lot of weight, and seemed very white—especially the hands and ears. It is said in Rome that he has cancer and will not last the year. That would indeed be sad—for he is a great man (in his own way) and has made a great impact on the world. He was very gay—talked incessantly in French and kept me for thirty-five minutes. I was

[1] 4 February 1963.

much touched. Almost the only sentence which I could get in referred to the Queen's decision to be personally represented at the Requiem Mass for Cardinal Godfrey. I explained to the Pope that this had not happened for four hundred years. He was much gratified.[1]

On our return from Rome we had to face the second of the important debates. The first, on the Nassau agreement, had turned out unexpectedly well. But the debate on the failure of the Brussels negotiations would open much wider opportunities for criticism and censure. I had given so much weight to the hopes for a united Europe over the last eighteen months and was so personally connected through my long support of the European movement that I felt my leadership could be seriously challenged. Already the Press were beginning to foresee, if not the fall of the Government, the end of my premiership. Much would turn not only on the division but on the effect on the Parliament and on the country of the arguments presented. I knew that the Opposition were much divided on the European question and would concentrate on the failure of the Government's general policies and the increasing difficulties at home.

The great question remains 'What is the alternative?' to the European Community. If we are honest, we must say that there is none—had there been the chance of a Commonwealth Free Trade Area, we should have grasped it long ago.[1]

On 5 February I

worked all day on the speech which I now seem condemned to make on 11 February (Monday) on the great Brussels post-mortem. I had a meeting after the division last night with some of my leading colleagues, but I did not feel that any of them had much stomach for this fight. Anyway, they expect me to lead off. After the exertions of last week—two major speeches in the House of Commons, with a T.V. appearance, followed by three days in Rome—I felt rather unwilling to undertake this task. But I must do so.[2]

[1] 4 February 1963.   [2] 5 February 1963.

General de Gaulle says 'No' at a Press conference, 14 January 1963

Heath, Soames and Sandys leaving Brussels on 29 January 1963, after the talks had collapsed

'I felt particularly sorry for Heath. No one could have been a better negotiator.'

Naturally, there had been some talk, especially by the old adherents of 'Empire Free Trade', of a new Commonwealth Prime Ministers' Conference. This I was determined to reject, for it would suggest that something could be done by reviving an obsolete concept. Yet I must tread carefully and devise some other method calculated to increase Commonwealth trade. On the first point I thought it best to meet the issue fairly in my speech.

The Commonwealth cannot be a single economic unit in the sense of any other trading community like, let us say, the United States or the Common Market. It is not only the mere separation by distance; this could be overcome. It is quite a different sort of obstacle. The different stages of industrial development, and the different sorts of trade which meet the needs of individual Commonwealth countries, make it impossible for them all to be unified with us in a free trade area.

Some have very high tariffs, some very low. Some are at the beginning of their industrialisation, some are far advanced. Some are determined to protect—as they have the perfect right to do—their nascent industries with high protective tariffs, and would not for a moment accept what they would call being flooded by cheaper products from Britain. This is true of Australia, Canada and, to some extent, of New Zealand.

That is not to say that trade between Britain and the Commonwealth countries cannot be extended. It must be. It is only to say that a uniform system cannot be applied between the Commonwealth countries because of those variations which, on the political and moral side, represent the strength of the Commonwealth. This is an attitude which is shared by all the Commonwealth countries. It means, therefore, that neither an immediate Commonwealth Prime Ministers' Conference, nor any other conference, could devise, either in their interests or in ours, a substitute for what we had hoped to obtain, for us and for them, from Europe. It is for this reason that it does not seem right at this stage to suggest a Commonwealth Prime Ministers' Conference.

It would be better, therefore, to concentrate upon the problems to the solution of which we could make a co-operative approach.

There is a special field in which we could work together and

N

that is the approach to some of the problems presented by the various world agreements. The main hope which we now have in this field is in making effective the so called Kennedy Round [of tariff cuts]. We hope that this can soon begin. We have, therefore, proposed a meeting of Commonwealth Trade Ministers shortly before the time of the coming ministerial session of GATT. It is hoped that the GATT session will take place in the early summer.

In the same way, the work of EFTA could be developed.

As the House knows, EFTA has two broad purposes. It already offers a wide area of reduced tariffs among an important grouping of trading nations. Beyond this, we have always seen it as a step towards a fully integrated European market. These objects are not inconsistent. In practice, the EFTA countries have pursued them simultaneously.

We should, by all practical means, strengthen the fabric of European trade

until such a time as the obstacles preventing the establishment of a market, fully integrated, are removed and in this task the support of our EFTA partners will be of the greatest value.

I then turned to the problems at home and the need for economic 'growth'. In addition to the monetary policies which we had been pursuing, we must make new efforts to deal with the special areas of unemployment, as we had already begun to do. At the same time, we must face the fact that the old industries could not of themselves provide full employment and prosperity. We must make special endeavours in new techniques, which would involve greater mobility of labour and a new emphasis on the proposals for industrial retraining, on which the Minister had already made a start.

I summed up therefore this part of my speech as follows:

First, we have proposed a conference of Commonwealth Trade Ministers. Secondly, we shall work for close co-operation with the Commonwealth, the United States, EFTA and we hope the Six, for the Kennedy Round. Next we shall maintain our

EFTA association. We shall work for world commodity agreements. At home we shall work for an expanding economy, without inflation, based upon an incomes policy.

I then turned to the European Story.

The end did not come because the discussions were menaced with failure. On the contrary, it was because they threatened to succeed. That the French Government, in their hearts, had long feared success I do not now doubt, but I had always hoped that they might be animated by two considerations: first, by the underlying good will that undoubtedly links France and Britain. This friendship is very deep between our peoples, and the links have been forged in the purging fire of war, twice in my lifetime, during terrible years when Britain and France suffered side by side.

Secondly, I had hoped that the French Government would be unwilling to place themselves in the public position of opposing the will of all their colleagues in the Community and, indeed, of disappointing the hopes of every country in the free world. Of course, they may have hoped that the responsibility for this decision would not have to be placed upon their shoulders. They may have felt that the British Government would not be able to carry their policy forward, either through their party or through the assent of the Commonwealth, or through the House of Commons. But when these expectations began to fail the head of the French Government decided to act.

It is right to point out that there had been some confusion as to the method which the French Government adopted.

So many different reasons were given for Britain's exclusion —that she is an island; that our people were not sufficiently European-minded; that we do not accept the Treaty of Rome—a statement wholly incorrect; that the Nassau Agreement on Polaris was a sudden and unexpected blow—equally incorrect. It was clear that none of these reasons was the real one.

It was common knowledge that the whole French Government had every expectation that the negotiations would be carried through successfully. M. Pompidou, the French Prime Minister, was reported in the French Press as having told a group of journalists as late as 11th January—that is, three days before the matter was brought to a sudden close—that France desired to see Great Britain join the Six and accede to the Common Market. Other French Ministers had given us similar assurances in private discussions at much the same time.

Nevertheless, the French Government had made their decision and we must face the reality. Now we must do all we could to keep alive the large assets of good will which we had been able to mobilise, and thus rally Europe for the future. I ended by saying:

> I do not mean that we look forward to an early resumption of these particular negotiations for Britain's entry into the Community. That is impossible. This is not a kind of business deal that, if it fails one week, can be taken up the next. It is, for good or ill, a great historic event. It cannot be disregarded, but its importance and, perhaps, its permanence, must not be exaggerated. While it would be absurd not to recognise with our heads that Britain's entry is not now capable of early realisation, we should surely strive to keep the vision in our hearts.

The debate went off well, and although my speech was, in parts at any rate, somewhat heavy, it was welcomed by the House and afterwards by the Press as impressive and suited to a great occasion. Of course, it was not possible for me to conceal my disappointment or frustration, yet I thought it right to continue to hold out the hope that sooner or later the unity of Europe would be reached. How long it would be I could not tell, yet never from that day did I waver in my faith.

It was therefore a moving occasion for me when, by the kindness of the Prime Minister of the day, Edward Heath—the man who carried on his shoulders the whole burden of this long and difficult negotiation—I was able to be present ten years later at the signing of the Treaty in Brussels, by which Britain and three other powers were admitted to membership of the European Community, with the full approbation of the French Government. The wheel had come full circle.

CHAPTER XII

Debits and Credits

I. THE SHADOW OF UNEMPLOYMENT

Mr. Baldwin is said to have made the reflection, at the end of his long political career, that there were three forces in conflict with which it was very unwise for a British politician to engage. These were the Vatican, the Treasury and the National Union of Miners. To this, at the time about which I am writing, might well have been added a fourth—Bretton Woods; that is the system of money management throughout the Free World set up by the agreements reached after the Second War. No doubt during the early post-war years this structure gave at least some degree of stability to a battered world. But it contained within it the seeds of its own decay. For the Bretton Woods system had been accepted without the vital proposals made at the time by Maynard Keynes. Had his plan for 'Bancor' been adopted, much sorrow and tribulation might have been avoided. It is one of the ironies of history that the Keynes plan was torpedoed and finally 'sunk without trace' by the efforts of an American Treasury official who was subsequently said to be a Communist agent. He certainly did his work well. This strange episode, which would hardly be plausible in a work of spy fiction, proves once again the truth that 'nature beats art every time'. Meanwhile, the almighty—and still convertible —dollar was to enjoy some thirty years of domination before its collapse.

For many years I had begun, in my own mind, to have doubts about a system which, from the British point of view, was doubly oppressive. It limited the liquidity of money and its role in financing the growing production of wealth at continually higher prices; it placed a special burden upon us, in comparison with our European competitors, because of the diverse roles of sterling. Consequently, when in preparation for my first meeting with President Kennedy, I sent him at the end of 1960 a letter setting out the main questions for discussion, I wrote:

> The first and most important subject is what is going to happen to us unless we can show that our modern free society—the new form of capitalism—can run in a way that makes the fullest use of our resources and results in a steady expansion of our economic strength. Therefore the problem of money, the problem of its proper use in each of the Western countries, and of securing that there is sufficient credit available to keep all our countries working to the full extent of the potential available, is really the prime question of all. If we fail in this, Communism will triumph, not by war, or even subversion, but by seeming to be a better way of bringing people material comforts. In other words, if we were to fall back into anything like the recession or crisis that we had between the wars, with large-scale unemployment of men and machines, I think we would have lost the hand. Of course, things are not as bad as that, but there are great dangers facing us. For one reason or another, I believe the total credit available is either not sufficient or improperly used and this makes it necessary to reconsider the whole basis on which it stands.[1]

About a year later, although the small cloud which I had seen on the horizon was now beginning to move steadily into view, little had yet been done. I was therefore glad to hear on 13 December 1961 from the Chancellor of the Exchequer, then Selwyn Lloyd, of some modest advance. He reported to me that at a meeting of the O.E.C.D. in Paris the discussions on the expansion of the resources available to the International Monetary Fund had gone well.

> The sense of urgency which we have so long hoped for has at last been apparent. We have reached agreement in principle on the plan to increase resources available by about six and a half billion dollars. The United States share (if the maximum amount is called up) is two billion dollars, ours one billion dollars, the Six two and a half billion dollars, and the rest a further half billion dollars plus something . . . from the Swiss.

[1] For the full text of this letter, see *Pointing the Way*, p. 310.

Yet by May 1962 my anxieties had not been relieved. Accordingly I sent a note to the Chancellor of the Exchequer on 22 May reiterating my fears.

> In the early months of 1961, I got into disgrace with you and the Treasury for telling the new American Administration that the easiest way to enlarge the credit base and get us out of our difficulties of trying to finance more and more production and trade with insufficient money was to raise the price of gold.
>
> For eighteen months we have all played about with various tentative approaches to the problem of world credit, and certainly these moves have helped. But interest in these different schemes (which went by the strange names of their inventors) has rather languished.

The same doubts were expressed by Lord Cromer, the Governor of the Bank, in a long talk on 20 June.

> He is very intelligent. He agrees with me. But, in reality, although 'sound', Lord C. has a nose. He is not a Baring for nothing—a long business and financial tradition. He realises that the new danger to the world is not world inflation but competitive deflation. (The impending collapse of the Canadian dollar is symptomatic. We are trying to get up an American—British—European consortium to lend Canada $750,000 m.)[1]

A few days later, on 23 June, I sent a further memorandum to Selwyn Lloyd.

> We spoke this morning about the financial and economic dangers which seem to be looming across the horizon. You undertook to consult your people as to the possibility of discussions with America on radical changes to meet the needs of the next period. I also suggested that you should consider with your experts and the Bank the possibility of unilateral action by us if the pound is strong enough, or by the Europeans with us, which the dollar could follow. In other words, if the Americans will not revalue gold in terms of the dollar, if the pound, mark and franc force them to, they will have to follow. However, it would of course be much better if all this was done by general agreement.

[1] 20 June 1962.

I only put these dangerous thoughts into your head because some-times it needs a brave man to set off a fuse.

The problem really is this; there ought to be a World Economic Conference with the Heads of Governments taking part. But if Heads of Governments take part there is a danger of creating a panic by the mere meeting of the Conference. This is the problem. Either Heads of Governments are not available to take part, or even Chancellors of the Exchequer and Finance Ministers find themselves unable to take revolutionary decisions because they are hamstrung by their more orthodox advisers.

How then do we get over this? Apart from your studies under paragraph one, I should be glad were you to consider whether we could not disguise a World Economic Conference under the machinery of O.E.C.D., with Heads of Governments taking a part behind the scenes. It might be possible, by extending the range of discussions from merely money to commodity and development matters, e.g., relieve the Canadians, Australians and even the Americans of their troubles by selling or giving a lot of food to the people who have none. This would of course itself involve an increase in the liquidity of the world and the availa-bility of larger sums necessary to finance these larger operations.

All this, which I foresaw coming a year ago, seemed then to your advisers the ravings of a kind of political King Lear. But now the storm is clearly approaching.

At the same time I tried to get the Foreign Secretary to work through the American Secretary of State, with whom we were going to have some talks in London.

I should like to talk to him about the world economic situation, which worries me greatly. The collapse of the Canadian dollar may be as serious in 1962 as the collapse of the Credit Anstalt thirty years ago. I should like to ask Rusk whether the American Administration take the economic situation as seriously as I do, and what he thinks the President proposes to do about it. Of course, the logical course would be to have an economic con-ference at Heads of Government level, but this might merely create a panic and may in any case be an unsuitable forum for detailed economic discussion. Nevertheless, there must surely be some concerted moves by the Western countries to avert the threat of a major slump. I will ask if the Americans have considered using O.E.C.D., and whether there is anything which could be done in the field of commodities.

I feel that this economic question is really the most important immediate one which faces us.

I also wrote to our Ambassador, David Ormsby Gore, on 3 July 1962.

For your private information, I have it in mind to start a movement to bring some rational system of international credit into being. You may remember that this was one of the subjects of my first letter to the President in the winter of 1960, and we discussed it in some detail at my first meeting with him in the spring of 1961. Although some progress was made and there have been, of course, some improvements in technique (e.g. the help given to us last summer and the help recently given to Canada) yet the more ambitious plans ran into the sand. . . . Is the President still interested in all this, or would there be any chance of my getting him interested? I quite realise that he cannot politically do anything about the price of gold *on his own*, but does he intellectually take the view that something must be done to widen the base upon which increasing world trade is to be carried on? If not, the superstructure cannot reach the size which it ought to. As you know, my views here are regarded as heretical and dangerous by the orthodox and by what one might call the economic establishment; but they are shared by very many people whose intelligence I rate higher. I would greatly value any thoughts you have about this. At present, the signs are that all the developed countries will begin to deflate or desire to preserve their gold; Germany, France, Japan, are all talking the same language. We are doing it a bit. America is running on high unemployment and under-used industry, and in the end, by taking a course which might be defended for any individual country, we shall collectively move slowly (I do not think this time with the rapidity of the inter-war crisis) towards the decay of capitalism.

The Ambassador, in a most helpful reply of 11 July, reported his feeling that the President was certainly not happy about the existing international monetary system. Yet it was almost certain that he could not himself increase the price of gold, although he held views very similar to mine. However, the Ambassador felt that the political

N2

pressure upon the American Administration for an inflationary policy and an unbalanced budget, rather than accept the stagnation which would follow any serious deflation, might be relied upon to arrest the worst dangers. He added his own view that the time was coming when 'what was decided at Bretton Woods should be reviewed in the light of our experience over almost two post-war decades'. In a further letter David Gore told me that he proposed, during the course of a private visit to the President, to raise the whole question informally.

Although these and similar ideas were being discussed in many quarters and in every country, little progress could be made. The British Government had prudently repaid all its debts to the International Monetary Fund arising from the crisis in 1961, thus protecting itself against a possible devaluation of the dollar and at the same time increasing the liquidity of the Fund. But this was of minor importance in the larger scene.

The ministerial changes in July 1962 involved the Treasury, and Maudling now succeeded Selwyn Lloyd.

> To my great pleasure (and surprise) the Treasury are now adopting my views about the need for increasing world 'liquidity'. This after 18 months—nearly two years—of battling with them. . . . The Bank of England have also come round to this view. Since it is clear that the President still refuses (or is unable) to raise the price of gold, the Bank have devised a scheme of their own. Of course the real problem is to get public opinion to recognise that there is nothing more 'immoral' in an international Bank creating credit—or money—out of nothing than a national bank doing so. Internationally we are still in the early nineteenth century.[1]

Unluckily, at this rather critical moment, when both our American and our European partners seemed to be moving towards a more forward policy, Per Jacobsson, the Managing Director of the International Monetary Fund, delivered a speech which had the most deplorable effect. At the meeting of the Fund on 17 September, he presented a report which exuded confidence. He dismissed fears of a scramble for international liquidity as exaggerated and professed

[1] 10 August 1962.

to see signs that the industrial countries were now approaching 'a state of equilibrium'. In other words, 'God's in his heaven, all's right with the world.' I immediately sent an urgent message to Maudling.

> I have read with considerable anxiety and distress the latest speech by Mr. Jacobsson. I hope that this will not in any way deter you and that you will put forward your views with unabated vigour. I am sure that President Kennedy does not share the views of this man. Would you like me to send him a personal message urging the importance to the whole free world of both our countries keeping free from the toils of the old régime? It is not an exaggeration to say that Mr. Jacobsson threatens to turn out to be the reincarnation of Montagu Norman.

Within a few weeks,

> even Jacobsson and the Bank pundits have realised the danger of world *deflation* (more dangerous, really, than inflation). But there has been no action by President Kennedy or by the Europeans. It is the most urgent question of the day. I am (as usual) a helpless Cassandra on all this.[1]

With the Common Market negotiations still continuing and with the apparent inability of Washington to take a lead—the feebleness of their Treasury representatives was of so vigorous a character that it seemed likely to totter on almost indefinitely—I could see little chance of progress. Indeed it was not until after the troubles of a whole decade that some steps were at last taken to loosen the bonds which Bretton Woods had fastened on the world.

But if we could make little progress in the international field, what were we to do? How were we to stimulate the British economy, which clearly required the loosening of some of the remaining brakes on expansion and at least 'a touch on the accelerator', without incurring all the troubles of balance of payments, pressure on sterling and inflation from which we had suffered so often? I was concerned as to

> how we can handle this effectively so long as sterling remains (with inadequate reserves) a reserve currency for the world. But we made little progress at New York with our new approach to

[1] 18 October 1962.

the question of providing, on a world basis, a wider foundation for world trade. First, the Americans, then the Germans, and now the French—in turn, these have collected too much of the money.[1]

Yet, with growing unemployment and disappointing investment we must somehow take the risk. Meanwhile, something could be done by a vigorous campaign for the 'modernisation of Britain' and the improvement of our industrial methods at home as well as our techniques of export. But more—much more—was needed. Thus, in the second half of October 1962, I began a series of discussions with Maudling to see whether, even if we could get little response on the international front, by taking some chances at home, we could at least stimulate the economy.

> Like the Governor, the Chancellor seems against lowering the Bank Rate—at any rate for the present. But he will concentrate on trying to reduce the long-term rate of interest. This is made possible by the rise in gilts. (Unfortunately, I feel that the rise in gilts is only the reflection of the recession.) But even here, we must try to bring more pressure on Building Societies to lower their rates. Another measure (which I think should have a quick effect) to which I agreed, was an immediate cut (to be announced when Parliament returns) in Purchase Tax on Motor Cars from 45 per cent to $33\frac{1}{3}$ per cent. It will 'cost' the Revenue £30 m. But I believe it will have a good effect all round. I had already put to Maudling some ideas of mine about 'depreciation' (affecting the Initial and Investment allowances). My fear is that in view of the uncertainty as to (a) Europe, (b) General Election, we have little chance of getting any natural increase in private investment during the next year, unless we can stimulate it by some such means as I have proposed. Maudling is considering my plans and hopes to have an answer shortly.[2]

A few days later the Chancellor of the Exchequer proposed further Purchase Tax reductions, to which I readily assented.

After recovering from the somewhat hectic Cuba week, when the destruction of the civilised world by nuclear bombs seemed a more

[1] 10 October 1962.   [2] 19 October 1962.

urgent danger than that of monetary maladjustment, we returned to our immediate difficulties. Unemployment now stood at half a million, a low figure compared with the distant past, but alarming to a generation who were beginning to regard full employment as a permanent and indeed natural feature of industrial life. Moreover, although in some areas it was as low as two per cent, in others it had risen to five per cent. This seems today a moderate burden; but for us, full of memories of the past, it struck at that time a note of alarm. Yet I knew that we must still guard against an undue rise in wages and prices.

What is needed now is a stimulus not to *all* consumption (such as use of regulator would do—including whisky and tobacco) but to *selected consumption*, which (*a*) has wide effect on other industry; (*b*) good export history. Chancellor of Exchequer came at noon today, to settle final plans for a little scheme which we have been talking about and minuting each other about for some weeks. We settled the 'package' this morning. It will be (*a*) new concessions on either initial *or* investment allowances; (*b*) accelerated 'write off' for *heavy* plant; (*c*) inducement to investment on science and research; write off in *one* year, if desired; (*d*) reduction of tax on motor cars from 45 to 25 per cent. This will cost a lot (£90 m.) but should have a very good effect on the economy all round.[1]

These changes were duly announced on 5 November and well received.

Taken as a whole, the relaxations made during this autumn were substantial. The repayment of post-war credits would amount to an injection of £42 m. in spending power. Public investment was increased by £70 m. The rate for special deposits by the London clearing banks was reduced from two to one per cent; this 'package' would, in a full year, amount to £165 m. But, although these were all useful to stimulate an economy as a whole, the 'black spots' were becoming steadily darker. Work on the modernisation campaign continued; further relaxation in Purchase Tax was agreed on 11 December. Yet little that we could do seemed likely to have an immediate effect on the old 'special areas', in Scotland and the

[1] 26 October 1962.

North of England. Meanwhile the Government was subject to widespread attacks in the Press and on the television. At any rate, Ministers were not idle on the last day of the year.

> Home Secretary and Chancellor of Exchequer all the morning. We discussed various *general* measures for the Economy. The Treasury are now quite in [an] expansionist mood. The reduction from 45 to 25 per cent Purchase Tax of *all* remaining items in the 45 per cent category will be announced tomorrow. Another half per cent reduction (from $4\frac{1}{2}$ to 4 per cent) in Bank Rate on Thursday. We discussed plans for N.W. and N. East and some special measures.[1]

There was little more that could be done before the Budget, except for minor adjustments in social benefits. For instance, increases in unemployment pay and retirement pensions were announced on 23 January 1963. Meanwhile, apart from other troubles with which we were beset in this 'winter of our discontent' – a period which comprised all the difficulties about nuclear armaments and the final and brutal conclusion of the Common Market negotiations by General de Gaulle–we were now to be afflicted by three months of the worst weather since the terrible winter of 1947. During January the temperature continued to fall and the numbers of unemployed to rise.

> The cold weather continues, although there has been no more snow, at least on any extensive scale. But the construction industry is almost at a standstill.[2]

On the next day I recorded:

> Snow is not now expected, but intense frost–a bleak outlook, for comfort, for production, and for employment. Added to this, the news about the Power position is rather worse today. The trade union leaders seem to be losing out to the Communist shop-stewards. A serious situation is upon us.[3]

The Power dispute added a man-made difficulty at a moment when we were suffering from 'natural causes'.

> The 'go-slow' combined with the extreme cold (which still

[1] 31 December 1962.   [2] 11 January 1963.   [3] 12 January 1963.

persists) is playing havoc with our industrial life as well as with the comfort of almost every home. The Press (including, happily, the *Daily Mirror*) is very critical of the shop-stewards and of the weakness of the official trade union leaders. The problem is what more, if anything, the Electricity Council can or ought to do. The trade unions have an arbitration agreement which they refuse to implement on the ground that since the summer of 1961 arbitrators have been subservient to the Government's Incomes Policy! How I wish it were true! A meeting with the Chancellor of the Exchequer, Minister of Labour, Home Secretary, and Minister of Power. We agreed on the general line which we would take with the Electricity Council. They showed a certain tendency to refuse any further negotiation 'under duress'—that is, until the unofficial 'go-slow' movement stopped. This would not really be wise. It would encourage rather than discourage the extremists.[1]

Naturally, the weather, as well as every other hardship, was charged to the Government's account, the Press becoming more and more hostile and the Party increasingly restless.

The weather is still cold; the last fortnight has been a nightmare on this account alone. The snow and ice have dislocated all our life—there has been nothing like it since 1947. In my view, the authorities, all kinds, have done remarkably well. The streets and roads have been cleared, and in spite of delays, trains and buses have kept on running pretty well. The public (who are in a very peevish mood—or at least the Press) do not take this view and seem to criticise everyone very sourly. Anyway, we managed to settle the Electricity dispute *without a defeat*. (Indeed, the extreme trade unions and the shop-stewards complained bitterly about the agreement reached—three-year agreement, and about 4 per cent rise a year—*very* good from the Incomes Policy point of view.) The Communist shop-stewards [have] lost out. But the E.T.U. remains very disgruntled and threatens to re-open the settlement, to which I feel some of the other four unions will not agree. The effect of the 'go-slow', together with the tremendous load on electricity owing to the weather, has been trying—'cuts', 'blackouts', etc. (On Friday night we had a breakdown [at Chequers] from midnight till 4 p.m. Saturday, owing to the peculiar effect

[1] 14 January 1963.

of frost and fog on the insulators, which upset the grid from Birmingham to Buckinghamshire.) . . . However, the thaw looks like coming and the strike has been foiled. This has meant a tremendous [number] of meetings with Ministers. We have tried *not* to interfere with the Chairman of the Electricity Council (Professor [Sir Ronald] Edwards) except to back him up.[1]

It was during this month that a somewhat novel step was taken. Early in the year I had held prolonged discussions with Maudling and the Chief Whip regarding plans for the North-East coast and Merseyside.

> We have been arguing backwards and forwards about a 'Special Commissioner' or some such character to help N.E. coast, where quite a radical approach seems now to be required. After a lot of thought, I decided on a *Minister* (not a Ministry) and on a Minister of first rank (not an Under Secretary or Minister of State as had been proposed and generally agreed).[2]

Accordingly, on 5 January, I sent a memorandum to Lord Hailsham in the following terms:

> I have been considering how we might best adapt our machinery of government to deal with the special problems of the North-East. I have reached the conclusion that, if the Cabinet are to be assisted to take a comprehensive view of these problems, it is desirable that a Minister of Cabinet rank should be invited to accept, in relation to the North-East, the type of responsibility which is exercised by the Secretary of State in relation to Scotland, by the Home Secretary in relation to Northern Ireland and by the Minister of Housing and Local Government in relation to Wales. I should be glad if you would accept an additional and temporary assignment for this purpose.
>
> Our aim must be to promote the conditions for long-term economic growth in the area and so to raise its employment level nearer to the national average. It is essential that this question should be treated as a whole, in the sense that all the inter-related issues—the choice of 'growth areas', the development of housing and other public investment, the adaptation of communications, etc.—should be brought to a central point and dealt with as an

[1] 28 January 1963.   [2] 11 January 1963.

integrated complex. An inter-departmental group, which is just setting to work on these problems, will be at your disposal.

You will no doubt agree that your first act should be to visit the North-East in order to acquire first-hand experience of the local problems and to acquaint yourself with the personalities involved, particularly the North-East Development Council under the Chairmanship of Mr. [George] Chetwynd. I hope that, in the light of these consultations, you will prepare a definite plan for the whole area, which you can present to the Cabinet. It will then be possible for the Cabinet to weight the claims of the North-East against the claims of other areas in need of special assistance and to reach an informed judgement on the proper priorities. I shall also welcome your advice on the best means of ensuring that the measures which we adopt may be promptly and effectively executed.

With characteristic loyalty, Hailsham accepted this exacting and politically unremunerative task.

The reception [of Hailsham's appointment], when it came out on Wednesday, was pretty good. Anyway, the Opposition are very angry, so they must be afraid that he may do some good.[1]

Hailsham's speech, some weeks later, in the House of Lords made it clear that he had succeeded, in the words of an impartial commentator, in carrying

the debate on regional planning, growth points, and local communications into the higher echelons of Whitehall. Addressing the House of Lords on 19 February, Lord Hailsham seemed anxious to accept the portfolio of minister for the 21st century, calling for a 'radical experiment in social engineering' throughout the depressed areas.[2]

On 9 January I took the opportunity of the 150th annual dinner of the Birmingham Chamber of Commerce—at which there were six or seven hundred guests—to restate the Government's broad philosophy. One of the speakers, a clever and even brilliant man, delivered

a reactionary, witty, Liberal *laissez-faire* kind of speech attacking

[1] 11 January 1963.   [2] *Annual Register*, *1963*, p. 7.

the Local Development Act and the attempts to help the North, etc. . . . But he gave me a chance which I took. I discarded a great part of my speech, and plunged into a fierce reply, sometimes indignant, sometimes sentimental. By the end, I got all these Brummagem types to a standing ovation lasting several minutes. I was proud of this; they . . . seemed a bit ashamed.[1]

This was particularly helpful to me for much of the murmurings in the Party arose from misgivings in the industrial and commercial world. Moreover, I was glad to be able to preach progressive doctrine in the home of the great radical reformer, Joseph Chamberlain, whose authority had swayed Birmingham for so long, and was not yet forgotten.

In looking into the details of the dispute in the Electrical Supply industry, I had noticed the long hours which are constantly worked. I accordingly sent a minute to the Minister of Power on 21 January, suggesting that some dilution of labour could be effected.

I do not understand why in the Electricity Generating and Supply Industries 40-hour weeks are agreed and praised as a sign of industrial advance (you will remember that leisure was the thing we were supposed to learn to enjoy). Yet it seems to be generally agreed that everybody works 55 hours a week. Since there are a great number of fairly unskilled jobs as well as some more skilled ones and quite a lot of unemployed all over the country, why cannot the industry take on and train if necessary enough men to prevent continued overtime on this scale. Overtime is meant to be an occasional method of dealing with an extra flow of orders. It should not settle down into a routine. Will you talk to your people about this? I also feel that these hours of work probably tend to produce a slightly nervous situation among the men. Of course they get the extra money but they are also unduly fatigued. At least they ought to be if 40 hours is supposed to be the right working week.

Some steps were taken; but it still seems somewhat of a paradox to pride ourselves as a modern community on short hours if they are merely to be a means of increasing take-home pay by long overtime.

[1] 11 January 1963.

All through January the freeze-up continued.

> The result of the cold weather has been to add an immense
> figure (perhaps 150,000–170,000) to the registered unemployed.
> The total is now about 800,000 – the largest since 1947. Naturally,
> the Opposition are jubilant and we are to have a vote of censure
> next week.[1]

At the end of the month this was my assessment of the situation:

> The economy is not *yet* responding to the Chancellor of the
> Exchequer's measures. The pound is strong; exports not bad;
> imports lower and so balance of payments good; production
> increasing slowly. But there are bad prospects for shipbuilding,
> for heavy steel and engineering – that is, for Scotland, N.E. coast.[1]

These topics were discussed at a conference with members of the
Scottish Trades Union Congress, which went off very well. I found
them practical and helpful and not at all inclined to denigrate the
efforts which we were making. I was especially struck by the good
sense of the Secretary, George Middleton.

But the winter was still against us.

> The weather has deteriorated. The thaw is over, more snow
> (blizzards in South and South-East England) and temperatures
> low. I'm afraid this is going to put us back a lot. Our affairs are not
> properly arranged for cold weather, so I fear that there will be
> further falls in production and employment.[2]

At this time an unexpected stroke of fate removed one of the
chief figures in our parliamentary life. Hugh Gaitskell, the leader
of the Opposition, died suddenly on 18 January, following only a
short illness. This was a disaster, both for the Labour Party, which
he led with conspicuous talent, and for Parliament, of which he was a
leading ornament; equally it was a loss to the whole country.

> Poor Hugh G., who has been ill for some weeks with a
> mysterious germ or virus, died on the night of Friday 18th. It
> was apparent from the bulletins that he was unlikely to sur-
> vive. . . . It is very sad . . . he was a man of *high* quality and his
> death is a real loss to the nation.[1]

[1] 28 January 1963.   [2] 4 February 1963.

On the next day I thought it appropriate to deliver a broadcast tribute, as Prime Minister.

Hugh Gaitskell's death, after a very short illness, at the comparatively early age of 56, is a grievous loss to the whole nation. It will be felt all the more poignantly because during the last few days there is hardly a family in the Kingdom which has not seemed to be sharing in the wonderfully gallant fight which he put up on his sick bed, right to the end. Even now, it seems almost unbelievable. Just a month ago, he was in his place in the House of Commons. On Tuesday, when we return from our Christmas recess, his place will be empty. We shall be making on that day our tributes to his life and work as a Parliamentarian. He has died prematurely; but he will leave behind him a record of achievement of which any man may be proud. Tonight I would like to say a few words about him as a man.

I remember first meeting Hugh Gaitskell during the war when he was in the Ministry of Economic Warfare, as a temporary civil servant, under Mr. Dalton. His reputation as an economist was already high and he had added to it by his work in Whitehall. As soon as the war ended he went into active politics. His career in the House of Commons was spectacular. Within six years he had risen from Private Member to Under Secretary, then to Minister and finally to Chancellor of the Exchequer. Why this rapid rise? There was a wide field to choose from in the 1945 Parliament, with the large Labour majority. How did he outclass his rivals? Primarily, of course, because of his clear brain and intellectual power, his gift for lucid exposition, and his unsparing application to work. But he had something more. He had that indefinable thing, character. So, we, on our side of the House, were not surprised when he was later elected Leader of his Party and Leader of the Opposition. For he had the qualities most needed for a particularly difficult job—courage and patience. These are what matter most. He had another quality—more subtle—not always readily recognised (at least on first acquaintance) either by supporters or opponents. He had real humanity—not paraded but genuine. He wasn't just, as many people thought, a fine intellect; he was a man of warm heart, with a real affection for his fellow men—not just for mankind in general, but for individual men and women. He was courteous, sympathetic and understanding, even with bores. He had no hatreds—except a deep and genuine hatred of injustice in any form.

In some ways, political life has always been cruel; success or failure are so chancy; public favour or disfavour so capricious; the work so hard and pitiless, so that physical strength becomes almost as important as intellectual or moral pre-eminence. But there are great compensations. One of them is the fact that there can be strong conflicts without resentment. Another is the sense of sympathy which binds together sincere men of all parties in a sort of comradeship which is a unique and living thing. In this company, Hugh Gaitskell was both distinguished and respected, and, among his intimates, loved. His death will leave, of course, a great gap in our public life. What his devoted wife and family may be assured is that it leaves an equal gap in the private lives of a very wide circle of friends, in all parts of the country and in all ranks of society, who will mourn him sincerely.

Although, according to precedent, it was only for the death of a former Prime Minister that the House of Commons customarily adjourned for a whole day, I thought it right to follow this course in honour of Gaitskell. This courtesy was much appreciated by the Labour Party. Formal tributes were made in the House of Commons on Tuesday, 23 January. On 31 January I attended the memorial service in Westminster Abbey.

There was a large attendance—the Cabinet, the Corps Diplomatique—in the choir—the transepts full of M.P.s, etc., and the nave also full. The singing was exquisite. I thought the lesson oddly chosen—it was the sheep and the goats—('goats to the left, sheep to the right' one might almost hear St. Peter calling, in Parliament's last division).[1]

The consequences of Gaitskell's death upon the Labour Party were not easy to assess.

Of course, he had become both experienced and respected. . . . He was the sort of upper-middle class leader which a party of the Left requires in *normal* times—Asquith, or Attlee. He moved in many circles, and attracted the academic, the literary and artistic, and . . . some of the 'smart' society of London. He was

[1] 4 February 1963.

thought much of abroad in 'progressive' circles – both in America and (to a less extent since his anti-European Market attitude) in Europe. He was a distinguished man, with considerable political courage. . . . He held his Party together. His successor (with an election approaching) should be able to do this easily.[1]

I felt that the Labour Party had done right from their point of view in their choice of a successor to Gaitskell.

> Wilson is an able man – far more able than Brown. He is good in the House and in the country – and, I am told, on T.V.[2]

Although I heard that a new Tory group called the Monday Club, which had been founded by Lord Salisbury and others of the Right Wing, was now demanding my resignation, my own feeling throughout this difficult period was that the bulk of the Party was remaining remarkably firm. Of course, I had a number of strong critics in the House of Commons, composed largely of Ministers who had resigned or had been omitted from administrations over which I presided.

> This . . . is reaching quite formidable dimensions. 'Macmillan must go' is the cry. Faced with Wilson (47 or so) we must have a young man (Heath or Maudling). This line of approach leaves out poor Butler as well as me.
>
> Of course, there's something in it. We have had a run of bad luck. Once this starts, everything seems to go wrong. Really, everything that would have been passed over as a minor contretemps when things are good is elevated into a major crisis when things are bad. Nevertheless, apart from spite, this is mostly defeatism. If I were to resign *now*, it could be of no benefit to anyone. We *must* go on at least till May, perhaps to October 1964, in the hope that our economic measures will have produced their results. So we must stick it out.[2]

Fortunately, at this moment, much attention was concentrated on a meeting of the Young Conservatives Conference, attended by fourteen hundred delegates. It was here, above all, that, according to the Press, I would have to face a critical audience.

[1] 28 January 1963.   [2] 17 February 1963.

I tried a new (or rather old) technique. No prepared speech and no 'text'—a few notes, and the rest 'off the cuff'. (Actually, I spent nearly two days dreaming about this speech—composing it and getting it fixed in my mind.) It was a *huge* success. I have never had such a reception or such prolonged and enthusiastic support *after* the speech in my lifetime. I came back to Admiralty House at 7 p.m. tired, but relieved. Even the Press today find it difficult to conceal the triumph which I had. Since there were a good many M.P.s there, this will get about I hope. But if things do not improve (particularly the unemployment figure) it will not be easy, and the pressure for a 'sacrificial victim' . . . will begin to grow.[1]

On the day after this meeting, I had two important visitors.

A long talk with Butler, about the position of the Government and the Party. He seemed fairly confident that the opposition groups [in the Party] would not be able to coalesce effectively, since each distrusts the other.

Sir W. Haley (Editor, *Times*) called at 6 p.m. He was enthusiastic about my speech. I was enthusiastic about his leading article. This mutual 'buttering' was agreeable and may be useful.[2]

At the same time the Opposition had their own difficulties.

Harold Wilson is already in trouble. A Private Motion on Steel has forced him to come out strongly in favour of nationalisation. As the election approaches, this will get more difficult for the Socialists. Brown has disappeared (like a man in a detective story) and the *Guardian* is very pontifical about it all. My announcement (by implication) on Saturday that there is to be no General Election in 1963 will, I hope, steady things a bit.[2]

The mid-February unemployment figures had now risen to 3.9 per cent throughout the country. Unhappily, it reached 7 per cent in the North-East. These were alarming figures to those who had been accustomed to full, or rather over-full, employment. It was in this atmosphere of conflicting difficulties that we had now to

[1] 17 February 1963.   [2] 19 February 1963.

approach the problem of the Budget. Much would clearly turn on its character.

The arguments for and against an expansionist Budget were as usual nicely balanced. Many leading economists, of which perhaps the most notable was Professor F. W. Paish, recommended caution. The balance of payments was satisfactory; production was increasing slightly; the present rates of taxation would show a surplus 'above the line'. There would perhaps be room for some minor concessions, including the abolition of Schedule A (the income tax on the assessed rental value for owner-occupiers). So long as the Americans refused to give the lead to other European countries for some modification of the present international monetary system which would enable all-round expansion to take place in the industrial countries, was it not safer to wait—to rest on our oars? It is true that there were now some six hundred thousand unemployed, but these figures were misleading. Many of them were out of work for only a few weeks; were changing jobs rather than out of a job. Moreover, even the patron saint of the welfare state, Lord Beveridge, had declared (and Gaitskell had agreed) that figures of unemployed ranging from 3 to $3\frac{1}{2}$ per cent overall were to be regarded as full employment. It was true that in some of the old 'distressed areas' in the North-West and North-East, and above all in Scotland, the situation was far worse. Nevertheless, we should trust to the laws of supply and demand. The movement of population would follow available employment. We would do more harm than good by trying to tinker with natural forces which we could not control.

Against this cold but not unimpressive deployment of what was in effect the old *laissez-faire* doctrine of classic Liberalism, I reacted instinctively and violently. In so doing I felt I had the sympathy of the mass of the Conservatives as well as of the nation. Apart from any reasons of humanity, it was clear that in modern conditions with the rigidity which had entered into the economic system since the increased power of the trade unions and the buttressing forces of social benefits, which prevented the harsh pressure of poverty acting as it had in the past, some degree at any rate of state interference—or *dirigisme*—was both necessary and in conformity with traditional

Tory philosophy. To my mind (and here the Chancellor of the Exchequer and other colleagues were in full-hearted agreement) it was really a question not of dogma but of degree. The National Economic Development Council (NEDDY) declared at the end of February that a 4 per cent annual growth in the period 1961 to 1966 was still obtainable, but that the stagnation of 1961 to 1962 now required an effort of some 5 per cent to reach the target. Most experts certainly regarded national wage increases of some 3 per cent as the maximum which the economy could stand. If wage-restraint on something like these lines could be achieved, then it would surely be right to 'prime the pump'—in other words to make an increase of purchasing power available on Keynesian lines over a wide field, to stimulate both consumption and investment.

Before the Budget some further steps, in addition to those already described, had been taken to help the most affected areas both by Admiralty orders for Tyneside and by authorising the Tay Bridge at Dundee as well as approval of various public works in Merseyside, Scotland and the North-East. But much would depend upon the degree to which we could safely inject new money into the economy without falling into the danger of inflation. On this, many Minutes passed between my office and the Treasury, and long discussions were held. I found Maudling both flexible and ingenious; and the decisions ultimately reached, although not quite so daring as I had hoped, were bolder than I had expected. For I knew from experience how strong were the orthodox opinions prevailing in the seats of power. Certainly the expansionist nature of the Budget and ancillary measures in 1963 were not the cause of difficulties which were to follow at the end of 1964. I have no means of judging whether, in the period after I had left office, expansion was pressed too far. I am certain that during the time for which I was responsible, even if we could not hope for a more imaginative policy to be followed in Washington, we did not overstep the limits of prudence. When the final decisions were taken, the relief in taxation amounted to some £269 m.; to this had to be added certain Government expenditures such as £30 m. for the shipping industry, and some other similar grants. Since the highest figure that I had dared suggest was some £400 m. I was not disappointed at the result.

But before the Budget could be introduced on 2 April, there was still a trying period to be endured. This horrible winter continued.

> More snow, ice on roads, and no sign yet of a real thaw. We were lucky that the unemployment figure has remained under 900,000—for all work on roads, building, etc., has stopped for over two months.[1]

Yet, on the same day I was pleased by the progress that I was making with the Treasury:

> A very good talk with Maudling. We are in broad agreement on the general outline for economic recovery. We must face the risks in relation to sterling. If the nation will accept in practice (as well as in principle) the need for a reasonable 'incomes policy' I believe we can have another 'go' without an inevitable 'stop'.[1]

All the political indications were still against us.

> The Gallup Poll is bad—Socialists well ahead, 12–15 points, and my 'popularity' sinking fast. However, we have had it all before. Harold Wilson has started being rude to me—with all the old stuff about dukes, relations in office, etc. This will not wear well.[2]

I was encouraged, also, two or three days later.

> Harold Wilson made a very clever broadcast last night. But he fell into one or two traps. The people don't want more taxes; they want less taxes.[3]

The sense of uncertainty continued.

> The Press is still full of stories about my resignation and of intrigues in the Party against me. But I think this is just a sort of delayed result of the talk that was going on some weeks ago. Everything now depends on the Budget and the possibility of getting expansion without inflation. This means that the 'brake' must be the general acceptance of a reasonable incomes policy.[4]

The next day, however, our hopes for a good incomes policy were 'rather dashed by a settlement in the Electrical Industry, amounting

[1] 21 February 1963.   [2] 25 February 1963.
[3] 28 February 1963.   [4] 3 March 1963.

to 6 per cent rise'.[1] It must seem strange to a new generation to reflect how modest were the figures which caused us such alarm in a previous decade. The economists of that time argued like Mr. Micawber; three or four per cent was tolerable; five or six per cent would lead to national bankruptcy. I could never be wholly persuaded of this truth, which had little regard to the rising costs in competitive countries. However, more as a gesture than from any hope of reversing the agreement, we decided to refer the Electrical wage settlement to the National Incomes Commission (NICKY), who duly delivered a critical judgement:

Parallel with the question of injecting further money into the economy, whether for consumption or investment, was the important concept of 'modernisation' in British industry, for which we now began a great campaign. This was pursued with increasing effort and with some success during the spring and summer. Yet the immediate task was undoubtedly expansion as far as possible without inflation. I tried to summarise the situation on 11 March in a letter to the Queen, on her return to England from a visit to Fiji, New Zealand and Australia:

Everything, from our point of view and indeed the country's, depends on whether we can re-expand the economy without disaster to the balance of payments and sterling. In other words, can we have a boom without busting? To this sixty-four thousand dollar question the pundits are contributing a tremendous flow of words in every journal, popular and serious. They are usually divided into three parties. One says, 'Boom and do not mind busting', i.e. devalue the pound or alternatively let it float. The second says, 'Expand and throw everything you have into the battle if sterling is attacked. Borrow all you can and fight it out.' The third says, 'Expand but restrict imports either by physical controls on all imported goods or alternatively by some form of surcharge.' But behind the pundits lie the people. Your Majesty's Government are determined to expand the economy. The measures that we have already taken and the further measures which will be revealed in the Budget should produce this effect. But we are going to continue with our efforts to persuade the people to accept a reasonable incomes policy as the price for

[1] 4 March 1963.

expansion. The great battle for two years has really been about this, and I am persuaded that the lesson has been partly learned, if not altogether digested. The Trade Union and even the Labour leaders do not now reject an incomes policy as such. Indeed they all declare that they will have an incomes policy of their own. No doubt they will ask for many concessions from the so-called rich or the employers, possibly the proposed capital tax is connected with this. But the fact that an incomes policy is talked about, even in Labour and Trade Union circles, makes me hope that we may be able to carry the expansion without an undue increase in wages, salaries and dividends. Moreover, the expression 'undue' means something different to what it implied in 1961. Then we were leading the race towards expansion. Our competitors in Europe and America were well behind us. Now the price level in Europe, especially France and Germany, is ahead of ours and is rising rapidly. The French are risking a general strike at this moment to try to restrain it, in spite of the unpopularity. It proves what importance the French Government give to trying to hold down their rapidly rising cost of living and of production. Therefore, if we can keep our rises to 4 per cent, or even 5 per cent a year, I think we may be able to carry the expansion we require without inflation. In other words, we can boom without busting. In addition, if we can concentrate a good deal on the expansion in Scotland and the North-East coast, since there are unused resources there, I hope we may be able to expand without the inflation that follows from full or over-full employment. So we shall try to concentrate a good deal on these areas. But fundamentally, as we have been preaching for two years and I think we can now emphasise with great effect, if we can begin the expansion, and if we are to put aside the old Adam of monetary control – all the things the Bank of England makes us do – then we must put on the new man of self-control, which really means not asking too much. Whether Your Majesty's subjects will now be in the mood to accept what is so simple that it is almost ridiculous that one should have to preach it I cannot tell. But I think they are in a somewhat chastened mood and may be more ready to wait for the golden eggs and spare the goose.

During my visit to Scotland, I had got on to good terms with George Middleton, the Secretary of the Scottish Trades Union

Congress. Accordingly I wrote to him on 15 March to summarise what we were doing and hoped to do in Scotland.

Thank you for your letter of February 28. I had intended anyway to write to you about now to let you know what progress we have been able to make on the points we discussed when your delegation came to see me on January 22. Like you, I felt it was a valuable meeting.

One of the schemes you urged on me, the Tay Bridge, was announced the next day. I won't pretend that this was a direct result of what you urged upon me but at least it was a good start.

I think it would be convenient if I first summarised what has already been done and then gave you an account of the progress we are making on some of the other proposals.

Your delegation argued that more could and should be done to speed up social development by increasing the level of expenditure on houses, roads, schools and hospitals. Since we met the following projects have been announced;

Smaller capital projects in selected areas—£2 m.

Additional road work—£2½ m.

Three vehicle ferries of Macbraynes—£1¼ m.

Expenditure by the two Electricity Boards on transmission and distribution—£6¼ m.

An expansion of teachers' training colleges—£1 m.

A reservoir for Glasgow—£1 m.

This, with £4¼ m. for the Tay Bridge, adds up to some £20 m. of new capital expenditure in Scotland.

Then you raised with me the gas turbine generator at Townhill, Dunfermline, for the South of Scotland Electricity Board. This is to go forward at a cost of £1¾ m. I am told that this will provide new peak load capacity quickly for the winter of 1964–5 to fill in a gap before bigger schemes like the pumped storage scheme at Loch Awe come into operation; but the station will be expensive to run, and the Board must be careful about overloading the cost of electricity by extending this method of generation.

One of your delegation asked for more to be done on site improvements at industrial estates. The Board of Trade is to spend some £300,000 on this notably at Donibristle, Blantyre and Vale of Leven, Fife. More programmes of rehabilitation in our listed industrial areas are being considered.

Then the proposed new coal-fired power station. There are many complicated technical problems here which we are pressing forward. I hope that a decision can be reached in May.

The problems of the shipbuilding industry must, as I know you understand, be considered as a whole. The Scottish yards have basically the same problems as those in England. The points you put to me are being considered and of course some orders under Government control have already been brought forward.

These are all in the main projects which will help in the short term. The long-term problem is that of reinvigorating the Scottish economy. I said at our meeting that we could not solve this by simple or short-term measures. But we are determined to grasp this problem and carry out those measures within the Government's control which are necessary to solve it.

May I add a personal note. I was very sorry to hear of your impending retirement and I wish you a long leisure in which to enjoy it.

On 2 April, the Cabinet met at 10.30 a.m.

The Chancellor of the Exchequer gave an outline of the main Budget proposals in a masterly exposition—clear and convincing. After all the work we have done on it, the result is better than I had hoped. The proposals to attract industry to and expand industry within Scotland, N.E. coast, etc., are imaginative and should be effective. I am sure it is right to use the Income Tax as the main method of expansion, and within I.T. to use the allowances rather than standard rate. The whole Budget is on one simple theme—expansion without inflation—this means a real partnership between Government, Employers and Trade Unions. To this end, the allowances changes amount—for a married man with two children earning £15 a week—to a rise in wages of $2\frac{1}{2}$ per cent, *without adding to costs*. Ministers were pleased and impressed.[1]

When the Budget was introduced next day, on the lines already described, including relief amounting to nearly £300 m., together with the additional expenditure on Government works and the like in various directions, the reception was good, although the professional economists disagreed, sometimes with us, more often with

[1] 2 April 1963.

one another. The Labour Party were hampered by having already committed themselves to an increase rather than a reduction of taxation. Moreover, the redemption of Selwyn Lloyd's pledge of the previous year to abolish the Schedule A tax was welcomed by the many millions of owner-occupiers.

> Chancellor of Exchequer spoke from 3.30 to 5.15–an admirable performance, which both in manner and matter delighted the Government benches and won reluctant admiration from the Opposition. Wilson's rather cheap sneers were not effective. The scene is set–Expansion without Inflation. Will trade unions play? It all depends on them.[1]

A few days later Dorothy and I made a visit to South Wales. In spite of, or perhaps because of, the mounting attacks upon me personally, the visit proved a remarkable success. There were very large numbers both at the meeting and at an informal party given afterwards–perhaps five thousand in all. 'I have never had a more enthusiastic welcome. It was quite touching.'[2]

At this time I took the opportunity of the annual luncheon of the 1922 Committee at the Savoy to make it quite clear that I intended to lead the Party in the next Election. This decision was underlined by the announcement a few days later of the return of Lord Poole to act as Joint Chairman with Iain Macleod of the Party. Lord Poole was known as one of the organisers of victory in 1959. His return was welcomed as an omen that equal success lay before us. The luncheon was in itself a remarkable event.

> It was an occasion of special importance for me, for *two* reasons. (1) After all the rough weather of the last year or more, can I claim that we are moving into better weather conditions? Shall I put all doubts at rest, and announce my determination to continue as P.M. and to lead the Party in the next General Election? (2) The luncheon was to be the occasion for presenting me with a picture of quite remarkable interest and importance. It represents (the artist Mr. [A. R.] Thomson, R. A.) the interior of the House of Commons on the Debate on the Address in 1960– I am speaking; Maurice (who moved the Address) is behind me.

[1] 3 April 1963.   [2] 6 April 1963.

Winston in his corner; Gaitskell rising slightly to intervene; and
the familiar faces of leading Ministers on front and back benches.
It is really *very* well done, in the style of similar efforts made
occasionally in the last century. The speech was made by John
Morrison. The picture was 'unveiled' and examined by M.P.s.
My reply tried to thank them with sufficient warmth and grace
combined (I was indeed much moved by this unique mark of
affection) and also to rouse them for the future. After discussion
earlier with Chief Whip, I announced my intention (d.v.) of
leading the Party in the next Election.[1]

With the coming of spring there was an improvement in the
Gallup Poll and a growing sense of confidence in the Party and the
country. Neddy was working well, with employers and trade
unionists combining on constructive proposals for new training
schemes, liaison between academic and industrial scientists, regional
development programmes and other valuable plans. If Nicky
criticised the agreements reached in the construction industry as
likely to be inflationary, there was a general feeling that this degree
of inflation, like the housemaid's baby, was a very little one.

When therefore I convened a gathering of Ministers at Chequers
on 27 and 28 April to study Commonwealth and foreign policy,
industrial and economic policy, social services and the machinery of
government—a large order indeed—we settled down to our work in a
not unhopeful mood. I had returned from Glasgow

> after a tremendous programme including (*a*) opening an indus-
> trial development exhibition, with the socialist Lord Provost;
> (*b*) luncheon with 30 Scottish editors, from all over the country;
> (*c*) television interview; (*d*) opening Memorial Library (Walter
> Elliot) in Glasgow University; (*e*) mass meeting—over 3,000
> people; (*f*) dinner with Scottish Unionist notabilities. The whole
> day went off well. The T.V. was said to be very good.[2]

The gathering of Ministers—all those in and out of the Cabinet—
lasted over two days.

> The first night, we had leading Ministers—chiefly on Foreign
> and Commonwealth affairs and during Sunday all the rest (32 in

[1] 10 April 1963.   [2] 5 May 1963.

Adenauer and de Gaulle, the old men of Europe, January 1963

An audience with Pope John

'I was shocked by his appearance . . . He was very gay – talked incessantly in French.'

all). There were three sessions—one in the morning and two in the
afternoon. The 'openers' in each case had prepared their notes—
the rest contributed extempore. It was a very useful as well as
quite an enjoyable exercise. Naturally, it created quite a stir in the
Press, and (equally naturally) Mr. M Lipton (a very sour
Socialist) asked me on the following Tuesday what had been the
'charge on public funds'. I was able to say *none* (we had taken
steps to see to this).[1]

Nor were the losses in the local elections at the beginning of May
any great surprise. These are not uncommon in the mid-term of a
Parliament and are partly due to the apathy of supporters of the
Government. On 14 May I

> began the first of my weekly meetings with Lord Poole and Iain
> Macleod, the two Chairmen of the Party. We shall call in others
> to help on different aspects of the work. It lasted nearly two
> hours, and was very helpful. I think we may now begin to see
> some progress. The Local Election results are what we expected—
> neither worse nor better.[2]

As the terrible winter of 1962–3 drew to an end, there was a
marked improvement, both in the economy and the temper of the
nation. To quote the same impartial critic,

> the economy was shifting into higher gear, to vindicate Mr.
> Maudling. The gold reserves rose by £29 million in May and
> unemployment came bumping down. At the mid-May count
> unemployment was just 2.4 per cent of the labour force and at
> mid-June 2.1 per cent. However, these figures were patchy. In
> London and the South-East the rate (1.2 per cent) was remini-
> scent of the days of 'over-full' employment; but Scotland and the
> North-East were still stuck at 4.3 per cent. The best sign of all
> was that exports were moving well. March had been a record
> month (£349 million) as trade thawed out from the winter and
> an American dock strike; now May's exports rose unassisted to a
> figure of £341 million.[3]

The coming of spring and the broad improvement in conditions in
the special areas reflected itself in the spirit of the Party, both in the

[1] 5 May 1963.   [2] 14 May 1963.   [3] *Annual Register*, 1963, p. 17.

O

House of Commons and in the country. Sometimes I myself suffered from an onset of depression, no doubt due to mere physical exhaustion. In these moods it seemed to me that the British public were

> becoming more and more cynical and satirical. I read a most depressing account, based on question and answer, of what the young intelligentsia are supposed to be thinking. The number questioned was 7,000 or so; the questions very detailed and very well devised. Religion, morality, patriotism, honour, all these are at a discount. Envy (although concealed) is a strong emotion, and a rather doleful highbrow concept of a good time. How to appeal to this type is not an easy problem to resolve.[1]

Yet in the joyous atmosphere of May, even the most morose of my Conservative critics began to relax and I felt that from the Party point of view we were now through the worst. Employment and production continued to rise. Given the rigidities of the international money system, we had taken considerable risks; but there was no sign yet of exports falling or any pressure on the balance of payments or on sterling. This continued all through the summer, indeed up to the end of my administration. We had therefore somehow struck the right balance. I can only record my gratitude to those, above all Maudling, Chancellor of the Exchequer, who steered us through these treacherous shoals.

11. DEFENCE ORGANISATION

AMID the many disappointments of this period there was at least one cause for satisfaction. At the very beginning of my premiership, I had begun to consider the question of a central organisation for Defence. This problem had been obscured during the war, when Churchill, without legislative sanction but with the full consent of the nation, appointed himself Minister of Defence

[1] 20 May 1963.

and by his sole authority was able to impose a system of centralisation which could not be sustained by his successors. Even during his last administration, Conservative Ministers of Defence, like their Labour predecessors, suffered from the inherent weakness of their position. I knew this from bitter experience, having found the few months during which I held that office a period of painful frustration.

The Act of Parliament which established the Ministry of Defence after the war clothed the Minister with doubtful authority and gave him insufficient means to fulfil even the functions which he was supposed to carry out. A new Ministry, staffed not with the highest commanders but with subordinate, if devoted, officers, could with difficulty assert its will against the long tradition of the armed forces of the Crown. Their Lordships of the Admiralty, with their hierarchy of Admirals under the First Lord; the War Office with its Secretary of State and Army Council; even the later-created Air Ministry, again with its Secretary of State—it was in these historic bodies that rested the real, practical control. Moreover the responsibility of their political heads to Parliament had scarcely been altered by the emergence of the Minister of Defence. Even so strong a character as A. V. Alexander was unable to overcome the inherent weakness of his position. Meanwhile, our experience in the field showed that, apart from organisation at the centre, actual operations of any kind required that the three Services should be under a single commander. We had followed this plan throughout all the great campaigns of the Second War; and every practical soldier, sailor and airman knew the benefits that had followed this close tactical and even strategic unity which the Supreme Allied Commander could exercise, whether in Africa, Italy or Western Europe. After the war, this structure of command, with a soldier, sailor or airman acting as chief of all the forces, was gradually instituted in our remaining colonies and bases.

At the beginning, therefore, of my administration, I took the first moves towards improving the position of the Minister of Defence.[1] A few months later, on 16 May 1957, I wrote to the Minister of Defence, Duncan Sandys:

[1] See *Riding the Storm*, pp. 240–5.

The broad shape and size of the Armed Forces has been settled in the Defence White Paper, and we are to consider later in the month some of the main problems of their equipment. We ought thereafter to turn our attention to the problems of organisation.

The separate traditions and *esprit de corps* of the three Services must be preserved. At the same time I think we ought to examine the possibility of combining their headquarters administration and policy control in a single integrated Defence Department, which would also take over the functions of the Ministry of Supply.

I should be glad if you would consider this and let me have your views.

I am sending copies of this Minute to the Service Ministers and the Minister of Supply.

This plan would mean a completely new 'set-up' under a real Minister of Defence. As so often happens with major but not immediately pressing issues, discussion proceeded and papers were circulated in a leisurely way. But by the end of the year there had been no decision on the basic principles.

In March 1958, a group of Ministers were appointed to discuss plans for defence reorganisation, but, as I noted at the time,

there will be a great row over this. Neither Chiefs of Staff nor Service Ministers will like it.[1]

A few days later the Chiefs of Staff and Service Ministers attended a meeting at which the difficulties of the present system were explored and proposals for the future were outlined. The real problem had still to be faced. My directive in 1957 had at least given the Minister authority to give decisions on all matters of policy 'affecting the size, shape, organisation and disposition of the armed forces' together with matters of supply, equipment, and so forth. This was some advance. At the same time, the Secretaries of State and the First Lord could plead their constitutional authority and responsibility. No directive of mine or any other Prime Minister could override their historic duties, certainly in time of peace. No doubt some objections to a more logical system arose from a conflict

[1] 14 March 1958.

of personalities; the strong and powerful character of the then Minister of Defence, Duncan Sandys, was resented by some of the Service Ministers, urged on by their professional advisers. But there were fundamental, sincerely held principles involved. All through the spring of 1958 there was a kind of smouldering fire in Whitehall. The Chiefs of Staff were divided; Air Marshal Sir William Dickson, the Chairman of the Chiefs of Staff Committee, and Lord Mountbatten, the First Sea Lord, were keen and loyal supporters of reform; but the others were highly critical.

In the summer the matter was discussed by the full Cabinet, the controversy having by then found its way into the Press. I observed at the time, and have noted since, that any inter-service debate of this kind is more rapidly taken up by the newspapers and develops a greater heat and even acrimony than is aroused by mere civil questions. Nor was this unnatural; for the latter disputes are often ephemeral, the former involve the devotion of a lifetime and the ideals of a service deep-rooted in history. The White Paper, which was considered in draft by the Cabinet, was modest enough in its final version.[1] Published in July 1958, this was in the main a formal confirmation of the redefinition, which I had made by directive the year before, of the functions of the Minister of Defence. The system was to remain basically one of co-ordination of four separate, independent Ministers; the fourth being at that time the Minister of Supply, two years later to be renamed Minister of Aviation. In the 1958 version there were three changes of detail. First, the Defence Committee, over which the Prime Minister normally presided, would have a variable membership determined by the Prime Minister in accordance with the nature of the subject involved. Secondly, there would now be a new post of Chief of the Defence Staff, replacing the 1957 position where one of the three members of the Chiefs of Staff acted as Chairman. This was a substantial advance, because it gave an independence to the Chairman which would enable him to advise the Minister of Defence from an impartial position. Finally, a Defence Board was set up to assist the discharge of the responsibilities set out in the 1957 directive.

Even to these changes there was strenuous opposition and at one

[1] *Central Organisation for Defence*, Cmnd. 476 (H.M.S.O., 1958).

time the threat of certain resignations. But, partly by exhaustion, partly by good will, partly by the tireless effort of Sir Norman Brook, but mainly perhaps because of the acceptance of the doctrine that the new Chief of the Defence Staff was to have no 'control' of his own, leaving all the machinery of operations in the hands of the three Chiefs of Staff, agreement was finally reached and the White Paper duly published. I felt that it had been rather a Pyrrhic victory, and the atmosphere in which our discussions were conducted had been at certain periods so disagreeable, in spite of my own good relations with the officers concerned, most of whom I had known well during and since the war, that I felt unwilling to reopen the question with so many other pressing decisions facing us.

It was not until the end of 1962 that I felt able to revive the subject. Peter Thorneycroft was now Minister of Defence, and Lord Mountbatten had been appointed Chief of the Defence Staff. I knew that both these men would be sympathetic, indeed enthusiastic, supporters of reform. Equally important, Admiral Sir Caspar John, an officer of outstanding intelligence, who favoured the proposed changes, had now become First Sea Lord. Finally, the fact that the nuclear deterrent would in future no longer be exclusively entrusted to the Air Force, but, through the Polaris submarine, would pass increasingly to the control of the Navy, seemed a further reason for the unification not merely of command but of organisation and control in the three Services. We believed that this could be made effective in the area of staff and command, without in any way affecting morale or infringing upon the tradition of any individual corps or unit or of any Service as a whole.

As a result of these talks, I addressed a long Minute to the Minister of Defence, setting out the general plan of reorganisation. My letter to the Queen of 13 December sets out both the problems and the plan in some detail.

> Your Majesty will by now have seen a copy of a Minute which I have sent to the Minister of Defence about the reorganisation of our Defence structure.
>
> The problem of the proper relationship between the three Service Departments and the Minister of Defence has been getting increasingly difficult. The need for the Service Departments to

consult together and help one another is growing greater as each year passes. Moreover the growing complexity and expense of modern weapons makes it essential that the demands which the Defence Departments as a whole make on the economy shall be shaped and balanced to achieve the most efficient result with the least waste.

There are some who feel that the right course now is to strengthen the Ministry of Defence and transmute the three separate Services into a single Armed Force of the Crown. Just as all Civil Servants are the same in whatever Department they serve, so all fighting men would be in one Service whether it was on sea, land, or in the air. There would be one Staff and one Minister answerable in Parliament. All the money would be on one Vote, and all recruitment, training, pay, discipline and appointments would be, like planning, operations and weapon development, a single responsibility.

There is a lot to be said for this if these were matters to be dealt with by logic and materialism only. But of course when dealing with fighting men the most important factor of all is morale. The soldier is more interested in the Regiment than he is in the Army; and the sailor's loyalty is to his ship and not to the Board of Admiralty. The airman, as the youngest of the three Services, is perhaps even more anxious than his fighting comrades to identify himself with his own show, the Squadron, or the Wing, or the Group.

Somehow we have got to meet the two needs. We must unify to be efficient and avoid waste. And we must diversify to keep alive the spirit of the men.

Many of the opponents of any closer integration of the Services derive the strength of their feeling from their opposition to the complete unification of all three Services. This often explains why otherwise sensible men may be driven into adopting positions which, viewed in a limited context, appear ridiculous. There are a number of activities which the Services could easily share; stores, hospitals, transport, communications, Chaplains, and others. If the will to co-operate were there much useful co-ordination could be brought about. But at present the feeling of antagonism towards the wide concept of the single Service is operating against the narrower but quite practical arrangements at the working level.

In 1958 the Service Departments were not ready for any significant measure of reform, and at the end of the day the Minister of Defence and I were defeated. In spite of the Defence White Paper and the new Defence Board, and the transfer of operational responsibility to the Minister of Defence, the underlying situation did not alter. There were still three entirely separate Services: three Staffs, and three competitors for the resources we could allocate to Defence. The unity and coherence of the Services was expressed in their loyalty to the Crown but not in their willingness to work with one another.

But in the last four years feelings have changed. This is partly due to the pressure of events, and partly due to change in personalities amongst the Chiefs of Staff. Lord Mountbatten has long been an advocate of much closer integration between the Services. Sir Caspar John sincerely believes that this is right. General Hull is ready for some move, and even the Chief of the Air Staff is now prepared to agree that the Ministry of Defence should be strengthened. So I feel it possible to try and make another move forward with better hope of success.

My idea is to try to combine the good features of both the single Service concept and the existing three separate Services. I am sure it is right to centralise responsibility for planning, operations and weapon development in the Ministry of Defence and as a direct responsibility of the Minister. And in order to give him the necessary control over the Services I think it is right for him to have the responsibility for promotions and appointments in the senior ranks of the Services, hence my idea of the Common List from Major General upwards. At the same time the three separate Services will continue separate existences up to Brigade level. After all, some 95 per cent of officers never rise higher than Brigadier and the ordinary fighting man does not look much beyond the Colonel—most indeed are content to focus their attention on the Captain or Lieutenant.

The Common List would not mean that above Major General there would only be one Service. There would still be three uniforms; Generals would not sit in the Admirals' day cabin in the flag ship. But the Minister of Defence would from the Common List appoint the right man to the right job within the appropriate Service. Recruitment, training, pay, discipline, etc., would be dealt with by the three Services under the general directions of the Minister of Defence. But I do not think it would be right to make the Minister responsible in Parliament for these questions. Quite apart from anything else it would be an impossibly onerous task; nor do I think it would be effective. I believe it to be right that there should be a Minister for each of the three Services. Not a Secretary of State or someone of that rank. That is clearly outdated. But perhaps a Minister of State would be right. It remains to be decided what should be done with the existing managing Boards or Councils, and we shall also need to settle the title of the senior professional post in each of the three Services. But these are questions that can be considered when the main outline of my plan is being discussed.

The Ministry of Aviation will also have to be considered since the research and development programme is now an important and, alas, expensive part of our Defence arrangements. It will have to be brought in to the new scheme. The right thing might be to have a Minister responsible for logistics, who would carry out all procurement functions at present exercised by the War Office and the Ministry of Aviation; and a Minister responsible for weapon development, who would carry all the responsibilities at present exercised by the different scientific branches in the three Services.

There would thus be a Secretary of State for Defence, a Minister for procurement, a Minister for weapons development, and three Ministers in charge of the Services. There would probably need to be a deputy to the Secretary of State for Defence, and perhaps one or two Parliamentary Secretaries.

Your Majesty will see that under these arrangements we would have central direction of defence and the three Services. But that so far as the fighting units were concerned they would still be a member of Regiments and ships and groups which have a long history and tradition and which are an essential part of the make-up of the morale of the Services.

I will be having further discussions on my plan with Ministers after the Christmas holiday, and I will report to Your Majesty how matters develop.

On my return from Nassau, I received the Chiefs of Staffs' comments on the plan, which, as I expected, were somewhat critical.

However, I think all that has happened recently in the defence field (especially as between the bomber and the submarine) really strengthens the arguments for defence integration, at any rate at the higher levels.[1]

On 31 December the argument was taken up at a full meeting.

2.45–5 p.m. with Service Ministers, who are putting up a strong reactionary fight (aided by Chiefs of Staff) against reform of Service and Defence organisation.[2]

In order to gain the confidence of the fighting Services, I asked Lord Ismay and Lieutenant General Sir Ian Jacob to make an enquiry and write a report upon the higher organisation of Defence. These two officers commanded the respect and admiration of all who had known them in the war, because they had acted as the liaison between Churchill and the Chiefs of Staff. No two men had their experience or could bring greater knowledge, imagination and good sense to the solution of the problem. The report, when it was received towards the end of February 1963, was circulated to the Cabinet. It analysed the defects of the present machinery for the higher direction of defence policy and proposed certain remedies; the next step should be to incorporate the three Service Ministries as subordinate departments of the Ministry of Defence, leaving the Services intact. While they believed that in the end the Ministry would be organised on a functional basis, they recommended that for the present a Minister of State, serving under the Minister of Defence, should be responsible for each Service. Whether or not the final stage would be reached, the course they recommended was a logical first step. Similarly, it could be hoped that the end would be a unified Service at the rank of Rear-Admiral, Major-General or Air Vice-Marshal, with a single promotion list above that rank.

When the Service Ministers and Chiefs of Staff discussed the plan with me on 26 February, they seemed quite ready to accept it in the form proposed, leaving any further development for the future. The great thing now was to make a start. On the next day the Cabinet discussed the plan and gave general approval. Naturally, since the Queen has a special position in regard to the Armed Forces, I wrote again at some length about our proposals.

[1] 26 December 1962.　　　　　[2] 31 December 1962.

On 4 March, Peter Thorneycroft, in the course of a general Defence debate, set out the plan:

> His speech on the reorganisation (which has caused us such months of work and worry) went very well. The Opposition were completely taken by surprise. Our boys (some of the more important of whom had been warned) were satisfied.[1]

The Ministry of Aviation posed a special problem because the Research and Development which it handled had both civil and military importance. A final decision on this point had yet to be taken.

When it came, however, to working out the details for the new Ministry of Defence, with all the problems of votes of supply, accounting officers and the like, I sensed at the beginning of April that we were running into difficulties. Accordingly, I sent a minute to Thorneycroft on 8 April as follows:

> Thank you for your Minute of March 22 reporting progress on the implementation of the Cabinet's decision to establish a unified Defence Department.
>
> I look forward to a further report. As we wish to publish a White Paper towards the end of June we ought to take action on the details during May. The time-table is going to be pretty tight.
>
> As I understand it, the main danger lies in the fact that we may be forced by the terrible weight of inertia of the Service Departments into doing nothing. This will look very bad. The Government will have been made to appear foolish.
>
> If we have to decide between two possible courses of action we must always choose the more radical. It is no longer a question of balancing the niceties of two possibilities. Once we start doing this we shall end up by doing nothing.
>
> I am relying on you to see that we do not fall into this trap again as we did in 1958. I rather fear that just being in one building and getting used to working near one another may not be enough. Thus I very much fear that if we are to have four Votes instead of one we might just as well not have embarked upon this exercise.

[1] 4 March 1963.

One can approach this in a number of different ways, but if we do not create a new structure our successors will. We might as well get the credit for doing it, since it is what we believe ought to be done.

On 29 April, I followed this up with a further Minute.

I received your Minute of April 26, which I have read with the greatest apprehension and alarm. There ought to be certain clear principles.

The staff should be cut by at least 20 per cent as a result of the exercise. 25 per cent would be better. All the principles in your paragraph 5 should be accepted. A clear line of command should be laid down. There should be one accounting officer, and not four. If there are four accounting officers the whole thing is hopeless. Permanent secretaries should be Deputy secretaries. Everybody should go down, nobody should go up. I would rather drop the whole idea than say that we have been defeated by the Service Departments. Pray take no notice at all of any obstruction. You should approach this the way Lloyd George used to approach problems with dashing, slashing methods. Anyone who raises any objection can go, including Ministers. The Service Ministers are not in a very strong position anyway, politically or in any other respect. I beg you to take an axe to all this forest of prejudice and interest.

In the first weeks of May I continued to feel anxious. 'The new plan is gradually taking shape, but there is a lot of resistance.'[1] A few days later,

Minister of Defence and I had a long talk about the Reorganisation Plan, which is making rather slow progress. In spite of their 'acceptance', the Service Departments at various levels are putting up a sort of 'go-slow' resistance.[2]

Finally, on 14 May, I thought it right to clarify precisely what was needed.

I was most interested in your oral report of progress with Defence Reorganisation. I was glad to hear that you are getting on with the preparation of the White Paper.

[1] 5 May 1963.   [2] 9 May 1963.

I hope that the White Paper will reflect the following principles:

(*a*) There must be a fully integrated single Ministry of Defence, not a collocation of semi-autonomous sub-Departments. This does not necessarily imply complete functionalisation, but I was glad to see from paragraph 5(ii) of your Minute of April 26 that you intend that the new Ministry should, whenever possible, carry out its functions on a defence basis rather than a single-Service basis.

(*b*) All powers must be vested in the Secretary of State for Defence. We may find it necessary that, e.g. certain judicial authority should be vested elsewhere; I hope that this can be kept to the minimum.

(*c*) There must be clear channels of command and responsibility from and to the Secretary of State.

(*d*) No other authorities must block or obscure these channels.

(*e*) The Secretary of State must be free to delegate and distribute responsibility as he wishes. This must include the power to alter the organisation of the Department from time to time as may prove desirable.

(*f*) There must be no increase in the total numbers of civilian and military personnel employed in the Defence Departments and, if possible, there must be reductions. This principle is to apply at all levels. There must be no question of substantial increases in general officers and Under-Secretaries compensated by reductions in other ranks and clerical grades.

I am sending copies of this Minute to the three Service Ministers and to Sir Laurence Helsby and Sir Burke Trend.

The work on the White Paper continued, Thorneycroft showing remarkable patience and being splendidly supported by Lord Mountbatten. On 11 July,

a very long Cabinet 10.30–1.30 but a *very* good one. The Defence White Paper was the main subject, and approval was given to the Reorganisation scheme.[1]

The Defence White Paper was accordingly published, setting out the whole plan, on 16 July.[2] The debate took place on 31 July, and

[1] 11 July 1963.
[2] *Central Organisation for Defence*, Cmnd. 2097 (H.M.S.O., July 1963).

the Minister gave a clear and impressive exposition. We had succeeded on all the major issues; we had defeated the attempts to
weaken the powers of the new Secretary of State for Defence. For
instance, there was to be only one Permanent Under-Secretary, who
would have under him four Second Permanent Under-Secretaries,
one for each Service and one for the Defence Secretariat. Nor was
there left any doubt that the new Ministers of State would be of
secondary rank. In the same way, the Chief of the Defence Staff
would be the adviser to the Minister, although, naturally, in the re-
organised Defence Committee the Chiefs of Staff would attend as
and when required. They would also—this was a point to which they
attached great importance and which it seemed wise to concede—
retain their traditional right of access to the Prime Minister, and
their position as head of their Service. The problem of the Ministry
of Aviation was solved by retaining a separate Ministry in view of
the very heavy commitments on civil as well as on Defence matters—
for instance supersonic transport. In order to facilitate close co-
operation, the Minister and his top staff would be in the same
building as the Secretary of State for Defence.

The legislation necessary to carry out this revolutionary change
was introduced in November, obtaining the Royal Assent in
March 1964, coming into effect on 1 April of that year. Although
I was not able to take part in the concluding stages of this large
enterprise, the matter was in fact settled by the debate in July 1963,
and I had the great satisfaction of being able to complete a project
for which I had worked for many years. Steps providing for a
functional organisation for the Ministers of State were not taken
till later; nevertheless the great principle was gained in 1963. Not
merely command in the field but also study, preparation and
planning in their widest sense would cease to be the responsibility
of separate Service departments at the Admiralty, the War Office,
the Air Ministry; instead, they would take place in the Ministry of
Defence, and, in the words of the White Paper, would be organised
'on a defence rather than a single-Service basis'. This system seemed
to offer the advantages of unified authority and responsibility at
the centre, while recognising that the fighting spirit of individual
men in battle depended mainly on their loyalty to their ships, their

units or their squadrons. The traditions and battle honours of individual Services and units were retained; but for the difficult, complicated and exacting tasks of devising the machinery of modern armaments and planning effectively any operations, great or small, which the Services might be called upon to perform, a modern, effective instrument had at last been provided.

CHAPTER XIII

Security and Scandal

THE Security Services, although administered by the appropriate Departments of State, have in recent years come to be regarded as the special responsibility of the Prime Minister of the day. Since even their most spectacular successes must be veiled in secrecy, while their occasional failures receive widespread and hostile publicity, this new convention has proved generally acceptable to other Ministers. Nevertheless, in spite of the deep respect which I felt during these years for the officials who headed these Services, I found my duties painful and frustrating. In dealing with other matters, whether of policy or of administration, one can generally form a view based on experience or knowledge. But in considering the intricate and specialised problems which are involved under the broad term 'security' an amateur is at a great disadvantage. Nor had I a wide knowledge of detective fiction. Accordingly, I confined myself to two tasks—first the appointment to the chief posts of men of experience and integrity; secondly, the scrupulous enforcement of the recommendations resulting from the various expert enquiries following a serious failure. From my first introduction to this painful subject, I realised the peculiar difficulties with which the security forces are faced, especially in time of peace. In the autumn of 1955, it was my duty, as Foreign Secretary, to deal with the case of two Foreign Office officials, Burgess and Maclean, who had defected to Russia. Although the events had taken place under a former administration, I had to unfold the story to the House of Commons.[1] I have always personally been somewhat sceptical as to the real value of the information brought by such defectors when they are merely political officials and have no technical knowledge. I have often wondered

[1] *Tides of Fortune*, pp. 680–6.

which in the end become the most disappointed—the defectors or the tempters. Nevertheless I was determined to use every possible means to protect ourselves in the future. At the same time I did not claim that the measures which we were taking would make the recurrence of such an event impossible. We had to balance the advantages and disadvantages of any security practices which might prove a menace to individual liberty, and had said at that time, 'It would, indeed, be a tragedy if we destroyed our freedom in the effort to preserve it.' This is, and must always be, a dilemma facing the governments of free nations.

Fortunately, for the next few years we were not plagued by any serious security troubles. It was not until the beginning of 1961 that I was informed of a dangerous conspiracy to obtain important information of a highly secret character regarding modern submarine methods. This, generally known as the 'Portland case', involved 'Lonsdale', believed to be a Russian; the Krogers, Polish Jews formerly resident in America and friends of the Rosenbergs; Houghton and Gee, two Britons employed· in the Underwater Weapons Establishment. They were all arrested on 7 January, and the trial was brought to a conclusion on 22 March, when they received heavy sentences. Although I immediately informed the House of Commons that the First Lord of the Admiralty, Lord Carrington, would set up a committee of enquiry to investigate the circumstances, there was great public concern over what seemed an inexplicable affair. Fortunately, I was able to say that there was no ground for thinking that any information affecting the United States or any other NATO country was compromised. Gaitskell, quite rightly, pressed me regarding the security procedures which had been agreed in 1956. Were they adequate today? Was there not a public loss of confidence, not only in our counter-espionage system but in the 'security vetting' system? I admitted that we might have to look again at the method that was called 'positive vetting'—that is, a procedure by which those employed in delicate fields should be submitted to an especially rigid scrutiny. Accordingly, the Home Secretary announced on 29 March the setting up of a committee under Sir Charles Romer to investigate what had happened and particularly to consider what weaknesses had been revealed in the existing procedures. I was naturally concerned at the criticism in Congress about the Portland case; but the President refused to be rattled and accepted our assurance that no American secrets had been betrayed.

While we were awaiting the report of the Romer Committee, a new blow fell. George Blake, an employee of the Security Services, was tried and found guilty of treachery on a formidable scale. It was not then possible and still would not be wise to give the full details. The extent of his crime can perhaps be judged by the sentence which so humane a judge as Lord Chief Justice Parker imposed upon him—imprisonment for forty-two years. At first I took the view that we had better wait for the Romer Committee report before taking any further steps; but Gaitskell, not unnaturally, pressed hard for a more complete enquiry. After seeing him, I sent a note to Butler on 4 May 1961:

> I saw Mr. Gaitskell tonight. He originally wanted to bring five colleagues with him—Lord Alexander, Lord Morrison, Mr. Gordon Walker, Mr. Shinwell and Mr. Brown. He has agreed to cut it down to three, omitting Lord Morrison and Mr. Gordon Walker. . . . Gaitskell also agreed with me that after the first meeting, he and I might perhaps have a talk alone to discuss the next steps. . . .
>
> On our side I said that I would ask the Home Secretary, the Lord Privy Seal and Sir Norman Brook to attend.

A few days later at a full meeting of Ministers,

> I stated firmly that in my opinion (whatever officials might say) we could not avoid *some* enquiry. In the end, we might gain from it.[1]

All through this affair, Gaitskell behaved not only correctly but considerately, and I was grateful to him for his balanced view. But the newspapers were not so reserved.

> The Press has been terrible, without any sense of responsibility. They want sensation. Also, since the Press is tired of me and the Government. . . . We are said to be exhausted, ageing and practically *in articulo mortis*. Against this, the Local Borough

elections show a great swing to the right. We have captured Liverpool, Nottingham and several other large cities.[1]

I was now able to announce that a fresh review would be made of the security procedures and practices, and the findings of the Romer Committee made available to the new body. Much to my relief, Lord Radcliffe agreed to act as Chairman.

When the Romer Committee reported on 13 June, it disclosed a certain lack of 'security mindedness' on the part of the officials in the Underwater Weapons Establishment. George Brown seized upon this and wished to know what Minister would be held responsible and what penalty he would pay. Fortunately, in spite of some awkward moments at Question Time, by the beginning of July I felt that the House was becoming rather tired of Brown's insistence. 'We have got through the immediate Parliamentary row and I have been able to save the First Lord.'[2] There was now a welcome interval, and it was not until the beginning of 1962 that Ministers were able to consider at length Lord Radcliffe's full and vitally important recommendations.

On 26 January 1962, a Committee of Ministers appointed to deal with security held a long meeting to discuss what should be done. The situation which Radcliffe revealed was in some respects alarming and involved us in difficult and delicate problems. A disturbing number of the paid officials of the Civil Service unions were Communists.

What a state of affairs, and how repugnant to the real views of the masses of respectable Civil Servants. It is the Electrical T.U. story all over again.[3]

The first thing to do was to consult with Gaitskell and his colleagues. Rather complicated negotiations followed. The Leader of the Opposition throughout remained affable and courteous; but his tail (for, like a Highland chief, he never came without a large attendance) included more combative figures, such as George Brown and Emmanuel Shinwell. Some delay followed, for it was also necessary to discuss with the responsible members of the Press that part of the report which dealt with the so-called 'D-Notice system'. The

[1] 14 May 1961.   [2] 8 July 1961.   [3] 26 January 1962.

report did not mince words, and it was clear that full publication might raise many difficulties both at home and abroad. However, Ministers approved the plan to publish the report in as complete a form as possible. As I explained to my colleagues, the report, while suggesting several ways in which our security measures should be intensified, disclosed no radical defect in the system as a whole. Moreover, it not only revealed the extent of the espionage threat but also demonstrated, in convincing detail, the difficulty of countering it effectively in a free society. Publication would therefore help to secure a better public understanding of both the importance and the complexities of the whole problem.

The Radcliffe Report was duly published on 5 April 1962. The chief findings were as follows. The threat to security arose from two main sources. First, from the intelligence services of foreign powers —the Russian Intelligence Service made use not only of ideological sympathisers, but also of any who could be bought or bullied; secondly, from subversive organisations which meant, in effect, the Communist Party and its fringe bodies. The Conference of Privy Councillors in 1956 had put the main emphasis on identifying Communists. The Radcliffe Committee thought this inadequate— it was also necessary to guard against those who, for defects of character or other reasons (such as relatives behind the Iron Curtain), were particularly vulnerable to Russian pressure. The Committee, in seeking to promote a maximum awareness of the problem and a sense of responsibility towards it throughout Whitehall, confirmed the practice whereby the prime responsibility for security in its broadest sense rested upon individual departments. At the same time they defined more precisely the duties of the Security Services themselves and suggested improved forms of liaison. They made recommendations on both the action to be taken and the staff to be employed to ensure security in departments and out-stations. They drew attention to the problem created by the extensive penetration of Civil Service staff associations and trade unions by Communists, suggesting that 'it would be reasonable to establish the right of any Department in respect of establishments or staff employed on secret work to deny access to or to refuse to negotiate with a named trade union official whom it had reason to believe to be a Communist'. The

Committee recommended a reappraisal of the application of security classifications, to prevent material being given an unnecessarily high classification, and they asked for more effective de-classification of ephemeral secrets, so as to minimise the quantity of material requiring special handling. To avoid the risk of employing spies on secret work, the Committee considered that, where persons were under some suspicion of being Communists, positive steps should be taken to ascertain the truth; in addition, periodic checks on character should be applied to all those in sensitive posts—a once-for-all 'positive vetting' was inadequate. Those for whom clearance was denied were, if they were accused as Communists, provided with a channel of appeal; in addition improved rights of appeal should be accorded for those denied clearance on other grounds. In either case, it would be the responsibility of the Civil Service to find them non-sensitive work provided they were not 'inefficient or in breach of accepted standards of discipline'. Some detailed recommendations were made about the selection of staff for service abroad, the application of security to industrial contracts, education and training for security, and about the physical security of documents, including advice on how to prevent conditions in which unsuspected employees might have opportunities to photocopy documents. Finally, the Committee investigated the 'D-Notice system', and, subject to a discussion of certain detailed points, advised its continuation.[1]

The most striking revelation, which alarmed the public more than the occasional breakdown of individual employees under pressure, was the definite statement that the Communists had achieved a 'higher degree of penetration' of the Civil Service staff associations and trade unions 'than in almost any other sector of the trade union movement'. Yet officials of these associations and trade unions, although not themselves civil servants, might in servicing their members become aware of delicate and secret operations.

The Radcliffe Report was well received by the Press, and it was felt that the Government had handled the affair with wisdom and good sense. The close association of the Labour leaders with the decision to publish the Report and with some of the steps that were to be taken, especially in the trade union world, was regarded as

[1] *Security Procedures in the Public Service*, Cmnd. 1681 (H.M.S.O., April 1962).

wise and prudent. In presenting the Report to the House, I could not refrain from dwelling once more on the inherent difficulties of a free society in trying to counter the vast organisation operated with ruthless efficiency by the communist states. In the Committee's own words, 'security weaknesses . . . are part of the price we pay for having a social and political system that men want to defend'.

The so-called 'Portland case', of which 'Lonsdale' was the protagonist, and the Blake case were serious and damaging breaches of our defences. Although I was assured by the experts that even in the first no serious leakage had taken place of methods or mechanisms of which the Russians were not broadly aware, yet I had an uneasy feeling that either the Underwater Weapons Establishment served no very useful purpose or that what went on there were secrets of the highest possible importance. Nevertheless, so rapid are the changes in technique and tactics that I could only hope that the leakage would produce no real effect upon the balance of power in the NATO and Warsaw Pact countries. The Blake case was almost unique, and its results were damaging to our intelligence system in certain areas for many years. In addition, Blake's treachery led many who had trusted him to imprisonment or death. Nevertheless, as regards Blake himself, it seemed to be a case not of yielding either to blackmail or to bribery but of genuine conversion. In the war of rival economic and social ideologies, as in the wars of religion, it may be comparatively easy to trace the perversion of a man who yields either to pressure because of some moral defect or to the temptations of affluence. But Blake asserted he had yielded to no material pressure or advantages but had been genuinely 'converted to Communism while a prisoner of war in Korea'. With the ideological spy we were faced with a phenomenon such as had hardly appeared in these islands for some four hundred years. I could only find comfort in the fact that these cases were rare at any high level of importance – they were more likely to occur not among engineers or technicians, who lived in the world of practical application of science to weaponry, but rather in the vaguely idealistic circles, where men or women might yield to flattery but in fact would not be in a position to part with information of any substantial value.

Had the whole of this matter of security ended with the Radcliffe

Report, whose recommendations we began rapidly to carry out, all would have been well, and the remainder of my administration would not have been darkened by this cloud which, always threatening, had not hitherto been the prelude to a dangerous storm. But it was not to be; and the last year of my premiership was overshadowed by a series of difficulties starting with some genuine apprehensions as to security and spreading rapidly into the much wider area of scandal, more easily comprehensible and more generally enjoyable.

On the morning of 12 September 1962, I was sitting quietly in the Cabinet Room meditating upon a number of high matters including a first draft of my speech to the Conservative Party Conference on the Common Market, when I received a message that Thorneycroft, the Minister of Defence, and Lord Carrington, First Lord of the Admiralty, were asking to see me urgently. Knowing that no Minister ever asked for an urgent meeting except on something very troublesome, I asked Sir Norman Brook to be present at the talk. What they had to tell me was indeed distressing in the present nervous atmosphere. A certain J. W. C. Vassall, an executive officer in the Admiralty, had been arrested as a spy and would shortly come up for trial.

> There has been another espionage case—and a very bad one in the Admiralty. An executive officer, homosexual, entrapped by the Russian Embassy spies and giving away material (of varying value) for five or six years. . . . There will be another big row.[1]

Yet even with some experience I could not anticipate the full malignity of some of the attacks which were to be delivered on Ministers and others of the highest reputation. Yet so it was to prove. Vassall was duly tried and sentenced to eighteen years' imprisonment on 22 October. On the advice of Sir Norman and others, I thought that we might be able to deal with this matter within the Civil Service, without invoking the ponderous machinery of an outside tribunal. After all, we had the Radcliffe structure on which to work. The best thing seemed to be to make an initial investigation as to whether there had been any divergence from the

[1] 28 September 1962.

system as strengthened and reformed in accordance with Lord Radcliffe's recommendations. The next stages may perhaps be described in the words of the *Annual Register*.

> By the start of November a passionate parliamentary row had broken out over Admiralty security. . . . The Prime Minister (with the Cuba crisis on his hands) decided that, rather than set up another full scale enquiry into security procedures, the Vassall affair could be dealt with by a more informal review by a committee of three senior civil servants, on whose report he would take action personally. The Labour Party, with Mr. George Brown in the vanguard, hotly declared that this was totally inadequate in view of previous Admiralty lapses. Meanwhile a whispering campaign developed in some circles purporting to connect Vassall with a former Civil Lord of the Admiralty, Mr. Thomas Galbraith, who had since become an Under-Secretary of State for Scotland. On 7 November letters that had passed between Mr. Galbraith and Vassall were published as a White Paper, revealing nothing more damaging than the former Civil Lord's interest in his office carpets, crockery, and paper clips. The most that could be said against Mr. Galbraith was that he had suffered a socially pressing and plausible junior colleague a trifle too gladly.[1]

These sentences describe in a few words what was beginning to prove a most painful and difficult situation for me and my principal colleagues.

> The Vassall case is getting more embarrassing. I'm afraid the Minister of Defence took the debate last Friday with too Palmerstonian a touch—in a word, a little flippantly. When it was said that Vassall lived *above* his income in Dolphin Square, he said, 'We are all living above our incomes in all the London squares'—which was good. I feel that the people really to blame were the Ambassador and Head of Chancery in Moscow. One ought to know the private life of a staff in Moscow in a way which is quite impossible in London. What seems odd is that this man can write his memoirs and sell them to the Press for an immense sum *after* conviction.[2]

[1] *Annual Register, 1962,* p. 48.   [2] 5 November 1962.

The attacks now became even more fantastic. A journalist actually informed a Conservative M.P. that Mr. Galbraith and Vassall had planned to escape to Russia. In addition, the First Lord, Lord Carrington, was accused of sheltering traitors in the Admiralty and almost of treachery itself. At this point,

> I had to admit . . . that a Committee of Civil Servants would not do and propose a Tribunal under the 1921 Act, over which Lord Radcliffe has agreed to preside–Mr. Justice Barry and a Q.C. will make up the court. This manoeuvre was not very easy to execute, and caused me infinite trouble to prepare.[1]

While these events were boiling up, I had been engaged in facing what seemed the opening phase of a Third World War, involving not merely the intellectual strain of constant talks with the President, but the physical disadvantage of scarcely sleeping more than one or two hours each night. Yet, so strangely is the human brain constituted, this terrible danger seemed to distress me less than the personal and human anxieties.

> I do not remember a more worrying time–and so wasteful of effort. I suppose I would have done better to have had a Judicial Enquiry of some kind at the start. Had I known that all this mud would be thrown about, I would have done so. But we cannot have a tribunal every time we catch a spy. Now that the net is closing, we shall probably have some more cases. The public does not regard catching a spy as a success, but as a failure. Unhappily, you can't bury him out of sight, as keepers do with foxes. Maurice [Macmillan] has been a great help all through, and knows the feelings of the Party very well. In a curious way, I may have gained by this incident, as it has helped to re-establish my ascendancy over the House of Commons.[1]

Perhaps the most distasteful part of this whole affair was the suggestions of impropriety against Galbraith; and I refused to accept his resignation until this matter had been cleared up. The Radcliffe Committee submitted an interim report, published as a White Paper, dealing with the correspondence between Galbraith and Vassall, completely vindicating the Minister. On looking back,

[1] 15 November 1962.

I feel that it was a mistake on my part to accept Galbraith's offer of resignation at this stage. But he was very insistent, and did not wish to return to office until the full enquiry had been completed. He particularly wished the freedom to take legal action against his libellers. I appreciated his feelings, although I remember telling him that while I should, from my own point of view, rather see him stick to his post (he was now Under-Secretary at the Scottish Office) I could see that he would be better placed by resignation, at least temporarily, to hit back and confound his enemies.

When I came to propose the motion setting up a formal tribunal on 14 September the public seemed to accept that I had good grounds for changing my position. A Committee of Civil Servants could have dealt with questions which could arise as to the internal organisation in the foreign or home services, but accusations of the gravest kind had now been made against individuals standing in high places.

> The public confidence must be restored, either by the exposure of guilt or by public proof that those who pose as the protectors of the public have themselves been guilty of trying to destroy private reputations from motives either of spite or gain. This is not a question for a . . . committee. It . . . can be tried only by a tribunal . . . armed with the power of subpoena, armed with the power to put witnesses on oath . . . pursue them for perjury if they tell untruths.

I felt strongly that not only should the truth be searched, but also that the purveyors of lies should be punished. It was important that an incipient McCarthyism should be stemmed without delay. Of course, this would involve trouble with the Press. Indeed, during the debate, Gaitskell, who was clearly distressed by the violence and brutality of some of his colleagues, expressed the view that the journalists would refuse to disclose the sources or the alleged sources on which they based their slander. This was later to prove an important issue, and the firmness of the judges infuriated those who believed in a kind of divine authority, even infallibility, of Fleet Street. In all our later difficulties, the Press was still actuated by rancour at the mere suggestion that they could be held responsible for the statements they printed. I have never understood this position, which is, however, sincerely held by many editors and journalists of high standing. The Press, in demanding full protection for their 'sources', have even claimed the privilege of the priesthood. But this is a false analogy, for the secrets of the confessional are not normally made available in newspaper headlines. In the event, two journalists, one from the *Daily Sketch* and one from the *Daily Mail*, were sent to prison by the judges in March 1963 for refusing to disclose to the tribunal their sources of information. The Press represented them as martyrs, but the man in the street was more sceptical.

While waiting for the final stages in the Vassall case, a number of other events affecting 'security' caused some public misgiving. In December 1962 a senior official of the Central Office of Information was sentenced to two years' imprisonment for passing information to her Yugoslav lover, apparently in the somewhat naïve attempt to convert him to the Western way of life. I felt myself that hers had been an act of folly rather than treachery.

Early in the following year there was a strange development affecting a famous, almost historic, case of defection.

> We think we have at last solved the mystery of who 'tipped off' Burgess and Maclean. It was a man, much suspected at the time, but against whom nothing could be proved—one Philby. He was dismissed in 1951 from the service and has lived since in the Middle East, chiefly in the Lebanon, where he writes for the *Observer* and the *Economist*! In a drunken fit, he confessed everything to one of our men, so the whole thing is now clear. . . . He has now disappeared from Beirut, leaving £2,000 in cash for his wife. Whether he will appear in Russia or not, we do not know. Anyway, it means more trouble.[1]

On 29 March, Heath, on behalf of the Foreign Office, announced the disappearance of Philby from the Lebanon, and on 1 July he stated definitely that we were now satisfied that Philby had been the so-called 'third man' who had 'tipped off' Burgess and Maclean. Philby was now presumed to be 'behind the Iron Curtain'. This statement led to a spate of questions, involving every variety of

[1] 19 February 1963.

suggestion and innuendo. It was even insinuated that the Foreign Office were using Philby in the Middle East for 'secret work'.

> The Philby case has been very difficult, chiefly because of the problem of answering the questions asked by the Press and public without injuring and even hamstringing the work of the Secret Service.
>
> I had an hour with Harold Wilson and tried to explain to him how the so-called Security Services really worked. It seemed to me right to do so, and he took it quite well.[1]

I also had

> a good talk with Mr. Wilson and Mr. Brown about the Philby case. I think W. will 'play up'.[2]

The result of this approach was satisfactory. When on 16 July a new volley of questions was launched, which could not be answered without considerable injury to the work of the Security Services, I made an appeal in the following terms:

> We lead from one question to another and one question leads to another. It is dangerous and bad for our general national interest to discuss these matters. It has been a very long tradition of the House to trust the relations between the two parties to discussions between the Leader of the Opposition of the day and the Prime Minister of the day. I ask the House now to revert to the older tradition [Hon. Members: 'No'] which I think is in our real interests. Otherwise, we would risk destroying services which are of the utmost value to us.

Mr. Wilson responded nobly. He said:

> Is the right hon. Gentleman aware that I can confirm what he has just said? In the two meetings which we have had, he has given my right hon. Friends and me a very full and frank account of this case, which raises a number of issues which, frankly, cannot be discussed across the Floor of the House. While we still have some grave anxieties about the way in which it has been handled, which I think it best we should pursue in further confidential discussions with the right hon. Gentleman, we feel that in

[1] 11 July 1963.   [2] 15 July 1963.

the public interest this is a matter which should now be left where it is and not made the subject of further public discussion or public enquiry.

At a period when I was very hard-pressed, I was grateful both for the courtesy and the high sense of responsibility shown by the Leader of the Opposition.

On 12 April, a few days after the Radcliffe Tribunal had reported on the Vassall case, there was an incident which was more irritating than dangerous. 'Spies for Peace', a Left-wing organisation fostered by the C.N.D. and the Committee of a Hundred, were able to distribute to Aldermaston 'Easter marchers' duplicated sheets claiming to give the location of the regional seats of government which had been prepared in the event of an 'emergency'.

> It is *not* very serious from a practical point of view, but it's *another security failure* of the Government, and the Press – smarting under Vassall – has grasped eagerly at a new chance of attacking me and the Home Secretary.[1]

It will be seen, therefore, that during this period, by an extraordinary combination of circumstances or an exceptional run of ill-luck, Parliament and the public were being continually stimulated into a sense almost of hysteria. Nor did our critics distinguish between the failures and the successes. Indeed, from my point of view, life would have been easier if the counter-espionage work had been less effective. Yet, on the really serious issues, the Government was completely vindicated in the Vassall case. Lord Radcliffe showed me the draft of his report at the beginning of April, and I was very happy to learn from him that in his view there were no radical deficiencies in the security system, although there were one or two minor improvements which would be of help. On the vital question, Lord Radcliffe and his colleagues were clear and decisive: Lord Carrington, who had been grossly slandered, was completely vindicated. Galbraith was equally cleared of any complicity with Vassall's espionage or his homosexual activities. The whole flood of rumour and suspicion was therefore swept away in respect of these two Ministers by a man whose authority in these matters could not

[1] 16 April 1963.

be challenged. He was supported by the other members of the Tribunal. I felt, therefore, fully justified in regarding this complete vindication as a criticism of those who had made these vile accusations so lightly and pursued them so ruthlessly. Wilson, as Leader of the Opposition, had been careful to restrain his more loquacious and perhaps less scrupulous colleagues. Indeed, throughout all this painful period, the Leader of the Opposition seemed to realise the responsibilities which lay on anyone who might aspire one day to preside over a British Government.

But if the triumph in the case of Vassall was complete, undoubtedly the firmness with which the judges had refused to accept the doctrine of Press infallibility, although satisfactory from one point of view, was dangerous from another. It infuriated Fleet Street, at every level of activity, and made the newspapers anxious to seek and exploit any possibility of counter-attack. Meanwhile, I had the satisfaction of appointing Galbraith on 3 May as Parliamentary Secretary to the Minister of Transport.

Unhappily, another wave of painful and damaging rumours had begun to circulate. This time, however, although cloaked under the cover of security, they were moving into the realm of scandal. This was the beginning of a strange and even fantastic episode of which it is almost impossible, many years later, to give any coherent account. I do not propose to weary my readers with the detailed story of the 'Profumo case'. Much has been written and published, accurately and inaccurately. It is only necessary for me to give the broad outline of this sad series of events in order to explain the still stranger sequel, a general attack launched on the probity and moral character of almost the whole body of Ministers, with a ruthlessness and disregard for all semblance of truth unequalled since the days of Titus Oates.

On 4 February 1963, on my return from an official visit to Italy, I was informed by my Private Office that while I was away a newspaper had reported to us a 'story' involving an important, though not a Cabinet, Minister. It appeared that Jack Profumo, then Secretary of State for War, had, in the language of the police, 'compromised himself' with a girl of doubtful reputation, whom he met at a somewhat raffish party at Cliveden, to which she had been brought by a Mr. Ward. She had sold or was about to sell her story to the Press. It had, or was to be given, a security angle, for the lady in question was said to share her favours with the Russian Naval Attaché, a certain Ivanov. My Private Secretary, Tim Bligh, had in my absence passed this information to the Security Service, and it had been agreed that Profumo should be asked whether there was any truth in it. Bligh and the Chief Whip accordingly saw Profumo. He admitted having been acquainted with the woman involved, a Miss Christine Keeler, during 1961 and knew of her approach to the newspapers. But he denied all allegations of impropriety and said that on the advice of his solicitors he was awaiting the opportunity to take legal action to refute them if anything were published on which he could issue a writ. On the question of security, Profumo explained that he had been warned in 1961 to see as little as possible of Stephen Ward, because there was a security problem involved, and he had heeded that advice. I was satisfied with these assurances. No doubt Profumo had frequented circles in which, in my youth, it would have been thought inappropriate for a Minister to move. But times had changed, and although I had not myself much knowledge of this new social world I recognised that the distinctions which had ruled in the past no longer obtained. Respectable and disreputable people now seemed to be all mixed up together.

On 14 March the name of the lady in the case was mentioned in the courts. She had been cited as a prosecution witness in the trial of a West Indian accused of trying to murder her, but had failed to appear. Not unnaturally, in view of the charge, the police regarded her as an important element in obtaining a conviction. Her disappearance, therefore, began to be talked about in the whispering galleries of the London which enjoys this kind of scandal as proof of her having been spirited away by powerful protectors. The 'romantic' element in this story was particularly appealing.

I was forced to spend a great deal of today over a silly scrape [over a woman] into which one of the Ministers has got himself. It's Jack Profumo—Secretary of State for War. It would not matter so much if it was just an affair of morality. But unfortunately, among the frequenters of this raffish and disreputable set, which centres round Lord Astor (Bill Astor), was the Russian

Military Attaché! This is the new Cliveden set!... I must decide what I ought to do.... All this is very bad for the reputation of the Party and of the Government.[1]

I had not forgotten the case of Galbraith, impugned by rumour, whom I felt I had allowed to suffer some injustice. I was determined not to let this happen again.

A few days later the matter became embroiled in the operations of the Vassall Tribunal. By now the two reporters involved in that investigation had been imprisoned.

> The Press continue to be very hostile to the Government. This is largely due to the Vassall case, the Tribunal and the anxiety about what Lord Radcliffe will say. The imprisonment of the two reporters for contempt of court, for refusing to disclose to the Tribunal the source of their information ... has been treated by the Press (or most of it, with the honourable exception of the *Guardian* and to some extent *The Times*) as if these men were martyrs. Meanwhile, the popular Press gets sillier, dirtier and more degraded than ever. The *Guardian* has a very good article today ridiculing the *Mirror*. (Freedom of the Press is freedom to bribe a 'char' to tell lies about her employer.)[2]

On 21 March, during a debate on the imprisonment of the two journalists for contempt of court, George Wigg, a Labour M.P., who had by then begun to take upon himself the role of unofficial keeper of morals and protector of security, made a definite charge, which he alleged it was his duty to do since the Press were muzzled by the Vassall Tribunal. He declared that rumours were going round which involved a member of the Government, who ought to admit or deny the accusation made against him. I was not present during this part of the debate. Wigg's speech was made on the Consolidated Fund Bill, on which, according to our rules, any matter could be raised without notice, and I had already left the House.

> The M.P.s who raised the matter in Debate really helped Profumo. Conferences were held in the middle of last night and early this morning I was asked to approve a 'personal' statement after the House met (at 11 a.m.) today. I went through text with

[1] 15 March 1963.   [2] 20 March 1963.

A meeting of Ministers at Chequers, 27–28 April 1963, photograph by Lord Hailsham

Lord Hailsham marshalling us for the photograph

Attorney General and Chief Whip and went to the House to give Profumo my support. His statement was clear and pretty convincing. He had met Ward at Cliveden originally and had called at Ward's flat where the girl was living. He (and his wife) had been friends with both, but he had actually not seen the girl since the end of 1961. Profumo has behaved foolishly and indiscreetly, but not wickedly. His wife (Valerie Hobson) is very nice and sensible. Of course, all these people move in a raffish, theatrical, bohemian society, where no one really knows anyone and everyone is 'darling'. But Profumo does not seem to have realised that we have—in public life—to observe different standards from those prevalent today in many circles.[1]

Profumo's declarations were more specific than I recorded in my diary. He had not seen Miss Keeler since December 1961; he had first met her in July 1961 and again on half a dozen occasions between then and December 1961; he had nothing to do with her absence from the Old Bailey; there had been no impropriety in their behaviour, and he would issue a writ for libel and slander if any such allegations were made outside the House. This categorical statement in my eyes settled the matter.

The only new development was that Wilson, no doubt at the prompting of Wigg, came to show me a letter written to him in November 1962 by Ward. In this, Ward admitted, or claimed, that he was the intermediary who had handed a letter from the Russians to the Foreign Office during the Cuba crisis. There was nothing improper or any breach of security in this. I therefore ignored it. It was a common practice of all Embassies to use unorthodox methods on occasion.

My confidence in Profumo was strengthened by two libel actions which he immediately brought against *Paris-Match* and the Italian paper *Il Tempo*, and their distributors in London. In the first, the defendant retracted immediately; in the second, costs and damages were awarded. Had I any doubts about Profumo's integrity, I could hardly believe he had both misled the House of Commons and perjured himself in the courts.

On 9 April, Wilson sent me a memorandum compiled by Wigg,

[1] 22 March 1963.

based on rather rambling accounts of the social lives of Ward and his friends. But the deduction was that, whatever criticisms might be made of Profumo's wisdom in mixing with such people two years ago, there was no question of his being a security risk. So the days passed on and, engrossed in far more important problems, I trusted that we would hear no more of this particular episode. Even when Ward, aware that the police were enquiring into his moral activities, suspecting him of being a procurer, obtained an interview with one of my Private Secretaries and declared that Profumo had not told the truth to the House of Commons, there did not seem any serious cause for alarm. It was obvious that his purpose was to put pressure on the Government to stop police enquiries into his nefarious life. On 14 May I told Wilson that the 'material' supplied by Wigg had been studied, but that no particular action seemed necessary beyond that already taken. On 24 May Wilson sent me a letter enclosing a long communication from Ward, in which he alleged that Profumo had not told the truth in his statement to Parliament. In a following meeting, I told Wilson I would look into the matter again, but that it seemed to me that Ward was more anxious to exculpate himself than help us, whether on security or on any other problem involved. All through this period the Leader of the Opposition acted with complete propriety, and when the final collapse of Profumo's case came, with all the ensuing publicity, he was the first to assert that no question of security was involved. Naturally, moral scandals damaging the Government might not be unwelcome to any Opposition; but he did not take part in the wild mud-flinging that was soon to follow.

On 29 May, I had a visit from the Head of the Security Service, who told me that, according to Miss Keeler, Ward had asked her to find out from Profumo some information concerning atomic secrets. But she denied having acted on his instructions. The evidence was too slender to permit of a prosecution of Ward. Indeed, it seemed a ridiculous story, for Profumo had no information on 'atomic secrets' and it was doubtful whether Ward was really an 'agent'. The police were convinced that Ward was not a spy—he was a disreputable man and probably a pimp, but he was far too open and lax in his methods to be an agent. Nevertheless, I did not feel that these new developments could be wholly disregarded. I therefore asked the Lord Chancellor to look further into the matter, and informed Wilson, who continued to press me, of my action.

Dorothy and I then left for a short holiday in Scotland.

> I am handing over to Butler for a week (the first time I have done so since I became P.M., except for my longer visits abroad). I am to get only the minimum of telegrams and papers. It should be a real rest.[1]

Alas! the few days of repose were quickly and rudely ended.

> When I was at Oban, I was told by telephone that Profumo had admitted that he had lied to me, to the House, and to the courts. Although we managed to finish our Scottish holiday and go to Iona and Gleneagles as planned, from the day I got back till now (when there is a slight pause) there has been a serious and at times dangerous crisis, which seemed likely to involve the fall of the Government as well as my resignation.
>
> I do not remember ever having been under such a sense of personal strain. Even Suez was 'clean'—about war and politics. This was all 'dirt'.[2]

What had happened was simple. On 4 June Profumo suddenly 'came clean'. Over-burdened no doubt by a guilty conscience, he confessed to the Chief Whip and Bligh that Miss Keeler had been his mistress and that, in this respect, his statement to the House had been untrue.

This was unforgivable. Profumo had definitely, purposefully, and after careful warning from his friends and colleagues, lied both to the House of Commons and in the Courts of Law. I accepted his resignation by letter the next day. Since Parliament was not sitting, I did not think it necessary to return immediately.

Before I got back, there had been some new developments. Yet another West Indian was on trial at the Old Bailey for attacking Miss Keeler. More important, on 8 June, Ward was arrested and charged with living on the immoral earnings of women. On 9 June, triumphing over their rivals, the *News of the World* began the

---

[1] 31 May 1963. [2] 7 July 1963.

serialisation of Miss Keeler's life story, for which literary gem the newspaper was said to have paid the sum of £23,000.

I got back to London on 10 June. Parliament was to meet on the 16th, but M.P.s were already in London, holding meetings, etc. Every part of the Profumo story, now only a ramification of the 'Ward case' (a sort of Stavisky case) was used against the Government by an exultant Press, getting its own back for Vassall. *The Times* was awful—what has since been called a 'Holier than thou' attitude, which was really nauseating. The 'popular' Press has been one mass of the life stories of spies and prostitutes, written no doubt in the office. Day after day the attacks developed, chiefly on me—old, incompetent, worn out.[1]

Of this time of trouble I have one especial, among other pleasant memories. Lord Shawcross sent to me, by hand, the following letter:

> I cannot refrain from telling you how much I sympathise with you in the ill-luck of this miserable business. I only wish there were some way in which I could help, for it really is frightening to think that the course of politics might be affected by such an irrelevant, however personally tragic, incident.

The Cabinet were staunch throughout; but we had, of course, to face the House of Commons, distracted and excited.

In the debate (on 17 June) I had the most difficult and wearing task. I had to tell the whole story—from 1 February (when Profumo denied and continued to deny any but the most perfunctory acquaintance with Ward and Miss Keeler) to his confession. I had to defend the police, the Security Service, and Civil Service and myself. Meanwhile, the Parliamentary Party was undergoing one of those attacks of hysteria which seize men from time to time. In the end, twenty-seven of our Conservatives 'abstained'—that is, not only the usual malcontents . . . but a lot of worthy people, who had been swept away by the wave of emotion and indignation. What made the debate of 17 June more difficult [for me] was the week preceding it, which was particularly full of ordinary (but fatiguing) engagements such as degree at University of Sussex; visit of President of India

[1] 7 July 1963.

(Radhakrishnan) with usual banquets, reception, etc. All the time, the Government was generally believed to be tottering.[1]

When it came to presenting our case on 17 June, I had naturally to open the discussion.

> I set out to prove three propositions. First, that I had acted honourably; second, that I had acted justly; third, with reasonable prudence. One comfort to me was that the first two were accepted by all the House and even by the Press.[1]

After the debate, it was generally agreed that I had succeeded, at any rate in narrowing the accusations against me. The last one remained doubtful. Had I been wise in accepting at their face value Profumo's statements? I felt that even on this count those who thought the matter over with any detachment would accept my argument. The whole of our public life is based upon complete confidence within Parliament, within a Party, and especially within a Government. Formal statements such as Profumo had made 'on his honour' were regarded as absolutely binding. More especially was this true of matters affecting personal issues. No doubt, on public questions great and small, a certain amount of prevarication is pardonable—what Churchill called 'terminological inexactitudes' are not uncommon. But these refer to the various political arguments with all their uncertainties and confusion, their woolliness and their frayed edges. When it comes to a direct statement on a single issue, to lie to the House of Commons is unpardonable and has never been forgiven. Was it then unreasonable to have accepted this declaration?

There now followed the second week of the crisis, broadly from 17 June, when the debate ended, to 22 June, when I announced the decision of the Government to set up a judicial enquiry, headed by Lord Denning, into all the vague rumours and scandals charging all and sundry with every kind of depravity.

> In addition to the Profumo–Ward scandal, a kind of Titus Oates atmosphere prevailed, with the wildest rumour and innuendo against the most respectable Ministers. Altogether, partly by the blackmailing statements of the 'call girls'; partly by the stories started by or given to the Press; and partly (I have no

[1] 7 July 1963.

doubt) by Soviet agents exploiting the position, more than half the Cabinet were being accused of perversion, homosexuality and the like. This week ended by my speech at Bromley, where I said that I would 'act neither in panic or obstinately'. I would do what was best for the country and the Party. This was interpreted to mean (as I intended) that I would hold on.[1]

Accordingly, on 21 June, I made the formal announcement about Lord Denning's appointment to an important though distasteful task, which he accepted out of pure patriotism. This led to at least some check in the flood of accusation and rumour. On the same day all Ministers were informed by a memorandum in the following terms:

> You will have seen from my Statement in the House today that Lord Denning is undertaking a Judicial Enquiry into the security aspects of the circumstances leading up to the resignation of Mr. Profumo and that he is also being asked to investigate any information on material which may come to him in this connection which may endanger national security.
>
> As I said in my Statement, many rumours and allegations are circulating which are damaging to Ministers and other people in public life. If these rumours had any substance they might demonstrate that the persons concerned were in some degree a security risk.
>
> It is important that this cloud of innuendo should be dispersed.
>
> I think it right, therefore, that all members of the Administration should report such rumours. This should be done, as soon as possible, in a minute to the Home Secretary indicating the time and date when the rumour was heard and from whom, its nature and substance, and from whom it is said to have originated in the first place. The Home Secretary will take the necessary action in forwarding these to Lord Denning.
>
> If Ministers come across scandalous allegations about themselves they should consider with their legal advisers whether to issue a writ (and it may well be that in many cases this would be appropriate). However, in order to make sure that in any such situation Ministers take common action I should be grateful if

[1] 7 July 1963.

you would arrange for the Attorney General to be consulted before any decision is taken in a particular instance.

Attached is a form of press guidance which Ministers should use during any period when Ministers may be considering how to deal with a publication. Copies of any publication affecting them in respect of which they are contemplating taking legal action should be sent to the Prime Minister (with a consent to refer it to Lord Denning when appropriate) and to the Attorney General.

I thought it right also to give an account of the situation to Her Majesty, which I did in the following letter on 23 June:

Although I am to have the honour of an Audience with Your Majesty on Thursday next, I feel I should not like to delay so long before expressing to Your Majesty my deep regret at the development of recent affairs. . . .

Looking back upon all this tragic affair I can see, as one always can with hindsight, moments when one might have acted differently and perhaps thus avoided so many troubles. Nevertheless, I have always felt it was important to act justly as well as wisely, and it was perhaps to this consideration, following the unjust attacks upon Lord Carrington and Mr. Galbraith, that I may have given too much weight. Moreover, I had of course no idea of the strange underworld in which other people, alas, besides Mr. Profumo have allowed themselves to become entrapped. We do not know the precise role that Dr. Ward has played, but I begin to suspect in all these wild accusations against many people, Ministers and others, something in the nature of a plot to destroy the established system. It is interesting that the whole of the *Sunday Mirror* today is addressed not so much against me as against poor Lord Normanbrook and the Civil Service.

All these are very distressing affairs. But I am confident that they can be overcome and that when Your Majesty looks back upon them, in the course of what I trust may be a very long and successful reign, they will appear no more than the irritations which have, from time to time, been of concern to Your Majesty's predecessors. What is so painful to me is to think that, whether by some action or inaction on my part, I may have contributed to your burden.

During the third week of the crisis, beginning 24 June, a

> massive reaction began. I have had telegrams, letters, messages, etc., on a scale never equalled (I am told) in the history of No. 10. This has come from people in *all* walks of life and who have either had some association with me (e.g. a Platoon Sergeant at Loos) or who knew me only by reputation. Workmen in the streets call out 'Stick it, Mac!' ... I had to go to New College on the Wednesday of this week to open a new building. ... Next day was Encaenia, with all the usual engagements—the procession from Lincoln College to the Sheldonian; the ceremony in the Sheldonian; All Souls; Garden Party at Balliol; Dinner in Christ Church. At every stage, and in different ways, people of all kinds went out of their way to express their sympathy. It was very moving and encouraging.[1]

The week ended with a meeting at Wolverhampton with nearly three thousand people present representing sixty Midland constituencies.

> It was the most extraordinary demonstration of loyalty and affection. I did a broadcast also. ... The M.P.s who are working against me were rather knocked off their guard. All this week, the constituencies have been reacting *against* the disloyal members, and are putting a lot of pressure on them.
> So ended the *third* week of the crisis.[1]

Meanwhile, the unfortunate figure, round whom these waves of confusion and indignation were beating, had paid the full penalty. He was forced not merely to resign his position in the Government but to renounce his membership of the Privy Council and vacate his seat in Parliament. He therefore paid a dreadful forfeit for his lapse from honour and truth. It is right that I should pay tribute to the courageous way in which he has set about rebuilding his life by social work for others and thus in due course regaining not only his own respect but that of his fellow men.

Meanwhile, Lord Denning carried out his painful task with skill and rapidity. On 16 August, I gave my own evidence in order to clear up some doubtful points.

[1] 7 July 1963.

He took the opportunity to raise certain problems which he had in finishing his report. I suggested that he might perhaps discuss them with the Lord Chancellor (as head of the Judiciary). I felt that I must be able to say (with absolute truth) that I had taken no part and had not discussed report (other than my own evidence) with Lord D. He agreed that this was right.[1]

On 10 September I had a discussion with a number of Ministers including the Lord Chancellor, Butler, Macleod, and the Attorney General, as to how to deal with the publication of the Denning Report, which was to be received in a few days' time. The difficulties were technical but troublesome.

I must submit it to the Security Committee (for any excisions on Security). I must discuss it with my legal advisers (for any excisions on the ground of 'contempt of court', in view of trial of Miss Keeler for perjury). I must discuss it with Wilson, on these two aspects. It will take ten days to print. There is then the question of 'privilege'. This could be done (if Opposition agree) by recall of House of Lords. But they probably will not agree. We cannot recall House of Commons, because of the two Party conferences. So it may not be possible to get the necessary Parliamentary immunity until Parliament meets on 24 October, for the Prorogation.[2]

On 17 September, the Report came into my hands.

All the libellous 'rumours' against various Ministers are dismissed. The rest of the story is told as I told it to the House of Commons.[3]

There was only one paragraph which might cause some anxiety. Lord Denning, perhaps rightly, thought that a measure of blame could be laid upon Profumo's colleagues for having been deceived. But I was not unduly concerned at this—it was an old story. I naturally expressed my sincere thanks to Lord Denning for his help so generously given.

Sir Peter Rawlinson, who had been specially concerned with Profumo's statement in the House, generously offered his resignation, but I was quite unwilling to accept this. I felt that if there was

[1] 16 August 1963.   [2] 10 September 1963.   [3] 17 September 1963.

P2

blame in our handling of this difficult situation we must all share it. The major responsibility at any rate lay upon me.

When the Cabinet met on 19 September, Ministers were naturally relieved, although not surprised, at the complete and final answer to the wild rumours which had been circulating. Nevertheless, there was much concern over this awkward question of 'privilege'. This arose simply from the fact that in view of Miss Keeler's trial, and since Parliament was adjourned, there might be an unwillingness of the newspapers to publish the report in full, because 'privilege' could not be claimed. Secondly, there might be incidental statements which would prejudice justice in any action being taken against Miss Keeler and others. There was

> a long discussion about the problem of publication of the Denning Report ... [particularly on] the question of 'privilege' – absolute or qualified – the need to recall one or both Houses of Parliament – the drawbacks and even dangers of this course – the worse alternative of waiting till 24 October. After a bit, the idea emerged of 'publish and be damned'. Why not? What could happen to anyone? After all, newspapers and others reproducing the text of the Report only get 'qualified privilege' anyway. (They are secure unless 'malice' can be proved, and obviously 'malice' can't be proved against a newspaper that merely reproduces a command Government paper.) Who then gains from 'absolute privilege' and what is the gain? Prime Minister and Stationery Office gain (Lord Denning has, it is thought, 'absolute privilege' anyway). What is the gain? Well, with 'absolute' a writ cannot even be issued or an *ex parte mandamus* sought. With 'qualified' a writ can be issued, and be used to delay things or even prevent further publications, though it is *very* doubtful if any court would sustain it.
>
> So, it was left to me to decide, if I wished, for 'publish and be damned'.[1]

There were one or two other points where, on security grounds, minor omissions were necessary; but on the question of affecting a fair trial for Miss Keeler,

> the Law Officers gave later in the day a written opinion that there

[1] 19 September 1963.

was really nothing about Miss Keeler in the Report which had not already been published *by* her or *about* her.[1]

Wilson came to see me in the afternoon.

> I told him . . . of the only omissions on security grounds which seemed at all desirable. I explained to him the position about Miss Keeler. We had a short talk about this, but he said he would leave decision to me and support publicly whatever I decided. Then about publication. I explained about privilege, and said my inclination was to publish immediately it could be printed. He seemed very startled and said, 'And not call Parliament to get absolute privilege?' I said I thought it almost impossible (because of our two Party conferences) to call House of Commons. There would be difficulties about the Lords, I said, smiling sweetly![1]

Later the same day, after discussion with a few Ministers,

> I decided to publish *in full* . . . and to publish *as soon as possible*. As for Parliament's recall, it was quite out of the question.[1]

Later in the day, the Leader of the Opposition, as was indeed his right, put out to the Press his demand for the recall of Parliament. He did not, however, send me any formal application, and we decided to let it be known

> that if a formal request is sent, it will be refused. All precedent is against such a recall. I think Labour are upset at the course events have taken.[1]

The rest of the day was devoted to the wider but hardly more explosive subject of nuclear power.

When the Report was published on 26 September, it proved an overwhelming answer to the campaign of scandal and obloquy which had raged throughout the summer. The Press, without remembering Lord Chesterfield's dictum 'that in a case of scandal, as in that of robbery, the receiver is as bad as the thief', were

> so disappointed by the lack of scandals in Denning, that they all turn on me. It was to be expected. The leading articles are less hysterical than the news pages.[2]

[1] 19 September 1963.   [2] 26 September 1963.

However, the tables were soon completely turned.

We had, I think, a splendid counter-attack on Profumo case. Hailsham and Macleod were *excellent* on T.V. My broadcast on sound radio was said to be good. Lord Shawcross was very effective—a *very* friendly neutral![1]

In reflecting upon this strange episode, I have found it difficult to explain the reasons or the motives which led to the public being excited almost to a state of panic by this distressing build-up of accusations against leading men of unblemished integrity. There have, of course, been many such cases in history, in our own and other countries, but generally based on some stronger foundation. In retrospect, the causes seem to have been twofold. The unlucky series of security trials had shaken the public confidence in the work of the Security Services. This was quite unjust because, although some of these arose from weaknesses in the general system, it was due to the extreme vigilance and skill of our defensive forces that the criminals were finally brought to justice. Naturally, the more successful our counter-espionage and the narrower the net closing around foreign agents, the larger became the number of cases which became public. Yet, these were not regarded as triumphs but rather as failures. Nor was full weight given to the immense difficulties facing the work of counter-espionage with all the protection of a legal system rightly exercised in favour of the accused. Anyone who knew the details of this battle of wits and the handicaps under which our loyal servants worked understood the problem; yet it was not known by and could not be explained to the general public. Secondly, the unprecedented disgrace and fall of a leading Minister proved—and rightly—a grave shock to the great body of the general public. That a Minister should be found incompetent was pardonable. That he should deceive his leader, his colleagues and his fellow-members was a wound to the whole body politic.

It was in this atmosphere that the case of Stephen Ward, with all its salacious details, was built up into a *cause célèbre* and revealed a curious social feature of the new permissive age. It was, I must admit, as much a surprise to me as to ordinary folk to hear of this strange

[1] 26 September 1963.

environment in which men of some importance, sometimes even holding high positions, were led to mingle with crooks, charlatans, pimps and courtesans. In my youth, good manners, although not necessarily good morality, made such a confusion impossible. The *monde* and the *demi-monde* were kept strictly apart. But now it seemed that among a small but notorious group of people a new system prevailed. I therefore sympathised with those who felt ashamed at the decadence revealed by these scabrous accounts of certain aspects of modern life in London. I could even understand (although I thought it hysterical) the emotion of the Editor of *The Times*, brought up like me in a respectable upper-middle class home in which all this kind of thing was not only distasteful but unthinkable. Yet, to disapprove was one thing; to turn this incident into an extravagant campaign, which by its very lack of proportion became ridiculous, was to destroy rather than sustain respect for all established government.

Perhaps also some of the people who were affected by these revelations had themselves a certain sense of shame at the apparent weakening of the old ties. They required a sacrifice to appease the offended gods, if not of morality, at least of convention. What could be a more convenient victim for this purpose than an elderly but respectable Conservative Prime Minister? There is a passage in one of Macaulay's essays which admirably describes the course of these occasional outbreaks of emotion in British life:

We know no spectacle so ridiculous as the British public in one of its periodical fits of morality. In general, elopements, divorces, and family quarrels, pass with little notice. We read the scandal, talk about it for a day, and forget it. But once in six or seven years our virtue becomes outrageous. We cannot suffer the laws of religion and decency to be violated. We must make a stand against vice. We must teach libertines that the English people appreciate the importance of domestic ties. Accordingly some unfortunate man, in no respect more depraved than hundreds whose offences have been treated with lenity, is singled out as an expiatory sacrifice. . . . He is, in truth, a sort of whipping-boy, by whose vicarious agonies all the other transgressors of the same class are, it is supposed, sufficiently chastised. We reflect very complacently on our own severity, and compare with great pride the high standard of morals established in England with the Parisian laxity. At length our anger is satiated. Our victim is ruined and heart-broken. And our virtue goes quietly to sleep for seven years more.[1]

This whole affair was naturally a great trial to me. I was conscious of the mistakes which I had made in handling some of its aspects. I should have pressed Profumo harder myself rather than leaving it to his contemporaries and colleagues. I should perhaps have taken a stronger stand when the first stream of accusations started to rise like a river in flood around the feet of the Government. Nevertheless, I could claim that in the method adopted, the putting of our whole lives and careers in the hands of a judge, we took a risk which showed confidence in our own integrity. It was fully justified, and although it left marks upon my physical strength and was perhaps one of the causes of my later illness, I look back in pride upon the loyalty and affection which was shown to me on every side. Above all, without the constant daily affection and support of my wife I might have succumbed to melancholy brooding in the midst of all these troubles. As always in times of stress, her calm serenity radiated confidence.

[1] Lord Macaulay, 'Moore's Life of Lord Byron', *Critical and Historical Essays* (London, 1851), p. 296.

CHAPTER XIV

Breakthrough in Moscow

THE Cuba crisis ended on 4 November 1962. But there were some intricate and detailed points still to be resolved on which it was necessary for Washington to exert considerable pressure on Moscow. Meanwhile I began to reflect upon the probable results of the failure of Khrushchev's dramatic coup. Would his power in the Kremlin, by no means absolute, be seriously shaken? Would he retort by some dangerous move on Berlin? Or would he accept the situation and revert to the comparatively moderate policy which he had taken before this dangerous experiment on the very doorstep of the United States?

> Khrushchev and Hitler are very different characters. Hitler *had* to act with frantic haste. He could not wait, for he was putting on Germany strains which such a country could not stand for more than a short time. Moreover, since we *have* 'stood up' to the Russians for fifteen years; since Khrushchev may be the best type of Russian leader we are likely to get, there *is* a strong argument for trying now to negotiate either some limited agreements or over a wider field.[1]

On 27 November, Alexander Soldatov, the Russian Ambassador, delivered a long letter from Khrushchev. In all the circumstances, it was a somewhat unexpected document. On Cuba he contented himself with saying:

> The Cuban issue still retains its top priority. It is now necessary to focus attention on the final elimination of the crisis that arose. Steps have been reciprocally taken which have diminished the acute danger of the situation in the Caribbean area and it has proved possible to avert the sliding of the world into a precipice.

[1] 27 November 1962.

Thus is history written in the Soviet Union. Nevertheless this long missive was essentially constructive. On Berlin he would ask the Ambassador to have further discussions with Lord Home. But the greater part of his plea was directed to the possibility of an agreement on nuclear tests. He argued that there was now in effect an agreement between the three nuclear powers to stop underwater, atmospheric and outer space explosions. However, a proper agreement should go further than this. *All* tests should be banned, including underground tests. There was no need for inspection teams; modern science could devise mechanisms by which automatic, unmanned seismic stations could do the necessary monitoring. On the next day, the Foreign Secretary informed me that, although the Ambassador's proposals on Berlin were not new, they seemed to indicate a genuine desire 'to talk'. However, both de Gaulle and President Kennedy believed that it would be best to leave things to develop on Berlin and similar issues while keeping open the possibility of negotiations. We should in any event wait for the Russians to make a formal move.

While we were at Nassau, the President received a letter from Khrushchev on nuclear tests. It was very similar to that which he had sent to me, but it added an important point and a real concession. Although repeating the argument that underground tests could be detected by unmanned stations, he stated that the U.S.S.R. would now be willing to consider two or three on-site verification inspections each year. Although Kennedy did not regard two or three inspections as adequate and observed there were limitations as to the areas which would be made available, nevertheless he agreed that this offer marked a substantial advance.

On 8 March 1963, the news came that both the 17-Nation Disarmament Committee and the Sub-Committee consisting of the three nuclear powers had reached a total stalemate at Geneva. I at once called into conference the Foreign Secretary, Joseph Godber (Minister of State), Harold Caccia and Philip de Zulueta. It was – horrible phrase – a 'working luncheon'. My purpose

was to discuss a plan by which [we] might try to break the deadlock which has occurred at Geneva over the Test Ban agreement. We worked at this till 3.30 or so. Then Sir William Penney came, to explain . . . the precise situation from the scientific point of view, which he did with his usual clarity. He is quite clear that it's not science but politics which holds back the President. I am very anxious that we should take some initiative, and we decided to draft a message which I might send and also consider what action I might take if the Americans (as I fear) are stubborn or frightened of the internal political pressure.[1]

On 11 March, at a further meeting, the Foreign Secretary

agreed entirely with my idea of a direct letter to President Kennedy about the Test Ban position. I doubt whether I shall move him and may be forced to act alone. However, the first thing is to try a discussion with Kennedy. I worked out text of (a) message to President (b) covering message to David Gore. When I have got Gore's comment, I will prepare final text and inform Cabinet *after* I have [the Ambassador's] reply.[2]

David Gore saw every advantage in my making a further approach to the President on nuclear tests but he felt that the political situation was not encouraging. Dean Rusk's last letter to Alec Home showed how despondent the Americans felt at the moment, and this feeling was fully shared by the President. Moreover, Congress, especially the Senate, were in a hostile mood. If I was going to suggest a new Summit Meeting, he felt bound to point out that the President would not be prepared to consider such a plan unless there was a virtual assurance of a constructive outcome. It was therefore important to devise some means of discovering whether Khrushchev would be seriously interested in a 'package deal'. Gore did not feel that it would be much good relying on normal diplomatic channels, either through Foreign Secretaries or through Ambassadors. 'I suspect', wrote the Ambassador, 'that Khrushchev judges Rusk's importance in the light of his own importance to Gromyko; that is to say, as someone who is a competent post-boy'. If, therefore, anything was to be done, it would be better to send special emissaries, one from Washington and one from London. This last proposal turned out to be highly fruitful.

[1] 8 March 1963.   [2] 11 March 1963.

Fortified by David Gore's suggestions, I redrafted my message to the President and on 16 March sent it on its way by diplomatic bag. It covered the whole field; and although some of my hopes were to prove outside our grasp, yet it was the basis on which the Test Ban Treaty was founded. It has, therefore, some historic interest.

I was very glad to get your message about the whole problem of the nuclear forces.

The more I think of it, the more constructive I believe our Nassau declaration was. In whatever form our plans ultimately emerge, the spirit in which they were launched has undoubtedly been more and more understood as the weeks have passed. . . .

With the signature of the technical agreement between our countries arising from Nassau, the foundation of one part of our work will be well and truly laid. Nor do I think it will ever be abandoned by any Government here. After long experience I have found that we are all of us apt to say things when we are not in authority which we do not feel either willing or able to carry out when we succeed to responsibility.

But thinking so much about all these matters has led me, and I expect you, to turn back to another part of this nuclear problem, far more constructive in reality; for it might open the path to something better for the world than merely building vast forces which if not used are wildly expensive, if used are wholly destructive to mankind, and which at the best keep a kind of uneasy peace by a balance of horror. So, after much thought, I am impelled to write to you to give you my ideas about the question of nuclear tests and the possibility of an agreement to ban them.

You and I both remember well the background of our meeting at Bermuda. Then the agreement, which had seemed in our grasp two or three years before, when we had a moratorium—informal but nevertheless very welcome to the world—had been frustrated by the massive Russian tests in the previous autumn. How far Mr. Khrushchev made these for internal political reasons, or how far he wished to frighten and impress the neutral and unallied world with his power, is only a matter for speculation. But it was certainly a great shock to us all. When we met in Bermuda in December, 1961, I had the feeling that you were as anxious as I to avoid having to reply with another series of tests, American and British—yours of course on a far greater scale than ours. I remember well the discussions and the difficulty of getting any very clear picture from the experts. Incidentally, the more I discuss this problem, the more I find that we laymen talk about the technical aspect and the experts always tell us that it is a political problem. Perhaps there is some lesson to be drawn from this.

At Bermuda, we resisted the temptation to hold a new series on political grounds as an answer to the Russians, although we were, with some difficulty, persuaded that it was necessary to do so on military grounds in order to protect the vital interests of the Western Alliance. This was the theme of our announcement at Bermuda. It was on this basis that I was able to persuade my colleagues and Parliament to give their consent to the joint operation and to the use of Christmas Island.

All the same in the Christmas atmosphere of that year I felt impelled to write to you an inexcusably long letter to set out my thoughts and feelings.

After some exchange of messages, we decided to accompany our announcement of tests by a rather novel approach to the question, which made a considerable impression, in both our countries. We sent joint letters to Mr. Khrushchev on February 7, 1962, followed by two sets of letters in broadly similar terms.... The point, you will remember, was that although the Western tests had to be made, we hoped that this series would be regarded as the end of a definite round and that we should all try to concentrate on the Disarmament Conference about to open in Geneva—to this body the subject of the Test Ban had been transferred at the request of Russia. We both promised to take a personal interest in this and to try to bring matters to a head whenever the moment seemed right. The words that I used to Mr. Khrushchev on February 25 were:

'As I told you in my letter of February 14, I am also very ready to take part personally in these negotiations, when it seems that the presence of Heads of Government can be of positive value. Two situations might arise in which this method might be fruitful. The first is if the Conference is making satisfactory and definite progress. In such a case a meeting of the Heads of Government might well serve to consolidate what had been achieved and to take a further step towards an actual agreement.

'The second situation is one in which certain major and clear points of disagreement have emerged which threaten to hold up further progress. In that case the Heads of Government should perhaps meet in order to try to break the deadlock.'

On February 24 you sent a message to Krushchev in which you said:

'The Heads of Government should meet to resolve explicit points of disagreement which might remain after the issues have been carefully explored and the largest possible measure of agreement has been worked out at the diplomatic level.'

The fact that both Dean Rusk and Alec Home went to Geneva for the opening Conference to start it off was intended to underline the importance which you and I attached to the meeting.

During recent months the negotiations have made considerable progress. The Russians have now publicly accepted the principle of inspection. It is true that they seemed to accept this three years ago, but they had afterwards very definitely rejected it. They have now accepted it definitely and have also accepted three annual inspections. The West has moved down from twenty inspections to seven. So, from the man in the street's point of view, the two sides have come a great deal nearer. Indeed, to the layman, we would seem so near that it would be almost inconceivable that the gulf could not be bridged. There are, of course, a number of other points to be settled in connection with these inspections so as to ensure that they are a reality and not a farce. But I do not feel that the Russian refusal to discuss them until the number is settled means that they will use these points as a way of bringing the negotiations to an end. If they were to do so after an agreement on numbers had been reached they would be in a very bad posture before the world.

I have wondered in my own mind and tried to find some answer to the question as to why Mr. Khrushchev suddenly moved forward on the inspection issue. So long as he stood upon the principle that any form of inspection involved espionage he had at least a logical position. We may think it ridiculous but it is in conformity with the well-known Russian sensitiveness to contacts with the outside world and with the almost Oriental xenophobia which has been traditional in Russia whether Tsarist or Communist. But, having abandoned this position, it is difficult to argue that three inspections do not endanger security while four, five, six or seven might. I wonder perhaps whether there was some real misunderstanding in his mind over this, and whether he somehow got it into his head that if he moved on the principle, you would accept a quota of two or three. Mr. Khrushchev, like an old elephant, has a very tenacious memory. For example, in conversation in Moscow in 1959 when this matter was first under discussion I casually mentioned various figures for annual inspections, from twelve down to three, as an illustration of my general argument in favour of a test agreement. Since then he has affected to regard this chance observation as a substantive proposal by the British Government. Of course he should know that it was not. But that is the way he has learned to think—or double-think. Similarly, something must have happened recently to explain Khrushchev's apparently genuine mood of exasperation and distrust. However, whatever may be the explanation, that is the position, and there now appears to be a deadlock based upon the question of number.

What, then, are we to do? Of course, there are very strong arguments for doing nothing. Strong logical arguments, strong political arguments. But this is not the spirit in which you, who carry the largest responsibility, before God and man, have faced your duty, nor that in which I have tried to do the same. I have a feeling that the test ban is the most important step that we can take towards unravelling this frightful tangle of fear and suspicion in East—West relations—important in itself and all the more important for what may flow from it. All the same, strictly it is the Russian turn to move. They have come from nothing to three; you have come from twenty to seven, and it is up to them to make a bid. If they want a Treaty they can get one—and, it will be argued if they do not want one, why negotiate at considerable risk. Why is it that the West always have to move? Why is it that all the concessions seem to come from us? And so on. Then of course there are quite strong groups of opinion who are really in favour of tests. Some scientists think it is a pity not to know all you can know. It seems almost restrictive and reactionary not to blow things up to find out what would happen when they go off. Others are very fearful as to whether in some way or another important lessons might be learned by the Russians from a clandestine series of disconnected tests. I assume that this is the old question of yield for weight, which may have some bearing upon the development of the anti-missile missile in its most sophisticated form. On the other hand, there are equally strong bodies of opinion that feel that from a purely scientific point of view on the figures we are discussing there is not very much more danger in the small number of inspections than in the larger one.

I have just been reading a short account of this whole story from the beginning and I am impressed by the fact that whenever we seem to get near a solution somebody finds out a new scientific theory. The 'big hole' was itself a good example of this, and in that hole are likely—unless we are careful—to be buried the hopes of mankind. All the same, the arguments against moving can be powerfully put forward, and I have no doubt are very strong politically with you. To those that I have mentioned can be added that if we do sign a Test Ban the French and the Chinese will stand out and so in the end we may not be so very much further on. Finally, it is alleged that there is not very much pressure on either side to start a new series of tests.

However, since it seems to take a couple of years or more to evaluate one set of tests and to make the necessary preparation for the next, this lull may prove very deceptive. We may within a year or two be faced with the same situation which confronted us in 1961 in Bermuda. Apart from avoiding the practical difficulty that hangs over us in the near future, I am sure you will agree that we would gain enormously if this Treaty could be made. First, it would stop the contamination of the atmosphere. We have been thinking so much about the underground tests that we tend to forget the injury done by atmospheric testing. While it might not stop the Chinese and the French tests altogether, it would certainly drive them both underground, which is a good thing from this angle. Secondly, I am quite sure that it would have a very considerable effect upon some countries which may be hesitating about what to do. For instance, Sweden, India and Israel, and other countries which will be almost bound to enter the nuclear race unless they can find an excuse not to do so. Thirdly, the effect on the world of an agreement solemnly entered into by our two countries with Russia would be enormous. It would give a tremendous new sense of hope. We could probably succeed in giving a new impetus to the Disarmament Conference and might also give a lead on other fronts.

It would be a great gain, of course, if Sweden, India, Israel and the rest would undertake not to test; but I have a feeling that if we get the test ban agreement, there would be another prize just as important to be secured. We ought to be able simultaneously to get a non-dissemination agreement; an undertaking, that is, from non-nuclear countries not to accept nuclear power at the gift of others, for their sole use, and from nuclear powers not to give nuclear weapons or knowledge to non-nuclear countries. To me this seems the real key to the German problem; one which gives a good deal of anxiety both to the Russians and to us, and, to be fair, to many Germans, who are genuinely anxious lest in due course they or their successors will be forced to become a nuclear power. It is quite true that Germany is bound by all kinds of agreements and undertakings. But these could easily be represented by a bad German in the future as the modern counterpart of Versailles. We know—only too well—what might follow from all that way of thinking. Indeed, speaking frankly, the most attractive part of clause 7 of the Nassau Agreement[1] is that it may give the Germans a sense of participation without incurring these dangers. But I feel that a test agreement accompanied by a non-dissemination agreement would serve to underline clause 8 if we are able to bring clause 7 into operation, and anyway would be effective in itself. No Germans could then say that Germany had been forced into this abnegation in a period of weakness just after the war when the present treaties or agreements were made.

On the contrary the Germans could claim with pride that, with other great States, Germany had entered into this undertaking as a contribution to the solution of one of the gravest problems which confronts the world. At the same time, this is a prospect which must appeal equally to the Russians. The countries of the West have, thank God for it, decided to rebuild their bridges with Germany. We have tried to forget about the two wars and the Hitler persecutions and all the rest. This is true of your country and mine, and to be fair, of the French. All this is good. But then without being cynical, we all have an interest, because the Germans are our Allies against the Communists. The Russians both hate and fear the Germans. They hate them, inspired by the cruel memories which we have decided to blot out; they fear them as an efficient, hard-working, brave and determined people. Nor can they fail to be conscious of the pressure which they put continually upon German patience

[1] See Appendix 4.

by the obstinacy with which they enforce the division of Germany. For all these reasons, then, I think the tests ban, followed by adherence of other countries not to test, accompanied by a non-dissemination agreement which was reasonably well supported, would have a profound effect in removing the present state of tension in the world.

Of course whatever agreement is made, the Russians might be able to evade it and we might not be able to catch them. From our point of view, if there are some twenty-five unidentified events of Magnitude 4 or over annually in Russian then of course with seven inspections we have nearly a one in four chance of catching them out; with five we have a one in five chance, and with only three we have one in nine. Naturally, if they make a definite series, we have a better chance of finding them out. There is also the possibility that they might so arrange the tests at the end of the year that we would have exhausted our right of inspection. However, this and other difficulties might be got over in negotiation, not merely by splitting the difference between seven and three but by some arrangement to carry over unused inspections to an agreed extent, from one year to another. Since our machines, whether operated overtly or covertly, will continue to improve we are likely to need fewer annual inspections as time goes on, and an arrangement of this kind for carry-over of inspections might be one way of allowing ourselves enough inspections at first without over-ensuring for the future.

So much for the chances of our catching them if they cheated. However I am bound to say that I think they would be at great risk if they did cheat after signing the Treaty. Although they might have no moral inhibitions in breaking their word, I think they would be abashed at being publicly shown up before the world; and, what is more important, they would lose the great benefits of a non-dissemination agreement, with all that this implies in Central Europe.

So we come to the problem of how we are to renew the negotiations with a view to bringing them to a satisfactory conclusion. Looking back to our declaration in 1962 I am bound to say that I feel myself under an obligation to act in accordance with what I then said. Certainly in my statement, which perhaps went further than yours, I undertook to do something about it in either of two situations, one of which is now approaching.

There are various possibilities:

(*a*) I can see the disadvantage in merely offering five inspections through the Geneva negotiators with no certainty that this would be accepted. A rejection would be very bad politically for you, although not so much for me.

(*b*) I can see the dangers involved, although I think the advantages might well outweigh them, in simply suggesting that we all three should meet and try to settle the matter. If the West then offered five and Khrushchev stood out, our position might not be very dignified but it would not be ignoble.

(*c*) We could summon a conference on the understanding that the conditions of the inspections were first brought near to a conclusion, so that we should only have to settle the final steps to be taken on these together with the question of numbers. But it would still be a risk.

(*d*) Or, if it was better for you, I could write to you and Khrushchev either privately or publicly or both, suggesting that we should all meet at Geneva. If he refused, it would be a great disappointment and we should not get the agreement, but again it would not be discreditable.

(*e*) Before suggesting either jointly or separately a conference of the Heads of Governments, we might make some further soundings.

In this connection, I still feel there is something queer about Khrushchev's move towards accepting the principle of inspection. There may have been some genuine misunderstanding in his mind, or perhaps some misunderstanding or misrepresentation by those Russians who reported to him what they picked up in Geneva. Possibly therefore you could send some personal message to Khrushchev on this matter or perhaps some emissary such as Averell, or even your brother Bobby, who would both clear up any misunderstanding and find out whether there was a chance of settling round about five or by some juggling with the numbers, including the conception of bisques and the limit for any one year, coupled of course with what I think could be made very attractive to Khrushchev, the non-dissemination aspect.

Some of my telegrams report that he is supposed to have lost interest in the nuclear test ban but if that is so, it may well be because he has not had the non-dissemination aspect sufficiently impressed upon him.

I am sorry to inflict so long a letter on you, but I feel this very deep personal obligation upon me, and it is one which in some form or another, I must discharge, before it is too late. I do not, as you know, want to trouble you on the telephone but I would be very glad to hear first from you either through David Gore or by teleprinter message, and then perhaps we could have a talk to clarify any outstanding points.

I am sending this letter to you through David who is fully conversant with all our ideas and whom I know you trust as much as I do.

It will be seen that I based my appeal on Khrushchev's acceptance of the principle of 'on-site' inspections, under certain conditions. In the event, partly due to American intransigence as to the number to be claimed and partly because of Russian limitation of the areas to be available, this whole concept proved abortive. But it helped to start the ball rolling. If in the end we had to be content with a partial ban, omitting underground tests, compared to the immense gain to the world the loss was trivial.

On 28 March the President sent his reply. Although he was doubtful about the wisdom of dealing at the same negotiation with the Test Ban and the question of a non-dissemination treaty and was unwilling to hold another Summit Meeting until the technical matters had been disposed of by our representatives, his answer was not unhelpful. He proposed that we should send a joint letter to Khrushchev and forwarded me a draft.

For some days drafts and amendments to drafts passed between us. Kennedy began to have doubts as to the willingness of Khrushchev to negotiate in view of his difficulties with China. To this, I replied that if he were in difficulties with China he should be all the more likely to come to terms with us. On 11 April, Kennedy and I had a long conversation by telephone and I noted:

> Another reply from President about our proposed approach to Khrushchev. He is moving nearer and I had a useful telephone talk with him this afternoon. Then a lot of telegraphing to Gore became necessary. I am encouraged.[1]

[1] 11 April 1963.

The President repeated his anxieties about offering what was virtually a Summit Meeting—would it not be wiser to stick to the special emissaries? When I sent him a further draft he was still anxious about any suggestion of a meeting.

> We must try to answer President Kennedy's last proposal. We are so nearly agreed that I would like to [settle] it with the President while he is at Palm Beach for the Easter holiday and before the rats get at it.
>
> During the morning, after Philip de Zulueta had talked with Foreign Secretary, we agreed (over the telephone) telegrams to Washington in reply to President. I have accepted *two* of his amendments and suggested a slight change of order in the *vital* sentence (the method of negotiation leading to a Summit Meeting) which I hope he will accept. If David Gore can get these last points settled, we might get instructions to our Ambassadors to deliver the message by tomorrow or the next day. However, 'there's many a slip . . .'.[1]

The President was sympathetic, but he reminded me in a letter of 15 April that

> memories . . . of May 1960 are very strong in this country, and in my own mind, and I believe that on the historic evidence it is not likely that Khrushchev would make major changes at a Summit from positions put forward under his direction.

Finally, I accepted his modified text and instructions were prepared for our Ambassadors in Moscow.

Although these days of telegrams and telephone messages were not prolonged, yet for me the tension was great. I was desperately anxious to achieve a modicum of success, and I felt instinctively that at least some agreement was within our grasp.

Khrushchev was away from Moscow for a few days, and it was not therefore until 24 April that the letter was delivered. Meanwhile,

> the State Department (after being sceptical, not to say hostile)

[1] 13 April 1963.

have suddenly become enthusiastic about the joint approach to Khrushchev. I suppose this means that the President's Press boys are getting ready to represent it as entirely an American initiation, with the young New Frontiersman in the van and the old British P.M. being dragged reluctantly at his heels. It is really rather amusing.[1]

The text of the joint letter to Khrushchev as finally sent on 15 April ran as follows.

You will recall that in February and March 1962, we had some correspondence about the Geneva Disarmament Conference, and in particular about the possibility of reaching agreement on the text of a treaty to ban nuclear tests. Both President Kennedy and I pledged ourselves to take a personal interest in the progress of this conference on which so many of the hopes of mankind have been fixed. Last October we both indicated in messages to you our intention to devote renewed efforts to the problem of disarmament with particular reference to the proliferation of nuclear weapons and the banning of nuclear tests.

Since then the Geneva meeting has continued but it has not reached the point of definite agreement. Nevertheless, some encouraging advance has been made. For example, your acceptance of the principle of on-the-spot verification of unidentified events has been of great value. Equally, the Western countries have been able to reduce the number of annual inspections for which they felt it essential to ask, from about twenty to seven. The difference remaining is of course real and substantial, if only because it presents in practical form the effects of two different lines of reasoning. At the same time the actual difference between the three inspections which you have proposed and the seven for which we are asking, important though this is, should not be impossible to resolve. As regards the automatic seismic stations, the difference between us appears to be fairly narrow.

We all have a duty to consider what are the needs of security; but we also have a duty to humanity. President Kennedy and I therefore believe that we ought to make a further serious attempt by the best available means to see if we cannot bring this matter to a conclusion with your help.

[1] 17 April 1963.

We know that it is argued that a nuclear tests agreement, although valuable and welcome especially in respect of atmospheric tests, will not by itself make a decisive contribution to the peace and security of the world. There are, of course, other questions between us which are also of great importance; but the question of nuclear tests does seem to be one on which agreement might now be reached. The mere fact of an agreement on one question will inevitably help to create confidence and so facilitate other settlements. In addition, it is surely possible that we might be able to proceed rapidly to specific and fruitful discussions about the non-dissemination of nuclear power leading to an agreement on this subject. Such an agreement, if it was reasonably supported by other countries, would seem to us likely to have a profound effect upon the present state of tension in the world. If it proved possible to move promptly to an agreement on nuclear weapons and on the proliferation of national nuclear capability, an advance to broader agreements might then open up.

The practical question is how best to proceed. It may be that further discussions would reveal new possibilities from both sides as regards the arrangements for the quota of inspections. But if we attempted to reach this point by the present methods both sides may feel unable to make an advance because this would appear to be surrendering some point of substance without obtaining a final agreement on a definite treaty in exchange. It may be that we could make some progress on this question of numbers by exploring an idea which has been mentioned by the neutral nations in Geneva—the idea that a quota of on-site inspections might be agreed upon to cover a period of several years, from which inspections could be drawn under more flexible conditions than an annual quota would permit.

But at the moment it is not only the question of numbers which holds us up, but we also have to agree on the final content of the draft treaty and in particular to decide certain important questions as to how inspections are to be carried out. You have taken the view that once the quota is agreed the other matters can easily be settled, whereas we feel that the final agreement about the number of inspections is unlikely to be possible unless most of the other matters have been first disposed of. Thus we have reached an impasse.

We should be interested to hear your suggestions as to how

we are to break out of this. For our part we should be quite
prepared now to arrange private tripartite discussions in whatever seemed the most practical way. For example, our chief
representatives at Geneva could conduct discussions on the
questions which remain to be settled. Alternatively, or at a later
stage, President Kennedy and I would be ready to send in due
course very senior representatives who would be empowered to
speak for us and talk in Moscow directly with you. It would be
our hope that either in Geneva or through such senior representatives in Moscow we might bring the matter close enough to a
final decision so that it might then be proper to think in terms of
a meeting of the three of us at which a definite agreement on a
test ban could be made final. It is of course obvious that a meeting
of the three of us which resulted in a test ban treaty would open a
new chapter in our relations as well as providing an opportunity
for wider discussions.

We sincerely trust that you will give serious consideration to
this proposal. We believe that the nuclear tests agreement and
what may follow from it is the most hopeful area in which to try
for agreement between us. The procedure which we have
suggested seems to us the most practical way of achieving a result
which would be welcomed all over the world.

Khrushchev replied on 8 May. His arguments followed familiar
lines. All tests, he alleged, could be detected without recourse to
inspection. Modern science made this possible. Yet the West
continued to harp on inspection. Why? For purposes of espionage.
The only reason why the Soviet Government agreed to the symbolic
number of two or three inspections a year was because they thought
it a political necessity for the President to satisfy the United States
Senate. Yet, instead of accepting this offer in the spirit in which it
was put forward, the West had started to haggle. Now we talked
about seven or eight inspections, covering up to five hundred square
kilometres each.

Our people would be quite right to take their Government very
severely to account if it entered into negotiations about how many
spies we will admit on to our territory per year, and what sort of
conditions we will create for these spies.

Nevertheless, the Russians were prepared to continue to seek agreement and 'to receive your highly-placed representatives'.

The position had, of course, been complicated by the American proposal for the so-called 'Multi-Manned NATO Force'. This we had accepted in principle at Nassau, but it seemed unlikely ever to be clothed with any reality. There followed now a number of conferences at Chequers.

> David Ormsby Gore flew back for these conferences and has been of the greatest help. We have had Foreign Secretary, Minister of Defence, C.D.S. (Mountbatten), Solly Zuckerman, William Penney, and other officials like Caccia (F.O.) and Scott (Defence). The two great questions have been:
>
> (1) Khrushchev's reply to President/P.M. letter on nuclear tests.
>
> (2) U.S. proposal for so-called 'multi-manned' force—twenty-five ships and two hundred Polaris missiles.[1]

I was very glad that I had brought the Ambassador back, for

> in the course of all the expositions and arguments about these two issues with our delicate relations with U.S.A. and President Kennedy, David Gore has been quite invaluable. He has established a remarkable position with Kennedy, an intimate and trusted friend. It is most fortunate—and almost unprecedented—for a British Ambassador to have this position and is based on old pre-war friendships between various Kennedys and Cavendishes and Gores. I was very impressed with his wisdom as well as his wit and gaiety.[1]

As a result of our discussions, by Sunday night,

> I was able to compose two replies to the President's two letters. On the first, I have strongly urged him not to be discouraged by the rather negative side of Khrushchev's reply to our letter. It does not, in spite of all the rather specious and irritating arguments, reject our main proposal—viz. to send two high-powered emissaries, known to be in our special confidence, to Moscow to carry on the talk and see whether we can somehow get closer together. The Americans will not like this, but David Gore is confident that the President will agree—if only to please me.[1]

[1] 20 May 1963.

On the second issue, I played for time.

By 29 May, after some interchange of telegrams, the text of a reply to Khrushchev was agreed.

> We are rebutting some of his arguments, but (I hope) not in an arrogant or provocative way. But we *are* welcoming his willingness to receive our 'two emissaries'.[1]

On 8 June, Khrushchev's further answer was received. Although it restated in rather tough language his views about espionage, with a side-blow at West German 'revanchists' and the proposed creation of a NATO nuclear force, it expressed a clear agreement to open the negotiations. This was publicly welcomed by the President in a major speech in Washington in which he announced that high-level discussions would shortly begin in Moscow on the test ban problem. He also declared that the United States would carry out no more atmospheric tests so long as other states did not do so.

I now decided to send Lord Hailsham as our representative. Fortified with the help of so able an Ambassador as Humphrey Trevelyan, I felt sure he would do well. He had qualities of energy and imagination which might appeal to Khrushchev. At the same time I was very glad to learn that the President had decided on Harriman to act for the United States. I have always regarded Averell Harriman as one of the ablest Americans with whom I have had to deal. For a task of this kind, he had every quality—infinite patience, tact, courage and complete independence from any political or even administrative pressure. His authority was so great that in a crisis he could act upon his own, relying upon the ultimate support of the White House and the State Department.

I now sent to Kennedy a memorandum prepared by our scientists. The choice appeared to be either no treaty at all or a treaty which involved the risk of clandestine underground tests. What could such underground tests achieve? Already each side was capable of destroying the other, and the various refinements that could be made would not affect the general balance of power. The only thing that could affect this would be the successful development of an

[1] 29 May 1963.

Kennedy arrives at Gatwick Airport
'combining that indescribable look of a boy on holiday with the dignity of a
President and Commander-in-Chief.'

Home signs the Nuclear Test Ban Treaty, 10 October 1963
'So was realised at least one of the great purposes which I had set myself.'

anti-missile missile. But the final testing of any anti-missile missile did not seem to be entirely dependent on underground nuclear tests. The major problems involved in the successful and reliable functioning of such a system would be questions of interception, of jamming of the complex radar systems and all the rest. So one must ask whether we were not assigning too great a significance to underground tests in themselves and their positive identification as man-made events rather than natural seismic events. We were also appalled by the possibilities of exploding multimegaton warheads at considerable heights from which they could devastate thousands of square miles on the ground. Something similar might be done by large explosions at sea causing devastation by tidal waves. Underground tests then seemed irrelevant to the further development of these appalling threats. If a partial test ban treaty would prevent all these horrors, why should we worry about underground experiments?

An opportunity for discussing these grave matters was fortunately afforded by a short visit which the President paid to me at Birch Grove House on 29 June. It was, in addition, an agreeable change from our troubles on the home front.

The President flew in from Ireland (where he had made a sentimental journey to 'the home of the Kennedys' and a rather foolish speech about Liberty). With a characteristic change of plan, he decided to stop in Derbyshire, go to Chatsworth, and see his sister Lady Hartington's grave. (By a strange irony she is buried next to Lord Frederick Cavendish, murdered by the Irish.) This made him a little late. However, after this slight delay all went according to plan.

Jack Kennedy—his valet and security man were in my mother's [bedroom] and [my father's dressing room]. Dean Rusk and Mr. Bundy in No. 3 and No. 4. No. 5 our secretaries. The nurseries put up others of the party. David Gore and some Americans were at Pooks [my son's house].

Mrs. Bell and our few servants excelled themselves. We got butler, etc., from Government Hospitality.

Although Saturday was a nasty wet day, Sunday was better with a lovely afternoon.

Q

The President and his party were here for twenty-four hours; about twelve hours was talk. . . . I gave the Americans the smoking room as their office. My sitting room was for the British. Lord Home, Lord Hailsham, Peter Thorneycroft, Duncan Sandys; Ted Heath came and went. (Alec Home stayed in the house.)

Altogether, it was a *great* success from our point of view . . . We got all we wanted.

(1) Full steam ahead with Moscow talks – Test Ban to be No. 1 Priority.

(2) Go slow on Multi-Manned.

On other difficult but really less important matters we were in agreement. . . .

The Security men (in hundreds); the Communication men (with vast apparatus); British Police (in hundreds) made the whole place a sort of armed camp. But it was all very well done, and vanished (after the President left) as suddenly as it had appeared. The Press . . . are rather uncertain about the meeting. Of course, the fact that we got exactly what we wanted is not agreeable to those who wish to attack me by all methods.[1]

This brief and hurriedly written extract from my diary gives an incomplete picture of the fantastic, even romantic, atmosphere that prevailed during these thrilling hours. From the very first moment when the President's helicopter flew in and landed in the park until his departure there was a feeling of excitement combined with gaiety which has left an indelible memory for all concerned and indeed for the whole neighbourhood. I can see him now, stepping out from the machine, this splendid, young, gay figure, followed by his team of devoted adherents. Never has a man been so well or so loyally served. Until he left, the whole of our little world was dominated by the sudden arrival and equally sudden departure of leading figures in the drama. My own house and my son's were made available; but of course they were not large enough to contain Secretaries of State, Ambassadors, members of the Foreign Office and State Department, secretaries, typists and all the protective apparatus which constituted his immense court. Hotels were taken

[1] 7 July 1963.

in the neighbourhood, inns commandeered; a communications centre was set up in Brighton with a forward post in my son's house. In addition, there was a permanent *va-et-vient* of helicopters between London or the Brighton centre and our landing ground.

Naturally, reporters appeared in great numbers, but caused us no trouble; for they were admirably shepherded by Harold Evans on my side and the President's Press Secretary, Pierre Salinger, equally efficient but operating upon somewhat cruder lines. Afterwards I read full, if varying, accounts of everything that we had said to each other and all the conclusions reached. In view of the paucity of information, journalists and editors did their best. At any rate the photographs were genuine.

In our immediate neighbourhood the excitement was intense, and the impression left was lasting. To greet Kennedy on his arrival I invited children from neighbouring schools (including boys from a preparatory school near by), neighbours, tenants, servants and estate staff. All were delighted by his happy acceptance of their simple but genuine welcome. The roads were packed outside the front gates and the crowd included a hundred C.N.D. marchers, with banners demanding that we should abolish nuclear tests. Since it was the main purpose of our meeting to achieve this, the demonstration seemed hardly necessary. However, the President took it all in very good part. When he drove early on Sunday morning to Mass at Forest Row, the roads outside the drive and on the corner of Chelwood Gate (by Ashdown Forest) were packed with people who had come from far and near. In Forest Row there was, I was told, an equally enthusiastic crowd. All seemed to be inspired by a single spirit. To them, Kennedy meant youth, energy, idealism and a new hope for the world. When the tragedy came, both these communities set up their own special memorials.

Inside the house it seemed more like a play or rather the mad rehearsal for a play, than a grave international conference. There was none of the solemnity which usually characterises such meetings. After all, we were all friends and many of us intimate friends; and the whole atmosphere was that of a country house party, to which had been added a garden party and a dance. There were the residents in the house itself, and there were those who came from outside. There seemed a perpetual flow of diplomats and politicians and their staffs. They all sat and talked to each other, and I hope were adequately entertained and refreshed.

The President seemed in the highest spirits and was particularly charming to Dorothy and the children and gave us lavish presents which gratified us at the time, and which I value still more now. It was of course sad to realise how illness and pain had already laid their hands on this buoyant and gallant figure. His specially constructed bed had to be brought, on which alone he could get comfort. I obtained, and still cherish, a rocking chair which he used throughout our talks. But none of these disabilities seemed to have the slightest effect upon his temperament. Of our party, as doubtless of many others, he was what is called 'the life and soul'.

All the serious discussions took place between him and me alone, with sometimes Private Secretaries to record decisions. This seemed to be much the most effective way for reaching rapid and full agreement. But at the end of the day I suggested that since this mass of experts had been assembled in the house and in neighbouring residences and hotels, we really ought to give them a show. Kennedy, with his usual puckish humour, had rather enjoyed teasing Rusk and others of his devoted friends by keeping them out of the picture. But he readily agreed to my proposal. We therefore staged a rather formal conference on orthodox lines, the two protagonists facing each other with a circle of their supporters behind—something like a prize-fight. This took place in the drawing-room, and since we had already settled all the important points it was necessary to think of a subject. The President suggested a general discussion on the future of NATO. This seemed to me all right, and we accordingly embarked on a formal interchange of views, chiefly for the benefit of our advisers. Kennedy was in a mischievous mood, nor could I resist reacting in the same spirit. For instance, he asked at one moment whether I thought the other countries in NATO would like to break the succession of American Commanders-in-Chief by having a Canadian, French, Italian or British officer. I could not resist the temptation. 'Yes, I agree, Mr. President. Or perhaps a Russian.' There was some confusion amid the advisers behind me, and one called out, 'I don't think the Prime Minister quite means that'. 'Oh, yes, I do. You see it would work very well. The forces of the Western powers already face East. The Russians would only need to "about turn" and the NATO and Warsaw Pact amalgamate in defending Europe from any Chinese threats.' In the gravest manner and without a smile the President observed, 'Mr. Prime Minister, I think that is a proposition that needs much serious consideration.'

Far too soon, the visit drew to an end. It was time to go. He went, as he came, by helicopter. Before he said goodbye we discussed once more our plans for frequent communication, by telegram or telephone; with another meeting before Christmas or, at the latest, in the New Year. Hatless, with his brisk step, and combining that indescribable look of a boy on a holiday with the dignity of a President and Commander-in-Chief, he walked across the garden to the machine. We stood and waved. I can see the helicopter now, sailing down the valley above the heavily laden, lush foliage of oaks and beech at the end of June. He was gone. Alas, I was never to see my friend again. Before those leaves had turned and fallen he was snatched by an assassin's bullet from the service of his own country and the whole world.

On 2 July, Khrushchev, speaking in East Berlin, seemed to suggest the possibility that the Russians would accept a partial Test Ban Treaty; previously they had wanted all or nothing. I informed the Governments of the old Commonwealth countries about this development and continued to discuss by telegram with the President how best to influence the French and Germans. De Gaulle would, of course, gain little from a Test Ban Treaty and the Germans were always nervous about any agreement between the West and East.

On 12 July, Harriman came to luncheon with me on his way to Moscow and I had a good talk with him alone.

He is certainly 'on our side' and will do all he can to get a Test Ban agreement of some kind with the Russians. He was very sound about Germany and France, and how to handle them. I had a special message from the President, which encourages me. But what will Mr. Khrushchev do? We do not know the answer. Does he want an agreement or not? The situation is dramatic and vital for me. If there is any chance of our agreement and a Summit Meeting afterwards, I will fight on in home politics. If not, I shall feel inclined to throw in my hand.[1]

The talks opened in Moscow on 15 July and were finally concluded on 25 July. Although this period was short, it was certainly agitated. In Hailsham's first message he reported a talk with Khrushchev in which he made it clear that the earlier offer of two or three on-site inspections a year was now withdrawn. The obsession about espionage, whether genuine or affected, seemed to dominate his thoughts. On the other hand, he did not insist upon linking a settlement of the German problem with any possible Test Ban Treaty.

On 16 July, rather to my surprise in view of our recent meeting, with that sudden change of direction which has been such a marked feature of American policy in recent years, the President started an altogether new hare. He proposed, in order to pacify de Gaulle and induce France to sign any treaty on tests which might be reached, to release the vital nuclear information which had been so long and so jealously withheld, first from us and then from the French. This unexpected offer was apparently to be made without conditions and without any *quid pro quo*, except to abstain from tests, which would, in any case, have been rendered unnecessary. As may be imagined, this new move was received with mixed feelings in Whitehall. Had the Americans armed me with this powerful weapon six months before, it might have made the whole difference to Britain and to Europe.

On 18 July

we had a short meeting before the Cabinet, and I felt in almost total disagreement with the F.O. view. Why be so cautious, when the President was so imaginative? Why bother about the President going 'far beyond what his advisers feel'? That is an American affair. The only thing that matters is—does the President's attitude to France—that is, to try to use the gift of nuclear information as an instrument of policy—suit us? As it is what I

[1] 12 July 1963.

have been trying to do—and failed to get American agreement—for a long time, why should I object? We might even revive Europe (Common Market, etc.) and start a new and hopeful movement to straighten out the whole alliance. So I left the Cabinet (which had mostly routine items that pile up at the end of the session) to Butler and concentrated on the answer. . . . By 1 p.m. we had a good draft, which Foreign Secretary and Minister of Defence saw and accepted after Cabinet.[1]

My message to the President on 18 July ran as follows:

Thank you for your message of July 16. As I promised on July 17, my colleagues and I have been reflecting on this and can now send you our considered thoughts.

Let me say first of all how much we welcome your approach and the bold sweep of your proposals. We entirely agree that there is a great opportunity here with profound consequences for East–West relations and also for restoring the full unity of the Western Alliance by bringing France back into partnership. We want to co-operate with you fully in doing our best to make use of this opportunity. At the same time I know you will agree that the very magnitude of the opportunity calls for a most careful assessment and cautious handling.

It seems to us that our immediate object is fairly simple. It is to stop de Gaulle from destroying at least the moral effect of any test ban treaty which we may get with the Russians, by making some intemperate remarks immediately after the treaty is initialled or perhaps at his press conference at the end of July. The General is evidently in a difficult mood. In this connection I am asking David Gore to show you some recent telegrams which we have had from our Ambassador, Dixon, in Paris following on an interview with the General on last Monday, July 15. It is clear from these telegrams that de Gaulle is taking a tough attitude and is showing no disposition to compromise. This is all the more reason for concentrating in the first instance on the limited objective.

I would therefore suggest that the first approach to de Gaulle might be on the following lines. We would explain that, as he knew, the United States and the United Kingdom were hoping

[1] 18 July 1963.

that the Moscow talks would result in a treaty agreeing not to conduct nuclear tests. The talks in Moscow on this point seem to be going fairly well although it looks as if we can only think in terms of a treaty to cover tests in the atmosphere, in outer space and underwater, and that underground tests will be excluded. We do not of course yet know for certain whether even such a limited treaty can be concluded, but we attach importance to reaching agreement with the Russians on this if we can, not only because of the intrinsic value of a test ban agreement, but also because it might be the first step towards the *détente* with the Russians for which we know General de Gaulle has always argued. Because of the symbolic importance which such a treaty may have for all of us we hope that General de Gaulle will continue to keep an open mind as regards the value of such an agreement.

We would go on to say that if other countries are asked to adhere to a test ban treaty we quite see that France is in a special position. Adherence would present no great difficulties for countries which have not begun to develop nuclear weapons any more than it would for countries which have already got a fully tested range of weapons, but we are very aware of the problem which all this may involve for France. We would hope therefore that the French Government would agree to participate in private talks with the two of us designed to determine whether we could, without any injury to the French programme, find means by which the need for French tests at least in the three environments covered by the treaty could be avoided. We could say that if this idea appealed to him we would make specific proposals for private tripartite talks when the Moscow discussions had made more progress.

In your message you suggest that our two Ambassadors should call on President de Gaulle and make what I take to be a joint communication. Knowing as I do the General's suspicion of the 'Anglo-Saxons' which Dixon's latest reports show to be still so much in the forefront of his mind, we are not sure that this is the best method. I am inclined to think that it might be better if you and I each sent the General substantially similar personal messages somewhat on the lines of the above paragraphs and if you like this idea perhaps we could exchange drafts. This approach seems to us to be safer than putting to de Gaulle now a more definite offer which might risk either giving him every-thing that he wants without securing adequate commitments in return, or causing him to reject our approach out of hand on the grounds that we were seeking to tie him to unreasonable conditions.

A further consideration of great importance is that you and we ought to be quite clear in our minds before we enter into detailed discussions with the French about exactly what we are prepared to offer and about what we want to obtain in return. As regards any offer to the French we could consider arranging to provide them with nuclear information and perhaps also supplying them with fissile or other material in such a way as to save them time and money and of course above all to obviate the need for further French tests. On our side, we should consider what we might hope to obtain in return. For example, what do we want in NATO? What do we want in the European–Atlantic relationship? What do we want as regards European unity both political and economic? Above all can we use this opportunity to our advantage in at least paving the way towards a new era, in which France would play a full part, both as regards relationships in the Western world and relations between East and West? These and other related question should I feel be examined between us at the technical and political level before we make any further offer to the French beyond the initial approach which I have outlined. If you agree we would be very willing to send a suitable team to Washington or to receive your people here if you would prefer. Clearly we should get on with this work as soon as we reasonably can.

Even when we make our first limited approach to de Gaulle we shall I think have to consider carefully what we should say to our Allies. Presumably we can say that we are very conscious of the special nature of the French problem and of the importance of persuading the French if possible to make no further tests, at least in the environments covered by the treaty, and we shall be seeing what we can do to this end.

By now rivers of telegrams from Moscow were beginning to flow in.

We have not yet got to the crunch—but I feel a little worried by Khrushchev's talk in public. He may be playing for a break, in order to put the blame on the West. On the other hand, he has quarrelled so publicly and so bitterly with the Chinese, that it would seem more probable that he really seeks a *détente* with the West.[1]

The President's answer to my message was very satisfactory. He accepted our position and proposed that we should deliver separate messages through our two Ambassadors in Paris. At the same time, he sent a draft of his in which he expressed the hope that de Gaulle would not take a final decision about future action until he had discussed with the American and British Governments 'alternative means by which the necessary technical information could be made available for your programme'. On the next day I sent a draft of our proposed message, which was acceptable. Nevertheless, Kennedy now seemed to be concerned about the 'mounting evidence of the General's unfriendliness' and feared that he would say harsh things at his forthcoming Press conference.

Everything was ready so far as Paris was concerned, and for the next few days all turned on what would happen at Moscow. These were to me thrilling and exciting moments, and I can never be sufficiently grateful both to Hailsham and to Harriman for the energy and imagination with which they conducted this delicate negotiation. The Russian position was now slightly changed. They returned to the suggestion of a non-aggression pact to be signed at the same time as a Test Ban Treaty. The two Western representatives could only reiterate that, while they were ready to listen, they were not empowered to act on this proposal, which affected other members of the Western alliance. As regards inspection and 'identification', the Russians remained obdurate. For my part, I was anxious to obtain at the same time as the Treaty a non-dissemination pact. But Hailsham reported to me that the Americans were now moving against this idea. They thought that the Russians would anyway put sufficient pressure on China to make them adhere to a Test Ban Treaty (a view which has been proved completely mistaken) and they were frightened of the effect of such a pact on the members of NATO because they were still wedded to their favourite plan of the multilateral force.

[1] 19 July 1963.

Harriman now thought that in order to maintain momentum, we might propose a further but separate round of talks to cover not only the possible unmanned control posts (the famous 'black box' which was supposed to reveal seismic explosions, to which Khrushchev had referred in his speech of 19 July), but also non-aggression and other subjects. This, however, excited some alarm in the mind of the President, who was afraid that the Allies, presumably Germany and France, would deeply distrust any expansion of the Moscow talks into wider issues. He thought our representatives should leave Moscow the moment the Treaty was initialled. But Gromyko continued to press for a non-aggression pact. Except for the unpleasant memories connected with the term, because of Hitler's frequent negotiation and consistent breach of such treaties, I could see no objection. But the pundits of both sides of the Atlantic took alarm. All that Harriman and Hailsham could therefore do was to argue that we must have some proper consultation with our Allies. Nevertheless, Hailsham still assured me of his optimism. In a message of 22 July he explained that Gromyko had enquired about the attitude of the British and American Governments on wide questions irrespective of the views of their Allies.

> I stressed your anxiety to make the most of the opportunity for progress towards better East–West relationships, and your feeling that the opportunity might not recur. On the other hand the Soviet Government would achieve the worst possible results if our Allies thought that we were doing a deal in Moscow behind their backs. Harriman emphasised how important it was not to hold up the signature of the test ban, and I said that this would make a profound impression on public opinion in the West and all over Europe. If the Soviet Government wanted a Non-Aggression Pact, the signature of a Nuclear Test Ban would be a powerful argument in favour of further partial measures of agreement, perhaps including a Non-Aggression Pact. We ourselves would do our best to respond.

In the same message he said that he felt pretty sure that the Soviet Government would not insist upon a link between the two treaties. Perhaps some formula could be found in the final communiqué which would satisfy the Russians.

The whole day was spent in messages to and from Moscow and Washington. No one seems to know the exact position. The text of the Treaty is certainly agreed. But they are now arguing about the form in which reference is to be made to the 'non-aggression pact' which [the] Soviet Government have proposed. The Germans (encouraged by the French) are beginning to panic.[1]

The next morning there was the usual setback.

Bad telegrams from Moscow this morning. I have told Gore to stay in Washington, postponing his leave.[2]

David Gore continued to warn me that Congress, while ready to accept a Test Ban, partial or complete, were very concerned if the idea gained currency that we could only reach agreement with the Russians by including proposals objectionable to our allies. So we awaited the outcome. 25 July proved

a very long and tiring—but historic day. Messages from Gore in the night and telephone conversation between him and Lord Home showed that the President had decided to accept Lord Hailsham's compromise words to be put in the communiqué (*not* the Treaty) about the Russian proposal for a 'non-aggression pact'.[3]

There was, however, one final hurdle. Just as everything seemed to be clear, a new source of difficulty arose over a highly technical argument. It was proposed that the Test Ban Treaty should be open to adherence by all countries and that, if any country was ready to sign, this instrument should be 'deposited' with all three of the original signatories. But what was to happen, asked some ingenious lawyer, if Governments wished to adhere who were not in diplomatic relations with the three original parties?

The significance of the 'depository' clause is, in reality, negligible. But it amounts to this. If Formosa—or China as the Americans recognise the Government of Chiang to be—asks to adhere to the treaty, what happens? Russia will refuse to register a country whose government they do not recognise. Similarly, if East Germany want to accede, U.S. and probably U.K. will refuse. The absurd thing is that neither of these two countries

[1] 23 July 1963.   [2] 24 July 1963.   [3] 25 July 1963.

could, by any stretch of the imagination, develop the capacity
to make a nuclear explosion. The new American clause seemed
to go back on the compromise already agreed which was quite
sensible and said that no country *need* accept formal adherence
from a country with which they were not in relations. (They
could do so if they wished.) The other American clause was that
nothing in the Treaty could be taken to prevent the use of nuclear
weapons in war ! This was so absurd as to be hardly credible. The
title of the Treaty was 'Test Ban Treaty'. How could this
amendment or new clause be in order ?[1]

On 25 July the Moscow conference was due to resume at 4 p.m.
(2 p.m. our time).

> Hailsham foresaw a wrangle and perhaps a breakdown. Home
> spoke on the open telephone to Gore during luncheon hour here
> and Gore went off to see the President. At 3.15, I had to answer
> questions [in the House of Commons], including one about the
> progress of negotiations in Moscow, with no idea of what was
> happening.[1]

It seemed incredible that these last-minute difficulties should
prevent the signature of a Treaty which, even if not complete, would
be welcomed with enthusiasm by the whole civilised world. For,
after all, it was the atmospheric tests and the anticipated evil results
of their growing intensity which had caused something like panic.
If underground tests continued, they would probably be small and,
from the pollution point of view, negligible.

The rest of the story I should perhaps tell as I recorded it at the
time. The Cabinet, with a full agenda in the morning, met again in
the House at 4.30 p.m. to finish off a number of items. I then went
to Admiralty House and

> at last got a talk with the President at 5.30 p.m. He told me that
> he had abandoned the American position and had told Harriman
> not to insist. Indeed, he said that the Treaty was just being
> initialled ! (He might have told us before and saved us a lot of
> anxiety !) He said some lawyer had thought all this up ! However,
> considering the difficulty of conducting a tripartite negotiation
> and the time factor in the different capitals, I suppose we have

[1] 25 July 1963.

done well not to have had more confusion. At 6 I was back in the House. The news of the initialling of the treaty was on the tape about 5.40. At one time, I wondered whether I should get to the House or would have to go on arguing with [the] President. However, all's well that ends well.[1]

At 11 p.m., by permission, I made a short statement in the House of Commons.

> The House was very full. The statement was well received and the questions which followed were friendly and generous (especially from the extreme Left). When I left, the whole of the Conservatives stood up and waved their order papers. Many of the Opposition stood up also. It was like the greatest of my Parliamentary successes. No doubt, tomorrow, some horrible revelation on security or morals or what-not will threaten to destroy the Government, and I shall be down again. However, for the moment, it's up. I have learned (in a hard school) not to be affected too much either by good or rough weather.[1]

So was realised at least one of the great purposes which I had set myself. Nor had I any doubt that once the rivalry of tests between the great nuclear powers was brought to an end some progress would be made in the limitation of the ever-increasing number and complexity of nuclear weapons. After sending to all the Commonwealth countries an account of what had occurred, I was able to wait with confidence the formal signature of the Treaty, which took place between the three Foreign Ministers on 5 August.

Perhaps the story should end with a letter of 1 August which I asked Lord Home to deliver to Khrushchev.

> I was much touched by your kind thought in sending me the excellent caviare, crab-meat and wine which Lord Hailsham brought back. I hope that in return you will accept the modern English vase which I have asked Lord Home to take out with him and which I believe represents that peace and prosperity which all of us in our different ways desire. I hope too that you will try the English Stilton Cheese which I am also sending.

[1] 25 July 1963.

The conclusion of the Nuclear Test Ban Treaty was a great satisfaction to me as I know it was to you. I hope sincerely that this agreement, important in itself, will lead on to other understandings.

CHAPTER XV

The Stroke of Fate

As the parliamentary session came wearily to its end, I had the opportunity to reflect upon my own future and that of the Conservative Party. The Cabinet was staunch. But it seemed wise to hold a

> meeting of Ministers not in Cabinet, including Ministers of State, Under Secretaries, Parliamentary Secretaries, both of Lords and Commons. I talked to them for forty-five minutes, ending with a passage about myself and my future.
>
> This was a *very* important gathering and much depended on it. I heard later in the evening that it had been a great success.[1]

In the following week there was (or so the newspapers foretold) a more testing ordeal to be faced—the 1922 Committee.

> This much-advertised meeting turned out very strangely. I was received with great applause and banging of desks. I spoke for forty minutes, on broad policy, home and abroad. I had thought out the speech on Sunday and (except for one page of notes) spoke extempore. I followed (but in a more popular form) the general line I had used to the meeting of Junior Ministers. Of course, the news of the Test Ban Treaty was known to members and mentioned by John Morrison, Chairman. But I hardly mentioned it, except in its natural context in East–West problems. When I sat down, after simply saying about myself that my sole purpose was to serve the Party and the Nation and to secure a victory at the Election, there was great applause. There may have been a few abstainers at the end of the room (but very few). . . . Altogether, it was a triumphant vote of confidence.[2]

[1] 18 July 1963.   [2] 25 July 1963.

Nevertheless, after all these excitements, I began to

feel a strange reaction. We have worked so hard and so long for the Test Ban and it has (until a few weeks ago) seemed so hopeless, that I can hardly yet realise what has happened. When the President gave me (on the telephone) the news which we had not yet got, I had to go out of the room. I went to tell D. and burst into tears. I have prayed hard too for this, night after night.[1]

Meanwhile, I could sense the recovery of good feeling in the Party by their behaviour at Question Time.

Our M.P.s are now coming in heavily to support me and other Ministers. This confuses the Opposition and is also a healthy sign generally.[2]

Moreover, it was clear that the feeling in the country was swinging back to the Party, and to me personally.

The *Daily Mail* opinion poll has shown a tremendous swing back towards us. Only six per cent or so behind Labour (instead of eighteen to twenty per cent) and I have risen equally or more in public favour. How strange it all is.[3]

Apart from the final stages of the Malaysian agreement and a continual flow of telegrams about the Security Council and the sale of arms to South Africa, there was at least now a little respite. In the United Nations,

We all agree to *no arms for S. Africa for internal oppression*. We want to sell arms (such as submarines, warships, aeroplanes) against external aggression. But that's where the big money is. While Governor Stevenson was pontificating at U.N., American arms interests—with full support of State Department and Pentagon—were making a desperate bid against our exporters for some huge contracts.[4]

Dorothy and I now set out on a trip to Finland and Sweden which lasted from 6 to 13 August. I was determined to enjoy these visits

[1] 27 July 1963. [2] 1 August 1963.
[3] 2 August 1963. [4] 4 August 1963.

without worrying too much about our troubles, and both of us found in them a delightful and invigorating change.

It is over twenty-three years since I went to Finland (in February 1940) with Lord Davies–to try to help the Finnish Government by (*a*) volunteers, (*b*) munitions. They were then fighting the Russians, who had made a sudden and quite unprovoked attack. Marshal Mannerheim (with his Chief of Staff and main adviser, General Walden) had raised a considerable army which fought with great courage and tenacity. At first, they inflicted heavy defeats on the Russians. But finally they were overwhelmed by sheer weight of numbers. . . . The famous white hat (which I wore on my visit to Russia in 1959) was acquired then. Of course the Russians knew about my Finnish adventure, and anyway they knew that my hat was a Finnish hat. But they were very discreet about it. The Russians forced the Finns to surrender the whole of Karelia, including the town of Viipuri. Their object, of course, was to get a better defensive position for Leningrad. When the Russians marched in to take over the surrendered territory, they found it empty of inhabitants.[1]

Colonel Serlachius had been my host in 1940, and I was glad to meet his son at a party given in our honour. Naturally recent events culminating in the Test Ban Treaty gave great relief and renewed confidence to the Finns, who had a difficult and delicate role to play, balanced between East and West.

On the next day we had some rather strained talks with President Kekkonen and Prime Minister Karjalainen. Not unnaturally,

President K. plays his cards pretty close to his chest. He would not answer any question without a good deal of prevarication–especially about the quotas, etc., and the very unfavourable balance of trade which we have with Finland. He was equally cagey about Russian oil.[2]

Nevertheless, I felt much sympathy for the Finnish Government, who were showing both courage and skill. I formed a great affection for these people in the short time that I was there in the Winter

[1] 6 August 1963. See also *Blast of War*, pp. 28–59.   [2] 7 August 1963.

War; and as we drove about on various expeditions it was wonderful to find everything so clean, orderly and gay. We had

> a good reception and even an enthusiastic one. This was partly due to the local Press having 'written up' my small efforts in 1940; partly to relief at Test Ban Treaty and what this might imply.[1]

Altogether, it was a happy experience and we particularly enjoyed our drives through country villages and the beauty of lakes and woods.

> My impressions of Finland are rather confused. The Government is a coalition, rather uneasily dependent on President Kekkonen's skill in playing off the Communists and the Social Democrats against each other, and yet maintaining himself rather a 'fellow travelling' attitude towards Soviet Russia which keeps Moscow quiet. The 'Capitalist' class—that is the owners and managers of the industrial plants are rather uneasy, but on the whole are glad enough to avoid a truly Socialist or semi-Communist régime. The pressure exerted by Russia is felt everywhere, and it is especially severe on a country which has no real history. First a colony of Sweden, then—for a hundred years—of Russia, Finland is small in population but determined, somehow or other, to preserve her independence. She learned in the hard 'Winter War' that she could not really maintain herself by force of arms. But she now seems able to do so by a very subtle and very flexible diplomacy.[2]

On the afternoon of 9 August, we left for Stockholm. So far as there was any real business to be done, the Foreign Secretary, who had joined us there, took the load off me. The Swedish Ministers were particularly interested in his accounts of his visit to Moscow for the recent Test Ban negotiations.

> The Swedes have today largely lost their old sympathy for the Germans. The Nazi régime shocked them deeply. They are critical of Adenauer's intransigence on European policy, especially towards Russia. Naturally enough, C.D.U., with its Roman Catholic bias, does not attract Swedish Social Democrats. They seem, however, to have pretty close links with the German

[1] 7 August 1963.   [2] 9 August 1963.

Social Democrats. Apart from foreign policy, Mr. [Gunnar] Lange (Economic Minister) expressed his views and his anxieties about future of E.E.C. and EFTA.[1]

Apart from the usual sightseeing in Stockholm, including the remarkable Town Hall where we were given a formal luncheon, the most pleasant part of our entertainment was at the Harpsund, which one might describe as the Swedish Chequers. We arrived here about 5 p.m.,

> and walked or sat in garden and continued very informal discussions. Harpsund is a charming house—copy of an old Swedish manor house, on an old estate, with charming garden and farm buildings. Dinner at 7—crayfish and schnapps! an old Swedish custom to open the crayfish season. Songs, and a general mood of merriment. About 20 in the party, including Mr. and Mrs. Nilsson, the Swedish Ambassador and his wife, our Ambassador and his wife, the Conservative Party leader, a business man (Wallinger), etc. A very pleasant evening.[1]

Sunday was a splendid day, warm and sunny.

> Church at 11. A very fine church (northern aisle fourteenth century, rest modern). Church full. Singing very good. 'Ante-Communion' service, ending with sermon and hymn.
> Drove to Gripsholm castle—a beautiful little place—very old and interesting. In the evening, went by water from Stockholm to Drottningholm Palace. The theatre (recently discovered) is an eighteenth-century gem. An admirable performance of a charming operetta (*The Music Master*) followed by cold supper. Altogether a most agreeable day, with very little politics and plenty of sightseeing.[2]

The next day was largely taken up by a visit to the King. 'In spite of his eighty years, he is remarkably spry and well informed.'[3]

We received no news from London except routine Foreign Office telegrams. But, as this pleasant holiday drew to an end, I was faced with the necessity to make some definite decisions about the future. The Denning Report was not yet available but I felt little doubt that it would cause us no serious anxiety, at least as to its

---

[1] 10 August 1963.   [2] 11 August 1963.   [3] 12 August 1963.

content. When I had time to reflect, in my home at Birch Grove, the issues to be resolved seemed to be becoming clearer.

> The choice is between (*a*) *resigning* in [the] week before Parliament meets—about 22 October or so; (*b*) going on and fighting election and saying so at Conference. I don't particularly want a tiresome eight weeks from November to Christmas, with Party in House of Commons making trouble and then resigning at Christmas. Unless there was some great *international* prize the extra two months are not worth the trouble. So it is the choice between finishing my political life at end of October, or going right through to and including the election.[1]

However, this simple issue became complicated by a third possibility which was soon to emerge—that is, an announcement at the Conference that I would not lead the Party at the next election.

At this time I began to feel a serious physical reaction from all the troubles which I had been through. I did not seem to respond so quickly as in past days, and a kind of lethargy began to affect me, no doubt the symptoms of approaching disease. Fortunately I was able to enjoy a holiday of ten days in Yorkshire. I went first to Bolton Abbey, where there was a very agreeable party and plenty of grouse. The presence of David Gore among the guests gave me a chance of some talk about the probability of the President agreeing to seek a further *détente* with the Russians. It would need a strong effort, both by America and Britain if we were to push the French and the Germans into a new effort. Yet it seemed a pity not to follow up the success gained by the Test Ban Treaty. From Bolton Abbey I went to Swinton, where we had three excellent days' shooting. I had great confidence in Lord Swinton's wisdom and experience. Although he had a real affection for me, he was also completely impartial in his judgement. After much debate, we dismissed the possibility of immediate resignation, as a sign of weakness and almost an admission of failure.

My mind had been to some extent cleared by the healthy atmosphere of the moors. I was determined not to take any step which would bring my long premiership to an ignoble end or look

[1] 16 August 1963.

as if I was afraid of facing any difficulties which might still confront us. I did not wish to go down to history as a Prime Minister who had been drowned by the flood of filth which had seeped up from the sewers of London. It seemed clear, therefore, that there were now only two choices. First, to announce at Blackpool that I would resign in good time before the General Election, which must take place either in the spring or in the autumn of 1964. I would follow Churchill's example and leave my successor the choice of dates. Alternatively, I would declare my determination to continue in office and lead the Party in the next General Election. In favour of the first plan was the fact that I would be seventy in the following year, and in times when youth was so clamorous for recognition and there was little respect for age this might be thought a disadvantage. Churchill, of course, had been even older; but then Churchill was unique. I was also very tired and already had some troublesome symptoms of failing health. Against this and in favour of the second plan there were strong arguments. It would rally our supporters, both from the point of view of Party and personal allegiance. Moreover, it would avoid the difficult question of the future leadership. I was not so happily placed as Churchill, whose successor had been designated for many years and against whom there could be no serious candidate.

I spent most of the month of September at Chequers. Dorothy was still away in Scotland, and with the exception of occasional visits from members of my family I was alone with the Private Secretary on duty. During this period there was of course a continual coming and going of Ministers, especially those concerned with the problems arising from the publication of the Denning Report, which have already been described. But as the weeks passed I began to feel daily more depressed, and although there was plenty of routine work I allowed myself to brood moodily about the future. Yet, as every day passed, it became more necessary to reach a decision, for the Press speculation must, sooner or later, be resolved. On 5 September I recorded:

My mind is beginning to be clearer about my own position. I *must* stay to deal with Lord Denning's report and the debates in Parliament—say early November. But I cannot go on to an election and lead in it. I am beginning to feel that I haven't the strength and that perhaps another leader could do what I did after Eden left. But it cannot be done by a pedestrian politician. It needs a man with vision and moral strength.[1]

In writing to the Queen on 5 September thanking her for an invitation to Balmoral later in the year and giving her some account of the broad situation on the foreign and economic fronts, I added:

> The other main problem with which I have to deal lies in the political situation, the leadership of the Party and the life of the present Parliament. I have not yet reached a decision in my own mind as to how all these things ought to be handled and I should like to write a further letter to Your Majesty when my own thoughts are in a more orderly sequence than they are at present.

During these weeks I noticed that

> Harold Wilson is certainly running a good campaign—Price of Land, interference of Executive with Judiciary—all rather specious. But we are doing nothing.[2]

I therefore wrote to Iain Macleod, now Chairman of the Party, on 15 September:

> You were speaking yesterday about the Opposition. Baffled by the good state of the economy, full employment, the Test Ban and on the whole good news throughout the Commonwealth, they are turning to a lot of nonsense about the judiciary and personal attacks on me. In today's papers it is clear that both Grimond and Wilson have now started on this line in a big way. I think this is very good and just what the doctors ordered. It should help to rally our own people.
>
> At the same time a considered reply should be made, not by me, for I will reserve myself to the Party Conference, but by some of our supporters. Could not the Attorney or the Solicitor General or the Home Secretary make a good answer; or if you are speaking yourself anywhere, better still.

[1] 5 September 1963.   [2] 8 September 1963.

On the evening of 11 September, Butler came

> and we had long talks about the position before and after dinner. I was rather careful *not* to give him any idea about which of several alternatives I would choose. . . . But I get a good idea of his own position. He would naturally (if I resign) accept the Premiership if there was a general consensus of opinion for him. But he doesn't want another unsuccessful bid.[1]

One happy spark of humour now brightened the political sky.

> The Liberal Conference (with Mark Bonham Carter shouted down and Lady Violet refused a hearing) ended in *Opéra bouffe*.[2]

The next day, however, I noted:

> Harold Wilson is now launching a great personal attack on me—for 'debauching and corrupting public life'. I don't think it amounts to much. I suppose Sir William Haley will join in next.[3]

Except for some anxieties in South-East Asia, things were fairly quiet.

> I fear that the Indonesian Government will react against us, probably by confiscating our valuable investments (Shell, Unilever, etc.). But I doubt if they will risk war against Malaysia. They will, no doubt, try subversion, etc., especially in Sarawak and Borneo.[4]

When the Foreign Secretary came to see me on some of these matters, I had a talk with him about my own position. Lord Home

> was very distressed to think that I had any idea of retiring, but could well understand my reasons and thought them sound. . . . [He] fears that there will be complete disunity in the Party and that great troubles will follow. I may be forced to stay. I replied 'In that case I shall be "drafted"—not a "limpet". I don't want it to be thought that I am just clinging on.'[4]

This new plan was now taking shape and my chief colleagues had begun to understand its implications. It was not unnatural that if my

[1] 11 September 1963.   [2] 14 September 1963.
[3] 15 September 1963.   [4] 18 September 1963.

resignation was to take place in January or February of 1964 there would be intense speculation about a possible successor. On 20 September, I had an audience with the Queen in which, after telling her of the satisfactory state of the economy, with production rising and unemployment falling, I went on to explain my plan

of announcing on 12 October that I would *not* have an Election this year and that I would *not* lead Party at Election. This would involve a change in January or February. The Queen expressed her full understanding. But I thought she was very distressed, partly (perhaps) at the thought of losing a P.M. to whom she has become accustomed, but chiefly (no doubt) because of all the difficulties about a successor in which the Crown will be much involved. We discussed at some length the various possibilities. She feels the great importance of maintaining the prerogative intact. After all, if she asked someone to form a government and he failed, what harm was done? It often, indeed at one time almost invariably, happened in the first half of the nineteenth century. Of course, it would be much better for everything to go smoothly, as in my case.[1]

This was the course Bonar Law took in 1922

when he refused to accept the King's Commission until he had been elected leader of the Conservative Party. After all, there was considerable confusion at the time of the break-up of the Lloyd George coalition. Bonar Law had retired. Chamberlain was leader of the Conservatives. Even so, I feel that Bonar Law should *not* have made this condition or the King accepted it.[1]

I was determined at all costs to preserve the prerogative, which had been so useful in the past and which might be so valuable in the future. Shortly after this audience I wrote a note to Michael Adeane on 25 September in the following terms:

I will be writing to The Queen, as I promised her, before my speech at Blackpool on Saturday, 12 October. I understand, from what you said, that you will be away.

[1] 20 September 1963.

I went to Hughenden the other day. This is just to remind you that (as perhaps you know) there is a tablet in the Church with this inscription:

> To the dear and honoured memory of
> Benjamin, Earl of Beaconsfield
> this memorial is placed
> by his grateful sovereign and friend
> Victoria R.I.

'Kings love him that speaketh right' Prov. 26.13.

There is a nice, old Norman church in Horsted Keynes, Sussex – St. Giles. There would be room on the wall, when the time comes.

Meanwhile, I shall be available at any time to obey Her Majesty's commands. Presumably the audiences will take place in the normal way when the Queen returns from Scotland.

This plan – involving resignation early in 1964 – being more or less settled, at least in principle, I now began to turn to the problem of succession. It was soon clear that what seemed an easy solution, namely to resign quietly, leaving the new Prime Minister the choice of dates as was done by Churchill in 1955, had grave disadvantages. With Churchill the succession was clear, only the date had to be decided. With me, all would be confusion; and after the meeting of Parliament in October 1963 until the final date early in 1964 there would be continual dissension and intrigue. Moreover, the more I or any of my advisers reflected on this aspect of the problem, the more uncertainties seemed to develop. Many names were put forward, in the Press or in private conversation. I personally favoured either Hailsham or Macleod, preferably the former, for I felt that these two were the men of real genius in the Party who were the true inheritors of the Disraeli tradition of Tory Radicalism, which I had preached all my life. I regretfully had to admit that I did not feel that Butler could win an election or could receive the loyal support of the Party as a whole. I told Hailsham of my own views and hoped that he would become a candidate. But, of course, we both knew that if the Queen should ask for my advice I would adopt the same kind of system that had followed Eden's resignation in 1956, although the range of consultations might be extended.

Nevertheless, although this plan still held the field, I began gradually to doubt its wisdom. Even after the complete vindication of Ministers by the Denning Report,

I still feel that my decision *not* to fight the next election is right, although I hate doing it so near the Profumo trouble. But I hope that people will realise that my decision is nothing to do with this affair. All the same, I know that the Cabinet and the great mass of the Party will be greatly distressed and I feel rather tempted to change my mind. The date—12 October—(or really the Cabinet of 8 October) is drawing near. I brood about this all the time—but the period (three weeks or four) which I have had here at Chequers has given me the opportunity of thinking it all out quietly and calmly.[1]

During the first days of October, appeals reached me from every quarter—Ministers, ex-Ministers, private Members: I must stay on at all costs. On 6 October I noted in my diary:

I did not sleep at all last night. . . . There are so many factors—the chief one being that there is *no* clear successor. But there is also a growing wave of emotion in my favour, throughout the Party, especially the Party in the provinces. This will be evidenced at Blackpool. I have written the actual speech—leaving six or seven minutes at the end for the personal bit—to go or to stay? I *hate* the feeling that I shall be letting down all these loyal people, from highest to lowest, if I give up. On the other hand, I shall probably be humiliated if I stay and everyone will say that failure has been due to the old limpet.[2]

On that same afternoon, I had a long discussion of the problem with my son, Maurice.

I am beginning to move (at the last minute) towards staying on—for another two or three years. Maurice says that, although it would be difficult to win, for the fourth time, yet it *might* be done, by a sort of emotional wave of feeling. . . . After all, we have brought them both Prosperity and Peace.[2]

[1] 18 September 1963.   [2] 6 October 1963.

The same evening, I dined alone with Home.

We began with a discussion of whether or not there was any real chance of a good forward step in the East–West situation. He is *not* too hopeful; but reminds me of the situation last year, on the Test Ban. The French are, of course, against a *détente* (unless initiated and led by de Gaulle). The Germans under Schroeder are rather better–although Adenauer–even in retirement and von Brentano will certainly cause trouble. The real difficulties are (*a*) My power in G.B. is waning, as Parliament draws to its close; (*b*) President's ditto. Worse still, policies which are popular here (Test Ban, etc.) are not so very popular in U.S.A. The President has been very good about following behind our lead. But as his Election approaches, he will worry more and more about the electoral effects of his policies. All the same, we *did* have some success before, and we might again.[1]

When we turned to the personal question, while Home was on the whole in favour of the outlined plan to announce at Blackpool that there would be no election this autumn and that I would retire next year,

he (and I) have begun to wonder whether it can, in fact, be worked. It would mean from 12 October to (say) first week in January (three months) during which I am to be P.M. under (self-imposed) sentence of death. Would not the whole situation disintegrate? We felt that if I announced on Saturday that I would *not* fight the Election, it would be impossible to prevent the search for a leader from beginning at once, to the exclusion of everything else. On the other hand, if I announced my determination to go on, it would be accepted–and welcomed by a great majority. But there would still be a substantial and very vocal minority. It would be a great moral and physical strain to overcome them–and two or three months' bitter struggle.[1]

Dorothy and I were now back in London and had returned to Downing Street. Although Admiralty House had many advantages–finer rooms, more light and a greater sense of space–yet I was glad to be back in No. 10, now renovated and even improved, but retaining all the atmosphere of its historic past.

[1] 6 October 1963.

The agitation in parts of the Press and in certain sections of the Party was now renewed. Yet at the same time Tim Bligh, my Private Secretary, reported that a great majority of the Cabinet preferred my staying.

Motored to London in morning. I had first a talk with Bligh, who tells me that the Cabinet are rallying to me with great enthusiasm. Only one or two exceptions. In the course of the morning, I saw Butler—who would clearly prefer me to go on, for—in his heart—he does not expect the succession *and* fears it. Then came Lord Chancellor (Dilhorne) *all* for going on—'the call to battle'. The Chief Whip—very ready to fight, if he is given the order. Then Duncan Sandys—unhesitating and loyal.[1]

At 5.30 p.m. Oliver Poole came to see me. He was wonderfully helpful and resourceful throughout.

I told him that I was now beginning to think that I had no option but to see it through—and for the following reasons:

1. I should seem to be 'deserting' and this would especially affect the 'marginal' seats.

2. I would seem to have yielded to the group of malcontents, who are swayed either by personal or purely reactionary sentiment.

3. I should leave the Party in complete disarray—with some for Butler, some for Hailsham, some for Maudling.[1]

Poole, who was deeply moved, was not persuaded that this was the right course. If we were to lose the election, which was more than likely, while it would be

bad for my successor [it] would be humiliating for me. Why should I endure it? I could not save the situation and since I would have to spend the next three months in a tremendous row in the House of Commons, etc., there would hardly be time for a recovery.[1]

Later in the evening,

we were joined by Lord Chancellor, Butler, Home, Sandys. A long discussion brought out all the same points again. Duncan was *very* strong for me going on. Alec Home was balanced. . . .

[1] 7 October 1963.

Duncan stayed to dinner, and Chief Whip came in afterwards. It was clear that I would get *full support* of Cabinet if I decided to go on, but that several would be rather unhappy, partly for my sake, partly for that of the Party.[1]

There were one or two further messages from Butler and Home, but it was quite clear to me that all my colleagues would accept whatever course I proposed. The Lord Chancellor, as always, was encouraging and helpful.

On the night of 7 October I reached a firm decision to continue and fight the Election. I proposed to inform the Cabinet of my intentions the following morning. The Cabinet was to meet for routine business and to hear my declaration. After this, most of the Ministers would leave for Blackpool, where I would go later in the week.

On looking back upon these two or three weeks of hesitation I am surprised and shocked at my vacillation. I was not accustomed, even in the most difficult circumstances of my life, to shilly-shally or to seek unnecessarily the advice of others. During all this period— that is from after my return from Yorkshire at the beginning of September—I felt nervous, uneasy and with a curious lack of grip, combined with a tendency to drowsiness at inconvenient moments. This I put down to fatigue and did little about it. But I have no doubt that these weaknesses were symptoms of my coming illness. My doctor, Sir John Richardson, was on holiday, and I did not want to bring him back, nor did I consult any other physician. Nevertheless, when I had finally reached, after these unusual procrastinations and hesitations, the decision to continue and fight the Election, I felt immensely relieved. Naturally, my wife fully agreed. Although she had been doubtful of my physical strength (perhaps she had watched this strange apathy coming on me), she now seemed relieved at my new determination.

I went to bed last night determined to inform the Cabinet that I had now decided to stay on and fight the General Election and to ask for the full support of my colleagues. I would say that I fully realised the difficulties, but that I felt they could be overcome.[2]

[1] 7 October 1963.   [2] 8 October 1963.

Since much has been written, often inaccurately, about the events which followed, it is necessary for me to give the detailed story. It seemed indeed almost incredible that on the very day that I decided, and received the full support of the Cabinet, to continue my work, I was struck down. Some commentators thought the sequence of events scarcely believable. One famous columnist, Cassandra, alleged that I had invented my illness. I could only hope that he would never undergo anything so disagreeable himself. On the night of 7 October, I had determined to remain Prime Minister and seek again the suffrage of the people. Twenty-four hours later I was in hospital and had already undergone the preliminary attentions of the surgeons.

In the middle of the night (or rather earlier in the evening while our agitated discussions were going on) I found it impossible to pass water and an excruciating pain when I attempted to do so. I was seized by terrible spasms. . . . Dorothy came to my help and got a doctor—Dr. King-Lewis (Sir John Richardson was on holiday in Windermere). He finally arrived about 4 a.m. and managed to give me relief by inserting an instrument to drain the water out of the bladder. Unfortunately, the bladder kept filling up, and by about 8 a.m. it was worse. Dr. K.-L. came again and helped. He promised me that he would get Mr. [A.W.] Badenoch, the greatest surgeon in this line of business, by 1 p.m.

Cabinet at 10. A large number of items—rating relief, Robbins's educational report, etc., etc. At noon, I stopped further items; asked Cabinet Secretariat to leave (except Sir Burke Trend) and explained shortly the problem to the Cabinet and announced my plan. Since I realised (I said) that there could be no free discussion in my presence, I withdrew. (The 'plan', of course, was to announce at Blackpool that I would lead in the General Election.) At this point, I had no reason to think (from what Dr. King-Lewis had said) that my trouble would be very serious. He hoped that normal passing of water might be re-established in a few hours. Any treatment of a more radical character would be perhaps avoided or postponed. Of course, Dr. K.-L. was quite right to keep me quiet at the time and had no idea of the issues involved. He thought it only a question of going to Blackpool for the speech on Saturday. But during the

Cabinet, I had to go out twice with spasms, and felt pretty bad. At 12.45 p.m. Mr. Badenoch came. He re-inserted the instrument and drained the bladder. After consultation with Dr. K.-L., he told me that the cause was the inflammation of the prostate gland (by either a benign or malignant tumour) and that it would have to be dealt with. Sir J.R. had been told by telephone and would be in London by 4 p.m. or so. It was agreed that there should be a meeting at 6 p.m. to decide on a course of action. Meanwhile, I heard (at about 1.30) from Chief Whip that the Cabinet had (with one exception) agreed to back me to the full if I decided to go on through the General Election. . . .

The afternoon went on, with coming and going, some pain and some moments of relief. We were giving a party to our staff, to celebrate the return to No. 10, at 6.30–8 p.m. I managed to appear at this, *after* the doctors' conference and verdict. The decision was to go to hospital at once, for the operation.

The rest of the evening was rather confused. I telephoned to Lord Poole (at Blackpool). Butler came in to see me. I had talks with Maurice and my daughters.

At 9 p.m. I went to the Hospital (King Edward's Hospital for Officers) in excruciating pain. Mr. Badenoch came and I was taken at once to the operating theatre, where he put in a catheter, to drain the bladder. This gave me relief.

After the usual hospital doings, I was put to bed and got to sleep about 11.30 p.m.[1]

Before I had left No. 10 on the night of 8 October, Harold Evans rightly insisted that the true story be given to the Press. In the morning, therefore, it was 'headline news'. During the course of the next day, the Foreign Secretary and the Lord Chancellor came to see me. It so happened that Lord Home would take the chair at Blackpool as President of the National Union for the year. With their help and with that of my admirable private staff, we got a lot of work done.

1. Letter for Alec to read out on Friday, which makes it clear that although I had decided to go on through the Election, this is now impossible.
2. *Approval* of this letter by the Queen.

[1] 8 October 1963.

The Queen leaving King Edward VII Hospital on 18 October 1963
'She came in alone . . . she seemed moved; so was I.'

Saying goodbye to the Matron on leaving hospital, 27 October 1963

3. Letter in general terms about situation to the Queen.

4. I have had—before getting ill—a wonderful letter from the President about my part in getting the Test Ban. Could it be read to the Conference? Or published in some other way? David Gore will ask President. (It was read: 15 October.)

5. Some general plans about date of my retirement and successor taking over. If Hailsham is to be a competitor, he must at once give up his peerage and find a constituency.

I managed in the course of the day to finish all the outstanding routine work. Dorothy came in afternoon, Maurice in the morning.

A parade of doctors, etc., at 6.30 tonight—two surgeons, two physicians, a house doctor, an anaesthetist. Also during the day, blood test, heart test, lungs x-rayed, etc., etc., which was rather painful, since any movement is rather painful.

In the middle of the day the tube got blocked—either by a clot of blood or some impurity or by some technical hitch—and I had to have another rather tiresome clearing of it—which the house doctor did (and very well, I thought).

Wrote up the diary. Read Bible.[1]

It is best, perhaps, to continue from my own account, which I managed to write up on 12 October.

10 *October:* Operation performed successfully. I did not remember having been taken from my room to the operating theatre. It was all over by 1 p.m. But I remember little about the rest of the day, or the next day.

11 *October:* D. came in morning and afternoon. Others tried to come but failed. I can only just write a few words.

12 *October:* A horrible day—with perpetual 'spasms' which were very painful but happily not dangerous.

The *public* events of these days . . . are quite beyond my control. I decided nothing about myself, and gave no instructions about anything or anybody. The conduct of the Government I have handed over to Butler but I shall take this back as soon as I am able to do so. But I fear that all kind of intrigues and battles are going on about the leadership of the Party. Perhaps those who were so anxious to get me out will now see the disadvantages.

[1] 9 October 1963.

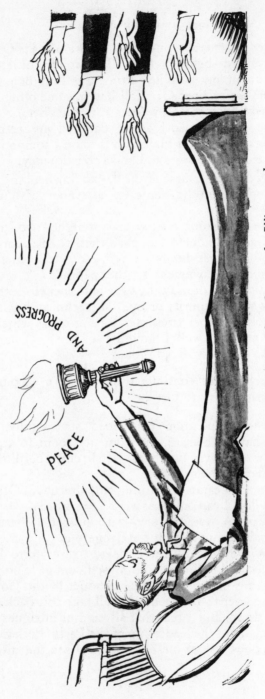

INTO WHOSE HANDS?—*Cartoon by Illingworth*

What I do profoundly hope is that the *image* of the Party is not injured by all this public disputing.

D. and Maurice came for short periods today—but I was very weak. The Queen has rung again—the third time. The surgeon was in the hospital, so he spoke to her. The Queen Mother has also telephoned. But it has been a bad day, and I can't understand what they are saying.[1]

This unhappy stroke of fate could not have come at a worse moment. Had it been a month earlier, the whole matter of succession might have been settled quietly in accordance with past precedents, without any reference to the Party Conference and all the excitement that was caused at Blackpool. Had it been a month later, the Party Conference would have been satisfactorily past; I would have announced my intention to continue; and on being struck down my resignation would again have followed in an orderly way. Finally, had there been any certainty as to the succession, such as was the case with Churchill and Eden, even this unfortunate timing might have produced no real trouble. But the combination of these events combined to cause the maximum of confusion and excitement and, alas, corresponding injury to the Party. This was, and has remained, a great source of grief to me. Political death is always uncomfortable; but in my case it could not have been more untimely.

The announcement was made by Lord Home, as President, that my resignation was now inevitable. I had given him this authority in the following minute, dictated the night before the operation.

I should be very grateful if you would tell the Conference assembled at Blackpool, of which you are the President, how sorry I am not to be with them this week. I was especially looking forward to the mass meeting on Saturday, which is a great annual event and on this occasion likely to have special significance.

It is now clear that, whatever might have been my previous feelings, it will not be possible for me to carry the physical burden of leading the Party at the next General Election. If the operation which I am to undergo tomorrow proves successful it is clear that I will need a considerable period of convalescence. I would not be able to face all that is involved in a prolonged Electoral campaign.

[1] 12 October 1963.

Nor could I hope to fulfil the tasks of Prime Minister for any extended period, and I have so informed the Queen.

In these circumstances I hope that it will soon be possible for the customary processes of consultation to be carried on within the Party about its future leadership.

I am writing to you as President of the Conference to ask you to announce this at the earliest opportunity.

A large number of candidates thereupon began to throw their hats into the ring.

At the same time I composed a farewell message to be read to the Conference on the last day:

I am very glad that the great mass meeting which is a feature of every Conservative Conference is to take place and I know that in the hands of Lord Home and Mr. Butler it will be a great success.

Naturally I am very sorry not to be there myself but I will be thinking about you, and there are just one or two thoughts which I would like to put before you through the mouth of the President.

It is just forty years since I first stood for Parliament. During all that time I have seen the steady progress of the Conservative Party towards realising the ambitions which, in the enthusiasm of youth, my friends and I who survived the first war formed for the Party. We then looked back to the memory of the great founders of modern Conservatism—Pitt, Canning and, above all, Disraeli. We recognised [that] there have been periods when Conservatism has succumbed to a rigidity unworthy of this great tradition. Even between the wars it was faced with problems of the modern world, internal and external, which it was unable to resolve. It is equally true that Labour Governments failed completely and disastrously. Only one great figure stood out—that of Churchill. But since 1945 I have lived to see the Party of our dreams come into being, democratic in the true sense of the word, with an organisation widely based upon the will of the constituencies, and with candidates chosen not for their wealth or position but for their merit. I have seen our policies develop into that pragmatic and sensible compromise between the extremes of collectivism and individualism for which the Party has always stood in its great periods. I have seen it bring to the people of our own country a degree of comfort and well-being, as well as opportunities for living the good life, both through increasing leisure and ever-spreading systems of education such as I and my comrades could not have dreamed of when we slogged through the mud of Flanders nearly fifty years ago. Thus the silent, the Conservative, revolution has come about. At the same time I have seen Britain face the changes brought about by the second war calmly and without faltering, organising confidently the transformation of her old Empire into the Commonwealth of today, and at the same time playing in the world a role of influence—always great and sometimes decisive.

Now, nearly twenty years after the end of the second war, and solidly based on twelve years of Conservative Government, I see a new vision—a changed Britain, a changed world. We must accept—indeed we must welcome—change. But not change for its own sake. Not change that means discarding moral and religious values which long experience has taught the British people to respect. The Conservative Party has always had the *faith* to honour the things that history has taught us to cherish and revere. But it has also had the *courage* to grasp what is new and fresh, so that a constant process of renewal and re-invigoration takes place in our national life.

Today, when so many responsibilities and so many opportunities face our country in a turbulent world we need this double inspiration if we are to ensure that the responsibilities are met and the opportunities seized. Let each and everyone of you resolve to prove equal to the challenge.

God bless you all.

Although the operation took place on 10 October, my formal resignation did not take place until 18 October. I was not yet able to have an audience with the Queen, but I knew enough of constitutional history to realise what were my duties and obligations. It was perfectly within her power to ask any Conservative statesman either to try to form an administration and then return to her with the result of his preliminary soundings, or to appoint him Prime Minister, in which case he would kiss hands immediately. Either of these courses she could adopt entirely by her own prerogative and without necessarily consulting the outgoing Prime Minister. The precedents were clear: Queen Victoria had not consulted Gladstone on his resignation of his last Government, when Lord Rosebery was appointed. Bonar Law made it clear that he was too ill to be consulted. Yet it was intimated to us quite clearly from the Palace that the Queen would ask for advice. After all, I had served her for nearly seven years and it was no surprise to me that she would wish for my help. It therefore became necessary for me to do what I would have preferred to avoid—become involved in the situation as it was after my colleagues had returned from the Blackpool Conference. Since I was, of course, still in bed and suffering considerably from shock and exhaustion, it would have been much easier for me to follow Bonar Law's precedent and refuse to give any advice. I seriously thought of this way of avoiding a most tiresome duty. Yet it seemed to me, on reflection, a mean evasion, unfair both to the Queen and to the Party. Yet I knew that whatever I did would lead to much recrimination and no doubt to all sorts of stories, some true and some untrue, about my actions. At any rate, with the help of my devoted staff, I would make sure that a full and accurate record should be made of the whole affair.

As I lay in the half-drugged coma of the first few days that followed my operation, some odd thoughts crossed my mind. The grave difficulty into which we were now to be plunged depended, by a curious irony, on the strangest chances. Had Mr. Wedgwood Benn been content to follow his father to the House of Lords; had a Joint Select Committee, appointed in 1962, not been able to make a rapid and unanimous report; had our Government been unwilling to give not only to those succeeding to a peerage but to all existing peers the right to disclaim their rank and privilege; had the Government's proposal, approved by the House of Commons, that the new system should only come into force at the dissolution of the present Parliament, been acceptable to the House of Lords, where an amendment to make the act effective from the day of the Royal Assent was carried by four to one against the front bench; had it not been possible to pass the bill through Parliament and obtain the Royal Assent by 31 July 1963, only ten weeks before the crisis—all our troubles would have been avoided. Neither Lord Hailsham nor

Lord Home could in practice have even been considered for the premiership. Butler must have succeeded, almost without challenge. Out of such slender threads are woven the fortunes of states and men.

My doctors and surgeons demanded absolute quiet and warned me of the dire effects of any disregard of their advice. Convalescence would be retarded and even endangered. They proved to be right. But it was impossible to wash my hands of the whole affair. Accordingly, on 14 October I was able to see the Chief Whip and Lord Poole. But I was too weak to do more than hear their impressions of Blackpool.

I had now determined on my course of action. On the occasion of Eden's resignation, members of the Cabinet, the Chief Whip, the Chairman of the Party and the Chairman of the 1922 Committee were each asked for their views by the Lord President (Lord Salisbury) and the Lord Chancellor (Lord Kilmuir).The result was made available to the Queen. In addition, Sir Winston Churchill was summoned to the Palace. There had been some feeling that this procedure was too restricted. I therefore proposed that Ministers outside the Cabinet and Under-Secretaries; regular Conservative supporters in the House of Lords; and all Conservative Members of the House of Commons should be consulted. In addition, advice should be sought from the various Party organisations. Accordingly, on the night of 14 October I drafted a minute which I sent to Butler and other leading colleagues as to the procedure which I thought should be followed.

I have been considering how best to proceed with the customary processes of consultation. You have kept me informed of the consideration which you have given to this matter and as you know I have today seen the Lord Chancellor, the Chief Whip and Lord Poole, as a Joint Chairman of the Conservative Party.

I think I should record my view that it is right that soundings should be undertaken as follows: the Lord Chancellor with Members of the Cabinet; the Chief Whip will see all other Ministers and Members of the House of Commons; Lord St. Aldwyn will see Members of the House of Lords who are regular supporters of the Party and Lord Poole will talk to Lord Chelmer and Mrs. Shepherd representing the National Union (and this should also include the candidates).

These consultations may take a day or two. I would like to be informed when they have been completed and I will at that time decide according to the state of my health what steps should then be taken.

I may see the people concerned myself or I may wish to make other arrangements for their advice to be co-ordinated. I will let you know.

I am much looking forward to our talk tomorrow, Tuesday, 15 October, but I thought it might be helpful if I sent you this minute tonight.

I am sending copies of this minute to the Lord Chancellor, the Chancellor of the Duchy of Lancaster, the Chief Whip, Lord St. Aldwyn and Lord Poole.

After this,

I had a better night and slept altogether nearly seven hours—moderate drugs. The various pains are settling down or changing their venue. I am surprised how bruised one is by these modern anaesthetics. They seem to put pins in all over one's body, and wherever there is a pin there is a bruise.[1]

Soon after 10 on the morning of 15 October, Butler called to see me. I showed him

the minute of instructions which I wished him to read to the Cabinet. He seemed to acquiesce willingly enough.[1]

Later in the day I received Butler's report.

Thank you for your minute of 14 October about the customary processes of consultation in relation to the leadership of the Party.

We discussed this when we met this morning and agreed that I should read it out to the Cabinet. I did this at the end of the Agenda today. They all agreed that this was the right procedure and I thought you would like to know this.

I am sending copies of this minute to the other recipients of yours.

[1] 15 October 1963.

On the same day, in spite of the protests of doctors and nurses, I completed another task:

> So that there may be no mistakes or argument in the future, I have dictated a record of events from last Monday onwards, in form of a letter to the Queen. Bligh is going to check this and bring it back later today.[1]

This document was completed and despatched by the evening. After giving a full account of what had happened up till my operation, I continued:

> Until Monday morning I was so much under continuous sedation of various kinds that it was difficult for me to make any clear analysis of what had happened in the intervening days. But on that day I was able to consider the position and decide that I must take the lead in order to get some order into what might end in complete confusion. Although Mr. Butler was able to preside over the Cabinet and other Cabinet Committees for me and to take certain decisions on my behalf this was not a matter with which he could deal since he was one of the possible successors. I therefore sent a minute to Mr. Butler on Monday night (copy attached). This set out certain steps to be taken to sound opinion in different quarters. . . . I hope to have the result of these by Thursday morning. When I have received them I will consider what best course to take. But I would venture to suggest that Your Majesty need not be troubled by the matter until these processes have been completed.
>
> I am anxious that everything done so far should be amply recorded in writing and not give rise to the kind of confusion by which previous crises have afterwards been poisoned with very ill effects to all concerned. I believe that all this can be documented from beginning to end. . . .
>
> I cannot end without once more expressing my great gratitude for Your Majesty's personal kindness to me at this very difficult time.

Having seen Butler, I could not refuse to see all the other Ministers who wished to come partly to discuss their experiences at the Conference, partly to give their views on the situation, partly out of

[1] 15 October 1963.

kindness and loyalty and to say goodbye. For they knew that their service in my administration was drawing rapidly to an end. This procedure was very tiring and I was, perhaps, foolish to have agreed to it. On the evening of 15 October there came Home, Macleod, Heath, Maudling and Hailsham. The next morning, 16 October, I saw Thorneycroft, Boyle, Soames, Lloyd, John Hare, Brooke, Keith Joseph and Sandys. The general impression that I received was that, while there was a good deal of division of opinion about who should succeed me,

> practically all of these Ministers, however, whether Hoggites or Butlerites or Maudlingites, agreed that if Lord Home would undertake the task of P.M. the whole Cabinet and the whole Party would cheerfully unite under him.[1]

On 17 October, I nerved myself for what would be the decisive day. I had to receive the reports from those whose advice I had sought.

> In the morning I saw (separately) the following:
> 1. Lord Chancellor.
> 2. Chief Whip and John Morrison—the latter I saw alone for some minutes.
> 3. Lord St. Aldwyn—Chief Whip in Lords.
> 4. Lord Poole; Mrs. Shepherd (Chairman National Union); Lord Chelmer.
> This was in accordance with the minute which I had sent to Cabinet and was approved by them.
> After luncheon (3 p.m. onwards) I saw Lord Chancellor; Chief Whip; Lord St. Aldwyn; Lord Poole *together*.
> All this tired me very much. It took two and a half hours in morning and two hours in afternoon. But after 6 p.m., the work began and I dictated memorandum for the Queen (should she seek my advice) and also signed formal letter of resignation. We finished at midnight! Tim Bligh has set up an office in the hospital, and two typists from No. 10 have been here all day.[2]

No wonder the doctors were disturbed. But I was determined that there should be, at any rate in the eyes of history, no misrepresentation.

[1] 16 October 1963.   [2] 17 October 1963.

Verbal advice might be forgotten or misrepresented. My memorandum to the Queen would remain among my own papers and in the Royal archives, to protect both my reputation and the constitutional position of the Monarch.

The remarkable and to me unexpected result of all these four groups of people asked to give their views was (rather contrary to what I expected) a *preponderant first* choice for Lord Home (except in the constituencies, who hardly knew he was a serious candidate but agreed that he would be universally acceptable if *drafted*). . . . There were *strong pro*-Butlerites; but equally violent *anti*. There were strong—very strong—*pro*-Hailsham—but very violent *anti*. On Maudling the feelings were not so strong in either direction.

In Cabinet, ten for Home; three for Butler; four for Maudling; two for Hailsham. Among three hundred M.P.s consulted, the largest group (not by much, but significant) were *pro*-Home. But, again, no one against. In Lords, two to one for Home. The constituencies were about sixty per cent for Hailsham; forty per cent for Butler, with *strong* opposition feelings to both. Mrs. S. and Lord C. were certain that everyone would rally round Home.

I drew up the memorandum, and my copy (which I shall keep in my personal records) will have all the documentation.[1]

The next day, destined to be the last of my premiership, was

a terrible day and very bad for me. The doctors protest, but I could see no way of shuffling out of my duty. At the end of the day, I can hardly hold a pen.

At 7.30 a.m. Bligh rang up to say that a critical situation had developed and that he and Chief Whip would be round at hospital at 8.30 a.m. to consult me. It seems that the news that the general choice favoured Home got out last night (leaked by someone). Meetings were organised. . . . The idea was an organised revolt by all the *unsuccessful* candidates—Butler, Hailsham, Maudling and Macleod—against Home. Considering their intense rivalry with each other during recent weeks, there was something rather eighteenth-century about this . . . and somewhat distasteful. Home rang up and felt aggrieved. He had only been asked to

[1] 17 October 1963.

come forward as a compromise candidate, from unity. He felt like withdrawing. I urged him not to do so. If we give in to this intrigue, there would be chaos.[1]

In this strange and somewhat unreal atmosphere, I decided to proceed with my plan unchanged. My letter of resignation was sent and delivered to the Palace at 9.30 a.m. I can hardly do better than complete the story in the words which I wrote in my diary that day.

The Queen came to the Hospital at 11 a.m. I was in bed, in the board-room. A high chair was put ready for her on my right. Dorothy, the Matron, Lady Birdwood (secretary of hospital), Sir J. Richardson, Mr. Badenoch received the Queen, who came with Sir Michael Adeane. All stayed outside; she came in alone, with a firm step, and those brightly shining eyes which are her chief beauty. She seemed moved; so was I. She referred to the very long time I had served her—nearly seven years—and how sorry she had been to get my letter of resignation. She then asked for my advice as to what she should do. I asked leave to read her a memorandum which I had written yesterday, and brought up to date this morning, after hearing of the so-called 'revolt' of certain Ministers. I said I was not strong enough to trust myself to speak without a text, and I also wanted my written memorandum in the Queen's archives, to be there as a full justification of any action she might take on my advice.

She expressed her gratitude, and said that she did not need and did not intend to seek any other advice but mine. I then read the memorandum. She agreed that Lord Home was the most likely choice to get general support, as well as really the best and strongest character. But what of the revolt? . . . I said that I thought speed was important and hoped she would send for Lord Home immediately—as soon as she got back to the Palace. He could then begin to work. She agreed. Before leaving, she thanked me again most generously for my thoughtfulness for her over this and over many other matters affecting her comfort during all these years. She gave me her hand and left, carrying the memorandum—in an immense envelope—which I could see (as the door opened) she gave to Adeane—which made him look . . . like the Frog Footman. . . .

[1] 18 October 1963.

One thing I should record ... I advised the Queen, both verbally, and in the second part of the written memorandum, *not* to appoint Home as P.M. at his first audience, but to use the older formula and entrust him with the task of forming an administration. He could then take his soundings and report to her. She followed this course.

So ended my premiership– 11 *January*, 1957–18 *October*, 1963.[1]

The memorandum to the Queen described the procedure adopted and the results flowing from the consultation with the different groups, with some comments in amplification. The document set out the conclusions as recorded in my diary for 17 October. An important addition which I made was the definite recommendation that, if Lord Home accepted the Queen's nomination, he should take advantage of the new Peerage Act and seek immediate election to the House of Commons.

Within a day or two, Home's administration was successfully formed and included the three main rivals, Butler, Maudling and Hailsham, who all behaved with splendid solidarity. I was sad that Macleod, for whom I had the highest regard, did not feel able to join.

Many other duties still remained to be performed, including an appropriate list of resignation honours. A vast number of letters had to be acknowledged, as well as a most touching telegram from Churchill. Perhaps the correspondence with Lord Beaverbrook is worth recording.

To the sadness that came with your resignation, joy has succeeded! For now every day the news of you is good and confidence is supreme that your recovery of strength and health will be swift and complete.

So among your friends happiness prevails.

Come back and take part once more in politics. Your withdrawal has only proved how much your presence is essential.

If you came back as the Prime Minister for Peace, I, for one, am persuaded that you would carry the country in the election, and perhaps by a fine majority.

[1] 18 October 1963.

Between us there lies only the shadow of the Common Market. But that is over now and, I hope, over and done with for ever !

Certainly I am not writing a political letter to you. This is simply an expression of my own joy and delight that you have surmounted your troubles so magnificently.

With every good wish.

I replied:

Many thanks for your very kind letter of the 16th.

It has touched me very much. I have never forgotten how kind you were to me when I was your Under-Secretary and that friendship has always remained. If ever I come back to play any part in politics it would be for the purpose of which you speak. It is the only thing that matters now. Russia has quarrelled with and fears China. We must turn the Russians into Europeans. In that role the British can play a special part.

Of course there were countless other messages, some of which could be dealt with by Private Secretaries, but the replies to many of which occupied me for several weeks. Among the most touching was that from the President, the last I was ever to receive from him and sent only a few weeks before his death:

As you lay down your great responsibility, I want to send you on our private wire one more message of affection and respect. In nearly three years of co-operation, we have worked together on great and small issues, and we have never had a failure of understanding or of mutual trust. I believe that the world is a little more safe and the future of freedom more hopeful than when we began, and I am certain that history will recognise your great role in this improvement.

Mrs. Kennedy joins me in the warmest of good wishes for your prompt and complete recovery, and for a future in which we hope to see you and Lady Dorothy often again as old and good friends.

With warm regards.

Only one minor matter remained to be settled—my own future.

The Queen has written to say that she did not offer me the Earldom when she came to the hospital, for fear I would be embarrassed, since she knew my disinclination. But she made it clear I could have it *on her authority* (that is, not 'on advice') if ever I wanted it. This was very gracious.[1]

However, I was not at all anxious to go to the House of Lords. I felt it more appropriate to accept the inevitable, and abandon a life in which I could play no effective part. I did not resign immediately from the House of Commons, for there was no need to burden the constituency with a by-election when a General Election must take place within a year. I spoke only on three occasions, and that with the greatest difficulty owing to my physical weakness. The first was in November 1963 after the murder of the President. The second was a short statement in December 1963 on the publication of the Denning Report. The third was in July 1964, when I added my tribute to Churchill, just before the dissolution of Parliament.

However, while lying in bed reflecting on all these events that had moved with such terrifying rapidity, I was comforted to receive a letter from the Queen.

> When you told me in September that you might cease to be my Prime Minister before the next General Election this seemed a long way ahead; but no one could have foretold the events which were to follow so soon on the heels of your decision and which were bound to make such a difference to it.
>
> Now that you have actually given me your resignation I must tell you, once more, how sincerely sorry I am that you are no longer my Prime Minister.
>
> I have the greatest confidence in Alec Home and this is re-inforced by his distinguished record at the Foreign Office and as Leader of the House of Lords; he will be greatly missed in both places as well as by the foreign Statesmen who have come to trust in his character and skill and I have not the least doubt that as the fourth Prime Minister of my reign he will lead my Government and our country with an equally firm and sure hand.
>
> Nevertheless, it is you who have held the highest office continuously for nearly seven years. I believe this is a record for the twentieth century and if it has been exceeded at other times their conditions cannot have been comparable with the arduous circum-

[1] 20 October 1963.

stances of modern political life. For me it means that for the greater part of my reign you have not only been in charge of Britain's policies but you have been my guide and supporter through the mazes of international affairs and my instructor in many vital matters relating to our constitution and to the political and social life of my people.

There is therefore no question of your successor, however admirable he may be, being able to perform exactly those services which you have given so generously and for which I am so deeply grateful.

During these years you have had to unravel a succession of major and intricate problems affecting the peace of the world and the very existence of Britain and the Commonwealth. History will witness to the masterly skill with which you have handled them. I suppose that the success which may give you the greatest satisfaction is the recent signature of the Nuclear Test Ban Treaty for which you and your colleagues have worked so long and so patiently and which has given new hope to people all over the world.

There have also been, I am afraid, a number of problems affecting my family—lesser perhaps in scope but not always in intricacy—which must have occupied a great amount of your time. I should like to put on record my appreciation and gratitude for the unstinted care which you have taken in giving me your advice about them and helping me to find solutions.

As you know, it is my hope that some day, later if not sooner, you may accept an Earldom and continue to take part in public life from the benches of the Upper House. But whether you are in the Lords or the Commons and though you are no longer Prime Minister I shall take comfort that, as a Privy Councillor and an elder Statesman of immense experience and accomplishment, you may sometimes be prepared to give me your advice should I be in need of it.

I send you and Dorothy my true good wishes on your retirement from office, and I hope that you will soon be out of hospital and completely well again.

It is difficult to conceive a more gracious and generous tribute from a Sovereign to a subject.

CHAPTER XVI

Epilogue

NEARLY ten years have passed since the events recorded in the last chapter of this volume.

My political life ended with my resignation in October 1963 from the office of Prime Minister. Nor have I sought to extend it artificially. I have long felt that 'enough was enough'. Forty years in the House of Commons, seventeen years in Ministerial office, including the exacting posts of Foreign Secretary and Chancellor of the Exchequer, and ending with nearly seven years as Prime Minister, should satisfy any normal man's ambition—and taste for punishment. I have therefore carefully abstained from any involvement in affairs since 1963. Moreover it has always seemed to me more artistic, when the curtain falls on the last performance, to accept the inevitable *E finita la commedia*. It is tempting, perhaps, but unrewarding to hang about the greenroom after final retirement from the stage.

Accordingly, when I reached the end of a long convalescence, I began to look through the mass of diaries, letters, papers and the like which I had collected in the course of a long life. In August 1964 I prepared a short outline of a possible volume, or volumes.

At the beginning of the next year, in 1965, I set about my task. Of course I did not then realize the large scale and terrifying length which my story would demand. For this I can only plead inexperience, coupled with the weight of available material.

For though I was only a spectator of events in the earlier volumes, yet, as the story unfolds, I become increasingly a participant. Besides, I have rather enjoyed the experience, however laborious; for I have lived again, with a new intensity, through the stirring issues and the dramatic conflicts which have filled the fifty years of my active life.

Naturally, there have been times when I have felt discouraged and tempted to abandon my self-imposed burden. The death of my wife, in the summer of 1966, all the more poignant because sudden and unexpected, has cast a shadow over my old age, which even the devotion of my family and the kindness of countless friends has not been able altogether to dissipate. It has been a comfort to me to realize how widely her qualities were recognized and how deeply she was loved by all who knew her or even were brought into contact with her in any capacity.

A second and serious operation in 1969 proved a further set-back. But, with the help of my old friend, Sir John Richardson, I have been able to regain and maintain the strength to complete my task.

I have tried, throughout, to rely on contemporary sources and wherever possible to give a picture based not on hindsight, but on documents—including letters, messages, memoranda—belonging to the date of the events described. For this reason, I have drawn largely on my own diaries, which record my own feelings at the time.

I have also tried to be as objective as possible in my account of various incidents. Naturally one must include, especially in an autobiography, a proper degree of subjectivity. But the balance should be, as far as possible, preserved.

Finally I am grateful for the friendly reception of the first five volumes of this massive work. I hope the sixth, and happily the last, will be as acceptable to critics and readers.

Talleyrand once said that no one who had not known France before the Revolution could understand, in its true sense, 'la douceur de la vie'.

The same is perhaps true of anyone who did not know England before the First World War. I do not, of course, refer to the social structure, which had many weaknesses, nor the distribution of wealth, which had many faults, nor the standards of health, housing, sanitation and education, which now must be judged as sadly deficient. I am thinking of the sense of peace and security which in the course of this century has been taken from us.

The invention of the internal combustion engine has destroyed our quiet. The breakdown of the international system which, with only minor exceptions, maintained the peace of the world from the Treaty of Vienna in 1815 to the German invasion of Belgium in 1914 has brought an end to the old concept of Europe–threatened the position of Europe and Europeans, by raising in the East and the West the Great Colossi, and now by a strange paradox resulting from the development of nuclear power, overwhelming but unusable, has Balkanised the world.

My childhood and early youth were spent in the horse age (hardly affected by the railways), when even London was something of a country town, and Oxford was proud of its horse-trams. All this repose and quiet has been drowned by a ceaseless roar on earth and in the sky.

At the same time in the early years of the century the inevitability of peace and progress seemed too assured and was regarded as almost a natural condition of life. Yet, during the years that followed, we have suffered ten years of war, and almost as many years in recovery from or preparation for war.

Nevertheless, such is the resilience of mankind that, in spite of these terrible handicaps, there has been, in almost every field, a degree of at least material progress which no one would have dared to prophesy in the old, quiet, secure country of my childhood.

In these volumes I have tried at least to give some picture of what I have called the 'fifty years of revolution'. For never, since the decline of the Roman Empire, have men and women been forced to adapt themselves to such vast changes as the people of Britain–and in so short a time.

The social revolution; the economic and technological revolution; the transformation of the old Empire into the new Commonwealth; the violent changes in the balance of world power–all these, and many similar changes, have inclined many to indulge in nostalgic reminiscence on the one hand, or equally exaggerated denigrations of our national aims and purposes on the other.

Yet perhaps the truth lies, as so often, between these extremes.

It is not easy for the British people, after their long sense of security and their supremacy in many fields–in trade, in industry, in monetary stability, and in undisputed naval power—the country of the Pax Britannica, with ever growing imperial and colonial responsibilities, to adjust themselves to the new conditions. Nor do they remember the comparatively short period of this unquestioned leadership.

Yet, through their long history, our island people have seen many and radical alterations in their fortunes. We were a small, isolated, but intensely dynamic nation from Elizabethan times to the early years of the eighteenth century, when Marlborough made us a great power. Even so, we could only meet and overcome Napoleon, the Kaiser, and Hitler as the centre of great coalitions.

Once more, it is in the new unity of Europe that we may, with full loyalty to our Commonwealth responsibilities, play our part to meet whatever unknown dangers and to exploit whatever new possibilities the next fifty years may bring.

Nothing in my long experience or in my observations of the youth of today makes me fear that the people of Britain, in every walk of life, will shrink from the new challenge or fail to rise to the level of events. But to do so they must restore and strengthen the moral and spiritual, as well as the material, base on which they have rested for so many generations through so many troubles and tribulations.

May 1973   H. M.

Appendix One

Harold Macmillan's speech at the opening of the Commonwealth Prime Ministers' Conference, 10 September 1962

Section I: Background

As I explained this morning in welcoming my colleagues to this Conference, I thought it would be convenient to devote this afternoon to an exposition of the situation as regards the European Economic Community as we in Britain see it. I would like, in this context, to pass in review the world situation which is the background against which we must discuss these matters and to say something about the general relationship between the Commonwealth, Europe and the United Kingdom. I will not, myself, go into details about the negotiations in Brussels, nor about the situation there reached. As you know, these are concerned with matters on which agreement must be reached if we are to preserve our honourable undertakings to our friends and our duty to our own country—Commonwealth countries, our partners in the European Free Trade Association and our British agriculturalists. But after I have given my general picture I would propose to ask the Lord Privy Seal, Mr. Heath, to give you a more detailed account of the discussions in which he has been engaged and which are, for the moment, adjourned for the holiday season. I would only say in this context that, whatever may be the outcome of the negotiations in Brussels, we in the United Kingdom are deeply grateful to Mr. Heath, and his carefully selected team of experienced and devoted officials, for the work which they have done. I believe this tribute will be shared by both Commonwealth Ministers and officials with whom they have been in the closest touch throughout. We believe that he is working not only to protect the short-term interests of us all but to provide the essential framework for expansion in the long term.

It is now seventeen years since the end of the second of those two terrible wars in which Europe involved not only herself but the whole world besides in the course of a single generation. It is fifteen years since, with the enactment of independence for India and Pakistan, there began the final stages of the transformation of the former British Empire into the present Commonwealth. This comparatively short period has seen the political map of the world redrawn in a most dramatic way. It has also witnessed great changes in the economic position of the countries of the world. Naturally in the vast upheaval caused by the Second World War it was difficult to foresee how the civilized world would shape itself. But now the mists are beginning to roll away and we can see more clearly the broad picture. We must now try to foresee and adapt ourselves to the new pattern.

The more sanguine hopes that following the foundation of the United Nations in 1945 we should be able to move under the guidance of the Security Council, fortified by the support of the Assembly, into something like a world system, have not been fulfilled. We must face that fact. From the point of view of sheer power the world is unhappily divided into two great blocs. On the one hand the United States and her allies; on the other the Soviet Union and hers. These two great groups together occupy a dominating position as regards both military and economic strength; each of them has at its disposal resources on a scale hitherto unknown in the world. In addition these are fortified by novel and terrifying forms of destructive power. In the East, China, which Napoleon once called a sleeping giant, has awakened now and with her enormous population and resources is bound to play an ever greater part in the world scene. In addition to the two great power blocs, there is also a third group of peoples, mostly in what are called the developing countries, which, primarily preoccupied with their own struggle to build up their political institutions and to advance economically and industrially, have striven to maintain their position as unaligned in the world struggle.

Even inside Western Europe a complete transformation has taken place since 1945, not so much politically as economically. In 1946, Sir Winston Churchill could say 'the awful ruin of Europe with all its vanished glories glares into our eyes'. But now Western Europe has achieved a remarkable economic recovery. It is on its way to forming an economic and—in one form or another—perhaps a political unit which could, in terms of population, skill and wealth, rival the United States or the Soviet Union. This is the background, familiar enough to you all, against which we in Britain have had to consider what we ought to do not only in our own interests but in those of the Commonwealth.

Let me say at once that I absolutely reject the view that Britain is today faced with a choice between the Commonwealth and Europe. This is not so—and for a very simple reason. The European Economic Community is an organisation totally different from the Commonwealth and one which is likely to continue to exist whether we join or not. We have in Britain indeed a choice of courses of action. But if we do enter the European Economic Community this will not mean that we can or shall neglect the Commonwealth; nor, if we stay outside the Community, will we be able to ignore Europe. The problem before us is how to reconcile the historic and living structure of the Commonwealth with the new and developing structure of the Continent of Europe. In a sense this is not a new situation for, with all our world-wide connections, Britain has always been part of Europe. What we must find are the modern ways of dealing with the present-day aspects of this historic position.

Section II: The Commonwealth

Let us look at the problem in two parts. First the Commonwealth. Unlike the Europeans we in the Commonwealth are not people whose history has been shared for the last two thousand years. Of course with some members the United Kingdom has special ties both of blood and of allegiance to the Monarchy. These are all the stronger for the memories of disasters and triumphs shared together. These are very special links which no British Prime Minister, certainly not I, would ever wish to weaken or injure. Nevertheless our Commonwealth association is not a political unity. Different members take different views on a whole range of international problems, they pursue different and sometimes conflicting policies, they even vote different ways in the United Nations. Still less are we a military alliance. For inside the Commonwealth some are members of regional pacts such as NATO, SEATO and CENTO; some have mutual defence arrangements and others prefer to remain without military commitments. In the financial and economic field, for most of us the sterling area and for all of us our trading arrangements, to which I shall refer in a moment, form perhaps a more concrete link. But the Commonwealth is not a single financial or economic unit. We do much trade of great importance with each other and share an interest in the stability of sterling as an international currency. While we have traded fruitfully together, we have also deliberately worked for the greatest possible freedom of world trade. In the past the members of the Commonwealth have not had any high degree of tariff discrimination in their trade. Even the level established 30 years ago has been steadily reduced. The Ottawa Agreements in the 1930s were in a sense contrary to previous trends in Commonwealth trade. They originated in the world slump and were a deliberate answer to the emergency of that time. These Agreements were certainly of great value not to the Commonwealth alone, but to the whole world since they assisted in its economic recovery. Nevertheless they were characteristic of a particular period which was already beginning to pass away by the late 1930s. When the Ottawa Agreements were signed, the industrialisation of the Commonwealth had not been developed very far; they envisaged a pattern of trade in which other Commonwealth countries exported mainly primary produce whilst this country exported manufactures. Since then industry in the other Commonwealth countries has proceeded very fast, while Britain herself has become a substantial producer of foodstuffs. This change, stimulated by wartime conditions but in any case natural and inevitable, has meant that over the years that proportion of Commonwealth trade done with other Commonwealth countries has fallen. Before the War it was about 40 per cent of total Commonwealth trade, in 1961 it was only 35 per cent. The pattern of course varies from country to country and from commodity to commodity. But to give you one example, before the last war we in Britain took five times as much wool from Australia as Japan, whereas today Japan takes twice as much as we do.

It has sometimes been suggested that the Commonwealth itself might form a closer economic unit, vast in population and natural resources and able on its own to equal the great economies of the United States, the Soviet Union or Europe. But I do not think that this idea has ever been a practical policy for the Commonwealth in recent years. None of the conditions exist for the creation of a common Commonwealth market or Customs Union without internal tariff barriers. It is clear that the situation varies too much between the different countries for such a scheme to be practicable. Wage conditions, labour costs and other costs are not comparable, nor are standards of living similar. Each Commonwealth country, quite rightly, is determined to use whatever methods are necessary to encourage and protect its local industrial development. In other words they are, with the exception of the United Kingdom, building up their own industries and have recourse to measures which even the great free traders, like Adam Smith, recognised as defensible in the early stages of industrial development. At the same time the United Kingdom cannot by itself supply adequate markets for the Commonwealth countries, either in primary or industrial products. Nor can the United Kingdom today supply the large amounts of capital which are one of the greatest needs of the developing countries. We do our best but the task is beyond us single handed.

It is clear therefore that neither for the purposes of trade nor for those of capital expansion can the Commonwealth be or become a unit of the character of the United States or the European Economic Community or the Soviet Bloc.

We have then to ask ourselves what in fact the Commonwealth is now. What does it represent? What should be its function in the world? It used to be fashionable to refer to the Commonwealth as a family. This simile was perhaps apt in the purely constitutional field in that the United Kingdom has tried to help Commonwealth countries to grow under her protection into independent sovereign states. But now that this process has been so largely accomplished we can best think of the Commonwealth as a group of friends and relations who, with different problems in all the various parts of the world, nevertheless hold in common certain beliefs and traditions and retain a continuing interest in and practical concern for each other's welfare. Looked at dispassionately, as I have been trying to do in the last months, I believe that perhaps the most important characteristic of our Commonwealth is its very diversity. Yet that diversity is matched by what we have in common. Each of us wishes to play a part in the life of our own area of the world and many of us belong to regional organisations. But the existence of the Commonwealth is a constant reminder to all of us and to the rest of the world that regional organisations, however good, however prosperous, however powerful, are in themselves incomplete and may become selfish. The Commonwealth provides each of us with the salutary lesson both of the differences in the world and also of the fundamental unity of the human race. We learn tolerance and understanding from our association and we derive mutual benefits from the desire which we all have to help and support each other in our difficulties. And however we may act in different questions we always try to consult with each other first. It is in these consultations and their influence upon our actions that the true spirit and value of the Commonwealth is to be found. The consultations we shall have at this meeting are an important example of this truth.

This interchange of information and our system of consultation are, I believe, of value to all Commonwealth Governments. Certainly we in Britain regard them as of the greatest importance. From them, we gain the benefit of your views on the great issues of the day and an interest in and an understanding of your own problems. Britain cannot, of course, speak for the Commonwealth in the discussions we have with other Powers. But we can often feel more confident that the views we express do represent something more than an insular judgement made in London. In New York, in Washington, in Geneva, even in the purely military organisations such as NATO and the rest, wherever, in fact, we meet with other countries outside the Commonwealth, we believe this to be helpful and in the general interest.

Let me give you an example. Britain can, perhaps, claim some success for our policies in the settlement reached two months ago on the Laos question. I think it is fair to say that our influence helped to avert what might have been a very dangerous situation. I am convinced that our views, and those of other interested Commonwealth Governments such as India, Australia and New Zealand, were heard with more attention because we were all speaking as members of the Commonwealth with great interests in that area.

So the Commonwealth remains for us in Britain a system and an association of great importance and practical value, quite apart from the sentimental and other ties which bind us. We believe that it is the duty of Commonwealth countries each in their own way to exert the maximum influence in world affairs and to contribute as far as they can to the welfare and well-being of the Commonwealth as a whole. An association such as ours depends for its influence upon the standing of its members. At the basis of all our policies lies, I think, the common determination to prevent that collision of the great world powers which is the major risk to the survival of us all. If we are to help in this task, we must be in a position to make our voices heard. This means that it is the duty of each of us, of the United Kingdom as well as of other countries, to maintain its economic and political strength and to develop its influence. If Britain becomes a member of the European Community, then in talking to us other Commonwealth countries would not be speaking just to Britain alone but also to a leading member in a new organisation. In such an organisation we in Britain would certainly exercise significant influence and perhaps decisive leadership. Through us, therefore, Commonwealth views would have an effect upon the policies of the whole European Community.

It is in this belief that the British Government has taken the view that it is in the interests of the Commonwealth as well as of the United Kingdom that we should join the European Economic Community if satisfactory arrangements can be negotiated.

Section III: Europe

I have spoken about the modern Commonwealth as I see it. What is the European pattern? I referred a few moments ago to the revival of Western Europe after the last war. In this development, the European movement, in which the leading figures of all parties in this country have played a role, has been a significant factor. With characteristic magnanimity Sir Winston Churchill out of office took the lead, but with equal foresight Mr. Bevin as Foreign Secretary brought about the Treaty of Dunkirk with France in 1947 and the Brussels Treaty with France and the Benelux countries in 1948. British Governments have made an important contribution to the new forms of international co-operation throughout Europe: the Council of Europe, the Organisation for European Economic Co-operation, the European Payments Union and Western European Union; all these mark different stages in this journey. I do not think that anyone has seriously questioned the wisdom of our co-operation with Europe in these ways. But the urge for unity in Europe was not satisfied by these developments. The determination to create closer organic forms of union faced us with a more difficult problem. We tried to solve this by the promotion of a European-wide free trade area on an industrial basis. After long negotiations these efforts failed. We were forced to stand aside and think again. We had to recognise that the European movement has caught the imagination of the young; transcended party politics and national barriers. Its impact has not been limited to economic affairs. With the development of the European idea there has come a resurgence and new vigour in all aspects of European life, in music, arts, science, industry. There is something here of that release of the spirit which lifted Europe out of the mediaeval period into the Renaissance and the modern world. Europe, which Spengler saw as decadent and declining, is once more seeing a great Renaissance.

We in Britain cannot stand aside from these developments. For, as I have said earlier, we are Europeans, and can play a leading part in Europe. Now it is quite true that in the latter part of the 19th century and the first half of the 20th century we have sometimes tried to ignore the continent of Europe. But we have never in reality been able to insulate ourselves from developments only 20 miles away. The fact that our people from this small island had spread themselves to other continents and throughout the seven seas made it a tempting delusion that we had ceased to be Europeans. But for this mistake both we and you, Gentlemen, have paid a heavy price. Twice in my lifetime we have been brought to the brink of destruction by this fallacy. Twice in my lifetime we have involved not only our own people but those dependent on us, almost the whole world, in a degree of destruction and misery unexampled in history. If we escape the positive guilt of those upon whom the deeper blame lies we cannot, if we are honest, put out of our minds the thought that if we had taken a more active part in Europe's politics before 1914 and before 1939 these tremendous calamities might have been avoided.

Therefore we can only welcome the determination of our neighbours to create a Community which seeks to bury for good the age-old European conflicts. But in creating this Community, Europe has profoundly changed our own environment. The world will never be the same again. Already the European Economic Community is beginning to pursue common economic policies towards the outside world; soon it may begin to do the same in foreign affairs. It is of the greatest importance to all of us in the Commonwealth that the policies which it pursues should take full account of the needs of other countries and that we in Britain should not be forced into a new phase of isolation from the European scene. We cannot expect to have any steady influence on the formulation of Community policy from the outside. And in my judgement we cannot expect the Community as at present constituted to be as sensitive to the interests of the world beyond Europe or to see matters in as broad a perspective as its strength and weight in world affairs really demands. We told you a year ago, when my colleagues made a series of visits to Commonwealth countries, that one of the reasons which prompted us to apply for membership was concern lest we would lose our influence in Europe. I believe that in the long run the isolation of Britain from the centres of European power would be very damaging for us all as well as for Europe itself. And while we have naturally had to take the most unfavourable situation into account in our discussions about the future, we must remember that Britain as a member of the Community would not be impotent. Surely it is reasonable to suppose that if we were members our influence would be important and perhaps decisive. I do not think that if we do not join the Community immediate disaster will follow. No. But in a period, perhaps not so long a period, we should run the risk of losing our political influence. Great as the loss would be to us, in this country, I am persuaded that this loss would be felt also by our Commonwealth partners.

We have, for instance, to think of the effect on our relations with the United States of this consolidation of power in Europe. Our present relations with America are close and fruitful; I do not believe that Commonwealth countries would wish them to be otherwise. But if we were outside the Community, it seems to me inevitable that the realities of power would cause the United States to attach increasing weight to the views and interests of the Six and of other countries which might accede to them. Inevitably too the United States and the Community would concert policy on major issues without the same regard for our views and interests such as our present relationship with Washington affords. To lose influence both in Washington and in Europe would seriously detract from our standing and gravely impair our usefulness to the Commonwealth.

There is another political aspect of this problem which I believe shows how our participation in the Community could be of direct interest to the Commonwealth. The European Community as it stands at present is concerned in a very acute way with the East/West conflict at its most emotional point, that is to say on the borders of Germany and Berlin. This is natural since Germany itself is an important member of the Community. But it would be a very unfortunate thing, and a very dangerous thing, if the Europe of the future were to become obsessed with the problems of the Eastern frontiers. It is important for world peace and for the prospects of any eventual reconciliation between the Communist and non-Communist worlds that Europe should take a broad view of these problems. I think we can fairly claim that in recent years Britain and the Commonwealth have always tried to work towards healing discords and bring about a reconciliation, or at least a *détente*, between the Communist and Western blocs. The visit which I made to Moscow; our attempts to settle affairs through Summit meetings, so tragically frustrated; our efforts to end the competition in nuclear tests and for comprehensive disarmament are all proofs of our intentions in this respect with which, I think, all the Commonwealth are in sympathy. I feel very deeply that this role is one of the main functions of Britain in the world today. If Britain is playing a full part in the Community, then it seems to me that we shall be able to fulfil this role more effectively.

Before developing the economic arguments I would say something about the obligations which Britain would accept if we acceded to the Treaty of Rome and about the further possibilities in the political field in Europe which might follow. Of course, like any other Treaty, accession to the Treaty of Rome must involve some pooling of sovereignty. But this would only apply to matters within the ambit of the Treaties and their scope could not be extended without unanimous agreement. In the prescribed field – as in any other economic field – we should be sharing some of our sovereignty. We should receive in return a share of the sovereignty of the other members. Our obligations would not, however, alter the position of the Crown nor fetter the broad independence of Parliament here.

It is true that the Governments of the Six are anxious to move forward from an economic to some form of political union for Europe. So far agreement has not been reached, but it seems clear that the approach of the six existing members of the Community is gradual and pragmatic. There is no grandiose supra national or federalistic plan. This prudence has of course been a disappointment to some enthusiasts. We in Britain welcome it. For, whatever the future of European institutions may be, we do not believe that they will flourish without relying on all that is best in national traditions. We are anxious to join in the task of building a greater political unity in Europe and the type of unity which we foresee as the most fruitful and possible will not be one which would be incompatible with Britain's position in the Commonwealth. In any event, we are not now concerned with the precise structure or the detailed development of the mechanisms by which a greater degree of unity may be achieved by the countries of Western Europe. All of this will need further consideration when the time comes.

Section IV : Economic

On the economic side there are strong arguments too. Although the United Kingdom market cannot take all the imports from other parts of the Commonwealth which you would like us to receive, we are still the largest single market after the United States for Commonwealth goods and we do 34 per cent of our trade with the Commonwealth. This existing trade and still more the prospects for increase depend so far as we are concerned on the prosperity of Britain. In the same way we are still able through the sterling area and through the City of

London to supply very large amounts of help and development capital to Commonwealth countries. Last year our overseas lending (Governmental and private) was £436 million, of which £300 million went to the Commonwealth. Nevertheless the amount that we can lend or give whether on private or public account depends upon our economic strength. In both these fields, therefore, both as a market for your goods and as a source of capital, if it is true that British accession to the European Economic Community would make us stronger, then it is clear that it must equally make us of greater help to the Commonwealth. Economically therefore the question then turns on this. Will British economic strength be increased or not by our joining Europe? This is the question which my colleagues and I have tried to study dispassionately and in some detail.

In considering it we must begin with the hard, but inescapable fact that Britain is a small island, heavily populated and with meagre natural resources. Our whole existence therefore depends on trade; if we are to be able to import the foodstuffs and raw materials which are essential to us, we must be able to find markets for our exports of manufactured goods. The competitiveness of our exports is the key to the healthy growth of our economy; and in recent years, I must be frank and say this, with the rapid development of secondary industry all over the world, we have found it increasingly necessary to rely on exporting more sophisticated goods, such as those requiring heavy capital outlay, where economies of scale are important. And of course competitiveness depends on the size of the market.

Separated from us by a few miles of sea, and perhaps soon to be joined to us by a tunnel or a bridge, is Europe and the rapidly expanding dynamic economic community already comprising some 170 million people. The resurgence of Europe's economy since the war is a matter of common knowledge, but the statistics are nevertheless remarkable. Between 1954 and 1960 industrial output in the E.E.C. grew by over 50 per cent as compared with our growth of 20 per cent. The figures for individual items are even more striking. For instance, the output of cars in the Community trebled in the same period. This dramatic growth in domestic production was accompanied by equivalent growth in international trade, imports into the Community rising by 61 per cent during the period. In 1960 alone Community imports from the rest of the world rose by 20 per cent and accounted for a fifth of world imports, while imports per head of population were more than those of the United States. Of these imports overseas Commonwealth items amounted to 10 per cent of the total and 9 per cent of the increase. It can of course be argued that expansion in Europe has not been due to the Common Market. Certainly it was well under way before the Treaty of Rome and was generated at first by the post-war reconstruction, including generous American capital aid and the supply of plentiful labour from Eastern Germany and Italy. But the formation of the Community has been a powerful factor. The Common Market is more than a free trade area or customs union, and its provisions for the removal of barriers will provide not only a fuller interchange of men and ideas but also powerful incentives for growth. These forces are already becoming effective. Intra-Community trade increased by over 50 per cent between 1958 and 1960 and the rate of foreign investment in the Community increased by 60 per cent in the same two years.

The trend towards a larger market is of course nothing new. It follows an age-old pattern. As communications, industrial techniques and so forth have developed so the organisation of economies and individual industries has been in larger and larger units. Originally our economies worked on the basis of the village. Then, in Europe three hundred years or more ago, municipal centres became the basis with each town still largely self-supporting. It was only in the 19th century that the development of communications, the railway and the steam ship, made it possible to organise international and internal trade on a far larger basis. In the 20th century the development of road and air transport has made it possible for the first time to organise economies on a continental scale, and to develop the hinterlands which previously could not be easily reached by sea and only partially by rail. Consequently economic power in the world has shifted towards continental economies. Let me give an example, perhaps rather a grim one. In 1940 and the following years Hitler was able to seize and hold practically the whole European continent. By this means he was able to withstand for five years almost alone the combined military and economic forces of the United States, the Soviet Union, Britain and the Commonwealth, which were able in their turn to command both their own resources and those of the neutral world. This illustrates the power of continental organisation and of any large market for the evil purposes of war. But the advantages are equally great and equally diverse for the beneficent operations of peace. In the first place there are simple economies of scale with longer production runs, mass production and a higher degree of specialisation. But, in addition to this, modern technology is making these large economic units essential for the newest industries. The later an industry develops the more complex the industrial structure required to support it. It is possible to have a very small economic base and still to have a cotton textile industry. It is possible to have a medium-sized economy and still have a modest steel industry. It seems probable however that no country with a population of much less than 20 million could have a fully fledged modern automobile industry—even though the example of Canada, Australia and Sweden shows that there could be exceptions in specially favourable circumstances. But if we move on from the motor car, which is now after all a development some 80 years old, the scale of economy required to support new industries goes up very sharply indeed. Obvious examples are the space industry, where we are already co-operating with Europe in the European Space Research Organisation, and the development of nuclear energy. There is therefore both a natural development towards larger industries and also a stage in that industrial development at which unless one's economy is large the development of new and complex industries may be prejudiced. This stage is particularly important because, if the technologies required for each new industry as it comes along are not developed, we suffer a double disadvantage. We fail to develop the new industries, but we also deprive ourselves of the new technologies which would strengthen our existing industries. The whole industrial complex, not just what we fail to develop but what is there already, tends to become relatively obsolete. And this is one reason why the United States has established a position relative to the rest of the world where despite much higher labour costs America can produce a wide range of things which people must buy and can sell them very cheaply.

Of course, while a larger and unified market provides opportunities it also ensures that there is greater competition; the less efficient will not survive. I do not think that we need fear European competition for British industry if we join. Anyway, in or out of Europe, we have got to face competition. The basic factor in competition is the cost of production. But there is now a very considerable similarity in the general cost structure including wage rates, between ourselves and the European countries. The true proof that we are competitive with Europe is to be seen in the trade figures. Up to 1960 Britain normally ran a balance of trade deficit with the Common Market powers. But our own exports to the Community have increased by over 50 per cent between 1954 and 1960. And our exports to the Community in the first six months of this year are 18 per cent higher than they were in 1961 and 35 per cent higher than in 1960. Meanwhile since 1960 there has been an increase of only about 5 per cent in our imports from the Community. This rather encouraging picture is, I think, accounted for in no small degree by the stimulating effect on British industry of the possibility of entering the Common Market. May I summarise it in this way. Assuming we are competitive, and I believe we are, assuming we have the will to make the best use of our manpower and energetic management, and I believe we have, if Britain enters Europe it means from the industrial point of view quadrupling the home market at one blow.

Naturally there will be serious difficulties in adapting our economy to the new system over a period of years. Yet, for the reasons I have given, my colleagues and I feel sure that the consequences of our joining the Common Market would benefit Britain from the economic angle. We are also convinced

s

that if we do not join there will be adverse effects not only on the British economy but on that of other Commonwealth countries as well. If this was the whole picture from the economic point of view there would have been no need for the prolonged negotiations which are still continuing in Brussels, but when we made our application to accede a year ago we were very conscious, as we still are, of the many immediate difficulties and even hardships which have to be overcome. And this has been our continuing preoccupation in Brussels throughout.

I shall not go into these matters in detail myself. I shall ask Mr. Heath to follow me with his analysis. I am deeply conscious of the legitimate anxieties of various countries regarding particular items in their trade. I thought, however, that it would be right, before proceeding to a detailed examination of the complicated but important particular questions, to give my colleagues this broad picture of the reasons that have actuated the Government of the United Kingdom. Of course, I do not wish to suggest that the British economy would collapse if we failed to achieve a satisfactory settlement allowing us to join the Community. No doubt we should get along—or jog along. But we should be deprived of the important advantages which I have outlined and which come from membership of a larger community. In addition—and this is the point I wish specially to emphasise—our ability to absorb imports from the Commonwealth and to provide capital for Commonwealth development would be correspondingly reduced. Moreover, if we are outside the Community, British industry would tend to duplicate its resources by investing within the tariff barrier and this would leave less capacity to help development in this country and elsewhere in the Commonwealth. There is another aspect of the problem which for an island depending on its foreign trade cannot be overlooked. In addition to the prospects of our share of the European market, what is at stake is our capacity to compete in third markets. I am persuaded that with the present tendencies in industrial development the size of the home base on which all exports are founded will be of growing significance.

I have already referred to the fact that the British market is no longer big enough to absorb the growing production of other members of the Commonwealth. An increasing proportion of Commonwealth trade is now with countries outside the Commonwealth, many of them inside the Six. Outside markets must, therefore, now be of increasing importance to you.

Britain's entry into the Community will almost certainly be only the first step in a fundamental reshaping of world trade. The possibilities of moving at last towards world-wide agreements should be greatly improved. We believe that our entry into the Community, together with some of our EFTA partners—Norway, Denmark and the rest—would decisively strengthen the liberal and outward-looking forces already at work in the Six. The Community, in co-operation with the United States, would then be able to carry further the gradual processes of freeing world trade. President Kennedy's bold and sweeping proposals for further tariff negotiations in the framework of the GATT have been generally welcomed. We would expect the opening of these negotiations to follow quickly upon our entry into the Community. Both the United States Government and the Six have made it clear that they are willing to consider constructively the negotiation of world-wide agreements on trade in agricultural products. Such agreements could be of decisive importance in themselves. At the same time, economic growth coming from reduced trade barriers should also facilitate the development of the proposals now being canvassed which would promote the disposal of food surpluses through aid programmes to under-developed countries.

Of course all these are difficult problems. Yet even the prospect of our joining the Community has proved a powerful stimulus to new ideas. But if we do not join, things will not remain as they have been. The Community will go on but those forces inside it which would prefer to see the Community develop in an inward-looking manner would be strengthened. The U.S. Administration would find it more difficult to carry President Kennedy's proposals for tariff negotiations against his own protectionist forces. The prospects of world-wide commodity agreements would be greatly damaged. Furthermore, the position as regards agricultural products would be extremely difficult. The Forces in favour of liberal agricultural policies in Europe would be seriously weakened. You know how European agricultural production has increased since the war and it can still go on. Technical advances, coupled with a high level of protection, would lead to increased surpluses. The pressure on the British domestic market would grow; and our present system of agricultural support would become intolerable. I doubt whether we could maintain our policies of free entry and cheap food; and, even if we could, the advantages which these policies have in the past offered to the Commonwealth might not continue.

Section V: Peroration

I have tried in this review to give my colleagues a broad picture both of the world scene against which we must reach our decision and of the political and economic arguments which have led us in the direction of accession to the European Economic Community. I hope I have said enough to convince you that membership of the Community will not be incompatible with the Commonwealth; the two associations being complementary.

If we decide to go forward, the way will not be easy. In the United Kingdom our own agriculture will have to go through a period of re-adjustment, many industries and trades will have to alter their ways, some injury will be done in different parts of the economy and to consumers as well as to producers. Perhaps the benefits will not appear as quickly as the difficulties: they will certainly not obtain equal publicity. For the rest of the Commonwealth, there will also be a period of re-adjustment and change. There is in fact no doubt that it would be much easier for us all, and certainly for someone of my age, to do nothing and reject the bold path of change. We should not suffer at once; we should get along. To do nothing would be easier in my view though it would be wrong.

Let me summarise the more practical political and economic arguments which I have tried to develop. On the economic side, Britain's value to the Commonwealth lies in the markets which she offers and in the capital which she provides. By ourselves we cannot increase our market except gradually through the increases in our population—and they are small. If we are to offer you better markets we must therefore increase our wealth. I believe that the prospects of our doing so inside the European Economic Community are better than if we stayed outside. I also believe that our influence and position in Europe will help to secure for the Commonwealth economic opportunities inside the Community which would otherwise be denied or restricted. On the political side the Community may of course break up—it is possible—or it may grow stronger. If it did collapse the situation would be most dangerous to us all. The economic dislocation would be harmful to world trade; the political consequences would be no less serious. The old rivalries and struggles would very likely begin again and Europe might well succumb to Soviet power which would then perhaps reach to the very Straits of Dover. So we desire to see the forces of unity in Europe grow stronger and banish for ever the fear of a return of the quarrels and destruction of the past. We believe that British membership of the Community would lend a new element of stability to it. And I believe that the European Community would be more likely to develop and to grow in political strength than to fall apart. But if this happened and Great Britain were to be isolated off the shore of a united European Community perhaps not six, but seven, eight or ten, our general political influence in the world would inevitably diminish. Moreover, there is a danger that without us the European countries would be excessively concerned with the problems of the European continent.

These seem to me and to my colleagues sound arguments, based upon our long experience of the past. But we have also to think at a deeper level about the probable course of the future. It is not good to go back in history. We in the United Kingdom have always stood for evolutionary and not reactionary policies. If this were not so we should not all be sitting round this table today. In the last few months it has been possible now for men to move out from the world's own sphere and look down upon our planet from outside. What a curious sight the world presents. There is the Commonwealth, the great United States, the developing Europe, the Soviet Union and its empire, the future colossus of China and all the rest. The value of these various groups will ultimately be judged by the contribution which they may make to the prosperity and progress of mankind. We, in Britain, feel it to be our duty as well as our interest to play our full role in these great world movements. As members both of the Commonwealth and of Europe, we are bound to have a special responsibility. We cannot refuse the great opportunity of playing our full part in the movement, slow or rapid as it may be, towards the ultimate world order into which mankind must move or perish.

Appendix Two

Harold Macmillan's Speech at the end of the
Common Market discussions at the Commonwealth
Prime Ministers' Conference, 17 September 1962

Gentlemen, it falls to me, as Chairman, to conclude that part of our discussions which deals with the question of the relations between Britain and the Commonwealth and Europe. Apart from the first three days of our discussion which were held in plenary session, and were pretty well available to the outside world, we have had three very useful days of detailed talk about a large number of practical questions in the economic field, ranging from commodities of overriding general importance and world-wide significance, to those affecting a particular locality or of special interest. I hope you will agree that we have all learned a great deal from these days. Although for ten months the British Government, through its Ministers and officials, have been in the closest touch with other Commonwealth governments, yet this is the first time that we have had an interchange on this scale—so comprehensive and so complete.

I do not intend, like a Government spokesman winding up a Parliamentary discussion, to make a kind of debating reply to all the points that have been raised with the appropriate quotations from speeches, or to employ any of the other methods of Parliamentary reply, with which most of us are familiar, and at which some of us are quite skilled. I would content myself with making one or two observations which I think it right to make from the point of view of the British Government, and in these I will concentrate on what I might call the general sense.

I believe that just as there is in our Commonwealth an immense variety—indeed, that is its main characteristic—of tradition, race, creed, so there is also a general sense, and it is on that general sense, that common feeling, that we must rely if we are not merely to rest contented upon the traditions of the past, but to face the changing perils of the future. Perhaps I might start with a reflection which has been much in my mind in recent days. There is hardly any human effort, certainly no creative human effort, that cannot be and that is not looked at from two absolutely opposing points of view. Thus, the same sets of proposals can be acclaimed as altruistic, imaginative, constructive, and as contributing to the forward movement of a united world. Turn over the page and it is equally possible to present them as deep intrigue, inspired by all the worst reactionary motives. I certainly wish, as I did in my opening speech to you, to treat these questions as impartially as I can. But while I am conscious of the strong and genuine feeling of many of the critics of European unity, I do not think it would be right to underrate the equally strong feeling of the promoters. Let us take all these motives and purposes at their best rather than at their worst.

On the constitutional and political side it is obvious that there is a sense among all our colleagues—whether representing some of those countries that have been longest in the Commonwealth, or those that are the newest arrivals—of genuine emotion and anxiety; some members fear a weakening of the Commonwealth's strength of purpose and, in a sense, a tarnishing of the brightness of the old shield. The Commonwealth, it is felt, will never be the same again. The truth is that it never has been. When I was a young man and joined the Army for the First War the Commonwealth consisted of the United Kingdom and five other countries of largely British origin, self-governing it is true, but with substantial powers still in the hands of the Westminster Government. The right of declaration of war rested with The Crown and Parliament at Westminster; no separate citizenship existed in the Commonwealth countries and so forth. At the opening phases of the Second World War when I was a young Minister, the Statute of Westminster had altered many of these conditions which appeared inappropriate to the modern age. But the Commonwealth still had the same restricted number of members. Now the Commonwealth has become as we see it, with some fifteen members, likely still to grow, covering the old British territories first occupied and now freely governed by men of British origin, Asian countries with histories of organised government extending through long centuries and many vicissitudes and new emergent countries whose outlines were only defined in the last century and are now springing into being, under the impetus of modern civilisation. I cannot help feeling that if it was possible for the Commonwealth in so short a time to undergo so great a transformation and be able to survive, then it will survive also the event of Britain's adherence to the Treaty of Rome.

But there are certain points which are specific points with which I would like to deal. The Prime Minister of Australia in a brilliant analysis of federal systems, though I was not sure whether he regarded himself as the beneficiary or the victim of this constitutional form, argued that by all historical facts any European grouping must either become stronger in structure or break apart completely. Of course it is quite right to have regard to these historical parallels. Nevertheless as Max Beerbohm wrote: 'History does not repeat itself; historians repeat one another'. I am bound to say that I do not think you can compare thirteen isolated British colonies on the Eastern Sea Board of North America separated from the whole world by three thousand miles of the Atlantic, searching for some way of life of mutual benefit after the long conflicts of a bitter parricidal struggle, with the Constitution of Europe as it is now today in the beginning of the 1960s. European countries are divided by language, history and tradition and are still trying to preserve their individuality.

Secondly, in defence, the Prime Minister of India seemed to think, although he did not press this point very strongly, that there was a danger of the new Europe in some way or another adding to world tension and that the Russians might not like it. It might be regarded as having implications in the defence field. Against this the Prime Minister of Canada appeared to feel a serious anxiety about the effect it might have on NATO. I am bound to say I do not see why it should have any more effect than the formation of the Western European Union which consisted of the Six plus Britain and which was formed largely for defence. Although wholly within the NATO field this was nevertheless loyal to the NATO concept. The truth is, Gentlemen, that all these problems depend upon what is going to be our purpose. For if the formation of groups and federations whether in the United States or in South America or Europe or Asia or Africa is judged and based on the old concepts of victory, conquests, exploitation, power, then each group must look askance at the other. But may we not hope that this conception in the modern world will be made obsolete if not impossible. If so, we must regard such groups from a new point of view. I think the whole question which has been round us the last ten days is whether we are going to look to the past or to the future. If so, then perhaps we need not be too anxious about the broad forms of organisation. What matters is the spirit in which they try to operate.

If these are the large issues that emerge from the political problem today, I have in a sense answered the particular point made by the Prime Minister of Australia and, I think, repeated by the Prime Minister of New Zealand which seems to me to be based upon conditions which do not now apply. They said in effect that if this island, so long separated by twenty vital miles of sea, should now join Europe were we not abandoning an age-long policy based upon the balance of power? The truth is that the power has moved and the balance has shifted. It is no longer true that Britain can by herself hold the balance or form an effective counterweight as perhaps she could when America was scarcely heard of and Russia was no more than France or Germany. But the world has much changed now from the days when the actual power pressure was to be measured in terms of France and Germany. The old concept of Balance of Power meant Balance of Power in Europe. But the growth and strength of the United States, the size and extension of Russia, the position of the new China based on a growing population ultimately to reach ten figures with the power that must inevitably follow, the similar development of South America, the future and change of the rest of Asia, the interdependence and, I hope, prosperity and strength Africa is destined to achieve; all this has completely changed the picture. The power has moved and a policy which has certainly been followed for three hundred years is no longer appropriate, and was indeed ceasing to be effective even in the first half of this century. If we want to keep a balance we must seek it by new methods.

If my colleagues have had an opportunity to study some of the discussions in the Press and outside which are now going on in this country, they cannot fail to be struck by the sense of idealism and enthusiasm which is being engendered, especially among our younger people, by the concept of a new role for Britain to play in the world. This is not, I repeat, alternative to our position in the Commonwealth. We believe that the whole future of the world may well depend upon the policies pursued by the European countries in the next generation or more. We see them abandoning their old internal and fratricidal disputes. We believe that they have it in their power to take the leadership in the concept of world unity which fascinates young people in every country. Many—of our younger generation especially—impatient of old disputes and intolerant of what seem to them obsolete conceptions, are anxious that our country should take the lead. They see in Europe not a protective wall within which those countries which have some of the advantages of modern civilisation can huddle together against an oncoming storm; on the contrary, they see it as an outpost of the future from which they can advance confidently beyond the confines of the present towards the frontiers of the future.

Now I pass to the economic side. There would be considerable dangers if the policies of Europe were carried on in a narrow or autarchic way. The dangers are of varying importance. I would not wish to underrate any of them but I think it would be fair to say that Canada's position as a producer of hard wheat is much stronger than Australia's as a producer of soft wheat. Moreover, in these discussions we have all recognised it, New Zealand has a special problem as regards, particularly, meat and dairy produce. This is certainly something which must be dealt with, if necessary by special methods. As regards the Asian nations, I would have said that broadly speaking the prospects of opening new markets in Europe to absorb imports of all kinds, and particularly of the manufactured goods, are favourable and should be encouraged. Of course, Europe's willingness to import, whether foodstuffs like meat or all manufactured goods, is still an uncertain quantity, but the limits of the British market can be very clearly discerned. For the African and West Indian countries on the economic side the offer is outstandingly good. Without any obligations

T

of any kind to counter-balance, they would have a preference for their products in a far larger market than at present—220 millions or more instead of 50—to say nothing of the great possibilities of development aid. In return they would not be asked to tie their trade or to abandon protection of their own nascent industries. We respect the desire of other Governments not to become politically committed. We have examined the proposed arrangements most closely and we cannot see any political commitment here. But we cannot judge for others; they must judge for themselves.

We had thought that the opportunity we had obtained for Commonwealth countries would be a help in their effort to secure African unity or at least to remove some of the obstacles to it. Again, this is for them to judge. I do not see how it can be a hindrance.

In listening as I did to the debates of the first three days I was struck by one thought on the economic side which seemed to be the main theme of almost every speech. If there has been a good deal of dispute as to method in this conference, there has as well been a striking unity as to purpose. I would put it in a single sentence: all of us are resolved to follow policies which will foster the harmonious development and steady expansion of world trading. The primary products and the other goods of the type mostly exported by the other Commonwealth countries will make up the great part of the imports of the developed countries in Europe or America for many years to come. We shall still need your raw materials and foodstuffs.

I quite understand my colleagues' anxiety in this respect. I believe that the chief worry is not even so much the question of sales of their products as the uncertainty about the terms of trade. It is true that for many years the prices of primary commodities have fallen in relation to manufactured goods. Why this should be is indeed something of a mystery. I had hoped that the increase in prosperity since the war would have produced good results. This is clearly one of the problems in which the world should force itself to reach agreement and the prospects of doing so would seem to me to be better if the negotiating partners are reasonably few. That is why I regard with hope the possibility of world commodity agreements in which a united Europe with the United States and possibly even Soviet Russia might join. There will, of course, also be major international negotiations following upon the passage through the Congress of Mr. Kennedy's new trade programme. There is, therefore, before us already a prospect of moving forward on the wider front of expanding world trade to which Mr. Diefenbaker has referred. Whether a Conference would be fruitful without precise proposals to consider is, I think, doubtful. But in all the efforts to expand world trade, Commonwealth countries can always be expected to take a leading part.

We hope that through the world commodity agreements prices can be stabilised and so the developing countries will receive real help in this field. Even so, there is still a further question to be resolved. If independence is to be fruitful, something more is needed than stability of earnings from primary products, even if these are reinforced by gifts or loans from outside. The developed countries of the world must take from outside a proper proportion of the industrial products of the under-developed countries. Much, of course, has already been done but the development of manufacture must not only serve home markets, but also find outlets in more advanced countries. This is perhaps the question of greatest importance which was raised on the first day by President Ayub. The Prime Ministers of India and Nigeria referred to it also, and so in one form or another did almost every other speaker. I fully realise how much importance all the Commonwealth countries attach to this problem.

Let us consider the position now. As it has been said, the Ottawa arrangements were based on the conditions of the day, which broadly speaking was for Britain to purchase primary products and to export manufactured goods in return. Raw materials were to be exchanged for processed goods; this was the agreement in broad outline, and undoubtedly it was of value to the Commonwealth and to the world. But the concept is now out of date. Of course, advanced countries like Australia, Canada and New Zealand, will continue to be large producers of food, but they will also make their own manufactures of motor cars and the like. I have only to suggest to you the possibility that they will not change the pattern existing in the 1930s for you to see how absurd the idea is. Indeed it has already changed. But it is not only out of date for these countries, but also for countries like India, Pakistan and Ceylon, all of whom export substantial quantities of industrial goods and confidently expect to increase their exports. It is not even true for dependent territories like Hong Kong who have become large exporters of manufactured goods. It will be increasingly out of date, as the Prime Minister of Trinidad has pointed out in his reference to the plantation system, for trade with the West Indies. It will become increasingly out of date as the African territories develop their own industries.

In any event, how can Britain, only a small country, maintain our free entry system in this country when there is a structure of tariffs being built up against it in many parts of the Commonwealth with protection for home industries? No doubt the Commonwealth countries would reply that we in Britain have ourselves increased our agricultural production. So we have but we could not leave our farmers to moulder in pauperism. It was not right or possible to leave agriculture in a depressed state while our industrial life was moving towards an affluent society.

Let us consider a particular problem, that of textiles. First of all, why is this manufacture developed so extensively? It is because it is a vital form of activity which is not too difficult to carry on once the right conditions can be established. It is a production which can be carried on in many different areas and in many different climates. It does not need a very experienced labour force. It has a firm basis in human needs and needs which are continually renewed. But let us consider what has already happened. At the time of the First World War the British textile industry not only provided almost the whole of the home market, it also exported $6\frac{1}{2}$ thousand million square yards. Now we only export some 300 million square yards and we import 40 per cent of our home consumption of textiles from the Commonwealth. The labour force in the textile industry has fallen since 1921 by about 450,000 and all the time mills are closing. Two important ones closed on the first day of this Conference. From all this I think it is clear that it could not be said that Britain has not tried or has failed in her duty. But there is a point at which we shall not be able to go on and continue our liberal policy without corresponding developments in other areas of trade to compensate us. I am afraid that European countries have not done as much to help in all this as we have. I am not sure that our American friends are doing all that they could. We in this country find ourselves in this dilemma. The goods on which we now rely in the textile field are the sophisticated high-quality cloths and woollens but we are prevented from exporting these to the United States by her trade policy at the same time as we try to take more of the Commonwealth production of cheaper lines.

I have said that it is quite true that our European friends have not always faced their responsibilities to the full. I must be frank and say that I cannot promise how Europe will develop, how far these pressures of self-interest and conscience will combine. I have no doubt that these responsibilities should be accepted. We are all really agreed on this and I believe that if nothing else comes from this Meeting at least some message to encourage the outward-looking elements in the developed world should go out from here. I might sum it up in these words—increased opportunities for trade are no less important than financial aid. We recognise the need for the less-developed countries of the world to be able to find outside markets for the products of their industries as they become established. If we agree on this message, we must decide how best we are to make it effective. How is Britain best to play her part—in or out of Europe? How are we to make our voice effective—in or out?

There is another aspect of this matter which is of equal importance. I think it was President Ayub and indeed others of the Prime Ministers who suggested that the developed countries should take the less sophisticated goods from the under-developed countries and concentrate their own work on sophisticated goods. Take textiles and rubber boots and so forth from abroad and concentrate on electronics. Well, I do not quarrel with this as an aim, but the electronic industry and other more sophisticated products are precisely those which require a very large industrial base, enormous quantities of capital and highly developed skills in production. If Britain is to take this line then she needs a larger home base; not 50 million people but 200 million or more. Or, to put it another way, if we only have a base of 50 million people as against the Europeans with 170 million, we shall not be in a position to compete effectively in these fields either in Europe or in third markets. It is not as though Britain had over Europe any particular advantages on which we can rely. So, if we have a much smaller market to absorb the high capital costs, then we shall have a far less favourable competitive position. In such a case it would be difficult for us to hold our own in the export of the more complicated manufactures. That must mean, and will certainly mean, not only that we shall not be able to import more of the less sophisticated products into our own market, but even that the opportunities now existing in Britain for such products will inevitably be restricted. There is one other matter that is bound to need elaboration. Of course, much of the trade of Commonwealth countries will remain in foodstuffs and perhaps largely in temperate foodstuffs. We are now agreed that on these subjects we must aim for world-wide, or almost world-wide, agreement. Everybody agrees on this—though without minimising the difficulties. May I put it in this way? We all support policies and initiatives designed to improve the organisation of the world market in a manner fair alike to producers and consumers. In particular we will support a fresh approach to the negotiation of international commodity agreements to this end. This is not limited to temperate foodstuffs; it extends to sugar and coffee and other tropical products. The problems of the future in this field are rather considerable, but commodity agreements seem the only way in which we can move out from the old concept of *laissez-faire* into the new field of a managed market, not just for one country or even one group of countries, but for all those who together form the major world market. We ought to press on, without delay, with such agreements—perhaps most of all a Wheat Agreement. Some of you have criticised our past attitude to international commodity agreements and particularly that of price policy as far as our imports are concerned. I think it is fair to say that we are less likely to be able to move in the direction which some of you desire if we have to stand alone. If we do not enter the European Community we shall not collapse, we shall do our best. The British people have too much spunk and fight to give in. But if Britain is not to have the benefit of a larger industrial base and we have to make the best of it in the economic field as we did militarily in the 1940s, then of course we shall have a free market, but we shall be forced to operate this with strict regard to our own self-interest. We shall have to rely far more than at present on buying in the cheapest market. But that is an approach to world trade to which personally I have been opposed all my life. I preached against it internally thirty years ago and now I am glad to feel that the Government of my own country accepts the view that we must make a move into a new stage. That is why I believe that we should have this second message from the Conference.

There is a further point that will come up. The old price system may have been brutal, but it was effective. If demand fell then production fell. That was in the chaotic days of *laissez-faire*. Now we want to move to a better organised market with more stable prices. That is absolutely right. We must do our best. We must aim so to arrange production as neither to stimulate it unduly nor to depress it so that agriculture is left in scandalous poverty and misery. We do not want to make mistakes, but there will certainly be some inequalities, some surpluses, some errors in prices. Of course surpluses are not evil in themselves, but only evil in so far as they are not used after they have been produced. It is a scandal to think of a shortage of food and even starvation in some parts of the world while surpluses of food are stored at vast expense in others. The concept should be that just as it is the duty of the developed countries to take a reasonable amount of manufactured goods from advancing countries, so the richer countries should combine according to their capacity to provide from their surplus production for those in want. 'We believe that in the disposal of any surplus of agricultural production opportunity should be taken to the fullest extent compatible with the legitimate interests of traditional suppliers to meet the needs of those people in the world who are in want.' This, I believe, should be the third message from this Meeting.

To return now to the main question—Britain's proposed entry into the Common Market. In the course of forty years in Parliament I have sometimes heard criticisms from Commonwealth countries of the United Kingdom, but at this meeting I have been greatly impressed by the anxiety so firmly stated lest we may somehow weaken now the connection with the Commonwealth. This is very gratifying to us. The members of the Commonwealth are all, of course, independent countries. And, as you have made clear, the responsibility for decision rests in this case with us. We shall exercise it with the deepest sense of our duty to the Commonwealth. We are determined to work together for all the things that we can together do to promote the principles in which we all believe, and to use every instrument which, in our different ways, we can hope to influence or control to that end.

I may sum it up in this way. We have listened with the closest attention to all that you have said in the general discussion and in the more restricted meetings. Everything that you have expressed we shall always bear in mind but we have to deal with the situation as it stands and not as it might be. We have here to face the position that the European Economic Community has come into being. It exists as a grouping of 170 million of the most skilled and advanced and developed countries in the world on our doorstep. This is an economic grouping which will certainly rival the United States and Russia. It has the largest export potential in the world, one of the largest industrial productions, and perhaps the largest basis of skilled men. It exists—we have to live with it and we have to do our duty for the Commonwealth in the best way we can as we see it. From our point of view, for the reasons I have explained, we believe that we should join it in order to increase both our political influence and our industrial strength. Our political influence to work for peace, disarmament and understanding; to avoid under Providence the fearful conditions that have so often led the world to misery and conflict. Our industrial strength so as to help us and to help you; to see that, so far as we can secure it, the growing European market with all its benefits and advantages should be extended to you. I believe it is right that we should join this Community on fair terms; right not just for ourselves but also right for you, and that is what concerns our people as well as, and perhaps more than, our own interests. We have to ask ourselves too what is the right thing to do for the world as a whole. Doubts have been expressed and indeed frankly stated that Europe will in fact be inward-looking and not out-ward-looking. These tendencies may exist. I do not know. But if they were to triumph, then Europe would be far less helpful to us and to you. If we stood aside this would be more likely to happen. We must not forget that our fellow members of EFTA, for whom arrangements with the Community must be made, will reinforce liberal trading tendencies. Nor should we forget the many far-sighted and broad-minded Europeans in the existing Community who fully share our view of things. My colleagues and I feel that our presence in this group of European countries will be beneficial and helpful to all that you most desire. The European structure as we see it now will change. As is always the case, the spirit of the times will be reflected in the leaders of the peoples. We firmly believe that if we can join we shall be able to do good. If we can do so we shall put all our influence into the attempt to work for the aims for which in general we at this Conference have declared in one form or another.

Our discussions have taken place at a point when certain principles have certainly been agreed and these covering a fairly wide field. This we owe to the pertinacity and skill of the negotiator, Mr. Heath, to whom universal tribute has been paid. But there are blanks to be filled in. There are also very large subjects—some of the great commodities—which have not yet been discussed. The question whether there are to be nil or minimum tariffs on many minerals and other imports from the Commonwealth into Europe. There are of course also problems affecting particularly British agriculture which remain to be discussed. There is the possibility of special arrangements to cover what is regarded by all as a very special position: that of New Zealand. In other words, there is much negotiation still to be done. And this will begin again within a few weeks. Certainly the British Government will study closely and bear continuously in mind all the views that they have learned from their Commonwealth colleagues. You have been able to put before us your anxieties and fears both upon broad and general issues and upon special but important points where each country is individually affected. I hope therefore that on consideration the fourth message which might come from this Meeting might be an expression of the hope that in the resumed negotiations in Brussels means will be found of enabling Britain to enter the Community on terms consistent with these objectives. Gentlemen, this is my attempt to summarise the position as I see it, and I believe that it is these messages of hope and determination for the future that we should somehow send out from this Meeting.

Appendix Three

Bermuda Communiqué, 22 December 1961

The President and the Prime Minister have had two days of valuable discussions surveying the world situation. The discussions centred mainly on the question of Berlin, on nuclear tests and on the situation in the Congo. The talks will form the basis of continued United States/United Kingdom co-operation during the coming months on a great variety of questions.

The President and the Prime Minister examined the situation concerning Berlin in the light of decisions taken at the meetings of the Foreign Ministers of the Four Powers and the NATO Council in Paris. In particular, they discussed the steps to be taken in regard to the renewal of diplomatic contact with the Soviet Union.

The President has agreed as a consequence of the Paris meeting that the initial contact would be made by the United States Ambassador in Moscow and the Prime Minister has indicated that the British Ambassador would be available to play whatever part might be desirable.

The President and the Prime Minister agreed that the purpose should be to ascertain whether a reasonable basis for negotiation could be found. Consultations with other Governments directly concerned are continuing.

The President and the Prime Minister considered the problems of the nuclear arms race. They took note of the new situation created by the massive series of atmospheric tests conducted in recent months by the Soviet Government after long secret preparations.

They agreed that it is now necessary, as a matter of prudent planning for the future, that, pending a final decision, preparations should be made for atmospheric testing to maintain the effectiveness of the deterrent.

Meanwhile they continue to believe that no task is more urgent than a search for a path towards effective disarmament and they pledge themselves to intensify and continue their efforts in this direction. Serious progress towards disarmament is the only way of breaking out of the dangerous contest so sharply renewed by the Soviet Union.

The President and the Prime Minister believe that the plans for disarmament put forward by the United States in the current Session of the United Nations

General Assembly offer a basis for such progress along with a treaty for ending nuclear tests, which the two nations have so carefully prepared and so earnestly urged upon the Soviet Government.

The President and the Prime Minister reviewed recent developments in the Congo. They noted with satisfaction that as an encouraging step towards understanding, a useful meeting had been held at Kitona between Mr. Adoula and Mr. Tshombe.

They expressed their strong hope that further progress will be made through the efforts of both parties. It seemed to them of first importance that the present discussions should be actively continued in appropriate ways. They agreed on the importance of avoiding any renewal of armed action while genuine efforts at consultation are going forward.

In a general discussion of the economic situation the President and the Prime Minister took note of progress in the negotiations between the United Kingdom and the European Economic Community and expressed the hope that this will be brought to a successful conclusion.

Appendix Four

Nassau Communiqué, 21 December 1962

The President and the Prime Minister met in Nassau from 18 to 21 December. They were accompanied by the Secretary of Defence, Mr. McNamara, and the Under-Secretary of State, Mr. Ball, and by the Foreign Secretary, Lord Home, the Minister of Defence, Mr. Thorneycroft, and the Secretary of State for Commonwealth Relations and Colonies, Mr. Sandys.

The President and the Prime Minister discussed a wide range of topics. They reviewed the state of East–West relations in the aftermath of the October crisis in Cuba, and joined in the hope that a satisfactory resolution of this crisis might open the way to the settlement of other problems outstanding between the West and the Soviet Union.

In particular, they reviewed the present state of the negotiations for a treaty ending nuclear tests, and reaffirmed their intent to seek agreement on this issue with the U.S.S.R., in the hope that this agreement would lead on to successful negotiations on wider issues of disarmament.

As regards Berlin, they reaffirmed their interest in arriving at a solid and enduring settlement which would ensure that Berlin remains free and viable.

The Chinese Communist attack on India was discussed with special consideration being given to the way in which the two Governments might assist the Government of India to counter this aggression. Defence problems of the sub-continent were reviewed. The Prime Minister and the President are hopeful that the common interests of Pakistan and India in the security of the sub-continent would lead to a reconciliation of Indian–Pakistan differences. To this end, they expressed their gratification at the statesmanship shown by President Ayub and Prime Minister Nehru in agreeing to renew their efforts to resolve their differences at this crucial moment.

The two leaders discussed the current state of affairs in the Congo, and agreed to continue their efforts for an equitable integration of this troubled country. They noted with concern the dangers of further discord in the Congo.

The Prime Minister informed the President of the present state of negotiations for United Kingdom membership in the Common Market. The President reaffirmed the interest of the United States in an early and successful outcome.

The President and the Prime Minister also discussed in considerable detail policy on advanced nuclear weapons systems and considered a variety of approaches. The result of this discussion is set out in the attached statement.

Statement on Nuclear Defence Systems, 21 December 1962

1. The President and the Prime Minister reviewed the development programme for the SKYBOLT missile. The President explained that it was no longer expected that this very complex weapons system would be completed within the cost estimate or the time scale which were projected when the programme was begun.

2. The President informed the Prime Minister that for this reason and because of the availability to the United States of alternative weapons systems, he had decided to cancel plans for the production of SKYBOLT for use by the United States. Nevertheless, recognising the importance of the SKYBOLT programme for the United Kingdom, and recalling that the purpose of the offer of SKYBOLT to the United Kingdom in 1960 had been to assist in improving and extending the effective life of the British V-bombers, the President expressed his readiness to continue the development of the missile as a joint enterprise between the United States and the United Kingdom, with each country bearing equal shares of the future cost of completing development, after which the United Kingdom would be able to place a production order to meet its requirements.

3. While recognising the value of this offer, the Prime Minister decided, after full consideration, not to avail himself of it because of doubts that had been expressed about the prospects of success for this weapons system and because of uncertainty regarding date of completion and final cost of the programme.

4. As a possible alternative the President suggested that the Royal Air Force might use the HOUND DOG missile. The Prime Minister responded that in the light of the technical difficulties he was unable to accept this suggestion.

5. The Prime Minister then turned to the possibility of provision of the POLARIS missile to the United Kingdom by the United States. After careful review, the President and the Prime Minister agreed that a decision on POLARIS must be considered in the widest context both of the future defence of the Atlantic Alliance and of the safety of the whole Free World. They reached the conclusion that this issue created an opportunity for the development of new and closer arrangements for the organisation and control of strategic Western defence and that such arrangements in turn could make a major contribution to political cohesion among the nations of the Alliance.

6. The Prime Minister suggested and the President agreed, that for the immediate future a start could be made by subscribing to NATO some part of the forces already in existence. This could include allocations from United States Strategic Forces, from United Kingdom Bomber Command, and from tactical nuclear forces now held in Europe. Such forces would be assigned as part of a NATO nuclear force and targeted in accordance with NATO plans.

7. Returning to POLARIS the President and the Prime Minister agreed that the purpose of their two Governments with respect to the provision of the POLARIS missiles must be the development of a multilateral NATO nuclear force in the closest consultation with other NATO allies. They will use their best endeavours to this end.

8. Accordingly, the President and the Prime Minister agreed that the United States will make available on a continuing basis POLARIS missiles (less warheads) for British submarines. The United States will also study the feasibility of making available certain support facilities for such submarines. The United Kingdom Government will construct the submarines in which these weapons will be placed and they will also provide the nuclear warheads for the POLARIS missiles. British forces developed under this plan will be assigned and targeted in the same way as the forces described in paragraph 6.

9. These forces, and at least equal United States forces, would be made available for inclusion in a NATO multilateral nuclear force. The Prime Minister made it clear that except where her Majesty's Government may decide that supreme national interests are at stake, these British forces will be used for the purposes of international defence of the Western Alliance in all circumstances.

10. The President and the Prime Minister are convinced that this new plan will strengthen the nuclear defence of Western Alliance. In strategic terms this defence is indivisible, and it is their conviction that, in all ordinary circumstances of crisis or danger, it is this very unity which is the best protection of the West.

11. The President and the Prime Minister agreed that in addition to having a nuclear shield it is important to have a non-nuclear sword. For this purpose they agreed on the importance of increasing the effectiveness of their conventional forces on a world-wide basis.

Index

Purchase Tax cuts, 67, 386, 387, 388

Radcliffe, Lord, 425
Radcliffe Report (1962), 425, 426–8
Radcliffe Tribunal (1962), 431, 435, 438
Radhakrishnan, Dr. Sarvepalli, 443
Rambouillet, author's talks with de Gaulle at (Dec 1962), 337, 340, 345–55, 367
Ranke, Leopold von, 221n
Rawlinson, Sir Peter, 447
Renison, Sir Patrick, 288
Reynaud, Paul, 368
Rhodesia, Northern: seeks independence, 297; proposal for African majority in Legislature, 299, 307–8, 310; Constitutional Conference (1961), 305, 307, 309–11; Welensky's objections to proposals, 307–308, 310; new scheme for Legislature, 310–11, 312; amended proposals, 314–15, 317, 318–20; violence in, 317; African coalition government in (Dec 1962), 323, 326; insistence on secession, 326, 328
Rhodesia, Southern: seeks independence, 297, 298, 313; Salisbury conference on (1961), 305; agreement on new constitution, 305–7; referendum on, 313, 316; bans National Democratic Party, 318; Rhodesian Front victory (Dec 1962), 324; insistence on independence, 326–31; attends dissolution conference (June 1963), 331
Rhodesia and Nyasaland, Federation of (Central African Federation), 280, 286; Monckton Commission on, 295, 298–301, 310; Welensky's belief in, 296; steps towards dissolution, 296–332; proposed constitutional changes, 299–300; Federal Review Conference (Dec 1960), 301–5; arrangements for separate territories (q.v.), 305–32; Butler appointed Minister for, 321–2
Richardson, Sir John, 144, 316, 501, 502, 503, 516
Robens, Lord, 43, 53
Roberts, Sir Frank, 178
Roll, Sir Eric, 28
Rome, author's visit to (Feb 1963), 373
Rome, Treaty of (1957), 1, 3, 12, 17, 18, 22, 23, 349, 377, 378, 532

Romer, Sir Charles, heads committee on security (1961), 423, 424, 425
Roosevelt, Franklin D., 353, 356
Rose, Michael, 284
Rusk, Dean, 89–90, 145, 164, 169, 172, 177, 239, 336, 382, 455; and Cuban crisis, 195, 219, 220; and test ban talks, 458, 471, 474
Russell, Bertrand, 200
Russia: and Berlin, 142, 143, 146, 150–1, 152, 161, 169, 177, 182, 187, 192–3, 199, 200, 203, 216, 218, 454; threat to sign treaty with East Germany, 142, 158; and nuclear tests, 142, 146, 152, 155, 156, 157, 158, 161, 165, 167, 172–4, 176, 177–9, 360, 454–85; and disarmament, 142, 143, 160–3; and German situation, 148–51; and Summit meetings, 157–8, 168–9, 170, 171, 175–6; objection to international inspection of explosions, 172–3, 174, 175–6, 355; proposes moratorium, 176; and Cuban missile crisis, 181–220, 453; build-up of arms and technicians in Cuba, 182–6, 188, 190–1; strategy admired by Kennedy, 193; turns back some of its ships, 198–9, 206, 208; denies existence of missiles, 196, 197, 219; attempt to bargain against American rockets in Turkey, 212, 213, 217, 219; signs of weakening, 213–14; capitulation, 214–15; possible motives, 216–17; strained relations with China, 222–3, 464; gives India fighter aircraft, 226–7; and Laos, 240, 243, 245; and Thailand, 244; renewed offer on nuclear tests, 454, 455–9, 463–4, 476; accepts principle of inspection, 454, 458–9, 463, 464, 468; and Test Ban Treaty, 459, 460–2, 470, 475–6, 479–85; hatred and fear of Germans, 461; suggests non-aggression pact, 480, 481–3; and Finland, 488, 489

St. Aldwyn, Lord, 509, 510, 513
Salinger, Pierre, 473
Salisbury, 5th Marquess of, 290, 301, 312, 313, 509; and Monday Club, 396
Sallal, Colonel Abdullah al, 266, 267, 269, 270, 273, 274, 275, 276, 277
Sanaa, 275
Sandys, Duncan, 8, 10, 12, 25, 227, 307, 355, 472; and Common Market, 8, 25, 28, 110,

1962

March 2	U.K. applies to join European Coal and Steel Community
March 5	U.K. applies to join Euratom
April 18	West Indies Federation dissolved
July 1	Commonwealth Immigrants Act comes into force
July 3–16	Reorganisation of U.K. Govt. Maudling succeeds Lloyd as Chancellor of the Exchequer
Aug. 6	Jamaica independent
Aug. 31	Trinidad and Tobago independent
Oct. 9	Uganda independent
Nov. 1	New Constitution for S. Rhodesia comes into force
Dec. 19	U.K. accepts Nyasaland's right to secede from Central African Federation

1963

June 4	Profumo resigns
Sept. 16	Federation of Malaysia established. Malaya, Singapore, Sabah, Sarawak
Oct. 8	H.M. to hospital
Oct. 18	H.M. resigns. P.M. : Sir Alec Douglas-Home
Dec. 10	Zanzibar independent
Dec. 12	Kenya independent
Dec. 31	Federation of Rhodesia and Nyasaland dissolved